MOZART

Mozart in Verona. Oil portrait by Saviero dalla Rosa, 1770.

MOZART

A LIFE

Maynard Solomon

HarperCollins*Publishers*

HarperCollins books may be purchased for educational, business, or sales promotional use. For information, please write: Special Markets Department, HarperCollins Publishers, Inc., 10 East 53rd Street, New York, NY 10022.

FIRST EDITION

Designed by George J. McKeon

Library of Congress Cataloging in Publication Data

Solomon, Maynard
   Mozart : a life / Maynard Solomon. — 1st ed.
      p.   cm.
   Includes bibliographical references (p. 593) and index.
      ISBN 0-06-019046-9
      1. Mozart, Wolfgang Amadeus, 1756–1791. 2. Composers—Austria—Biography. I. Title.
   ML410.M9S65   1995
      780'.92—dc20
[B]   94-42277

95 96 97 98 99 ❖/RRD 10 9 8 7 6 5 4 3 2

For Eva, Nathaniel, and Alexander, with love,
Joseph Kerman, in friendship,
and
Marianne Goldberger, with deep regard

"Consider well. He is a Prince!"
"More! He is a Man!"
—*Die Zauberflöte*

CONTENTS

ACKNOWLEDGMENTS

Portions of this book formed the basis for the Messenger Lectures that I gave at Cornell University in the spring of 1992. Other sections were presented as lectures at Brandeis University, the University of California at Berkeley, Peabody Conservatory of Music, Princeton University, Rutgers University, Smith College, Stanford University, the Woodrow Wilson International Center, the Biography Seminar of the Department of English at New York University, the New York Institute for the Humanities, the Muriel Gardiner Program in Psychoanalysis and the Humanities at Yale University, and the Royal Musical Association in London. "The Myth of the Eternal Child" was initially presented as an Albert Schweitzer Lecture in the Humanities at New York University at the invitation of Aileen Ward, now Schweitzer Professor Emeritus, and was subsequently published in *19th-Century Music* 15 (1991). Chapter 18, here entitled "Adam," appeared in the Festschrift for Georg Knepler, *Zwischen Aufklärung and Kulturindustrie,* ed. Hanns-Werner Heister et al. (Hamburg, 1993). A version of chapter 28, "The Journey to Berlin," appeared in the *Journal of Musicology* (1994). Chapter 22, "The Zoroastran Riddles," was written for a Mozart symposium at Rutgers University organized by Ellen Rosand and Douglas Johnson; it was published in *American Imago* 12 (1985) and is reprinted here, in revised form, by permission of Johns Hopkins University Press.

My thanks to the unfailingly helpful staff members of the music division of the New York Public Library, the libraries of Columbia, Harvard, and Princeton universities, and the Österreichische Nationalbibliothek. Also to the Berlin Staatsbibliothek Preussischer Kulturbesitz, the British Library, the Graphische Sammlung Albertina in Vienna, the Hunterian Art Gallery of the University of Glasgow, the Pierpont Morgan Library, the Museen der Stadt Wien, and the Mozart-Archiv of the Internationale Stiftung Mozarteum in Salzburg. Quotations from Emily Anderson, *The Letters of Mozart and His Family,* are used by permission of Macmillan Press Ltd. Photographs are by Maury Solomon. The reductions of the music examples were done by Scott Griffin and prepared for publication by Carl Johnson of Music Publishing Services, New York.

For materials, suggestions, collegial responses to queries, and exchanges of ideas, I am grateful to Wye Jamison Allanbrook, Rudolph Angermüller, Karol Berger, Bruce Cooper Clarke, Cliff Eisen, Joseph Kerman, William Kinderman, Richard Kramer, Lewis Lockwood, Robert L. Marshall, Josef Mančal, Max Rudolf, the late Gert Schiff, Elaine Sisman, Leo Treitler, Alan Tyson, James Webster, Robert S. Winter, and Neal Zaslaw. I owe a great deal to the members of my Mozart seminars at the State University of New York at Stony Brook, Columbia University, and Harvard University, where many of the chief ideas of this book were first elaborated. Professors Eisen, Kerman, Lockwood, Marshall, and Zaslaw all read the manuscript and made innumerable valuable suggestions for its improvement, sacrificing time from their own projects to assist a friend and colleague who now cannot find appropriate words to express his deep appreciation. I can only say that wherever possible I have gladly availed myself of their corrections, accepted their advice, and taken serious account of their objections. Perhaps a future edition will enable me to remedy any remaining errors of fact or infelicities of interpretation.

I am indebted to Aaron Asher for his enthusiasm for this project and for reading the manuscript with a keen musician's eye and an editor's tact; to my agent, Georges Borchardt, for his patience and sound advice; and to executive editor Hugh Van Dusen of HarperCollins, who deftly guided the book through its final stages with the able cooperation of Katherine Scott, Stephanie Gunning, Pamela LaBarbiera, Maureen Clark, and Elyse Dubin.

As always, my wife Eva has been my best critic, editor, and endlessly patient listener. My old teacher Harry Slochower died before he could see this book, but I hope that I have managed to remain faithful to his warning that "all absolutist explanations are bound to fail."

—New York, 1994

TABLE OF MONEY VALUES

1 florin [or gulden] = 60 kreuzer
1 ducat = 4 ½ florins
1 Reichsthaler = 1 ½ florins
1 friedrich d'or = 7 to 8 florins
1 sequin = 2.8 florins
2 English shillings = 1 florin
1 English pound = 10 florins
1 louis d'or = 9 to 10 florins

Rates vary somewhat owing to currency fluctuations.

A NOTE ON
KÖCHEL NUMBERS

Mozart's compositions are identified by the numbers assigned to them in the first edition of the chronological thematic list of his works by Ludwig von Köchel, followed by the revised numbers (if any) assigned to them in the sixth edition of Köchel's catalog (thus, Sonata in A minor, K. 310/300d). This procedure is followed as well for works that formerly were listed in an appendix (*Anhang*) to the first three editions of Köchel but now appear in the main catalog (thus, *Les Petits Riens,* K. Anh. 10/299b). K. *deest* designates a work that is not to be found in Köchel.

INTRODUCTION

Browsing in the stacks of a major university library, I come upon a two-volume guidebook to Salzburg and environs, published in 1792 and 1793, shortly after Mozart's death. It was written by Lorenz Hübner (1753–1807), a Munich editor who was called to Salzburg in 1783 by Archbishop Hieronymus Colloredo to run the city's main newspapers, the *Staats-Zeitung* and the *Salzburger Intelligenzblatt,* which he did until his departure from Salzburg in 1799. Hübner was on cordial terms with Leopold Mozart and was fully aware of Mozart's genius, his fame, and his stature as Salzburg's greatest son.

I leaf through Hübner's chapters on Salzburg's cultural life, its musical establishment and public institutions, churches, leading living citizens. I study the statistics on population, births and deaths, shops and industries, land ownership and agricultural output. And then, out of curiosity, and perhaps hoping to locate a previously overlooked reference to Mozart, I turn to the street listings, specifically to the two pages devoted to the Getreidegasse, where Mozart was born in 1756, where the Mozarts lived for the quarter century from 1747 to 1773, and where his birth house still stands.[1] Hübner gives measurements for the width and length of the street, lists the main houses and their architectural features, and mentions past and present inhabitants, among them several familiar figures, including the merchant Lorenz Hagenauer, the Mozart family's friend and landlord. The name Mozart, however, does not appear. Presuming a simple error of omission, I skim the pages and locate Hübner's brief description of the Tanzmeisterhaus ("dance-master house"); here again there is no mention of the Mozart family, which occupied that house from 1773 until the death of Leopold Mozart in 1787.[2]

Now somewhat puzzled, but having formed a working hypothesis, I turn to Otto Erich Deutsch's comprehensive *Mozart: A Documentary Biography* and its supplements, including Cliff Eisen's recent *New Mozart Documents,* in search of references to Mozart in Salzburg during his Vienna years and after his death. It is not long before my vague surmises are confirmed by an array of facts and, more poignantly, by the absence of other, expected facts.

When Mozart died, memorial gatherings and concerts were held in his honor in Vienna, Prague, Kassel, and Berlin, but not in Salzburg, although his friends, patrons, fellow musicians, and admirers there had once numbered in the hundreds.[3] Between 1792 and 1797, Mozart's widow, Constanze Mozart, held benefit concerts featuring his music in Vienna, Prague, Graz, Linz, Dresden, Leipzig, and Berlin, but no such concert took place in Salzburg. Beginning in May 1792, Mozart monuments were erected in various cities of Europe, but it was not until 1842 that Schwanthaler's bronze Mozart statue was unveiled in Salzburg.[4] In nearby Graz, where the first such monument was erected, an academy devoted to Mozart's music was founded as early as February 1793, and about seventy of his works were performed there between 1791 and 1797.[5] But in Salzburg no Mozart society came into being until 1841 (and no effective one until 1870), and few performances of his works took place in the decades after his death. Indeed, although there may have been others, we know of only one performance in Salzburg of a work by Mozart between 1784 and his death—a performance by Leopold Mozart's pupil Heinrich Marchand of the Piano Concerto in D minor, K. 466, at a concert on 22 March 1786.[6]

Apparently, a makeshift curtain of silence had begun to descend in Salzburg well before Mozart's death, beginning in the wake of his flight to Vienna in 1781, and intensifying as the years wore on. From the time of his defection until his death, there is only one recorded mention of his name in any Salzburg newspaper, a passing reference in the course of a review of an edition of a Dittersdorf opera.[7] When Hübner published Mozart's "Zoroastran Fragments" and one of his riddles in the *Staats-Zeitung* on 23 March 1786, he omitted Mozart's name and stressed that he was publishing the material only because the paper was "short of more important matters."[8] And although Mozart was one of the most frequently published composers in Europe during the 1780s, none of his publications was reviewed in Salzburg, and few (if any) were even announced there. Nor did news of his later activities and appointments reach the citizens of Salzburg through their own press.[9] They did, however, learn of his death: on 12 December 1791, an eleven-line obituary that had appeared in the *Wiener Zeitung* on December 7 was reprinted on the front page of Hübner's *Staats-Zeitung*.

> During the night of the 4th and 5th of this month Imperial Court Chamber Composer Wolfgang Mozart died here. Known from his childhood on as the possessor of the finest musical talent in all *Europe*, through the fortunate development of his exceptional natural gifts and through persistent application he rose to the level of the greatest masters; his works, loved and admired by all, bear witness to this, and are the measure of the irreplaceable loss that the noble art of music has suffered by his death.[10]

Four weeks later, on 7 January 1792, the *Salzburger Intelligenzblatt* published an anecdote about the anonymous commission Mozart received for the Requiem: "Some months before his death he received an unsigned letter, asking him to write a Requiem."[11]

The process of forgetting Mozart began in the aftermath of his rancorous quarrel with Archbishop Hieronymus Colloredo, who thereafter may have preferred not to be reminded of his former employee's continuing existence. The notorious kick in the rear by which the archbishop's chamberlain Count Arco sealed Mozart's resignation from His Grace's service in 1781 was a blunt way of saying, "And don't come back!" Of course, the "forgetting" of Mozart's name and memory was not a calculated policy of the archbishop, the Salzburg citizenry, or the local aristocracy, among whom were many people who were friendly to him or who loved him and his music. Indeed, Archbishop Colloredo displayed his magnanimity by attending the Marchand concert in 1786, just as, earlier, he had lent his presence at the 1784 performance of *Die Entführung aus dem Serail* and commented, graciously, "*Really, it wasn't bad at all.*"[12] But there were few Salzburgers who put friendship or love above accommodation to the community's displeasure with an unruly subject who had repudiated their native town in favor of the big city: "It seems," read the Mozart entry in a 1790 dictionary of composers, "as if his sphere of activity at Salzburg had become too narrow for this young man; for he again left his birthplace about 1780 and betook himself to Vienna."[13]

Voluntary migration had resulted in informal exclusion: Mozart had brought about his own exile. He was punished for leaving home, for preferring a different place, for dissatisfaction with a city that was good enough for everyone else. His departure seems to have been experienced as a mortification and a betrayal, his every triumph as one more reproach to those who remained behind. Thus, when Mozart left Salzburg, he was given up for dead, but he was not the only one who was mortally wounded. Blaming and grieving, those he had abandoned closed ranks, continued their orderly routines, and pretended that the void had been filled. Life in the old country goes on without the expatriate, and a kind of amnesia eventually engulfs the traces of his existence. If he returns home, as Mozart did in the summer of 1783, it is as a phantom visiting a place where he no longer really belongs. Indeed, Mozart dreaded to make that journey, fearing that he would be arrested by the authorities for having broken his employment agreement; and thereafter he avoided visiting Salzburg—even when his father died, even for his sister's marriage or the birth of her children.

A beloved son—a favorite son—was disinherited by his own city. And this same beloved son was effectively disinherited by his father as well—in more than a metaphoric sense—when he was no longer willing to play the part that had been scripted for him as a child. As in his conflict with Colloredo, Mozart was faced with extreme alternatives: submission to injustice or expulsion from his family. The issues were the same, capitulation or exile, a state of perpetual childhood or the anguish of enforced isolation: on the one hand, Mozart's yearning to continue as a dutiful member of a symbiotic family and hometown that offered the gifts of approval, love, and the validation of his identity; on the other, a sense of homelessness, a profound melancholy rising from the renunciation of responsibilities and the sundering of his closest human connections. After years of inner and outer conflict, Mozart at last made his choice and thereby became almost a nonperson in his birthplace—estranged from his sister, rejected by his father, and uncelebrated by his compatriots. We will want to know what were the compensations for these losses. In what follows we may come to see the disinheriting of Mozart as a source of his empowerment, as the emblem of a recalcitrant bravery, and even, perhaps, as a precondition of his creativity.

PROLOGUE

Mozart in gala dress, 1763. Unsigned oil portrait, attributed to Pietro Antonio Lorenzoni. Mozart-Museum der Internationalen Stiftung Mozarteum, Salzburg. © Mozarts Geburtshaus, Salzburg.

THE MYTH OF
THE ETERNAL CHILD

The child Mozart was examined by several eminent observers, who authenticated his gifts and issued glowing scientific reports describing his prodigious talents. The English magistrate and scholar Daines Barrington visited nine-year-old Mozart in London and put him to several tests, offering his conclusions to the Royal Society in London, which published them in its *Philosophical Transactions* of 1770.[1] After much initial skepticism, he confirmed that the child possessed what the music historian Charles Burney called "premature and almost supernatural talents."[2] "Suppose then," suggested Barrington in attempting to describe Mozart's sight-reading abilities, "a capital speech in Shakespeare never seen before, and yet read by a child of eight years old, with all the pathetic energy of a Garrick. Let it be conceived likewise, that the same child is reading, with a glance of his eye, three different comments on this speech tending to its illustration; and that one comment is written in Greek, the second in Hebrew, and the third in Etruscan characters. . . . When all this is conceived, it will convey some idea of what this boy was capable of."[3] In Paris, Friedrich Melchior von Grimm, a close associate of the Encyclopedists, exclaimed in amazement that the child was "such an extraordinary phenomenon that one is hard put to it to believe what one sees with one's eyes and hears with one's ears. . . . I am no longer surprised that Saint Paul should have lost his head after his strange vision."[4]

A Swiss philosophe and educator, Auguste Tissot, who observed Mozart in Lausanne in 1766, set down his astonishment at the superiority of Mozart's performances, at the "character of force which is the stamp of genius, that variety which proclaims the fire of imagination, and that

charm which proves an assured taste." But the phenomenon of young
Mozart, he avowed, transcended issues of genius or precocious virtuosity,
rising instead from a harmonious union

> . . . between moral man and physical man. A well-ordered mind appears
> to be made for a virtuous soul and sweet ways; experience has verified this
> in several great artists, and little Mozart supplies a new proof of it; his
> heart is as sensitive as his ear; he has modesty such as is rare at his age, and
> rare combined with such superiority; it is truly edifying to hear him
> attribute his talents to the giver of all things and to conclude from this,
> with a charming candor and an air of the most intimate conviction, that it
> would be unpardonable to pride himself on them.[5]

Thus, beyond the miraculous surface, Mozart was held to be, in the
words of Tissot's German translator, "not only a natural but a moral human
being; a splendid object, in truth, worthy of study," and his parents were to
be congratulated for knowing "so well how to unite and nurture in [him]
the moral and the natural man."[6] Leopold Mozart was regarded as God's
surrogate in this matter, guiding the development of his son—and his
daughter, Marianne, who had an important role in the early concerts—with
a benevolent, scientific, and loving disposition. "One cannot see without
emotion," wrote Tissot, "all the evidence of his tenderness for a father who
seems most worthy of it, who has taken even greater care over the formation of his character than the cultivation of his talents, and who speaks of
education with as much sagacity as of music; who thinks himself well
rewarded by success, and regards it as sweet for him to see his two lovable
children better rewarded by a glance of approval from him, which they seek
with tender anxiety in his eyes, than by the plaudits of a whole audience."[7]
Mozart was seen, then, as a superlative example of the child's unlimited
potentiality for creative and moral development, which could be unlocked
by enlightened upbringing. The most famous musical prodigy in history,
he was marked from the outset as the quintessential, perfect child. In an
extraordinary series of triumphs, he was received, feted, and honored by
the royal families of Europe—the king and queen of France, the empress of
Austria and her son Emperor Joseph, the king and queen of England—and
Pope Clement XIV himself. Mozart and his family were showered with
money and expensive presents. He was kissed by empresses and petted by
Marie Antoinette. And all because he was a gifted child, one who not only
could perform wonders and miracles but was the very incarnation of a miracle, one whose small body exemplified the infinite perfectibility of the
child and, by inference, of mankind.

The early literature about the child Mozart inevitably drew on a variety of rich traditions about other child heroes. There are tales in the Herculean mode of his endless labors and feats: he was undaunted by blindfolds and by keyboards covered with cloths; he emerged victorious from strenuous musical contests; it was claimed as a miracle that he was able to write down Allegri's *Miserere*—the Church was said to have forbidden copying it—after a single hearing at the Vatican. Legends of the Christ child readily attached themselves to him. "We have seen him for an hour and a half on end withstand the assaults of musicians," wrote Grimm, echoing Luke's narrative of the twelve-year-old who was questioned by the elders in the temple, "and while they sweated blood and had the hardest struggle in the world to keep even with him, the child came out of the combat unfatigued."[8] There is perhaps something of the youthful trickster in all this: While Mozart certainly had the capacity to write out the *Miserere* from memory, he may also have had prior access to a manuscript copy of Allegri's score;[9] and he professed to read at sight compositions of unlimited difficulty but sometimes, without missing a beat, substituted different passagework already in his repertory.[10] Many people—perhaps most—doubted his age, suspecting deception and even sending to Salzburg for his baptismal records.[11] In Naples, so they said, Mozart was accused of wearing a magical ring to aid his dexterous left hand.[12] It was reported—perhaps apocryphally, for the story has the sound of legend—that the archbishop of Salzburg, not crediting his young subject's abilities as a composer, "shut him up for a week, during which he was not permitted to see any one, and was left only with music paper, and the words of an oratorio," for which he triumphantly produced the music at the close of his incarceration.[13]

In a rare moment of self-revelation, Leopold Mozart let us glimpse the extent to which he himself identified the boy with the Christ child; he wrote to his friend Lorenz Hagenauer in 1768 that his son was "a miracle, which God has allowed to see the light in Salzburg. . . . *And if it is ever to be my duty to convince the world of this miracle, it is so now, when people are ridiculing whatever is called a miracle and denying all miracles. . . .* But because this miracle is too evident and consequently not to be denied, they want to suppress it. *They refuse to let God have the honor.*"[14] In the descriptions of Mozart there are hints, too, of Apollo and Hermes, of Dionysus and Ganymede. Primarily, however, he is seen as Eros, the divine child, the playful embodiment of love and beauty. And the preoccupations of Eros were his as well. "Who is this, that will not kiss me?" he is said to have asked imperiously when Madame de Pompadour rebuffed his embrace. "The empress kissed me."[15] He had indeed animated the Austrian empress to kiss him by jumping on her lap, hugging her, and "saying that he loved her with all his heart."[16] The Salzburg court trumpeter Johann Andreas Schachtner recalled, "He would often ask me ten times in one day if I loved him, and when I sometimes said no, just for fun, bright tears welled up in his eyes."[17]

To be sure, from the first there were also hints that the perfect child—so small, delicate, prone to illness—was somehow doomed, and might not survive to adulthood. Writing to him in 1778, his father recalled, "Why, even your expression was so solemn that, observing the early efflorescence of your talent and your ever grave and thoughtful little face, many discerning people of different countries sadly doubted whether your life would be a long one."[18] Grimm worried whether "so premature a fruit might fall before it has come to maturity."[19] Daines Barrington hoped that Mozart might attain "to the same advanced years as Handel, contrary to the common observation that such *ingenia praecocia* are generally short lived."[20]

Homer tells us that the child gods are timeless and unchanging: "They age not, they die not, they are eternal."[21] In the course of time, however, Mozart's physical appearance began to diverge from the world's image of him. It was as though the grown Mozart was a quite different person, one descended from but not identical with a legendary child Mozart. The boy faded from view, replaced by a somewhat strange and awkward adolescent and adult. Fanciful imaginings about the young Mozart materialized and remained frozen in time while another Mozart grew older, suffered, and died. The maturing historical Mozart became the porcelain-child Mozart's double, and the divine child survived his own death. A sickly infant with a large head and a tiny body, a winning youngster with an arch smile and unshakable confidence, a little magician gifted with marvelous powers, performed wonders before the crowned heads and elite of Europe, while everywhere were heard predictions of his early doom.

Adding to the sense of uncanniness was another picture, of a zealous father who had created a living instrument in the shape of a little boy to labor in God's service, producing things of beauty. On one side are the classical images of Apollo and Eros, on the other, hints of the medieval Faust and his homunculus, of Maelzel and his mechanical trumpeter, and even of Rabbi Loew and his golem.

To all appearances, Mozart was a happy child. He was perfectly compliant and undemanding, working for the commonweal, which is to say, for the ideal family of which he was so integral a part. He delighted in his role as virtuoso-magician-prodigy; he rejoiced in applause and caresses, in being able to bring honor and fortune to his family; he derived pleasure from his celebrity and its accompanying adulation. It was a seductive role for him: from the age of six he wielded extraordinary power over his audiences, moving them to enthusiasm and rapture. And though he may not have been altogether conscious of it, he held great power over his family, for he had become its main source of wealth and status, a breadwinner charged with contributing to the support of his mother, father, and sister.

But anyone who troubled to look could have perceived many early signs of Mozart's difficulty in sustaining his multiple burdens: he was quick to tears, stricken and often taken ill by the loss or absence of friends, bereft when his constant pleas to "love me" were not reciprocated. There was no indication that the child understood the extent to which he had been converted into an instrument of patriarchal ambition and subjected to the inevitable resentments that attach to a father's growing realization that he has become deeply dependent upon his little boy.

Leopold Mozart had gained esteem, even glory, from his role as begetter, instructor, and impresario of so noble a creature, and he had seized every opportunity to turn the labors of his miraculous child into a cash equivalent, reaping extraordinarily large sums of money from the family's European tours. More and more, his career, financial health, and hunger for recognition came to depend on his son, particularly when he began to neglect his duties as deputy kapellmeister to the Salzburg court and abandoned his activities as a composer and litterateur. And during years of almost nonstop travel, the Mozart family had grown accustomed to servants, private carriages, friseurs, and expensive clothing, and to the sense of superiority that attended their mingling with the highest levels of the nobility and intelligentsia. Not surprisingly, then, Leopold came to fear that Mozart would grow up, that is, would cease to be a child. He wrote to Hagenauer from Lyons in 1766, when Mozart was ten, "Surely you will agree that now is the time when my children on account of their youth can arouse the admiration of everyone."[22] He felt an urgent need to exploit his possibilities before they evaporated: "Every moment I lose is lost forever. And if I ever guessed how precious for youth is time, I realize it now. You know that my children are accustomed to work. But if with the excuse that one thing prevents another they were to accustom themselves to hours of idleness, my whole plan would crumble to pieces."[23] It is most telling that as Mozart was approaching his teens, Leopold asked bitterly, "Should I perhaps sit down in Salzburg with the empty hope of some better fortune, let Wolfgang grow up, and allow myself and my children to be made fools of until I reach the age which would prevent me from traveling and until he attains the age and physical size that no longer attract admiration for his merits?"[24]

From dreading Mozart's maturity Leopold eventually undertook to prevent it from coming to pass. Even in his adolescence and young adulthood, Mozart was not allowed to travel unless accompanied by his father, who made all the practical decisions and appraised every opportunity with a view to the family's interests. Beginning in 1772, Mozart held a modest post as a violinist in Salzburg, where he had uncertain prospects of advancement, let alone of fulfilling his ambitions as a composer, for these ambitions required a larger arena than was available there. Frustrated both personally and professionally, he asked his father to let him pursue his career elsewhere, but Leopold Mozart raised every conceivable objection. He sought to bar Mozart's departure by making it conditional on the entire family's accompanying him and even upon finding appropriate employment for himself. And he complained about the high travel expenses. But if Mozart countered that these expenses would be minimal for a single man traveling alone, living frugally, and earning something from his talents, his father would shift the ground to Mozart's helplessness and childishness. "I could not let you travel alone, because you were not accustomed to attend to everything or to be independent of the help of others and because you knew so little about different currencies and nothing whatever about foreign money. Moreover, you had not the faintest idea about packing nor about the innumerable necessary arrangements which crop up on journeys."[25] And when Mozart set out from Salzburg at the age of twenty-one and the archbishop refused to give Leopold Mozart leave to travel, Frau Mozart went along as her husband's agent, covertly pledged to report home any sign that their son was going astray.

Also following Mozart on his journey were Leopold's exhortations and remonstrances, transparent attempts to barricade his son within the family. Mozart was instructed to be wary of both the friendship of men and the love of women. "All men are villains" ("*Die Menschen sind alle Böswichter*") was a *basso ostinato* of Leopold Mozart's letters to his son. "Trust no one!" he warned, adding, "All friendships have their motives," and scoundrels hover about whose only intent is to "squeeze [you] dry."[26] "All men are villains!" he reiterated. "The older you become and the more you associate with people, the more you will realize this sad truth."[27] (Oddly, the Mozart scholar Hermann Abert sees this as Enlightenment pessimism, springing from the "dream of a more perfect world,"[28] but the contrast with Schiller's "*Alle Menschen werden Brüder*" ["All men shall be brothers"] could not be more striking.) In 1778, on Mozart's arrival in Paris, his father abjured him to avoid not only strangers, adventurers, and unbelievers but members of the musical and theatrical professions as well; from what he had heard about Paris, "You should be on your guard against its dangers and . . . should refrain from all familiarity with young Frenchmen, and even more so with the women, who are always on the look-out for strangers to keep them, who run after young people of talent in an astonishing way in order to get at their money, draw them into their net or even land them as husbands."[29] Obviously, women constituted a particularly dangerous class of creatures: "Where they are concerned, the greatest reserve and prudence are necessary, Nature herself being our enemy. Whoever does not use his judgment to the utmost to keep the necessary reserve with them, will exert it in vain later on when he endeavors to extricate himself from the labyrinth, *a misfortune which most often ends only at death.*"[30]

To Leopold Mozart's mind, the greatest hazard was that Mozart might form a family of his own to which he would owe his primary allegiance. "Suddenly you strike up a new acquaintanceship—with Herr Weber," he wrote, referring to the father of the young singer Aloysia Weber, with whom Mozart had fallen in love. "All your other friends are forgotten, now *this family* is the most honorable, the most Christian family and the daughter is to have the leading role in the tragedy to be enacted between your own family and hers!"[31] Distraught over Mozart's infatuation with Fräulein Weber and his attachment to her family, Leopold inveighed against the prospect of his son's marriage: "Now it depends solely on your good sense and your way of life whether you die as an ordinary musician, utterly forgotten by the world, or as a famous kapellmeister, of whom posterity will read—whether, captured by some woman, you die bedded on straw in an attic full of starving children, or whether, after a Christian life spent in contentment, honor, and renown, you leave this world with your family well provided for and your name respected by all."[32] Without significant exception, Leopold Mozart opposed or interfered with all of his son's love affairs, up to and including his marriage to Aloysia's sister, Constanze, in 1782, an event that rent the family fabric beyond repair.

Thus, when Wolfgang Amadeus Mozart first attempted to emerge from the bosom of his family, he discovered that his way was barred. His extraordinary family, rather than being a loving haven within which he could grow to maturity, had somehow come to resemble a kind of debtor's prison from which he could escape only by the most strenuous effort. Or, to shift metaphors, the family had come to resemble a miniature authoritarian society whose benevolent leader made every decision, organized all enterprises, and took complete responsibility, whose will was held to represent the interests of the commonweal. Within its tiny confines, the Mozart family illustrated the pathways by which a rationalist utopia may readily be transformed into a patriarchal autocracy.

Naturally, the Mozart children derived important benefits from their participation in the family covenant: approval, a sense of belonging, of being part of a greater enterprise. Control was exercised through a variety of techniques: the inculcation of guilt regarding desires for personal gratification; indoctrination of the idea of unlimited responsibility to the family as a whole; cultivation of tribal values—altruism and cooperation within, distrust and suspicion without; the alternation of caring, teaching, and nurturing with the threat to withhold love; and, at its most extreme, the threat of expulsion. At each sign of Mozart's resistance to family imperatives, the full weight of his father's coercive rationality was brought to bear upon him. And if this proved insufficient, his sister and his mother were conscripted to stand against him as well. Marianne Mozart did so unquestioningly, but Frau Mozart, with great qualms and mixed feelings, sought to shield her beloved son, and even, on occasion, like an inwardly recalcitrant servant of the state, to undermine her husband's instructions while appearing to carry them out. Nevertheless, when she perceived the possibility of losing her son to the Webers—"In short, he prefers other people to me," she wrote to Leopold—she helped to precipitate a series of events that had tragic consequences.[33]

Leopold Mozart had pictured his son as the ideal subject of an experiment in enlightenment, one he intended to record for posterity in a biography written by himself. Yet he would scarcely have acknowledged the justness of Rousseau's remark, in his *Discourse on Inequality,* that "by the law of nature the father continues master of his child no longer than the child stands in need of his assistance; that after that term they become equal, and that then the son entirely independent of the father, owes him no obedience, but only respect."[34] In contrast, true to the deep-rooted outlook of the artisan class from which he sprang, Leopold Mozart regarded his son as his personal economic resource and insurance against the calamities of old age.[35] Mozart was held to have an unlimited obligation to care for and support his family, to augment Leopold Mozart's salary, and to pay off the debt the father had supposedly incurred on his son's behalf. In the course of time, Mozart came to understand that his debts could never be paid in full.

"If you continue to pursue your empty hopes," Leopold Mozart wrote him, "you will make me and your sister into beggars."[36] He even came to imagine that his son had already brought him to poverty, and he did not hesitate to lay this charge upon him:

> I myself do not possess a kreuzer. I look like poor Lazarus. My dressing gown is so shabby that if somebody calls in the morning, I have to make myself scarce. My old flannel jerkin . . . is so torn that I can hardly keep it on any longer and I cannot afford to have either a new dressing gown or a new jerkin made. Since your departure I haven't had a single pair of new shoes, nor have I any black silk stockings left. On Sundays I wear old white stockings and during the week black woolen Berlin stockings, which I bought for 1 florin 12 kreuzer.[37]

There is no need to question Leopold Mozart's sincerity here: doubtless he felt abandoned, forlorn, and poverty-stricken as he faced the absence of his wife and son and the prospect of "losing" his son. But his claims of poverty were egregiously false. From Mozart's performances in earlier years, Leopold had been able to save very large sums, perhaps equivalent to more than fifty times his annual salary, and in light of his prudent stewardship there is no reason to believe that these sums had since been dissipated.[38]

Stunned by his father's lament, Mozart pledged to remain his loyal subject. "*Next to God comes Papa* was my motto or axiom as a child, and I still cling to it. . . . But I must tell you that I was absolutely horrified and that tears came into my eyes when I read in your last letter that you have to go about so shabbily dressed. My very dearest Papa! That is certainly not my fault—you know it is not! We economize in every possible way here; food and lodging, wood and light have cost us nothing, and what more can we want!"[39]

What more did Leopold Mozart want, indeed? As I will try to show, economic factors were only the surface of his motives, which also included an erotically tinged drive to dominate and a penchant for an almost Jamesian vicarious creativity, with Mozart serving as his father's sacred fount. And there may be a sense in which Mozart was appointed to assume the burden of his father's own earlier transgressions against God and family, both to repair past sins and to prevent future ones. Leopold's struggle to control his son was a desperate one, for he was seeking to preserve not merely the source of his surplus income but the integrity of his personality.

Leopold Mozart would not—indeed, could not—surrender his prerogatives, and he would try to thwart his son's every move toward independence and maturity. In the end, Mozart clearly understood that his father would never be reconciled to his departure for Vienna in 1781, his subsequent marriage, or even his brilliant career. He learned that his freedom would have to be purchased dearly.

It has become a commonplace of psychoanalytic aesthetics that art—on the Proustian model—seeks the reparation of loss, attempting to reconstruct a fragmented past, to memorialize and resurrect departed love objects. Whatever the partial validity of theories of art as restoration of the past, it seems clear that they are forms of piety to tradition and to ancestry, and often they are unmindful that recollection and forgetfulness are always intertwined, that creativity involves destruction as well as restoration, erasing and undoing as well as making and preserving. Surely, some part of the creative impulse aims to accomplish a separation from the dead, or at least from the paralysis of tradition.

That may be why the refusal of the past to stay put has often given rise to some bitterness: "All that has once lived clings tenaciously to life," wrote Freud in his last years. "Sometimes one feels inclined to doubt whether the dragons of primeval ages are really extinct."[40] From quite another perspective, Marx exclaimed, "We suffer not only from the living but from the dead. *Le mort saisit le vif!*"[41] The desire to alter or improve reality is the desire to give it over to a new generation, not only to restore it to an older one or to fulfill an ancient prophecy.

It may be that an impulse to recapture a real or fantasied era of personal bliss informed Mozart's creativity, though it seems equally likely that his elaboration of multiple alternative universes in his music was also powered by some discontent with the order of things. But throughout his life, Mozart struggled against the demands of his past, the survival of archaic patterns of behavior, and the incessant invocation of his childhood image, for these were largely insignia of the reenactment and perpetuation of ancient rites of submission. His father often lamented that Mozart neither respected the past nor considered the future: "The present alone engulfs you completely, and sweeps you off your feet."[42] In actuality, Mozart wanted to leave childhood and its subjections behind, to shatter the frozen perfection of the little porcelain violinist and to put in his place a living man, one with sexual appetites, bodily functions, irreverent thoughts, and selfish impulses, one who needed to live for himself and his loved ones and not only for those who had given him life. The altruistic impulse was too deeply rooted in him to be eradicated, but it desired to choose its objects freely and to expand beyond the tribal unit to larger entities; it wanted to demonstrate that not all men are malevolent, not all women bent upon ensnarement.

Though he ultimately founded his own family, attached himself to still other, idealized families, and joined what he viewed as the universal family of Freemasonry, Mozart nevertheless continued to yearn for the old relationships. In a sense, the pathos of Mozart is that of the freedman who discovers to his dismay that he still dreams of slavery, even with all its attendant terrors. Of course, a repetition compulsion is at work here—always returning to the scene of the crime, ever doubling back, going home, filled with disbelief, to confirm, to deny, and perhaps to revise a graven narrative, somehow symbolically to convert terror into beauty, dissonance into harmony, hostile attachment into unalloyed love. But also at work is the yearning to be needed, to be essential to the community, to be a child who labors eternally for the benefit of the family, whatever the cost.

The received view of Mozart as eternal child is the Mozart family's ideology writ large. It was inculcated in him by verbal force, contrived logic, and appeals to sentiment. Leopold Mozart repeatedly invoked their early relationship as a model of his expectations: "Those happy moments are gone," he wrote in February 1778, "when, as child and boy, you never went to bed without standing on a chair and singing to me 'Oragna fiagata fa,' and ending by kissing me again and again on the tip of my nose and telling me that when I grew old you would put me in a glass case and protect me from every breath of air, so that you might always have me with you and honor me."[43] He brought the child Mozart to bear against his mature self: "My son! You are hot-tempered and impulsive in all your ways! Since your childhood and boyhood your whole character has changed. As a child and a boy you were serious rather than childish and when you sat at the clavier or were otherwise intent on music, no one dared to have the slightest jest with you."[44] Now, he charged, Mozart permitted others "undue familiarity" and had become an easy prey to flatterers, "whereas as a boy you were so extraordinarily modest that you used to weep when people praised you overmuch."[45] The myth of Mozart as eternal child was utilized to perpetuate his subjection.

For a time the myth was also an impediment to his success as a mature composer and virtuoso, forcing him to contend with those who remained blinded by his fabulous career as a young prodigy. In 1770 Abbé Ferdinando Galiani wrote to Madame d'Épinay, from Naples, that "little Mosar is here, and that he is less of a miracle, although he is always the same miracle; but he will never be anything else than a miracle, and that is all."[46] Similarly, Mozart was described by Louis de Visme as "one further instance of early Fruit, which is more extraordinary than excellent."[47] In 1778 Mozart complained to his father about his reception in Paris: "What annoys me most of all here is that these stupid Frenchmen seem to think I am still seven years old, because that was my age when they first saw me."[48] His physical stature played into this perception. As late as 1780, at the last rehearsal of *Idomeneo,* the elector of Bavaria jested: "Who would believe that such great things could be hidden in so small a head?"[49] Mozart was not amused. And of Mannheimers who failed to treat him with respect, he observed, "They probably think that because I am little and young, nothing great or mature can come out of me," adding, with a touch of malice, "But they will soon see."[50]

Mozart's triumphs in Vienna put an end to these understandable misconceptions. But if, during his last decade, he had largely won the battle to be recognized as a man, his voice was stilled after his death while those of his father and sister dominated the discourse. "Wolfgang was small, thin, pale in color, and entirely lacking in any pretensions as to physiognomy and bodily appearance," reads an entry in Marianne Mozart's biographical notes and reminiscences in early 1792. "Apart from his music he was almost always a child, and thus he remained: and this is a main feature of his character on the dark side; he always needed a father's, a mother's or some other guardian's care. He married a girl quite unsuited to him, and against the will of his father, and thus the great domestic chaos at and after his death."[51] Mozart's first biographer, Friedrich Schlichtegroll, used these condescending formulations in his lengthy obituary notice, published in 1793, whence they made their way into many influential contemporary writings about Mozart.[52] The Mozart family's tendentious view of him prevailed with the publication of many of Leopold Mozart's voluminous letters in Georg Nissen's documentary biography of 1828. It was as though Leopold had posthumously managed to fulfill his ambition to write his son's biography, and in particular the story of their conflicts, from his own point of view. Mozart's widow, Constanze, who married Nissen and edited the biography, could have counteracted these trends, but instead elected to pose, in the words of Mozart's greatest biographer, Otto Jahn, "as a patient martyr, suffering from the thoughtlessness of a man of genius, who remained a child to the end of his days."[53]

Soon notions of Mozart's irresponsibility and childishness coalesced with other reports and fictions about the supposedly automatic, almost somnambulistic nature of his creative process. All this seemed to imply a channel between childhood and creativity that early Romantic aestheticians found irresistible, for it echoed their rediscovery in childhood of the mourned Golden Age.[54] Using Mozart as his primary example, and citing both Schlichtegroll and Nissen, Schopenhauer elevated this connection to a kind of principle of creativity, asserting that "every genius is already a big child, since he looks out into the world as something strange and foreign, a drama, and thus with purely objective interest."[55] Other purveyors of the Mozart-as-child myth viewed him not only as a child but as a simpleton or, to put it more kindly, a divine vessel. Hegel obviously had Mozart in mind when he wrote: "Musical talent declares itself as a rule in very early youth, when the head is still empty and the emotions have barely had a flutter; it has, in fact, attained real distinction at a time in the artist's life when both intelligence and life are practically without experience. And, for that matter, we often enough see very great achievement in musical composition and performance combined with considerable indigence of mind and character."[56]

This tendency to downgrade Mozart's character and intellect appeared quite early. By 1825 the violinist Karl Holz was writing of Mozart in Beethoven's conversation book, "Outside of his genius as a musical artist, Mozart was a *nullity*."[57] At century's end, the British composer and critic Hubert Parry declared that "Mozart was gifted with the most perfect and refined musical organization ever known; but he was not naturally a man of deep feeling or intellectuality."[58] And recently Wolfgang Hildesheimer has revived this antiquated but vigorous viewpoint, almost in Leopold Mozart's own words. Mozart, he writes, "was as great a stranger to the world of reason as to the sphere of human relations. He was guided solely by the aim of the moment."[59] Apparently, commentators feel the need to portray Mozart's nonconformism, his bohemianism, his liberated sexual attitudes, his critique of authority, his Freemasonry, as devoid of larger significance, as merely the reactions of a child to necessary constraints. "Don't take Mozart seriously" is their message, "he is only a child at play." It is but a short step from here to a denial of Mozart's capacity for feeling as well as reason: "Human ties, as we know them, were alien to him," says Hildesheimer. "He was relatively quick to get over human disappointments, and we do not know if they ever really touched him deeply at all."[60] Extending the claim that Mozart never felt the simple mortal pain that makes him our kin, the author of *Amadeus* is perplexed by references to Mozart's "suffering" and contends that "there is really not the slightest evidence, either in his own voluminous correspondence or in accounts of him by contemporaries, that Mozart ever suffered for his art."[61]

Nineteenth-century biographers found much to admire in the elder Mozart's exhortations to probity, piety, and family obligation, as well as in his descriptions of his own virtue, self-sacrifice, and wholesome influence upon his son, which, in Jahn's words, was "the foundation of [Mozart's] moral and social existence." Jahn pictured a Mozart who

> grew up in an atmosphere of conjugal and parental affection, of sincere religion and conscientious morality, and of well-ordered economy, which could not fail in its effect on his character. . . . We have seen, and shall see further, how fully Leopold Mozart deserved the trust reposed in him. It was absolute confidence, not timid fear, that bound wife and children to him, and candor and truth ruled all the family intercourse.
>
> Above all was the father's earnest devotion to duty, and his example gave weight to his unsparing demands on the labor and industry of his children. . . . He was not content to recognize in the wonderful receptive and productive powers of his son a passport to easy indolence, but strove to make him consider them as deposits to be turned to the best account by study and cultivation. He accustomed his children to work from their youth up, and made it his first object that their outer circumstances should afford them no excuse for idle hours.[62]

This became a dominant view, echoed to one degree or another in most conventional biographies of Mozart, but it was not the only one. Several influential scholars, unimpressed by Jahn's portrait of an exemplary life shaped within an ideal patriarchal family, read the Mozart correspondence in a quite different way. A few years after Jahn's biography was published, Ludwig Nohl wrote of Leopold Mozart's "unconscious feeling of mortification at his son's independence of action" and found it admirable that Mozart at last "shows his strength of character by no longer listening to his father's remonstrances."[63] In the first major revisionist biography, published in 1913, Arthur Schurig could not restrain his condemnation of Leopold; he described him as a "pedantic calculator" who sought to maintain Mozart "in unconditional slavery" and he observed that Leopold's "tyranny" had the unexpected result of forcing Mozart, against his own nature, to become "callous, reserved and, on occasion, even actually hypocritical" toward his father.[64] In England, at the same time, Edward J. Dent, in his now classic study of Mozart's operas, portrayed Leopold as a "rigid disciplinarian," a "disagreeable" personality who viewed any potential opponent as "a monster of jealousy and intrigue" and was incapable of grasping either his son's human dimension or his capacity for creative development: "Wolfgang was to be forced upon the world as a miraculous prodigy, and the iron was to be struck while it was hot; there was no reason to suppose that after he was grown up he would be anything more than a respectable professional musician like his father."[65] According to Dent, Leopold Mozart was "quite content to be a servant of the Archbishop himself and he could not understand why Wolfgang should be so rebellious. He was inwardly convinced that what really governed his son's actions was a love of pleasure and dissipation, and that once set free from paternal discipline he would merely lead a life of self-indulgence and extravagance."[66]

By the mid-twentieth century these antithetical opinions were still being reflected in Mozart scholarship. In an influential book, Alfred Einstein described Leopold as "no mean psychologist" and praised his patient handling of Mozart's "childish" tendencies.[67] But an equally outstanding musicologist of the same generation, Erich Hertzmann, believed that Leopold "tried to force Mozart into a position of emotional dependence." He wrote:

> The young Mozart idolized his father and tried to emulate him in every way; even his musical handwriting was the image of Leopold's. At the age of twenty-six he asked his father to write out the alphabet for him, in capital and small letters, so that he might continue to practice and improve his own hand. Only through the outward rebellion against the Archbishop was it possible for him to break loose from the strong domination of his father, whom he both loved and resented.[68]

It seems evident that, by this time, Hertzmann's view was not untouched by psychoanalytical thinking about fathers and sons. And indeed one has the sense of a digging of trenches on either side of an oedipal divide. Those who approved of Leopold Mozart's pedagogy necessarily found themselves supporting the view of Mozart as an eternal child, while those who were outraged by the father's actions understood Mozart's need and capacity for autonomy.

For the present, Mozart has largely lost the struggle to be regarded as something other than a child. The most venerable tropes have recently been revived, and to them we are even now adding new perceptions of Mozart the child, albeit now as the rebellious-patricidal-oedipal child or the polymorphous child of his bawdy letters to his cousin, the Bäsle, whom he loved so tenderly.

It is also true that the child images persist because Mozart himself often licensed them, with an ironic exaggeration usually lost on posterity. This shows itself in Mozart's comic attitude—his game playing, punning, riddling, obscenity, wit, and general propensity for outrageousness—which he could assume in a trice. In part this represented his "admission" that the family was correct to designate him an irresponsible child. It is as though he were saying, "You regard me as a child? Well, then, I *am* a child!" More interesting is that the comic seems to have opened for him a realm relatively free from compulsion, an arena in which he could—indirectly, mockingly—confront those who would infantilize him. No less than Hamlet, Mozart showed the world an antic disposition even as he pursued a momentous purpose whose fulfillment he would not long survive. But unlike Hamlet, Mozart eventually found the strength to stop playing his part, thereby establishing a zone of free will within which, however painfully, his creativity could come to fruition.

And so there may be something to be learned even from misreadings of Mozart's life. This is not altogether unexpected, for views of Mozart as a child waver between transcendence and tragedy, innocence and wisdom, and other extreme juxtapositions, covering much of the spectrum of mythic possibility. All of these are partial, one-sided, and reductionist, for they are attempts to understand a protean phenomenon by drastic simplification. As a "good child" Mozart knows his place in an orderly universe. As an "evil child" he ungratefully destroys his own father and mother. As "innocent child" his sexuality and darker impulses are sublimated into art and altruistic service. As "doomed child" and "ancient child" he symbolizes the transience of virtue, beauty, and life, the indissolubility of pleasure and pain. "What is a poet?" asked Kierkegaard in the opening words of *Either/Or:* "A poet"—by which he meant both himself and Mozart—"is an unhappy being whose heart is torn by secret sufferings, but whose lips are so strangely formed that when the sighs and the cries escape them, they sound like beautiful music. . . . And men crowd about the poet and say to him: 'Sing for us soon again'; that is as much as to say: 'May new sufferings torment your soul.'"[69] Finally, as the immortal "divine child," Mozart is the beloved of the gods, favorite of the muses, blessed with the genius to provide a temporary surcease from pain, a glimpse of felicity, a yearning for a remote horizon. It is ungracious to subject so consoling a view to close scrutiny. In the end, one wants to yield to the dreamlike image of Mozart that the young Schubert inscribed in his diary on 13 June 1816: "As from afar the magic notes of Mozart's music still gently haunt me. . . . They show us in the darkness of this life a bright, clear, lovely distance, for which we hope with confidence. O Mozart, immortal Mozart, how many, oh how endlessly many such comforting perceptions of a brighter and better life hast thou brought to our souls!"[70]

BEGINNINGS

Leopold Mozart, c. 1765. Unsigned oil portrait, attributed to Pietro
Antonio Lorenzoni. Mozart-Museum der Internationalen Stiftung
Mozarteum, Salzburg. © Mozarts Geburtshaus, Salzburg.

1

LEOPOLD MOZART

When Leopold Mozart died in 1787 at the age of sixty-seven, Lorenz Hagenauer's son, Dominikus Hagenauer, wrote in his diary that his father's late friend had been "a man of much wit and sagacity, who would have been capable of rendering good service to the State even apart from music," but that he "had the misfortune of being always persecuted here and was by far less beloved here than in other, greater places in Europe."[1] By several accounts, Mozart's father was a hard man to like. Nissen wrote, "In Salzburg he was regarded as a sardonic humorist."[2] His acerbic and dissatisfied nature was no secret to foreign observers either, among whom he acquired the reputation of being perpetually discontented. It is important to find the sources of this discontent, for it powered his restless, unrelenting search for fulfillment and thereby became central to his family's sense of purpose and obligation.

Leopold Mozart sprang from a family of artisans who had lived for generations in the South German city of Augsburg. His mother, Anna Maria Sulzer (1696–1766), was the eldest daughter of Christian Sulzer, a weaver from Baden-Baden who had come to Augsburg in 1695, and his wife Dorothea, née Baur, who was a weaver's daughter. On 1 May 1718 Anna Maria married Johann Georg Mozart (1679–1736), who came from a family of artisans and masons but had chosen to apprentice himself as a bookbinder. The entry in the town marriage registry reads, "Johann Georg Mozer, a bookbinder, widowed, and Anna Maria Sulzer, single, both of this place; his witness Johann Georg Mozer, master mason; her witness Christian Sulzer, weaver."[3] Mozart's grandfather, a master bookbinder, had succeeded to his employer's guild license by marrying his widow, Anna Maria Banegger, in 1708; childless, she had died earlier in 1718. Leopold Mozart was the newlyweds' first child; he was baptized Johann Georg Leopold Mozart at St. George's Church in Augsburg on 14 November 1719. Seven more children were born to the couple by 1735; three boys and two girls survived, and all but one of these lived long lives.

The Catholic Church was the center of the Mozart family's life. They were members of the congregation of the Assumption of the Holy Virgin, the larger of two congregations run by the Marian Brotherhood in Augsburg. From 1722 they lived in a house in the Jesuitengasse owned by the Jesuit Order. Johann Georg sent his two oldest sons, Leopold and Johann Christian, to the nearby Jesuit gymnasium of St. Salvator, one of the region's leading seats of humanistic education, drawing its pupils from Augsburg's aristocratic and bourgeois families as well as from "people of standing" in neighboring Bavaria, Swabia, and Austria.[4] Leopold, whose godfather was Georg Grabherr, a prominent churchman and canon at St. Peter's, was apparently intended for the priesthood. That may have been one reason he very early became a choirboy in the monasteries of Heiligen Kreuz and St. Ulrich.

The course and content of Leopold Mozart's education is important to understand because he was to be his son's main instructor in virtually every branch of learning. The St. Salvator Gymnasium offered a rigorous six-year program of instruction, followed, for those deemed capable of pursuing the study of philosophy, by a two- or three-year term in the St. Salvator Lyceum. The curriculum centered on logic, science, theology, and rhetoric; spoken and written mastery of Latin were required, as was sufficient Greek to understand the New Testament in the original. Students were taught mathematics and the physical sciences; it was doubtless at St. Salvator that Leopold Mozart acquired his abiding interest in telescopes and microscopes.

An outstanding singer and proficient violinist, he participated in many of the school's annual celebratory performances, appearing in at least eight theater pieces as actor and singer between 1724 and 1736.[5] After several years of preparatory studies, which began before he was five, Leopold was enrolled as a first-year student (*Principista*) perhaps as early as the fall of 1727 and graduated magna cum laude in 1735. Despite his intelligence, however, he seems to have been left back for one or even two years, so that it may have taken him seven or eight years to complete the six-year course at the gymnasium.[6] Perhaps he was ill, or perhaps this was an early sign of his resistance to being educated for the priesthood. Indeed, there is a striking mention of that resistance in the reminiscences of a schoolmate, court counselor Franziskus Erasmus Freysinger, whom Mozart met in Munich in

October 1777 and who vividly recalled Leopold Mozart's Augsburg days: "*Ah, he was a great fellow. My father thought the world of him. And how he hoodwinked the clerics about becoming a priest!*"[7] Even in Leopold Mozart's later years, he often had harsh and sarcastic words for the priesthood, drawing a sharp line between his faith and those who administered it.[8]

Leopold entered the St. Salvator Lyceum in October 1735, but the death of his father soon thereafter, on 19 February 1736, unexpectedly disrupted the orderly progress of his education. In June 1736, three months before the end of his first school year, he abruptly broke off his studies at the lyceum, and on 4 August he was granted a withdrawal certificate.[9] That brought him to a crossroads: he now had to decide whether to resume his education, to take some role in his father's workshop, or to pursue some other profession, perhaps in music, for which he had already shown so pronounced a talent.

Leopold chose to resume his education, and on 26 November 1737, after a hiatus of one year, he matriculated at the Benedictine University in Salzburg as a student of philosophy and jurisprudence.[10] But his formal schooling prematurely came to a dramatic conclusion, for in September 1739 the rector expelled him from the university for want of application and poor attendance.[11] His calm reaction was remarked by the authorities:

> Johann Georg Mozart, a Swabian of Augsburg, has from the beginning of the civil year hardly attended Natural Science more than once or twice, and has thereby rendered himself unworthy of the name of student. A few days before the examination he was called before the Dean and informed that henceforth he would no longer be numbered among the students. Having heard this sentence, he offered no appeals, accepted the sentence, and departed as if indifferent: therefore he was not called for further examination.[12]

Leopold Mozart promptly obtained a position as chamberlain and musician with a prominent Salzburg canon, Count Johann Baptist Thurn-Valsassina und Taxis.[13] And in 1740 he made his debut as a composer with six Trio Sonatas, op. 1, which he gratefully dedicated to his patron, the benevolent "paternal sun" who had rescued him from "the harsh darkness of necessity and smoothed the path to the horizon of good fortune."

His expulsion from the university together with his embrace of a musician's career in a foreign city surely was a stunning rebuff to Leopold Mozart's family, confirming the worst implications of his sudden withdrawal from the lyceum. We do not know what impelled this repudiation of his family's expectations, which followed so closely on his father's death.

Perhaps his faith had been shaken by the loss and he now entered into a quarrel with God and his earthly representatives. Perhaps his father's death liberated him from the compulsions of authority. Or perhaps he shrank from the prospect of assuming his father's place as head of the family. From the admittedly circumscribed perspective of his Augsburg peers, however, Leopold Mozart had served his family badly. He had shamed it by his expulsion and dashed its hopes that he might achieve a distinguished career in the church. Moreover, on a simpler level his actions could be interpreted as an abandonment of his mother, recently widowed and burdened with raising five children ranging in age from eight to seventeen. Whatever his inner motivations, the family's eldest son seemed to have shirked his responsibilities to his mother as well as to St. Salvator, the university, the church, and not least to the city of his birth, for he was to remain in Salzburg for the rest of his life.

Despite her son's defection, the widow Mozart survived and even prospered. Her two youngest sons took up their father's profession, eventually qualifying as master bookbinders; her daughters married well; and the family workshop remained active for many decades under the direction of her youngest son, Franz Aloys (1727–91). In 1744 her own father died, bequeathing to her some property in the Georgenstrasse. A strong-willed personality, she had a litigious streak, evidenced by conflicts with the owners of neighboring properties. In 1756 her complaint against the district inspector was dismissed by the court as "futile and ungrounded."[14] Leopold Mozart was to learn that she did not take perceived rebuffs any more lightly than he himself did.

It is amply clear that she did not approve of her eldest son's marriage in November 1747 to Anna Maria Pertl, the daughter of an impoverished family. And it may well be that he now attempted to gain her consent to the marriage—along with an anticipated dowry—by giving the impression that he might return to Augsburg, or at least that he intended to remain an Augsburg citizen. That was surely one of his motives in applying for a renewal of his Augsburg citizenship, which automatically lapsed for anyone residing in a foreign city for more than three years without official sanction. Of course, it was not the only motive: citizenship itself was an honor, so Augsburg citizenship would give him greater status in Salzburg while keeping the door open for a return home in case things went badly for him at the archiepiscopal court. In any event, in a petition of 12 December 1747 to the Augsburg Town Council he asked for confirmation of his citizenship, for permission to marry, and for the right to continue his residence in Salzburg. The petition is a breathtaking study in prevarication and concealment. He refers to himself as the son of an Augsburg burgher and continues:

My father is a still-living bookbinder, who recently posted me to Salzburg
for my studies, and which I assiduously attended to. Now, however, it
happened that in the aforesaid city, aided by the high recommendation of
the Princely Archiepiscopal Court and gracious authorities, I have been
engaged as a chamber servant [*Cammerdiener*]. . . . At the same time I have
the good fortune to marry a wealthy burgher's daughter and set up housekeeping. . . . Out of respect for my upright old father, [I petition] to
continue my nonresident dwelling and to maintain my citizenship with
payment in advance of the customary tax.[15]

We know, however, that his father was long dead and could not have
sent him to the Benedictine University in Salzburg. We also know that
Leopold had not diligently pursued his studies there, that he had not
resided in Salzburg for only a short time, that he was not employed at the
court as a chamber servant, and that his bride was not a wealthy burgher's
daughter. Moreover, he was evasive about the fact that he was already married (the marriage had taken place three weeks before the petition was
posted). The main purpose of this reckless string of falsehoods is not hard
to find: the laws denied citizenship not only to those who took up foreign
residence and failed to renew citizenship every three years, but also to
those who married without official consent. Furthermore, marriage consent for a citizen residing abroad was contingent on demonstrating ownership of household goods plus cash equivalent to 200 florins, as well as payment of a substantial license fee. Leopold Mozart accordingly painted a
rosy picture of his circumstances, concealing his ten-year residence in
Salzburg and his true status as a poorly paid musician married to a poor
young woman. There is no obvious explanation for the extraordinary
assertion that his father was still alive, for as Mančal points out, "If
Leopold's father were indeed then still alive, that fact would be wholly
unimportant, since Leopold would already have received citizenship at his
birth."[16] This was a flagrant and gratuitous falsehood, and the risk of being
discovered in this patent lie was extremely high.[17] We may wonder whether
Leopold Mozart was willing to take this chance in order symbolically to
bring his father back to life, thereby to conjure an approving paternal
presence at his wedding. Whatever his reasons, in decrees of 30 January
1748 and 6 February 1748 the Town Council and the Marriage Bureau
granted his petition in every respect, upon payment of a fee of nine
florins.[18]

Leopold Mozart's realistic agenda was clear: to gain consent for his
marriage from the Augsburg authorities and from his mother, who apparently was still willing to believe that her son would someday come home.
Called before the Town Council as a witness, she testified to his intent to

marry. Perhaps she was unaware that he was already married, for it is hard to believe that she was colluding with him in deceiving the town council on this point. Three years later, she presented another application to the Augsburg authorities for a renewal of his citizenship (again, the fee was 9 florins).[19] But she was not altogether trusting; perhaps in an attempt to hold him to a promise to return, she withheld the substantial dowry of 300 florins—more than a year's salary for him—that she gave to each of her other children upon their marriages.

This embittered Leopold Mozart. He wrote to an Augsburg friend, the printer Johann Jakob Lotter, on 21 July 1755, "All of my brothers and sisters have now married; and each has received 300 florins as an advance upon my mother's future legacy. . . . I have not received anything."[20] Wary and fearful of rejection, he asked Lotter, who was about to publish Leopold's *Versuch einer gründlichen Violinschule (Treatise on the Fundamental Art of Violin Playing)* at its author's expense, to let Frau Mozart know that the sum of 300 florins was needed to cover the printing cost. So tenuous had his connection with his mother become that he was unable to make the request himself, resorting instead to this indirect approach, which he called a "strategy of war." Indeed, in his agitated state, he stood ready to consign his mother to the devil if she rejected his transparent ruse, as he had every reason to anticipate she would; if she failed to pay the money, he wrote angrily, "she can go to Hell today or tomorrow."[21] Later on, he posed similar extreme choices of submission or damnation to his only son. As was often the case in his relationship to his son, money came to stand for a variety of emotion-laden issues: to be denied the legacy was to be disowned by his family, whereas its receipt would have signaled the acceptance of his marriage and his return to equal standing among the Augsburg Mozarts.

In September 1755 Leopold decided to travel to Augsburg to take up the matter once more. He informed Lotter of this in a letter of 11 September 1755, which shows his uncertainty about his reception: "I am thinking of staying with my [mother]. But who knows, perhaps she doesn't have room to lodge me, because not only my two brothers, but particularly also my two sisters are now married; so there certainly will not be any other beds left over except for herself and for one maid." Persuaded by his own argument, he added: "Perhaps you can find a good friend who will shelter me," a broad hint that Lotter put him up.[22] A postscript revealed the extent of his bad feelings about his siblings: "Don't talk too much about my arrival, *it has to do with my brothers and sisters,* they might spoil the business with my mother." He wanted to be reconciled with his mother, hoping she would make room for him, though fearing that his brothers and sisters had displaced him from the family home. But there was little prospect that he would succeed either at peacemaking or at obtaining the money, probably because he was unable to disentangle the two goals and make a simple appeal for forgiveness. His bitterness at presumed injustice prevented him from realizing that his mother felt she had sufficient cause for grievance.

After one more indirect approach through Lotter, he finally came to understand that the issue was closed for good. On 15 December he wrote Lotter, "It is unfortunately all too true, even though she remains my mother a thousand times over, that she is wretched and has very little sense. The latter is indeed not her fault and, similarly, the former is God's will. However, it is her fault if she gradually comes to a bad end; for she doesn't trust me, although I am her own child; meanwhile, however, she lets the other children do her out of what is hers."[23] A grim silence now separated a mother and her eldest son, for this was the last significant reference to Leopold Mozart's mother in the family correspondence.[24] She lived until 11 December 1766, but the rift between them was never healed. Indeed, it became absolute, affecting the entire family; of her children, only the amiable Franz Aloys maintained close ties with Leopold Mozart and his family. Her name does not appear in any family correspondence during Mozart's lifetime, and although she was still alive when Wolfgang and Marianne gave three public concerts in Augsburg in June and July 1763, she did not attend them, so deep was the estrangement. It is daunting to picture the Augsburg Mozarts remaining stubbornly at home during the concerts and to imagine their reactions when they read the newspaper reports telling how Leopold Mozart "afforded the inhabitants of his native city the pleasure of hearing the effect of the extraordinary gifts which the Great God has bestowed on these two dear little ones in such abundant measure; gifts of which the Herr Kapellmeister has, as a true father, taken care with such indefatigable zeal."[25] Clearly, his Augsburg family would not give Leopold the satisfaction of welcoming him as a returning hero. His disappointment was evident: "Those who came to the concerts were almost all Lutherans," he wrote, which is to say that the Catholic community as a whole evidently abstained from celebrating his triumphs.[26]

As far as we know, Leopold Mozart's mother never met her son's wife, nor did she ever see either of his gifted children, her grandchildren. Presumably Wolfgang and Marianne Mozart were told how their father had been wronged by his mother and deprived of his birthright; certainly they were never informed of his own responsibility for the family estrangement. In her biographical notes, Marianne Mozart wrote that her father "came to Salzburg to study at the university, then became valet to Count Thurn."[27] She evidently had no knowledge of his Augsburg education, let alone the details of his university attendance and expulsion. Understandably, Leopold left the matter discreetly vague in the data he furnished for the German critic Friedrich Wilhelm Marpurg's survey of the Salzburg musical establishment in 1757: "He . . . entered the archiepiscopal service in the year 1743 soon after completing his studies in philosophy and law."[28] When Mozart, by chance, learned that his father had resisted a priestly vocation while still a boy in Augsburg, Leopold was not pleased that the subject had surfaced: "So nothing can be kept secret. You know how often I have said to you: *No matter how tightly we weave, everything will come to light.*"[29]

Leopold Mozart's flight from Augsburg and his withdrawal from the university eloquently expressed both his refusal to submit to authority and his desire to make a career in music. After two years of service to Count Thurn-Valsassina und Taxis, during which he made his first appearance as a composer with such works as a passion cantata and a Latin school drama entitled *Antiquitas personata,* he began his upward progress as a musician in the employ of Salzburg's prince-archbishops, augmenting his small income by giving private violin lessons. In 1743 he was appointed fourth violinist in the court orchestra; in 1758 he rose to the post of second violin; by 1759 he was listed as one of Salzburg's three "court composers";[30] and in 1763 he was named deputy kapellmeister. This was to be his highest rank, for he was repeatedly passed over for kapellmeister. We may deduce from Dominikus Hagenauer's diary entry that this was largely due to his difficult personality, and perhaps also to his numerous absences, rather than to any defects in his capabilities as a musician.

Leopold Mozart's outwardly courtly manner was insufficient to mask his contempt for the powerful, which overflowed even into his treatise on violin playing, where a discussion of ornamented violin scrolls serves as a pretext to inveigh against the bewigged classes of society.

> The violin—who would believe it!—is a victim of the universal deception of external appearance. He who values a bird for its feathers, a horse for its blanket, will also inevitably judge a violin by its polish and the color of its varnish. . . . This course is taken by all those who judge with their eyes and not with their brains. The beautifully "curled" lion's head [scroll] can improve the tone of the violin just as little as a fancifully curled wig can improve the intelligence of its living wig stand. Yet in spite of this, many a violin is valued simply for its appearance, and how often does it happen that clothes, money, pomp, and especially the curled wig is that which turns a man into a scientist, counselor, or doctor?[31]

Elsewhere in the treatise, Leopold asked, "Are not the best and most gifted people often in the greatest poverty?"[32] Clearly, in addition to pro-

pounding the Enlightenment maxim that merit ought to prevail over prerogatives of wealth and of birth, Leopold Mozart had a deep sense of the
underlying unfairness of existing social privilege. It is difficult, however, to
regard these statements as a "radical philosophical critique" of absolutism,
as Mančal does,[33] for they primarily exemplify their author's corrosive attitude toward those in superior social positions, constituting a critique of
undeserved privilege rather than any altruistic vision of a more just society.
To be the son of a bookbinder in an Augsburg social milieu dominated by
patricians and their sons was, for Leopold Mozart, to be steeped in gall.
"Everyone knows about the beggarliness of the patricians and every honest
man there laughs about it," he wrote, after an incident in Augsburg where
Mozart and his uncle, Leopold's brother Franz Aloys, were treated conde-
scendingly; "That is why they are *in the pay of the rich merchants,* who can
get anything for money from their hungry superiors. . . . The sole privilege
that the young patricians have ever claimed and still do claim—to jeer at
others, whenever an opportunity presents itself. Therein consists their great
nobility."[34] He remained constitutionally incapable of simple obedience to
his superiors, and his deep resentment of authority frequently erupted in
imprudent words or actions.

On one dramatic occasion, his behavior bordered on heresy. In 1753
he was called before the magistrate of the Salzburg cathedral and charged
with having printed a libel of two prominent citizens, a priest named
Egglstainer and one of the counts of Thurn und Taxis. The cathedral
archives record that Leopold Mozart's offending pamphlet was "torn to bits
and scattered at his feet"; he was commanded to apologize, "failing which
the author of the invidious pamphlet will be remanded to prison for well-
merited punishment."[35] By then he had been in the employ of the archbishop for ten years and was a long-standing member of the Salzburg community, one who hoped for eventual advancement to the highest rank of
his profession, court kapellmeister. He surely understood that his prospects
in Salzburg had now been severely damaged and that it might be wise to
explore possibilities elsewhere. The depth of his rage at this public humiliation can only be imagined. Nor would he have had any reason to doubt
the resolve of his superiors to mete out a harsh punishment; after all, he
had arrived in Salzburg only a few years after the persecution and forcible
expulsion from the province of thirty thousand Lutherans, or one seventh
of the total population, by order of Archbishop Firmian.[36]

Indeed, as we encounter in his letters additional instances of Leopold
Mozart's disdain for Catholic priests, monks, Jesuits, canons, and other
clerics, and as we consider these in connection with his resistance to a
career in the church, we begin to wonder whether he had not perhaps
undergone a crisis of faith, or even contemplated conversion. It is clear that

he was a nonconformist, and it may be that he was drawn for a time to some form of Protestantism (possibly Lutheranism) before returning to Catholic orthodoxy, though the evidence for this is wholly circumstantial and inconclusive. We know that he maintained close friendships in Augsburg with only a few people, especially with the printer Lotter and the organ and clavier builder Johann Andreas Stein, both of whom were Lutherans. His contacts with Augsburg's musical life were largely with Lutherans, who made up most of the membership of the Collegium Musicum there and were the main supporters of the Mozart children's concerts in June and July 1763, as Leopold noted. (Possibly the Catholic community avoided the concerts not only out of solidarity with their Augsburg Mozart neighbors but also because Leopold Mozart's Catholic credentials were somehow suspect.)

In 1755 he ordered from Lotter works by two noted Lutheran literary figures—the poet, essayist, and playwright Christian Fürchtegott Gellert and the rhetorician and linguist Johann Christoph Gottsched.[37] Leopold's views of aesthetics closely parallel those of Gottsched, who himself echoed ideas of conventional French neoclassicism. And Gellert's works had a special resonance for Leopold, who wrote to the poet expressing his admiration in such glowing terms that Gellert, in a heartfelt response, thanked him for his expressions of "love and friendship" and for his "beautiful, eloquent, and sensitive letter."[38] In 1764 a Lutheran friend of Leopold's apparently gave Mozart a copy of Gellert's most famous book, *Geistliche Oden und Lieder* (Leipzig, 1757), perhaps in its third edition (Berlin, 1764).[39] This book of sacred verse appealed not only to Protestants but also to nominal Catholics attracted by the idea of an unmediated connection between believers and their God. (Beethoven set eight of Gellert's devotional poems, op. 48). In August 1763, Leopold made it a point to visit the church in Worms "where Luther appeared before the Council,"[40] and in Cologne a few months later he viewed an ancient pulpit at the cathedral, writing home that "Luther is supposed to have preached from this pulpit."[41] There is no way of knowing if these visits were pilgrimages or merely the detours of a cultivated sightseer who wanted to communicate the details of his passion for things historical to his compatriots in Salzburg.

In his later years, Leopold Mozart outwardly controlled his heretical tendency, if such it was, regulating his relationship toward his church "with the same strict exactitude with which he governed his household," in Abert's words.[42] There is no doubt about his later devotion to the Catholic faith: he attended Mass and regularly received Communion and went to confession. He urged minute observance upon his family: "Is it necessary for me to ask whether Wolfgang is not perhaps getting a little lax about confession?" he wrote in a letter of 1777 to his wife and son. "God must come first! From His hands we receive our temporal happiness; and at the same time we must think of our eternal salvation. Young people do not like to hear about these things, I know, for I was once young myself. But, thank God, in spite of all my youthful foolish pranks, I always pulled myself together. I avoided all dangers to my soul and ever kept God and my honor and the consequences, the *very dangerous consequences,* before my eyes."[43]

In the course of time, it seems, Leopold Mozart had learned lessons in caution and diplomacy. He had lost his appetite for unequal contests from which he could not emerge victorious. Nevertheless, his discontents were scarcely appeased and perpetually sought new outlets, which were always readily at hand, in the person of enemies and adversaries—"wicked liars, slanderers and envious creatures"—bent on thwarting his ambitions.[44] "You see how one has to fight one's way through the world," he wrote to Lorenz Hagenauer in 1768. "If a man has no talents, he is unhappy enough; but if he has, envy pursues him in proportion to his ability."[45] Leopold's broad education and contact with Enlightenment thought did not instill in him a Rousseauean belief in fraternity or in man's innate goodness. "Mark well, my son," he once wrote, "that *to find one man in a thousand* who is your true friend from unselfish motives is to find *one of the great wonders of this world.*"[46] Compounding his constitutional dissatisfaction and mistrust was his sense—pervasive, yet nonspecific—of having been deeply wronged, which in turn required that he find some means to restore his status and to pay back his persecutors.

Eventually, he came to feel that musical composition was inadequate to his ambitions. Whether or not he aspired to greatness as a composer, he did not achieve it, remaining a prolific and competent craftsman who composed large quantities of music as required by his employer, particularly between 1740 and the early 1760s. He wrote in many of the standard genres, both secular and sacred: passions and oratorios, theater pieces, symphonies, serenades, concertos for solo wind instruments, trios and divertimentos, and hundreds of smaller pieces. It speaks for the workmanship of his music that several incomplete masses by him—the Missa brevis in C, K. 115/166d, and the Missa brevis in F, K. 116/90a—were until recently attributed to his son. Also, the so-called "New Lambach" Symphony in G, which scholars have ascribed to Mozart on grounds of its advanced stylistic features, seems actually to have been written by his father.[47] Occasionally revived are some of his programmatic instrumental works, such as "Sinfonia burlesca," "Sleigh Ride" ("Schlittenfahrt"), "Pastoral Symphony," "Divertimento militaire," and "Peasant Wedding" ("Bauernhochzeit") which utilize realistic and imitative devices and embody a kind of rustic comedy that never quite attains to the level of wit. Abert, seeking works by

Leopold Mozart to praise, particularly admired the piano sonatas of 1759–63, modeled on sonatas by Wagenseil, Scarlatti, and C. P. E. Bach.[48] Einstein judged him to be an undistinguished composer, noting his diffi- culty in adjusting to the shift from the Baroque to the *galant* style.[49] In Cliff Eisen's sober appraisal, however, he was "a thoroughly up-to-date, compe- tent composer whose works were comparable in style and quality to Wolf- gang's earliest symphonies."[50]

Although he had sacrificed family ties and expectations in order to become a musician, Leopold Mozart did not find his true vocation in a musician's career. He resented having to play in the court orchestra and dis- dained giving lessons. After a while he composed only as a necessary com- ponent of his duties and as a means of advancement, and he absented him- self from his responsibilities at every opportunity. Clearly, he had difficulty in finding his calling. His letters show that he wanted status and renown, but he appeared to want these more for their own sake than as the by- products of an achieved creativity. In any event, whether from lack of com- mitment or lack of superior talent, his career as a court musician stalled. Apart from being repeatedly passed over for the post of kapellmeister, Leopold Mozart failed to make his mark as a composer. In Salzburg, writes Schmid, "despite his archbishop's court title, he always had to stand some- what in the shadows of [the composers] Eberlin, Adlgasser and Michael Haydn."[51]

By the mid-1750s, Leopold Mozart was casting about for opportunities outside Salzburg. In 1755 and 1756 he had hopes of finding success in Augsburg, where his music was cultivated by the members of the Col- legium Musicum, but performances of his "Peasant Wedding" and "Sleigh Ride" there in January 1756 had no sequels. Accordingly, he began to con- sider a change of direction. At the least, in the train of the Egglstainer scan- dal, he determined to augment his career as a musician and music teacher by becoming an author; in fact, the offending pamphlet may perhaps be regarded as his first known effort as a writer. His violin method, written mostly in 1755 and published in 1756, was very well received; it was trans- lated into Dutch (1766) and French (1770), and had two further German editions (1769, 1787) during its author's lifetime. As Eisen observes, it was primarily because of this book that from 1758 on, Leopold Mozart's name began to appear with some frequency in dictionaries and works on music and musical pedagogy.[52]

Over the next decades he occasionally referred to books in progress: in 1767 he first mentioned his plan to write a biography of his young son,[53] and in 1778 he declared his intention to prepare a comprehensive peda- gogic work dealing with voice, clavier, and composition.[54] In an epilogue to the third German edition of the *Violinschule,* issued in the very year of his death, he renewed his promise to publish such a work: "I shall perhaps venture to bestow upon the musical world another book. I should unfailingly have so ventured, had not my travels hindered me."[55] No outlines, notes, or drafts for this book survive. Leopold Mozart published nothing after 1757, failing to consolidate his career as a music theorist and pedagogue. Similarly, his period of productivity as a composer came to a premature end: allowing the widest latitude, the Mozart authority Wolfgang Plath notes that he "seems to have composed rarely after 1762 and not at all from 1771."[56] Eisen observes that although he continued to perform his works until 1771 or so, and occasionally to revise earlier compositions, "there is no unequivocal evidence that Leopold Mozart composed even a single completely new work after 1762."[57]

In a 1776 letter to the Italian composer Padre Martini, signed by Mozart but actually written by his father, this lack of productivity is disingenuously explained as resulting from discrimination: "My father is in the service of the Cathedral. . . . He has already served this court for thirty-six years and as he knows that the present archbishop cannot and will not have anything to do with people who are getting on in years, he no longer puts his whole heart into his work, but has taken up literature, which was always a favorite study of his."[58] Mozart's sister, too, felt the need to justify her father, recording that by the late 1750s, "He entirely gave up his violin lessons and his composing so as to devote all the time remaining to him after his princely duties to the education of his two children."[59]

Marianne was closer to the mark, for Leopold Mozart did eventually find his calling: to raise, to educate, and to become the impresario of his children, and especially of Wolfgang Amadeus Mozart, an occupation to which he devoted himself wholeheartedly and with fervor, for it offered him not only unimagined vistas of worldly success and personal fulfillment but a way to exact satisfaction for past injustices and humiliations. He was explicit about these expectations in his letters, writing on one occasion that his son "will certainly do his utmost to win glory, honor, and money in order to help us and to save his father from the scornful mockery and sneers of certain persons, whose names I dare not mention, but whose ridicule would, as you know, most certainly send me to my grave. Wolfgang's good fortune and success will be our sweetest revenge."[60] Even before Mozart was five years old, Leopold Mozart had glimpsed the possibility that his son's musical talent might serve as an instrument of his own ambitions and as a means of quenching the burning sense of injustice that had been engendered in him by the circumstances of his earlier life.

Interior courtyard of Mozart's birth house, Getreidegasse 9, Salzburg. Unsigned photograph. Mozart-Museum der Internationalen Stiftung Mozarteum, Salzburg. © Mozarts Geburtshaus, Salzburg.

2

....

EARLY DAYS

On 21 November 1747, after a courtship of considerable length, Leopold Mozart, twenty-eight, married the slightly younger Anna Maria Pertl—"I joined the Order of Patched Trousers" is how he put it in a letter to Lorenz Hagenauer.[1] We know about the extended engagement because in 1772, while far from home, Leopold wrote to his wife in Salzburg in his dry, humorous way, "Today is the anniversary of our wedding day. It was twenty-five years ago, I think, that we had the sensible idea of getting married, one which we had cherished, it is true, for many years. All good things take time!"[2] There is a deserved hint of self-congratulation in Leopold's letter, for it had indeed been a good match: the couple had come up in the world during the intervening quarter century, and had worked hard for their success.

Mozart's mother was born on 25 December 1720 in St. Gilgen on the shore of Lake Aber, near Salzburg.[3] Her father was Wolfgang Nikolaus Pertl (1667–1724); her mother was Eva Rosina Puxbaum, née Altmann (1688?–1755), who was a widow when she married Pertl on 22 November 1712. Her father and first husband had been church musicians. The marriage register records Anna Maria's parents' marriage, with minor inaccuracies: "United in matrimony the noble and industrious Nicolaus Wolfgangus Pertl, learned in both [canon and civil] law, secretary to the Salzburg Exchequer, and the noble Euphrosina Puxbaum, widow."[4] They had three girls, an infant who was born and died in 1713, Maria Rosina Gertrud (born on 24 August 1719), who died before she was nine, and Mozart's mother.

Nikolaus Pertl, born into an old Salzburg family of court servants and artisans, was one of the most talented of Mozart's ancestors and was the first in his family to pursue a higher career, one usually reserved for aristocrats or the sons of officials.[5] He attended the Benedictine University in Salzburg and in his younger years was active as a musician, singing bass at St. Peter's Abbey and teaching at the monastery school. After completing his university studies in jurisprudence he held several posts in Salzburg, Vienna, and Graz, but after his marriage he moved to the Carinthian town of St. Andrae, where he served as district superintendent until he was stricken by a near-fatal, disabling illness in 1715. When he recovered, he managed to obtain a lesser post as deputy superintendent of Hüttenstein near St. Gilgen, but at a reduced annual salary of 250 florins. Soon he fell heavily into debt, from which he never emerged; his debts totaled 1,141 florins upon his death on 7 March 1724, causing his effects to be confiscated.[6] Although a portion of the debt was forgiven, his family, which moved back to Salzburg, now had to lead a threadbare existence on a charity pension of only 8 florins per month, increased to 9 florins per month after 1727.

The second daughter's death in 1728 left Frau Pertl and Anna Maria as the sole survivors. Thereafter, as might be expected of so humble a family unit, the documentary record is a scanty one. In 1729 mother and daughter lived in the Tragassen-Viertel next to the town hall. It seems highly probable—"at least conceivable," writes Valentin—that they supplemented their tiny income by handiwork or domestic employment.[7] Anna Maria was described in a 1733 document as "constantly ailing" (*immerdar unbässlich*), a description repeated in 1739 in an imprecisely spelled official report that characterized her as "the constantly ill bedridden daughter" (*der immerdar krankh ligenten Tochter*), without further details.[8] By 1742 they were living at Getreidegasse 48, the same street on which, five years later, Leopold Mozart and Anna Maria Pertl, now Frau Mozart, started their first household as a married couple. The marriage is recorded in the cathedral parish records for 21 November 1747:

> The noble Leopold Mozarth [*sic*], violinist to the Court, legitimate son of the most virtuous Johann Georg Mozart, book-binder, of Augsburg, and of Maria Anna Sulzer his wife, to the noble and chaste maiden Maria Anna, legitimate daughter of the noble Nicolaus Pertl, Deputy Prefect at [Hüttenstein] and Eva Rosina Altmann his wife.[9]

That Mozart's mother should have elected to marry a musician appears no more surprising than that her husband's sisters both married bookbinders, members of their father's profession, or that her own mother, the daughter of a musician, successively married two capable musicians.

The Mozarts—presumably along with Anna Maria's mother, who died in December 1755—took up residence on the third floor of the wholesale merchant Lorenz Hagenauer's house at Getreidegasse 9. During their six-teen-year residence at that address, Frau Mozart bore seven children, five of whom did not long survive.[10] Following the death of her third child, in late July 1750, she was sent to the spa at Bad Gastein for a medicinal cure. With his customary total recall of family events, her husband remembered both her stay and its cost in a letter of 1786 to his daughter: "It cost 12 ducats to send her to the spa at Gastein, although I only earned a salary of 29 florins 30 kreuzer per month. Yes, I traveled there myself by carriage to fetch her."[11] He did not know that she had left a little rhymed couplet in the hotel's testimonial book for 12 August 1750:

> I thank the Almighty for what I found
> During ninety-five hours in this noble spa.[12]

Less than a year later, on 30 or 31 July 1751, Mozart's sister Maria Anna Walburga Ignatia, known as Marianne and familiarly as Nannerl, was born; she was to live a long life, dying on 29 October 1829 at the age of seventy-eight.

On 15 December 1755 Leopold Mozart wrote to Lotter, his friend and publisher in Augsburg, "I hope that your dear wife has by now happily delivered her burden. . . . My own wife, who has the same task ahead of her toward the end of January, also sends this wish from the bottom of her heart."[13] On 9 February 1756 he informed Lotter that his son had been born after a difficult confinement: "On 27 January, at 8 P.M., my own wife was happily delivered of a boy, but the *placenta* had to be removed. She was therefore astonishingly weak. Now, however (God be praised), both child and mother are well. She sends her regards to you both. The boy is called *Joannes Chrisostomos, Wolfgang, Gottlieb.*"[14] Named Wolfgang after his mater-nal grandfather, and Johannes Chrisostomos, after the saint on whose name day he had been born, Mozart was baptized "Johannes Chrysost[omus] Wolfgangus Theophilus" on 28 January.[15] Years later, Leopold Mozart recalled how perilously close to death his wife had come: "She was almost given up for lost."[16]

The survival prospects of the family's children were scarcely good. Mozart was obscurely troubled by this issue, to judge from a letter he wrote on 3 August 1782, a day after his own first child was born: "And now the child has been given to a foster-nurse against my will, or rather, at my wish! For I was quite determined that whether she should be able to do so or not, my wife was never to feed her child."[17] The letter bears signs of its author's agitation, even confusion, suggesting the resonance these events had for Mozart. The question of survival is of course uppermost: "I wanted the child to be brought up on water, like my sister and myself. However, the midwife, my mother-in-law, and most people here have begged and implored me not to allow it, if only for the reason that most children here who are brought up on water do not survive, as the people here don't know how to do it properly. That induced me to give in, for I should not like to have anything to reproach myself with."[18] Although he will not reproach himself, he does implicitly reproach his father and mother, who fed their infants on a diet of barley water (*Gerstenwasser*) or oat gruel.[19] Mozart's concern may have been magnified because on several early occasions he confronted the possibility of his own and his sister's death. It would not be surprising if he came to feel that his life often hung by a thread, and that his survival (five of his siblings having perished) was a fortuitous circumstance, a matter of God's unpredictable will.

Mozart was about three when his seven-year-old sister, Nannerl, began to receive keyboard lessons from their father, who gradually assembled for this purpose a music book (*Notenbuch*) consisting mostly of minuets and other short pieces by contemporary composers, arranged in progressive order of difficulty.[20] Drawn to the instrument, perhaps by a desire to emulate his sister and to win his share of their father's attention, Mozart spent endless hours at the keyboard, particularly delighting in "picking out thirds and sounding them."[21] At four he was using Nannerl's music book, which soon bore proud notations by Leopold Mozart next to several of the pieces such as "Wolfgangerl learned this minuet in his fourth year," or, with great exactitude and a dawning sense of historical import, "This minuet and trio were learned by Wolfgangerl in half-an-hour, at half-past nine at night on 26 January 1761, one day before his fifth birthday."[22] Within a few weeks, Mozart's first compositions, an Andante and an Allegro for clavier, K.1a and 1b, were entered in the music book in his father's hand, and several other little pieces followed before the end of 1761. Even earlier, when he was four, Mozart had already tried his hand at composing what he called a "concerto," inventing his own system of notation: "His father took it from him and showed me a smudge of notes, most of which were written over inkblots that he had rubbed out," recalled the court trumpeter, Schachtner, a family friend who was often in the Mozart lodgings during the child's earliest years:

> At first we laughed at what seemed such pure gibberish, but his father then began to observe the most important matter, the notes and music; he stared long at the sheet, and then tears, tears of joy and wonder, fell from his eyes. Look, Herr Schachtner, [he] said, see how correctly and properly

it is all written, only it can't be used, for it is so very difficult that no one could play it. Wolfgangerl said: That's why it's a concerto, you must practice it till you can get it right, look, that's how it goes. He played, and managed to bring out just enough to give us a notion of what he intended.[23]

Similarly, Mozart doggedly taught himself to play the violin at the age of six, insinuating himself into a trio rehearsal at home, playing second violin, and then managing the first violin part with wrong and irregular positioning but without ever actually breaking down. Again, Leopold Mozart's cheeks were moistened.

As a small child, Mozart was said to have had "a lively disposition for every childish pastime and prank," pursuing these with such absorption "that he would forget everything else, including his meals." But from the moment he discovered music, "his interest in every other occupation was as dead, and even children's games had to have a musical accompaniment if they were to interest him."[24] For example, Schachtner wrote, "If we, he and I, were carrying his toys from one room to another, the one of us who went empty-handed always had to sing or fiddle a march as we went."[25] Schachtner is not altogether consistent on this point, for he also says that Mozart's passion for learning as such was so great that it was "of little moment to him what he was given to learn; he simply wanted to learn."[26] But he leaves no doubt about Mozart's single-minded and wholehearted application: "Whatever he was given to learn occupied him so completely that he put all else, even music, on one side; e.g., when he was doing sums, the tables, chairs, walls, even the floor was covered with chalked figures."[27]

Mozart's sister confirmed her little brother's rage for knowledge: "Even as a child he was desirous of learning everything he set eyes on; in drawing [and] adding he showed much skill, but, as he was too busy with music, he could not show his talents in any other direction."[28] Evidently, early morning and late evening were wholly devoted to music: "From childhood on he liked best to play and to compose at night and in the morning," she wrote; "If he sat down at the clavier at 9:00 P.M. one couldn't take him away before midnight; I think he would have played through the whole night. In the morning between 6 o'clock and 9 o'clock he wrote, mostly while in bed; then he got up and didn't compose throughout the entire day, except when he had to write something quickly. At 8:00 P.M. he always played the clavier or composed."[29]

Leopold Mozart was a supreme teacher who understood how to inspire gifted children to great effort and achievement, instilling a drive for excellence and awakening in them a sense of unlimited devotion to his person and a desire to obtain his approval above all else. (Paradoxically, his authoritarian attitude may also have stimulated in his greatest student, his son, a rebellious urge to go beyond his example, to do even more than was expected of him.) Apart from Mozart's voice lessons with Giovanni Manzuoli in London, some counterpoint studies with Padre Martini in 1770, and his tutoring in English in the 1780s, there is no record that either of the Mozart children ever received instruction from a tutor or attended any school. Their father appears to have been their sole teacher.[30] Very early, Mozart learned reading, writing, arithmetic, history, and geography; an elementary manual in the latter two subjects was found among his father's effects.[31] Within a few years, during the family's extensive travels, Mozart became quite fluent in Italian and French, and he had as much Latin as a musician might require. Little attention was paid to the humanities outside of music. Clearly, Leopold Mozart had a practical goal in mind—the preparation of his children for careers as young virtuosos.

In particular, it had quickly become evident that Mozart's clavier artistry was of an unusual order, quite apart from his age. From the first his playing was remarkable for its accuracy, speed, and infallible sense of time. To this he brought a powerful sight-reading gift and an ability to improvise at great length with both taste and feeling in all of the prevailing styles. The Benedictine priest Placidus Scharl, who first came to know the Mozarts in Salzburg prior to their great European journey, described the child's playing as he recalled it decades later:

> Even in the sixth year of his age he would play the most difficult pieces for the pianoforte, of his own invention. He skimmed the octave which his short little fingers could not span, at fascinating speed and with wonderful accuracy. One had only to give him the first subject which came to mind for a fugue or an invention: he would develop it with strange variations and constantly changing passages as long as one wished; he would improvise fugally on a subject for hours, and this fantasia-playing was his greatest passion.[32]

Leopold Mozart was quick to understand his son's prodigious talent as a keyboard artist and its implications for reshaping the family's life. Before his sixth birthday, in January 1762, Mozart was taken by his father to Munich, where, during a three-week stay, he and his sister played for the elector of Bavaria, Maximilian III Joseph, and, we may be certain, for the leading music lovers of that city. The trip was sufficiently successful to prompt a lengthy visit to Vienna the following fall, from 6 October to 31 December 1762.

The Mozart family was en route to Vienna for almost three weeks, including six days in Passau and nine in Linz. Mozart played for Count Joseph Maria Thun-Hohenstein, bishop of Passau, and in Linz he and Marianne gave a public concert attended by several visiting Viennese nobles, whose reports home, it was hoped, would heighten the anticipation of the Mozarts' arrival. At a brief stopover at the Franciscan Church in Ybbs, Mozart played the organ "so well that the Franciscans . . . were almost struck dead with amazement."[33] Reaching Vienna on 4 October, the Mozarts found that the news of their performances en route had indeed preceded them. Leopold reported that Count Pálffy, who had "listened with astonishment" in Linz, "spoke later with great excitement of the performance to the Archduke Joseph [later Emperor Joseph II], who passed it on to the Empress. Thus, as soon as it was known that we were in Vienna, the command came for us to go to court," a command they fulfilled on 13 October.[34]

Leopold Mozart did not exaggerate when he wrote home, "Everyone is amazed, especially at the boy, and everyone whom I have heard says that his genius is incomprehensible."[35] Anecdotes of the visit to Schönbrunn confirm that the children put on a diverting entertainment: One of the ladies of the court assured the biographer Franz Niemetschek that both children made "a very great impression," recalling that "people could hardly believe their ears and eyes at the performance."[36] It was said that the emperor teased the little "magician," as he was dubbed: "It is no great art to play with all your fingers; but if you could play with only one finger and on a covered keyboard, that would be something worthy of admiration."[37] Naturally, Mozart was not fazed by this suggestion, which could not have been altogether unexpected, for he had brought along a bagful of keyboard tricks from Salzburg. He commenced "to play with one finger only, as precisely as possible; and then, he permitted the clavier keyboard to be covered and performed with marvelous dexterity, as though he had long been practicing this feat."[38] Mozart also charmed the assembly by insisting that court composer Georg Christoph Wagenseil be sent for: "Is Herr Wagenseil not here? It was understood that he would be here." The emperor obligingly fetched Wagenseil to take his place beside Mozart at the clavier, and the boy said to him: "I am going to play one of your concertos and you must turn the pages for me."[39]

The court showed its appreciation not only by its applause but in the manner that was most welcome—paying the Mozarts 100 ducats for providing so unusual an amusement. The empress also sent gala costumes for Mozart and his sister, inaugurating what was to become, for Mozart in particular, a lifelong love of elegant apparel. His costume was "of the finest cloth, lilac in color. The waistcoat is of moiré, and of the same shade as the coat, and both coat and waistcoat are trimmed with wide double gold braiding."[40] Other nobles sent a variety of gifts and money. By 19 October Leopold Mozart sent home to be banked the sum of 120 ducats, equivalent to 540 florins, or more than two full years of his Salzburg salary.

The high aristocracy, too, opened its doors to the Mozarts. In addition to appearances at Schönbrunn on 13 and 21 October, they made the rounds of the leading palaces and salons during their stay in Vienna, playing for Archdukes Ferdinand and Maximilian Franz, Prince Joseph Friedrich von Sachsen-Hildburghausen, Countess Kinsky, Count Collalto, Count Wilczek, Count Harrach, and Countess Eleanore Elisabeth Sinzendorf, among others. They also met with many important musicians, including the court kapellmeister, Georg Reutter, and attended various cultural events. It was a period of constant activity, interrupted only when Mozart fell ill with scarlet fever on 21 October—"pains in back and hips, rash, fever. New teeth coming in made his cheek swell"—and was confined to the house until 4 November, causing Leopold Mozart to remark, "This event has *cost me fifty ducats* at least."[41] He knew that his future rested precariously on his children's health. By early December, their opportunities in Vienna had been largely exhausted, and from 11 to 24 December the family stayed in Pressburg (Bratislava) at the invitation of members of the Hungarian aristocracy. There they purchased their own carriage, in which they set out on the return trip to Salzburg on the last day of the year.

Archbishop Sigismund Schrattenbach of Salzburg fully approved and encouraged the Mozart Vienna tour, which reflected so favorably on his archbishopric. The family's expenses were subsidized, and Leopold Mozart received his full salary during a four-month leave of absence. It was the beginning of a belated honeymoon period for Leopold Mozart and the archbishop, who—on the surface, at least—regarded each other with mutual amiability. The archbishop's Viennese representative assured Leopold that "His Grace would certainly grant an extension of a fortnight or three weeks," and Leopold in turn wrote to Hagenauer that "if by staying away I were to lose the favor of His Grace, I should be ready on the instant to leave by mail coach for Salzburg."[42] But Leopold Mozart did not refrain from pressing his advantage with a scarcely veiled threat to leave His Grace's service if his ambition to be named deputy kapellmeister was frustrated: "I am now in circumstances which allow me to earn my living in Vienna also. However I still prefer Salzburg to all other advantages. But I must not be kept back. . . . For otherwise I myself don't know what I may let others persuade me to do."[43] He was granted the post a few months later, on 28 February 1763, but it is doubtful that the archbishop appreciated the manner in which the award had been extracted. From Vienna, Leopold Mozart quietly exulted in his good fortune, but he wondered if his sudden success would continue: "If only I knew how it finally will turn out," he mused.[44] Meanwhile, he and his wife laid ambitious plans to take their children on an extended tour of Europe.

3

....

THE GRAND JOURNEY

In resolute pursuit of good fortune, the Mozart family—Leopold, Anna Maria, Wolfgang, and Marianne—toured the continent of Europe continuously from 9 June 1763 to 29 November 1766. The first four months took them through the chief cities of Bavaria, southern Germany, and the Rhineland, including Munich, Augsburg, Schwetzingen, Heidelberg, Mainz, Frankfurt, and Coblenz. On 4 October they arrived in Brussels, where they remained until 15 November; then they proceeded to Paris, where their stay was a long one, lasting from 18 November until 10 April 1764. At last, on 23 April, they reached London via Calais and Dover, and stayed there for more than fifteen months, the longest stop of their journey.

The circuitous return to Salzburg commenced when they sailed from Dover on 1 August 1765. At first they planned to "spend the month of August in Holland, to reach Paris toward the end of September and then move gradually homeward,"[1] but the return trip was extended to a year and a half, partly by illness, mainly by the emergence of new performance opportunities. They actually remained in Holland and Belgium until early May 1766, visiting and performing in Dunkirk, Lille, Ghent, The Hague, Amsterdam, Utrecht, Rotterdam, Antwerp, and Brussels. Similarly, their return visit to Paris, beginning on 10 May and including several days in Versailles at the end of May, was extended to a full three months. From Paris the Mozarts traveled to Dijon, staying for two weeks, and to Lyon for a visit of one month. The final leg of the journey was a two-month tour through Switzerland, with main stops at Geneva, Lausanne, Bern, and Zürich. At last, via Winterthur, Schaffhausen, Donaueschingen, Ulm, and

Leopold Mozart with his children, 1763–64. Watercolor portrait by
Louis Carrogis, known as Carmontelle. Musée Condé, Chantilly.

Augsburg, they arrived in Munich, where they remained until about 27 November, before setting out for Salzburg. They arrived in their home-town on 30 November 1766.

They had been on tour for three years, five months, and twenty days, and had traveled several thousand miles by coach, stopped in eighty-eight cities and towns (including repeat visits), and performed for audiences totaling many thousands. Leopold Mozart left home a musician of good, even noteworthy, reputation; by the time the family returned to Salzburg he was a figure of great renown. He and his children had written a new chapter in the history of music, and were celebrated throughout Europe beyond all expectation. For decades thereafter, those who had witnessed Mozart's performances recalled them as astonishing feats of virtuosity. As late as 1830, Goethe still spoke of having heard Mozart in his Frankfurt concert of August 1763, vividly remembering the "little man with his wig and his sword."[2] The image of the child Mozart had permanently entered the folklore of Western civilization.

Upon arriving in each city, Leopold Mozart customarily presented himself to those who were in a position to offer hospitality or to arrange perfor-mances—the leading nobles and most influential families, as well as musi-cians, connoisseurs, and impresarios. Often he bore letters of introduction and recommendation, but sometimes, in accordance with the usual practice for traveling artists, he merely announced his presence and the availability of his children to perform. Naturally, testimonials to the extraordinary capacities of the Mozarts were circulated.[3] It was a somewhat chancy enter-prise: they might be kept waiting for days or even weeks in expectation of a command performance, and then they would wait anxiously for a gift or cash payment, its size resting entirely on the generosity of the donor and not subject to prearrangement or mutual agreement. In Munich, Leopold Mozart wrote, "The charming custom is to keep people waiting for pre-sents for a long time, so that one has to be contented if one makes what one spends."[4] In Brussels they were idle for five weeks awaiting Prince Karl Alexander von Lothringen's decision: "It looks as if nothing will come of it, for the Prince spends his time hunting, eating, and drinking, and in the end it appears that he has no money."[5] But Leopold Mozart somewhat exaggerated the difficulties, for Brussels gave them a triumphal reception: "We have now received here, it is true, various handsome presents. . . . Little Wolfgang has been given two magnificent swords. . . . My little girl has received Dutch lace from the Archbishop, and from other courtiers cloaks, coats and so forth. With snuffboxes and étuis and such stuff we shall soon be able to rig out a stall."[6] Within a few days a major concert fulfilled his fondest hopes of hauling in large sums of money.

In the main capitals, they were feted by the royal families, the high nobility, and representatives of the best society. In Paris, they stayed at Hotel Beauvais, the residence of the Bavarian ambassador, Count van Eyck: "They gave us a most friendly welcome and have provided us with a room in which we are living comfortably and happily. We have the Countess's harpsichord, because she does not need it."[7] Eventually, they made the acquaintance of all the foreign envoys in Paris: "The English Ambassador, Mylord Bedford, and his son are very partial to us; and the Russian Prince Galitzin loves us as if we were his children."[8] At Versailles, the children were showered with snuffboxes and other exquisite gifts. "My children have taken almost everyone by storm."[9] The king's daughters not only permitted the children "to kiss their hands, but kissed them innumerable times. And the same thing happened with Madame la Dauphine." At the "grand couvert" on New Year's Eve, "Wolfgang was graciously privileged to stand beside the Queen the whole time, to talk constantly to her, entertain her and kiss her hands repeatedly, besides partaking of the dishes which she handed him from the table."[10]

From London Leopold reported, "At all courts up to the present we have been received with extraordinary courtesy. But the welcome that we have been given here exceeds all others."[11] On 27 April 1764 and again on 19 May they were received by the king and queen in Buckingham House, garnering 24 guineas per appearance. The royal family's favor made their public benefit concert of 5 June a major success: "I have had another shock, that is, the shock of taking in one hundred guineas in three hours," Leopold wrote. "To the amazement of everyone there were present more than a couple of hundred persons, including the leading people in all London; not only all the ambassadors, but the principal families in England attended it. . . . The profit will certainly not be less than ninety guineas."[12]

In some cities they performed only in the salons and palaces of the nobility, but wherever feasible they also gave concerts and entertainments for the general public, including music lovers of the middle and professional classes. And not only music lovers but novelty seekers were attracted by the sensational advance reports of Mozart's talents that were featured in public notices prepared by Leopold Mozart. Initially, these were somewhat restrained in tone, as in the first advertisement for their five concerts in Frankfurt, referring, fairly enough, to Mozart's "incredible dexterity," which had "astonished the Electoral Courts of Saxony, Bavaria, and the Palatinate" and provided "exceptional entertainment to his Imperial and Royal Majesty."[13] By the time he prepared the second advertisement for those concerts, Leopold Mozart had shifted the emphasis so that each event would seem as much a demonstration of astounding powers as of musical skill:

The boy will also play a concerto on the violin, accompany symphonies on the clavier, completely cover the manual or keyboard of the clavier, and play on the cloth as well as though he had the keyboard under his eyes; he will further most accurately name from a distance any notes that may be sounded for him either singly or in chords, on the clavier or on every imaginable instrument including bells, glasses and clocks. Lastly, he will improvise out of his head, not only on the pianoforte but also on an organ.[14]

Announcements of performances in London were the most colorful of the entire tour; the one for the concert of 5 June 1764 reads, "Miss Mozart of eleven and Master Mozart of seven Years of Age, Prodigies of Nature; taking the opportunity of representing to the Public the greatest Prodigy that Europe or that Human Nature has to boast of. Every Body will be astonished to hear a Child of such tender Age playing the Harpsichord in such a Perfection—it surmounts all Fantastic and Imagination [sic], and it is hard to express which is more astonishing, his Execution upon the Harpsichord playing at Sight, or his own Composition."[15] Toward the close of the family's London residence, in an attempt to reap his last harvests of British currency—"Once I leave England, I shall never see guineas again. So we must make the most of our opportunity"[16]—Leopold Mozart put his children on daily view to the general public in a manner not altogether consonant with refined taste: he advised prospective customers that they might "find the Family at home every Day in the Week from Twelve to Two o'Clock, and have an Opportunity of putting [Mozart's] Talents to a more particular Proof, by giving him any thing to play at Sight, or any Music without a Bass, which he will write upon the Spot without recurring to his Harpsichord."[17] Similarly, a notice of 8 July 1765 in the *Public Advertiser* stated, "Mr. Mozart . . . who . . . has been obliged by the Desire of several Ladies and Gentlemen to postpone his Departure from England for a short Time, takes this Opportunity to inform the Public, that he has taken the great Room in the Swan and Harp Tavern in Cornhill, where he will give an opportunity to all the Curious to hear these two young Prodigies perform every Day from Twelve to Three. Admittance 2s 6d each person."[18] A week later, a concert "for the Benefit of Master Mozart, the celebrated German Boy, Aged eight years, and his Sister" was announced to take place at the town hall in Canterbury, where the family stayed from 24 to 30 July.[19]

In March 1765 Leopold Mozart complained about the falling off of his income, wondering "why we are not being treated more generously."[20] In his eagerness for shillings and guineas, he may have failed to consider that he might alienate his noble patrons, who surely were not pleased to discover that the Mozart children's miraculous favors were promiscuously available to all who could raise the entrance fee, regardless of their social standing. Perhaps that is why the children were not again invited to Buckingham House, although the queen did respond generously to the dedication of Mozart's Sonatas, op. 3.

If the vaudeville character of the Mozart concerts is often evident in contemporary documents, their more serious musical content is difficult to fix with any precision. Marianne was said to have performed, on both harpsichord and fortepiano, "the most difficult sonatas and concertos by the greatest masters," but these are not specified.[21] Mozart was advertised as playing "sonatas, trios and concertos," in addition to playing accompaniments, but he apparently did not perform many well-known compositions; if he did, the notices make no mention of them, though perhaps composers' names were not a selling point.[22] As the main attraction of the concerts, according to Friedrich Melchior von Grimm's notice from Paris, Mozart would customarily "improvise for one hour after another and in doing so give rein to the inspiration of his genius and to a mass of enchanting ideas, which moreover he knows how to connect with taste and without confusion."[23] Grimm went on to describe the now obligatory playing on a cloth-covered keyboard and Mozart's reading at sight "whatever is submitted to him," as well as his facility at writing a bass part, improvising a figured bass, and adding intermediate voices to any music set before him.[24]

Mozart seems to have been content to provide on demand a spectacular entertainment for the wide-eyed general populace. Schachtner's report that Mozart was reluctant to play, "except his audience were great amateurs of music, or he had to be deluded into thinking them such," may therefore need modification, certainly in regard to the early years. But it also seems possible that Mozart soon came to resent performing for the gapers and gawkers, as was perhaps implied in Schlichtegroll's remark that the boy "would only play trifles when the audience consisted of people who didn't understand music."[25] Of course, trifles were precisely what the public expected to hear. An entirely different dimension of Mozart's creativity unfolded when he was in the presence of professional musicians or knowledgeable listeners; it was said that "he was filled with passion and attentiveness when connoisseurs were present."[26] In Donaueschingen, Mozart played almost daily over a twelve-day span for Prince Joseph Wenzeslaus von Fürstenberg. At Buckingham House, the king gave Mozart works by Wagenseil, Johann Christian Bach, Carl Friedrich Abel, and Handel to play at sight; he also played splendidly "on the king's organ," accompanied the queen in an aria, took the "bass part of some airs of Handel (which happened to be lying there) and played the most beautiful melody on it and in such a manner that everyone was amazed."[27] Also in London, Johann Christian Bach took Mozart on his lap and "they played alternately on the same keyboard for two hours together, extempore, before the King and the Queen."[28]

Such reports are illustrative of Mozart's growth as a musician during the Grand Journey: his musicianship soon began to outstrip the restrictive venues in which he was forced to perform. His extraordinary musicality increasingly became a topic of discussion and description. Naturally, Leopold Mozart was the first to remark on this. "What he knew when we left Salzburg is a mere shadow compared with what he knows now. It exceeds all that one can imagine," he wrote as early as May 1764,[29] and again, "My boy knows in this his eighth year what one would expect only from a man of forty."[30] Two years later the Swiss educator Auguste Tissot, cited earlier, rhapsodized on Mozart's artistry rather than on his musical athleticism:

His imagination is as musical as his ear: it always hears many sounds together; one sound heard recalls instantaneously all those that may form a melodious sequence and a complete symphony. . . . He was sometimes involuntarily attracted to his harpsichord as by a secret force, and drew from it sounds, which were the lively expression of the idea with which he had just been occupied. One might say that at these moments he is himself the instrument in the hands of music and one may imagine him as composed of strings harmoniously put together with such skill that it is impossible to touch one without all the others being also set in motion.[31]

In London, Daines Barrington was as impressed by Mozart's ability to improvise "vocal works in various affects, such as Song of Love, Song of Anger, Song of Rage," as by his skill at reading a five-part score at sight: "Nothing could exceed the masterly manner in which he sung."[32] The eminent music historian Charles Burney similarly was impressed by a performance at which Mozart imitated "the several Styles of Singing of each of the then Opera Singers, as well as of their Songs in an Extemporary opera to nonsense words—to which were [added] an overture of 2 Movements. . . , all full of Taste [and] imagination, with Good Harmony, Melody & Modulation, after which he played at Marbles, in the true Childish Way of one who knows nothing."[33]

In the course of the Grand Journey, Mozart made rapid strides as a fledgling composer, moving from the little keyboard pieces in Nannerl's music book (Notenbuch) at the outset of the journey to a large number of simple keyboard sonatas with violin or flute accompaniment and, by the close of the journey, to the composition of orchestral music, including several symphonies, four keyboard concertos, and a quodlibet serenade for harpsichord and orchestra entitled Galimathias musicum, K. 32. Four sets of accompanied sonatas appeared in three different capital cities as Mozart's first published works: opus 1 consisted of the Violin Sonatas in C and D, K. 6 and 7, published at Paris at Leopold Mozart's expense in 1764 with a dedication to Princess Victoire from the composer, "agé de Sept ans"; a companion set, opus 2, the Violin Sonatas in B-flat and G, K. 8 and 9, was issued by the same publisher and dedicated to Countess Tessé; opus 3, published in 1765 in London with a dedication to Queen Charlotte, consisted of Six Violin (or Flute) Sonatas, with cello obbligato, K. 10–15; finally, the Six Violin Sonatas, K. 26–31, appeared in 1766 at The Hague, dedicated to Princess Caroline Nassau-Weilbourg, née Princess of Orange. Donald Francis Tovey observes that these sonatas "are full of inventiveness, and technically as competent as most contemporary works," and he considers it "fortunate that the infancy of the sonata-forms coincided with the infancy of Mozart; for in no earlier or later epoch could his juvenile work have had so normal a relation to the musical world at large."[34] Of course, this compatibility also shows how closely the young composer followed his models, which were chosen for him by his father from those composers whose music was finding greatest favor in the European capitals of the day.

Mozart also wrote several symphonies in the prevailing style of the royal chamber musicians Johann Christian Bach and Carl Friedrich Abel to open and close his London concerts and perhaps also for use at these composers' acclaimed public concerts. Among these were the Symphonies in E-flat, K. 16, D, K. 19, and F, K. Anh. 223/19a, all composed in London. "Oh what a lot of things I have to do," wrote Leopold of his preparation for the 21 February 1765 concert. "The symphonies at the concert will all be by Wolfgang Mozart. I must copy them myself, unless I want to pay one shilling for each sheet."[35] Two more symphonies were written at The Hague, the Symphony in B-flat, K. 22, in December 1765, and the Symphony in G, K. Anh. 221/45a, in March 1766.

Mozart's father took a hand in the composition of some of his son's early works, but the extent of his participation cannot be fully determined because many autographs have not survived; for example, we lack those for almost all of the published works and for all the symphonies but K. 16, which is in Mozart's hand. In several instances where autographs do survive, they have been shown by Wolfgang Plath to be either partially or wholly in Leopold Mozart's handwriting, suggesting that he revised some works, or even collaborated with Mozart on a number of them.[36] For example, of the sixty small pieces in Nannerl's music book (*Notenbuch*), twenty-six are in Leopold Mozart's hand, but only one in his son's, and the music book also contains the keyboard versions of the three movements of the Violin Sonata, K. 6, in Leopold's hand. The only surviving autographs of the Violin Sonatas, K. 7–8, are in the father's handwriting.

The first section of the Kyrie in F, K. 33, written in Paris on the return journey, is another mixed autograph; its opening section is in Leopold's hand. The *Galimathias musicum,* K. 32, written to celebrate the installation of Prince William V of Orange in March 1766, is a thoroughly mixed autograph, with Leopold contributing much of nos. 5, 9, and 12, plus measures 45–132 of the fugue of no. 18, which replaced Mozart's own effort. Other passages are written jointly, though much of the work, which consists of a simple string of familiar tunes and characteristic styles culminating in the Dutch national anthem, "Willem van Nassau," is by Mozart.[37] Even after the return to Salzburg, when Mozart's powers as a composer were more highly developed, Leopold continued to collaborate with him on occasion. The "Pasticcio" Clavier Concertos, K. 37 and K. 39–41 of 1767, prepared in anticipation of their impending journey to Vienna and arranged from solo sonata movements by such fashionable composers as Hermann Raupach, Leontzi Honauer, Johann Schobert, Johann Eckard, and C. P. E. Bach, were jointly written down by the two of them, but with Leopold's share, according to Plath, "extraordinarily large."[38] And in Vienna, Leopold evidently contributed the Intrada to the singspiel *Bastien und Bastienne,* K. 50/46b, if only to help Mozart meet his deadline. That may also be why the keyboard parts for all three of the Concertos after keyboard sonatas by J. C. Bach, K. 107, composed probably as late as 1772, were copied out by Leopold, who also supplied sections of the figured bass, leaving the ritornellos and part of the accompaniments for Mozart.

While Mozart was rapidly emerging as a composer, absorbing influences, learning a variety of styles, and working within a range of genres, Leopold was hastening him along with assistance and instruction, which often merged into a collaboration that could scarcely be acknowledged. Leopold Mozart called attention to a series of three consecutive fifths in the second minuet of the Violin Sonata, K. 9, saying that he had corrected them but that they had been left in by an engraver's oversight and that this in turn was fortunate, for they constituted "a proof that our little Wolfgang composed them himself, which, perhaps quite naturally, everyone will not believe."[39] Clearly, he was concerned that the outside world might draw unwarranted conclusions from what was, to the Mozarts, only a manifestation of intimate cooperation within the family enterprise. In a work such as *Galimathias musicum,* which Leopold Mozart patently conceived as a tribute to Dutch patrons and whose mixture of rustic and courtly styles is so reminiscent of his own programmatic works, even including quotations from them, one can sense the naturalness of the collaboration and even imagine the delight father and son took in this opportunity to work together and thereby advance the family interests. If this, in the end, served to heighten the public's perception of the Mozart miracle and thereby to magnify the family income, well, so much the better.

The Mozarts began the journey in their own coach, drawn by four horses, and were accompanied by a personal servant, one Sebastian Winter, who functioned as their friseur and valet. When Winter left their service in early 1764 he was replaced by two servants, a friseur named Jean Pierre Potivin and an Italian named Porta, and the family's carriage to Calais now had seven post horses.[40] Although parsimonious by nature, Leopold Mozart did not stint on travel expenses, in part because the family needed to make a favorable impression: "To keep our health and for the reputation of my court, we must travel in the style of nobles or cavaliers," he explained.[41] In their dress, demeanor, and style of living, the Mozarts had rapidly undergone a metamorphosis into a quasi-aristocratic family, as every contemporaneous portrait of them confirms. Leopold did not disguise his elation at living like a patrician. "We do not associate with anyone except the nobility and other distinguished personages," he wrote from Coblenz, "and receive exceptional courtesies and respect."[42] In accordance with his new status, Leopold did not bother to contradict the general perception that he was kapellmeister to the Salzburg court. Years later, Mozart himself used slightly exaggerated titles, and he too demonstrated that he had grown used to the perquisites of living in an aristocratic style.

Leopold Mozart's voluminous letters home, addressed to Lorenz Hagenauer and his wife, show that he was an accomplished chronicler of manners, and even an authority on artistic, social, and historical issues. Indeed, as an observer he was equal in many respects to Baron Caspar Riesbeck, Charles Burney, and other noted contemporary chroniclers. In Louvain he visited the churches, "stood transfixed" before a Dierick Bouts triptych, and admired a painting by Rubens, and at the residence of Prince Charles of Lorraine he found much to praise in the Dutch tapestries, Chinese statues and porcelain, and "all kinds of natural history specimens. I have seen many such collections; but it would be difficult to find such a quantity and so many species."[43] He also furnished Frau Hagenauer with news of the latest Parisian fashions and trends: "In winter the women wear not only fur-trimmed garments, but also neck ruffles or neckties of fur and instead of flowers even fur in their hair and fur armlets and so forth." He frankly offered his opinion of French elegance: "I really cannot tell you whether the women in Paris are fair; for they are painted so unnaturally, like the dolls of Berchtesgaden, that even a naturally beautiful woman on account of this detestable makeup is unbearable to the eyes of an honest German."[44] All this was of great interest to his friends in Salzburg, and indeed, except for certain passages marked "something for you alone," the letters were written to be circulated; that is why many of them exist in the hands of various contemporary copyists.[45]

Leopold Mozart's letters also record the intrusion of social realities into the fantasy world of glittering courts and gilded concert halls. "You will hardly find any other city with so many miserable and mutilated persons," he wrote from Paris. "You have only to spend a minute in a church or walk along a few streets to meet some blind or lame or limping or half-putrefied beggar, or to find someone lying on the street who has had his hand eaten away as a child by the pigs, or someone else who in childhood fell into the fire and had half an arm burned off while the foster father and his family were working in the fields. And there are numbers of such people, whom disgust makes me refrain from looking at when I pass them."[46] A letter from London vividly describes the demonstrations of unemployed British weavers—"a great outpouring of the people"—seeking protection from the competition of French silk imports. "On the street on which I live, I saw over 4,000 people passing my lodgings." They were carrying "black flags" and "wearing green aprons," on their way to present their petition to the Crown, which responded with repressive force.[47]

If we cannot trace the impact upon young Mozart of constant reminders of poverty and injustice, we do have indications that other stresses were beginning to tell upon him. He wept when he learned that Hagenauer's son Cajetan had entered a monastery, and when questioned, wrote Leopold, "He said that he was grieved, as he believed that he would never see him again," remembering how the older boy used to play with him.[48] In Paris the mortal illness of their compatriot Countess van Eyck also brought Mozart and his sister to tears, for "Wolfgang loves the Countess and she loves him to distraction."[49] Illness and the danger of death were the Mozarts' constant companions on their travels. In Paris, in February 1764, Mozart was stricken with a high fever. Inoculation for smallpox was recommended, but Leopold demurred: "It depends on His divine grace whether He wishes to keep this prodigy of nature in the world in which he has placed it, or to take it to Himself."[50] Both Marianne and Wolfgang had their closest brush with death at The Hague in the fall of 1765. On 12 September Marianne caught a cold that appeared to be of no consequence: "But on the evening of the 26th she suddenly started to shiver and asked to lie down. After the shivering she had fever and I saw that her throat was inflamed. The following day she was no better and I sent for a doctor." She was bled, but to no avail, and her condition worsened in the weeks that followed.

> The doctor himself had given up hope and my poor child, feeling how weak she was, partly realized the danger. I prepared her to resign herself to God's will and not only did she receive Holy Communion but the priest

found her in such a serious condition that he gave her the Holy Sacrament of Extreme Unction [on 21 October], for she was often so weak that she could hardly utter what she wanted to say. Whoever could have listened to the conversations which we three, my wife, myself and my daughter, had on several evenings, during which we convinced her of the vanity of this world and the happy death of children, would not have heard it without tears. Meanwhile, little Wolfgang in the next room was amusing himself with his music.[51]

In his desolation, Leopold Mozart feared that his plans would have to be altered. "Now God has upset my calculations. If God spares her, I cannot expose her capriciously to the obvious danger of losing her life through an inopportune journey. It is easy to understand that I have derived no advantage, but the greatest loss from this accident."[52] Overcome by sadness at his sister's condition, Mozart himself succumbed to illness on 15 November and was deathly sick for two months. "He is not only absolutely unrecognizable, but has nothing left but his tender skin and his little bones and for the last five days has been carried daily from his bed to a chair."[53] At the beginning of December, beginning to recover, he lay for "eight days without speaking a single word."[54] Altogether, it was four months before the children were fully recovered and ready to resume the final leg of their journey. By then Mozart was nine years old. He spent the last weeks of his convalescence composing the Six Violin Sonatas, K. 26–31, which he dedicated to Princess Caroline of Nassau-Weilbourg, for whom he had twice performed in mid-September. "Deign to accept this fruit of my hard work," reads the dedication, "and deign to regard it as a mark of my genuine gratitude and the profound respect with which I am, Madame, Your Serene Highness's very humble, very obedient, and very small Servant."[55]

After a whirlwind tour through the Netherlands, Belgium, France, Switzerland, and southern Germany, in the course of which they performed for such eminences as Prince William V of Orange, Louis-Joseph de Bourbon, the Prince de Condé, Prince Ludwig Eugen of Württemberg, and Elector Maximilian III of Bavaria, they came home at last. As Marianne put it in her biographical notes, "They returned safe and sound to Salzburg at the end of the month of November 1766 after a three-and-a-half-year journey."[56] Leopold Mozart had some trepidation about what awaited him there. "But who knows what plans are being made for us after our return to Salzburg?" he wrote from Munich. "Perhaps we shall be received in such a way that we shall be only too glad to shoulder our bundles and clear out." It was a prospect he faced with a touch of defiance. "I am going to bring back my children to their native town. If they are not wanted, it is not my fault. But people shall not get them for nothing."[57]

4

···

THE FAMILY TREASURE

Anyone who reads the letters of Leopold Mozart will soon observe that money is a constant subject of his concern, even a profound preoccupation. Prices, discounts, interest rates, exchange rates—transactions of every kind were his specialty, and he had no need to give ground to any mathematician in the proficiency of his calculations. He knew the cost of everything and preached economy quite as fervently as he did religious devotion, exhorting his family to save money on every expense, no matter how small. Of course, it was no more than prudent to safeguard one's money in a society where impoverishment threatened any court employee who became ill or was otherwise unable to perform his duties. Mozart's maternal grandfather had suffered precisely such a precipitous decline in his fortunes after a serious illness, leaving his wife and daughters penniless at his death.

"What will become of Salzburg," wrote Leopold Mozart from Milan in 1770, "if some means are not devised of establishing a sound régime? With the small pay we get we shall in time all be beggars. The poor court servants have hardly enough to satisfy their hunger; and their children who learn nothing, because there is no money, will grow up to be idlers, and in about twenty years the town will be full of useless people living in misery, a burden both to the court and to the whole community."[1] The court, though benevolent in thought, was parsimonious in deed, justifying the extremely low wages it paid by asserting its charitable intent. The contemporary traveler Baron Caspar Riesbeck was told by one informant that two thirds of the Salzburg court's employees were superfluous and were only

Tea at the prince de Conti's residence in the Temple, 1766. Oil
painting by Michel Barthélemy Ollivier. Louvre.

kept on the payroll to provide employment to the maximum number of citizens.[2] This rationale was of little comfort to those who had to make do on meager wages. "Since you were born," wrote Leopold to Mozart, with some exaggeration, "or rather since my marriage it has been very difficult for me to *support* a wife, seven children, two maids and Mama's own mother *on my monthly pay* of about 20 florins, and *to meet the expenses* of childbirths, deaths, and illnesses. If you think it over, you will realize that not only have I never spent a kreuzer on the smallest pleasure for myself but that without God's special mercy I should never have succeeded in spite of all my efforts *in keeping out of debt.*"[3]

In the later 1770s, in the course of an epistolary onslaught designed to keep his son under his control, Leopold Mozart expressed an inordinate fear of poverty. During the 1760s, however, he seems to have been wholly preoccupied with making money rather than with the fear of losing it. "But now I must spare no money, for it will come back to me today or tomorrow. Nothing ventured, nothing gained," he wrote in 1768.[4] He pursued moneymaking single-mindedly, hoping to seize every possibility of magnifying his gains, but he did so in high spirits, with a sense that his hour of fortune had struck and he could not be denied. Always he measured his opportunities, forecast his results, and counted his takings. He was sometimes in an elated, rapturous mood, speaking with almost palpable anticipation of his prospects of raking in large amounts of Austrian florins, German thalers, English guineas, and French louis d'or. Naturally he also complained bitterly of every missed chance to make money. Often he lamented his children's illnesses for the loss of income they entailed: "I should have had at least twelve louis-d'or more, if my children had not had to stay at home for a few days," and "It will certainly be a week more before [Wolfgang] is quite restored to health. In God's name a hundred florins soon disappear."[5] Of course, the health of his children was paramount. "So heavy inroads are made on my purse. Basta! After all, what is money, if only I get away again safe and sound with my family?"[6] And again: "Expense must not be considered. The devil take the money if one only gets away with one's skin!"[7]

Despite all setbacks and misadventures, the money was indeed rolling in, in a rich stream of various European currencies. We cannot calculate precisely how much Leopold Mozart made on the early journeys, but it was a very large sum, befitting perhaps the most successful virtuoso concert tour in music history until then. It is known that on three separate occasions he was able to deposit with his bankers sizable amounts for transmittal to Salzburg—540 florins (October 1762), 2,000 florins (April 1764), and 1,000 florins (June 1764).[8] By March 1765, within a year after arriving in England, he reported that "we have made a few hundred guineas," a sum equal to 2,000 florins.[9] Gross income cannot be accurately tabulated because the letters contain only fragmentary data, even in the earlier years. For 1763, the letters show earnings only in five German cities and only for the period between 21 June and 18 September; known omissions include earnings from three public concerts in Augsburg, five in Frankfurt, one in Coblenz, and a "grand concert" in Brussels attended by Prince Karl Alexander, brother of Emperor Franz I.

In the first flush of success, Leopold Mozart did not hesitate to share with his friends his delight at the family's good fortune and his expectation of rich proceeds. He wrote from Brussels, "I hope that next Monday, when a big concert is being held, I shall haul in plenty of fat thalers and louis d'or."[10] After the successful London concert of 5 June 1764, which grossed one hundred guineas, he estimated that "the profit will certainly not be less than ninety guineas."[11] As reports of his earnings began to circulate in Salzburg, however, he curbed his enthusiasm, considering it best to keep such information to himself. In the later years of the tour, Leopold Mozart very rarely mentioned his fees in his letters home; there are only a handful of references to earnings in 1765 and 1766. On subsequent journeys he did not repeat his mistake of boasting about his income; rather, he refrained from giving details and made sure to emphasize the magnitude of his expenses, attempting to create the impression that, at best, he was doing little better than breaking even. Later, during the first Italian journey, he even withheld all financial information from his wife, who remained behind in Salzburg.

Despite his precautions, the size of the profits finally became a matter of speculation in Salzburg. The librarian at St. Peter's, Father Beda Hübner, recorded in his diary for 29 November 1766 that the Mozart family

> has now been absent from Salzburg for nearly four years and has traversed the greater part of Europe. . . . They were in France nearly a whole year, receiving countless honors and the most valuable appreciations. . . . From France they went to England, where they made very much money: they never cease to relate how dreadfully expensive everything is in England. . . . It is easy to imagine the amount of money this Herr Mozart must have made in England, where moreover all presents are given purely and solely in ready cash. . . . From England they went to Holland . . . where again they received very many presents and collected much money.[12]

A keen observer, Hübner was not impressed by Leopold Mozart's constant references to his high expenses. "The now-completed journey is said to have cost them something near 20,000 florins. I can well believe it; but how much money must he not have collected?"[13]

The figure of 20,000 florins appears to be exaggerated, though, and is contradicted by Leopold Mozart's own letters, which on several occasions set forth his expenses in various countries. Writing from Vienna in November 1762, he noted that "we only just manage every day on one ducat [about 4.5 florins] and that daily there are additional expenses."[14] On the 117th day of the tour, in 1763, he wrote, "we have already spent 1,068 florins," i.e., 9 florins per day, presumably including travel costs.[15] During sixteen days in Versailles, not counting the cost of new clothing, expenses were "about twelve louis-d'or," or approximately 7.5 florins per day.[16] From London Leopold reported that he had spent one hundred seventy guineas in about 150 days, or 11 florins per day,[17] and on a later occasion he calculated that it cost "300 pounds sterling a year" to maintain the family in London "with the strictest economy," an amount equivalent to 3,000 florins, or a bit more than 8 florins per day.[18] It bears repeating that Leopold Mozart may have had an interest in overstating his expenses in these letters. Even so, if we use the average of his per diem figure, 8 florins, the 1,269 days of the 1763–66 European tour would have cost 10,152 florins. Travel costs, where not included in Leopold Mozart's figures, might come to another 2,000 florins. Adding a 10 percent margin of error to allow for miscellaneous expenses and a higher per diem rate brings the total cost to 13,500 florins at most. By comparison, the young Johann Nepomuk Hummel's father reported that a very similar three-year tour of Europe with his son during 1788–91 cost 14,306 florins.[19] Furthermore, one must bear in mind that the Mozart family's early journeys were partly subsidized by the archbishop of Salzburg and that their lengthy stay in Holland was sponsored by the Dutch republic, so that a substantial portion of the expense was not borne by Leopold Mozart at all. For example, by the time they arrived in Coblenz after three months on the road, he calculated that they had already spent over 1,000 florins. "But other people have paid for all these expenses," he noted, a reference to an underwriting by the archbishop, which was well deserved because "such performances brought great honor to our Court."[20]

Moreover, apart from cash earnings, the family amassed large quantities of expensive gifts. Hübner related, "I afterward saw all the tributes and presents . . . : of gold pocket watches he has brought home 9; of gold snuffboxes he has received 12; of gold rings set with the most handsome precious stones he has so many that he does not know himself how many; earrings for the girl, necklaces, knives with golden blades . . . without number and without end. . . . It is just like inspecting a church treasury."[21] Among the gifts was a snuffbox from the king of France containing the written stipulation that should "Mozart be obliged by necessity to sell this snuffbox, he was to return it to the king to buy, and he would give him 100 *Louis d'or,* i.e. 1,000 florins for it." Dazzled by the haul, Hübner estimated its value at 12,000 florins, adding that Leopold Mozart "had bought very many things cheaply in these foreign countries, which he will sell here at a high price, and in this way make even more money on the spot!"[22]

In the absence of precise information about income, the detailing of expenses would seem of little use. However, inasmuch as the figure of 20,000 florins in expenses was probably bruited by Leopold Mozart to counter the assumption that he had enriched himself, it may also be taken as an acknowledgment that receipts equaled or exceeded 20,000 florins, for he never claimed to have lost money on the tour. Thus, if we assume minimum earnings of 20,000 florins against maximum expenses of 13,500, and if we put the resale value of the gifts at only 6,000 florins (half of Hübner's estimate), Leopold Mozart's profits would have been on the order of 12,500 florins. Of course, these calculations are extremely inexact and necessarily have a wide margin of error, but if we approach the matter from a totally different avenue, we arrive at rather similar results. If we assume that Leopold Mozart continued to bank money throughout the full three and a half years of the tour at the same rate documented for the first year— 3,000 florins—and that those sums represent profits rather than simply repayment of advances to his bankers, then total profits would be approximately 10,500 florins, plus the value of the gifts, for a total of 16,500 florins. Even if the sums were to be applied against monies advanced, any balance due would probably have been offset in substantial measure by the archbishop's and other subsidies. In assessing the reasonableness of this latter estimate of the annual profits, we must remember that Leopold Mozart exploited every opportunity to display his children in London, both publicly and privately, and that the family gave at least as many concerts on the return tour as on the journey out; moreover, the Mozart family's fame had increased with the passage of time, presumably increasing the family's fees as well.

In summary, by either method of calculation, Leopold Mozart's profit through the end of 1767 was somewhere between 12,500 and 16,500 florins—an amount equal to more than fifty times his annual salary of 250 florins, and a substantial fortune in a country where 500 to 1,000 florins was a very comfortable annual salary. It must, however, be noted that this estimate does not take into account the strong likelihood that Leopold Mozart's backers—in the first place the merchant Lorenz Hagenauer—were not merely his bankers in this enterprise but his partners, advancing the large sums required to finance a risky journey in return for a share in the profits. From Brussels in November 1763, for example, Leopold Mozart wrote Hagenauer a letter headed "something for you alone," authorizing him to take 200 florins in Bavarian currency out of a strongbox containing valuable gifts Leopold had shipped to Salzburg (he called them "Peruvian treasure"); perhaps the money was a payment owed to Hagenauer, for a full accounting was promised "in due course."[23] If Hagenauer was indeed a partner, then Leopold's net profits have to be reduced by some unknown percentage, although they would still be considerable.

The bulk of the funds generated by the Grand Journey remained intact, and in light of Leopold's thrifty stewardship and additional income from subsequent journeys, it is highly probable that the capital actually increased in later years, despite some failed ventures. (Leopold lost some of the Grand Journey money in connection with Mozart's aborted opera project in 1768 and in his subsidy of Mozart's tour in search of a position in 1777–78.) Until his death in 1787, Leopold Mozart continued to draw his official salary as deputy kapellmeister—raised to 450 florins in 1779—and to earn some money from private teaching. Moreover, although details are sparse, we know that he put his money to work for him, selling pianos and other musical instruments that were displayed in the large salon of his fine

Inscription by Leopold Mozart on a windowpane, Frankfurt 1763.
Historisches Museum, Frankfurt.

eight-room apartment, continuing the sale of his book, dabbling in music engraving and music copying, and on occasion lending money, presumably at appropriate rates of interest. All in all, he had done very well for himself.

Early in the Grand Journey, Leopold Mozart incised a message to posterity on a windowpane of their Frankfurt lodgings: "Mozart, Kapellmeister of the Salzburg Court, with his family, the 12th of August 1763" ("*Mozart Maitre de la Musique de la Chapelle de Salzbourg avec Sa Famile le 12 Août 1763*").[24] It was as though he needed to confirm the reality of recent events, to assure himself that he was in fact visiting one of the great cities of Europe, to leave a permanent, ineradicable mark of his extraordinary success—indeed, to magnify reality by unequivocally elevating himself to the rank of kapellmeister. In the space of a few short months, the family he headed with great dignity was on its way to achieving world acclaim. By virtue of his talent and charm, the child Mozart held within him the power to transform his family's life; he was a magical being, capable of making wishes come true. Mozart's father had discovered, nurtured, and harnessed his son's amazing powers, which proved an inexhaustible fount of benefactions and wealth. As the 1760s drew to a close, Leopold Mozart frankly described Mozart as a miracle:

> The extraordinary musical talent with which merciful God has blessed my two children in full measure was the cause of my traveling through the major part of *Germany* and my very long sojourn in *France, Holland* and *England,* &c. &c. I might here take the opportunity of entertaining the public with a story such as probably appears but once in a century, and which in the domain of music has perhaps never yet appeared *in such a degree of the miraculous;* I might describe the wonderful genius of my son; circumstantially relate his unbelievably rapid progress in the whole extent of musical science from the fifth to the thirteenth year of his age; and I might, in so incredible a matter, call to witness the unanswerable testimony of many of the greatest masters, indeed even the testimony of envy itself.[25]

It was truly miraculous that a poor Salzburg musician, seemingly condemned to a respectable but limited career in a minor court, chastised by that court as a blasphemer only a few years earlier, cut off without a penny by his mother, was now universally renowned, elevated in social status, and acquainted with the most eminent persons of the day, including the royal families of every major European nation. Marianne's role in all this was secondary: Mozart was the mainspring of his father's fame, wealth, and standing, the instrument by which his father's unfulfilled career was redeemed; he was the extension of Leopold's own self, the source of his power.

As we have seen, Leopold Mozart was convinced that he had been charged with the mission of presenting the miracle of his son to an unbelieving world. And as guardian of the miraculous, he had an ominous sense of malevolent opposition to his revelation, an almost messianic belief that persecution inevitably awaits those who seek to bring light to the world. When his plans went awry, as in his first venture, with his son, into opera in 1768, he readily slipped into *ad hominem* explanations: "They think that it is only a question of a few years and that thereafter [this miracle] will become natural and cease to be a Divine miracle. So they want to withdraw it from the eyes of the world. . . . But by patience and perseverance one must convince people that our adversaries are wicked liars, slanderers, and envious creatures."[26] Thus, in Leopold's mind, the unfolding of Mozart's genius somehow became entwined with obscure struggles between darkness and light. Any interference with Leopold Mozart's mission seemed to him to border on the sinful or heretical—even the child's own potential recalcitrance, for if he could grant wishes, he also had the power to deny them.

During Mozart's childhood, there was little danger that he might betray the family interests. On the contrary, all reports confirm that his profoundest desire was to please and that he reacted to requests and directives with an almost automatic, even excessive, obedience. "Not once did he show himself to be unhappy with his father's instructions," wrote Schlichtegroll, whose excellent informants were Marianne Mozart and Schachtner.[27] Mozart would perform upon command at any time: "Even when he had been practicing the entire day without rest, he would start playing once again, if his father wanted him to, without displeasure." He would even refuse to take nutrition without authorization: "He understood and obeyed his parents' every hint; and he carried his devotion to them so far that he would not risk accepting the smallest amount to eat which was offered him without their permission."[28] Schachtner reported that Mozart would learn whatever was asked of him, for he "simply wanted to learn, and he left the choice to his dearly loved father as to what field he was to work in."[29]

The young Mozart's submissiveness may have been a response to Leopold's pedagogy, which alternated reward and punishment to achieve maximum compliance. It was not always a compassionate tutelage. An example is provided by Schachtner, who recalled that the boy had an unreasonable and overwhelming fear of trumpets: "Until he was almost nine he was terribly afraid of the trumpet when it was blown alone, without other music. Merely to hold a trumpet in front of him was like aiming a loaded pistol at his heart."[30] His father reacted to Mozart's phobia with an extraordinary lack of psychological subtlety, seeing it as something to be rooted out by force and thereby magnifying its terror: "Papa wanted to cure him of this childish fear and once told me to blow [the trumpet] at him despite his reluctance, but my God! I should not have been persuaded to do it; Wolfgangerl scarcely heard the blaring sound when he grew pale and began to collapse, and if I had continued, he would surely have had a fit."[31]

Mozart's greatest reward was his father's approval, granted for high achievement and acquiescent behavior. To judge by an account left by his sister, his greatest fear was of his father's disfavor, which could be warded off only by ritual propitiation. Earlier we heard his bedtime routine described by his father. As Marianne recalled it:

> He loved his parents, and especially his father, so dearly, that he composed a melody which he would sing out loud each day before going to sleep, to which end his father had to set him on a chair. Father always had to sing the second part, and when this ceremony, which might on no occasion be omitted, was over, he would kiss his father most tenderly and go to bed very peacefully and contentedly. He continued this game until he was in his tenth year.[32]

We recall that "Next to God comes Papa" was Mozart's childish motto, which he continued to cling to even as a young man.[33] Throughout his life, Mozart's letters unfailingly and conspicuously declared his eternal affection for his father, even when relations between them were most strained.

Mozart's mother, it seems, was too much her husband's faithful help-mate—or too unwilling to risk his displeasure—to take exception to his pedagogical methods. Mozart probably had reason to feel that however much she doted on him, however valiantly she played the difficult role of peacemaker in the family—trying to defend her children while mollifying her husband—she owed her first allegiance to Leopold, or at the least she could not stand against him in a crux. Her role is difficult to assess, for there are few references to her in the anecdotal literature—she is all but effaced by Leopold Mozart's powerful presence—and no letters to her son. Her only surviving letters are to her husband, with occasional lines to her daughter, and these letters date only from her travels with Mozart in 1777 and 1778. Moreover, Frau Mozart's interests did not vary from her husband's in any significant way. She had known poverty, illness, and deprivation as a child and young woman; Leopold's slender income during the first fifteen years of their marriage provided only a minimal living standard. As the Grand Journey commenced, Frau Mozart, now in her mid-forties, recognized in her children's talents the prospect of a better life—perhaps even wealth—for herself and her family. Later, having grown accustomed to comfort and status, she would find it difficult to relinquish her gains.

As a child Mozart began to seek affection outside his own family, clamoring for kisses, embraces, and verbal assurances. In his last years, as we shall see, he compulsively sought even more tangible proofs of love. The source of his need is not entirely clear, but he certainly had sufficient reason to feel that his parents loved him neither disinterestedly nor unconditionally. From the first, Leopold Mozart's expressions of approval and fondness bore unmistakable signs of self-interest, intimations that became explicit in later years. His goal was to shape, guide, and animate his son's professional and moral life, that is, to instill in him a sense of purpose, whose main ingredient was to advance the family interest. For Leopold, parental approval was primarily a reward bestowed for fidelity to this enterprise.

Mozart's desire for approval might have led to utter docility, even obsequiousness. Instead, he was driven to go far beyond what was asked of him, to excel at all costs. He had felt the power of music—to bring approbation and love, to evoke admiration and applause, to harvest money and gifts. Here was a wondrous activity, one that gave him a sense of achievement, for it was a virtually unlimited means of developing and exhibiting his natural gifts. Schachtner saw the boy's own inner equation of music and magic on the occasion of his first compositional effort: Mozart, he recalled, had "the notion that to play a concerto and work a miracle must be one and the same."[34]

Perhaps because he was intoxicated by these capacities of music, Mozart wanted to move quickly—even more quickly than his father desired. Leopold Mozart did not start him on the violin; Mozart taught himself how to play and instantly moved to share (perhaps to usurp) his father's role as violinist. Similarly, at four or five Mozart tried to teach himself composition, inventing his own primitive system of musical notation. Wanting to proceed at a more deliberate pace, Leopold Mozart seems to have urged caution and patience on each of these occasions; even at that early stage, he may already have glimpsed that the boy had the potential to go in unanticipated directions, indeed to upset his plans for the future. For a long time, the existence of the so-called "Salzburg Study Book" (*das Salzburger Studienbuch*), a collection of lessons in strict counterpoint, was regarded as evidence that Leopold had trained his son in that subject, but recent research shows that Mozart himself prepared the book as a course of instruction for one of his own students in the 1780s. From this, Wolfgang Plath and Alfred Mann conclude that Mozart may not have received systematic theoretical instruction from his father. According to Plath, "there is not a single document that can attest to the father's purposeful contrapuntal instruction."[35] And Mann writes, "So far as the received sources indicate, Leopold Mozart set about to instruct his son not as a theoretical, but rather as an eminently practical musician."[36] Thus, recognizing that the available sources are limited, and without attempting to diminish Leopold Mozart's crucial role in his son's musical development, we may need to think of Mozart as being impelled almost from the first to become his own primary instructor.

Mozart found in music a two-edged power—both to please and to resist. The issue of resistance, however, had not yet arisen; during his preadolescent years, he gave no overt sign of dissatisfaction with his role. Willingly, even joyously, he performed his part within the family, unaware of the possibility, let alone the desirability, of pursuing a separate path. It seems clear that he had no need for, nor he could envisage, any alternative to his highly structured and rewarding existence. And yet one wonders why, in the private sphere of his own imagination, he spun fantasies of a kingdom in which he could reign supreme, free of outer compulsion. His sister relates how

> he would think out a kingdom for himself as we traveled from one place to another, and this he called the Kingdom of Back [das Königreich Rücken]—why by this name, I can no longer recall. This kingdom and its inhabitants were endowed with everything that could make of them good and happy children. He was the King of this land—and this notion became so rooted within him, and he carried it so far, that our servant, who could draw a little, had to make a chart of it, and he would dictate the names of the cities, market towns and villages to him.[37]

Whatever else can be said about Mozart's fantasy kingdom, on one basic level it surely represented a place where grownups were excluded, a good place where Mozart himself wielded the scepter of responsibility, thereby asserting dominion over his own life. In this world there was no room for rival monarchs; the elders were simply wished out of existence. It would not be surprising if Mozart's yearning for his own royal space, which is to say, the desire for the free expression of his own individuality, should have begun to stir even at so early an age.

5

....

A VIENNA SOJOURN

Leopold Mozart had reason to be uncertain of his reception in Salzburg. He had been away from his duties much longer than his employers had anticipated, having persisted in extending the Grand Journey for a full three and a half years. He may have been concerned, too, that reports of his large profits would not sit well with his superiors. However, his worries were not justified. The Mozarts' success had brought celebrity to their hometown and had reflected glory upon its prince-archbishop, whose wisdom in sponsoring his gifted subjects had been broadcast in all the major courts of Europe. The authorities showed their appreciation in the most appropriate manner, by allowing the family to take yet another journey only ten months after their return to Salzburg on November 19, 1766.

Clearly, Mozart was in great favor, for during his stay in Salzburg he was asked to undertake several important composing assignments, which he executed in an exemplary manner. His Recitative and Aria for tenor, "Or che il dover"—"Tali e cotanti sono," K. 36, was performed on 21 December 1766, the anniversary of the archbishop's consecration. Soon Mozart was invited to join with the senior Salzburg court composers Michael Haydn and Anton Cajetan Adlgasser in composing an Oratorio, *Die Schuldigkeit des ersten Gebots*, K. 35, his section of which was performed on 12 March 1767; for his efforts he received a gold medal worth twelve ducats. On 13 May 1767 Mozart's Latin comedy, *Apollo et Hyacinthus*, K. 38, was performed at the Benedictine University graduation ceremony; later that day, Mozart played for an enthusiastic university audience, giving "notable proofs of his musical art at the harpsichord," in the words of a contemporary report.[1] Doubtless

Emperor Joseph II. Oil portrait by Joseph Hickel, Vienna 1771.
Historisches Museum der Stadt Wien, inv. no. 104-680.

there were other occasions on which Mozart exhibited his powers as a musician for the edification of the better classes in Salzburg and their foreign guests, including a reception for the imperial ambassador on 29 March 1767. He also wrote a lengthy Passion Cantata (*Grabmusik*), K. 42/35a; the four keyboard concertos, K. 37, 39–41, based on sonata movements by other composers; and a fair number of smaller works that no longer survive—including six Divertimenti, K. 41a; various works for winds, K. 41b; and a variety of miscellaneous pieces, K. 41c–g—although they are listed in Leopold Mozart's thematic catalog (*Verzeichnis*) of Mozart's early works.[2]

Even as he arrived in Salzburg at the end of the Grand Journey, Leopold Mozart was planning further trips to exhibit his children's abilities. We know that a realistic appraisal of the situation had persuaded him that time was not on his side; he understood full well that his children's successes were founded on their youth and the novelty of their performances. Marianne was now seventeen, and Mozart was almost twelve. All the more reason, then, to move quickly. "There is a strong rumor that the Mozart family will again not long remain here," wrote Hübner in his diary, "but will soon visit the whole of Scandinavia and the whole of Russia, and perhaps even travel to China, which would be a far greater journey and bigger undertaking still."[3] But Leopold Mozart was planning another visit to Vienna instead, in expectation of a resounding reception from the royal family and the princely houses. And he was already looking beyond Vienna to Italy: "The trip to Naples is now definitely set for early next year," he wrote in late 1767.[4]

On 11 September 1767, the entire Mozart family, traveling in their own carriage with a servant named Bernhard, left Salzburg en route to Vienna. They stayed overnight at Vöcklabruck, had lunch at the monastery at Lambach, stayed in Linz at the Green Tree inn, drove to Melk, where Mozart played organ at the Benedectine abbey, slept at St. Pölten, and on the fifteenth arrived in Vienna, where they took lodgings in the Weihburggasse on the second floor of a house owned by the goldsmith Johann Schmalecker. Leopold Mozart was elated at his prospects and undaunted by the costs. He wrote to Hagenauer, "Do not be surprised if we draw four hundred or even five hundred florins. . . . Perhaps one single day will arrive which will repay it all."[5]

In Vienna, the imperial family was in no hurry to see the Mozarts. While they were awaiting the court's summons, a smallpox epidemic broke out, and Archduchess Josepha died on 15 October. When their landlord's children fell ill, Leopold took his family to Brünn (Brno) for safety, arriving on 23 October; there they visited Countess Herberstein and Count Franz Anton Schrattenbach, brother of Salzburg's archbishop. When they moved on to Olmütz (Olomouc) three days later, on 26 October, Mozart began to exhibit the first symptoms of smallpox: "Wolfgang was complaining of his eyes. I noticed that his head was warm, that his cheeks were hot and very red, but that his hands were as cold as ice. Moreover his pulse was not right. So we gave him some black powder and put him to bed. During the night he was rather restless and in the morning he still had the dry fever."[6] Apparently afraid of alarming Salzburg, Leopold withheld one of the worst details, Mozart's temporary blindness, which was only reported in 1800, by Marianne. "He caught the smallpox, which made him so ill that he could see nothing for nine days and had to spare his eyes for several weeks after his recovery."[7] He was better by 10 November, but then his sister came down with the disease and was ill for almost three weeks.

Nearly four months had been lost by the time the emperor and empress, along with Duke Albert of Saxony and the archduchesses, finally received the Mozarts on the afternoon of 19 January. "You cannot possibly conceive," reported Leopold Mozart with pride, "with what familiarity Her Majesty the Empress conversed with my wife, talking to her partly of my children's smallpox and partly of the events of our grand tour; nor can you imagine how she stroked my wife's cheeks and pressed her hands. Meanwhile, His Majesty the Emperor talked to little Wolfgang and to me about music, and many other things too, which often made Nannerl blush."[8] Alas, the imperial enthusiasm was not translated into coinage; despite their favorable reception, the Mozarts received only an inexpensive medal. The emperor "positively abhors everything that might entail any expenditure," complained Leopold, "and believes, no doubt, that he has paid us by his most gracious conversations."[9]

Thus, they had been in Vienna for a considerable time without any significant income. Leopold Mozart wrote, "We have spent so much of our capital that there is little apparent hope of our being able to recover it."[10] It was already amply clear that Mozart was not going to create the expected furor in the Austrian capital. Perhaps he was too old to play the infant prodigy; perhaps the novelty had worn off; perhaps he was now a subtler artist and subtlety was not what was needed to cause a great éclat in Vienna—or so Leopold Mozart asserted. "That the Viennese, generally speaking, do not care to see serious and sensible performances, have little or no idea of them, and only want to see foolish stuff, dances, devils, ghosts, magic, clowns, Lipperl, Bernardon, witches, and apparitions is well known; and their theaters prove it every day."[11] Furthermore, there were stirrings of active opposition to Mozart, and skepticism about his abilities was voiced. According to his father, many Viennese musicians claimed that *"it was all humbug and foolishness; that it was all prearranged; that he was given music which he already knew; that it was ridiculous to think that he could compose, and so forth."*[12]

Under the circumstances, Leopold Mozart considered cutting his losses and going home. Instead, a chance question from the emperor, asking whether Mozart would not like to write an opera, gave Leopold a sudden inspiration for a total change in strategy. "But as I was considering this matter as carefully as I could and thinking of how much money I had already spent and that if I were now to go home without waiting for anything more, it would perhaps be extremely foolish, something quite different occurred. . . . I decided to do something entirely out of the ordinary, that is, to get Wolfgang to write an opera for the theater."[13] Instantly, he was enraptured by triumphal visions: "Can you not imagine what a turmoil secretly arose amongst those composers? What? Today, we are to see a Gluck and tomorrow a boy of twelve seated at the harpsichord and conducting his own opera?"[14]

Leopold Mozart may well have been right to believe that since Mozart's appeal as a child virtuoso was fading, it would be wise to pursue other options, of which the most ambitious surely was for a boy of twelve to make his debut as an opera composer. Perhaps by now Leopold had also grasped the subtext of the skeptical reception: that serious musicians and music lovers resented his crass promotional approach and wanted something more from Mozart than dazzling displays. But though he understood that he would have to change his tactics, he made a series of miscalculations—not least, that Mozart could compose a successful full-scale opera buffa on his first try, especially in light of his youth and his imperfect command of Italian—and thereby suffered the most serious setback of his career as Mozart's impresario. He was misled by his boundless faith in his son's powers.

Using a libretto by Marco Coltellini based on a text by Carlo Goldoni, Mozart began the opera *La finta semplice* in late January; at the end of March, Leopold Mozart reported that it was "going well" and that they hoped to have it ready for performance upon the emperor's return from Hungary in June.[15] Unfortunately, though, the first rehearsal was a disaster: the singers said the work was unsingable, members of the orchestra complained that "they did not like a boy to conduct them," and reports spread that the music "was not worth a fig" and in any event had been written by the father rather than the son.[16] Most calamitous, after calling for various revisions, the impresario Giuseppe Affligio, who was the lessee of the two court theaters—the Burgtheater and Kärntnertor Theater—canceled the proposed production outright and declined to pay Mozart any fee for his work, which he now condemned as "untheatrical."[17]

It is remarkable that a man of Leopold Mozart's business acumen had obtained neither a written commitment nor an advance payment, and now was in the position of trying to enforce an undocumented verbal agree-

Autograph manuscript, *La finta semplice*, K. 51/46a, Act I, finale.
Biblioteka Jagiellónska, Kraków.

ment. Beside himself with embarrassment and chagrin, he petitioned the emperor on 21 September 1768, hoping to recover his expenses from Affligio for breach of contract and attempting to repair Mozart's seriously damaged reputation as a composer: he asked the emperor to investigate the "shamefully envious and dishonoring calumniators" who were endeavoring "to suppress and cause unhappiness in the capital of his German fatherland to an innocent creature whom God has endowed with an extraordinary talent, and whom other nations have admired and encouraged."[18] The emperor was unmoved. Following an investigation of the matter by the general theater director, Count Johann Wenzel Sporck, Leopold Mozart's petition was denied. Whatever the truth of his detailed bill of particulars, it surely did not help his cause that he attributed all of his reversals, which were quite normal in the theater world, to cabals and conspiracies by rival composers, perfidious Italians, and unspecified enemies. "Our adversaries are wicked liars, slanderers and envious creatures," he told Hagenauer, "who would laugh in their sleeves if we were to get frightened or tired out and, by going off in a huff, give them the victory."[19] Nor could the court have been encouraged when Leopold Mozart declined to press for a performance of the opera on the ground that if one conspiracy had aimed to suppress it, another conspiracy was ready to stage it "as wretchedly as possible."[20]

When things didn't go well for him, Mozart's father often reverted to primitive explanations; he wrote Hagenauer, "I could tell you a very long story of all sorts of the most deeply laid plots and malicious persecutions."[21]

To compound Leopold Mozart's difficulties, the Salzburg court finally began to show its displeasure at his absence, for the trip to Vienna was not supposed to be a long one. As early as 10 November 1767, in a letter to Hagenauer, Leopold Mozart voiced his "regret that he would have to arrive in Salzburg later than he had thought," pleading his children's illness as his excuse.[22] But after the children recovered and had their imperial audience there was no longer any reasonable explanation for the family's continued absence. The archbishop quickly came to see that Leopold Mozart had a private aim that did not coincide with the court's interests— namely, a position for himself in Vienna, in pursuit of which he extended his leave for more than a year and attempted to involve himself in opera production. Rumors about his personal ambitions circulated in aristocratic circles. On 27 April 1768 Madame Geoffrin wrote to Prince Kaunitz from Paris: "I have heard that someone named the little Mozart, called the little prodigy of music, was in Vienna with his father, who . . . has resolved to settle in Vienna under your Highness's protection."[23] Either the archbishop had already heard the same rumor or the Salzburg authorities had grown impatient with their deputy kapellmeister's perpetual absences, for Leopold Mozart's salary was abruptly withdrawn in March. The chief steward wrote laconically, "Our most gracious Prince has no objection to Herr Mozart's staying away as long as he likes and will pay him his salary for the month of March, but . . . in future when he is not actually in Salzburg he will be retained as before in the Archbishop's service but during his absence will not be paid his usual salary."[24]

Leopold Mozart now considered his options, telling Hagenauer that he would not plead for restoration of his salary. "How can I in fairness and honor obtain by begging something which I am not earning? For I am not performing my services in Salzburg. . . . On the other hand this is what makes it easy for me to get permission to make a journey to Italy, a journey which . . . can now be postponed no longer and for which I have received from the Emperor himself all the necessary introductions for Florence, the Imperial States, and Naples."[25] Clearly, he still had some cards to play in Salzburg.

The extent of Leopold Mozart's financial losses during the sixteen-month Vienna sojourn is difficult to specify. It is known that the family's expenses amounted to 6 florins per day, for a total of about 2,900 florins,[26] but his letters are resolutely silent about any income, leading Jahn to conclude that "receipts at Vienna could not but be insignificant."[27] Yet there must have been more than negligible income from Mozart's documented appearances in Olmütz and Brünn and from performances of portions of *La finta semplice* for members of the Viennese nobility. Leopold Mozart wrote, "My son was on various occasions asked by the nobility to perform one or other of the arias, and even the finale of the first act, at the clavier; and this was admired by them all."[28] At the end of March Mozart also gave a "big concert" at the residence of the Russian ambassador, Prince Dmitri Galitzin,[29] and tradition has it that his newly composed singspiel, *Bastien und Bastienne*, K. 50/46b, was performed at Franz Anton Mesmer's suburban mansion in the fall of 1768.[30] Many other performances took place for which we lack specific details; in one letter, Leopold Mozart mentions displays of his son's compositional skill at the houses of kapellmeister Giuseppe Bonno, court poet Pietro Antonio Metastasio, composer Johann Adolph Hasse, and such high nobles as the duke of Braganza and Prince Kaunitz.[31]

Doubtless it was for such private concerts that several of Mozart's new symphonies were composed and performed, notably those in F, K. 43, in D, K. 45, and in D, K. 48, works that give evidence of his absorption of rhetorical and structural elements from Viennese composers like Vanhal, Dittersdorf, Hofmann, Haydn, and Gassmann. These composers' four-movement symphonies featured greater theatricality of expression, expansive developments, and a more liberal use of contrapuntal textures than his earlier Italianate models. Mozart's youthful works always reflected influences he encountered on his journeys, though not through the largely involuntary process typical of composers in their formative period. Rather, under his father's expert guidance, he consciously set out to model his music on compositions popular in each city or region. Thus, the new symphonies were crafted primarily to please the aristocratic patrons of the Viennese symphonic tradition; *La finta semplice* was intended for the court audience, which favored stock Italian opera buffa; and for the enlightened connoisseurs who gathered at the Mesmer residence, he composed a pastoral singspiel based on a text by Rousseau celebrating rustic simplicity and the unspoiled virtue of a shepherd and shepherdess. The issue of a personal style was not yet on Mozart's agenda.

It is probable that Mozart's many patrons covered at least part of the cost of the family's stay in Vienna, in return for which he and his sister filled their salons with musical entertainment of a high order. Perhaps this widespread aristocratic patronage gave rise to the rumor, which greatly angered Leopold Mozart, "that little Wolfgang has received 2,000 florins for the opera."[32] Furthermore, even though the imperial court would eventually show its displeasure at Leopold Mozart's burdensome complaints, the Mozarts were not wholly out of favor there. Mozart was commissioned to preside over the music for the public dedication of a church on 7 December 1768. Marianne Mozart recalled, "At the consecration of the Orphan-

age Church [*Waisenhauskirche*] on the Landstrasse this 12-year-old boy conducted the service in the presence of the Imperial court."[33] Mozart's effort
was highly successful, as the *Wienerische Diarium* for 10 December reported:
"The whole of the music . . . has been newly composed for this solemnity
by Wolfgang Mozart, the little son aged 12 (but already well known for his
talents) of Herr Leopold Mozart, . . . [who] performed by himself to general applause and admiration, and conducted with the greatest accuracy;
and apart from this he also sang in the motets."[34] Of course, Leopold
Mozart was delighted; he wrote that the event had "restored that reputation which our enemies, by preventing the performance of the opera,
intended to destroy, and, as the throng was amazing, has convinced the
court and the public of the wickedness of our adversaries. . . . And, what is
more," he added with emphasis, "Her Majesty the Empress has sent us a
beautiful present."[35]

Despite serious setbacks, then, Leopold Mozart was able to correct his
course and to mend some fences. And he had learned a great deal, realizing
that Mozart would henceforth have to prove himself in more serious arenas
of composition, solo performance, and theatrical production. He continued to put Mozart's abilities on display, but no longer at cloth-covered keyboards. Nevertheless, he had not lost his flair for the dramatic: in Vienna,
visiting the great musical houses, he would ask someone to open the works
of Metastasio and to choose at random a text for an aria, whereupon
"Wolfgang took up his pen and with the most amazing rapidity wrote,
without hesitation and in the presence of several eminent persons, the
music for this aria for several instruments."[36] Leopold Mozart was already
formulating a campaign strategy adequate to the altered circumstances.

Teatro Regio Ducale, Milan. Engraving by Marco Antonio Dal Rè.

6

··

THE ITALIAN JOURNEYS

Mozart and his father went on three journeys to Italy between December 1769 and March 1773. The second and third were of relatively short duration (four months and less than five months, respectively) because each was for the specific purpose of fulfilling a major commission in Milan. But the first journey was an extended tour, lasting more than fifteen months, from 13 December 1769 to 28 March 1771, and covering almost forty cities and towns, with triumphant appearances in Verona, Mantua, Milan, Bologna, Florence, Rome, and Naples. The tour gathered momentum with Mozart's acclaimed public concerts in Verona and Mantua on 5 and 16 January 1770, which prepared the way for his conquest of Milan; there he played frequently at the palace of Count Karl Joseph Firmian, the governor of Lombardy, giving a major concert on 18 February in the presence of the duke and princess of Modena, and another, on 12 March, where, Leopold wrote, "over 150 members of the leading nobility were present, the most important of them being the Duke, the Princess and the Cardinal."[1] Mozart also mounted a public concert in Milan on 23 February and was commissioned to compose an opera to be performed at the Teatro Regio Ducale during the next carnival season.[2] In late March he spent five days in Bologna and presented another memorable concert on the twenty-sixth at the villa of Count Gian Luca Pallavicini, attended by 150 aristocrats, church dignitaries, and other notables, including the prolific composer and renowned theorist Padre Giovanni Battista Martini, who instantly became Mozart's friend, teacher, and powerful advocate. From Bologna, father and son proceeded to Florence, giving private concerts for Grand Duke

Leopold of Tuscany, the younger son of Maria Theresia and later to become emperor, at the Palazzo Pitti and at his summer palace.

In Rome, where they stayed for a full month, Mozart gave no public concerts but appeared frequently at the residences of the highest nobility and various ambassadors. A report from there on 2 May observed that "the son of the Kapellmeister of Salzburg has been here for some time and is admired by all for his extraordinary and precocious musical talent."[3] On 15 April, Easter Sunday, Leopold and his son were received at St. Peter's by Pope Clement XIV, who subsequently conferred on Mozart the cross of the Order of the Golden Spur. The papal order read in part, "Hearkening to the supplications humbly submitted to us on thy behalf in this matter, we hereby make and create thee—whom we understand to have excelled since thy earliest youth in the sweetest sounding of the harpsichord— Knight of the Golden Order."[4] Leopold Mozart wrote home to his wife, expressing both his excitement and his sense of disbelief: "Tomorrow we are to hear a piece of news which, if it is true, will fill you both with amazement. For Cardinal Pallavicini is said to have been commanded by the Pope to hand Wolfgang the cross and diploma of an order. Do not say much about this yet. If it is true, I shall write to you next Saturday."[5]

From Rome they proceeded south to Naples, where they stayed for six weeks, until 25 June, providing musical entertainment for grateful princes, princesses, duchesses, and ambassadors—including William Hamilton of Britain, whose wife, Emma's predecessor, was a keyboard player—and enjoying excursions to Pozzuoli, Baia, Vesuvius, Pompeii, and Herculaneum. The summer season intervened, and there were relatively few performances during the remainder of the year, which was largely devoted to the composition of the opera for Milan, *Mitridate, rè di Ponto,* to a libretto by Vittorio Amedeo Cigna-Santi, based on an Italian translation by Giuseppe Parini of Racine's *tragédie* on that subject.

Mindful of his misadventure in Vienna, Leopold Mozart did not fail to negotiate a written contract with a guaranteed payment of 100 ducats. The libretto was delivered to them in Bologna on 27 July, exactly a week after their arrival, and Mozart immediately began work on the recitatives. But the main work on the opera, which premiered on 26 December 1770, was done in Milan during an extended stay starting on 18 October. Characteristically, Leopold Mozart saw malevolent forces arrayed against *Mitridate;* he wrote to Padre Martini, "My son's opera has been received most favorably in spite of the great opposition of his enemies and detractors, who before hearing a single note had spread the rumor that it was a barbarous German composition. . . . The calumniators kept on spreading most evil reports."[6] But the calumniators were routed; the opera ran for twenty-two consecutive performances, with Mozart directing the first three from the harpsichord.

"Our son's opera is still running, is still winning general applause and is, as the Italians say, *alle stelle!*" wrote Leopold to his wife on 5 January.[7]

Several weeks in Turin beginning 14 January and a month in Venice, where Mozart gave a major concert at the Maffei residence, brought the first Italian journey to a close. Leopold Mozart was in no hurry to go home; the return trip took them by way of Padua, Vicenza, Verona, and Innsbruck, and they arrived in Salzburg on 28 March 1771. A few days later, Mozart received an imperial commission to compose a theatrical ser-enata—"really a short opera," noted Leopold[8]—entitled *Ascanio in Alba,* intended to celebrate the marriage the following October of Empress Maria Theresia's son, Archduke Ferdinand, to Princess Beatrice Ricciarda. The wedding was to be held in Milan, so Mozart's second journey to Italy was assured almost before the first had been concluded.

This second journey consisted of a three-and-a-half-month stay in Milan, lasting from 21 August until 5 December 1771, with brief stops in several cities and towns en route to and from Salzburg. On 29 August Mozart received the text for *Ascanio in Alba,* written by Giuseppe Parini, and immediately set to work; by mid-September the overture, the recita-tives, and the choruses had been completed, and the first rehearsal took place on 14 October. Mozart's work was scheduled as a climax of the spec-tacular marriage festivities, which featured a flock of theatrical productions, masquerades, horse races, and other events. According to newspaper accounts, the entire city was "magnificently lighted" and "each day three hundred persons will dine at court, where there will be masked balls, and at the theaters masked balls will also take place." At a public ceremony, 150 young couples were to be married and given dowries by the royal bridal pair. "Two fountains will flow with wine instead of water, various orches-tras with musicians will perform, and, finally, a *serenata teatrale* entitled *Ascanio in Alba,* composed by Abbate Parini and set to music by Herr Mozzart, will be performed."[9] The work was presented so successfully on 17 October that a repeat performance was given two days later: "We are constantly addressed in the street by courtiers and other persons who wish to congratulate the young composer," Leopold Mozart wrote to his wife.[10] He proudly reported that the archduke and archduchess "showed their gra-cious approval by calling out 'Bravissimo, maestro' and clapping their hands."[11] The composer Johann Adolph Hasse, who had written the prin-cipal opera for the wedding festivities, supposedly exclaimed, "This boy will consign us all to oblivion!"[12] Hasse had good reason to be concerned, for the notices emphasized the superiority of Mozart's serenata over Hasse's work: "The opera has not met with success, and was not performed except for a single ballet. The serenata, however, has met with great applause, both for the text and the music."[13]

The third journey followed a now familiar routine. *Mitridate, rè di Ponto* had been so well received that Mozart was commissioned to write another opera for the Milan carnival season of 1773.[14] After ten months in Salzburg, he and his father returned to Milan, arriving there on 4 November 1772 for a stay of four months almost entirely devoted to writing *Lucio Silla* to a libretto by Giovanni de Gammera, and preparing it for performance. Mozart had started the recitatives in Salzburg and then rewritten them to account for changes in Gammera's libretto. He wrote the choruses and overture soon after arriving in Milan, but as late as 5 December he still had fourteen numbers to compose and was feeling pressed: "I can think of nothing but my opera."[15] The premiere was so chaotic that it is difficult to credit Leopold Mozart's optimistic report: "The first hitch was that the performance . . . started three hours late. . . . Thus it did not finish until two o'clock in the morning. . . . For three hours singers, orchestra, and audience (many of the latter standing) had to wait impatiently in the heat for the opera to begin."[16] Later on, though, he remarked that "the opera has gained daily in popularity and has won increasing applause" during its scheduled run of twenty-six performances.[17]

Mozart was extremely productive during the Italian journeys, in addition to his stage commissions. In Milan during February and March 1770 he composed two Soprano Arias, "Misero tu non sei," K. Anh. 2/73A (lost), and "Fra cento affanni," K. 88/73c, as well as a Soprano Scene, "Misero me"—"Misero pargoletto," K. 77/73e, for use at concerts there. Two additional arias for soprano, "Se ardire, e speranza," K. 82/73o, and "Se tutti i mali miei," K. 83/73p, were written at Rome in April and May for use in Naples. All the foregoing had texts by Metastasio. Mozart wrote home from Rome, highlighting his industriousness: "When I have finished this letter I shall finish a symphony which I have begun. The aria is finished. A symphony is being copied."[18] In August he wrote, "In the meantime I have composed four Italian symphonies, to say nothing of arias, of which I must have composed at least five or six, and also a motet."[19]

Apart from opera, he was most prolific in the symphony genre, because symphonies were in demand as curtain-raisers and finales at musical and theatrical events. Evidently he brought some symphonies from Salzburg for the earlier Italian concerts, but starting in April 1770, he set to work writing new ones. Although autograph scores are lacking for all of these but K. 74, in G, many experts are willing to take it on faith that Mozart composed four other symphonies during the first Italian journey: K. 81/73l, 97/73m, 95/73n, and 84/73q, all in the key of D.[20] Here again he adapted his symphonic style to local tastes, employing the melodies, formal structure, orchestration, and buffa character of the Italian symphonic tradition.

As Stanley Sadie observes, "The manner of these symphonies shows Mozart influenced by the music he encountered in Italy, and keen to please Italian audiences, or both."[21] To these symphonies, one ought to add the Symphony in C, K. 73, written in anticipation (or even at the beginning) of the first journey, and several symphonies written for or during the second journey, K. 110/75b, 96/111b, and 112.[22] At home between late December 1771 and August 1772, either for Salzburg occasions or as part of a portfolio for the third Italian journey, Mozart composed eight more symphonies, all well authenticated: K. 114, 124, 128–130, and 132–134.

Keyboard music was notably absent from the works of Mozart's Italian period, though it seems possible that the concertos after sonatas by J. C. Bach, K. 107, were written to provide keyboard vehicles for use in his Italian concerts. Starting in 1772 he made his first contributions to the string quartet genre, apart from the lone String Quartet in G, K. 80/73f, written mostly in 1770. The three Divertimentos (so titled on the autographs, but the designation is not in Mozart's hand) in D, B-flat, and F, K. 136–38/125a–c, which have become staples of string orchestra programs, are probably string quartets rather than orchestral works. Mozart's major efforts in this genre, however, are the six String Quartets, K. 155–60, which date from the third Italian journey and take their inspiration from Italian models exemplified by the outstanding Milanese composer Giovanni Battista Sammartini, a congenial influence because of his connection with Mozart's London mentor, J. C. Bach, during the latter's Milan years. All are in three-movement form, and are composed as a set, Mozart's cyclical intentions signaled by his choice of successive keys at downward intervals of a fifth—D, G, C, F, B-flat, and E-flat. Inasmuch as they date from autumn 1772 to early 1773, the last months of the last journey, they may not have been intended for specific performance but as a hopeful applicant's offering to a potential Florentine employer, Grand Duke Leopold of Tuscany. Mozart's father perhaps tried to divert attention from this possibility by informing Salzburg that "Wolfgang is . . . at the moment writing a quartet to while away the time."[23]

Rounding out Mozart's Italian compositions are several sacred works, including an incomplete Miserere, K. 85/73s, and an Antiphon, "Quaerite primum regnum Dei," for four voices, K. 86/73v, which was required to test his suitability for membership in the Accademia Filarmonica of Bologna. (Until recently it was believed that during the summer of 1770 Mozart worked on academic exercises in *stile antico* counterpoint for Padre Martini and the Marquis de Ligniville, including a Canon for five voices in A, K. 73i, a Kyrie in G for five sopranos, K. 89/73k, four Riddle Canons, K. 73r, and fourteen Canonic Studies for voices, K. 73x, but Plath's handwriting analyses make it conceivable that these works really belong to 1772 or later.)[24]

After this quantity of sacred works, Mozart wrote no other religious music in Italy until just before his final departure in January 1773, when he composed the brilliant Motet for soprano, "Exsultate, jubilate," K. 165/158a, a condensed three-movement vocal concerto written for a performance by the castrato Venanzio Rauzzini. In Salzburg, however, during the intervals between journeys, he was very much occupied with sacred music. In 1771 he wrote a "Regina coeli" for four voices, orchestra, and organ, in C, K. 108/74d, and a *Litaniae Lauretanae BVM* in B-flat, for four voices, two violins, three trombones, bass, and organ, K. 109/74e. In 1772 he composed another "Regina coeli," in B-flat, K. 127; a *Litaniae de venerabili altaris sacramento* in B-flat, K. 125; a fragmentary Osanna for four voices, strings, and organ, K. 223/166e; several unfinished Kyries, in C, K. Anh. 18/166f, and in D, K. Anh. 19/166g; and three Church Sonatas for two violins and basso continuo, K. 67–69/41h, i, k; and a Kyrie for four voices and figured bass (organ), K. 90, whose authenticity has been questioned. Also from this period is *La Betulia liberata*, K. 118/74c, an Italian heroic oratorio to a Metastasio text, completed by the summer of 1771 and intended for a concert performance that perhaps never took place. Despite Mozart's long absences in Italy, the Salzburg authorities were getting good value from their young composer.

In Italy, Leopold accomplished the main goal he had set himself two years earlier: to establish Mozart's reputation as a serious composer worthy of operatic commissions and consideration for a post as kapellmeister at a major court. At the same time, with boundless energy and extraordinary diplomatic skill, Leopold exploited every opportunity to exhibit his son's keyboard artistry for an admiring audience of musicians, music lovers, and connoisseurs. It was a fortunate moment in Mozart's development: he had not quite outgrown his wunderkind years and thus was greeted everywhere as a prodigy; in addition, he was in the first flowering of his abilities as a mature composer who, though he had not yet established a personal style or learned to extend the boundaries of tradition, was already composing characteristic and even exemplary works in the existing styles and genres, including opera seria, the most highly regarded genre of the time. The widespread recognition of his talents as a composer and his powers as a virtuoso made the first Italian journey the climax of Mozart's career until that time. That the venue was Italy, the center of Europe's musical life, transformed a personal triumph into a historic event as well, one consistent with a shift of musical supremacy from Italy to the north during the maturing of the classical style.

In the eighteenth century, Italian musicians and composers occupied countless positions in the musical establishments of the great European courts, including those of Austria, Germany, England, Russia, and France. At various times, Italian kapellmeisters were in full charge of music at the courts in Bonn, Salzburg, and Vienna. An Italian, Pietro Metastasio, was the imperial court poet at Vienna. Italian performers dominated many of the touring companies that presented operas throughout Europe. J. C. Bach, Gluck, and Grétry studied with Italian masters. With all due recognition of the internationalization of eighteenth-century culture, the musical balance of trade was everywhere heavily in favor of Italy, which was Europe's leading exporter of music, performers, and composers. Mozart's storming of the Italian musical citadel and his stunning acceptance there was thus a startling reversal, a master stroke of Leopold Mozart's promotional genius, and a tribute to his sense of history.

Mozart's reception was also a tribute to Italian taste and tolerance, and by no means simply to Italian indulgence of one so young. Musicians in virtually every city he visited in Italy were initially skeptical of his abilities, putting him to the most rigorous tests before they would acknowledge his gifts; unlike audiences in prior years, they would not accept virtuoso artifice as a substitute for musical substance. (Of course, public tests of his son's prowess continued to be part of Leopold Mozart's strategy, nor did he scruple to deduct a year or two from Wolfgang's age.)[25] In Verona, it was reported that Mozart overcame "the most arduous trials . . . with an inexpressible skill, and thus to universal admiration."[26] The tests ran the gamut of his abilities: first he played a harpsichord concerto and several sonatas at sight; then a party of "distinguished professors" from the Accademia Filarmonica submitted four verses to him, to which "he composed on the spot an aria in the best of taste"; he closed with a demonstration of his powers of improvisation "according to the best rules of the art."[27]

The report from the Accademia Filarmonica of Mantua described a similar series of public trials in composition, improvisation, and accompa-

Verona: View of the Roman amphitheater. Unsigned color engraving.
Österreichische Nationalbibliothek, Vienna.

niment, as well as performances on various instruments, followed by private examinations at the homes of the local "masters and professors of music," who in the end could not find "words sufficient to express their feeling that this youth appears to them to be born to confound all the experts in the art."[28] They agreed that Mozart "*is a miracle in music, and one of those freaks Nature causes to be born, a Ferracina to humiliate the Mathematicians, and a Corilla to degrade the poets.*"[29] In Milan, too, where the Mozarts arrived on 7 February 1770, Mozart was subjected to "tests of his knowledge" in the presence of a brilliant assembly that included Sammartini, and Leopold Mozart wrote home of how his son "amazed them."[30] (So impressed were the experts that he was offered the commission for *Mitridate, rè di Ponto* after they received from him several sample arias, K. Anh. 2/73A, K. 88/73c, and K. 77/73e.) And from Bologna Leopold wrote: "Wolfgang is admired here even more than he has been in all the other towns of Italy; the reason is that Bologna is the center and dwelling-place of many masters, artists, and scholars. Here too he has been most thoroughly tested."[31]

The series of Herculean trials continued in Florence, where in Marianne Mozart's account "the Marchese Ligniville, the music director and a great contrapuntist, placed the most difficult fugues before the son, and gave him the most difficult themes, which he immediately read at sight and then worked out."[32] It culminated in Bologna, where Mozart underwent rigorous formal examinations in October in connection with his petition for admittance to the Accademia Filarmonica. "He was locked up quite alone," wrote his sister, but completed the task of composing the required four-voice antiphon within half an hour.[33] He was judged competent and accepted for membership on 9 October 1770, and the diploma was presented to him on the following day. Not to be outdone, Verona's Accademia Filarmonica named him an honorary "maestro di capela" on 5 January 1771.[34] By then, the Italians had already christened Mozart "Il Signor Cavaliere Filarmonico."[35]

The Italian triumph was not accomplished automatically or without a struggle. While Mozart contended with the musicians, Leopold Mozart had to counter political opposition and gather allies in his son's cause. The opposition showed itself most powerfully at the start, in Mantua, where several of the aristocratic directors of the Accademia there greeted the pair with conspicuous ungraciousness.[36] A rebuff by Prince Michael II von Thurn und Taxis was unmistakable, although they carried a letter of recommendation to him from Salzburg's eminent Lodron family. "Today we went to the Prince von Taxis but he wasn't at home," wrote Leopold Mozart on 11 January 1770, suspecting but not yet certain that they had been snubbed.[37] The next day they went again, and finding the prince and his family in church, "we likewise went to the church and afterward went home after them, following the cook at about 50 paces. . . . However, the prince now had to perform necessary devotions, and was unable to speak to us; we should come on some other occasion. The demeanor and the shaking voice of the servant and his half-broken words showed me clearly that the prince had no desire to see us."[38] Erich Schenk suggests that Leopold Mozart's clumsy attempt to involve the imperial court in his quarrel over *La finta semplice* in 1768 may have "blighted matters" for him in Habsburg Italy.[39]

Leopold succeeded in warding off this early threat to his plans. He and Mozart sought and found warm welcomes from other Mantuans, including Count Francesco Eugenio Arco (a cousin of Salzburg's Count George Anton Felix Arco, the archbishop's chief chamberlain) and the cultured Bettinelli family. By winning the protection of the powerful Milanese aristocrats, chief among them Count Karl Joseph Firmian, the governor-general of Milan, he quickly gained the day.[40] In addition to the gala concerts at his residence in Milan and his sponsorship of the Mozarts there, Count Firmian (and through him, the Bolognese Count Pallavicini) furnished letters of recommendation to prepare the Mozarts' visits to Bologna, Parma, Florence, Rome, and Naples, thereby giving them access to all of Italy.[41] It was only in Naples that their expectations were at all disappointed, and here again the hand of the Habsburg imperial court may have been at work, for the Mozarts were unable to obtain an audience with Empress Maria Theresia's son-in-law and daughter, King Ferdinand and Queen Maria Carolina of Naples. "We did not get beyond the stock compliments which the Queen paid us wherever she met us," wrote Leopold Mozart to his wife. "She has no influence and what sort of a fellow the King is it is perhaps wiser to speak of than to write about."[42] Nevertheless, as in Mantua, the Mozarts showed their mettle by cultivating favor with the high nobility and the diplomatic corps, making contacts that led to a splendid concert and several glittering private appearances.[43]

Naturally, Leopold Mozart reaped a substantial financial harvest during the first journey, considering Mozart's many public concerts and the extraordinary number of private salons and gala appearances before the highest nobility. Concert expenses were minimal, so far as we know, and halls were customarily supplied without charge. Everywhere, Mozart's celebrity brought full houses and the generous payments usually accorded to the latest popular idol. Mozart's father seems to have renewed his resolve to furnish only minimal financial information in his letters home, so that it is difficult to assess the final balance sheet. In a letter written for his wife's eyes only, he bluntly explained, "You will be very much disappointed that I do not send you more details about our takings, but I refrain from doing so on purpose, because in Salzburg only the earnings are considered and the expenses ignored and because there are very, very few people who realize what traveling costs are. Let it suffice if I tell you that, thank God, we lack nothing that is necessary to enable us to continue our travels in an honorable fashion."[44]

In letters intended for circulation in Salzburg, he again stressed his great expenses and minimized his takings. He claimed that little money could be made in Mantua and Verona because the nobles and other eminent citizens had free season tickets, omitting to note that such music lovers often gave performers valuable presents. Constantly he sounded the refrain that he merely hoped to break even. From Milan he wrote, "Next Friday there will be a concert for the general public and we shall then see what profit we shall make. But on the whole we shall not earn much in Italy. The main thing is that there is the greatest enthusiasm and understanding here. . . . Otherwise one must generally accept admiration and bravos as payment."[45] After the Milan concert of 23 February, however, he could not quite contain himself, and communicated his satisfaction to his wife in guarded but fairly transparent language: "Our concert, which took place on Friday, went off in the same way as our concerts have done everywhere, and therefore no further description is necessary. We are well, God be praised, and although we are not rich, yet we always have a little more than what is barely necessary."[46]

Occasionally, Leopold Mozart's letters give us a glimpse of substantial financial success. Private concerts at aristocratic residences generally brought in close to 100 florins. At a major private concert in Milan, "Count Firmian gave Wolfgang a snuffbox set in gold" and worth about 90 florins;[47] in Innsbruck, at a salon for Count Leopold Franz Künigl, Mozart received 12 ducats, about 50 florins; in Bologna he received the equivalent of 90 florins;[48] and for his 2 April 1770 private concert in Florence at Villa Poggio Imperiale, he received the equivalent of 112 florins.[49] Mozart probably gave no fewer than twenty-six such concerts during the first Italian journey, earning as much as 2,000 or 2,500 florins. For *Mitridate, rè di Ponto* he was paid 1,625 lire, or 450 florins, and free lodging during three months in Milan.[50] By way of comparison, the successful opera composer Baldassare Galuppi was paid only 110 lire more than Mozart for an opera, and for *Lucio Silla* Mozart received about 500 lire more than Galuppi.[51]

Leopold did not record the profit from public concerts, but he hoped that the Naples concert of 28 May would bring "at least 150 zecchini" (675 florins);[52] afterward he reported, "Yesterday we gave our concert, which turned out very well," so we can assume that his goal had been achieved if not surpassed.[53] "Indeed we need money," he added, "for, if we leave, we shall have a long journey during which we shall not be able to earn anything, and, if we remain, we shall have to hold out for five months. It is true that here we should always be able to earn enough for our needs."[54] It may safely be estimated that the public concerts in Milan, Naples, and Venice brought in at least 2,000 florins. Thus, even without including any income from the public concerts in Mantua and Verona, and leaving aside numerous costly gifts from patrons and admirers, the Mozarts probably grossed about 5,000 florins on the first journey.

In a letter written shortly after arriving in Milan, Leopold Mozart gave his expenses for the first six weeks as 70 ducats, including travel, or 7 florins per day.[55] Writing from Bologna on two separate occasions, he mentioned expenses for food and lodging that work out to 4.5 florins per day: "I shall hardly get away from this inn under twenty ducats, if that does the trick!"[56] Multiplying Leopold Mozart's highest expense figure by the full 470 days of the journey gives a total of 3,290 florins, leaving a potential minimum profit of about 1,700 florins. But there were long stretches when their lodgings were paid for, including those three months in Milan, and many other weeks when friends put them up at little or no cost, for example in Rome at the Scatizzi Palace from 14 April to 8 May 1770, and again from 26 June to 10 July. Similarly, from 10 August to 1 October they were guests at the Villa Pallavicini outside Bologna; in Venice, too, they lodged with the Ceseletti family from 11 February to 12 March 1771. And there were other times—e.g., Milan between 23 January and 15 March 1770, Naples from 14 May to 25 June 1770—when they stayed in monasteries at negligible cost, as low as 18 florins per month. If one makes allowances for these factors and assumes an average daily cost of 4.5 florins, itself a fair sum, the potential profit rises to almost 2,900 florins. In either case, a substantial sum was made on Mozart's first Italian journey. And whatever the margin of error in these calculations, it is surely offset by the fact that on 27 November 1769 the archbishop of Salzburg presented Leopold Mozart with 120 ducats (600 florins) as a subsidy "for the journey to Italy."[57]

Somehow, Leopold Mozart had contrived a success that rivaled the financial yield of the Grand Journey and surpassed it in musical accomplishment. It was his finest hour, and on the evidence of his letters to Salzburg, perhaps his happiest. He delighted in the unbroken string of musical triumphs and in the accompanying monetary rewards. And he delighted in his own reception, in being greeted by Sammartini, Martini, and Nardini, in being interviewed by Burney, in being called a kapellmeister, a title even Mozart granted when he referred to himself in a letter home as "the kapellmeister's son."[58] The pair moved with absolute ease among the highest nobility of Italy—princes, princesses, governors, counts, grand dukes, and church dignitaries, up to and including the pope himself. For example, Leopold wrote from Rome, where they lodged at the residence of Signor Uslenghi, the papal courier: "We all dine together and we have a large room which, as it gets the morning sun, is very healthy. When friends come to see us, all the other rooms are at our disposal and . . . we have a harpsichord too."[59] From Pallavicini's villa he wrote, "Our sheets are of finer linen than many a nobleman's shirt; everything is of silver, even the bedroom sets, and the night lights and so forth. . . . We have two servants to wait on us, a footman and a valet. The former sleeps in our anteroom in order to be at hand in case of necessity. The latter has to dress Wolfgang's hair."[60]

Luxury and distinguished company appeared to feed a grandiose strain in Leopold, most obviously in Rome. "I announced everywhere that I was the steward of the Imperial Ambassador, because in these parts the stewards of such personages are very highly respected."[61] At the Vatican he even encouraged the perception that Mozart was a high noble: "Our fine clothes, the German tongue, and my usual freedom of manner, which led me to make my servant order the Swiss guards in German to make way for us, soon helped us through everywhere. They took Wolfgang for some German courtier, while some even thought that he was a prince, which my servant allowed them to believe; I myself was taken for his tutor."[62] Their expensive manner of dress did nothing to diminish such perceptions; from Naples Leopold reported that they had left their fine cloth suits in Rome and had now donned their "beautifully braided" summer costumes: "Wolfgang's is of rose-colored moiré . . . it is trimmed with silver lace and lined with sky-blue silk. My costume is of the color of cinnamon and is made of piquéd Florentine cloth with silver lace and is lined with apple-green silk."[63] Mozart was no less enchanted: "We put on our new clothes and we were as beautiful as angels," he wrote to his sister in May 1770.[64] For the premiere of *Mitridate, rè di Ponto* later in the year, the tailor was again set to work: "Picture to yourselves little Wolfgang in a scarlet suit, trimmed with gold braid and lined with sky-blue satin."[65] For the Milan carnival in 1770 the tailor made them new cloaks and cowls. "I looked at myself in the mirror as we were trying them on," wrote Leopold, vainly trying to conceal his elation, "and thought of how *in my old age I too have had to take part in this tomfoolery. The costume suits Wolfgang amazingly well."[66]

Leopold Mozart's high spirits led him to propose that Mozart prepare a copy of Allegri's *Miserere*:

> You have often heard of the famous Miserere in Rome, which is so greatly prized that the performers in the chapel are forbidden on pain of excommunication to take away a single part of it, to copy it or to give it to anyone. *But we have it already.* Wolfgang has written it down and we would have sent it to Salzburg in this letter if it were not necessary for us to be

there to perform it. . . . So we shall bring it home with us. Moreover, as it is one of the secrets of Rome, we do not wish to let it fall into other hands.[67]

Later, when Frau Mozart expressed concern, he added, "There is not the slightest cause for anxiety. . . . All Rome and even the Pope himself knows that he wrote it down. There is nothing whatever to fear; on the contrary, the achievement has done him great credit."[68]

At every stage of the journey Mozart gave evidence in his letters to his sister and mother of his own high spirits and good cheer. From Wörgl, en route to Italy, he wrote: "Dearest Mama! My heart is completely enchanted with all these pleasures, because it is so jolly on this journey, because it is so warm in the carriage and because our coachman is a fine fellow who, when the road gives him the slightest chance, drives so fast."[69] From Naples he wrote, "I too am still alive and always merry as usual and I simply love traveling." From Bologna, "I . . . am . . . as merry as can be. I had a great desire today to ride on a donkey."[70] He formed tender friendships with two boys his own age, in Bologna with the gifted young Giuseppe Maria Pallavicini (1756–73) and in Florence with the English violin prodigy Thomas Linley (1756–78), who "wept bitter tears" upon Mozart's departure.[71] He participated in the carnival celebrations, learned to play boccia in Rome, and tirelessly visited the sights, from the art treasures of the northern cities to the ancient ruins and excavations in southern Italy.

His loving letters to his sister overflow with puns, scatological humor, and lightly disguised amatory references to Salzburg girls. He related his staunch resistance to temptation in Venice, during a visit to the Wider household and its six daughters: "Tell Johannes [Hagenauer] that he must soon come back to Venice and submit to the *attacco,* that is, have his bottom spanked when he is lying on the ground, so that he may become a true Venetian. They tried to do it to me—the seven women all together—and yet they could not pull me down."[72] It may not be coincidental that Leopold expressed his concern about Venetian morality a few weeks later: "I know what is good and what is bad for young people, especially in Venice, the most dangerous place in all Italy."[73]

The bond between father and son had never been more secure, based as it was on mutual and total devotion to common goals. Leopold Mozart was single-mindedly dedicated to his son's welfare and career. There was truth in his posing as the tutor of a young prince. By his efforts and by his precepts, he saw to it that Mozart completed his education in Italy: that he learned Italian with such fluency that he could almost flawlessly compose the recitatives to an opera seria within a few months; that he improved his knowledge of counterpoint with Padre Martini's assistance during their visits to Bologna; that he strove for admission to the academies of Bologna and Verona; that he perfected his ability to move in the highest ranks of society. Doubtless under his father's direction, Mozart also continued his lessons. He asked his sister to send him his arithmetic tables; he read *The Arabian Nights* in Italian, and *Les Aventures de Télémaque, fils d'Ulysse,* a rationalist utopian novel by François de Salignac de la Mothe-Fénelon, whom Leopold Mozart adored.[74] And of course the tours themselves, the contemplation of Italy's art treasures, monuments, and landscapes, were the culmination of Mozart's education.

Mozart was engaged in a continuing romance with the world, which unfolded its wonders to him and rendered him its tributes. With an inner conviction reinforced by his father's utter belief in him, he was discovering his enormous gifts as a composer, writing his first successful operas, surmounting every challenge to his abilities, enrapturing audiences through the beauty and inventiveness of his music, meeting great personages and important musicians, receiving the golden spur of a chevalier. All these achievements and honors belonged to the Mozart family as an entity. Affectionately and obediently, Mozart redoubled his efforts to enhance the collective enterprise. In their joint venture, Mozart and his beloved father spent virtually every moment of the fifteen-month journey together, always sleeping in the same room, often in the same bed. From Rome, Mozart jested about taking his mother's place: "Oh, I am having a hard time, for in our rooms there is only one bed and so Mama can well imagine that I get no sleep with Papa."[75]

The depth of their connection was intensified not only by their physical proximity but by their separation from the Mozart women. The whole family had embarked on every previous trip, but Leopold Mozart refused to take his wife and daughter on any of the Italian journeys. This became a point of contention, increasingly so as the journeys continued. "I often thank God that I left you at home," he wrote from Milan in January 1770. "Firstly, you would not have been able to stand the cold. Secondly, it would have cost us a great deal of money and we should not have been so free to live the way in which we now do; for here *we are staying at the Augustinian monastery of S. Marco.*"[76] From Rome he wrote, "Though I am glad that neither of you undertook this journey with us, yet I am sorry that you are not seeing all these Italian towns, and especially Rome."[77] It was particularly ungenerous of him not to let them come for the performances and festivities in connection with Mozart's Milan commissions, and it was grievous that the Mozarts' twenty-fifth wedding anniversary in 1772 was marked only by a line or two in a letter written from afar.

From the start, Frau Mozart felt left out and let her husband know it, as we may deduce from his letters to her. She was familiar with travel expenses and evidently pointed out that a carriage for four did not cost much more than a smaller one, and that they could save money by eating in their lodgings instead of at expensive public inns. Leopold was not pleased: "A carriage for four persons would not eat up much money," he acknowledged, "but the rooms would be a very heavy item. Of course I could take one room for both of us. In the circumstances we should have to camp like soldiers for a short time and have our meals cooked at home."[78] Deftly and unyieldingly he fended off her complaints, alternating references to the high expenses with allusions to the extreme discomforts—earlier too cold, now too hot. "The expense of the outward and return journeys alone would have meant a difference to me of at least sixty ducats. But really you need not feel any regrets, for you would have had to put up with a heat which is incredibly trying. It is true that arrangements are being made for some remarkable entertainments, but they are all shows which you have already seen better performed elsewhere."[79] It irked him to be so often reminded that Marianne was "sighing so deeply for Milan."[80] And on one occasion he impatiently retorted that his wife could come if she wished, but without his approval: "If you are so keen to travel to Italy, we invite you to the opera at Milan."[81] In the end Frau Mozart and Marianne had to be content with promises of expensive new clothes and of a future Italian journey (which never materialized). "*Italy can always be visited,*" wrote Leopold Mozart from Milan, adding, a week later, "You will both see Italy more pleasantly later on than you would now during this horrible rush."[82]

Leopold's obduracy may have been motivated by more than frugality or a desire to have his wife attend to his business affairs in Salzburg, which included the distribution of the second edition of his *Violinschule*. While there is no indication that he blamed her for the failure of the Viennese trip, it seems certain that he wanted to maximize his freedom of action and minimize his encumbrances. It was not the first time Leopold Mozart had emancipated himself from restraints and obligations. Now, moving from triumph to triumph, living like a noble, examining art treasures with a connoisseur's eye, he did not have to carry out his unwanted duties at the Salzburg court, or give wearying lessons to untalented pupils, or bow to the whims and wishes of those whom the fates had chosen to place above him in the social hierarchy. It is difficult to tell whether he was also in flight from family and conjugal responsibilities, difficult to assess how he felt about the extended periods of sexual abstinence. Perhaps it was a sense of having been released from economic and biological imperatives that led him to write rather obscurely, from Bolzano, at the beginning of the second journey, "Thank God, we are both like two deer, but, I should add, we are not in heat."[83] Evidently, however, he was forced to pay a price in mental pain for his freedom; a few weeks after arriving in Milan on the third journey in November 1772, he confessed, "I drop into thinking about Salzburg and, without noticing it, I go on brooding for some time. However, I quickly banish these thoughts or at least try to do so, just as I used to drive out all those wicked ideas which in my youth the devil suggested to me."[84]

Leopold's mood on the third journey was splenetic and petulant; usually prolix, he now found that there was no interesting news: "You want me to write very fully, but what is there to write about?"[85] He perked up only when Mozart's opera was performed, but soon afterward he was plagued with vertigo and other complaints. On earlier occasions, too, he had revealed troubled feelings, though without specifying their nature: "When I was laid up with my foot my old melancholy thoughts came to me very often," he wrote in August 1770.[86] From the same letter we learn that he had forgotten to congratulate his daughter on her name day, an unusual omission for one who placed great emphasis on such observances. On failing to receive timely congratulations on his own name day a few months later, he made his displeasure clear: "Nannerl, I suppose, could not think of a motto, for she too wrote nothing. . . . Indeed, it would not have killed Nannerl if she had written to me."[87] Mozart was saddened at this outburst; his father quoted him as saying, *I am truly sorry for Mama and Nannerl, because in his last letter Papa wrote such cutting remarks in jest.*[88]

The acknowledgment of Mozart's distress on this occasion was uncharacteristic, for Leopold Mozart was wont to stress his son's perpetual good spirits. "He is fat and cheerful and gay and jolly all day long," he wrote from Milan.[89] But Mozart's longing for his mother and sister could not be permanently disguised: "I only wish that my sister were in Rome, for this town would certainly please her," he wrote in a postscript to one of Leopold's letters.[90] He missed them and wanted news from home. "I beg you to send me a letter every post-day," he wrote from Naples, "even if you have nothing to write about. I should like to have one merely in order to receive some letter every time the post comes in."[91] And as the first journey drew to a close, he finally gave expression to his homesickness: "Mama, I beg you to pray for me, that my opera may go well and that we may be happy together again. I kiss Mama's hand a thousand times and I have many things to say to my sister, but what? . . . If it is God's will, I shall soon, I hope, be able to tell them to her myself."[92] To Marianne he wrote separately, "Dearest Darling little sister . . . I burn with eagerness to see you both in Salzburg soon again."[93]

Doubtless, Leopold Mozart sorely missed his wife and daughter, but in compensation he had his son all to himself—perhaps the main reason that Italy had become an Edenic summer for him, one he could not easily forsake and hoped would never end. He began to lose any sense of the urgency of time. "I cannot yet say how long we shall stay here," he wrote from Naples. "The matter is entirely out of my hands. It may be five weeks or five months, but I think that it will be five weeks."[94] He wanted to delay the return to Salzburg as long as possible. In his last letter from Milan, at the end of the third and final journey, he admitted, "You cannot think into what confusion our departure has thrown me. Indeed I find it hard to leave Italy."[95]

Certainly Leopold Mozart knew that an era in his life was over. Perhaps he had a foreboding of difficulties to come, of conflict over a young man's need for independence, of more problems with the Salzburg court. Perhaps, too, he knew that he had failed to accomplish what turns out to have been his great purpose: to resettle his family in Italy. And here he faced the opposition of Empress Maria Theresia herself, something he could not overcome by strategic maneuvers, for the posts he sought were located at the courts of Lombardy and Tuscany, whose thrones were occupied by two of her own children. In a letter to her son, Archduke Ferdinand of Lombardy, written at the end of 1771, the empress made her views about the Mozarts devastatingly plain:

> You ask me to take the young Salzburger into your service. I do not know why, not believing that you have need of a composer or of useless people [*de gens inutiles*]. If however it would give you pleasure, I have no wish to hinder you. What I say is intended only to prevent your burdening yourself with useless people and giving titles to people of that sort. If they are in your service it degrades that service when these people go about the world like beggars [*quand ces gens courent le monde comme des gueux*]. Besides, he has a large family.[96]

Apparently, it was not only Leopold Mozart's bothersome petition about *La finta semplice* that troubled the court, but his reputation as an unreliable, peripatetic employee whose money- and job-seeking activities were considered to be in bad taste. The composer Hasse wrote: "The father, as far as I can see, is equally discontented everywhere, since here too he uttered the same lamentations."[97] Leopold's widely advertised dissatisfaction, which cast the Salzburg court in a pinch-penny light, surely did not endear him to prospective employers. On 8 December 1771, Leopold wrote home guardedly: "The affair is not quite hopeless," but it was already becoming clear to him that he had to look elsewhere than Lombardy.[98]

A year later, in December 1772, nearing the end of the third journey and armed with strong recommendations from Count Firmian and other supporters, he applied to Archduke Leopold of Tuscany for an appointment for Mozart. "I hear from Florence that the Grand Duke has received my letter, is giving it sympathetic consideration and will let me know the result. We still live in hopes."[99] Soon, however, a pessimistic note entered his letters. "There is little hope of what I wrote to you. God will help us. But do save money and keep cheerful, for we must have means, if we want to undertake a journey. I regret every kreuzer which we spend in Salzburg. Up to the present no reply has come from the Grand Duke, but we know from the Count's letter to [Milan court official Leopold] Troger that there is very little likelihood of our getting work in Florence."[100] Leopold sent the grand duke a copy of *Lucio Silla*. "Even if there is no hope of obtaining anything from him, I trust that he will recommend us."[101] He did not give up completely until the very end, and he delayed his return to Salzburg by claiming to be "plagued with acute rheumatism," which forced him to remain in bed.[102] In the next letter, though, he confessed, "What I wrote about my illness is all quite untrue. . . . You must, however, spread the news everywhere that I am ill. You should cut off this scrap of paper so that it may not fall into the hands of others."[103] On 6 February he wrote in the cipher the family customarily used when writing of sensitive matters, "I cannot travel, because I must await a courier from Florence."[104] Finally, however, he was compelled to acknowledge defeat: "As for the affair you know of there is nothing to be done. I shall tell you all when we meet. God has probably some other plan for us."[105] By now he saw there was some invisible barrier to his application, that he could not overcome the forces arrayed against him.

Thus, if the journeys to Italy were the culmination of Leopold's abilities as an impresario, his greatest triumphs, they closed with a great failure, for he did not succeed in settling Mozart and himself in secure and prestigious posts. Furthermore, despite the critical and popular success of his Italian operas, Mozart was not again invited to write an opera for Milan, and he received no commissions from other Italian centers, perhaps indicating that his father's bid for a permanent position in the face of the empress's opposition had diminished his marketability. Or it may be that *Lucio Silla,* despite its run of twenty-six performances, which had been scheduled in advance, did not really please the Milanese. It is noteworthy that within a few years the librettist revised the text for presentation in Turin with new music by Michele Mortellari.

For the time being, Mozart's career as a virtuoso was at an end, for he was too old to be a wunderkind and had not yet created the musical vehicles—in particular, the Mozart piano concerto—that would open to him the concert halls and salons of the Habsburg nobility. Leopold Mozart once again had to draw new blueprints. "But if it is all in vain, we shall not go under, for God will help us. I have already thought out some plans."[106]

SALZBURG

View of Salzburg, late eighteenth century.
Color engraving by Anton Amon after
a drawing by Franz Naumann.

7

....

THE FAVORITE SON

An eighteenth-century traveler approaching Salzburg from the south became aware, by degrees, of the more varied landscapes, the neater habitations of the peasants, and the improved cultivation of land in the Salzburg region. At least that was the impression of the contemporary traveler Caspar Riesbeck. "About half a mile from this town," he wrote,

> there is one of the prettiest prospects I have ever met with. Conceive to yourself a vast amphitheater; the background of the picture is occupied by high rocks lifting up their heads to heaven. Some of them, which are rather on the side, are in the shape of pyramids. These vast masses terminate by degrees in wooded mountains to the back, and in beautiful and cultivated hills to the side of the prospect. Precisely in the midst of this scene stands the town, which is commanded by the castle standing on a high rock.

As for Salzburg, he continued:

> The town itself is very handsome—the houses are high, and built all of stone. The roofs of the houses are in the Italian taste, and you may walk out upon them. The cathedral is the handsomest building I have seen since I left Paris. It is built of freestone, and is an imitation of St. Peter's at Rome. . . . This town contains many more excellent buildings and statues, which remind you that the borders of Italy are not far distant.[1]

Mozart's ultimate break with Salzburg and the bitterness of his departure have cast a shadow over the years he spent within these agreeable surroundings. He returned from Italy to Salzburg on 13 March 1773 and lived there for much of the next seven and a half years. Mozart had spent more than two thirds of the preceding eleven years on tour; by contrast, Salzburg became home to him for all but twenty-five months of the next seven years, until November 1780, with three uninterrupted stays, of fifteen months, of two and a half years, and of a year and a half. During that time he was paid an annual salary of 150 florins, a small sum that nevertheless compared favorably with the salaries of other Salzburg musicians, including his father's 250 florins as deputy kapellmeister. As was customary, he received little additional reward from the court for his compositions. But if he was not paid sums in Salzburg remotely approaching what he might have earned elsewhere as a virtuoso performer or free-lance composer, he was still much appreciated in his hometown, particularly when his youth is borne in mind. Indeed, contrary to his own perception of the matter, it may fairly be said that during his years in Salzburg he achieved the status of favorite son, bathed in approbation and goodwill. At Salzburg in the 1770s, to judge only by the evidence of the works he composed there and his widespread performance opportunities, Mozart was understood, encouraged, and given extraordinary leeway to exhibit his abilities as a virtuoso and to develop his powers as a composer. It is true that there were drastic limitations to what Salzburg could offer him—in the way of opera, concerts, and great musicians—but within those limitations Mozart's access to Salzburg's musical life was highly privileged.

From the moment of his first triumphs at the Viennese imperial court in 1762, the boy Mozart was regarded as the shining jewel in Salzburg's crown, and the Mozarts had become quasi-official cultural ambassadors of the Salzburg archbishopric, on whose behalf they had delighted audiences in all the major capitals and courts of Europe. Everywhere on their travels they were identified as citizens of Salzburg and as employees of Salzburg's prince-archbishops, whose wisdom, benevolence, and aesthetic sensitivity were thereby confirmed. Press reports and concert announcements consistently reminded the rulers and notables of Europe where the Mozarts came from. In November 1769, Mozart was named concertmaster (*Konzertmeister*) of the court chapel so that he could carry an official Salzburg title with him to Italy. And in Italy he continued to serve his employer and his city well: his selection to compose two operas and music for an imperial wedding in Milan reflected most favorably on the Salzburg court.

The Mozarts received special treatment from the Salzburg authorities, particularly during the reign of Archbishop Schrattenbach. The family's tours to London, Paris, and Italy were significantly underwritten by the court, both through direct cash subventions and through Leopold Mozart's extended leaves with pay. But the best evidence of Mozart's favorite-son status lies in commissions and performances of his music in his hometown. It is striking that after the cancellation of the Viennese production of *La finta semplice* in 1768 and Leopold Mozart's fruitless appeal to the emperor, the opera was mounted in Salzburg on 1 May 1769, only a few months after the family's return from Vienna. The program read, in part:

> La Finta Semplice, Comic Drama in Music,
> To be performed at Court by order of His Most Reverent Highness
> Monsignor
> Sigismund Archbishop
> and Prince
> of Salzburg.
> Prince of the Holy Roman Empire
> Hereditary Legate of the Sacred and Apostolic See
> Primate of Germany and of the most ancient family
> of the Counts of Schrattenbach . . .
> The Music is by Sig. Wolfgango Mozart, aged Twelve Years.[2]

The production was an expression of the archbishop's unswerving support for Salzburg's young prodigy, and, by implication, a vindication of Leopold Mozart's complaints to the Viennese court.

Archbishop Schrattenbach died on 15 December 1771, and his successor, Count Hieronymus Colloredo, was elected by a badly divided committee of his peers on 14 March 1772, on the forty-ninth ballot.[3] Henceforth, the relationship between the archbishop and the Mozarts was to be significantly altered, but though they would not be cherished as dearly as they had been under Schrattenbach, neither would they be ignored, and under the new regime Mozart continued to receive valuable commissions, including his share of dramatic and theater works, which were infrequently required. To celebrate the installation of Colloredo, he revised a dramatic serenata, *Il sogno di Scipione,* K. 126, to a text by Metastasio, which had been intended for Schrattenbach and may have been performed at the archbishop's residence in late April.[4] In early 1775, in honor of the visiting Archduke Maximilian Franz, he wrote another dramatic serenata in two acts, *Il rè pastore,* K. 208, which was performed on 23 April and followed by a concert at court featuring Mozart's improvisations at the keyboard. And in January 1776, Mozart's incidental music to the drama *Thamos, König in Ägypten,* K. 345/336a, an earlier version of which had been performed in Vienna in April 1774, was given in Salzburg. He composed large quantities of instrumental and choral music for the leading institutions of Salzburg—the church, the court, the university, and the theater. A contemporary journal took note of the "particularly beautiful and agreeable

music" he provided for a High Mass at Maria Plain, a pilgrimage church in
the environs of Salzburg, in 1774:

> It was produced almost exclusively by the princely court musicians, and
> especially by the older and younger, both famous, Motzarts. The young
> Herr Motzart played an organ and a violin concerto, to everyone's amaze-
> ment and astonishment. And in general there was exceedingly exquisite
> music at today's High Mass.[5]

Mozart also wrote numerous works for his own use as a keyboard artist and
violin soloist at concerts and musicales in the best homes as well as in the
large salon of the Mozarts' fine apartment in the impressive house known
as the Tanzmeisterhaus, where they moved in the fall of 1773. The variety
of his commissions and performance opportunities was such that he was
able simultaneously to pursue many of the main genres of secular and
sacred music, including masses, symphonies, concertos, chamber music,
sonatas, divertimentos, serenades, and dances.

Mozart kept up a substantial rate of productivity in his post-Italian
Salzburg years. In 1773, even after allowing for fragments, doubtful works,
and some uncertain datings, he composed six or seven symphonies, four
divertimentos, a serenade, six string quartets, a string quintet, a piano concerto, a set of keyboard variations, eight minuets for keyboard, sixteen minuets for orchestra, and a mass. In 1774 he wrote three symphonies, a piano
sonata, two church sonatas, a set of variations, a serenade, two concertos, two
masses, and several other sacred works, his efforts capped by the opera buffa
La finta giardiniera, to a libretto by Giuseppe Petrosellini, which occupied him
for more than four months beginning in September. In 1775 his main works
were a set of six piano sonatas composed during a journey to Munich, five
violin concertos, four or five masses (some, perhaps, dating from the following year), and *Il rè pastore,* plus a divertimento for winds, a serenade, five arias,
and a church sonata. Divertimentos and serenades were his main genres in
1776, with a total of eight in those forms, but he also composed two piano
concertos and a concerto for three keyboards, several arias, four church
sonatas, a litany, and an offertory to round out the year. Although his productivity declined somewhat in the first nine months of 1777, perhaps
because of his impending departure from Salzburg, he nevertheless produced
a piano concerto, two divertimentos, a "notturno," an oboe concerto, an
aria, one or two masses, a gradual, an offertory, two church sonatas, and several minor works (including as many as twenty dances written in 1776–77).

We can also survey Mozart's productivity by genre during these four
years. He remained active as a symphonist in 1773 and 1774, with four
symphonies (in E-flat, K. 184/161a; G, K. 199/161b; C, K. 162; and D, K.

181/162b) written between 30 March and 19 May 1773, either for local performances or possibly in preparation for the journey to Vienna in July. Two more, in B-flat, K. 182/173dA, and G minor, K. 183/173dB, were completed by the first week in October, within ten days of his return, suggesting that they may have been written in fulfillment of a Viennese commission. A Symphony in C, K. 200/189k, may date from November 1773, perhaps as the third of these post-Vienna symphonies, though it may belong in November of the following year. The Symphonies in A, K. 201/186a, dated 6 April 1774, and D, K. 202/186b, dated 5 May 1774, were perhaps composed for Salzburg gala occasions, but such occasions became increasingly rare, and Mozart wrote no more symphonies until his stay in Paris in 1778.[6] His positive appraisal of several of these works is confirmed by his asking that their scores be sent to Vienna during the 1780s. Curiously, Leopold's strongest known reservations about any of Mozart's works were expressed in reference to the symphonies, which he urged his son to refrain from offering to Parisian publishers in 1778:

> It is better that whatever does you no honor, should not be given to the public. That is the reason why I have not given any of your symphonies to be copied, because I suspect that when you are older and have more insight, you will be glad that no one has got hold of them, though at the time you composed them you were quite pleased with them. One gradually becomes more and more fastidious.[7]

The numerous divertimentos and serenades of this period fall into several distinct genres: Among the orchestral serenades that Mozart composed for various celebrations, often outdoors—weddings, graduations, ennoblements—were the Serenade in D, K. 185/167a ("Andretter"), of July–August 1773, the Serenade in D, K. 203/189b ("Colloredo"), of August 1774, Serenade in D, K. 204/213a, dated 5 August 1775, the Serenade in D, K. 239 ("Serenata Notturna"), of 1776, and the Serenade in D, K. 250/248b ("Haffner"), composed in July 1776. All of these are for winds and strings except the "Serenata Notturna," which is scored for timpani and strings. Other Mozart divertimentos functioned as *Tafelmusik* (table music), including the Divertimentos in B-flat, K. 186/159b, and E-flat, K. 166/159d, composed in March 1773, and five divertimentos for wind sextet (two oboes, two horns, two bassoons) in F, K. 213; B-flat, K. 240; E-flat, K. 252/240a; F, K. 253; and B-flat, K. 270, composed between July 1775 and January 1777.[8] The first of his six piano trios, composed in August 1776, is titled Divertimento in B-flat, K. 254.

Among his greater works of chamber music are three divertimentos scored for string quartet and two obbligato horns, composed between June

1776 and June 1777, in F, K. 247; D, K. 251 (with added oboe); and B-flat, K. 287/271H, a series continued several years later with the Divertimento in D, K. 334/320b. A significant precursor of these works is the Divertimento in D, K. 205/167a, probably written in July 1773 for the name day of Maria Anna Elisabeth von Andretter, wife of Johann Ernst von Andretter, and perhaps performed at a concert at the Mesmer residence in Vienna on 18 August 1773. Several lesser divertimentos and numerous marches associated with the larger works round out Mozart's efforts in these genres, which found so receptive an audience in Salzburg.

Embedded within four of Mozart's serenades—K. 185/167a, 203/189b, 204/213a, and 250/248b—are miniature two- or three-movement violin concertos, and the divertimentos, too, often feature important passages for solo violin, which Mozart himself presumably performed in connection with his post as court concertmaster. It was during this period that he came forward as a violin soloist, performing in Vienna, Munich, and Augsburg as well as Salzburg. From Munich, after a performance of the Divertimento in B-flat, K. 287/271h, in October 1777, he wrote, "I played as though I were the greatest fiddler in all of Europe."[9] Nevertheless, perhaps because his gifts as a string player did not match his virtuosity as a pianist, or because string instruments offered fewer possibilities for improvisation, his performances on violin and viola in later years were limited to chamber music.

Climaxing his efforts as a composer of violin music, Mozart wrote five violin concertos—in B-flat, K. 207; D, K. 211; G, K. 216 ("Strassburg"); D, K. 218; and A, K. 219 ("Turkish")—between 14 April and 20 December 1775, which are closely related to the serenades in style and atmosphere.[10] Several independent movements for violin and orchestra, an Adagio in E, K. 261, and a Rondo in B-flat, K. 269/261a, which may have been substitute movements for several of the concertos, complete Mozart's efforts in this genre, which were inaugurated with his Concertone for two violins in C, K. 190/186E, of 1774. The Violin Concertos in D, K. 271i, and E-flat, K. 268, are of doubtful authenticity. Mozart's only other concertos of this Salzburg period are the Bassoon Concerto in B-flat, K. 191/186e, dated 4 June 1774, and an Oboe Concerto in C, K. 271k, written in 1777 for the oboist Giuseppe Ferlendis. Long thought to be lost, it turned out to be the original version of the Flute Concerto in D, K. 314/285d, written at Mannheim in the winter of 1777–78.

Salzburg was less receptive to chamber music for strings or to solo piano music; both the set of six String Quartets, K. 168–173, and the set of six Piano Sonatas, K. 279–283/189d–h and K. 284/205b, were composed during visits to foreign cities, the former in August and September 1773 in Vienna, the latter in Munich between 14 January and 6 March 1775. It is not known what occasioned Mozart's first string quintet, in B-flat, K. 174, composed in 1773; perhaps he was inspired by Michael Haydn's efforts in the genre, but it remained his only Salzburg string quintet. He composed no piano sonatas in Salzburg except the two Sonatas for piano four hands in D, K. 381/123a, of mid-1772, and B-flat, K. 358/186c, of spring 1774, which were needed for joint appearances with his sister. Apparently, his solo keyboard performances in Salzburg featured improvisations of various kinds rather than sonatas or even sets of variations; his only sets of variations from this period are the Six Variations in G on a theme by Salieri, K. 180/173c, written in Vienna in the autumn of 1773, and Twelve Variations in C on a theme by Johann Christian Fischer, K. 179/189a, written during the second half of 1774.

Mozart's first piano concertos, apart from the earlier ones based on transcriptions of other composers' music, were written during the Salzburg years. Perhaps connected to the impulse that gave rise to his violin concertos in 1775, a cluster of keyboard concertos appeared during the first four months of 1776, the Concertos in B-flat, K. 238, and C, K. 246 ("Lützow"), along with the Triple Concerto, K. 242 ("Lodron"). Even earlier was the Concerto in D, K. 175, bearing a date of December 1773, but it was revised about 1777 or 1778; in fact, the earliest surviving authentic manuscript for it postdates Mozart's removal to Vienna.[11] The epochal Concerto in E-flat, K. 271 ("Jeunehomme"), composed in January 1777, completes the list of his Salzburg concertos.

In Salzburg, Mozart was a prolific and proficient composer of church music, writing nine of his fifteen or sixteen Salzburg masses during the four years following his return from the last Italian journey. Most of these were of the *missa brevis* type, composed largely in the required prevailing style, including Missae breves in F, K. 192/186f, D, K. 194/186h, C, K. 220/196b ("Sparrow"), C, K. 258 ("Piccolomini"), C, K. 259 ("Organ Solo"), and B-flat, K. 275/272b, the last completed shortly prior to his departure for Mannheim and Paris in the fall of 1777. His other Salzburg masses were the Missa in C, K. 167 ("Holy Trinity"), composed in June 1773; the Missa longa in C, K. 262/246a, written in June or July 1775; and the Missa in C, K. 257 ("Credo"), of late 1776 or early 1777. In addition, he wrote a Dixit and Magnificat in C, K. 193/186g, a fragment of a Kyrie in D, K. 91/186i, the *Litaniae de venerabili altaris sacramento* in E-flat, K. 243, a gradual, "Sancta Maria, mater Dei," K. 273, and three offertories, "Misericordias Domini" in D minor, K. 222/205a, "Venite, populi" in D, K. 260/248a, and "Alma Dei creatoris" in F, K. 277/272a.

Although Salzburg patrons did not place a premium on individuality or originality of expression in church music, Mozart thought well enough of two of his masses, K. 192/186f and K. 220/196b, to bring them, along with the Offertory, K. 222/205a, on his 1777 journey. In 1780 he wanted to demonstrate his skill as a church composer with three of his later Salzburg masses, including the Missa brevis in B-flat, K. 275/272b. "I should also like people to hear some of my compositions in this style," he wrote, deeming them superior to the local product, which "one could easily turn out at the rate of half a dozen a day."[12] As late as the summer of 1791, he performed the Missa brevis in B-flat, K. 275/272b, in Baden, and in September of that final year of his life several of his Salzburg masses were evidently performed under Salieri's direction at the Prague coronation of Emperor Leopold II.

Some of Mozart's works were composed for friends, family, and fellow musicians: the Divertimento in D, K. 251, for his sister on her twenty-fifth birthday; the Recitative and Aria "Ah, lo previdi"—"Ah, t'invola agl'occhi miei," K. 272, on the occasion of the Prague soprano Josepha Duschek's visit to Salzburg in August 1777; the Alto Recitative and Aria "Ombra felice"—"Io ti lascio," K. 255, for castrato Francesco Fortini in September 1776; the oboe concerto noted for oboist Giuseppe Ferlendis; and the Piano Concerto in E-flat, K. 271, written in January 1777 for Mademoiselle Jeunehomme, a French pianist visiting Salzburg.[13]

Many works are associated with the most eminent of Salzburg's citizens. To celebrate the name day of Countess Maria Antonia Lodron, who maintained Salzburg's leading musical salon, Mozart composed the Divertimenti K. 247 and K. 287/271H, and for the countess and her two daughters he wrote the Triple Concerto in F, K. 242. One of Mozart's masses in C (most likely the Missa longa, K. 262/246a) was written for the ordination of Count Friedrich Franz Joseph Spaur on 17 November 1776,[14] and Countess Antonia Lützow was the aristocratic recipient of the Piano Concerto in C, K. 246, composed in April 1776.[15]

Other members of the high nobility counted among Mozart's friends and patrons, including the Firmians, Arcos, Kuenbergs, and Czernins. "He had free entry into their houses," writes Jahn, "played at their entertainments, and gave lessons to their daughters, all the ladies, old and young, vying with each other in attentions to the distinguished virtuoso."[16] As for the apex of the Salzburg hierarchy, we may assume, even in the absence of documentary confirmation, that Mozart's music was often heard at the archbishop's palace as well as in his court and cathedral; presumably the divertimenti for wind sextet were written as *Tafelmusik* to lend atmosphere to the archbishop's meals. We have already seen that Mozart's playing graced religious ceremonies at Maria Plain in 1774.[17] And Archduke Maximilian Franz's journal mentions an occasion where Mozart rubbed elbows with the elite at an entertainment at the palace in 1775:

In the evening . . . Countess *Lüzau,* a niece of the Archbishop's, as well as another lady, performed on the clavier, and were accompanied, apart from the Archduke [Maximilian], by the Archbishop and by Counts Ugarte, Czernin and Hardegg. Also, at the end of the *musique,* the famous young *Mozart* was heard on the clavier and played various things by heart with as much art as pleasantness.[18]

It did not hurt Mozart's cause that several of his noble patrons were linked by ties of blood; for example, Count Johann Rudolph Czernin was the brother of Countess Lützow, and they in turn were nephew and niece of Archbishop Colloredo. Doubtless, on special occasions Mozart was able to supplement his tiny salary with the usual array of gifts and gratuities from these patrons, and Count Czernin apparently persuaded his father, Count Prokop Adalbert Czernin of Prague, to settle a small annuity of 20 ducats on Mozart in 1776, in return for some compositions. Perhaps this is why he delivered to the count one or two sets of Contredanses, K. 269b and K. 267/271c, that year or the following one.[19]

Mozart also had numerous supporters and friends among the lesser nobility, the bureaucracy, and the wealthy burghers of Salzburg. The "Haffner" Serenade, K. 250/248b, was composed for the wedding of the former mayor Sigmund Haffner's daughter Marie Elisabeth in July 1776

Sigmund Haffner and Ignaz Anton von Weiser.
Lithographs by Sebastian Stief. Reproduced from Maria Vinzenz Süss,
Die Bürgermeister in Salzburg von 1433 bis 1840 (Salzburg, 1840).

and was performed at the Haffner summer residence. (Later, Mozart wrote a famous symphony to celebrate the ennoblement of Sigmund Haffner the younger.) Haffner's successor as mayor, the textile merchant Ignaz Anton Weiser, who was also a literary man, wrote texts for works by both Mozarts, including Mozart's first oratorio, *Die Schuldigkeit des ersten Gebots,* K. 35, of 1766–67.[20] Other middle-class supporters and friends were the merchant-manufacturer Robinig von Rottenfeld, for a member of whose family Mozart wrote his Divertimento, K. 334/320b;[21] Silvester Barisani, physician to the archbishop; Johann Bernhard Zezi, a textile and fancy goods dealer; Johann Lorenz Hagenauer, a banker and merchant and the Mozarts' longtime landlord and close friend; and Giovanni Battista Gusetti, a merchant and amateur musician at whose home Mozart's music was performed. The names of many lesser noble families, including Mölk, Heffner, Amann, Kürsinger, and Schiedenhofen, are frequently mentioned in the Mozart correspondence. Naturally, Mozart was also friendly with dozens of fellow musicians, both performers and composers, such as Johann Andreas Schachtner, Joseph Leutgeb, Joseph Nikolaus Meissner, Franz de Paula Deibl, Anton Cajetan Adlgasser, Johann Eberlin, and Michael Haydn, to name only a handful. To these may be added numerous amateur players who performed his music informally or in such assemblages of dilettantes as the orchestra headed by Count Czernin.[22] All in all, the Mozarts in the 1770s led a rich sociable existence, exchanging visits with friends, regularly participating in congenial entertainments, and attending the theater, concerts, and public balls.

Salzburg had always represented home to Mozart. When he was seven, he awoke one morning in a strange city and started to weep. His father "asked him the reason and he said that he was sorry not to be seeing Herr Hagenauer, Wenzel, Spitzeder, Deibl, Leutgeb, Vogt, Cajetan, Nazerl and other good friends."[23] Fifteen years later, writing from Mannheim shortly after leaving Salzburg, Mozart compiled an alphabetical list of dozens of friends whom he missed and to whom he sent his best regards: excluding fellow musicians, household acquaintances, and some wholly invented names, the list is a virtual roll call of Salzburg luminaries, indicative of the extent to which the young composer was deeply rooted in the life of his city.[24]

Nevertheless, almost from the moment of his return from Milan in 1773, Mozart longed to leave Salzburg, as we learn from the family correspondence. It may even be that the essential feature of the Salzburg years is that he regarded them as transitional: restless, eager to resume his travels, Mozart was ready to pack his bags on a moment's notice, and now he wanted to relocate permanently. This was not an irrational desire. Having known Europe's main musical centers at first hand, he was keenly aware of

Salzburg's deficiencies and in particular felt the absence of any significant musical theater there, especially after 1775, when the court theater was closed and its replacement, the Ballhaus on the Hannibalplatz, reserved almost exclusively for use by visiting troupes. Mozart felt that he had exhausted the opportunities available to him at Salzburg, in terms of both creative growth and financial reward.

He continually pressed his father to let him leave Salzburg. But of course Leopold Mozart objected strongly, for he could not countenance the possibility of their being separated. We learn the details of the conflict between them from a letter by Leopold Mozart written to Mozart in December 1777, after Mozart's departure:

> You know that for many years certain people in Salzburg have been trying our patience and you know how often you and I have longed to clear out. No doubt you still remember what objections I used to raise to our doing this, and how I would point out that it would be impossible for us all to leave Salzburg. You now realize these difficulties, that is, the great expenses of traveling and the impossibility of making enough money to defray them, especially with a whole family.

Leopold went on to stress Mozart's inexperience with such matters as packing and exchange rates: "You were not accustomed to attend to everything or to be independent of the help of others." He argued that Mozart was too helpless and immature to leave Salzburg, and that Mozart could relocate only if the entire family went along. Always he urged more careful consideration, trying to deal with the issue by perpetual postponement.

> I used to point out to you that, even if you were to remain in Salzburg until you were a little over twenty, you would not necessarily be wasting your time, which you could spend in dipping into other useful branches of knowledge and in training your reason by reading good books in several languages. Further, I used to remind you that it takes time for a young man, even one of such extraordinary gifts that he surpasses all other masters, to win the esteem which he deserves. Indeed several years are necessary; and as long as the young man is under twenty, his enemies and persecutors will certainly attribute his possible lack of success to his youth and *slight experience*.[25]

Under mounting pressure from Mozart, Leopold energetically tried to find a new patron. Together they made two forays in search of alternative employment, one to Vienna from 14 July to 26 September 1773, and a second to Munich in the winter of 1774–75. Naturally Leopold hoped to conceal the purpose of these trips: "There are many matters about which one cannot write. Moreover we must avoid anything which might create a stir or provoke any suspicion either here or, in particular, at Salzburg, or which might give someone an opportunity to put a spoke in our wheel," he warned in a letter to Frau Mozart from Vienna, where Court Kapellmeister Leopold Gassmann's illness held out the prospect of a coveted vacancy for him.[26] Although Leopold's letters home could not be explicit, he managed to let his wife know that their goal had not been achieved: "Her Majesty the Empress was very gracious to us, but that was all. I am saving up a full account until our return, for it is impossible for me to give it in writing."[27] And again: "Herr Gassmann has been ill, but is now better. I do not know how this will affect our stay in Vienna. Fools everywhere are but fools!"[28]

He still had no idea of the opposition to employing them at the Viennese court, nor did it help that Archbishop Colloredo spent the first half of August in Vienna and was there on the very day of their audience with the empress. Although they pursued other possibilities for several more weeks, performing both privately and in local churches, they returned home empty-handed at the end of September. The four symphonies (K. 184/161a, K. 199/161b, K. 162, and K. 181/162b), assorted divertimentos or serenades, and other works Mozart must have brought to Vienna as his display portfolio surely won him many admirers there, but they did not win him a post in the Austrian capital, nor did the six string quartets he composed soon after his arrival (K. 168–173), utilizing an unaccustomed, pathos-filled style favored by Emperor Joseph II. Evidently Mozart thought to advance his prospects by incorporating some of the formal designs, rhetorical devices, techniques, and textures of such imperial composers as Ordoñez and Gassmann; the influence of Joseph Haydn's string quartets, especially opp. 17 and 20, has often been noted as well in Mozart's thematic materials, rhythmic patterns, and his use of fugal finales—though the last is not surprising, since the string quartet in the 1770s and 1780s was a testing ground for "learned" contrapuntal techniques.[29]

The Vienna campaign had been well planned and executed, but it did not achieve its purpose. Leopold's bitter disappointment overflowed into his letters. "I am very much obliged to the citizens of Salzburg who are so anxious for my return. In that case I shall go back with greater pleasure and shall walk about the whole night in the illuminated town, so that the lights may not burn in vain."[30] Leopold Mozart had miscalculated once more, failing to grasp the deep antipathy that he aroused in the imperial court and underestimating Archbishop Colloredo's Viennese connections, ties so strong that it was widely believed that his post had been "procured for him by the court of Vienna."[31]

The journey to Munich, which lasted from 6 December 1774 to 8 March 1775, accomplished at least one of its central aims, to fulfill the commission for *La finta giardiniera*. Mozart himself reported to his mother on the success of his opera at its premiere on 13 January:

> It is impossible for me to describe the applause to Mama. In the first place, the whole theater was so packed that a great many people were turned away. Then after each aria there was a terrific noise, clapping of hands, and cries of "Viva Maestro." Her Highness the Electress and the Dowager Electress . . . also called out "Bravo" to me. After the opera was over and during the pause . . . people kept on clapping all the time and shouting "Bravo." . . . Afterward I went off with Papa . . . and I kissed the hands of the Elector and Electress and Their Highnesses, who were all very gracious.[32]

The reception was somewhat more mixed than Mozart knew. The secretary of the Saxon legation wrote that "the music was generally applauded,"[33] and the correspondent for Schubart's *Deutsche Chronik* reported, "Flashes of genius appear here and there; but there is not yet that still altar-fire that rises towards Heaven in clouds of incense—a scent beloved of the gods. If *Mozart* is not a plant forced in the hot house, he is bound to grow into one of the greatest musical composers who ever lived."[34]

As in Vienna, the family's hopes for employment at the electoral court were not realized, nor was Mozart invited to compose the grand opera for the following carnival season, as his father had expected.[35] Nor did Leopold's efforts to exhibit his own abilities as a composer and conductor of church music bear fruit. At the canonical hours on New Year's Day, 1775, he conducted performances of two *Litaniae de venerabili altaris sacramento*—one by himself and the other Mozart's K. 125. On 12 and 19 February 1775 he conducted Mozart's Missa brevis in F, K. 192, and the Missa brevis in D, K. 194, at the Munich court chapel. Although there is no direct evidence of an approach to the elector, rumors multiplied in Salzburg, leading Leopold to exclaim, "That the gentlemen of Salzburg are gossiping so much and are convinced that Wolfgang has entered the service of the Elector, is due to our enemies. . . . You know well that we are accustomed to these childish stories and that such talk leaves me quite cold. So you can tell that to everyone. . . . They rightly fear in Salzburg lest one bird after another may fly away."[36] He added, disdainfully, "Write everything that you hear, so that we will have something to laugh about, for we know these fools."[37]

Mozart's longing to leave Salzburg is broadly hinted in his letter of 14 January, the day after the premiere of *La finta giardiniera,* when he wrote meaningfully to his mother that she should not wish for his early return, "for she knows how much good it is doing me to be able to breathe freely."[38] Even before their return to Salzburg a rift had opened between the Mozarts and the archbishop; a few days after the premiere Leopold Mozart wrote to his wife, "Picture to yourself the embarrassment of His Grace the Archbishop at hearing the opera praised by the whole family of the Elector and by all the nobles, and at receiving the enthusiastic congratulations which they all expressed to him. Why, he was so embarrassed that he could only reply with a bow of the head and a shrug of the shoulders. We have not yet spoken to him."[39] It was only to be expected that their relationship had deteriorated, for by this time there could be no doubt that the archbishop was well aware of the Mozarts' fickle allegiance to him and to Salzburg.

The wariness between the Mozarts and the Salzburg authorities had a long history, predating by several decades Archbishop Colloredo's installation in 1772. As though unwilling to commit himself to Salzburg, Mozart's father had maintained his Augsburg citizenship through 1754, and the Egglstainer affair in 1756 had caused his employers to regard him as a troublesome personality. As early as 1762 he had come close to forsaking Salzburg for Vienna. "Perhaps you have long ago come to the conclusion that *everyone who comes to Vienna, is charmed into staying here.* So it has almost been with us."[40] Toward the end of the Grand Journey, when the Salzburg court expressed its displeasure at his constant requests to extend his leave, he yielded gracelessly: "I have taken my decision. I have promised to go home and I shall keep my word."[41] And we have already seen that the usually indulgent Archbishop Schrattenbach withheld his deputy kapellmeister's salary in 1768, perhaps acting upon rumors of Leopold Mozart's intent to remain in Vienna.

There is every reason to believe that the Salzburg court learned of Leopold Mozart's ongoing efforts to leave its employ, and had heard of his rejections in Vienna, Milan, Florence, and Munich through family connections and diplomatic channels. For example, both Count Firmian and Count Arco of Milan had close family ties in Salzburg—indeed, in the archbishop's court—so that the intervention of Empress Maria Theresia to block Leopold's application to her son the Archduke Ferdinand surely was known by the archbishop even as it remained a secret to Leopold Mozart himself. And it may even be that the empress actually forestalled the appointment at the behest or on behalf of the Salzburg court, which behind the scenes maneuvered to keep its favorite son from clearing out.

The court had to regard the Mozart family's attempted defection as poor repayment for its many favors. Surely it must have felt that Mozart ought to be overcome by feelings of gratitude and ought patiently to look forward to eventually gracing the court as kapellmeister, after a necessary period of apprenticeship. Instead, he turned out to be an unhappy and ungrateful youth, belittling Salzburg's cultural life, broadcasting calumnies on the archbishop and his retainers, and accusing them of tyranny, backwardness and, perhaps worst of all, stinginess. They might have protested, rightly, that Salzburg was scarcely a backward city, for it offered its citizens an extensive range of social services and public institutions—eight hospitals and sanatoriums; numerous schools, seminaries, and an outstanding university; several almshouses and orphanages; major libraries and museums, ranging from the libraries at the court, the university, and the abbey of St. Peter's to a dozen collections devoted to the natural sciences and five to the fine arts.[42]

As for the cultivation of the arts and sciences, Riesbeck found that "there is very good company to be met with amongst the nobility, particularly amongst the canons, several of whom are distinguished for knowledge of various kinds."[43] He particularly singled out Count Virgilius Maria Firmian, a canon of the cathedral, and his brother Count Franz Lactanz Firmian, who was lord high chamberlain to the archbishop, for their libraries and portrait collections; Count Anton Willibald Wolfegg, for his knowledge of botany; Count Leopold Kuenburg for his wit and sociability—and for his library, which contained all the best modern authors, including works on the Catholic Church's *Index librorum prohibitorum*.[44] The Firmian brothers, too, were interested in rationalist and Enlightened thought; in earlier days they had founded a reading society at the university that had drawn strong opposition because of its "free scientific tendencies."[45] Archbishop Colloredo himself was an adherent of reform and secularization policies paralleling those advocated in Vienna by Emperor Joseph, and his reign was marked by a notable increase of scholarship and the encouragement of freedom of inquiry in Salzburg. "They converse here upon religious and political topics," wrote Riesbeck, "with a freedom that does honor to the place; and with regard to books, you may have almost every thing which the German presses produce, without any restraint."[46]

Nevertheless, the relatively prosperous Salzburg musical establishment that Archbishop Colloredo inherited was significantly affected by his curtailment of instrumental music at court and in the cathedral, by drastic reforms of the liturgy, by limitations upon the length of court concerts, and by the closing of venues for theatrical music, including of the university theater in 1778.[47] Where Count Firmian's musicales often lasted for six hours and Dittersdorf was known to give twelve violin concertos by Benda at one court concert, Colloredo cut back the length of Salzburg court concerts. On 17 September 1778 Leopold Mozart wrote, "Yesterday we started at 7:00 P.M. and when I left it was striking *a quarter after eight*, thus a total of an hour and a quarter. At most only four pieces could be played: *a symphony, an aria, another symphony or concerto,* then *another aria,* and *Addio!*"[48] And it was, after all, in the musical sphere that Mozart's complaints centered. In September 1776 he signed his name to the letter drafted by his father to Padre Martini in Bologna, emphasizing his own proficiency as a composer of church music and implicitly asking for help to obtain a position. Enclosing his offertory "Misericordias Domini," K. 222/205a, for Martini's opinion, Mozart underscored his dissatisfaction with Salzburg and did not fail to mention his employer's lack of liberality:

> I live in a country where music leads a struggling existence. . . . As for the theater, we are in a bad way for lack of singers. We have no castrati, and we shall never have them, because they insist on being handsomely paid; and generosity is not one of our faults. Meanwhile I am amusing myself by writing chamber music and music for the church. . . . My father is in the service of the Cathedral and this gives me an opportunity of writing as much church music as I like.[49]

Later on, Mozart elaborated his complaints in a letter to a close family friend, the tutor Abbé Bullinger: "Salzburg is no place for my talent. In the first place, professional musicians there are not held in much consideration; and, secondly, one hears nothing, there is no theater, no opera." He went on to criticize the quality of the musicians and singers and to present his own grandiose ideas for transforming Salzburg musical life, including the hiring of an outstanding kapellmeister and somehow persuading Metastasio to leave his post in Vienna as imperial court poet or, at least, to "write a few dozen opera texts" for Salzburg.[50]

The issue of Mozart's departure was, therefore, very much on the surface, and inevitably the matter eventually came to a head in an acrimonious series of exchanges with the archbishop. On 14 March 1777 Leopold Mozart addressed a petition to Colloredo, asking permission to travel once again, but permission was denied.[51] A subsequent petition was also refused in respect of the father; the archbishop suggested that Mozart might travel alone, but then apparently made some further objection to this as well, drastically limiting Mozart's options—either to submit to the princely will or to resign his post altogether.[52] Caught now between his son and the archbishop, Leopold Mozart drafted an intemperate letter that quoted the Gospel in support of Mozart's decision. To this Mozart affixed his signature:

> Most Gracious Sovereign Prince and Lord! Parents take pains to enable their children to earn their own bread, and this they owe both to their own interest and to that of the State. The more of talent that children have received from God, the greater is the obligation to make use thereof,

in order to ameliorate their own and their parents' circumstances, to assist their parents, and to take care of their own advancement and future. The Gospel teaches us to use our talents in this way.[53]

Having now instructed the archbishop in matters of morality and filial piety, the petition continued: "May Your Serene Highness graciously permit me, therefore, to beg most submissively to be released from service. . . . Your Serene Highness will not take this most submissive request amiss, inasmuch as when I begged for permission to travel to Vienna three years ago, Your Highness was graciously pleased to declare that I had nothing to hope for [in Salzburg] and would do better to seek my fortune elsewhere."[54] The archbishop, recognizing the hand and the voice of Leopold Mozart in the petition, was angered sufficiently to dismiss both Mozarts from his service: "Father and son have permission to seek their fortune elsewhere," adding, caustically, "according to the Gospel."[55] A few days later, Schiedenhofen visited the Mozarts, "where I found the father ill, because he and his son are dismissed from the service because of the request which the latter made to His Grace for permission to travel."[56]

Leopold Mozart had never intended that Mozart leave Salzburg without him, but he was no longer able to prevent it. Circumstances—the boy's intransigence, the archbishop's refusal to permit any further joint travels, Leopold's repeated failures to obtain dual posts elsewhere—had conspired to force Mozart's resignation and now to separate the father from his son. And so, on the twenty-third of September, Mozart, accompanied by his mother, set out for southern Germany and then for Paris in search of a new position. Salzburg had lost its favorite son.

Leopold Mozart recounted to Mozart a conversation between Count Firmian and the archbishop, who commented, "'Now we have one man less in the orchestra.' Firmian replied, 'Your Grace has lost a great virtuoso.' 'Why so?' asked the Prince. The reply was: 'Mozart is the greatest clavier player whom I have ever heard in my life; on the violin he rendered very good services to Your Grace; and he is a first-rate composer.' The Archbishop was silent, for he had nothing to say."[57] Later on, to justify himself, he fell back on the empress's argument, in almost precisely her own words, indicative either of a close convergence of attitude or some joint consultation. "To excuse himself for having refused us leave last year," wrote Leopold, "he said that he could not tolerate people going about the world begging."[58] The court seemed to be seeking scapegoats for its loss, for the rumor spread that Franz Xaver Duschek, husband of the singer Josepha Duschek, had encouraged his friend Mozart to leave, and, reported Leopold, "this suspicion has now been extended to Counts Hardik [Hardegg] and Lützow."[59] In late September Leopold reported to his wife that a

Mozart violin concerto was performed at a concert, where Kolb, the soloist, announced, "You have been hearing the compositions of a good friend who is no longer with us," whereupon everyone cried out, "What a pity that we have lost him!"—and then they all got drunk and smashed the large chandelier that hung in the hall.[60]

It was not long before Leopold Mozart petitioned for reinstatement; with ill grace and a touch of vindictiveness, the archbishop restored him to his post, but only on condition that he mend his ways and show appropriate humility toward his superiors: "In gracious confidence . . . that the petitioner will conduct himself calmly and peaceably with the Kapellmeister and other persons appointed to the court orchestra, His Grace retains him in his employment and graciously commands him to endeavor to render good service both to the Church and to His Grace's person."[61] Leopold Mozart's cup of bitterness was filled to overflowing: henceforth, if he wished to earn his salary, he had to render his ordinary services as a musician, as clavier teacher of the Salzburg choirboys, as occasional director of the court music, and as chief purchaser of music and instruments. And his glorious years as an illustrious traveler were over—apart from a single trip to Vienna in 1785, he never again ventured beyond Munich.

On the whole, the court had until now been extraordinarily lenient with a deputy kapellmeister who, in his son's (or his own) words, "no longer puts his whole heart into his work."[62] Despite occasional rebukes, the court regularly granted him special favors and extraordinary leaves because young Mozart was so valuable an asset; his son's genius gave the father license to avoid his responsibilities as an employee of the court. His reluctance to carry out his official duties was well known and years later was recounted as legend by a contributor to the *Allgemeine Musikalische Zeitung,* who recalled that "age, domestic sorrows" and the parsimoniousness of his prince "combined finally to make Mozart's father exhausted and worn down. He no longer composed, he simply withdrew from that which was legitimately required of him, and let the rest go as it would."[63]

Leopold Mozart's protracted flight from authority and responsibility, which had begun when he quit the lyceum in Augsburg and which for the past fifteen years had carried him throughout Europe in the dress and equipage of a gentleman, was now at an end. He had seized on the potentialities of Mozart's talent to inaugurate the journeys that became the vehicle of his rebellious impulse and of his quest for fulfillment. Now, all at once, his career as a bourgeois impresario had collapsed, and he had fallen once again into feudal service for a prince who deeply resented him. Naturally, however, his resources were not yet completely exhausted. Somehow, he would have to try once again to restore himself to the good graces of his serene highness.

8

....

A COMPOSER'S VOICE

At a certain point in his development, a gifted young composer becomes more than the sum of the influences he has absorbed from tradition, more than simply an amalgamator of other composers' styles, more than an imitator, more than a disciple, more than a transmitter of conventions. He becomes an adept, he speaks in a tongue that has not previously been heard, he finds his voice. He has discovered a style; or, perhaps, a style has discovered him. Henceforth, a recognizable portion of our musical language will be identifiable as his language, embodying his rhetoric, his devices, his formal structures. On closer examination, however, we see that there is no such fixed point, no single work or cluster of works representing Mozart's epistemological break with an imitative past and the forging of his personal identity. Instead of a clear dividing line we see a process that has long been adumbrated. And when it comes, it takes him, and us, unawares. Only afterward does one realize that it has happened, and still, one is not quite sure exactly when and how it occurred.

Relatively little attention has been paid to the individuality of Mozart's style. Perhaps this is due to the inherent difficulties of defining any musical style, let alone the idiosyncratic style of a composer whose greatness consists, at least in part, in his seeming purging of subjectivity in the service of a perfected, classical objectivity.[1] For many, indeed, Mozart has exemplified the supreme artist whose works transcend issues of personality, of self-revelation, of originality. T. S. Eliot would have been delighted to find in Mozart so lapidary an example of an artist's subordination of self to tradition—"a continual self-sacrifice, a continual extinction of personality." Eliot wrote:

Autograph manuscript,
Symphony in A, K. 201/186a, Allegro moderato.
Robert Owen Lehman Collection, on deposit
in the Pierpont Morgan Library.

We dwell with satisfaction upon the poet's difference from his predecessors, especially his immediate predecessors; we endeavour to find something that can be isolated in order to be enjoyed. Whereas if we approach a poet without this prejudice we shall often find that not only the best, but the most individual parts of his work may be those in which the dead poets, his ancestors, assert their immortality most vigorously.[2]

In this view, perfection, beauty, and universality issue from the suppression of individuality. Hegel, who worshiped Mozart as music's model of classical objectivity, had said something very similar a century earlier: "To have no 'manner' was ever the one great 'manner,' and in this sense alone can we ascribe originality to Homer, Sophocles, Raphael, and Shakespeare."[3]

As Mozart's music increasingly came to represent the classical norm against which all other music was measured, it became difficult to think of his works as products of subjectivity, for they seemed to have been always in existence, to have issued from an ideal sphere. Mozart's music was scrubbed of the labor that went into its creation, cleansed of the blood and pain that had been sublimated in it. Mozart's creativity came to be considered as the product of forces external to him; he was regarded as a receptive, neutral instrument or vessel of a vital, perhaps divine, force; he was thought to have written music automatically because that was his instinctive nature, to make music as a silkworm spins silk, to shake masterpieces out of his sleeve without conscious effort or volition. As early as Niemetschek's 1798 biography it was reported that Mozart "could see the completed work clearly and vividly when it came to him. . . . We rarely find anything corrected or altered in his concerto scores. . . . In his mind the work was already complete before he sat down at his desk."[4] This became the point of departure for a notable forged letter attributed to Mozart by the Leipzig editor Friedrich Rochlitz, in which the composer was alleged to have written that an entire work, "though it be long, stands almost complete and finished in my head, so that I can survey it in my mind, like a fine picture or a comely form at a glance. . . . The committing to paper is done quickly enough, for everything is . . . already finished; and it rarely differs on paper from what it was in my imagination."[5]

Whether he is seen as an aloof Olympian or, more currently, as a crude buffoon or idiot savant, tropes of Mozart's creativity propose an unbridgeable split between the individual and his work. Even the tradition that proposes a "demonic" element in Mozart—a tradition begun by Goethe in the early 1830s—merely transferred the external source of his inspiration from the celestial to the realm of the subterranean. Goethe asked Eckermann, "How can one say, Mozart has *composed* Don Juan! Composition! As if it were a piece of cake or biscuit, which had been stirred together out of eggs, flour, and sugar! It is a spiritual creation, in which the details, as well as the whole, are pervaded by *one* spirit, and by the breath of *one* life; so that the producer did not make experiments, and patch together, and follow his own caprice, but was altogether in the power of the demonic spirit of his genius, and acted according to his orders."[6] Really, like the silkworm trope, this too conveys the idea that an external power wholly controls Mozart's creativity.[7]

The supposed externality of Mozart's inspiration and the receptiveness of his musical nature were also posited by a powerful musicological tradition. Several influential music historians have elaborated the premise that his evolution can best be understood as an unfolding of constantly shifting musical influences from a wide variety of sources, and often the history of Mozart's style has been seen as the documentation of his derivation from other composers and compositional schools.[8] His own works are regarded as an amalgam of influences rather than as products of an active personal creativity: indeed, by a curious lapse of logic, it is sometimes tacitly understood that the composers who influenced Mozart were carriers of a high degree of originality that was denied to him until his full maturity. Thus, Théodore de Wyzewa and Georges de Saint-Foix's influential five-volume *W. A. Mozart: Sa vie musicale et son oeuvre* (published in the years 1912–46) is devoted to uncovering the sources of Mozart's style—in the compositions of every European composer whom he heard or might have heard, including Leopold Mozart, Wagenseil, J. C. Bach, Abel, Schobert, Honauer, Vanhal, Gluck, Holzbauer, Mysliveček, Nardini, Tartini, Martini, Sammartini, Gossec, Eberlin, C. P. E. Bach, Michael Haydn, Joseph Haydn, Paisiello, Martín y Soler, Piccinni, and others—rather than to demonstrating the compositional originality or the unprecedented expressivity of his work. In a pathbreaking article they wrote, "Perhaps never in any art has there been any man of deep personal originality who has been as susceptible to external influences as Mozart, of whom one can really say that, during his entire life, his work was subject to the effects of other works which he had the occasion to hear or to read."[9] Successors to Wyzewa and Saint-Foix, including the authors of several standard encyclopedic surveys of Mozart's music, have in the main accepted their methodology, though they have called attention to additional influences that need to be taken into account, such as the influence of the Salzburg composers on Mozart's instrumental and church music, of the Viennese composers on his string quartets of the 1770s, and of various Italian operas on his own later operas.

Mozart was indeed a master imitator, capable of working in a large variety of styles. As we have seen, scholars like Daines Barrington and Charles Burney who met the young Mozart during the Grand Journey were astonished at his ability to extemporize vocal compositions in any of the prevailing opera seria styles. Mozart took pride in his mimetic powers, writing to his father, "As you know, I can more or less adopt or imitate any kind and any style of composition." Leopold saw this ability as a sure way of enhancing his son's career: "I know your capabilities. You can imitate anything."[10] Even more than most apprentice composers—perhaps because of his wide travels—Mozart absorbed various influences, learned the full range of current styles in the same way that he mastered the main foreign languages, and used procedures of modeling and parody to great effect. He had no hesitation about using models; from Munich in 1777 he sent his sister six duets for keyboard and violin by Joseph Schuster. "They are not bad," he noted. "If I stay on I shall write six myself in the same style, as they are very popular here."[11] On one occasion, in 1778, he described how he could so thoroughly transform a given model that his own work's derivation was concealed, a reminder of Lichtenberg's aphorism: "To do just the opposite is also a form of imitation, and the definition of imitation ought by rights to include both."[12] Writing to his father, Mozart declared:

> For practice I have also set to music the aria "*Non so d'onde viene,*" etc. which has been so beautifully composed by [J. C.] Bach. Just because I know Bach's setting so well and like it so much, and because it is always ringing in my ears, I wished to try and see whether in spite of all this I could not write an aria totally unlike his. And, indeed, mine does not resemble his in the very least.[13]

It should be self-evident that one composer's appropriation of external style characteristics of another is not necessarily an indication of deep affinity. Nevertheless, in narrating Mozart's compositional history as a series of successive encounters with and absorption of the music of other composers, critics have often exaggerated the extent of surface influences, and have mistaken his simple use of mannerisms, themes, or techniques—even where these were commonplaces of early classical style—for more fundamental influence. Similarly, the fund of historically evolved characteristic topics and rhetorical devices that the eighteenth-century music theorists described and upon which Mozart often drew for portions of his musical vocabulary is regarded as fixed and unchanging; Mozart's unprecedented contributions to those topoi are regarded merely as skillful manipulations of preexisting materials. Thus, Mozart is folded into his sources and his genius is defined as his gift for coherence and design and the deftness of his synthetic powers—his ability, as Leonard Ratner puts it, "to incorporate and synthesize elements from the various styles of 18th-century music."[14] Or, in Wye Jamison Allanbrook's words, "In general, nothing is ever wholly 'new' in Mozart's repertory, but is instead a brilliant combination of existing compositional materials."[15]

Alfred Einstein offered a somewhat different model of Mozart's absorption of influences: "One continues to marvel equally at his receptivity and at his powers of resistance—his talent for appropriating what was congenial and rejecting whatever was opposed to his nature."[16] Using an outmoded gender metaphor, he saw Mozart as a receptive traditionalist who "yielded to an influence quite ingenuously, quite in feminine fashion," who refined materials bequeathed to him by his predecessors and contemporaries. "What he derived from others was for him a fertilization. . . . It did not occur to him to do something new at all costs. He wanted to do it not differently, but better."[17] Friedrich Blume, too, regarded Mozart's development as a "youthful assimilation of innumerable other models [that] resulted in an amalgam from which everything disproportionate and characterless was little by little eliminated. . . . One gets a general impression of a constant simplification, clarification, and refinement."[18] He saw Mozart's period of imitation as carrying forward into the last Salzburg years, and even into his Vienna decade, so that it is only in his very last years that "we come to works highly individual and personal."[19] This is not very far from Saint-Foix, who held that Mozart outgrew influences only with the Prague Symphony. "Mozart here no longer speaks the language we have met in his former compositions; we get the impression that this language is entirely his own creation, and we know of no musician who might have been able to reveal its materials to him."[20]

Although the materials of every artist—forms, genres, language, vocabulary, techniques, and ways of looking at the world—are bequeathed by tradition, that is no reason to give excessive weight to the ancestral factor in creativity, to collapse the poet into his sources or into the period style— here the Classical style—to which his works belong. To the extent that the poet is able significantly to modify the inheritance and contribute something essential to the language he or she will have forged a style, and thereby earned a place among the poets and makers. Mozart is not lessened by the uncovering of correspondences and influences, any more that it diminishes Shakespeare to locate his sources in Holinshed's *Chronicles,* Plutarch's *Lives,* or even in the plays of Robert Greene or Christopher Marlowe. Greene thought otherwise, calling Shakespeare "an upstart Crow, beautified with our feathers," for he was naturally insensible of the distance between himself and a young rival poet.[21] And we, too, need to keep in mind the distance between Mozart and J. C. Bach or Schobert, whose talents were insufficient to daunt or intimidate the younger master. Admirable as they may have been, they did not fully engage his powers, let alone intimidate him by the force of their imaginations.

That may be why Mozart, though highly competitive by nature, never seriously came under the sway of the anxiety of influence, not even in his "Haydn" Quartets. For him, creativity was scarcely a perpetual struggle with his precursors and contemporaries. He had been taught to model himself upon other composers and he did so freely, without trepidation, without feeling that he would thereby inhibit his own creativity. As Rosen observed, "An artist is in many ways free to decide what will influence him."[22] Certainly, in his youth Mozart did not view the musical past as a melancholy burden but rather as an opportunity to be grasped. He approached contemporary masters—Wagenseil, J. C. Bach, Michael Haydn, Padre Martini, Joseph Haydn—as a precocious and trusting child, placing himself in their care, asking their assistance, confident in their loving responses. It may be overly simple constantly to see the live poets contending with the dead ones, projecting the family agon onto the screen of creative tradition. Frequently, a young poet or composer actually finds allies in such symbolic oedipal contests precisely among his or her colleagues, past and present, who strengthen the will to resist and lend courage to defy taboos against being a separate individual, to prove that one has the capacity to leave a mark upon the world.

Indeed, Mozart may have been possessed of a quite different kind of anxiety—an anxiety of originality—rooted in family prohibitions about becoming a mature person and a distinctive composer. As we shall see, those prohibitions did not center on tradition itself, but on modernity and the sphere of the imaginative. Because he had been empowered to imitate traditional models without transcending them, Mozart's musical personality split along the fault line of his father's grudging and ambiguous authorization: perhaps quite unconsciously, he gave the impression of adherence to tradition even as he subverted it. As a result, he did not initially lay claim to his own originality. And it is even possible that he himself was for a long time unaware of the extent of his capacity for originality; certainly he did not allow it open expression in much of his Salzburg music, which, unlike works of his Vienna years, never was charged with eccentricity, bizarrerie, or excessive learnedness. An apparently conformist manner, however, may often serve to conceal a subversive cast of mind, so subtly concealed in convention that it neither disturbs nor gives offense. It is only later on, in Vienna, that Mozart fully acknowledged the extent of his confidence in his powers, writing to his father in 1784, "I guarantee that in all the operas which are to be performed until mine is finished, not a single idea will resemble one of mine."[23] By then, he had overcome what he feared most—the prospect of remaining an imitator rather than a creator, a deputy kapellmeister rather than a master composer. To be condemned, like the Salzburg composers, to a career of routine accomplishment was unacceptable.

Mozart achieved a distinctive individual voice at different times in different genres. The major theatrical and liturgical genres—opera seria, *festa teatrili,* oratorio, school drama, and church music in all its forms—placed no special value upon originality. A composer's goal in fulfilling commissions in those genres was to meet expectations rather than to change sensibilities, to exhibit mastery of approved styles rather than to explore previously unplumbed potentialities. Thus, originality of style or uniqueness of voice was not an issue for Mozart in his Milan operas or his Salzburg church music; this may explain why several masses written by his father or other Salzburg composers were for long attributed to him, a confusion that could never have arisen with the C-minor Mass of 1783. It was not until the later 1770s that a characteristically lyrical Mozartean flavor is to be found in the Missa brevis in B-flat, K. 275/272b, and in the C-major Mass, K. 317 ("Coronation").

In the genres that are the main carriers of classical sonata-form evolution, Mozart began to achieve a marked degree of independence from his models toward the end of 1773 in such works as the String Quintet in B-flat, K. 174, the Piano Concerto in D, K. 175, the G-minor Symphony, K. 183, and the A-major Symphony, K. 201/186a of the following April.[24] These are works that are studied for the ways in which they bear upon the evolution of classical style in general and the sonata forms in particular, seen primarily in terms of such issues as formal symmetry, thematic development, harmonic trajectory, cyclic integration, coherence, organicism, and motivic work. Many music historians regard the two symphonies as the first unalloyed evidence of Mozart's genius.[25] Rosen, who sees Mozart's string quartets of 1772–73 as still embodying a "struggle to assimilate Haydn's language," finds the String Quintet in B-flat, K. 174, "astonishing" in its "breadth of conception, which goes far beyond any of the string quartets" of that time.[26]

Mozart and Haydn themselves valorized sonata-form cyclic works— Haydn in his unique announcement, in a set of letters to distinguished potential subscribers, that the String Quartets, op. 33, of 1781 were "written in a new and entirely special manner," thus signaling that he regarded them as a stylistic turning point,[27] and Mozart in his equally unique dedicatory letter published in the first edition of the string quartets he inscribed to Haydn in 1785. In Mozart's sonata-style works of later 1773, one often senses a certain restraint, even stiffness, as he seeks to subordinate his melodic impulse to formal restraints, as though he is reluctant to limit his imaginative vision and compositional spontaneity to accommodate structural issues or to illustrate "learned" techniques. These compositions are not yet unified Mozartean works; rather than marking the achievement of a personal style, there is in them a sense of searching for one—a brusque dramatic theatricality in the G-minor Symphony, an ethereal lyricism in the first movement of the A-major Symphony, a deep inwardness and interest in contrapuntal possibility in the slow movement and finale respectively of the String Quintet, K. 174. The Piano Concerto in D, K. 175, originally closed with a "learned" finale, which was replaced by an unproblematical rondo in ca. 1782.

It is in still another group of works that Mozart's characteristic style becomes fully realized for the first time. These are the Salzburg serenades, divertimentos, and violin concertos of 1772 to early 1776, whose connection to the evolution of the sonata style is precarious, tangential at best, although they are not wholly untouched by problems of sonata form. The serenade itself, which became a designation for a multimovement cycle, originated as an amorous musical offering, an open-air work sung by a lover to his beloved. This earlier meaning is retained in several of Mozart's operas, in arias usually with simulated guitar or mandolin accompaniments in *Bastien und Bastienne, Il rè pastore, Die Entführung aus dem Serail* (Pedrillo's Romance), *Don Giovanni* ("Deh, vieni alla finestra"), and *Le nozze de Figaro* ("Deh, vieni, non tardar"), Example 8.1.

Example 8.1. *Le nozze di Figaro*, Act IV (No. 27), Aria,
"Deh, vieni, non tardar," mm. 1–9.

The violin takes the vocal part in the instrumental equivalents, the most famous of which is the serenade from the "Haydn" (evidently Roman Hofstetter) String Quartet, op. 3, no. 5; two notable Mozart examples occur in an episode in the finale of the Violin Concerto in G, K. 216, and

in the Serenade in D, K. 185/167a, the former a pavanelike melody with
pizzicato accompaniment, the latter an *aria amoroso* with simulated guitar
strumming in the lower strings (Examples 8.2, 8.3).

Example 8.2. Violin Concerto in G, K. 216. Rondeau, mm. 252–64.

Example 8.3. Serenade in D, K. 185/167a. Menuetto II,
trio I, mm. 38–45.

Without ever altogether losing its original denotation, which came to
be reserved for the andantes and adagios, the serenade's function expanded
so that it became a multimovement instrumental musical homage rendered
on a celebratory occasion, including weddings, betrothals, promotions, ele-
vations, and graduations.[28] As a contemporary music theorist put it:

> The title "serenade" is also used for purely instrumental compositions,
> which, to honor or congratulate specific personages, are performed at
> dusk in front of their houses; such pieces are generally called Ständchen in
> German. The composer must strive to write simple, flowing melodies, set
> primarily to consonant rather than dissonant harmonies.29

The predominant character of the serenade style is pastoral, and the
serenades show Mozart's capacity for finding endless variety within the
standard pastoral tropes—allusions to nature sounds, quotations from folk-
songs, use of drones and horn calls, simulation of fretted and wind instruments, musical references to the hunt, the pervasive presence of dance
forms—musettes, gavottes, sicilianos, contredanses, gigues, and ländler—
with powerful associations to the pastoral.[30]

The serenade partakes of ritual, celebrating the old ways, the simple
ways. It is Rousseauean in outlook: we are born good, free, loving, and
sharing. It is aesthetic—seeking beauty and finding it in nature, in the features of a beloved person, in the comfortable ratification of communal feeling implicit in marking the stages of life with appropriate musical tribute. It
celebrates not only arrivals but leave-takings as well: the Mozart letters
often generically refer to serenades as *"Finalmusiken,"* for sometimes such

works marked the end of the school year, therefore embodying the concept of music as ritual farewell. Michael Haydn, in his Serenade, P. 87 (= Sherman 84), included a spoken (or shouted) "addio" just before the closing march. There is, of course, no funeral music here; that function is reserved for the enclosures of the church. Death is present in the serenade's implied Arcadian setting only in the form of the sadness, longing, and the sense of unfulfillment aroused by languorous and amorous music played outdoors in the evening, in quietude, in the afterglow of the day, or even under the stars. But the listeners are not isolated or alone, for the community surrounds them, sharing their feelings, celebrating the continuity of existence. It may also sometimes be a peripatetic music, a movable festivity inaugurated by a march that leads to the house of the honoree, moving through town to the locale of the main celebration, and ending with another march as the guests and musicians disperse. "On the 9th the *Finalmusik* was presented," wrote Mozart's sister in her diary for 9 August 1775 of his Serenade in D, K. 204/213a, composed for academic festivities and presented first at the archbishop's residence and then at the university: "At 8:30 it started out from our house for the Mirabell [Castle] where it lasted until 9:45, and from there it went to the university where it lasted until after 11:00."[31]

Mozart initially established his creative individuality in the great variety of serenades, serenade-divertimentos, and related works that he composed to order for his Salzburg patrons and friends, a "social" music that simultaneously represented the composer's ties to his community and his powerful attachment to feelings associated with pastoral and idyllic states of being. But although the idyll remains central to Mozart's conception of the serenade, his serenades are no ordinary idylls whose picturesque descriptions of country life convey simple moods of tranquillity, contentment, cheerfulness, and grace, as were the serenades of his predecessors. In a penetrating study, Günter Hausswald has shown how Mozart transformed the amiable and unproblematical character of the Salzburg serenade, modifying its naive psychological atmosphere, sharpening its contrasts, and deepening its expressivity.[32] He describes how Mozart's outer movements take on a new character, the opening movements now exhibiting an exuberant, festive brilliance and the slow movements conveying an unaccustomed inwardness of expression, with occasional darkenings through use of minor keys, underscoring a thoughtful pathos while retaining the expected qualities of grace and tenderness. The dance movements, too, acquire an unencumbered freshness and solidity, with Mozart highlighting the burlesque and folkish elements (including striking folksong quotations), without a hint of the coarseness we met in his earlier exercise in rusticity, *Galimathias musicum*. The best of these works are filled with a "subjective tension, giving up diffuse psychological indifference and developing in the direction of a deepened world of feeling."[33]

To this we may add that Mozart throughout assumes his characteristically ironic stance—an elegant sublimation of the "archness" that Daines Barrington found him to display—so that one can never be certain about how fully one ought to credit the music's apparent depth of feeling. Clearly, Mozart wanted simultaneously to appropriate the idyllic mode while disrupting the sentimentalities and insipidities of Arcadian/pastoral formulas and undermining the idealizations of aristocratic portraiture. The serenade was a vehicle in which he could participate in the rough-and-tumble of the world, give vent to erotic yearnings, focus attention on loss and mourning, show the interpenetration of opposing deep feelings that lie just beneath the green Arcadian turf. Always viewing the world from novel perspectives, Mozart cannot help but reshape traditions, however comforting they may be; he cannot help probing beyond the gentle longings of the serenader, who keeps his darker passions at bay, hidden within the lulling rhythms of the simulated lute accompaniment.

Serenade music was intended for immediate consumption: according to Marpurg, writing in 1757, a serenade, like much other music of the period, was "only performed once."[34] That may be why virtually all of the instrumental serenades of Salzburg—where the form had a vigorous life dating back to the Baroque, such as the suite-derived examples by Heinrich Biber in the later seventeenth century—have disappeared without a trace.[35] In 1757, Leopold Mozart reported that he had written "more than thirty grand serenades, in which solos for various instruments are introduced," but only one of them, a recent discovery at that, has survived.[36] Similarly, only four of Michael Haydn's numerous orchestral serenades—he wrote them rapidly, turning each of them out in a fortnight or less—are extant. Indeed, although many Austrian, German, Bohemian, and Italian contemporaries of Mozart's wrote instrumental serenades, none have left any particular imprint on the genre, so that Mozart's works remain as the form's most illustrious and influential examples, just as his "Deh, vieni alla finestra" remains the exemplary model of the vocal serenade.

The greater examples of Mozart's Salzburg works in the serenade genre include the Serenades, K. 185/167a ("Andretter"), K. 203/189b, K. 204/213a, K. 239 ("Serenata Notturna"), K. 250 ("Haffner"), and K. 320 ("Posthorn"). In their most characteristic form, they contained up to eight or nine movements, not counting the customary entrance and closing march, and included several minuets and two or three slow movements. Several concertante movements for one or more solo instruments were often embedded in the middle movements, and these were sometimes later extracted for separate use. The customary scoring was for strings, with added winds, totaling between half a dozen and a dozen instruments. The serenade style also constitutes the formal and expressive core of a cluster of works titled divertimentos, notturnos (serenades meant to be performed after nightfall), and cassations, for the descriptive terminology did not always clearly discriminate among these forms.[37] Among Mozart's purest serenades from the standpoint of form and function are the Divertimentos for strings and horns obbligato in F, K. 247, D, K. 251, B-flat, K. 287/271H, and D, K. 334/320b, all composed for leading families, except K. 251, which was written to celebrate his sister's twenty-fifth birthday. A significant precursor of these works is the Divertimento in D, K. 205/167a, probably written in July 1773 for the name day of Maria Anna Elisabeth von Andretter. Perhaps the earliest serenade-style work in which we clearly hear Mozart's voice is the so-called Divertimento in D, K. 131, of June 1772, scored for flute, oboe, bassoon, four horns, and strings. (The word "Divertimento" on the autograph score is not in Mozart's own hand.) It may well have been composed as wedding music, for the Adagio has the character of a serenader's love song, with strummed accompaniment simulated by the lower strings (Example 8.4).

Example 8.4. Divertimento in D, K. 131. Adagio, mm. 1–2.

Although Mozart wrote several serenades after he left Salzburg, including the Serenade in B-flat ("Gran Partita"), K. 361/370a and the *Eine kleine Nachtmusik* (literally, "a short serenade"), K. 525, it is sometimes said that Mozart's serenade style was so closely bound up with the conditions of Salzburg life that it could not survive transplantation. Paul Henry Lang believed that when Mozart ultimately left Salzburg, he "lost his faith in the music which symbolized it," seeing the serenade as incompatible with Mozart's growing interest in "symphonic concentration."[38] Of course, although sonata-style issues were to predominate in Mozart's mature instrumental music, we will find serenade style there as well as in several of the late operas, in pastoral and *amoroso*-style movements such as the Adagio of the "Hunt" Quartet in B-flat, K. 458, wherever he seeks to represent currents of nostalgia, elegy, and longing by employing what Allanbrook calls "the artifacts of *temps perdu*."[39] Already in his Salzburg music the serenade style was far from limited to use in serenades, divertimentos, notturnos, and cassations; rather, serenade characteristics eventually spilled over into several adjoining instrumental genres, infusing them with the rich vocabulary of classico-pastoral imagery that Mozart had developed and refined in his instrumental serenades as well as in such pastoral stage works as *Bastien und Bastienne, Ascanio in Alba,* and the mid-1775 opera, *Il rè pastore,* which contains diversified examples of Mozart's serenade style at its most developed.

In *Il rè pastore,* the shepherd-king Aminta's first-act aria, composed to a pastoral text, plainly contains a first draft of the Violin Concerto in G, K. 216 (Examples 8.5, 8.6).

> Tranquil air and serene days
> Fresh springs and green fields
> These are the prayers to fortune
> Of the shepherd and his flocks.

Example 8.5. *Il rè pastore,* Act I (No. 3), Aria, "Aer tranquillo," mm. 1–6.

Example 8.6. Violin Concerto in G, K. 216. Allegro, mm. 1–4.

Clearly, serenade style now had begun to move freely beyond any confining borders of musical genre. As we have already noted, interior movements of four of Mozart's Salzburg serenades—K. 185/167a, 203/189b, 204/213a, and 250/248b—form miniature violin concertos, and it was in these that Mozart's characteristic violin concerto style ripened. The three Violin Concertos, K. 216, 218, and 219, of 1775 are not so much examples of Mozart's move to annex increasingly structured forms as they are the highest examples of his serenade style after it has been detached from the serenade proper and reconstituted within a separate genre. The unpredictable consequence of this shift is the surprising emergence of serenade style as a universal style that is no longer subject to the limited expectations of the social setting within which it had been confined. Cut loose from its sociological function as a celebratory *Gebrauchsmusik* and integrated into a legitimate concert-music genre, serenade style now revealed new implications. Thus, what had formerly been viewed merely as conventions of idyllic rusticity viewed through the condescending lens of aristocratic self-congratulation are converted into representations of an ideal pastoral world, even of the classical image of Arcadia itself, and what had been a readily consumable festive music linked to a particular celebration now becomes a stylistic resource of extraordinary affective range, celebrating broad areas of human experience, centering on nature, love, and play.

A. Hyatt King remarks on the "sheer speed of the musical thought" in the violin concertos, and H. C. Robbins Landon writes of their "*embarras de richesse*," where "melody is piled upon melody, and new ideas succeed each other in blissful insouciance of each other and of any strict formal pattern."[40] Mozart has no need here for the constrictions and conventions of sonata forms, permitting the free play of fantasy to lead him into a variety of unexpected, even exotic, episodes (Examples 8.7a, b).

Example 8.7a. Violin Concerto in A, K. 219. Rondeau: Tempo di Menuetto, mm. 132–40.

Example 8.7b. Violin Concerto in A, K. 219. Rondeau: Tempo di Menuetto, mm. 165–72.

★   ★   ★

Freely limning his landscapes out of the materials of serenade style, Mozart is apparently unbounded by formal constraints, unfettered, free-associational. At the opening of this concerto, following the festive Allegro aperto orchestral tutti, which itself has the character of a miniature potpourri overture, the violin soloist unexpectedly unveils a six-measure adagio that has the character of a lyrical recitative, telling in pure pastoral/*amoroso* style of inward longings. Against murmuring strings meant to simulate the sounds of breezes and flowing brooks, the violin at last emerges from its interior space to join the orchestra in an arpeggiated celebratory mood (Example 8.8).

Throughout the violin concertos, Mozart experiments with irregularities of structure and whimsicalities of invention, and in the finales, only surprises are predictable. Though he does retain in broad outlines the traditional features of concerto form—the three-movement cycle, approximations of sonata form in the opening movements along with the conventional alternation of four tutti and three solos, da capo aria form in the slow movements, and closing rondo-type finales—the formal structures of the three concertos are loose, unsymmetrical, generous, yielding. Mozart understood that these qualities were not altogether compatible with newer trends towards concision and concentration. "If I have time," he wrote his father from Paris in September 1778, "I shall rearrange some of my violin concertos, and shorten them. In Germany we rather like length, but after all it is better to be short and good."[41]

If the serenade style's dominant procedure is that of constant metamorphosis, its central organizing image is the image of plenitude, springing from an overflowing abundance of unsullied idealism as yet untouched by any hints of morbidity, cynicism, or disillusionment. Embodying a desire to embrace the world, it is a youthful music of yearning but not of grief, imbued with an innocent utopianism, a faith in perfectability, beauty, and sensual fulfillment. It is music of unbounded possibility and imaginative fertility, representing the first cresting of Mozart's own creative powers. It is the paradigm of expectation in music, a carrier of hopeful possibilities. It is music that renders the poignant fusion of yearning and fulfillment, of unease and contentment, music that conveys the sense of an untested eroticism seeking in reality the object its fantasy has conjured up. That may be why Mozart's serenade-style concertos have the character of an amorous quest tinged with melancholy, like Watteau's "Embarkation for Cythera," in which a contingent of graceful young men and women, clothed in the garments of Arcadia, patiently gather to board the barque that will carry them to a good and happy place, a place already prefigured in what Ernst Bloch describes as the "wishful landscape" in which they are assembled.[42]

Perhaps there are also biographical parallels here: Mozart continues to

Example 8.8. Violin Concerto in A, K. 219. First movement, mm. 40–47.

"The Embarkation for Cythera," by Jean-Antoine Watteau. Louvre.

seek a personal fulfillment (one that he cannot quite define) that, especially in view of the almost unbroken string of triumphs climaxing in the Italian years, he has every expectation of achieving. The essential optimism that accompanied the initial crystallization of Mozart's personal style corresponds to his outward acceptance of the goals of the family enterprise and of his own protected position within the social and familial universe. Thus, his yearnings have the hopefulness of youth in quest of love and the confidence of great talent awaiting its day, nourished by the knowledge of being a favored son. A composer has discovered within himself shaping powers, imaginative powers, the power to visualize a musical structure before creating it in reality, the power to transmute inner feelings into objective forms. Mozart becomes a separate individual in his music before he becomes one in reality: his music forecasts his own future. As wish, his music tells of the landscapes he wants to inhabit, modeled out of the mythic imagery of the pastoral and Arcadian. As memory, his music tells of what he has experienced. As desire, his music tells of what he wants to enfold in his arms.

Mozart as a Chevalier of the Order of the Golden Spur.
Anonymous oil portrait, Salzburg 1777. Civico Museo
Bibliografico Musicale, Bologna.

9

·······································

A FOOL'S ERRAND

In September 1777, almost twenty-two years old, Mozart left his post as concertmaster to the archbishop of Salzburg and, accompanied by his mother, set out to make his fortune. Eighteen months later, dejected and unhappy, he returned to Salzburg at his father's insistence, having accepted a position there as court organist to the archbishop at a salary of 450 florins and pledged to devote himself wholly to the welfare of his father and sister and to repay the costs of his journey. The intervening time was spent in an unsuccessful search for an appropriate position in Munich, Mannheim, Paris, and Versailles. Mozart and his mother were en route to Paris for six months. They arrived in Munich on 24 September 1777, in Augsburg on 11 October, and in Mannheim on 26 October, remaining there until mid-March 1778, and finally arriving in Paris on 24 March 1778, following a ten-day coach ride. Mozart remained in Paris for six months. He commenced his return journey on 26 September—alone, for his mother had died in Paris—and after stays in Nancy, Strasbourg, Mannheim, Kaisheim, and Munich that lasted from a few days to a little more than a month, arrived home in the middle of January 1779.

The reasons why the most gifted and multitalented musician of the age was unable to secure a position bear exploration. In part, it had to do with Mozart's youth and inexperience as a director of musicians, which clearly made improbable his selection for any prestigious post, let alone that of kapellmeister. In Munich, where he offered his services to the electoral court, Elector Maximilian III Joseph was sympathetic but said, "Yes, my dear boy, but I have no vacancy. I am sorry. If only there were a vacancy."[1] Privately, he suggested to Mozart's advocate, the bishop of Chiemsee, that Mozart's hope for a major post was premature. "It is too early yet. He ought to go off, travel to Italy and make a name for himself. I am not refusing him, but it is too soon."[2] Mozart reported this to his father, commenting bravely that in a year or two he "would be sought after by the court instead of having to canvass them."[3] Indeed, the elector was reported to have said that Mozart "would *certainly* be taken into the Court service, but added that things could not be done quite so quickly."[4] Mozart was also led to believe that during the interim he would be able to obtain a substantial guarantee—perhaps 600 florins annually—from a consortium of connoisseurs, plus several hundred florins from Count Joseph Anton Seeau, manager of Munich's Residenztheater, for whom Mozart hoped to write operas. "Now what does Papa think of this idea? . . . It seems perfectly satisfactory to me. I should be near Salzburg, and if you, my dearest Papa, should feel inclined (as I heartily wish that you may) to leave Salzburg and end your days in Munich, the plan would be delightful and quite simple. For if we have had to live in Salzburg on 504 florins, surely we could manage in Munich on 600 or 800?"[5] But Mozart's father was not impressed, finding the scheme "quite inconceivable," and urged Mozart to move on: "*If the arrangement is immediately practicable, well and good, and you ought to accept it. But if it cannot be made at once, then you simply must not lounge about, use up your money and waste your time.*"[6] Mozart acknowledged that it would take some time to form the consortium, but he was willing to begin work in Munich at once, even without substantial guarantees of his economic security. "If I were here alone," he wrote, "it would not be impossible for me to manage somehow, for I should ask for at least 300 florins from Count Seeau. As for food, I should not have to worry, for I should always be invited out."[7] He calculated, not unreasonably, that he could earn an additional 500 florins from his compositions and performances.

With this suggestion, Mozart had now raised a most crucial—and sensitive—issue: that he could begin to build his career straightaway provided that he postpone the expectations of filling a distinguished position and instead seek work as a free-lance composer with the support of the music-loving aristocracy. Leopold Mozart firmly closed the door on this option: "I quite agree that if you were alone, you could live in Munich. But it would do you no honor, and how the Archbishop would laugh! *You can live in that way anywhere, not only in Munich. You must not make yourself so cheap and throw yourself away in this manner, for indeed we have not yet come to that.*"[8] Mozart's sister, Marianne, chimed in, tracking her father's argument: "It would not do you any credit to stay on in Munich without an appointment. It would do us far more honor if you could succeed in obtaining a post under some other great lord. You will surely find one."[9]

As events soon made clear, it was far from likely that Mozart would find such a post. Perhaps the best he could hope for was a position as court organist or court composer. Certainly it was improbable that he could instantly obtain a guaranteed post that would provide sufficient income to support the entire family. It was plainly the case that in order for Mozart to build the foundations of his career he needed to be on his own, living frugally, fulfilling commissions, making salon appearances, promoting concerts, and giving lessons. By repeatedly dissuading Mozart from pursuing a free-lance route, Leopold Mozart foreclosed the most simple, logical, and practical pathway to establishing his career. Mozart reluctantly obeyed his father, but not without resentments that have left their traces in his letters. "If I had been alone" became a leitmotif of his letters home: "That we stayed so long in Munich was entirely due to *me*," he wrote subsequently, "and if I had been alone, I should most certainly be there still."[10] Again, later on: "Now if I had been alone, this would have been an excellent opportunity for me."[11]

Nevertheless, he continued to look for a significant position, and indeed there now appeared to be some reason for optimism about his chances to be appointed a court composer in Mannheim, the seat of the elector of the Rhine Palatinate and one of the main centers of European musical life—"a paradise of musicians," as one contemporary put it.[12] Mozart's father underlined what Salzburg's Countess von Lodron had told him, "*Mozart will go to Mannheim and, whatever happens, I am persuaded that the Elector will retain him.*"[13] Leopold himself confidently wrote, "I do not doubt but that the Elector will keep you for the winter and perhaps even longer. . . . If you do spend the winter there, I feel sure that you will be appointed permanently and with a good salary."[14] In a subsequent letter, he reiterated, "If you can only remain there for six months and show what you can do in all styles of music, you will certainly be appointed."[15]

The Mozarts were on pins and needles, alternately optimistic and anxious, as they eagerly awaited the decision of the Palatinate's highly regarded elector, Karl Theodor, to whose four natural children Mozart gave keyboard lessons during his stay. Frau Mozart wrote home on 7 December, listing the extraordinarily high salaries for Mannheim's leading musicians, ranging from 1,400 florins for the concertmaster to 3,000 florins for composer Ignaz Holzbauer. "It makes your mouth water," she wrote, adding judiciously, "Things are moving a bit slowly. We must just wait and see, and be grateful for the time being that he has not refused altogether."[16] To his newly acquired supporter Count Louis Aurel Savioli, manager of the Mannheim orchestra, Mozart revealed his eagerness: "I begged him to persuade the Elector to grant me a permanent appointment. . . . 'He ought,' I said, 'to give me some work. I like work.'"[17] The governess of the elector's children twice assured Mozart that the elector had told her that "Mozart is staying here for the winter."[18] In a letter of 3 December, he described how he finally met his prospective employer in person and used the opportunity to promote his cause; seeing the elector approach, the governess told one of Mozart's royal pupils hastily to seat herself at the clavier. Mozart described the scene to his father:

> I placed myself beside her and gave her a lesson; and that was how the Elector found us when he came into the room. We stood up but he told us to go on. When the Countess had finished playing, the governess was the first to speak and said that I had composed a very fine Rondo. I played it and he liked it very much. At length he asked: "But will she be able to learn it?" "Oh yes," I replied, "I only wish that I might have the good fortune to teach it to her myself." He smiled and said: "I should like it too. But would not her playing be spoilt if she had two different masters?" "Oh no, Your Highness," I replied. "All that matters is whether she has a good one or a bad. I hope Your Highness will not doubt—and will have confidence in me." . . . "How long are you going to stay here?" *My reply:* "As long as your Highness commands."[19]

On 8 December Mozart was informed by Count Savioli that the elector had decided against hiring him. Overcome by disappointment, Mozart could not hide his sorrow during his lesson with Rosa Cannabich, daughter of the court music director, Christian Cannabich, so that she, her mother, Mozart, and another friend were all weeping while Rosa played the Sonata in C, K. 309/284b, which had been composed for her a few weeks earlier. "I must say," wrote Mozart, "that I have some very kind friends here. Indeed it is at times like these that one gets to know their worth."[20]

Having lost his great opportunity at Mannheim, Mozart showed his resilience by instantly drafting a plan to reduce expenditures so that he could make a living as a free-lance composer for several months before moving on to Paris accompanied by the oboist Friedrich Ramm and the flutist Johann Baptist Wendling. He would add two more pupils, compose some violin and piano duets and engrave them by subscription, lodge free at the home of Court Councillor Serrarius, and eat supper gratis with his friend Wendling. Inexpensive lodgings were to be found for Frau Mozart and she was to return home to Salzburg after the winter.[21] As for the elector, Mozart intended to provide evidence of his unswerving devotion by composing for him a grand mass.

The plan was immediately instituted. Frau Mozart wrote that Mozart began to give lessons to Councillor Serrarius's daughter in exchange for "free lodging, including wood and light. Wolfgang has his meals at Monsieur Wendling's and I go for mine to young Herr Danner's, who in return for this takes lessons in composition from my son."[22] Moreover, Mozart claimed to have obtained a commitment of 200 florins from the music-lover Ferdinand Dejean in return for a substantial number of flute concertos and flute quartets; this commission gave rise to several works, among which may have been the Flute Concertos in G, K. 313/285c, and D, K. 314/285d (arranged from an oboe concerto), an Andante in C for flute and orchestra, K. 315/285e, and the Flute Quartets in D, K. 285, and in G, K. 285a.[23] Mozart did work on the grand mass for the elector, but only a few fragments survive (probably K. 296a–c). He made good progress on a set of six sonatas for keyboard and violin, which were engraved and dedicated to the Electress Marie Elisabeth toward the end of 1778; four of these, K. 301/293a, 302/293b, 303/293c, and 305/293d, were completed at Mannheim.[24] While there he also composed the Piano Sonata in D, K. 311/284c, and the Violin Sonata in C, K. 296.

"You cannot imagine in what high favor Wolfgang is here both with the orchestra and with other people," wrote his mother.[25] Within just a few days Mozart had established himself as a busy free-lance musician, and he described his new life to his father:

> We can't get up before eight o'clock, for until half past eight there is no daylight in our room. . . . I dress in haste and at ten I sit down to compose until about twelve or half past twelve. Then I go to Wendling's, where I again compose a little until half past one, when we have lunch. Thus the time passes until three, when I go off to the Mainzischer Hof [an inn] to a Dutch officer to give him a lesson in galanterie and thoroughbass, for which I receive, if I am not mistaken, four ducats for twelve lessons. At four I must be home again to instruct the daughter of the house. . . . At six I go to Cannabich's and give Mlle Rosa her lesson. I stay there to supper, after which we talk or occasionally someone plays.[26]

"He has so much to do," commented his mother with evident pride, "that he really doesn't know whether he is standing on his head or his heels; what with composing and giving lessons he hasn't time to visit anybody."[27]

Steady work, a little ready cash, and the prospect of being entirely on his own had rapidly changed Mozart's outlook and demeanor. When, on 11 January 1778, he asked his father to look into a rumor that in Vienna Emperor Joseph was seeking "a young kapellmeister" to head a German-language opera program, he expressed his interest with a certain imperiousness that was indicative of his new confidence in himself and his unwillingness to be exploited: "It would be a good thing for me, provided of course that the pay is good. If the Emperor will give me a thousand florins, I will write a German opera for him; if he won't have me, it's all the same to me."[28] And when the suggestion came back, via a third party writing to Leopold, that Mozart write a German-language opera as a sample of his abilities and submit it "to the imperial judgment and then . . . await a decision,"[29] it caused Mozart "more annoyance than pleasure," for he considered himself too well established to write an opera on speculation: "Perhaps he thinks that people remain twelve years old for ever?" he asked.[30] He now considered his mother's departure a certainty and began to treat his father with a touch of ironic disrespect: "As for Mama's journey home, I think it could most easily be arranged during Lent. . . . That's merely what I think; what I know beyond all question is that what meets with your approval will be the best for us, for you are Court Kapellmeister and a paragon of intelligence!"[31]

More fatefully, he had fallen in love with Aloysia Weber, a sixteen-year-old singer and the daughter of the Mannheim singer-musician Fridolin Weber, and, heedless of the consequences, Mozart pledged to devote himself to furthering her career. (We will look at this in more detail later on.) Thus, unknown to his father, who was busily mapping the details of the trip to Paris, Mozart had decided to stay on in Mannheim instead, and then accompany Aloysia on a concert tour of Italy and perhaps of Switzerland and Holland. He spent from 23 January to 2 February in close company with Aloysia and her father on a journey to Kirchheimbolanden to perform at the court of the Princess Caroline von Nassau-Weilburg, with a side trip to Worms, where they visited a relative of Herr Weber. There, the relationship blossomed and Mozart decided to announce his new plans. With a straight face, he informed his father on 4 February that he could not carry out his plan to travel to Paris with Wendling and Ramm because he had discovered them to be immoral and irreligious. "I propose to remain here and finish entirely at my leisure that music for De Jean, . . . " he wrote. "I can stay here as long as I like and neither board nor lodging costs me anything. In the meantime Herr Weber will endeavor to get engagements here and there for concerts with me, and we shall then travel together."[32] Knowing exactly what her husband's reaction would be and seeking to soften the blow, Mozart's mother wrote her secret postscript to Mozart's letter on 5 February, in which she offered to sacrifice her return trip to Salzburg and to accompany Mozart to Paris.

The twin prospects of being displaced by a surrogate father and of being deprived of his son's future income naturally enraged Leopold Mozart, who now vehemently insisted that his wife and son leave immediately for Paris; in this way he would firmly separate Mozart from the Webers and set Frau Mozart to guard against further dangers and temptations. "I have read your letter of the 4th with amazement and horror," he wrote to his son. "For the whole night long I was unable to sleep and am so exhausted that I can only write quite slowly." With heated rhetoric he marshaled his arguments into a dramatic narrative of innocence corrupted yet capable of redemption. He recalled the "happy moments" of earlier times when the boy Mozart unquestioningly loved and obeyed him; he described their difficulties in Salzburg—"my wretched income, why I kept my promise to let you go away, and all my various troubles"; he reminded Mozart of their agreement concerning their goal: "The purpose of your journey was twofold—either to get a good permanent appointment, or, if this should fail, to go off to some big city where large sums of money can be earned. Both plans were designed to assist your parents and to help your dear sister, but above all to build up your own name and reputation in the world." In a striking passage quoted earlier, he alerted his son to the hazards of marriage and urged him to avoid ending up in a garret full of starving children. And now he pronounced judgment and offered deliverance: "*Off with you to Paris!* and that soon! Find your place among great people." In the end, Leopold stressed, altruistic feelings must be subordinated to family obligation:

> Your desire to help the oppressed you have inherited from your father. But you really must consider first of all the welfare of your parents, or else your soul will go to the devil. Think of me as you saw me when you left us, *standing beside the carriage in a state of utter wretchedness.* Ill as I was, I had been packing for you until two o'clock in the morning, and there I was at the carriage again at six o'clock, seeing to everything for you. Hurt me now, if you can be so cruel! Win fame and *make money* in Paris; then *when you have money to spend,* go off to Italy and get commissions for operas. . . . Nannerl has wept her full share during these last two days. Addio.[33]

To us it appears inevitable that Mozart's proposal would touch off Leopold's anger and precipitate the journey to Paris. Why, then, did he write it? Surely he could more diplomatically have postponed the journey on a pretext instead of declaring that he intended to go traveling with a family of strangers to whose welfare he would henceforth devote himself. Perhaps he yearned to relive through the Webers the golden days of his own family's journeys, with a somewhat revised cast of characters. For he undoubtedly regarded Herr Weber as a father substitute, and after their ten-day journey to Kirchheimbolanden he overflowed with good feelings about him as a new edition of Leopold Mozart: "When I am with him, it is just as if I were travelling with you. The very reason why I am so fond of him is because, apart from his personal appearance, he is just like you and has exactly your character and way of thinking. . . . I must confess that I much enjoyed traveling with them. We were happy and merry; I was hearing a man talk like you."[34] Mozart was so genuinely overjoyed that Aloysia's "father resembles my father and the whole family resemble the Mozarts,"[35] that he may not have consciously foreseen that his father would not share his enthusiasm. Seemingly unaware of the devastating effect of his words, he even wrote the fateful line, "I have become so fond of this unfortunate family that my dearest wish is to make them happy; and perhaps I may be able to do so."[36]

It was as though he had been weaving a pleasant daydream—a daydream in which he rescued a talented young maiden, helped a needy family, revived his own youth, took on his father's roles of pedagogue and impresario, and, not least, accomplished all of these while enjoying his father's loving approval. Rudely awakened from the daydream, Mozart wrote, "I always thought that you would disapprove of my undertaking a journey with the Webers, but I never had any such intention—I mean, of course, *in our present circumstances* . . . In the intoxication of the moment I forgot how impossible it is at present to carry out my plan, and therefore also—to tell you what I have now done."[37]

Stunned by the intensity of his father's response and embarrassed by the revelation of his own petty deceptions, he tried to reassure Leopold Mozart that he would now submit to his will. "Do rely on me. I shall do my very best to bring honor to the name of Mozart. . . . I do entreat you never to allow the thought to cross your mind that I can ever forget you, for I cannot bear it. My chief purpose was, is and ever shall be to endeavor to bring about our speedy and happy reunion! But we must be patient. . . . How can you doubt me? Surely it is to your interest that I should work as hard as I can, so that I may have the joy and happiness (the sooner the better too) of embracing with all my heart my most beloved and dearest father?"[38] Frau Mozart, too, tried to mollify her husband—"We are both awfully sorry that our letter horrified you so,"—and then she protested gently against his wrathful tone. "On the other hand, your last letter of the 12th distressed us greatly. I implore you with all my might not to take everything to heart in the way you do, for it is bad for your health. Why, everything can be made right again and we have lost nothing but bad company. We shall do our very best to make arrangements for our journey to Paris."[39] Thereafter she tried to calm her husband by warranting that they would follow his orders: "Rest assured that everything will be done in accordance with what you want and prescribe."[40] Mozart was now reduced to defending himself against the charge that he had succumbed to libertinage: "I am no Brunetti! no Mysliveček!," he exclaimed, referring to two musicians who were ravaged by venereal diseases. "I am a Mozart, and a young and clean-minded Mozart."[41] He fell ill, perhaps in reaction to his troubles. "I have been confined to the house for two days . . . as I have had catarrh, a cold in the head, headache, a sore throat, pains in my eyes and earache."[42]

Mozart's last weeks in Mannheim were clouded by sadness that he now must part from so many close friends and colleagues. In a subsequent letter he remarked that it had always been his misfortune "to leave people, countries, and cities, and with no great hope of soon, or ever again, seeing the kind friends whom I had left behind."[43] On 13 February and 12 March concerts were held at Christian Cannabich's home featuring Mozart's compositions, performed by himself, Rosa Cannabich, his student Therese Pierron Serrarius, Aloysia Weber, and Ramm. At the first, Fräulein Cannabich played his Concerto in B-flat, K. 238, Ramm performed an oboe concerto (probably K. 314/285d), Aloysia Weber sang several arias from Lucio Silla, and Mozart himself played his early Concerto in D major, K. 175. At the second, his Concerto in F for three claviers, K. 242, was performed and Aloysia Weber sang the scene that he had just completed for her, "Alcandro, lo confesso"—"Non so, d'onde viene," K. 294. "Mlle. Weber sang two arias of mine," he wrote home. "With the latter my dear Mlle. Weber did herself and me indescribable honor, for everyone said that no aria had ever affected them as did this one; but then she sang it as it ought to be sung."[44] He also wrote concert scenes, both dated 27 February 1778, for two other leading Mannheim singers: "Se al labbro mio non credi"—"Il cor dolente," K. 295, for the tenor Anton Raaff, and "Basta, vincesti"—"Ah, non lasciarmi," K. 486a/295a, for the soprano Dorothea Wendling. On the thirteenth he bid farewell to the Webers, receiving from Herr Weber a German translation of Molière's comedies and from Aloysia "two pairs of mittens knitted in filet as a remembrance and a small token of her gratitude."[45] "When I left, they all wept. Forgive me, but my eyes fill with tears when I recall the scene. Herr Weber came downstairs with me, and remained standing at the door until I had turned the corner and called out after me—Adieu!"[46]

In truth, there was no reason for Mozart to leave Mannheim, except that to remain there would have meant giving up his quest for the grand position his family had envisaged. But Mozart did not have the courage to confront the issue head on, to call into question his father's central assumption. Partly, this was because that assumption played into his own sense of his greatness, the importance of his calling: "I am a composer and was born to be a Kapellmeister," he now wrote. "I neither can nor ought to bury the talent for composition with which God in his goodness has so richly endowed me."[47] And so, on 14 March, despite having so quickly planted the seeds of a successful career in Mannheim, Mozart and his mother set out for Paris by way of Metz and Clermont, arriving, in Paris at four o'clock in the afternoon on the twenty-third of March.

The six-month Paris sojourn, which lasted from 24 March until 26 September 1778, did not solve Mozart's career problem either, despite his strenuous efforts to establish himself there. In Paris, with the composition of the Violin Sonatas in E minor, K. 304/300c, and D, K. 306/300l, he completed the set of six for the Electress of Mannheim. Shortly after his arrival he composed the Flute and Harp Concerto in C, K. 299/297c, for the Comte de Guines and his harp-playing daughter; he wrote a fair amount of keyboard music, including the Sonata in A minor, K. 310/300d, and two sets of variations, including Twelve Variations on "Je suis Lindor," K. 354/299a, and Nine Variations on "Lison dormait," K. 264/315d.[48] He hoped for a commission from the Académie Royale de Musique (the Paris Opéra) but had to settle for furnishing ballet music for the pantomime *Les Petits Riens,* K. Anh. 10/299b, which was presented on 11 June and repeated six times to great applause during the summer. His arrangement of Holzbauer's *Miserere,* K. Anh. 1/297a, was heard at the Concert Spirituel, a prestigious series of concerts, in early April. A lost Sinfonia Concertante in E-flat for four winds and orchestra, K. Anh. 9/297B, was also intended for the Concert Spirituel.[49] The Symphony in D, K. 297/300a ("Paris"), dated 12 June 1778 and performed at the Concert Spirituel on the eighteenth of the same month, was his only major symphonic composition. A few lesser works round out the list, which Mozart acknowledged was not a long one: "I am not bringing you many new compositions, for I haven't composed very much."[50] (He exaggerated his productivity in letters home, inventing a second "Paris" Symphony that for a long time baffled historians.)[51]

Modern scholarship has sharply reduced the number of his Paris compositions, stripping away not only the piano variations K. 265/300e and K. 353/300f, but the Capriccio, K. 395/300g, and the four piano sonatas K. 330–332/300h, i, k and K. 333/315c. Paris, however, did give rise to several masterpieces, especially the A-minor Piano Sonata, the E-minor Violin Sonata, and the "Paris" Symphony, reflecting Mozart's determination to make his mark with his most original works.[52] As the performances at the Opéra and Concert Spirituel attest, Mozart had begun to find appreciative listeners and had made a fair start upon a free-lance Parisian career, should he choose to pursue one. And, as we shall see, while there he even received an offer of a secure and prestigious position, but he left France without the employment he had come in search of.

It is my view that Mozart's quest for employment failed not because he was unemployable, unproductive, or untalented, but because his father pursued a private agenda that Mozart ultimately could not live with. In earlier years, at Milan, Florence, Munich, and Vienna, it seems reasonable to conclude that Leopold Mozart had bargained for a post of his own as a precondition to his son's employment.[53] That may have been what the empress meant when, in advising Archduke Ferdinand not to hire "the young Salzburger," she stressed that "he has a large family."[54] Leopold Mozart's dream of double employment even survived Mozart's departure from Salzburg. On 23 October 1777, Marianne Mozart wrote excitedly, "I only wish that what Herr Cassel came to congratulate us about were true, that is, that you and Papa were appointed to Munich and were to draw 1,600 florins."[55] It is clear, however, that Leopold's employment was not seriously contemplated at either Munich or Mannheim in 1777–78. He designed his scenario in more realistic terms: Mozart was to obtain a secure post that would anchor the family's economy, and after relocation, Leopold and Marianne would supplement Mozart's primary income by their own activities: "If . . . you could count on a monthly salary from some prince in Paris, and, in addition, do some work occasionally for the theater, the Concert Spirituel and the Concert des Amateurs, and now and then have something engraved par souscription, and if your sister and I could give lessons and she could play at concerts and musical entertainments, then we should certainly have enough to live on in comfort."[56] This is the most explicit statement of Leopold's plan for Mozart to support the relocated family, although it is often implied in other letters. From Mannheim, for example, Mozart's mother wrote, "I do hope that Wolfgang will make his fortune in Paris quickly, so that you and Nannerl may follow us soon. How delighted I should be to have you both with us, for nothing could be better."[57] Writing from Paris in May, Mozart showed that he perfectly understood his presumptive role: "I pray to God daily to give me grace to hold out here with fortitude and to do such honor to myself and to the whole German nation as will redound to His greater honor and glory; and that He will enable me to prosper and make a great deal of money, so that I may help you out of your present difficulties; and that He will permit us to meet again soon, so that we may all live together in happiness and contentment."[58] Later, in a letter of 31 July 1778, he described how eagerly he awaited the moment "when we are happily reunited and can live somewhere together (which is my sole ambition) . . . "[59]

Thus, with Mozart's outward agreement Leopold Mozart had framed the purpose of the journey in such a way that Mozart must secure a prestigious position that could support the entire family, the best case being that he would obtain a double appointment for himself and his father. In order to make this plan workable, Mozart had to limit his options. He had to secure a base of operations in a city to which the family could relocate. He had to have sufficient money guaranteed to him to warrant the expense of the relocation and to offset the loss entailed by Leopold Mozart in surrendering his Salzburg post. For similar reasons he could not be an itinerant composer or virtuoso musician. And he apparently did not consider renewing his efforts to gain a position in Vienna, for reasons that are not altogether clear. But perhaps he had learned of the empress's disfavor and thought it futile to pursue prospects there while she was still alive.

Curiously, unknown to Mozart, prior to his departure from Salzburg an advantageous proposal did come from Vienna that could have altogether mooted the long and frustrating quest for a position and given Mozart a three-year start on his career in Vienna. The wealthy and influential Viennese educator Joseph Mesmer offered to maintain Mozart gratis for as long as necessary while he established himself at the capital. We learn of this from a letter of late January 1778 in which Leopold Mozart asserted that he had never received Mesmer's initial letter containing the offer—a rare failure of the dependable postal service in those days; now, in the interest of full disclosure, he copied out Mesmer's follow-up letter. "Why did you not send your son at once to Vienna?" asked Mesmer; "Or why are you not sending him even now?" and he reiterated the details of his offer: "I promise you faithfully that he can have free board, lodging, and everything else with us as long as he likes, and that all your friends in Vienna, myself included, will endeavor to obtain some good appointment for him."[60] There is no longer any way of knowing whether Leopold Mozart suppressed Mesmer's original offer, and perhaps he should be given the benefit of the doubt. Now he wrote to Mozart, "If you decide to take this path, it is still open to you,"[61] but the entire matter was engulfed in the tumultuous events of early February.

In fine, as I understand it, Mozart was to be dissuaded from going on his own as a free-lance musician because the imponderables and fluctuating fortunes of that occupation would have undermined Leopold Mozart's master plan; further, it would have meant Mozart's separation from his family under unsupervised circumstances where he was apt to neglect his family obligations. The worst possibility, of course, was that Mozart might marry and thereby pledge both fealty and earnings to his wife and offspring; that is one reason why his sudden attachment to the Webers was sufficient to arouse his father's and mother's deepest anxieties.

In Munich and Mannheim, under his mother's watchful eye, Mozart had diligently pursued his father's business, seeking guaranteed court positions in congenial and attractive German cities and abandoning his excellent free-lance prospects in both cities out of deference to his parents. It was not for want of trying that he failed to achieve the family's purposes. But a new recalcitrance emerged following his rejection by Elector Karl

Theodor: he wanted to remain in Mannheim by himself and, later on, to travel with the Webers to various countries, pursuing precisely the kind of free-lance, itinerant career that would have defeated all of Leopold Mozart's expectations. His Mannheim dream shattered, Mozart had been shipped off to Paris, but it seems clear that he developed increasingly serious qualms about fulfilling his pledge of family allegiance. The prospect of being indefinitely subjected to his father's discipline, of being barred from marriage, of being the perpetual economic mainstay of a family that was not incapable of supporting itself had by now eroded his capacity for filial obedience.

Mozart's refusal to play his part became apparent in May, when, through his friend the court horn player Jean Joseph Rodolphe, he was offered the post of court organist at Versailles at a substantial salary and under favorable terms. In a letter of mid-May 1778 he coolly set forth his objections, juggling figures and translating the proposed salary into various currencies so as to disguise the attractiveness of the offer:

> The salary is 2,000 livres a year, but I should have to spend six months at Versailles and the other six in Paris, or wherever I like. I do not think that I shall accept it, but I have yet to hear the advice of some good friends on the subject. After all, 2,000 livres is not such a big sum. It would be so in German money, I admit, but here it is not. It amounts to 83 louis d'or, 8 livres a year—that is, to 915 florins, 45 kreuzer in our money (a considerable sum, I admit), but here worth only 333 thalers, 2 livres—which is not much. It is frightful how quickly a thaler disappears here.[62]

There may be several reasons why, after so much time spent in search of such an offer, Mozart now rejected this post: because he longed to return to Mannheim and Aloysia Weber; because he thought he could do better elsewhere; because he had quickly developed a marked antipathy to France. In the last analysis, however, it seems to me that its acceptance would have set in train a series of irreversible events, namely the resignation of Leopold Mozart from his Salzburg post and the relocation of the Mozarts to Versailles, thus making the family utterly dependent upon Mozart for the indefinite future.

Not surprisingly, and with much underscoring for emphasis, Leopold Mozart marshaled several reasonable arguments in favor of accepting the post:

> You must not throw that away so lightly. You should bear in mind that *you would be earning 83 louis d'or in six months—and that you would have another six months in which to make money in other ways.* Further, it is probably *a life appointment,* I mean, that you hold it whether you are well or ill—and,

moreover, that *you can always resign it. . . . You would be at Court. . . ; that*
when there is a vacancy, *you might obtain one of the two posts of kapellmeister;*
that in due course . . . you would become clavier-teacher to the young princes,
which would be a very remunerative post; that nobody could prevent you from com-
posing for the theater and the Concert Spirituel and so forth, from having music
engraved and dedicating it to your patrons . . . ; that Versailles is a small town in
itself and has many distinguished residents, among whom you would surely
find one or two pupils—and finally that an appointment of this kind *would*
be the surest way to win the protection of the Queen and make yourself
popular.[63]

Mozart's father did not quite credit the implications of Mozart's refusal,
and even chose to "regard the whole affair as a *pious wish* on the part of
Rodolphe."[64] But it was not a phantom offer, as Mozart made clear in a letter in which he repeated his objections: "As for Versailles, I never thought
of going there. I asked Baron Grimm and some other good friends for
their advice and they all thought as I did. The salary is small and I should
have to pine for six months of the year in a place where nothing else can
be earned and where my talent would be buried. Whoever enters the
King's service, is forgotten in Paris—and then, to be an organist!"[65] In closing, with what may have been some veiled sarcasm, he reminded his father
of their original grandiose plans: "I should very much like a good appointment, but it must be a kapellmeister's and a well-paid one too."[66] Moreover,
it is questionable whether Mozart would have accepted any Parisian post,
no matter how prestigious and lucrative, for he was extremely unhappy
there, revealing to Fridolin Weber that he wanted to pursue his fortune in
Mannheim or Mainz: "You have no idea what a dreadful time I am having
here. . . . You may have gathered that I am not very happy, and that
(between ourselves) I am trying to get away as quickly as possible"[67] And
he did not conceal from his father his feelings about life in Paris, which, he
wrote, "is totally opposed to my genius, inclinations, knowledge and sym-
pathies. . . . God grant only that I may not impair my talents by staying
here; but I hope that it won't last long enough for that."[68]

Thus we now enter a time of broken promises by both Mozart and his
father. Faced with a decision—to accept the Versailles post—that would
irrevocably commit him to the heaviest responsibilities, Mozart decided
that he would not accept the position he had gone in search of, and
thereby he reneged on the agreement with his father. And earlier, Leopold
Mozart had frankly conceded that if the search for a permanent appointment should fail, he would honor his pledge that Mozart could pursue a
free-lance career in a major musical center ("some big city where large
sums of money can be earned").[69] The moment to test that understanding

had arrived, but Leopold Mozart now fixed on a contrary course of action, one that he had held in reserve for some time, and even, it seems, from the very beginning. Having noted Mozart's failure to secure a lucrative appointment elsewhere, and perceiving his son's resistance to pursuing the family scenario, he intended to force him to return to Salzburg, where Leopold Mozart could continue to play out his dream of a dual appointment and the pooling of Mozart's income with his own.

The revised plan began to take shape as early as 21 December 1777, when, within hours after the death of Court Organist Adlgasser, Count Franz Lactanz Firmian asked Leopold Mozart "whether he ought not to put [Mozart's] name forward to the Archbishop for the post of organist."[70] Leopold Mozart reported to his son that he naturally declined, saying to Firmian, "It was quite out of the question."[71] Within a few days, however, elated that "we are already tasting" some of the sweetness of revenge, he gleefully told of a conversation between Count Arco and Count Starhemberg, in which Arco rebuked the court: "You are in a fix, are you not? Young Mozart would now have rendered you good service."[72] And a few weeks later Leopold and Michael Haydn were asked "whether we knew of a *very good organist* who must, however, be a *first-rate keyboard artist,* and at the same time *of good appearance and presence, as he will be giving lessons to the ladies.*"[73] To this, Leopold allegedly replied: "I know nobody who has all these qualities," but he added, with a modicum of malice, "*If there is such a person in Mannheim, then he can make his fortune.*"[74] Predictably, although Mozart knew what his father was about, he did not rise to the bait: he studiously avoided any reference to the matter of Adlgasser's replacement, as though it could be of no conceivable interest to him. He understood perfectly, however, that Leopold Mozart had now prepared the ground to ask him to return to Salzburg.

In June, Leopold Mozart casually told Countess Lodron of Mozart's Versailles offer: "I told her quite coolly and rather hastily (for I was hurrying back to lunch) that you were both in good health and that, if you chose, you might perhaps have one of the two posts of Royal organist," whereupon she expressed the desire to "have you back in Salzburg; that she would make sure that *later on you should certainly become kapellmeister,* but that this was at the moment out of the question, seeing that you had resigned from the Prince's service; that you could, however, be appointed Konzertmeister and organist . . . at fifty florins a month."[75] So negotiations of conditions on which Mozart might become Salzburg court organist were now under way without his consent: "I am not writing all this, my dear Wolfgang, in order to persuade you to return to Salzburg," Leopold wrote on 29 June. "They must come to me—and, before I agree to anything, the conditions they offer must be very favorable and advantageous—all of which is extremely unlikely."[76] Even as this letter reached Paris, Frau Mozart died there, on 3 July, and Mozart was in no condition flatly to refuse his father; instead, he equivocated by placing what he knew to be impossible conditions: he would not return "unless the Prince will trust you or me and give us full authority *as far as the music is concerned*—otherwise it's no good. . . . If I were to undertake it, I should have to have complete freedom of action. The Chief Steward should have nothing to say to me in musical matters, or on any point relating to music."[77] He continued in the same vein, "You know that there is nothing I desire more than a good appointment, good in its standing and good in money—no matter where—provided it be in a Catholic country. . . . I should still prefer to be anywhere than in Salzburg. But I need not worry, for it is highly improbable that all I ask will be granted, as I am asking a great deal."[78] His back to the wall, Mozart tried to justify his distaste for Salzburg by referring to "those coarse, slovenly, dissolute court musicians. Why, no honest man, of good breeding, could possibly live with them! Indeed, instead of wanting to associate with them, he would feel ashamed of them. It is probably for this very reason that musicians are neither popular nor respected among us."[79] And, to make his reluctance amply clear, on 18 July 1778 he notified his father that he had recommended another musician to apply for the post of Salzburg organist.[80] Somehow, he hoped to wriggle out of the net.

On 31 August Leopold announced that he had struck a deal with the archbishop: "Well, thanks to my brave perseverance . . . , the Archbishop agreed to everything, both for me and for you (you are to have five hundred florins), but he has even apologized for not being able at the present moment to appoint you kapellmeister; you are, however, to take my place if I am tired or indisposed. . . . And you will be appointed concertmaster as before. So together we shall receive *an official salary* of a thousand florins a year. . . . Everything now depends on whether you believe that I am still in possession of my mental faculties, whether you think that I have served your best interests, and whether you want to see me dead or alive."[81] He added that it was agreed that Mozart would be granted periodic "leave to travel where you like for the purpose of composing an opera," which is to say that Mozart could travel for no other purpose, certainly not on a concert tour or in pursuit of a position. Thus Leopold Mozart had negotiated and concluded the contract in contradiction to Mozart's explicit conditions, and in the face of his aversion to serving in Salzburg. Leopold neglected to mention that he had extracted an additional 100 florins in salary for himself as part of the arrangement, a sum which apparently was subtracted from the 600 florins that Mozart had initially been promised; and in the end, Mozart's salary was further reduced, to 450 florins.[82] In return for what the court must have regarded as an exorbitant salary, Mozart was to fill two positions, those of court organist and concertmaster, and to substitute for the deputy kapellmeister on occasion as well. Only gradually was it revealed that Mozart—whose outcry was, "I will no longer be a fiddler"—would have to provide some services as violinist and even to give keyboard lessons to the choristers who were maintained and educated at the archbishop's Kapellhaus.[83]

It now remained only to deliver the recalcitrant employee to the archbishop, to which end Leopold Mozart orchestrated his campaign for Mozart's rapid return, enlisting Baron Grimm (with whom Mozart was living) to press his boarder to hasten home and Abbé Bullinger to remind Mozart of his filial responsibilities. Grimm urged him depart within a week, saying, "It is your father's wish." When Mozart proposed to lodge elsewhere in Paris Grimm replied, in a rage, "Look here. If you leave my house before you leave Paris, I shall never look at you again as long as I live. In that case you must never come near me, for I shall be your worst enemy."[84] Mozart held his tongue, but complained to his father: "I should have . . . gone to a less boorish and stupid household, where people can do you a kindness without constantly casting it in your teeth."[85] In his response to Bullinger, as we have already seen, Mozart offered a lofty critique of Salzburg's musical establishment, to which he added his personal reservations: "You, most beloved friend, are well aware how I detest Salzburg— and not only on account of the injustices which my dear father and I have endured there . . . To live respectably and to live happily are two very different things, and the latter I could not do [there] without having recourse to witchcraft."[86] Bullinger's response was to append an ecstatic postscript to a letter from Leopold Mozart to Mozart: "O how I rejoice! What a rapturous pleasure will it be for me when I can embrace you in Salzburg."[87]

Meanwhile, Mozart's father continued his own barrage of commands, recriminations, and inducements: he warned Mozart that should he fall ill in Paris he would have to depend, "like a beggar, on the alms of goodhearted people. . . . Do you still want to live in Paris in beggary from day to day, in a place where you are not happy? . . . If you now want to leave Paris, who will give you the travel money? Me, perhaps? Who will pay when you are currently in debt?"[88] He painted the attractions of Salzburg life in bright colors: "Here we can now go to the Carnival balls at the Rathaus; the Munich theatrical company is arriving at the end of September and will remain the entire winter presenting comedies and operettas; every Sunday is our shooting party and if we want to be with company, we can now do so because we have a better salary, which changes everything."[89] In an access of magnanimity, he dropped his opposition to Mozart's friendship with Aloysia Weber. "As for Mlle. Weber, you should not think that I would be opposed to this acquaintance. All young people must run on a fool's string. You can still continue your exchange of letters as hitherto."[90] He even promised to refrain from reading their correspondence. He swore that he never again would leave his son exposed to arbitrary power: "I swear to you most solemnly that . . . I only remained tied to Salzburg in order that, whatever happened, your poor mother might have been sure of a pension. Well, that is all over now, the pension is no longer needed, and so we shall not stand any tyranny but be up and away."[91] Having exhausted these pathetic allurements, he resorted to emotional pressure, describing his own shocking appearance, his illness, his heavy burdens and his "distressed soul."[92] Similarly, he wrote that "the entire city praises your decision to return home to come to the aid of your father, who has lost his wife, and give him necessary support in his old age."[93]

Mozart's resistance began to crumble under his father's assault. In his letter of 11 September, he confessed that he "trembled with joy, for I fancied myself already in your arms," adding, "There is one place where I can say I am at home, where I can live in peace and quiet with my most beloved father and my dearest sister, where I can do as I like, where apart from the duties of my appointment I am my own master, and where I have a permanent income and yet can go off when I like, and travel every second year. What more can I desire?"[94] But in the next breath he described his "disgust" with Salzburg, and although he accepted the inevitable, his subsequent letters continued to express his unwillingness to go home. "I am truly committing the greatest folly in the world. . . . If my father knew of my present circumstances and excellent prospects . . . he would surely not have written to me in such a strain that resistance to his wish was out of the question."[95] By means of such vacillations he delayed his return, arriving in Salzburg only in mid-January 1779, traveling by way of Nancy, Strasbourg, Mannheim, Kaisheim, and Munich. He spent several productive weeks in Strasbourg, giving a solo subscription concert on 17 October and two additional orchestral concerts at the Strasbourg theater on 24 and 31 October. He then went to Mannheim, against his father's express order ("your idea . . . is absolutely impracticable"), arriving on 6 November.[96] During his month there he wrote—or considered writing—music to Otto Heinrich Gemmingen's melodrama *Semiramis,* K. Anh. 11/315e (not extant) and composed a lengthy fragment of the first movement of a Concerto in D for piano, violin, and orchestra, K. Anh. 56/315f. Einstein called the failure to complete this work "one of the great losses of art."[97] These, and the Soprano Scene "Popoli di Tessaglia"—"Io non chiedo, eterni Dei," K. 316/300b, dated 8 January 1779, constituted the sum total of his meager production during the five months he was en route home.

"God be praised that I am back again in my beloved Mannheim!" he wrote. "Since I came here I have not been able to lunch at home once, as there is a regular scramble to have me. In a word, Mannheim loves me as much as I love Mannheim. And I am not positive, but I believe that I may yet obtain an appointment here—here, not in Munich."[98] This prospect was calculated to, and did, drive Leopold to the edge of distraction. "I shall go mad or die of a decline. The very recollection of all the projects which since your departure from Salzburg you have formed and communicated to me is enough to drive me crazy. They have all amounted to proposals, empty words ending in *nothing whatever.*" He was wild at the thought of Mozart's remaining permanently in Mannheim. "You must not take an appointment at present either in Mannheim or anywhere else in the world. I will not hear the word *appointment.* . . . The main thing now is that *you should now return to Salzburg.* I do not want to hear anything more about the forty louis d'or which *perhaps* you may be able to earn. Your whole intention seems to be to ruin me, simply in order to go on building your castles in the air."[99]

His capacity for persuasion almost exhausted, Leopold Mozart ultimately reduced the entire matter to its simplest form: Mozart owed him money—he listed 863 florins as the amount—and therefore had no choice but to return to Salzburg, "*to take an appointment for a couple of years, as then I might have some prospect of paying off these debts.*"[100] Doggedly he reiterated: "The 863 florins must be paid. . . . I know that I can pay [the debts] in two years. However, I alone can not pay them . . . In brief! *My debts must be paid,* upon the *receipt of this letter you must start back.* I will not be the laughing stock of the town."[101]

Although, as we have seen, Leopold Mozart had accumulated considerable capital from the proceeds of the early concert tours, he attempted—probably with doubtful success—to conceal his good fortune both from the Salzburg citizenry and from his own family. In his letters of 1777 and 1778 to Mozart he claimed that he had gone into debt to finance the journey, picturing himself as almost wholly without funds, forced to borrow substantial sums that he could repay only with great difficulty, and constantly hovering on the edge of paupery. Jahn took him at his word. "He had no private property; the profits of the first journey had already disappeared; he was obliged to borrow, and debt was abhorrent to so conscientious a man; but his friends Hagenauer and Bullinger readily came to his assistance."[102] According to Leopold, the trip was initially financed by loans of 300 florins from Bullinger and 100 florins from Weiser, and (perhaps) by a further sum from Hagenauer, but there are no letters, promissory notes, or other documents to confirm these "loans," which may merely have been sums withdrawn from his own savings.[103]

In any case, there is no doubt that financing the journey was a great expense to Leopold Mozart. From the start, he regularly summarized and lamented his mounting outlay of cash: "*It is solely on your account that I am in debt to the extent of 450 florins,*" he wrote on 4 December 1777, "and you think perhaps to put me in a good humor by sending me a hundred silly jokes."[104] By the following week the sum had grown to "more than six hundred florins,"[105] and by early February it had increased by another 100 florins, and he asserted that he was unable to pay his bills or even the smallest household expenses. "I am now in very deep waters," he wrote. "As you know, *I am now in debt* to the extent of about 700 florins and *haven't the faintest idea how I am going to support myself, Mama and your sister on my monthly salary. . . .* So it must be as clear as noonday to you that the future of your old parents and of your good sister who loves you with all her heart, is entirely in your hands."[106] He continued, "If you think it over, you will realize that not only have I never spent a farthing on the smallest pleasure for myself but that without God's special mercy I should never have succeeded in spite of all my efforts *in keeping out of debt;* and yet *this is the first time I have got into debt.*"[107] On a later occasion he did acknowledge having modest savings, though barely enough to cover his debts. "If with the little bit of money which I still have *I now pay our debts,* then your Mama and your sister would not have a farthing *after my death* and, further, I could not assist you in any way."[108]

Although he had accumulated large sums of money, Leopold Mozart feared to let anyone know of his wealth, lest others seek to take it from him. Mistrustful of mankind, suspicious of the motives of others, he genuinely dreaded poverty and even believed that he was on the verge of impoverishment. Earlier, in an incautious moment, he revealed that he had calculated the money he advanced to Mozart as an investment on which he hoped to reap a considerable return; he wrote, in November 1777, "I am willing, if you really wish to go to Paris, to arrange for you to draw there *an advance of twenty or thirty louis d'or* in the hope that this sum will come back to me doubled and trebled."[109] Now he had abandoned his expectation of making a profit and would be content merely to get his money back.

In November 1778, Leopold Mozart summarized what his son owed him for the costs of the journeys until that date, reminding him

that on your departure from Salzburg I provided	300 florins
that I arranged for you to draw in Mannheim	200 florins
that I paid for money which you drew from	
Geschwender in Paris	110 florins
that I owe Baron Grimm fifteen louis d'or	165 florins

that you drew eight louis d'or in Strasbourg   88 florins
so that in fourteen months *you have plunged*
me into debt to the extent of   863 florins.[110]

By a combination of his own frugality and modest earnings, Mozart's indebtedness had increased by only 163 florins since February, even with the expense of traveling to Paris. Nevertheless, this was still a considerable sum. Turning a blind eye to his earlier substantial earnings from his son's labor, and ignoring the fact that half of the costs were attributable to Frau Mozart's expenses, Leopold Mozart had decided that the debt would have to be paid, and he had fixed upon the surest method of repayment: "I am old. I can not know when God will call me to eternity. I will not die in debt. . . . I will not have it that in order to pay the debts our things will be wretchedly sold after my death. . . . Only with your salary included can I be assured of taking in 100 florins per month, so that, even with accidents, and including the sale of my books, I can pay off everything in a few years and die peacefully: and *that I must* and *that I will do!*"[111] Unmercifully he pressed Mozart to submit or to accept responsibility for acting so as to bring about his father's death. "If, when you return, you do not lift this heavy burden from my heart, it will crush me utterly."[112]

It is remarkable to contemplate how drastically Leopold Mozart had now lowered his sights for his son's future as a creative musician and composer: he was willing to have him accept a combined court organist and concertmaster's post at 450 florins per year; to remain in provincial Salzburg, which had no significant indigenous theatrical or operatic life; to work in the service of a minor ecclesiastical prince as a court musician with at best an occasional opera-composing visit to Munich or Italy. This would have been a satisfactory career for many a lesser composer (*Kleinmeister*) such as Adlgasser, Eberlin, Michael Haydn, or Leopold Mozart—but scarcely one suitable for Mozart.

On the surface, it appeared that Leopold Mozart had done this so that he could continue the old practice of pooling his son's income with his own, so that, in effect, he could eventually subsist on a double pension—one from the Salzburg court, the other provided by his own son. The conflict between father and son had thereby been reduced to the lowest common denominator, but it had not reached bedrock, for underneath the struggle about money, the matter was rich in implications. Unable to confess that he loved his son and that he could not bear to be separated from him, he resorted to the crudest sort of coercion, ordering Mozart to return to him as his duty, as a sacrificial necessity, and finally as the obligation of an ordinary debtor to his creditor. He wrote bluntly, "If it is God's will, I want to live a few years longer, pay my debts—and then, if you care to do so, you can run your head against the wall."[113] Clearly, Leopold Mozart was at his wit's end. "I am heartily sick of composing these long letters and during the last fifteen months have almost written myself blind."[114]

Under the pressure of these harangues, Mozart began to feel that he had become estranged from his father. "I really cannot write—my heart is too full of tears. I hope you will write to me soon and comfort me," he wrote on 29 December from Munich, where he had arrived on Christmas Day, and he enclosed a letter from his father's old friend, the flutist Johann Baptist Becke, transmitting a plea for compassion that he could not bring himself to write. "Never have I seen a child who carried more feeling and love for his father in his bosom than does your son," wrote Becke to Leopold. "He is assailed by some fear lest your reception of him may not be as tender as he wishes. . . . He surely deserves to enjoy all love and happiness at his father's side: his heart is so pure, so childlike. . . . Pray write to us soon and assure us of your true fatherly love: . . . do but make his stay at Salzburg truly agreeable and friendly."[115] Mozart thereby revealed his pain at his father's harshness and his guilt over wanting to gratify his own needs, but he was asking for more than forgiveness and forbearance: through Becke he asked his father for the plain sign of unalloyed, selfless love that he so longed for. But just after mailing this appeal he received another hurtful letter, that of 28 December: "If you had travelled straight to Salzburg, I should have paid, or rather I *could have paid off* one hundred florins of our debts. So I command you to leave at once. . . . Good God! How often have you made a liar of me!"[116]

Mozart now tried to harden his own heart, describing how Becke had so persuaded him of "your tender paternal love, your indulgence towards me and your complaisance and discretion when it is a question of furthering my future happiness, that my heart melted within me!" and adding pointedly, "From your letter of the 28th I see only too clearly that Herr Becke in his conversation with me was inclined to exaggerate. Well, let's be frank and plain."[117] Therewith, Mozart suggested that he, too, would put their connection on a business basis, setting aside issues of love and sentiment. "It would be to my interest to remain here a little longer, but I will sacrifice that for your sake and in the hope that I shall be doubly rewarded for it in Salzburg."[118] In his final letter to his father before returning to Salzburg, written on 8 January 1779, Mozart remarked plainly that he did not wish to return to Salzburg and openly disclosed "the sadness which in the end I could no longer conceal." At the same time he defended his virtue: "As far as I know, I have done nothing to cause me to fear your reproaches. I am guilty of no fault." He also expressed his anger against his father, disguised as antipathy toward Salzburg, although as always he drew back with a (partial) disclaimer: "Please believe that I have the most aching longing to embrace you and my dear sister once more. If only it were not in Salzburg!"[119]

As a result of this process of extreme simplification, whereby the issue had been reduced to one of debt and repayment, Leopold Mozart actually succeeded in making matters somewhat easier for Mozart, undermining the filial impulse and in effect placing a rough time limit on Mozart's obligations. There was now a finite amount that Mozart owed, which, at the rate of 450 florins per year less the cost of his room and board, would take him about two years to work off. That, at least, was one of the implications of Leopold Mozart's estimates: "I am not in circumstances to pay off a debt which runs in totality to 1,000 florins, if the burden is not lightened by the income from your salary, by which I can then certainly pay off each year over 400 florins, and still live magnificently with the two of you."[120] On other occasions he offered different figures, once estimating that the debt could be retired at the rate of "a few hundred florins" per year, and at another time suggesting that "we can can live grandly and still put aside over 300 florins each year."[121]

In the end, after his long search for a position, Mozart fully understood that his best option—far better even than a kapellmeister's post that would result in the family's relocation—was to work off the debt in Salzburg and try to write *finis* to his financial responsibilities to his father. It did not quite work out that way, for Leopold Mozart never conceded that the debt had been repaid and Mozart was constantly drawn to a resumption of his customary sacrificial role. But increasingly, his compulsion to sacrifice himself was undermined by his inability to elicit from his father either a frank avowal of paternal love or a simple statement of gratitude for a son's superhuman efforts on behalf of the family enterprise.

In some way, the relationship between father and son had taken on the character of a dispute between debtor and creditor. Mozart had entered into an unwritten contract, under the terms of which he acknowledged receipt of certain monies, goods, and services the value of which was to be repaid in full within the lifetime of the lender. The parties agreed that Mozart owed his father for the gift of life, for his education and upbringing, and for the successful furtherance of his career. In addition, Mozart was to compensate his father for setting aside his own career and sacrificing his own ambitions as composer and litterateur so that he might dedicate himself to the rearing of his gifted child. In addition to reimbursing his father for monies actually expended, Mozart additionally agreed, obediently, lovingly, and without complaint, to care for his father during the term of the agreement, which was to endure until death. It was an exclusive contract: no third person was to obtain any portion of the debtor's earnings or affections, which were to be devoted solely to the discharge of the debt.

Mozart struggled for many years somehow to fulfill the terms of the agreement, but in the end he unilaterally canceled it as unduly onerous, thus placing himself in the position of a guilt-ridden debtor who has absconded to a distant city and been publicly declared insolvent. He may thereby have circumvented the literal payment of his debt, but he was unable to avoid judgment or to receive the indemnity from continuing prosecution that he so deeply craved.

10

....

MOZART IN LOVE

Eager to justify himself, Mozart offered many rationales for his resignation from Salzburg court service in 1777: the small salary he was paid as violinist, the inadequacy of compensation for his compositions, the restrictions placed on his travels, and other perceived examples of unjust treatment by the archbishop. Clearly, too, he needed a larger arena for the exercise of his abilities, and he was genuinely dismayed by the restrictiveness of musical life in his native city. Of equal force was his sense that he needed to be on his own, free from his father's guiding hand and from family responsibilities. Mozart always sought to deny the latter motives, but he could never refrain from alluding to them indirectly, in words whose wounding implications were clearly understood by Leopold Mozart, who was ever alive to the subtlest nuances of his son's letters. But it did not take great subtlety to grasp Mozart's implication when he wrote, just before his return home in 1779: "I cannot bear Salzburg or its inhabitants (I mean, the natives of Salzburg). Their language—their manners are quite intolerable to me."[1]

In addition to these powerful motivations to be free of Salzburg, there was another plain reason—his hunger for sexual expression and for a fulfilling love relationship. So far as we can tell, he had never been able to establish any serious or enduring love interests in Salzburg. Now almost twenty-two years old, he was more than ready to fall in love and his needs were so urgent that they would not brook further delay. Only six days after Mozart and his mother arrived in Augsburg on 11 October 1777, where they were met by Leopold's brother Franz Aloys Mozart, his wife, and his only daughter, Mozart's cousin, Maria Anna Thekla, Mozart delightedly wrote

Maria Anna Thekla Mozart (the Bäsle). Self-portrait. Pencil drawing, 1777 or 1778. Mozart-Museum der Internationalen Stiftung Mozarteum, Salzburg. © Mozarts Geburtshaus, Salzburg.

his father, "On the morning of this day, the 17th, I write and declare that our little cousin is beautiful, intelligent, charming, clever, and gay; and that is because she has mixed with people a great deal, and has also spent some time in Munich. Indeed we two get on extremely well, for, like myself, she is a bit of a scamp [*ein bischen schlimm*]. We both laugh at everyone and have great fun."[2]

In the same envelope, Mozart's cousin enclosed a warm letter to Mozart's father, evidently hoping for a closer relationship with the Salzburg branch of her family. "It is impossible for me to express the great pleasure which we have felt at the safe arrival of your wife and of such a delightful cousin and we only regret that we must again so soon lose such special friends, who show us so much friendship."[3] Leopold Mozart, sensing that a love affair could be in the making, was instantly on his guard: "I am altogether delighted to hear that my niece is beautiful, sensible, charming, clever and gay, and so far from having any objection to make, I should like to have the honor of meeting her." But he continued in an ironic, cutting tone: "Only it seems to me that she has too many friends among the priests. If I am mistaken, I shall be charmed to beg her pardon on bended knee. . . . I am quite pleased to hear that she is a bit of a scamp, but these ecclesiastical gentlemen are often far worse."[4] Mozart was thus immediately put on notice of his father's opposition to any closer connection with her. Nevertheless, he and his cousin, who was known affectionately within the family as the "Bäsle" ("little cousin," from *Base*, female cousin), appear to have fallen in love instantaneously and to have made the most of the few days that were available to them. On the twenty-fifth of October, the evening of his departure for Mannheim, Mozart wrote in her album:

> If you love that which I love,
> You will have to love yourself,
>> Your very affectionate cousin,
>> Wolfgang Amadée Mozart[5]

Maria Anna Thekla Mozart (1758–1841) was the only surviving child of Franz Aloys Mozart (1727–91) and Maria Victoria, née Eschenbach. Franz Aloys had successfully pursued the family's traditional occupation, bookbinding, with an occasional venture into publishing religious tracts. Like most daughters of the middle class, his child received only a limited formal education, but her few surviving letters, though uncultivated in style and orthography, are brimming with natural intelligence. As the recipient of arguably the most famous set of off-color love letters in cultural history, it is clear that she was alive to puns, riddles, and to every variety of wordplay, in fact, she was the joint originator of many of the verbal formulations that constituted a private code between herself and Mozart. They had met twice, briefly, as young children, during the family's continental tour, in June 1763 and again in November 1766. When Mozart and his mother arrived in Augsburg in 1777, they stayed at the inn called The White Lamb (*Zum Weissen Lamm*), located only a few steps from Franz Aloys's house in the Jesuitengasse, behind the cathedral; Maria Anna Thekla was not yet twenty years old.

Mozart's letters to the Bäsle are famous for their exuberant comic language, which is rich in obscenities and obscurities, many of which have yet to be decoded. But often the language is fairly straightforward in its acknowledgment of an uninhibited sexuality. On 3 December 1777, writing from Mannheim, Mozart assured his cousin that he has been faithful to her: "Since I left Augsburg, I have not taken off my trousers, except at night before going to bed."[6] In the same letter, pretending that he is speaking of his handwriting, he offered her a choice between something that is "fair, straight, and serious" and something that is "untidy, crooked, and jolly." It was now up to her. "So all depends now on what you prefer. You must make the choice (I have no medium article to offer you). . . . I expect to hear your decision in your next letter."[7] In another letter he writes, "I kiss your hands, your face, your knees, and your— finally, all that which you permit me to kiss."[8] More blatantly, in his letter of 10 May 1780, he spins a rapid series of sexual puns, enjoining his cousin to "blow into my behind. It's splendid food, may it do you good"; he refers to her "fascinating beauty (visibilia and invisibilia)"; describes himself as "very soft, and I like mustard too, particularly with beef"; and writes that "one has the purse and another has the gold," the interesting idea being, of course, to put the one into the other.[9] The letters abound in excremental humor, obsessively combining sexual and scatological imagery: "Write at once, the sooner the better, so that I may be sure to receive your letter, or else if I'm gone I'll have the bad luck, instead of a letter to get some muck. Muck!—Muck!—Ah, muck! Sweet word! Muck! taste! That too is fine. Muck, taste!—muck!—lick!—o charmante! muck, lick! That's what I like! Muck, taste, and lick! Taste muck and lick muck!"[10] Rollicking references to oral sex recur at the end of the same letter: "Whoever doesn't believe me, may lick me world without end, from now to all eternity. . . . He can go on licking for ever . . . for I fear that my muck will soon dry up."[11]

Mozart had long reveled in crafting double meanings out of apparently innocent words and phrases, as in a 1770 letter to his sister, where the verb *thuen* ("to do") serves double-duty as *facare* and *cacare*.[12] "*Do* keep well and *do* not die, so that you may *do* another letter for me and that I may *do* another for you and that we may keep on *doing* until we are *done*.

For I am the man to go on *doing* until there is nothing more to *do*."[13] (A later chapter will touch on how the deciphering of Mozart's obscene implications leaves intact still deeper issues that are "hidden" beneath a comic surface.) Hildesheimer, who has understood Mozart's linguistic usage and verbal acrobatics better than anyone, discloses a similar strategy in one of the Bäsle letters, where Mozart plays with the verb *schicken* ("to send") in order to call up its rhymed substitute *ficken* ("to fuck") in his cousin's imagination:

> I must ask you, why not?—I must ask you, dearest dunce, why not? . . . Why should I not . . . beg [Fräulein Josepha] to forgive me for not having sent her the sonata? . . . Why not?—What?—Why not?—Why should I not send it?—Why should I not despatch it?—Why not?—Strange! I don't know why I shouldn't—Well then, you will do me this favor.—Why not?—Why should you not do it?—Why not?—Strange! I shall do the same for you, when you want me to. Why not? Why should I not do it for you? Strange! Why not?—I can't think why not?[14]

The incessant "Why not?" requires less elaborate decoding, with the phrase "to do it" here bearing its commonplace implication. Hildesheimer writes that "the question must have occurred to the cousins often enough at the beginning of their relationship, until they came to see that there was no reason why they should not 'do it.' "[15]

Fragments and phrases do not give the remarkable flavor of several of these letters, which are sometimes like a thesaurus gone mad or a pre-Joycean frenzy of free-associational fragments rendered alternately in low comedy and in elevated mock-rhetoric:

> Bless my soul, a thousand curses, Croatians, damnations, devils, witches, sorcerers, hell's battalions to all eternity, by all the elements, air, water, earth and fire, Europe, Asia, Africa and America, Jesuits, Augustinians, Benedictines, Capuchins, Minorites, Franciscans, Dominicans, Carthusians and Brothers of the Holy Cross, Canons regular and irregular, all slacks, knaves, cowards, sluggards and toadies higgledy-piggledy, asses, buffaloes, oxen, fools, nitwits and dunces! What sort of behavior is that, my dears—four smart soldiers and three bandoliers! . . . Such a parcel to get, but no portrait as yet! . . . Perhaps you doubt that I shall keep my word? Surely you do not doubt me? . . .
>
> Forgive my wretched writing, but the pen is already worn to a shred, and I've been shitting, so 'tis said, nigh twenty-two years through the same old hole, which is not yet frayed one whit, though I've used it daily to shit, and each time the muck with my teeth I've bit.[16]

The Bäsle letters can be seen as doorways into an alternative cosmos within which the correspondents could be free, loving, and guiltlessly dedicated to the pursuit of pleasure. Theirs is the private language of a self-enclosed world, remote from real events, from which third persons are permanently barred or are admitted only as benign characters in an exotic mythology. However, the exuberant, fantastic style and sensational comic-scatological passages of Mozart's letters to his cousin may have obscured their plain significance as love letters. Indeed, the bizarre mode of expression of these letters serves to conceal the deepest feelings, as when Mozart sandwiches a tender remark—"Do go on loving me, as I love you, then we shall never cease loving one another"—between a scatological passage and a comic flourish. In the same letter, Mozart's salutation, "Ma trés chére Niéce! Cousine! fille! Mére, Soeur, et Épouse!"[17] suggests that he viewed his cousin as the fused embodiment of all women who were or could be related to him by blood or marriage, a multilayered, condensed transference-image of extraordinary resonance. She is dissolved into a variety of female figures: she stands for herself and is simultaneously the archetypal representative of all women. Mozart's use of the word "épouse," although distanced somewhat by being rendered in French, makes one wonder if there had not already been some talk about marriage. Now they arrange for an exchange of portraits, a sure sign of loving commitment. When Maria Anna Thekla's portrait arrived in Salzburg a few months later, Leopold Mozart was alarmed and wrote a caustic letter: "In Augsburg too you had your little romance, you amused yourself with my brother's daughter, who now must needs send you her portrait."[18] Mozart denied the charge: "What you say so cuttingly about my merry amusement with your brother's daughter has hurt me very much; but since matters are not as you think, it is not necessary for me to reply."[19]

And in this Mozart was not altogether lying, for despite his evident love for his cousin, despite their intimate rapport, he forsook her for Aloysia Weber, whom he met in nearby Mannheim only days after he left Augsburg on 26 October 1777 to continue his journey. A gifted singer, then sixteen or seventeen, preparing for a solo career on the operatic stage, Aloysia has been anointed as Mozart's grand passion by most of his biographers, eager to find for him a talented, dutiful, and virginal mate. On 17 January 1778 Mozart somewhat disingenuously informed his father about her: "I don't know whether I have already written about [Herr Weber's] daughter or not—She sings indeed most admirably and has a lovely, pure voice."[20] But he neglected to mention other details—such as that he was enamored of her and was ready to devote his life to the advancement of her career.

Mozart soon began to think about marrying Aloysia. In a letter to his father of 7 February 1778 he ruminated about marriage; referring to a money match, he tried to play on his father's egalitarian beliefs:

> I should not like to marry in this way; I want to make my wife happy, but not to become rich by her means. So I shall let things be and enjoy my golden freedom until I am so well off that I can support a wife and children. . . . People of noble birth must never marry from inclination or love, but only from interest and all kinds of secondary considerations. . . . But we poor humble people can not only choose a wife whom we love and who loves us, but we may, can and do take such a one, because we are neither noble, nor highly born, nor aristocratic, nor rich, but, on the contrary, lowly born, humble and poor; so we do not need a wealthy wife, for our riches, being in our brains, die with us.[21]

However, all plans involving Aloysia—whether of marriage, travel, or even of simply remaining near her in Mannheim—were rudely set aside with the emphatic outcry that issued from Salzburg in early February: "*Off with you to Paris!*"[22] The prospect of being displaced by Herr Weber's impecunious family was not one that Leopold Mozart could countenance.

Seeking to overcome his distress, Mozart turned to the Bäsle on the twenty-eighth of February, his first letter to her since 3 December. "Perhaps you think or are even convinced that I am dead?" He asked her forgiveness, tried to charm her into overlooking his neglect, and said nothing about Aloysia. He did not conceal his longing for the joyous simplicity of their old relationship. "How I wish I were with you so that we could run about together."[23] Then, contented at having connected to his cousin once again, he told her a lengthy fairy tale set in a village whose name might be Tribsterill, "where muck runs into the sea," or perhaps Burmesquik, "where the crooked ass-holes are manufactured." A shepherd there fell asleep on a riverbank and dreamed he had lost his sheep; in terror, he awoke to find the sheep still there, whereupon he walked on and drove his flock across a bridge. "Now," he asked his patient cousin, as though to pledge that their relationship would endure for a very long time, "please be so kind as to wait until the eleven thousand sheep have reached the other side and then I shall finish my story."[24]

One can scarcely recognize the Mozart of the Bäsle letters in his sole surviving letter to Aloysia, written on 30 July 1778 from Paris. It is a constrained and inexpressive letter, with far too many notes.

> Dearest friend! I hope that you are in excellent health—I beg you to take great care of it—for good health is the best thing in the world. Thank

God, I am very well, as far as my health is concerned, because I watch it. But my mind is not at rest—nor will it be until I have heard (and what a comfort that will be) that your merits have received their just reward. Yet my condition and my situation will be the happiest on that day when I shall have the infinite pleasure of serving you again and embracing you with all my heart. . . . You know that everything that concerns you interests me very greatly. . . . I never stop talking about you. . . . I am very anxious to get a letter from you. So please do not keep me waiting and do not make me suffer too long.[25]

His tone verges on the overbearing and self-important. "Be so good as to re-read my letters now and then and to follow my advice," he writes. And he continues to coach her from afar: "I advise you to watch the expression marks—to think carefully of the meaning and the force of the words—to put yourself in all seriousness into Andromeda's situation and position!—and to imagine that you really are that very person."[26] His courtship of her continued, but it is clear that there had been neither an intimate relationship nor a reciprocal commitment.

When Mozart left Mannheim, the Webers had been overflowing with gratitude toward him: "Indeed our best friend, our benefactor, is about to leave us," said Herr Weber to Frau Mozart, according to a letter from Mozart to his father. "Yes, that is certain, we owe everything to your son. He has done a great deal for my daughter and has taken an interest in her and she can never be grateful enough to him."[27] The feeling of gratitude did not long endure. Mozart had promised the Webers that he would make their daughter's fortune through their joint journeys, but soon they discovered that he was not his own man; on his father's orders, and accompanied by his mama, he must leave them with his good intentions intact but his promises unfulfilled. And when he wrote to Herr Weber from Paris he at last was compelled to acknowledge the limitations of his purse—"My friend, if I had the money which many a man, who does not earn it, squanders so disgracefully—how gladly would I then help you!"—and to admit his futility: "If I hadn't a father and a sister, to whom I must sacrifice everything and whom I must try to support, I would completely renounce my own interests with the greatest pleasure—and consult your interests only."[28]

Not surprisingly, therefore, when he reappeared in Munich in the closing days of 1778, he was coldly rebuffed by Aloysia, who now had bigger fish to fry, for in the interim she had obtained a long-term engagement at the Munich court opera. Nissen described the end of Mozart's courtship of Aloysia: "Mozart, upon his return from Paris, mourning for his mother in the French style, dressed in a red robe with black buttons, found that

Aloysia's sentiments for him had altered. When he entered, she appeared no longer to know him, for whom she previously had wept. Accordingly, he sat down at the piano and sang in a loud voice: 'Ich lass das Mädel gern, das mich nicht will' ('I gladly give up the girl who doesn't want me')."[29] So reads Nissen's book, but his manuscript shows that what Mozart actually sang was an old, traditional quatrain: "Leck mir das Mensch im Arsch, das mich nicht will"—"The one who doesn't want me can lick my ass."[30] On the occasion of their break he at last permits himself an obscenity in connection with Aloysia, but it is not a loving one.

Mozart may have been heartbroken, but he was not without resources. On 23 December 1778, he wrote to his cousin, inviting her to meet him in Munich before the New Year and boldly promising, "Perhaps you will have a great part to play."[31] He overflows with high spirits, elated at the prospect that they will soon be reunited:

> Come to Munich, that fine town. Make a point of being there before the New Year, mind, and I shall take a good look at you in front and behind; I shall take you round the town and, if necessary, wash you down. . . . Come for a bit or else I'll shit. If you do, this high and mighty person will think you very kind, will give you a smack behind, will kiss your hands, my dear, shoot off a gun in the rear, embrace you warmly, mind, and wash your front and your behind, pay you all his debts to the uttermost groat, and shoot off one with a rousing note, perhaps even let something drop from his boat.
>
> Adieu, my angel, my sweetheart. I am aching to see you.[32]

Mozart's tender feelings for his cousin had reemerged from their long sleep.

Their meeting in Munich was undoubtedly a happy one, for Mozart asked the Bäsle to come home to Salzburg with him from there. Evidently it was indeed a "great part" that he wanted her to play. In fact she did come to Salzburg, either traveling with Mozart on 13 or 14 January or following him by coach a week later. Sadly, their reunion did not end as joyously as it had begun.

We don't know what went wrong in Salzburg, but we do know that the affair came to an end there and then. Things started off badly, with Leopold Mozart frigidly ignoring his niece's letter from Munich asking him to receive her in Salzburg; instead, he tried to discourage her from coming, suggesting—through Mozart—that she wait in Munich for her father's permission, which he knew would come too late for the cousins to travel together. "If my niece wants to honor me with a visit, *she can follow on the 20th by the mail coach.*"[33] Mozart's return to Salzburg represented a massive surrender to his father's domination, and it must quickly have become clear to the Bäsle—as it already had to Aloysia and Fridolin Weber—that Mozart was not yet prepared to resist Leopold Mozart on an issue as momentous as marriage. That is surely why, in his two remaining years in Salzburg, although Mozart was not without a flirtation or two, he did not find a serious successor to Aloysia or the Bäsle.

We know that Maria Anna Thekla Mozart returned to Augsburg sometime before May 1779, for her name is absent from Marianne's diaries from May onward.[34] The old playful feelings flamed up for a moment in Mozart's letter of 10 May 1780, but the correspondence then declined into an almost embarrassed stiffness, and into a purposeful distancing. Mozart, his father, and sister may have visited Augsburg in March 1781, after the premiere of *Idomeneo* in nearby Munich, but it isn't known whether he and his cousin met on that occasion.[35] Six months later, in October 1781, he penned his very last letter to her, evidently in response to rumors about him and Constanze Weber, which he disdained either to confirm or to deny. "Let me tell you that the gossip which people have been so kind as to circulate about me, is partly true and partly false. That is all I can say at the moment. But let me add . . . that I never do anything without a reason."[36] In a chiding tone, he advised her that she ought not to listen to gossip: "If you had shown more confidence and friendship and had applied to me direct (and not to others . . .) you would certainly have heard more than everyone else." His expressed hope "that our correspondence, dear little cousin, will now start off again!" does not ring true, and he added insult to injury by a postscript request that she make inquiries on his behalf in Augsburg about a certain portrait of Aloysia, now Frau Lange.

In May 1782 Mozart glancingly referred to someone who was in love with his cousin; a few months later, after his marriage, he asked his father, "Should you be writing to my cousin, please give her kind regards from us both."[37] By the time the Bäsle gave birth to an illegitimate child several years later, an event that gave Leopold Mozart some obscure satisfaction, the once-beloved cousins had grown far apart.[38] Eventually she returned Mozart's letters to him or, more probably, to his widow, who preserved what she described as "the frequently tasteless but nevertheless very witty letters to his cousin."[39] Maria Anna Thekla's own letters to Mozart were not preserved.

On the testimony of the letters, the Bäsle loved Mozart for himself, for his person, his wit, his body—not for his earnings, possessions, or worldly position. And, it seems, she loved him selflessly, without restrictions, without strings, and gave him the kind of disinterested love that he always longed for. By her love and her responsiveness, she unlocked for him some of the mysteries of the feminine, helping him to overcome the usual—and perhaps some unusual—fears and prohibitions. The unembarrassed poly-morphousness of their connection opened upon a zone of freedom. In that zone Mozart is both master and servant: the lovers lick each other clean; they explore all of the cavities and convexities of their bodies; they delight in the release and the flow of their bodily fluids; they delight also in the innocence of their sexuality and its attendant scatology.

All this implies a mutual fixation on a quasi-infantile stage of develop-ment. Perhaps, then, Mozart's polymorphousness bears in part on his need to remain an eternal child, within an infancy Eden of imagination or memory, ruling over a private kingdom, unhindered by paternal injunc-tions or external restraints. Unfortunately, however, Mozart apparently could not quite manage to keep the polymorphous zone free of guilt, of authoritarian intrusion, of the punitive and dominating. Always pursuing his quota of freedom, Mozart constantly drew back and returned to condi-tions of bondage. Perhaps because of their close consanguinity, there may have been more than a trace of incest fear in his attachment to the Bäsle: she was his uncle's daughter, his father's niece, his sister's cousin, and as Maria Anna she bore both his mother's and his sister's names. Her image may have cut too close to the bone because it resonated with a variety of prohibitions. Later, in Constanze Weber, Mozart found another woman with some of the Bäsle's emancipated characteristics but without the close blood tie.

When all is said and done, Mozart may have needed to give up his beloved cousin because she was too good to be true. It was not Mozart's father who forced him to abandon the Bäsle in favor of Aloysia: it was Mozart who betrayed his cousin because he somehow needed to deny himself the physical and emotional fulfillment that she represented. In Aloysia Weber he found the ideal instrument of denial. In her he was drawn to one whom he could serve and who would, in turn, exploit him, so that he could once again play out the fundamental engrained pattern of his earlier family life. She encouraged Mozart's attentions only for so long as she thought he could be of use to her and her family; she spurned him when it became clear that his utility was limited. Turning from the accessi-ble Bäsle, Mozart cleaved to the untouchable Aloysia, whose virtue was assured and with whom he might safely repress his own troubling sexuality and neutralize his disconcerting erotic stirrings, with their incestuous implications. Clearly, he respected Aloysia, admired her as a singer, was drawn to Herr Weber as a surrogate father—but in relation to her there is no joyousness, no private language, no verbal exhibitionism, no rapturous flights of fancy. In the Bäsle/Aloysia dichotomy, Aloysia served to demon-strate Mozart's purity of intention to control the unruly sexual hunger that his relationship with the Bäsle had unleashed.[40] With Aloysia love was sub-ordinated to duty, and his goal was simply to help a young artist get estab-lished, to assist a worthy and needy family; his motives were now properly altruistic, purified.

Aloysia and the Bäsle represented two different escape routes from Salzburg. The Bäsle was beyond realization, too daring a departure. Mozart accordingly retreated to Aloysia as a "reasonable" and realizable alternative, through whom he simultaneously escaped from and returned to Salzburg and his father. With her, Mozart could play the instructor-impresario Leopold Mozart to her Mozart, subordinating his creativity to her own. Evidently he thought that by imitating his father he could evade the father's prohibitions. Aloysia was simultaneously a compromise and a mis-calculation: surely by dint of her talent, her virginity, and her hardworking family background (so congruent with the Mozart family ideal) she should have been acceptable to Leopold Mozart. But in the end, Mozart learned once again that his intimacy with any woman would not meet with his father's approbation.

Mozart could not irrevocably give himself to a liberated, joyous sexu-ality. By dedicating himself to Aloysia he positioned himself to serve another (and her family) as he had always served his father, mother, and sister. He was torn by dualities of this kind: enjoyment was subverted by a need to be dominated; selfless, magnanimous love gave way to care-worn responsibility. Hints of this duality had appeared earlier in his life: we have already seen how, during a stay with a large Venetian family, at age fifteen, Mozart valiantly resisted having his rear end spanked by the daughters of the family. Later on, he promises his wife that, upon his return from a journey, she "may count on" some thorough spankings on her "dear little kissable ass."[41] Representing a very different side of his personality is his very first surviving letter, written when he was about thirteen, which tells us of his preoccupation with duty and responsibility. "Forgive me for taking the liberty of plaguing you with a few lines," he wrote to a girl whose name is not given, "but as you said yesterday that you could understand everything, no matter what Latin words I might choose to write down, curiosity has got the better of me and I am writ-ing down for you a few lines made up of various Latin words. When you have read them, please do me the favor of sending me your answer by one of Hagenauer's maids, for our Nannie cannot wait."[42] The Latin proverb read: "I should like to know for what reason idleness is so popu-lar with most young people that it is impossible to draw them from it either by words or by punishments." This is all remarkably restrained, proper, and inhibited. Though the hand is the hand of Mozart, the voice

Aloysia Lange. Undated oil portrait. Private collection.
Reproduced from Selma Krasa et al.,
Zaubertöne: Mozart in Wien (Vienna, 1991).

is the voice of Leopold Mozart, telling of duty, virtue, and submission to
the performance principle, a father's voice warning his young son against
the pulls and snares of pleasure and sexuality. Ultimately, one cannot tell
whether Mozart's love for Aloysia represented his attempt to unite with
his father through identification with his values or to escape from him by
reenacting the family pattern.

Leopold Mozart had offered numerous explanations for his unwillingness to let the twenty-one-year-old Mozart travel alone in search of a posi-

tion, but beneath his expressed concern over his son's health and welfare was a deeply rooted fear of his sexual awakening. As Jahn noted, Leopold hoped that his wife's presence on the journey would preserve Mozart "from any dangerous or immoral intercourse,"[43] and she was ready to report home on any unwelcome liaisons. Leopold's fear that Mozart would find sexual opportunities was a central reason why he would not let Frau Mozart return home to Salzburg from Mannheim as planned. The thought that Mozart might have his own room preyed on his mind, and he insisted that his son and wife sleep in the same room: "That Mama should have to live alone, *that I simply will not have.* As long as Mama is in Mannheim, you and she must live together. *You should not and must not* leave Mama alone and at the mercy of other people. . . . However small her room may be, space can surely be found for a bed for you."[44]

At the outset, Leopold's warnings centered upon Mozart's piety and the observance of his devotions, but as the journey progressed, the sexual subtext of these warnings revealed itself. Only a few days after receiving Mozart's first letters about the Bäsle and her own simple letter to him, from which he deduced that an affair was in progress, Leopold Mozart wrote, taking the occasion of Mozart's name day to remind him of his religious obligations and of the need for diligence "in fulfilling the duties of a true Catholic Christian."[45] He went on, "You know me. I am no pedant and no praying Peter and still less am I a hypocrite. But surely you will not refuse the request of a father, that you should take thought for your soul's welfare so that in the hour of his death you may cause him no anxiety, and that in that dread moment he may have no reason to reproach himself for not having watched over your soul's salvation."[46] Mozart's response was a brave and defiant one: "Papa must not worry, for God is ever before my eyes. I realize His omnipotence and I fear His anger; but I also recognize His love, His compassion and His tenderness towards His creatures. He will never forsake His own."[47] Thus, to his father's injunction that he must not sin he countered that God will forgive his sins.

Unable to suppress his anxiety, Leopold wrote on 15 December, "Is it necessary for me to ask whether Wolfgang is not getting a little lax perhaps about confession? God must come first. . . . Young people do not like to hear about these things, I know, for I was once young myself."[48] Again, Mozart was "upset" by this "inquiry as to whether I wasn't perhaps getting a little lax about this. I have nothing to say to this; but just let me ask you one thing, and that is, not to have such a bad opinion of me. I like to enjoy myself, but rest assured that I can be as serious as anyone else can."[49] A few days later Leopold began to suspect, wrongly, that Mozart and his mother had taken separate rooms and suddenly he was beset by fantasies of his son's fall into perdition.

By February 1778, after learning of Mozart's infatuation with Aloysia Weber, Leopold no longer troubled to cloak his concerns and warned Mozart of the dangers of the female "labyrinth," adjuring him to maintain "the necessary reserve" with women. "Live like a good Catholic," he wrote, "Love and fear God. Pray most ardently to Him in true devotion and put your trust in Him; and lead so Christian a life that, if I should see you no more, the hour of my death may be free from anxiety."[50] Now he listed all the women with whom he feared Mozart had taken up during his absence from Salzburg: "the little singer at the theater" (a certain Mlle Kaiser in Munich); then, the Bäsle, whose unwelcome portrait had just arrived at home; "Next, Herr Cannabich's daughter was smothered in praises, her temperament was recorded in the Adagio of a sonata, in short, *she* was now the reigning favorite"; and he could not disguise his horror at the prospect that Mozart proposed "to travel about with Herr Weber and, be it noted, his two daughters—it has nearly made me lose my reason!"[51] Although Leopold Mozart now compelled Mozart to separate himself from Aloysia, this scarcely set his mind at ease, for his most "extreme anxiety" now focused on his son's journey to Paris, to him a latter-day Sodom among cities. He cited several authorities to bolster his warnings about the voraciousness of Frenchwomen: "God and your own good sense will preserve you. Any such calamity would be the death of me!"[52]

The end of the affair with the Bäsle in the first months of 1779 coincided with the close of Mozart's long westward journey in quest of independence and his abject return to Salzburg and the status quo ante. The latest stage in a cycle of rebelliousness and submission had terminated in renunciation. It was not merely the hope for a post that he had surrendered, but a portion of his manhood as well, for surrender to his father had strong implications of enforced celibacy. At his father's insistence, Mozart had earlier given up Aloysia; now he yielded up his cousin on the altar of filial obedience. He had lost a crucial engagement in the ongoing war between his sacrificial impulse and his drive for personal fulfillment. For the time being he had set aside hopes for sexual fulfillment and marriage, slowed the development of his career, and once again tried to pay off a debt that—he had yet to realize—could never be fully satisfied.

Mozart had struggled valiantly against his father's view of women as ensnaring and labyrinthine. Very possibly his explosive, joyous exploration of every fold of the Bäsle's body was his way of awakening from the view of women that his father tried to instill in him. Inevitably, however, he was driven to revert to early patterns, to partial identification with his father's outlook. That may be why he twice betrayed the Bäsle—first by preferring Aloysia and then by failing to stand against his father in early 1779, leading to her humiliation and withdrawal. Nevertheless, in his love affair with the Bäsle he had caught a glimpse of felicity and would not soon forget it, let alone give up its "promesse de bonheur."

Mozart, letter to Maria Anna Thekla Mozart (the Bäsle), 10 May 1780. The British Library: Department of Manuscripts—Collection of the Heirs of Stefan Zweig 67.

11

A MOTHER'S DEATH

Every child harbors thoughts of leaving home and finding, beyond the horizon, a beautiful kingdom where all wishes may come true. Mozart's exuberance at the start of the journey to Mannheim and Paris surely reflected his sense of liberation from compulsion, stultifying responsibilities, and limited opportunities. "I am always in my very best spirits, for my heart has been as light as a feather ever since I got away from all that humbug; and, what is more, I have become fatter."[1] But his exulting first letter home also has an admixture of oedipal merriment: "We are living like princes," he wrote. "Only one person is wanting—and that is Papa. Ah well, it is God's will. . . . I am most attentive to my duty. I am quite a second Papa, for I see to everything. . . . Why, I am sitting here as if I were a prince. . . . Well, I must stop. Mama has now finished undressing. We both of us beg Papa to take care of his health, not to go out too early and not to worry, but to laugh heartily and be merry."[2] Frau Mozart shared her son's exuberance and she too had the sense of having stumbled into a child's fairy-tale world in the company of her beloved son: "We lead a most delightful life—up early—late to bed, and visitors all day long. We live like the children of princes, until the hangman comes to haul us away."[3] The touch of gallows humor tells us that she knows the spell will not last forever, but meanwhile, she and Mozart may be prince's children together, brother and sister, enchanted, two innocents amazingly freed from every compulsion, embarked on a wonderful adventure.

It was not long before reality engulfed their transparent fantasies. Mozart needed to find a suitable post; they were spending Leopold Mozart's money; he reminded them that he was daily sinking further into debt. They quickly

Anna Maria Mozart. Unsigned oil portrait, ca. 1775. Mozart-
Museum der Internationalen Stiftung
Mozarteum, Salzburg. © Mozarts Geburtshaus, Salzburg.

learned to deemphasize the pleasures of the journey, to stress their scrupulous adherence to the family's purpose. Dutifully they described their Spartan existence and their letters took on a somber aspect. Mozart no longer told of his merriment or of the good food. In December, his mother described her own pathetically dreary condition: "I am at home alone, as I usually am, and have to put up with the most horrible cold. For even if they light a small fire, they never put any more coal on it, so that when it burns out, the room gets cold again. A little fire of this kind costs twelve kreuzer. So I make them light one in the morning, when we get up, and another in the evening. During the day I have to put up with dreadful cold. As I write I can hardly hold my pen, I am freezing so."[4] Naturally, she continued, entertainment was beyond their means: "Up to the present we have not been to any balls and only to one gala play, for the tickets are very expensive."[5] She stressed her discomfort, which was real, not only to emphasize their economy but because by now she wanted to go home. On the tenth of December Mozart proposed to send her home while he went on to Paris. "Mama is quite satisfied with this arrangement and it only remains for you to give your consent."[6] Frau Mozart marshaled the arguments for her return: "I myself do not like to let him go, nor do I like to have to travel home alone, it is such an awful distance. I can't bear to think of it. But what can we do? I am too old to undertake such a long journey to Paris and besides it would cost too much."[7] Her husband's insistence that they watch every kreuzer is turned against him; she even tells that she cannot go out because she has "no umbrella to put up when it snows or rains."[8]

Leopold Mozart was not to be pushed into a hasty decision: "I pity you, my dear wife, for having to suffer so from the cold, although you pay 24 kreuzer a day for heating." He recommended that she visit somebody with a warm room and that, when at home, she lie in bed, covered up.[9] He pointed out, "Mama cannot leave Mannheim now that really cold weather is setting in." And he asked, "How are you going to travel? In our chaise? And quite alone? This all requires very careful consideration."[10] A few weeks later, however, he appeared to be reconciled to the proposal, suggesting various routes for her return; and on 26 January he wrote, "It is high time that Mama got ready for her journey."[11] Unfortunately, as we have seen, by her confidential postscript to Mozart's letter of 5 February 1778, in which he detailed his plans to travel with the Webers instead of proceeding on to Paris, she irrevocably committed herself to the Paris journey. She wrote:

> You will have seen from this letter that when Wolfgang makes new acquaintances, he immediately wants to give his life and property for them. True, she sings exceedingly well; still, we must not lose sight of our own interests. . . . As soon as he got to know the Webers, he immediately

changed his mind. In short, he prefers other people to me, for I remonstrate with him about this and that, and about things which I do not like; and he objects to this. So you yourself will have to think over what ought to be done. I do not consider his journey to Paris with Wendling at all advisable. I would rather accompany him myself later on. . . . I am writing this quite secretly, while he is at dinner, and I shall close, for I do not want to be caught.[12]

Mozart's mother understood well that her son needed to pursue his own path in life, to discover his own potentialities, to make his own friends. But what she saw as Mozart's preference for Aloysia Weber and her family overwhelmed her best intentions; she was not ready to yield her son to another woman, another family. She herself felt betrayed, so she betrayed him to her husband, knowing that he would intervene forcefully. Naturally, she was not insensible of her son's needs. Although her letters to her husband were intended to convey that she was protecting their mutual interests, she clearly worked to mediate between the two men and to present Mozart's actions in a favorable light. But she had to be careful not to go too far, for Leopold Mozart accused her of being in collusion with Mozart against him. In the last analysis, however, she would inevitably submit to her husband's will, not, I suspect, primarily out of her own self-interest, but because she could not refuse him.

Frau Mozart knew that she could not readily endure the stresses of a prolonged tour. Repeatedly she informed her husband of her hardships, which began on the journey itself: "We were nearly choked by the wind and drowned by the rain, so that we both got soaking wet in the carriage and could scarcely breathe."[13] Arrived in Paris she was discouraged and lonely: "As for my own life, it is not at all a pleasant one. I sit alone in our room the whole day long as if I were in jail, and as the room is very dark and looks out on a little courtyard, I cannot see the sun all day long and I don't even know what the weather is like. With great difficulty I manage to knit a little by the daylight that struggles in."[14] Mozart was away during the days, because there was no clavier in their lodgings and he went to compose each day at the house of Joseph Legros, director of the Concert Spirituel: "I never see him all day long and shall forget altogether how to talk."[15] Leopold ignored her *cri de coeur*, responding only to her secondary complaint about the quality and expense of food. He was sorry that she was "having such a bad time with your food" and suggested she locate a German cook or do her own cooking.[16] For her loneliness, illness, and malaise he expressed no word of sympathy. Perhaps he suspected her of exaggerating these in the hope that he would ask her to come home, so he emphatically closed off that option: "You will have in the end to make some other arrangement, as you are not in Paris for just a few months—seeing that Paris is at the moment the safest place to live in, both from the money point of view and because it is untouched by fear of war."[17]

During their next weeks in Paris, Mozart's mother continued to describe her discontent and ailments. On 1 May, she asked Leopold to send her a supply of medicines: "All this long while, about three weeks, I have been plagued with toothache, sore throat, and earache, but now, thank God, I am better. I don't get out much, it is true, and the rooms are cold, even when a fire is burning. You just have to get used to it."[18] Although she never directly asked permission to come home from Paris, Leopold continued to view her complaints with suspicion and made it clear that he would not countenance any change in their plans. "You must realize that I cannot help you with money—and that without money Mama cannot come home nor can you go to Italy," he responded.[19] Meanwhile, he gave her medical advice at a distance: "My dear wife, do not forget *to be bled*. . . . Perhaps you can get the black powder at some chemist's shop."[20] After this, she evidently saw no further point in complaining, for although her condition worsened, she maintained a generally cheerful outlook in her letters, as though trying not to worry anyone. In her last letter home, dated 12 June 1778, she told of friendly social visits from the musicians Anton Raaff and François Heina, of walks in the Luxembourg gardens, and a tour of the Louvre; without fanfare, she let it be known that she had been bled the day before and that she "was frightfully tired," but she wrote nothing to alarm her husband or daughter. "Please give our compliments to all our good friends," she wrote. "Every day we talk about our friends in Salzburg and wish that they could be with us. Many of them would stare and gape if they saw the things we see here. Addio. Keep well, both of you. I kiss you several thousand times and remain your faithful wife, Frau Mozart."[21] A postscript indicated the strain of her effort: "I must stop, for my arm and eyes are aching."

Mozart's mother died shortly after ten P.M. on 3 July 1778 and was buried the next day in the cemetery of Saint-Eustache. The church register reads: "On the said day, Marie-Anne Pertl, aged 57 years, wife of Leopold Mozart, *maître de chapelle* at Salzburg, Bavaria, who died yesterday at Rue du Groschenet, has been interred in the cemetery in the presence of Wolfgang Amédée Mozart, her son, and of François Heina, trumpeter in the light cavalry in the Royal Guard, a friend."[22] The cause of her death is not given. According to Mozart, a few days after being bled on 11 June, "she complained of shivering and feverishness, accompanied by diarrhea and headache," and she stayed in bed from the nineteenth on, unable to speak and having lost most of her hearing: "I had to shout to make myself understood."[23] On the twentieth she developed chills and fever, and Mozart gave her an antispasmodic powder, while trying to persuade her to get a doctor. As she had no confidence in French physicians, it was not until the twenty-fourth that she was seen by a doctor, a German one that Heina fetched who prescribed "a rhubarb powder in wine."[24] Mozart had no faith in the doctor but did not know where to turn: "I had to leave her in the hands of the doctor," but when, on the twenty-sixth, the doctor "said to me quite unexpectedly, 'I fear she will not last out the night. . . . You had better see that she makes her confession,'" he arranged for Heina to bring a priest and then sought help from Baron Grimm and Mme d'Épinay. "They were distressed that I had not told them sooner, for they would have sent their own doctor at once. I had not said anything to them before, because my mother would not have a French doctor—but now I was at my wit's end. They said therefore that they would send their doctor that very evening."[25] Baron Grimm's physician was likewise unable to help Frau Mozart.

Meanwhile, unable to reveal to his mother that she was going to receive the last rites, Mozart instead told her that a German priest who was eager to hear him play would visit them on the next day. "She was quite unconscious at the time of her death," Mozart continued in his letter to Abbé Bullinger. "Her life flickered out like a candle. Three days before her death she made her confession, partook of the Sacrament and received Extreme Unction. During the last three days, however, she was constantly delirious, and today at twenty-one minutes past five o'clock the death agony began and she at once lost all sensation and consciousness. I pressed her hand and spoke to her—but she did not see me, she did not hear me, and all feeling was gone. She lay thus until she expired five hours later at twenty-one minutes past ten. No one was present but myself, Herr Heina, . . . and the nurse."[26] "As long as I live I shall never forget it," he wrote. "You know that I had never seen anyone die, although I had wished to. How cruel that my first experience should be the death of my mother! I dreaded that moment most of all, and I prayed earnestly to God for strength."[27] At the moment of his mother's death, Mozart too wanted to die: "Indeed I wished at that moment to depart with her."[28]

That night Mozart wrote two letters—one to his father and another to Bullinger. He asked Bullinger to prepare his father and sister for the news. "Do not tell them yet that she is dead—just prepare them for it. Do what you think best—use every means to comfort them—but act so that my mind may be relieved—and that I may not have to expect still another calamity."[29] The second letter described his mother's illness but withheld the news of her death: "I have been hovering day and night between hope and fear—but I have resigned myself wholly to the will of God—and trust that you and my dear sister will do the same. . . . I do not mean to say that my mother will and must die, or that all hope is lost."[30] By this strategy he hoped to ease the blow to his father and sister—perhaps as his mother might have wanted him to do.

Perhaps, too, in his grief, he was somehow denying—at least, postponing—
her death by an imaginative act of will. But this strategy did not long endure.
On the ninth of July he acknowledged to his father that his mother "was
already enjoying the blessings of Heaven" when he had written his earlier letter and he asked his father's forgiveness "for this slight but very necessary
deception; for . . . I could not indeed bring myself suddenly to shock you
with this dreadful news!"[31] Attempting to ease his own sorrow, Mozart wrote
at length of the consolation he found through accepting the will of God:
"Weep, weep your fill, but take comfort at last. Remember that Almighty
God willed it thus—and how can we rebel against Him?" He took consolation too from "the thought that she is not lost to us for ever—that we shall
see her again—that we shall live together far more happily and blissfully than
ever in this world."[32] He begged for understanding of his own torment: "You
will easily conceive what I have had to bear—what courage and fortitude I
have needed to endure calmly as things grew gradually and steadily worse. . . .
I have, indeed, suffered and wept enough—but what did it avail?"[33]

Leopold Mozart did not, however, spare his son further grief. He reproached
Mozart with having contributed to his mother's death, indeed with having
completed a deadly sacrificial process that had been set in motion many years
before, at the very moment of his birth. The recriminations began on the
thirteenth of July, even before Leopold was certain that his wife was dead. By
way of preamble he wrote, "I have complete confidence in your filial love,
and know that you have taken all possible care of your *devoted* mother, and if
God still spares her, you will always do so; for she is a *good* mother and *you
were the apple of her eye.*"[34] But then he charged both of them with neglect
causing her death: "As she fell ill a few days after the blood-letting, she must
have been suffering since June 16th or 17th. Surely you waited too long. She
hoped to cure herself by resting in bed—by dieting—by treating herself."[35]
Continuing to seek a culprit, he asked, "Perhaps she wasn't bled sufficiently?
It is quite certain that she trusted too much to her strength and called in the
doctor much too late. In the meantime the internal inflammation must have
gained the upper hand."[36]

In his letter of 31 July, Mozart rejected his father's implication: "First
of all, I must tell you that my dear departed mother *had to die.* No doctor
in the world could have saved her this time—for it was clearly the will of
God; her time had come—and God wanted to take her to Himself. You
think she put off being bled until it was too late? That may be. She did
postpone it a little. But I rather agree with the people here who tried to
dissuade her from being bled—and to persuade her to take a lavement."[37]
(Here Mozart is implicitly taking issue with his father, who had suggested
bleeding as a remedy.) On 3 August Leopold returned to the issue of negligence: "I am sure that my dear departed wife neglected herself and on that

account was neglected by others. For she was extremely economical, she would put off doing things from one day to the next and therefore would not call in a doctor, as she was convinced that she would get stronger in time. . . . I told you in May that she ought not to postpone being bled. . . . Yet she put it off until June 11th. . . . The day before this treatment she took far too violent exercise, and got home exhausted and overheated; she was probably bled too little; and finally the doctor was called in far too late, for . . . she was already in danger."[38] All at once, Leopold Mozart raised the stakes considerably: "You had your engagements, you were away all day, and as she didn't make a fuss, you treated her condition lightly. All this time her illness became more serious, in fact mortal—and only then was a doctor called in, when of course it was too late."[39]

And now, in a dramatic condensation, Frau Mozart's death caused her husband to recall Mozart's birth, as though the two events were inextricably interwoven, indeed that the one was the direct consequence of the other: "Well, it is all over. God willed it. The unbreakable chain of Divine Providence preserved your mother's life when you were born, though indeed she was in very great danger and though we almost thought that she was gone. But she was fated to sacrifice herself for her son in a different way."[40] To Leopold Mozart, then, his wife's death was the delayed playing out of a matricidal scenario whose first act had been Mozart's emergence from the womb. An infant is held to be implicitly responsible for endangering his mother's life; now, twenty-two years later, a young man is held to be responsible for her actual death. The overt accusation of matricidal neglect is linked with the original sin of placing his mother's life in danger by the act of being born.

The accusatory scenario quickly takes shape: "She readily agreed to leave Salzburg with you. When I was hoping to have her back from Mannheim . . . I received a letter from you which caused me astonishment, bewilderment, and distress. In that very letter she wrote to me (without your knowledge) that, for certain reasons and out of love for you, she wanted to travel with you to Paris."[41] In his letter of 27 August 1778, Leopold quoted directly from Frau Mozart's confidential postscript to the 5 February 1778 letter, in which she warned against Mozart's association with the Webers and suggested that she would, if her husband so decided, accompany Mozart to Paris instead of returning to Salzburg. Leopold presented his indictment with ineluctable logic. First, "she was to have returned home from Mannheim"; second, in order to protect Mozart against his own foolish impulses and hare-brained schemes, she was forced to change her plans—"If your mother had returned home from Mannheim, she would not have died"; in summary, "She had to leave home with you and, owing to your new friendship, her return had to be abandoned."[42]

Of course, we know that it happened quite differently. It was Leopold

Mozart who insisted that Mozart could not travel alone; it was he who abruptly canceled his wife's planned return from Mannheim to Salzburg in early 1778 and sent her on to Paris instead: "Mama is to go to Paris with Wolfgang, so you had better make the necessary arrangements."[43] It was he who would not hear of her coming home in the spring when she began to ail, he who ignored her complaints, he who excluded the possibility of her returning alone to Salzburg. Conveniently, Leopold Mozart had forgotten that Mozart never wanted his mother to accompany him in the first place; that he was eager for her to return home from Mannheim; that he did not even want to go to Paris, preferring to remain in Mannheim with the Webers and then to travel elsewhere with them; that it was Leopold who raged, "Off with you to Paris!" and thus indefinitely prolonged his wife's absence from home.

On some level, Leopold Mozart sensed that he had his full share of responsibility in her death, for he knew her age, her health, her psychological inability to be away from home. And self-reproach may be implicit in his remark that his wife would have remained alive if she had returned to Salzburg. Understandably, he could not acknowledge that he, if anyone, was to blame for exposing his wife to the hardships and hazards of the Paris sojourn. Fully aware of his vulnerability on these issues, Leopold sought to shift the responsibility—to his wife, to God, and, primarily, to his son. His revisionist history was intended as much to persuade himself of his own innocence as to persuade Mozart of his own culpability. There is no sign that Mozart was matricidal, but we do know of Leopold Mozart's bitterness against his mother for having denied and disinherited him, and we recall how he had once consigned her to hell for rejecting him. Moreover, signs of conflicted feelings about women run through his letters, in which he obsessively warns Mozart against the perils of feminine entrapment. Perhaps these troubling sentiments were now stirred up by the death of his wife, whose steadfast devotion to him had helped to keep such feelings at bay. In the aftermath of her death, having lost her loving protection and beset by old demons, he tried to deflect onto his son his own unacceptable impulses, to externalize them through projection, and thereby to absolve himself of guilt.

Mozart was innocent of his mother's death. But did he know it? Although he had done his best to save her, she had died nevertheless. He had been present at the deathbed, he had been deeply occupied with career matters and personal affairs when she fell ill, he had tried to treat her with home remedies and faith, then belatedly had summoned a hapless doctor. It would be natural for him to wonder whether he might have acted more decisively, whether he had paid sufficient attention to his mother's earliest complaints, whether there was something more that he could have done, such as seeking Baron Grimm's assistance at an earlier date. Perhaps that is why he, too, crafted a scenario of self-absolution, assigning chief responsibility to the will of Providence, while reserving auxiliary roles for Paris and its doctors. (In a letter of 8 January 1779, referring to a woman who had died in childbirth, Mozart commented, "She too has been done in by these doctors.")[44] Despite the most extreme provocation, however, he did not seek to defend himself at his father's expense; knowing his father's vulnerability, he did not mount a wounding counterattack. At the most he permitted himself to say: "Would that I had never come to Paris—but so it is."[45] He wanted to seal the matter with a prayer and a truce: "Let us therefore say a devout Paternoster for her soul and turn our thoughts to other matters, for all things have their appropriate time."[46]

The issue, then, was how Mozart was to survive the loss of his mother. At first he dealt with her death by denial: she hadn't died at all; she was ill but might yet recover. Then he internalized his grief, sealing it off from further reproaches: "I hope you have safely received my last two letters. We will not talk any more about their chief contents. It is all over now and were we to cover whole pages, we couldn't alter it!"[47] Of course, he did try to alter it, by seeking her again in other women, by founding his own family, and, after his marriage, by poignantly trying to shield his wife from harm at all costs. He courted women of simple background: unlike Beethoven, he never sought love among the women of the aristocracy, but among ordinary folk and musicians. We have seen how he took pride in saying, "The last thing I want is a rich wife," and with what eloquence he expressed his determination to marry a woman who was "lowly born, humble, and poor."[48] So it may not be accidental that when he returned to Salzburg it was with a woman named Mozart whose given names were Maria and Anna—the Bäsle, his dear cousin from Augsburg.

Characteristically, Leopold Mozart sealed his brief for Mozart's matricidal guilt by enjoining him to avoid the twin crime of patricide: "I hope that you, after your mother had to die so inappropriately in Paris, that you will not also have the furtherance of your father's death on your conscience."[49] The stakes were never reasonable in Mozart family contests: the slightest deviation from the father's will was taken as an act of treachery. For Mozart to pursue his own interest was to betray the family trust; to frustrate or thwart the father was equivalent to slaying him. For the time being, however, his main task was to carry out his mother's injunction, which had always been the family's central imperative—to provide comfort, solace, and care for a needy and unappeasable father. Thus, Mozart returned to Salzburg, downcast, defeated, having postponed both his need for love and his ambition for greatness, but determined to save his father if he could, as a way of doing what Mama would have wanted.

12

··

TROUBLE IN PARADISE

In several of Mozart's most characteristic adagios and andantes a calm, contemplative, or ecstatic condition gives way to a troubled state—is penetrated by hints of storm, dissonance, anguish, anxiety, danger—and this in turn is succeeded by a restoration of the status quo ante, now suffused with and transformed by the memory of the turbulent interlude. This dramatic compositional pattern appears in the A-minor Piano Sonata, K. 310/300d, composed in Paris in 1778, when Mozart was twenty-two. The slow movement is marked Andante cantabile con espressione, a designation intended to describe the singing, expressive opening section (Example 12.1). We have entered a self-contained, windowless, protected space within which, moving at a measured tempo, we quietly experience sensations of surpassing intensity—oceanic, comforting, and rapturous. These feelings are then reinforced through an unhurried, patient repetition of the entire initial section. But now, without raising his voice or quickening his pace, Mozart opens a trapdoor through which flood disturbing and destabilizing powers, threatening to annihilate what has gone before (Example 12.2).

We note the striking contrasts, the darkening of mood, the piercing, almost Schubertian dissonances, the brooding intensity, the relentlessness of the rapid modulations through a shifting sequence of major and minor keys. Mozart has no intention of giving way to chaos and disruption, however. Instead, after this outburst has spent its force, he moves to reinstate

Andante cantabile con espressione

Example 12.1. Sonata in A minor, K. 310/300d. Andante cantabile con espressione, mm. 1–14.

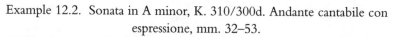

Example 12.2. Sonata in A minor, K. 310/300d. Andante cantabile con espressione, mm. 32–53.

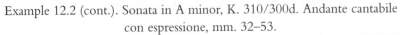

Example 12.2 (cont.). Sonata in A minor, K. 310/300d. Andante cantabile con espressione, mm. 32–53.

the original, Edenic condition, which is now heightened by melodic ornamentation and figurative elaboration (Example 12.3).

Mozart prolongs the descent to homecoming by swerving from the tonic key of F major soon after he has rediscovered it, so that it will have to be found once and for all before we can rest easy at the final cadence. In the end, and not without a renewed struggle, he has set the demons to rest, and they persist thereafter only as memory.

In this movement, Mozart invented, or at least made fully explicit for the first time, an important model of what later became the Romantic mood-piece form—of Schubert's impromptus and *Moments musicaux*, Chopin's nocturnes, Brahms's intermezzi. Although precedents may be sought in earlier music, perhaps in certain *da capo* arias of Italian opera

Example 12.3. Sonata in A minor, K. 310/300d. Andante cantabile con espressione, mm. 54–61.

seria, in Gluck's *Orfeo,* in the innovative Paris composer Johann Schobert's harpsichord sonatas, or in several of Haydn's dramatic symphonies, it was Mozart himself who established this form as a profoundly new, expressive archetype in instrumental music, and its closest precedents are actually to be found in his own music of the Salzburg years, in slow movements of his serenades and concertos, in one or two of the piano sonatas that he composed while on a brief journey to Munich in 1775, and in the String Quintet in B-flat, K. 174, written in 1773. In the serenades, concertos, and sonatas of the earlier 1770s Mozart unfolds a wide assortment of untroubled states (Examples 12.4, 12.5). In such works, however, the full significance of the idea of contrasting these passages with states drenched in pain or anxiety has not yet dawned on him, and it is in such juxtapositions that the startling novelty of the Andante of the A-minor Sonata consists, a novelty most presciently anticipated in the Adagio of the B-flat String Quintet (Example 12.6, 12.7).

Musical imagery resides in all of the referential materials that a composer weaves into his work—topics, characteristic styles, quotations, parodies,

Example 12.4. Serenade in D, K. 203/189b. Andante, mm. 1–6.

Example 12.5. Sonata in F, K. 280/189e. Adagio, mm. 1–8.

theme types, rhetorical devices, or procedures—to all of which are attached conventionally accepted connotations and historically evolved associations. Imagery is often evoked by the titles, expression marks, and other auxiliary indications by which a composer may try to lead a listener to sense extramusical possibilities. And music's metaphoric inferences also inhere in analogies between tone and language, many of which eventually become codified into musical vocabularies. Nevertheless, we grow impatient with readings that do not let us discover ever-unfolding meanings for ourselves but that compel us to channel our interpretations along restricted

Example 12.6. String Quintet in B-flat, K. 174. Adagio, mm. 1–8.

Example 12.7. String Quintet in B-flat, K. 174. Adagio, mm. 24–28.

lines, even if those lines of intentionality are laid down by the composer. Eventually, we all feel the impulse to remove the river from Smetana's "Moldau," the hero from Beethoven's "Eroica," the "Jupiter" from Mozart's symphony, so that we may respond openly and without limitation to other, perhaps equally resonant implications of those works. For there is an imagery in music that is beyond literal referentiality and extramusical indications. It is an imagery that is embedded in the formal design of musical compositions, which can appear to us as a composite image capable of evoking models from a very wide variety of sources. In other words, there may be an "image in form" that speaks to us and that we perceive, whether we know it explicitly or not.[1] Certainly, however, it does not speak a simple, denotative language. That is why the possible "meanings" of what we may want to call Mozart's "adagio/andante archetype" are wide open, overflowing with potentialities of every kind, limited only by our own intuitive responses and imaginative capacities, for these slow movements are capable of symbolizing vast realms of experience and feeling.

Although some of us may want simply to give ourselves to this music rather than to tax it with bootless questions, others may want to speculate about the sources and meanings of this strange mixture of beatitude and terror. In pursuit of these meanings, we may want to look for some of the ways in which musical structures may stand for recurrent natural, cosmic, and biological phenomena, connecting to the universal rhythms and periodicities of nature such as those described by the philosopher John Dewey as providing underlying patterns of artistic form: the "circular course of the seasons, . . . the ever-recurring cycles of growth from seed to . . . maturity, . . . the never ceasing round of births and deaths, . . . the rhythms of waking and sleeping, hungering and satiety, work and rest."[2] Dewey went on: "Because rhythm is a universal scheme of existence, underlying all realization of order in change, it pervades all the arts. . . . Underneath the rhythm of every art and of every work of art there lies, as a substratum in the depths of the subconsciousness, the basic pattern of the relations of the live creature to his environment."[3]

Or we may want to consider the overdetermination of significance that aesthetician Susanne Langer found characteristic of nondiscursive symbolic forms such as music: "Whereas the assignment of meaning to an acknowledged symbol (e.g., of literal or accepted hyperbolic meaning to a word) precludes other possibilities in its given context, the significance of a pure perceptible form is limited by nothing but the formal structure itself."[4]

Or we may find it fruitful to pursue the varieties of myth criticism, to emulate Northrop Frye and M. H. Abrams by showing how musical forms, like literary narratives, can also suggest the shapes of journeys, mythic quests, circular or spiral movements through space and time, celestial ascents, universal dreams, passages from darkness to light, processes of birth, death, and resurrection, and the ways music resonates with issues of flux and metamorphosis.[5] Possibilities can be further multiplied by drawing on imagery from every sort of duality: life and death, sound and silence, struggle and mastery, pleasure and pain, confinement and liberation, destruction and restoration, sleeping and waking, inspiration and exhalation, permanence and change. Thinking along these lines, Rudolf Arnheim wrote that expression in art "refers to the universality of the patterns of forces experienced in the particular images we receive: to expansion and contraction, conflict and concordance, rising and falling, approach and withdrawal. When these dynamisms are understood as symbols of the powers that shape human destiny, then expression assumes a deeper meaning."[6] Musical meaning is inexhaustible, and interpretation can become a process of perpetual semiosis, the endless unfolding of legitimate implications.

Clearly, at such a crossroads of intersecting possibilities, we will need both a road map and a compass. Without losing sight of the galaxy of possibilities, however, there may be something to be learned about Mozart's adagio/andante archetype from a more restricted, psychological perspective. The felicitous states that frame Mozart's excursions into anxiety may represent a variety of utopian modalities, and the impinging, disturbing materials may be taken to represent a variety of fearful things—the hidden layers of the unconscious, the terrors of the external world, a principle of evil, the pain of loss, or the irrevocability of death. An argument can be made, however, that in the last analysis we bring to the entire continuum of such states derivatives of feelings having their origin in early stages of our lives, and in particular the preverbal state of symbiotic fusion of infant and mother, a matrix that constitutes an infancy-Eden of unsurpassable beauty but also a state completely vulnerable to terrors of separation, loss, and even fears of potential annihilation, a state that inevitably terminates in parting, which even under the most favorable circumstances leaves a residue of grief and melancholy, engendering a desire—wrapped in the likelihood of further disillusionment—to rediscover anew the sensations of undifferentiated fusion with a nurturing caretaker. Not without good reason, the British psychoanalyst D. W. Winnicott described a baby as "an immature being who is all the time *on the brink of unthinkable anxiety*,"[7] an anxiety that is kept at bay only through a mother's ongoing, mirroring validation of the infant's existence. It may be such a precarious moment where inexpressible ecstasy collides with unthinkable anxiety that we sense in the Andante of Mozart's A-minor Sonata, which, reduced to its simplest essence, tells a story about trouble in paradise.

The burning ambivalence that characterizes the earliest years remains the emotional yardstick by which we measure all later experiences of fusion and loss, of loving and dying, of desire and fear, of safe havens endangered by the fear of impermanence. And reciprocally, life's subsequent vicissitudes revive, however faintly and imperfectly, those early feelings. Thus, Mozart's music resonates with every impulse toward and every failure of symbiosis, with every act of falling in love and every rejection, humiliation, or disappointment. It speaks not only of the long ago but of the here-and-now, and of what may be to come, for chronological time is irrelevant in the timeless, nonverbal world of the symbiotic adagio or andante. Seeking an outlet, these impulses, which were originally bonded to the physical senses of vision, touch, and hearing, may attach themselves to objects of art, trying to recover in the aesthetic dimension those supernal feelings of blurred boundaries between the I and the other, parent and child, lover and beloved.

In this way, the blend of intense emotions in heightened aesthetic reactions may reawaken echoes of the preverbal period, reactivating a longing for fusion. If a primary model of aesthetic feeling is indeed that of symbiotic merging, it would be little wonder that we perceive works of the greatest beauty—paradigmatically these slow movements of Mozart's—as pervaded by a heavy sadness, a knowledge of loss, a touch of fear, a sense of transience, a whiff of mortality. For it is clear that we cannot discover states of bliss without rediscovering pain. The repetition compulsion cannot readily distinguish between ecstasy and trauma. Thus, to relive early states of fusion inevitably is to rediscover the traumas that suffused those states or, at the least, accompanied their termination and attended the expulsion from the good place in which we once rested. If such art is an analogue of the refinding of the symbiotic experience, its potential for triggering painful, even psychotic, reactions needs to be harnessed—by limiting the

Autograph manuscript, Sonata in A minor, K. 310/300d, end of Allegro
maestoso and beginning of Andante. Robert Owen Lehman
Collection, on deposit in the Pierpont Morgan Library.

entry of anxiety-ridden materials, by structure and design, by classicism's symmetries, delicate balances, and ultimate closures. For reasons such as these, the formal rounding off of Mozart's adagios and andantes may be emblematic, not only of a return to innocence, but of the repair of every possible kind of fractured wholeness—a healing of woundedness, a balm to a convalescent soul, a reparation of injustice, a resurrection of those whom we have lost. Perhaps that is why Ernst Kris called art "the preservation of that which vanishes."[8] And why Ella Freeman Sharpe, who had read Proust and was perhaps the first to make the psychoanalytic connection between art and restoration, wrote that art "is a bringing back of life, a reparation, an atonement, a nullification of anxiety. It is an omnipotent phantasy of control, of security from evil."[9] Mainly, however, like a raging transference or the experience of being in love, these adagios and andantes have the power to mobilize both the memory of and the yearning for a fusion that we can never recapture in reality, but that we can experience symbolically through the measured movement of tones, thereby partially undoing an archaic separation and momentarily fulfilling an ancient wish. Through the image in form, the listener no longer experiences the regressive pull toward fusion as potentially annihilating, because the composer has provided a consoling structure that does not accept loss or separation as a tragic finality.

Mozart continued to elaborate the adagio/andante archetype, constantly changing its emphasis and details while retaining its fundamental strategy. Further examples and variants of it may be found in his most mature works in several genres, notably in the G-minor String Quintet, K. 516; the Violin Sonatas in B-flat, K. 454, E-flat, K. 481, and A, K. 526; and in many of the late piano concertos, including those in C, K. 467, C-minor, K. 491, and B-flat, K. 595. In these slow movements Mozart tries to summon up every gradation of emotion—from terror to vague feelings of unease, from unbearably intense pleasures bordering on ecstasy to a floating placidity and contentment. And every new edition of the archetype has its own individuality, not only of mood and feeling, but of design as well. In his restlessness, Mozart was not content here to repeat a successful formula. Instead, imbued with a spirit of inquiry and an impulse to represent in music what had never previously been represented, he sought to work out the potentialities of this new vehicle of musical expression, creating an array of differentiated slow-movement types whose unity lies in their exploration of the alternation and/or fusion of pleasure and unpleasure.

Some of these depart from the basic design in the most subtle way, as in the Andante cantabile of the Piano Sonata in B-flat, K. 333/315c, which features pungent chromaticisms in its middle section, followed by a lavishly ornamented recapitulation that emphasizes the reaching of a transformed and heightened state rather than a simple return to an antecedent condition (Examples 12.8, 12.9). The closing movement of the two-movement Violin

Example 12.8. Sonata in B-flat, K. 333. Andante cantabile, mm. 1–5.

Example 12.9. Sonata in B-flat, K. 333. Andante cantabile, mm. 51–56.

Sonata in E minor, K. 304/300c, marked "Tempo di menuetto," which was written almost simultaneously with the A-minor Sonata, uses a notably different narrative model. Instead of alternating blissful and fearful modalities, this model seems to describe a three-stage descent—from an ideal outer reality to a troubled inwardness, with the moment of symbiotic fusion reserved for the trio section at the movement's very center. At the opening, the social order is implicitly represented as an aristocratic state of grace, beauty, and decorum (Example 12.10).

Example 12.10. Violin Sonata in E minor, K. 304/300c. Tempo di menuetto, mm. 1–8.

Example 12.11. Violin Sonata in E minor, K. 304/300c. Tempo di menuetto, mm. 59–66.

This order is soon undermined, with agitated forces contending for expression and soon exhausting themselves in a declamatory peroration (Example 12.11). In the E-major trio, what Einstein calls "a brief glimpse of bliss," is, in our terms, a moment of symbiotic fusion, a discovery of the inmost retreat, providing release from strife (Example 12.12).[10]

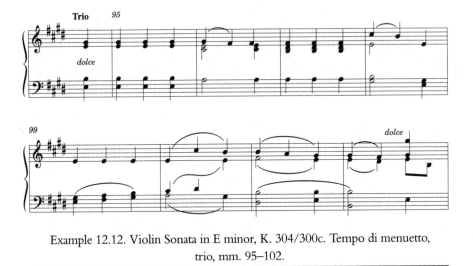

Example 12.12. Violin Sonata in E minor, K. 304/300c. Tempo di menuetto, trio, mm. 95–102.

The movement then closes with a return to the social framework, but the minuet is now heard as lament or imperfect consolation, because we know the pain through which we have passed since this same material opened the movement in such apparent innocence.

Inevitably, Mozart would sooner or later decide to turn the entire narrative inside out, in a stroke of daring whose implications for musical expressivity and extramusical denotation stirred Haydn and Beethoven to emulation. The opening bars of the String Quartet in C major, K. 465 ("Dissonance"), marked Adagio, immediately plunge into the center of symbiotic terror (Example 12.13). Here, Mozart has simulated the very process of creation, showing us the lineaments of chaos at the moment of its conversion into form. He has created an unprecedented network of disorientations, dissonances, rhythmic obscurities, and atmospheric dislocations. Without knowing precisely where we are, we know that we are in an alien universe. Laocoön is in the grip of the writhing serpents. Reality has been defamiliarized, the uncanny has supplanted the commonplace. In this introduction, Mozart has simulated the transitions from darkness to light, from the underworld to the surface, from the id to the ego. For, whatever our metaphoric frame, this music is ultimately about confinement and emergence. And now the Allegro theme emerges soaring and liberated, having already achieved release, transcended the fear of annihilation, freed itself from a burdensome confinement, shed the harmonic ambiguities,

Example 12.13. String Quartet in C, K. 465 ("Dissonance").
First movement, Adagio, mm. 1–22.

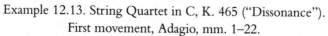

chromaticism, and pungent dissonances of the Adagio in favor of the simple brightness of an achieved C major (Example 12.14).

Example 12.14. String Quartet in C, K. 465 ("Dissonance"). First movement, Allegro, mm. 23–30.

Thus, the adagio/andante archetype fans out into alternative narrative pathways. But it is not purely a narrative strategy. The constant factor in every edition of the archetype is the re-finding and representation of a primal ambivalence, and to this end Mozart uses two main modes of representation—the narrative and the dialectical—which we separate only for taxonomic purposes. In the former, which we have been describing here, Mozart composes states that succeed each other in time; thus, the Andante of the A-minor Sonata is a simple narrative sequence, a circular or spiral journey from birth to expulsion to homecoming, or a progression from fusion to anxiety to fusion, if we prefer the psychological to the mythic metaphor. In the dialectical mode, however, he composes states of ambivalence that do not unfold successively, but occur at the same time, achieving the effect of simultaneity by chromaticisms, rhythmic shifts, modulations, registral contrasts, and a host of other compositional procedures that imply affective juxtapositions. Mozart specialized in the representation of amalgams of opposed affects, of beauty and sadness, of consolation and terror, of longing and anger, of pleasure and pain, teaching us what it may mean when the object of desire is simultaneously the source of fear.

Mozart's autograph score of the A-minor Sonata contains the superscription, "Sonata di Wolfgango Amadeo Mozart, Paris 1778." On 20 July he announced that he would soon forward to Salzburg several works, including "a few of my clavier sonatas," and again, on 31 July, he informed his sister that he would be sending "a few other sonatas of my own composition."[11] The sonatas are not further identified, but it seems probable that Leopold Mozart had already seen the A-minor Sonata (and perhaps the Violin Sonata in E minor as well), to judge from his alarmed letter of 13 August 1778, decrying Mozart's propensity to compose arcane music utilizing "harmonic progressions, *which the majority of people cannot fathom,* or pieces which have pleasing melodies, but which are *difficult to perform.*"[12] We cannot be certain whether the A-minor Sonata was written just prior to or just after his mother's death in Paris in July 1778, but in either event the issue of maternal/filial fusion and separation dominated the period of its composition no less than the issue of a rupturing paternal/filial symbiosis. The adagio/andante archetype, whose first stirrings date from 1773, when the Mozart family structure began to disintegrate, thus found its exemplary form during the stormy process of Mozart's attempt to separate from both his mother and his father, and from the combined parent figure that confronted him in fantasy as a monolithic entity.

It would be surprising if the events of the Mannheim/Paris journey, which were so thickly clustered around the harrowing issue of symbiosis and separation, had not set in motion impulses to recapture happier times, when the links between a gifted child and his benevolent, nurturing parents were as yet intact and seemingly indestructible. Nor would it be surprising that these longings were permeated by fears of loss, terrors of engulfment, and sensations of rage. Mozart was trapped in the dilemma of longing for the remembered ecstasies of an infantilized past even as he strove to escape from the bondage of being an eternal child. This dilemma may have found both its expression and its symbolic resolution in the creation of his adagio/andante archetype. Perhaps, buried deep within the fabric and structure of the A-minor Sonata, are the precipitates of the struggle over these insoluble issues of fusion and individuation, obligation and autonomy, love and guilt, and exile and return.

★   ★   ★

The most basic "narrative" variants of the archetype may have been too predictable to preoccupy Mozart's creative energies for long: certainly the dialectical variants, with their infinite possibilities of characterizing fused feelings, were more interesting than a simple musical equivalent of successive *tableaux vivants*. However, another pristine example of Mozart's original adagio/andante archetype, perhaps the most familiar of them all, and one that might well be overlooked if it were not placed in this context, arises a decade after the journey to Paris. It is the Andante of the C-major Sonata, K. 545, entered in Mozart's handwritten thematic catalog of his works on 26 June 1788 with the notation, "Eine kleine klavier Sonate für anfänger" ("A short piano sonata for beginners"). The slow movement opens in Eden—or Arcadia, or Elysium, or some equivalent geography of achieved desire—but does not remain there permanently, instead embarking upon a voyage into a troubled *Innerlichkeit* ("inwardness"). This movement has the remoteness of recollection rather than of palpable experience. There is a weariness about it, a current of nostalgia perhaps in keeping with its having been dated ten years to the day after he was told that his mother would not last the night (Example 12.15).[13]

Example 12.15. Sonata in C, K. 545. Andante, mm. 1–8.

Unlike the starkly dramatic A-minor Sonata, the contrasting section does not reach extreme levels of turbulence or dissonance, but rather is imbued with a tone of melancholy acceptance, as though its terrors and traumas had now receded into a distanced past, or were more deeply buried, or had been softened by the passage of time. When the trapdoor opens, Mozart ironically undermines the rococo surface as though to subvert not only the vision of tranquillity, but the aristocratic order it is customarily intended to validate. Thus, emotions having their origin in deep layers of the psyche overflow their psychological borders and spill into the social sphere as well. The development is in G minor, indelibly associated in Mozart's music with his use of chiaroscuro techniques and with the darker, tragic, passionate affects (Example 12.16).

Example 12.16. Sonata in C, K. 545. Andante, mm. 33–40.

The closing codalike section momentarily resists the pulls to serenity, now yearning upward in stepwise progressions as though to recapture the recollections of strife and pain. In the end, however, with the receding posthorn call, we have returned to Eden, laden with memories of exile but relieved to have gained so felicitous a homecoming.

★ ★ ★

We tend to valorize origins and goals, beginnings and endings, first and final causes. That may be why we often want to view the slow movement of the classical sonata cycle as tangential or transitional, as a meditative or affective interlude that happens to lie on the route between the fundamental complicating narrative of the opening sonata-allegro and the transcendent, simplifying strategies of the finale. It is of course characteristic of the slow movements of many paradigmatic sonata-form cycles (including most of Haydn's works and Mozart's pre-1788 symphonies) that we withdraw temporarily from the main narrative line into a contemplative haven, one that serves as a contrast to the predominant character—or "idea," as it was once called—of the composition. Through the impact of Beethoven's "heroic-period" music, the valorization of endings became profoundly embedded in our musical expectations, so that we are often impelled to perceive the classical slow movement as a transitional stage in an overarching narrative that terminates in an apotheosis or other transcendent state of being. Beethoven experimented with conceptions of the slow movement quite different from those of Haydn and Mozart, adapting French Revolutionary celebratory styles to impart a "public" character to the slow movements of the "Eroica" and Fifth symphonies; avoiding slow movements and their fundamental subjectivity altogether, as in the Eighth Symphony; and even setting aside a completed Andante in favor of a vastly compressed *Introduzione* to a climaxing finale in the "Waldstein" Sonata.

It may be because we often read Mozart's music with lenses adjusted to Beethoven's "heroic-style" paradigms that we sometimes overlook that Mozart's slow movements are conceived as the gravity center of many of his sonatas, piano concertos, and other instrumental cycles, that they are indeed "central" in the most fundamental sense. Issues of interiority are reserved for these slow movements, while the framing movements are briefer in length and lighter in texture; some opening movements are crafted to serve as prologues to an exploration of feeling and subjectivity and the weight of the composition resides in the slow movement, which sometimes is longer than the outer movements put together. In some of these works, the opening movement is a commedia dell'arte overture to the slow movement, and the rondo-finale issues from the slow movement, returning to the ludic dimension where all weighty issues are dissolved in irony. Such works trace a trajectory that arches from an overture, through the central experience of inwardness, concluding with an emergence into the light. Strategies of distancing—irony, a comic style, and a masquerading stance—are foreign to such slow movements, which speak the language of the heart, reflect upon the imagery of the interior, recall nostalgic beauties, and predict future moments of fulfillment.

Of course, Mozart's slow movements are extremely various, not only in covering an enormous affective range of inner experience, including every aspect of subjectivity, but in form and function as well. One pervasive slow-movement model—often in C minor, e.g., the String Quartet, K. 157, the Piano Concerto in E-flat, K. 271, and the Sinfonia Concertante in E-flat, K. 364/320d—is derived from opera seria, using copious dramatic gestures and recitativelike interjections to impart a somewhat objectified sense of the tragic or pathetic. In Mozart's serenades and violin concertos, the slow movement is primarily the locus for the expression of amorous feeling in a conventional Arcadian setting. Like Haydn and Beethoven, Mozart constantly experiments with the relative weight of various movements in the cycles; not in every work are the corner movements lightweight entrance and exeunt music. Thus, whereas the slow movements are forced to carry a heavier freight of meaning in less heavily weighted contexts, in the A-minor Sonata Mozart increases the weight of the first movement to an unprecedented extent, as though to counteract the extraordinary impact of the Andante.

Finally, in one of the most astonishing of all compositional strokes, the G-minor String Quintet places two profound adagios back to back—a full-scale slow movement in B-flat, Adagio ma non troppo, *con sordino,* followed by another Adagio, *senza sordino,* now in the quintet's tonic key of G

Autograph manuscript, String Quartet in C, K. 465, first movement, Adagio-Allegro. The British Library: Department of Manuscripts—Add. MS 37763, f.57ʳ.

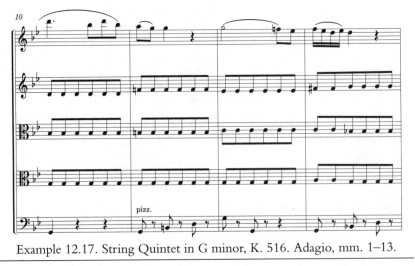

Example 12.17. String Quintet in G minor, K. 516. Adagio, mm. 1–13.

minor. It is as though Mozart were saying that tragedy, loss, and yearning are too great to be encompassed in a single adagio, or that after this sadness, there is another sadness that must be addressed, and it must be addressed without mutes, for it presses urgently for utterance—and resolution. Or, that an intermediate stage—begun by a solo recitativelike cantilena, which anticipates dissolution into G major—must be traversed before we can awaken from inwardness (Example 12.17). Thus, the Adagio *senza sordino* is not merely an introduction or transition to a finale, like those Haydn composed on several occasions. Mozart's twin adagios tell of many things, and among them may be the endlessness of our longing to return to sources, to start over, to find once again the place where it all began.

The Mozart family, 1780–81. Oil portrait by Johann Nepomuk della Croce. Mozart-Museum der Internationalen Stiftung Mozarteum, Salzburg. © Mozarts Geburtshaus, Salzburg.

13

....

PARALLEL LIVES

By now, the reader will have noticed a curious series of parallels in the life stories of Mozart and his father. Leopold Mozart too had refused to travel the road his parents had mapped out for him; like Mozart, he wanted to make his own way as an independent musician in a foreign city; and by his rebellious actions he, too, brought family opprobrium upon himself. Unknowingly, Mozart was repeating, under duress, a narrative similar in its basic outline to one long ago played out by his father. Equally unaware of the analogy to earlier events, Leopold Mozart tried to control Mozart as his mother had wanted to control him, attempting to compel his own son to remain in or return to his native city. Later on, like his mother, he refused to approve his son's marriage and, at the end, effectively disinherited him.

In some way, the Salzburg Mozarts were now reenacting a drama of sacrifice and atonement, unconsciously staged by Leopold Mozart to come to terms with the earlier events, the memory of which continued to grieve him. For Leopold Mozart was sorely wounded by his mother's repudiation of him and burdened with guilt over his own actions. He was at once driven to avenge the injustices he believed had been visited upon him and to repair the damage he himself had caused. Mozart became an instrument to accomplish these ends, an instrument by which Leopold Mozart endeavored to even some archaic scores and cast out some devils. By an arcane process, Mozart came to represent his father's own younger, sinful self, to serve as a scapegoat for his father's transgressions, whether of thought or of deed. Mozart was appointed to assume the burden of a father's offenses against God, city, and family: now it is he who is charged with neglect and abandonment of his parents, with frivolity, impiety, and irresponsibility, with his mother's death, and with a host of lesser faults and crimes, even though it was actually Leopold Mozart who had been the object of these charges, leveled against him by his family, the Augsburg Catholic elders, by the Salzburg authorities, and, not least, by his own conscience, stricken but unacknowledged. The deputy kapellmeister insisted that Mozart adhere precisely to those principles of obedience to law, father, and God which he, as a young man, had repeatedly breached. His endless complaints were reiterations of his mother's real or imagined warnings. To set his son on a righteous path was thus to avoid self-punishment and mortification, to prevent his own rebellious and heretical tendencies from once again gaining the upper hand and leaving him powerless, melancholy, bereft. Above all, he offered up his own son—but now obedient, compliant, overflowing with filial devotion—to the internalized image of his mother, thereby reliving and repairing his flight from Augsburg.

To achieve these ends, Leopold Mozart monitored his son's moves toward independence and maturity. Thus, it is he who will shape every detail of his son's career, he who will try to keep him celibate and unmarried. Thus, Mozart may not leave his parents' house or his home town; he may not separate from his parents because he is required to care for them and provide for their old age; he may not be placed in any position where others might gain influence over him; he cannot attend school or university, for these were the locus of his father's temptations; thus his primary teacher must remain his father, who thereby can supervise the boy's behavior and guarantee his adherence to precepts of order and rationality.

Leopold's actions are not merely reparative, but also involve a compulsion to repeat the rebellion against his own parent, the flight from home, the expulsion from his family. Ironically, however, he thereby brings about a repetition of his own crushing rejection. Reenacting the old events, he now takes his mother's role and, by his inflexibility and irrationality, makes it a certainty that his son will flee Salzburg. Leopold Mozart's clamorous assertions that a parent's welfare must take precedence over that of the child now seem to express his belated agreement with his mother's ancient complaint against himself. There is, of course, a fluid interchange of roles and a perplexing web of contradictory aims at work. Leopold has managed partially to purge his own guilt by repudiating himself in the guise of his own son. At the same time, Leopold's harsh treatment of Mozart is a form of self-scourging; he aims to punish himself as his mother should have been punished for disinheriting him and for withdrawing her love from him. Finally, Leopold's mother has gotten her just deserts for withholding her love and her money. Not surprisingly, issues of debt, payment, and obligation are once again predominant, and money becomes a universal solvent of this tangled drama: by perpetually extracting cash from Mozart's labor Leopold Mozart makes a son pay for his father's sins; by piling up money from him he may hope finally to obtain the legacy that had been denied him.

It goes without saying that all of this was a delusory process. In the end, therefore, Leopold Mozart's strivings for relief from inner torment were incapable of being satisfied. He and his mother died without forgiving each other; unbending and pitiless, he could not forgive himself.

Upon the departure of his wife and son from Salzburg in September 1777, Leopold Mozart slipped into a deep melancholy—"I was ill, confused, out of humor, depressed and very sad . . ."[1]—within which he stormed against what he perceived as frustrating objects in the outer world, objects that he did not see clearly, objects whose only purpose, he believed, was to aggrieve him. He is persuaded that his wife and son are hiding things from him: "I hinted in my last letter that there must be secrets which I am not allowed to know. . . . Whether they turn out well or ill, I shall hear them soon enough."[2] Victim of a disordered imagination, he masked his emotional malaise with an apparent superrationality, grimly using his analytic powers as a way of maintaining contact with the world. An orderly world was one that he could control or in which he could predict behavior; the alternative was free fall into the chaos of helplessness, an unacceptable choice. He needed to maintain order, to stop the world from changing. Thus, his melancholy never gave way to quiescence; his decline into sadness was always countered by a determination to act, to shape events, to try to rearrange things by sheer force of will.

Mozart had become the object of a melancholiac's fantastic grievances against the world. Leopold Mozart complained that he had been reduced to poverty by his son's improvidence and that soon he and Marianne could become indigent and be forced to beg on the streets. Most harrowing for Mozart, he was accused of causing by his negligence the death of his mother, and to the list of Mozart's sins Leopold Mozart suggested that he was capable of patricide. Repeatedly, obsessively, Mozart was charged not just with heartlessness but with seeking to destroy his own father: "Just think whether you are not treating me more cruelly than does our Prince. . . . You know what I have endured for more than five years—yes—and what a lot I have had to swallow on your account. The Prince's conduct can only bend me, but yours can crush me. He can only make me ill, but you can kill me."[3] Partly, it seems clear, these extravagant fantasies were elements of a strategy to bind his son to him, but they were more than simple tactics in a manipulative and domineering campaign. To Leopold Mozart, his son was indeed all-powerful, capable either of killing him or of keeping him alive: "If you stay away, I shall die much sooner, and . . . if I could have the joy of having you with me, I should live several years longer."[4] His belief, and Mozart's burden, was summarized in a single phrase: "You alone can save me from death."[5]

Leopold Mozart's feelings toward Mozart are a fierce bundle of contradictory impulses, and sometimes we may sense in his fears about his son's safety a hint of a morbid imagination: failing to receive a letter for a few days, he dramatically relates his fantasy that Mozart had fallen ill, or been robbed or even murdered en route from Nancy to Strasbourg: "*A frightful death-blow.* . . . I am still in this dreadful state of anxiety. . . . Whenever Bullinger appears, I watch his features with the greatest attention, lest he should be bringing my sentence of death. I have now spent four sleepless nights—*such ghastly nights, my son!* I dread them; and I am glad when the day breaks. . . . I have confessed and received Communion together with your sister and I have prayed God most earnestly to preserve you."[6] Throughout his letters one encounters, beyond his impatience, a fury against his son for refusing to play the multiple roles that he had scripted for him and for doing that which is forbidden—rebelling against reason as personified in the father. A strain of embittered submissiveness runs deep within Leopold Mozart; he has crushed his own rebelliousness, but in so doing his rancor has overflowed against his son, who still retains his defiant attitude, his refusal to submit.

In the last analysis, Mozart became a screen upon which Leopold Mozart projected his own repudiated impulses; accordingly, the boy must be controlled, for he bore within him his father's buried potential to violate fundamental taboos. That is why, without sensing any contradiction, Leopold Mozart's patricidal charges against Mozart are interwoven with invocations of him as an endangered child: somehow the patricide is himself helpless and can only be saved if he will submit, as in the past, to a father's benevolent protection. Mozart is told that he cannot survive without his father, that he is incapable of caring for himself, that, without the father's keen spur, he is heedless and unproductive. To judge from his letters, Leopold Mozart never grasped, even for a moment—even in the face of Mozart's greatest triumphs—how contradictory and wildly untrue these charges were. Mozart had not reduced his father and sister to poverty; he had not caused his mother's death or acted so as to endanger his father's life; he was far from unproductive; he was fully able to earn his own living. But even in his most irrational moments Leopold Mozart insisted upon his rationality. "It has ever been my habit to reflect and *ponder,*" he wrote in praise of his own mental acuity, "and but for this I should not have got on as well as I have, for I never had anyone to advise me; and, as you are aware, from my youth up I have never confided wholly in anyone until I had definite proofs of his sincerity. Just look at my brothers and myself; when you consider the difference between us, you will realize how valuable has been my reflection and meditation. Well, . . . from my early youth I have been accustomed to think things over."[7]

The family was well aware of Leopold Mozart's sadness and his pain, aware that in some respects he could no longer clearly distinguish fantasy from reality, aware of the depth of his delusions. Vainly, Mozart and Frau Mozart tried to cope with his breakdown—by reminding him of reality, cajoling him, jesting with him, enduring his rages and his complaints, and, usually, by agreeing with him and submitting to his unending demands. Always, they tried to pacify and reassure him. "Meanwhile do not worry and shake off all your troubles," Frau Mozart wrote. "Everything will come right in the end, when the hooks and eyes have been put on."[8] She advised him to tell Marianne "to take care that you have no worries and to help you to pass the time so that you do not get melancholy."[9] She tried to awaken his sense of humor by her loving earthy concern about his physical well-being: "Keep well, my love. Into your mouth your ass you'll shove. I wish you good-night, my dear, but first shit in your bed and make it burst."[10] She did not conceal her fears: "Somehow I am dreadfully anxious lest you should be unwell. . . . Do write to me soon and relieve me of my anxiety."[11] Mozart, too, often asks his father to calm himself: "Please don't worry, I will certainly make good. And I have one request to make, which is, to show in your letters a cheerful spirit," and again, "I must really beg you once more not to worry so much, not to be so anxious; for now you have no reason to be so."[12] Predictably, such recommendations to put on a sunny face only succeeded in bringing Leopold's censorious tendencies to the fore: "*You would like me to be very cheerful in my letters.* My dear Wolfgang! . . . My good spirits depend, my dear son, on your circumstances, which indeed can restore me to health. . . . Once you have made your father's happiness your first consideration, he will continue to think of your welfare and happiness and to stand by you as a loyal friend."[13]

The insuperable difficulty, I believe, was that Mozart could not turn for relief to the maternal image that he had internalized, for, though his mother's presence had been loving and protective, at bottom her vision of Mozart's family role did not essentially differ from Leopold Mozart's. Long ago in Salzburg, a little girl's main experience of the world had been to observe the physical deterioration (combined, it should be noted, with serious mental confusion and disorientation), financial impoverishment, and death of her once-distinguished father,[14] and, for more than twenty years after his death in 1724, she had felt the shame and deprivation of being, with her mother, wards of the state. We saw how she reacted to her losses with illness when she was in her late teens, and with fortitude when she was a woman, determined to repair her losses and to work to prevent such events from overcoming her new family, which came to consist of a husband, a daughter who was named after her, and a son, to whom they gave her father's name, Wolfgang. She imprinted upon the consciences of her two children an urgent sense of family responsibility and, above all, the injunction that their father—who was beset by both choleric and melancholic tendencies—be shielded from harm and provided with comfort. Just as Leopold Mozart was in the grip of a compulsion to repeat ancient hurts, Anna Maria Mozart had a compulsion to repair such hurts, to prevent the return of a childhood catastrophe. She placed herself and her children in her husband's hands, secure in her trust of his judgment and guidance. And he, without ever questioning his own assumptions, demanded and received from his children a devotion to his own person that placed intolerable strains upon them. Thus, by drastically different routes, a husband and a wife had formulated virtually identical roles for their children to play, so that, in the end, the messages reduced themselves to one, to save papa at any price.

The true family enterprise, then, was not so much the making of money nor the glorification of two gifted children but the providing of emotional assistance and supplies to its neediest member, Leopold Mozart. Frau Mozart taught the children that their main function was to do as she did—to take care of the *paterfamilias,* to preserve him from sadness, soothe his melancholic temper, calm his rages. Marianne took her mother's role literally, becoming Leopold's housekeeper, nurse, daily companion, and defender of the faith; Mozart, too, tried to take the mother's role, but his father's demands on him went beyond his capacity for self-subordination. His attempts to continue placating and nursing Leopold ran aground because his father's demands were insatiable. Eventually, Mozart had to give up his struggle to aid his father, because to continue would have meant surrendering his individuality, smothering his sexual needs, and setting severe limits upon his creativity. He needed to leave his father in order to survive as a person and as an artist.

Perhaps, Mozart also needed to leave his father to maintain his own mental equilibrium. For Mozart himself began to slip into despondent states of mind, and he struggled to keep his own predispositions to melancholia under control. On 31 July 1778, in the aftermath of his mother's death, he wrote: "From time to time I have fits of melancholy—but I find that the best way to get rid of them is to write or receive letters, which invariably cheer me up again. But, believe me, there is always a cause for these sad feelings."[15] Seeking his father's compassion, he confessed the extent of his unhappiness: "I often wonder whether life is worth living," he wrote; "I am neither hot nor cold—and don't find much pleasure in anything."[16] But his father didn't want to hear this; to him, it smacked of turning the tables. Surely, he wrote, "you were *discontented* or annoyed at the time or . . . you were writing in a bad humor. I don't like it."[17] Instead of extending sympathy he reminded Mozart of his, Leopold's, real worries, "which I have had to cope with during *thirty years* of married life, in order to support a family, *worries* with which I shall be saddled until the hour of my death."[18] Later on, in response to another of Mozart's pleas for understanding, Leopold summed up his limited view of the reciprocity of their relationship: "You say that *I ought to comfort you,* while I say, *come and console me.*"[19] In his narcissistic anguish he could not understand that his son also had feelings, let alone that he could know pain. On one occasion he derided his son's ambitions, calling them "your gay dreams."[20] Here he went too far, for Mozart, even as he had accepted the necessity of sacrificing himself once again to the family interests, knew that he must hold fast to the hope of some future moment of freedom. "What do you mean by 'gay dreams?'" he asked. "I do not mind the reference to dreaming, for there is no mortal on the face of this earth who does not sometimes dream! But *gay dreams!* Peaceful dreams, refreshing, sweet dreams! That is what they are—dreams which, if realized, would make my life, which is more sad than cheerful, more endurable."[21]

Faced with demands that were both global and annihilating, Mozart remained in Salzburg as long as he was able, and when he departed, it was sadly, in mourning, because he knew that no partial sacrifice would have been acceptable. And he departed, knowing that he would be branded as having abandoned his family and renounced his filial responsibilities. Thus he would leave with the consciousness that he had been cut adrift rather than liberated. Now he must either survive as a separate individual or go under. The poignancy of his striving for independence is that it entailed the severing of the ties to his own past, over which a pall of bitterness had been cast and which was to be forever permeated by an awareness of the extent of his exploitation and the devastating thought that he had not been loved.

In this he was wrong, for Leopold Mozart indeed loved his son. Even the pathological domination, the mercenary exploitation, the endless recriminations, the piling up of guilt, and the insistence that Mozart was an eternal debtor had one main root: they were a father's desperate maneuvers to keep the symbiotic relationship intact, for to lose his son was to lose the integrity of his being, to lose that which gave meaning to his life. He loved Mozart so profoundly that he needed to swallow him, to keep him within himself, to prevent him from getting out. He tried to keep Mozart from establishing a separate existence because, he was convinced, he himself had no separate existence without Mozart.

Sara Sheftel trenchantly observed that Leopold had an "unsatisfied earliest need, the need to be taken care of," and that Mozart "was expected as an adult to become his father's parent and, indeed, the parent and caretaker of the whole family."[22] From the earliest age, of course, Mozart had truly served as the family's breadwinner as well as the source of its status and fame. Indeed, without minimizing the fervor and skill with which Leopold Mozart served as Mozart's impresario during the early years, it might be said that the father had long been a kind of figurehead, believing himself the omnipotent ruler but in actuality utterly dependent upon the whims, health, and abilities of a little child to accomplish his purposes. Mozart, then, had to play the child while actually carrying the heaviest responsibilities. Mozart's abiding role was to heap money and fame upon his father and to provide for him in his old age. Leopold Mozart's parsimonious character—his passion for accumulation, his preoccupation with waste—masked a voracious oral character, drawing sustenance from those around him, receiving constant nourishment from his wife, his son, and his daughter. If Leopold acted the willful tyrant, it was the raging willfulness that comes from feelings of downright helplessness. In a sense, then, it was he rather than his son who had really been the eternal child of the Mozart family.

The Mozart family had evolved from four separate individuals into a single, indivisible organism. At least, that is how, in the course of time, its members came to view themselves—as a collective entity within which every member played an assigned role. Theirs was a productive association characterized by mutual aid, altruism, the balancing of interests, and the subordination of personal desire to rational leadership. They felt the strength that flows from united effort and the warmth of mutual acceptance. Uncomplainingly, even joyously, each recognized that the family enterprise entailed a sacrifice of individuality to the greater good. They experienced the ecstatic sensations, the inexpressible feelings of fusion and symbiosis that accompany the erosion of physical and mental boundaries between individuals.

The family's view of itself developed during the early journeys, where each member played an important, indeed a crucial, role in the family *Gestalt*. But the inroads of time altered that reality without diminishing

Leopold's passionate wish indefinitely to continue repeating the family's triumphs. Marianne, after 1768, was no longer a viable professional performer. By 1773 or 1774, when Mozart became a young man, the family enterprise was effectively defunct. External reality had changed, and the lives of the family's constituent members had changed. The plain truth was that Leopold Mozart was no longer needed to direct Mozart's affairs. The devastating conflict between Mozart and his father that climaxed with the flight to Vienna in 1781 hinged not merely on Mozart's drive for independence but on Leopold Mozart's inability to acknowledge that he was no longer central to the family enterprise that he had founded and commanded for a quarter century. He would never accept the possibility that Mozart could continue without him, for that would signify that he himself had become redundant. He struggled valiantly to confirm that he existed, that he had a reason for being. Unwilling to accept superfluity or lessened status, he raged at being cast aside. In the end, he became a Captain Ahab declaiming to his crew, "Ye are not other men, but my arms and my legs," in the face of impending destruction, a Joshua seeking to stop the sun from setting.

It was at this point that the family mythology at last turned utterly delusional: Mozart was stamped as an eternal child who must submit to the protection of the father; an eternal child, who can never grow up, because his life must be dedicated to the preservation of the family organism. The child must remain a child so that his father may continue to be his impresario. To complete the delusional fabric, it became the task of the family to pretend that nothing had changed. The family organism colluded to enact a collective charade, with complex levels of deception founded upon a central illusion—of Leopold Mozart's continuing centrality long after his guiding role had become obsolete.

In leaving Leopold Mozart, it seems, Mozart renounced his own pretensions to omnipotence, acknowledging that there was a limit to his ability to aid his father. Dramatically, his departure bespoke his insistence that his father become an autonomous individual, stand on his own feet, make his own living, give up his humiliating dependence on his son. Simultaneously, of course, Mozart had affirmed the cycle of the generations, the inevitability of the mortality of parents, the necessity of children leaving home, going into the world, naked and fearful, trading the protection of the hearth for the emblems of personal fulfillment and creative achievement. Leopold Mozart should have understood this well, for, in the end, his son did no more than he had before him: given up his dependency upon the family and sought his place as a creative individual in a distant city.

14

··

FAREWELL TO SALZBURG

During Mozart's last years in Salzburg, 1779 and 1780, his sister, Marianne, kept a diary, really a bare-bones log, recording the weather and the homely events of the unfolding days. Typically, on 28 May 1780, the diary pictures an eventful Sunday, with activities from early morning until late at night:

> ... the 28th from 5:30 to 6:30 with my brother to confession at Holy Trinity Church. At midday Mr. Eck and his son, [third organist] Paris and Catherl ate with us; [at the shooting contest, the] prize-giver [was] Zahlmeister [Franz Lankmayr], Catherl won, afterwards three quartets were played, played tarok and afterwards everyone went to the court; at night the Mssrs. Ecks, returned home with the Ecks, they ate with us and left at 11 o'clock.[1]

Other days were less eventful, but the basic rounds of morning Mass, lunch, social visits, dinner, and evening diversions remained fairly constant. "On the 11th around 8:00 o'clock, went to church, afterwards at Fräulein and Frau von Mayer; in the afternoon Captain Hermes's wife visited us, afterwards we went to the concert at the Town Hall; afterwards we went for a walk."[2] During extended visits of theatrical troupes, Marianne would list every performance with a brief description—and even a rare comment.[3] But, for the most part, the entries documented a life of simple routines and simpler pleasures, with the days, weeks, and months imperceptibly merging into each other.

Illustration for shooting contest. Embroidery on parchment. Mozart-
Museum der Internationalen Stiftung Mozarteum, Salzburg. © Mozarts
Geburtshaus, Salzburg.

Mozart occasionally wrote the entries in his sister's diary, almost always referring to himself as "my brother," and sometimes he would give the impression that he was straightforwardly transcribing events from her dictation or in her own voice. For example:

> Rained the whole day.
> On the 16th about 8 o'clock at church, afternoon at Lodron, around 4 o'clock Feigele played tarok at our house. Like April, inconstant weather and very brisk.
> The 17th around 7:30 in church. At Lodron and Mayr's. Around 2:30 the Barisani girls, Nannerl, Therese, and Louise, visited us. Around 5 o'clock to 6 o'clock the second Mademoiselle Hartensteiner visited us and around 6 o'clock Fräulein Josepha arrived. Feigele was also there, we played "Hineinschauen." Around 7:30 Herr von Mölk arrived and immediately went away again. Around 9 o'clock my brother accompanied the girls home. Inconstant weather, like yesterday.[4]

Sometimes, however, he would spice the entries with wordplay, parodistic comments, bawdy references, and obscene phrases. He told how they watched the Corpus Christi Day procession in 1780: "The 25th around 7:30 to Hagenauer's to see the horses shitting. My brother threw down a tin candlestick on the procession. Later to the Cathedral."[5] Or again: "On the 20th . . . around 10 o'clock it rained, with a pleasant stench; . . . the clouds lost themselves, the moon let itself be seen, and a fart was heard, giving hope of good weather on the next day for which we are all so anxious."[6] A zany, hyperbolic character surfaces in some of these entries, reminiscent of the style of the Bäsle letters.

> About shitting, my humble self, a jackass, a hernia, again a jackass, and finally a nose, went to church, stayed home with blow into my ass, blow into my ass, feeling a bit out of sorts. After lunch Catherl visited us and also Herr Foxtail, whose ass I thereupon licked to a turn, I did, O priceless ass—Doctor Barisani also came over, it rained the whole day.

This apparently meaningless passage turns out to be a code for a conventional diary entry, its meaning revealed by taking the first letters of the nouns in the German entry, so that, decoded, it reads, innocently: "Around 7:00 went to church. Papa stayed home, feeling a bit out of sorts. After lunch Catherl visited us, also Herr Fiala."[7] Here, as in several similar passages in Mozart's letters from Munich, there is also a note of carnivalesque defiance, flouting authority by encoding the names of the powerful in a string of obscenities, the archbishop naturally taking pride of place among these. In Mozart's diary entry, his own father is not neglected as an object of encoded ridicule, with "Papa" represented inelegantly by "*Pf*eif mir im *a*rsch, *pf*eif mir im *a*rsch."

Were it not for such aggressively obscene eruptions, we might imagine that Mozart was quite at peace with the world, as in a multilingual entry for August 62 (26) 1780:

> Den 62:^ten apud die contessine de Lodron. Alle dieci e demie war ich in templo Posteà chés le signore von Mayern. post prandium la sig^ra Catherine chés uns. Wir habemus joués colle carte di Tarock. À sept heur siamo andati spatzieren in den horto aulica. Faceva la plus pulchar tempestas von der Welt.

> The 62nd. At Countess Lodron's. Around 10:30 to church. Then with the von Mayr women. After lunch Catherl visited us. We played tarok. Around 7:00 o'clock we went for a walk in the court garden. It was the most beautiful weather in the world.[8]

And indeed, viewed from Salzburg's standpoint, Mozart's life there did have an idyllic cast. "Everyone is longing to see you again!" his father had written, telling how, in anticipation of his return, Count Firmian offered him the use of his horses, and Dr. Prex his "beautiful chestnut mare," and the cook Theresa—who loved Mozart dearly—was eager to prepare the many capons "which have been ordered in advance to celebrate your return."[9] "What more could you want?" asked Leopold Mozart, and did not wait for an answer. As in earlier days, Mozart moved in a wide circle of friends—fellow musicians, connoisseurs, and aristocrats—and participated in the family's regular rounds of visits, cardplaying, skittles, air-gun contests, musical performances, and theatergoing. His duties at court, although extensive—combining the posts of organist and concertmaster at both court and cathedral, with some additional services as keyboard teacher to the choirboys in the Kapellhaus[10]—were not especially onerous.

After the tumultuous love affairs with the Bäsle and Aloysia Weber, Mozart expressed some quietly romantic interest in Therese Barisani (born 1761), daughter of the court physician, to whom he had sent warm greetings in his letters as early as the Italian journeys. From Munich in late 1780, Mozart asked his sister to give "My most devoted greetings to Fräulein Therese von Barisani," who at that time had become Marianne's clavier pupil. "If I had a brother," he continued, "I should ask him to kiss her hands with the deepest respect, but as I have a sister, it is even better. So I ask her to embrace her most affectionately for me."[11] A few weeks later, Mozart asked, "Has my sister delivered those compliments?" and again, "My greetings to all my good friends, and particularly to your beautiful and clever pupil."[12] Finally, Marianne responded: "I have delivered your message to my beautiful pupil, who sends you her greetings in return."[13] Despite these affectionate exchanges, when Therese Barisani disappeared from Mozart's letters in early 1781, she did so without leaving any permanent imprint, let alone any deep sense of loss.

Mozart was able to maintain a steady level of productivity during 1779 and 1780, but in a fairly restricted array of genres. His orchestral works included three symphonies—the Symphony in G, K. 318, the three-movement Symphony in B-flat, K. 319, to which he added a Minuet movement later on, in Vienna, and the Symphony in C, K. 338, which is dated 29 August 1779; the "Posthorn" Serenade in D for winds and strings, K. 320, dated 3 August 1779 (given its date, intended probably for graduation ceremonies at the university); the Divertimento in D, K. 334/320b for strings and horns, written for the Robinig family; and the Sinfonia Concertante in E-flat for violin, viola, and orchestra, K. 364/320d. There is no chamber music from this period, except perhaps one violin sonata, in B-flat, K. 378/317d, which belongs either to 1779 or 1781, and there is only one keyboard concerto, the Concerto for two pianos in E-flat, K. 365/316a. As court organist he wrote Church Sonatas, K. 328/317c, 329/317a, and 336/336d, and several masses, the "Coronation" Mass in C, K. 317, completed in March 1779 and arguably his finest Salzburg composition in this genre, and the Missa solemnis in C, K. 337, of the following year. Other major church works included two vespers, *Vesperae de Dominica,* K. 321, of 1779 and *Vesperae solennes de confessore,* K. 339, of 1780. His only two theater works during this Salzburg period were the unfinished exotic singspiel *Zaide,* K. 344/336b, which he worked on from 1779 through the summer of 1780, and a revision of incidental music for a drama, *Thamos, König in Ägypten,* K. 345/336a, begun several years earlier.[14]

Documented public performances of music by Mozart were less frequent than in the earlier Salzburg years, and several of these were of older works, e.g., the Litany, K. 243, given at the cathedral on 30 March 1779, and the "Haffner" Serenade, K. 250/248b, played on 24 September 1779 in the Kollegienplatz and again at a concert probably held at the Tanzmeistersaal in the Mozart residence on 18 March 1780. (That concert, surely given under Mozart's own direction, also included an aria either from *La finta giardiniera* or from *Zaide,* a "rondeau" [perhaps the Scene, K. 255] sung by a male soprano, and a finale "with trumpet and kettledrums," very possibly the closing movement of the "Posthorn" Serenade.)[15] Rounding out the meager list of his known performances were appearances at court on three successive days in early September 1780. On one of these days Marianne joined him in playing a concerto for two keyboards (either an arrangement of K. 242 or the newly composed Concerto in E-flat, K. 365/316a) and a Sonata for piano four hands in D, K. 381/123a. Presumably there were performances of his most recent orchestral and choral works, but the total was not an imposing one for a composer in his prime and a virtuoso of world rank.

Despite the surface amiability of his existence, Mozart was leading a life of anxious desperation, ever conscious of the enormous disparity between his powers and his opportunities. Not long before, he had expressed his supreme confidence in those powers; of the Elector Karl Theodor he wrote, "He has no idea what I can do," and suggested, "I am willing to submit to a test. Let him get together all the composers in Munich, let him even summon a few from Italy, France, Germany, England, and Spain. I undertake to compete with any of them in composition."[16] He felt his calling as a composer and despaired that his gifts were being wasted. To be a teacher in the salons of the wealthy, a fiddler in the orchestra, an organist in the choir loft, or even a keyboard virtuoso in the concert halls and palaces of the nobility aroused in Mozart a mixture of anger and resentment because he felt that his abilities were being held in check.

Mozart's great ambition was to be a composer, and, in particular, a composer of operas, for the theater was in his blood. "I have an inexpressible longing to write another opera," he had once written to his father, trying to make him understand the depth of his hunger. "I am happier when I have something to compose, for that, after all, is my sole delight and passion. . . . I have only to hear an opera discussed, I have only to sit in a theater, hear the orchestra tuning their instruments—oh I am quite beside myself at once."[17] Even more urgently, he wrote, "Do not forget how much I desire to write operas. I envy anyone who is composing one. I could really weep for vexation when I hear or see an aria."[18] Nevertheless, he had not composed or staged an opera since La finta giardiniera in early 1775. He eagerly gravitated to the two theatrical troupes, headed respectively by Johann Heinrich Böhm and Emanuel Schikaneder, that successively took up residence in Salzburg during his last years there, for they offered a partial outlet for his theatrical passion. And he was not alone in his enthusiasm. "The rage for the theater" in Salzburg was such, reported Riesbeck, that Salzburgers "look for the coming of a company of strollers with as much eagerness as the inhabitants of Siberia look for the return of spring."[19] The archbishop, who had only recently closed down stages at the court and university, saw to it that his subjects were regularly supplied with theatrical productions by visiting companies at the 700-seat Ballhaus, which was reconstructed and reopened on the Hannibalplatz in September 1775. Böhm's company was resident in Salzburg in April and May 1779 and then for a full season, from September 1779 to March 1780; Schikaneder's company was there for the following season, from mid-September 1780 until the end of February 1781. Inasmuch as Mozart left Salzburg for Munich in early November 1780 he missed much of Schikaneder's season, his only musical contribution to the troupe being a single recitative and aria. His association with Böhm was far more enterprising.

Böhm's company, which gave three or four performances per week, numbered more than forty performers, augmented by local musicians who formed a theater orchestra consisting of strings, oboes or flutes, bassoons, horns, and sometimes trumpets and timpani. Its programs were devoted almost exclusively to theatrical works with music, including singspiels and light operas, as well as numerous translations of French operettas and a sprinkling of comedies, tragedies, and dramas without music. It presented plays by, among others, Shakespeare, Corneille, Voltaire, Goldoni, Gozzi, Marmontel, Gottlieb Stephanie, and Johann Jakob Engel, and musical works by Gluck, Piccini, Philidor, and Guglielmi, with multiple offerings by Grétry, Monsigny, and Paisiello.[20]

It was for Böhm that Mozart revised and expanded his incidental music for Gebler's *Thamos, König in Ägypten,* the choruses for which had been drafted as early as 1773 and the instrumental pieces in ca. 1777. Apparently Böhm never performed *Thamos,* but over the years he used its music with Karl Martin Plümicke's play *Lanassa,* and Mozart himself heard it performed in September 1790 in Frankfurt. *Zaide* (originally titled *Das Serail, oder, die unvermutete Zusammenkunft in der Sclaverey zwischen Vater, Tochter und Sohn*), K. 344/336b, to a libretto by Schachtner after a play by Friedrich Josef Sebastiani, may also have been composed for Böhm's troupe—though more likely it was intended to win Emperor Joseph's approval for the Viennese National Singspiel—but it, too, was neither completed nor performed.[21] These two stage works are known primarily for their anticipations of *Die Zauberflöte* and *Die Entführung aus dem Serail* respectively. A fulfilled collaboration was Böhm's production of Mozart's 1775 opera *La finta giardiniera* in a German translation titled *Die Gärtnerin aus Liebe;* it was first presented in Augsburg on 1 May 1780 and, under various titles, became a fixture in Böhm's repertory. Mozart's Augsburg cousin, the Bäsle, served as his intermediary with Böhm during the preparation of the performance (which Mozart did not attend). He wrote to her, "It is now a fortnight since I replied to M. Böhm. . . . Give him a thousand greetings. Tell him that as soon as I get a sign from him, he shall have his aria. . . . Well, my dear, you too are probably going to the theater every day, hail, rain and sunshine, the more so as you have free entry."[22]

In Salzburg, the members of the Mozart family had passes to

Schikaneder's performances, for his was a generous and friendly nature. Soon after his arrival in September 1780 he became a fixture of the Mozart circle, participating with them in their shooting and skittles parties, being selected as "Bestgeber" (bestower of the prize) for at least one of the air-gun contests, and being made the affectionate object of satire within the group. He was present at a concert of 13 December 1780 at the Tanzmeistersaal in which several of Mozart's sonatas were played by Marianne and the violinist Sieger. Upon Mozart's departure for Munich, his father remembered Schikaneder warmly, "Why, that honest fellow ran after the mail coach in order to say good-bye to you when you left."[23] Mozart promised Schikaneder an aria and Leopold Mozart felt so indebted to him that he urged his son, even when he was extraordinarily busy composing *Idomeneo* against an imminent deadline, to complete it. (The aria, K. 365a/Anh. 11a, now lost, was used in *Schlaflose Nächte,* based on a play by Gozzi.)

Schikaneder's troupe, which numbered thirty-four and gave four performances per week, offered quite different theatrical fare from Böhm's players. Of its ninety-three performances, only thirteen were of singspiels or music dramas, these composed by Piccini, Umlauf, Hiller, E. R. Duni, Georg Benda, and Schikaneder himself, who wrote words and music of the popular *Das lustige Elend oder die drei Bettelstudenten*—also given as *Die Lyranten (The Minstrels).* Although the repertory leaned heavily on broad comedies and plays on exotic subjects—*Die indianische Wittwe, Englands Spion, Die Westindier, Das Winterquartier in Amerika, Soliman der Zweite*—it also featured Lessing's *Emilia Galotti* and translations of *Hamlet, Macbeth,* and *King Lear* and of Italian plays by Gozzi, Goldoni, and Metastasio. Among the most frequently staged were works by lesser German playwrights such as G. F. W. Grossmann, Johann Christian Brandes, Stephanie, Gemmingen, Paul Weidmann, and Schikaneder.[24] Each night also featured a ballet, often on a mythological theme, drawn from a repertory of several dozen. The troupe's greatest success was the tragedy *Agnes Bernauer* by Count Törring, which had its premiere on 18 January 1781 before a packed house with two hundred turned away; it grossed 186 florins, and was repeated five times. And there was one disastrous flop, *Rache für Rache (Revenge for Revenge),* which according to Marianne was so dreary that most of the audience, starting with the archbishop, had departed well before it ground to a weary conclusion.

It was within this strolling-player tradition that Mozart learned much about stagecraft from two of the era's foremost directors and glimpsed the potentialities of an indigenous musical theater built upon French and Italian models, one that would expand the traditional audiences for operatic performances, that would serve as a vehicle for bourgeois and aristocratic tastes alike. Certainly the desire to contribute to the formation of a popular national theater, which he expresses so strongly in later years in Vienna, is already implicit in his projects for the Böhm troupe. Mozart's great ambition, however, remained to be a composer of Italian opera, and to this end he had been seeking commissions outside Salzburg. His main efforts centered on Munich, which now had replaced Mannheim as the seat of the Palatinate, where Elector Karl Theodor and his musical-theatrical retinue (which included many Mozart advocates, including Christian Cannabich and Count Seeau) were in residence.

The result was the commission for *Idomeneo*, issued in the late summer of 1780, the opera to be presented in January 1781. The subject was chosen by the Munich court, and Mozart engaged Abbate Gianbattista Varesco, court chaplain in Salzburg, to prepare an Italian-language libretto after *Idomenée*, a French lyric tragedy by Antoine Danchet that had been set to music by André Campra in 1712 and last revived in 1731. Mozart started work on the opera in October and left for Munich on 5 November 1780, having obtained a six-week leave to complete the opera and supervise its production. Leopold Mozart acted as his intermediary with Varesco in Salzburg to complete and revise the libretto and then to supervise Schachtner, who was to render a German translation to be printed alongside the Italian.

Once again, we can sense Mozart's elation at leaving Salzburg, his readiness to confront fresh challenges and opportunities. "My arrival here was happy and pleasant—happy, because no mishap occurred during the journey; and pleasant, because we could hardly wait for the moment to reach our destination, on account of our drive, which though short was most uncomfortable. . . . Why, that carriage jolted the very souls out of our bodies—and the seats were as hard as stone! . . . I really believed that I should never bring my behind to Munich intact. It became quite sore and no doubt was fiery red."[25] Within hours he was fully involved in Munich's cultural whirl, renewing his friendships with Count Seeau and the flutist Johann Becke, appraising singers, attending the Hoftheater, going to vocal concerts, enjoying his reunion with many Munich and Mannheim friends even as he prepared to complete his opera. "I had almost forgotten my best news," he writes. "Last Sunday after the service Count Seeau presented me en passant to His Highness the Elector, who was very gracious to me and said: '*I am glad to see you here again.*' On my replying that I would do my best to retain the good opinion of His Highness, he clapped me on the shoulder and said: '*Oh, I have no doubt whatever that all will go well.*' "[26] Mozart commented to his father, "*A piano piano, si va lontano*" ("Slow and sure wins the race").

Clearly, then, Mozart's aim from the start was to use the commission to obtain a position in Munich. To bolster his prospects, he apparently assembled a portfolio of other works to bring with him, just as he had on earlier trips to Munich and Vienna. Probably, the main compositions in the portfolio were two mature masterpieces—the Divertimento in D, K. 334/320b, and the Sinfonia Concertante, K. 364/320d, plus the Symphony in C, K. 338, with its brilliant opening fanfare.[27] After his arrival, hoping to display additional strengths as a composer of sacred music, he requested scores of several of his masses, probably K. 317 and K. 337, plus the Mass in B-flat, K. 275/272b, for he knew he could easily improve on Munich's current religious fare: "I should also like people to hear some of my compositions in this style. I have heard only one mass by [Italian composer Paul] Grua. Things like this one could easily turn out at the rate of half a dozen a day."[28]

The actuality of being in Munich, attending the brilliantly illuminated Residenztheater, watching beautifully mounted ballets, attending recitals by leading artists, and writing a major opera for a fine company and a great orchestra only heightened Mozart's desire to leave Salzburg. And Elector Karl Theodor's favorable remarks after the second and third rehearsals stimulated Mozart's most optimistic hopes: "After the first act the Elector called out to me quite loudly, Bravo! When I went up to kiss his hand he said: '*This opera will be charming and cannot fail to do you honor.*'"[29] Mozart was delighted to learn that on the next day the elector communicated his enthusiasm to whomever he met: "I have heard too from a very good source that on the same evening after the rehearsal he spoke of my music to everyone with whom he conversed, saying: '*I was quite surprised. No music has ever made such an impression on me. It is magnificent music.*'"[30]

His son's brilliant prospects did not raise Leopold Mozart's spirits. On the twentieth of November he wrote a doleful letter, implicitly blaming Mozart for his aches and pains, his melancholy state of mind, and his distress: "You no longer need to sleep in a cold room. I now must again have medical attention and with 61 years on my shoulders and although I simultaneously for several days have had a bad cold, must constantly drink barley water, take hot foot baths. . . . Enough! So long as it goes—it goes! On this earth I will not have the good fortune to live out my life in peace and without cares, least of all my last days, to live them out with pleasure, although and notwithstanding that I have earned it."[31] He closed his letter with a morbid and guilt-inducing reference to Mozart's mother and his own sorrow: "*Tomorrow is the anniversary of my wedding-day,* which is now but a sad memory—a thing you will not understand—for the present!"[32]

"Pray do not write any more melancholy letters to me," Mozart answered, "for I really need at the moment a cheerful spirit, a clear head and an inclination to work, and one cannot have these when one is sad at heart."[33] But at the same time he was unable to suppress his terrible inner conviction that he had somehow failed his father:

> I know and, God knows, I deeply feel how much you deserve rest and peace, but am I the obstacle?—I would not willingly be so and yet—alas! I fear I am. But—if I attain my object—if I succeed in getting a good appointment here, then you must leave Salzburg immediately. You will say—that will never be. At all events, industry and effort will not be wanting on my part.[34]

Mozart still carried the heavy weight of a responsibility to care for his father and to keep him free of melancholy. He tried to calm Leopold's constant fears that they were surrounded by enemies: "Do not worry, dearest father, about my opera. I trust that all will go well. No doubt it will be attacked by a small cabal, who in all probability will be covered with ridicule; for the most distinguished and influential families of the nobility are in my favor, and the leading musicians are one and all for me."[35] Even now, he renewed his pledge to relocate the family to the place of his new appointment. Thus, the contentious issues had not changed very much in two years, except in one fundamental respect: it was now clear that Leopold Mozart had no intention of moving from Salzburg. He complains that he no longer has the strength or the inclination to work; he wants both to be taken care of and to live out his last days in peace and quiet, i.e., in Salzburg. He doesn't want to hear about Mozart leaving home. His son's obstinacy and discontent are bidding to disrupt an altogether satisfactory existence, for Leopold is perfectly content to remain where he is, comforted by his son's presence and earning power.

Ignoring what had inspired Mozart's complaint, Leopold responded testily, "You ask me not to send you any melancholy news. Why, all I said was that your sister was ill, and surely I had to tell you that. Well, be honest and do not worry about me. But should you fall ill, *which God forbid,* do not hide it from me, so that I may come at once and look after you."[36] Angered by Mozart's request that he desist from burdening him with his cares, he conjured up a fantasy of rescuing his son from mortal danger, and this caused him to recall his wife's death, and then to revive the old matricidal charge: "If I had been with your mother during her illness, she might still be alive; but no doubt her hour had come and so I had to be absent."[37] Thus was Mozart reminded of what he owed his father.

Mozart made no reply and for several weeks his letters avoided troublesome matters, focusing instead on the progress of *Idomeneo.* At last, however, as his leave from the archbishop was about to expire, he could no longer suppress his deep yearning for breathing space and openly avowed that he could not bear the prospect of returning to Salzburg.

> Next Monday [18 December] I shall have been away from Salzburg for six weeks. You know, my dear father, that it is only to please you that I am staying on there, since, by Heaven, if I had followed my inclination, before leaving the other day I would have wiped my behind with my last contract, for I swear to you on my honor that it is not Salzburg itself but the Prince and his conceited nobility who become every day more intolerable to me. Thus I should be delighted, were he to send me word in writing that he no longer required my services; for with the great patronage which I now have here, both my present and future position would be sufficiently safeguarded. . . . But I would do anything in the world to please you. Yet it would be less trying to me, if I could occasionally clear out for a short time, just to draw breath. You know how difficult it was to get away this time: and without some very urgent cause, there would not be the slightest chance of such a thing happening again. To think of it is enough to make one weep. . . . Join me in Munich soon—and hear my opera—and then tell me whether it is wrong of me to be sad when I think of Salzburg![38]

In his letter of the eighteenth, Leopold assiduously avoided alluding to this outburst, saying only, "As to the *six weeks' leave of absence* I shall reply by the next post."[39] He did not want to hear about Mozart's dissatisfaction with Salzburg. And thereafter, until the end of Mozart's stay in Munich, there were no further laments or complaints on either side. Immediately after his outburst, Mozart assured his father, "You will have noticed from my letters that I am well and happy. One is indeed glad to be rid of such a great and laborious task—and—that, too, with honor and glory. For the work is almost finished."[40] Subsequent letters are filled with reports about his daily routine, rehearsals, and compositional activities, with much joshing back and forth. Leopold reported that the archbishop has cut his finger and Mozart responded with mock concern, "Thank God that the cut in the Archbishop's finger was of no consequence. Heavens! How frightened I was at first."[41] Mozart signaled, using a bawdy encoded passage, that Countess Baumgarten is the "favourite" of the elector: "It is she who has a *fox's* tail sticking out of her *a*ss and, oh *v*anity, an *o*dd-looking watch-chain hanging *u*nder her ear and a fine *r*ing; *I* have seen it myself, though death should *t*ake me, unfortunate fellow, without a nasal *e*xtremity, sapienti pauca."[42] Father and son look forward to a reunion: "I hope that we shall soon be able to have some fun together," Mozart wrote.[43]

Leopold Mozart becomes compulsively concerned that Mozart has caught cold, and gives him detailed medical advice. "*Keep yourself warm,* don't drink any wine, and before sleep take a little black powder with a small knife's point full of Margraf powder along with it, have tea for breakfast but no coffee."[44] In a letter of 4 December he goes on at great length and in extraordinary detail about pharmaceutical matters, signing this lengthy excursus "*ita Clarissimus Dominus Doctor Leopoldus Mozartus,*" and ending with, "Take care! *Rest now and then when you are composing!* Go to bed early! Do not catch cold! Perspire a little every morning! Be careful with your diet! Good night!"[45] In several letters he tells Mozart a cautionary tale about the castrato Ceccarelli, who pretended that he had left Salzburg "because he does not want to help his poor father and prefers to spend his money on an unnecessary number of clothes and, as you know, on all kinds of silly trifles."[46] In other letters he jests somewhat inappropriately about sexual matters, in one volunteering to act as Marianne's substitute in embracing Therese Barisani on Mozart's behalf, in another implying that he is aroused by her presence: "Now is the great question, whether it was the . . . *elderblossom* tea or *Therese Barisani* which drove out the perspiration, or whether I have both of these desirable agencies to thank?"[47] He tells of a visit from Madame Maresquelle—an actress in Schikaneder's company—to congratulate him on his name day, and how he was overcome with embarrassment when she held out her cheek to be kissed: "I felt as bashful as I did in my youth when I kissed a woman for the first time, or when after the ball in Amsterdam the women forced me to kiss them."[48] He has lost his sense of the physical boundaries between himself and his children, jesting about subjecting his testicles to the rigors of the bumpy road to Munich: "I shall certain not travel by mail coach, for I am rather careful of my two damson stones," he writes;[49] and as his and Marianne's departure for the opera premiere nears: "Your sister and I can sleep in the alcove and you can sleep outside. Why, we can live like gypsies and soldiers." He seems oblivious to any possible need for modest seclusion on her part.[50] (Mozart had offered, "I have a large alcove in my bedroom which has two beds. These would do capitally for you and me.")[51]

In their exchanges about the libretto of *Idomeneo* we see Mozart and his father at their best, collaborating easily and intelligently, both deeply interested in exploring and solving issues of characterization and dramatic action. Their letters breathe a sense of joyous creative collaboration and eager anticipation of the premiere. Clearly, Leopold had a large emotional investment in his work on the libretto—when Mozart decided to shorten a section, he objected that Idomeneo and his son Idamante "should not recognize one another too quickly. And now you want to make it ridiculous by making them recognize one another after they have exchanged only a few words."[52] The older composer even showed a touch of competitiveness, or at least of wanting to participate in the composition of the work. "I assume that you will choose very deep wind instruments to accompany the subterranean voice. How would it be if after the slight subterranean rumble the instruments *sustained, or rather began to sustain, their notes piano and then made a crescendo such as might almost inspire terror, while after this and during the decrescendo the voice would begin to sing?* And there might be a terrifying crescendo at *every phrase uttered by the voice.* . . . Why, I seem to see and hear it."[53] Mozart responded laconically to this suggestion: "The accompaniment to the subterranean voice consists of five instruments only, that is, three trombones and two French horns, which are placed in the same quarter as that from which the voice proceeds. At this point the whole orchestra is silent."[54]

Title page of piano arrangement, *Idomeneo, rè di Creta*, K. 366. Breitkopf & Härtel, 1798. Music Collection of the Österreichische Nationalbibliothek, Vienna, S. A.67.A.33.

By a curious process of substitution, the issue of Mozart's musical style had come to stand for the fundamental, disquieting issue of separation. Over the years, Leopold repeatedly urged Mozart to write conventional and popular music, to compose in the preexistent styles rather than in learned or experimental ones. Leopold's advocacy of the "popular style" was scarcely a new development; in Mannheim several years earlier he suggested that if Mozart obtained a commission for a German opera he ought

"to imitate the natural and popular style, which everyone easily understands. The grand and sublime style is suited to grand subjects. Everything
in its place."[55] This may have been reasonable enough advice. But when
Mozart arrived in Paris, his father hastened to advise him to *be guided by
the French taste. If you can only win applause and be well paid,* let the devil
take the rest."[56] Lest he be misunderstood, he reiterated, "I implore you,
before you write for the French stage, to listen to their operas and find out
what above all pleases them. Well, you will now become a thorough
Frenchman and you will endeavor, I hope, to acquire the correct accent."[57]
He wrote straightforwardly, "Your object is to make a name for yourself
and to get money."[58]

Although Mozart often indeed followed similar advice, he responded
defiantly on this occasion, for this philistinism touched the core issue of his
artistic individuality, his capacity for originality, his ability to create something that had never previously existed, and thereby to express his personal
feelings, social perspectives, and aesthetic principles. Concerning his just-
finished Symphony, K. 297/300a ("Paris"), he wrote, "I cannot say whether
it will be popular—and, to tell the truth, I care very little, for who will not
like it? I can answer for its pleasing the few intelligent French people who
may be there—and as for the stupid ones, I shall not consider it a great
misfortune if they are not pleased. I still hope, however, that even asses will
find something in it to admire."[59] His father was far from persuaded, and
not long thereafter he reformulated his argument against "difficult" or
arcane music in terms of aesthetic principle rather than commercial interest. He recommended that Mozart seek out an engraver and furnish him
with some easy chamber music:

> Let it be something short, easy and popular. . . . Do you imagine that you
> would be doing work unworthy of you? If so, you are very much mis-
> taken. Did [J. C.] Bach, when he was in London, ever publish anything
> but similar trifles? *What is slight can still be great,* if it is written in a natural,
> flowing and easy style—and at the same time bears the marks of sound
> composition. . . . Did Bach lower himself by such work? Not at all. Good
> composition, sound construction, il filo—these distinguish the master
> from the bungler—even in trifles.[60]

And now, even as Mozart was completing his first operatic masterpiece, Leopold Mozart again proposed that he not aim too high: "I advise
you when composing to consider not only the musical, but also *the unmusical public,*" he wrote. "You must remember that to every *ten real connoisseurs*
there are a *hundred ignoramuses.* So do not neglect the so-called *popular* style,
which tickles *long ears.*"[61] What seems to have prompted this highly inap-

propriate advice at this particular juncture was a letter from Leopold's Munich friend, the flutist Becke, who after hearing the rehearsal of Act I of *Idomeneo* wrote to Leopold (who transmitted the report to Mozart) that "*tears of joy and delight came into his eyes when he heard it, and that all the performers maintained that this was the most beautiful music they had ever heard, that it was all new and strange and so forth.*"[62] In all his admonitions to avoid the "new and strange," as in his maneuvering to keep Mozart in Salzburg, even in a relatively minor post, Leopold Mozart pressed his son to settle for considerably less than his potentialities. In order to keep him by his side he did not shrink from holding him back. Of course, it is clear that he was trying to impose his own limited neoclassic aesthetic upon his son, and it seems likely as well that he had decidedly mixed feelings about his son's having transcended his own accomplishments. But his advocacy of conventional styles was not simply a matter of generational competitiveness between a father and his son. Leopold Mozart had long understood that Mozart's rebelliousness had to be held in check everywhere it showed itself: in his music, his erotic life, or his career ambitions. A breach in any of these areas would eventually undermine his willingness to submit to the family mythology.

On 26 January 1781, Mozart's father and sister arrived in Munich, where they joined several other Salzburgers who had arrived earlier to celebrate Mozart's opera—for, on the basis of the rehearsals, it was already anticipated that *Idomeneo* would be a triumphal event. The dress rehearsal took place on the twenty-seventh and the opera had its first performance on the twenty-ninth at the Residenztheater under Cannabich's direction, with repeat performances given on 3 February and 3 March. No letters, diaries, or serious reviews describe the work's performance and reception. A Munich newspaper praised the scenery and reported that "the text, music and translation—all are by natives of Salzburg," but neglected to give the composer's name.[63] A report in a Bavarian literary annual wrote, "The music for this season is by the younger Herr Mozzard of Salzburg."[64] There is much else that we do not know about the aftermath of the *Idomeneo* premiere: how the Mozarts participated in carnival festivities in Munich or how they spent three days in nearby Augsburg between 7 and 10 March. Above all, we don't know why Mozart's expectations of a Munich post were not fulfilled, whether the elector ultimately found him wanting or whether he himself drew back from taking a decisive step. Once again, it seemed, his strivings had ended in a deadlock. Or perhaps he had already decided on another course, one that he could not yet openly acknowledge.

Now Mozart rested from his exertions and pondered his options: *Idomeneo* had been almost his sole compositional preoccupation for four months; his only other confirmed Munich works were two Lieder, K. 349/367a and K. 351/367b, the Soprano Scene, "Misera, dove son!"—"Ah! non son' io che parlo," K. 369, and the Oboe Quartet in F, K. 370/368b, written for Friedrich Ramm in early 1781. Einstein believes that another Soprano Scene, "Ma che vi fece, o stelle"—"Sperai vicino il lido," K. 368, was intended for the Munich singer Elisabeth Wendling, but Plath places it earlier, in Salzburg.[65] The Serenade for winds in B-flat, K. 361/370a ("Gran Partita"), once thought to have been started in Munich and completed in Vienna, is now assigned by Tyson entirely to the early Vienna years.[66] To complete this diminished picture of Mozart's Munich productivity, Tyson also conjectures that the great Kyrie in D minor, K. 341/368a, for which no autograph exists, may have been written during Mozart's later Vienna years and not in Munich, as previously thought.[67]

On 12 March Mozart left Munich for Vienna at the behest of the archbishop, who had gone to Vienna with part of his retinue to visit his ailing father and who wanted to show off the abilities of his musicians to the Viennese nobility. On the same day, Mozart's father and sister set out for Salzburg along with Leopold's young student, Heinrich Marchand, the son of Theobald Marchand, who directed the German court theater under Elector Karl Theodor. Mozart arrived in Vienna on 16 March 1781 after a four-day journey. He would live there for the remaining decade of his life.

VIENNA

The Michaelerplatz with view of the old Burgtheater, Vienna, ca. 1783.
Engraving by Karl Schütz. Historiches Museum der Stadt Wien,
inv. no. 51.611.

15

....

ARRIVAL

From the moment of his arrival in Vienna, Mozart was in a state of agitation, for he was attempting once again to steel himself to take a decisive, irreversible action. He was sensitive to perceived slights, complaining, even belligerent: feeling maltreated, he was ready to fight. Perhaps he had already made up his mind to leave the service of Archbishop Hieronymus Colloredo and was only seeking a suitable pretext to justify his decision. Perhaps he needed to convince himself—and his father—that the defense of honor, not self-interest, was his guiding purpose. Everywhere he looked he found reasons to believe that Archbishop Colloredo was an unworthy ruler, benighted, parsimonious, and unjust. Mozart wanted extra compensation for his appearances in the salons of the aristocrats where the archbishop had placed on display his best musicians—Mozart, the castrato Ceccarelli, and the violinist Antonio Brunetti—as testimony to his connoisseur's taste. On the very day of his arrival in Vienna, 16 March 1781, Mozart took part in a concert before an audience consisting of twenty members of the highest nobility, and on the next day the archbishop's players performed for the Russian ambassador, Prince Dmitri Galitzin. Before the month was out Mozart gave at least two more performances, one at the home of Privy Councillor Johann Gottlieb von Braun and one at the residence of the archbishop's father, Prince Rudolf Colloredo. On 8 April, a second concert there featured three new compositions by Mozart: the Rondo in C for violin and orchestra, K. 373, played by Brunetti; a Scene for male soprano, "A questo seno deh vieni"—"Or che il cielo," K. 374, performed by Ceccarelli; and the Violin Sonata in G, K. 379/373a, with Mozart at the keyboard.

"I shall go to the Archbishop," wrote Mozart to his father as early as 17 March, "and tell him with absolute frankness that if he will not allow me to earn anything, then he must pay me, for I cannot live at my own expense."[1] But this was somewhat exaggerated, for Mozart received four and five ducats, respectively, from the archbishop and Prince Colloredo following two of these appearances, and there may have been additional gifts from other nobles. Furthermore, Mozart claimed that his freedom of access to potential Viennese patrons was being severely limited, with the archbishop acting as "a *screen* to keep me from the notice of others."[2] He was frustrated that he could not accept an invitation to the residence of Maria Wilhelmine, Countess Thun, for there, he claimed, he not only could have earned fifty ducats but could have met the emperor, who was in attendance: "My chief object here is to introduce myself to the Emperor in some becoming way, for I am absolutely determined that he shall *get to know me*. I should love to run through my opera [*Idomeneo*] for him and then play a lot of fugues, for that is what he likes."[3]

Not unreasonably, though, the archbishop didn't want Mozart to give concerts for his own benefit, nor did he want him to perform indiscriminately, for that would dilute the effect of his appearances for the Salzburg court. Furthermore, well understanding Mozart's personal ambition and observing how he was visiting or lunching with various counts and countesses almost daily, the archbishop tried to prevent his reluctant employee from gaining a foothold among the movers and shakers of Viennese society. Accordingly, he refused permission for Mozart to participate in a charity concert for the Tonkünstler-Societät (Musicians' Society) and when permission was eventually granted (under pressure, for "all the nobility" had "made a grievance" of it)[4] the composer felt no gratitude: "Well, how much do you suppose I should make if I were to give a concert of my own? . . . But this arch-booby of ours will not allow it."[5] Mozart bitterly calculated the money he was losing by virtue of his Salzburg employment: "The Archbishop is a great hindrance to me here, for he has done me out of at least a hundred ducats, which I would certainly have made by giving a concert in the theater."[6] Were he to leave the archbishop's service he would "give a grand concert, take four pupils, and in a year I should have got on so well in Vienna that I could make at least a thousand thalers a year."[7]

Increasingly, however, finding his father unmoved by estimates of the substantial sums to be earned in Vienna, Mozart relied less upon the economic argument than upon the appeal to honor. He showed great consciousness of class distinctions, complaining of being seated at table with the valets and cooks; he demanded an artist's respect, for he was unwilling to be treated like a common servant, as were his fellow musicians. Invited to a concert at Prince Dmitri Galitzin's, he "went there alone on purpose, because I really feel ashamed to go anywhere with them. When I got upstairs, I found Angerbauer [the archbishop's valet] standing there to direct the lackey to show me in. But I took no notice, either of the valet or the lackey, but walked straight on through the rooms into the music room, for all the doors were open—and went straight up to the Prince, paid my respects and stood there talking to him."[8] The negligent hauteur displayed by Beethoven in the presence of aristocratic arrogance is already character-istic of Mozart's demeanor as well. So in the letters justifying his resigna-tion from his post, Mozart stressed the humiliations and affronts he had endured, how he had been ordered about like a common servant, how the archbishop repeatedly heaped verbal indignities upon him, calling him "a rascal and a dissolute fellow," "the most dissolute fellow he knew," and "a scoundrel, a rascal, a vagabond," until at last "my blood began to boil, I could no longer contain myself and I said, 'So your Grace is not satisfied with me?' 'What, you dare to threaten me—you fool? There is the door! Look out, for I will have nothing more to do with such a miserable wretch.' At last I said: 'Nor I with you!' 'Well, be off!' When leaving the room, I said, 'This is final. You shall have it tomorrow in writing.' "[9] Mozart felt that his honor was now at stake: "I had twice played the cow-ard and I could not do so a third time."[10] A few days later he wrote, "I did not know that I was a valet—and that was the last straw."[11] At last, with the archbishop's "Well, be off!" he had obtained the necessary pretext: he could quit his position because—he would claim—he had been discharged.

The archbishop's chief chamberlain, Count Karl Joseph Felix Arco, tried to mediate the quarrel, refusing to accept Mozart's letter of resigna-tion or his tender of his traveling expenses for the return to Salzburg: "He refused to take either and assured me that I could not resign without your consent, my father."[12] Now for a full month Mozart endured the harshest recriminations from his father, who was resolved that his son's resignation must be rescinded. Mozart pleaded for his father's forbearance; he told how the stresses of his struggle with the archbishop had made him "very fever-ish" and how he "was trembling in every limb, and was . . . staggering along the street like a drunkard," so that he had to take to his bed. He begged for his father's acquiescence: "If you wish to see your son well and happy, you will say nothing to me about this affair and . . . you will bury it in the deepest oblivion," he wrote, cautioning, "for one word about it would suffice to embitter me again and—if you will only admit it—to fill you too with bitterness."[13] Again, a week later: "I implore you, I adjure you, by all you hold dear in this world, to strengthen me in this resolution instead of trying to dissuade me from it, for if you do you will only make me unproductive. My desire and my hope is to gain honor, fame, and money."[14] But, summoning up all his powers, Leopold Mozart was remorseless, for he recognized that Mozart's actions had brought them to the point of permanent separation.

None of Leopold's letters to Mozart following his removal to Vienna are preserved, but their contents are reflected in Mozart's own responses. The charges run the full gamut of recriminations: he accused his son of acting "merely out of hatred for Salzburg and an *unreasonable* love for Vienna," of once again allowing the now widowed, fatherless Webers—who had moved to Vienna and with whom Mozart was boarding—to ensnare him, and of abandoning his father (Mozart responded, "God knows how hard it is for me to leave you").[15] He reminded him of a financial debt (Mozart replied, "By the next occasion . . . I shall send you a sum with which to pay the debt to which you refer"),[16] and he insisted that Mozart must reverse his decision. Mozart responded to this onslaught on 19 May, stoutly defending himself.

> I must confess that there is not a single touch in your letter by which I recognize my father! I see a father, indeed, but not that most beloved and most loving father, who cares for his own honor and for that of his children—in short, not *my* father. But it must have been a dream. You are awake now and need no reply from me to your points in order to be fully convinced that—*now more than ever*—I can never abandon my resolve.[17]

He asserts that his father has "most cruelly assailed" his honor and character:

> You say that the only way to save my honor is to abandon my resolve. How can you perpetrate such a contradiction! . . . Such a recantation would prove me to be the basest fellow in the world. . . . Everyone knows that it was because my honor was insulted. . . . Am I to make myself out to be a cowardly sneak and the Archbishop a worthy prince? . . . You say that I have never shown you any affection and therefore ought now to show it for the first time. Can you really say this? You add that I will never sacrifice any of my pleasures for your sake. But what pleasures have I here? . . . You seem to think that I am reveling in pleasures and amusements.

And so that his father ought not to mistake his sensitivity for a lack of resolve, he repeats, in closing: "Dearest, most beloved father, ask of me what you will, only not that—anything but that—the mere thought of it makes me tremble with rage."[18]

The Salzburg authorities were unwilling to accept that Mozart's decision was irrevocable. Count Arco met with him and they discussed their differences "in a very calm tone and . . . without irritation on either side. In short, he put everything before me in so friendly a manner that really I

could have sworn that what he said came altogether from his heart."[19]
Mozart tried to make clear that no reconciliation could long endure, for
his dissatisfactions were so varied, but he ended up asking for more money
and hoping that "the Archbishop does not take me at my word."[20] Count
Arco then sought unsuccessfully to inform Mozart about the fickleness of
Viennese taste, warning him that "a man's reputation here lasts a very short
time."[21] The discussion turned acrid when Count Arco brought up
Leopold Mozart's name. "When he told me that you had written to him
and had complained bitterly about me, I immediately interrupted him and
said: '*And have I not heard from him too? He has written to me in such a strain
that I have often thought I should go crazy.*'"[22]

At last, at a meeting toward the end of May, Mozart's persistence in
demanding his written release from employment so provoked Count Arco
that he called him "clown" and "knave" and literally booted him out of
the room—"with a kick on his ass," Mozart reported to his father.[23] "So
now, the affair is at an end. . . . How easy it would have been to persuade
me to remain! By kindness, but not by insolence and rudeness."[24]
Exhausted, Mozart once again asked for an end to any further discussion
of the matter. "I am so sick of the whole affair that I never want to hear
anything more about it. . . . I implore you, dearest, most beloved father,
for the future to spare me such letters. I entreat you to do so, for they
only irritate my mind and disturb my heart and spirit; and I, who must
now keep on composing, need a cheerful mind and a calm disposition."[25]
Though he never reconciled himself to Mozart's actions, Leopold Mozart
now had to recognize that his son's permanent departure from Salzburg
was a fait accompli. With all his trembling and trepidation, with his evasions and equivocations, his pretexts and prevarications, Mozart had
finally broken the pattern of submission. Rejecting his father's "impossible" premise that he could leave Salzburg only if he were called to a great
post, and rejecting the archbishop's implication that he was not hardy
enough to endure the vacillations of Viennese taste, he had opted for a
free-lance musician's life in the Austrian capital. At last, at the age of
twenty-five, he was on his own, emotionally drained but eager to
demonstrate his mettle.

We understand better by now the ties that bound this son to his father.
Mozart had a fateful goodness rising from a sense of filial responsibility
similar to that which Goethe saw in Hamlet: "A beautiful, pure, noble, and
most moral nature, without the strength of nerve which makes the hero,
sinks beneath a burden which it can neither bear nor throw off; every duty
is holy to him—this too hard. The impossible is required of him—not the
impossible in itself, but the impossible to him."[26] Inevitably, one wants to

understand how Mozart was able to surmount these impossibilities at this particular moment of his life, after years of wavering, indecision, defeats, and repeated failures of nerve. (Mozart's task was harder than Hamlet's, who at least had his father's spectral authorization, whereas Mozart had to defy both his father and the head of state.) It was not merely a matter of opportunity, for Mozart had earlier enjoyed similar opportunities to begin an independent career in Mannheim, Munich, and Paris—indeed in Vienna as well, had he simply accepted Mesmer's offer of 1777–78. Partly, of course, it was a matter of readiness: with the passage of time had come a deepening sense of wasted months and years, and a vision of unfolding years spent in an endless repetition of futile Salzburg patterns. A lifetime of events that could be entered into his sister Marianne's homely diary was not what Mozart envisioned for himself. Certainly, the process of cumulative frustration—artistic and libidinal—had now brought him to a breaking point. For too long he had endured feelings of humiliation, been forced to give up his ambitions (even if his father was right that they were grandiose and utopian, even if they were only "gay dreams"), compelled to delay his fulfillment as a physical being, asked to temper his drive for originality of expression, urged to write in conventional styles, to regard the making of money and the tending of his family of origin as his life's goals.

Furthermore, through the alliance between his father and the Salzburg authorities (whose embodiment was Archbishop Colloredo) he was additionally asked to submit to unfair treatment by his employer. Mozart could not fathom this, or, rather, he could not understand how his father might fail to recognize the injustice of it: "So, for the sake of a malevolent Prince who plagues me every day and only pays me a lousy salary of four hundred florins, I am to kick away a thousand?"[27] This seemed so self-evident to him that he continued to ask the same question in different forms: "I am liked and respected by the greatest families. All possible honor is shown me and I am paid into the bargain. So why should I pine away in Salzburg for the sake of 400 florins? . . . What would be the end of it?"[28] Whatever the cost, he had always accepted the idea of allegiance to the family as an unassailable commandment. To sacrifice himself for the family was one thing—after all, it was his own family, to which he owed so much; but to be asked, even compelled, to sacrifice his manhood and his opportunities to the archbishop and his bureaucrats was quite another thing, objectifying the sense of unfairness that he could not fully permit himself to feel toward his own kin.

That his father should, in effect, subcontract Mozart's services to the archbishop and fail to perceive, let alone to protest, the unjustness of his treatment was bewildering to Mozart. He wanted to attribute it to fearfulness, so he asked his father to assert himself, to join him in resisting maltreatment with dignity, confronting tyranny without cringing. "I beg you, most beloved father, not to crawl too much [*zu viel zu kriechen*]."[29] Although the imputation of cowardice was transparent enough to be wounding, Mozart pursued it repeatedly: "You really are too fearful, and yet you have nothing whatever to fear. . . . All I insist on, and nothing else, is that you should show the whole world that you are not afraid. Be silent; but when it is necessary, speak—and speak in such a way that people will remember it."[30] Like all of us, Mozart wants a heroic father, one who scorns servility: "I can well believe that the Court flunkeys are eyeing you askance, but why should you worry about such miserable menials? The more hostile these people are to you, the more proudly and contemptuously you must treat them."[31] He wants his family to wear its superiority as he does, as a badge of honor; reckless of the consequences, he suggests that when performing at court his sister "*demand* two ducats" each time she plays. "For, as we have always been utterly different *in every way* from the other court musicians, I trust we shall be different in this respect too."[32] If he had known of it, he would have been pleased that in a letter of 10 August 1781 to Breitkopf & Son, Leopold Mozart loyally described the conflict with the archbishop from his son's point of view: "As His Grace the Prince treated my son extremely badly . . . he was easily persuaded to resign a service to which a miserable salary was attached, and to remain in Vienna."[33]

Much as he might resist acknowledging it, Mozart surely knew that it was not timorousness but his father's self-interest that drove his alliance with the archbishop. And that may be why feelings of humiliation and guilt were now giving way to a sense of rage, rage to which he could at last give full voice. He has been robbed—of time, of money, of love, of opportunity. His creative life has been shortened. He has been financially exploited, his body used to generate cash surpluses. He has been spiritually exploited, his mind used to generate reflected glory for others. His long-held resentment of the archbishop has for too long siphoned off the anger he felt against someone closer at hand. Now he has pierced the veil of the archbishop and seen behind it the features of his own father. When he cried out, in a lonely appeal to basic principles, that he has an "*undeniable right to leave him,*"[34] he was speaking, not only of the archbishop, but of his father. The merging of two oppressive images unleashed a great anger, which at last authorized him to renounce the family imperative.

It was a life-affirming, revolutionary step. Finally, Mozart had learned the concise language of the Great Refusal, learned to say no to patriarchal domination, to hierarchical injustice, to unfairness, exploitation, and subjection. He refused to shoulder an unreasonable burden of guilt; his letters resound with variations on the recurrent, heartfelt outcry, "It is *not* my fault, you *know* it is not my fault." Perhaps, too, he sensed, and no longer could countenance, the mounting danger to his creativity, which had sustained him until now, for his letters tell that his father's reproaches and melancholy complaints were having a destructive effect.

A volatile mixture of humiliation and rage contended with Mozart's desire to maintain a distanced, ironic sense of decorum. Later, of Osmin's rage in *Die Entführung aus dem Serail,* he observes, "For just as a man in such a towering rage oversteps all the bounds of order, moderation, and propriety and completely forgets himself, so must the music too forget itself." But then he draws back, fearful of overstepping the bounds of moderation, and affirms the need to hold on to some restraining principle: "Passions, whether violent or not, must never be expressed to the point of exciting disgust, and . . . music, even in the most terrible situations, must never offend the ear, but must please the listener . . . in other words must never cease to be *music.*"[35]

And so in the end Mozart's rage, having served its immediate purpose, was again internalized, reined in, channeled into a variety of alternative outlets. After all, who was there to understand his pain? Not his father, his mother, his sister, Bullinger, Grimm, nor the patriarchal legion of Leopold Mozart's friends who sympathized with a father's "natural" expectation to receive comfort and support from a pampered son. Nor could Mozart reveal his pain to his friends, for that would have been a betrayal of the family's solidarity. Instead, he reinstated older patterns of compromise, maintaining contact with his father, perpetuating archaic illusions—however frayed and tattered—that he would yet bring about a happy reunion of the family and dedicate himself to its support. To mitigate the pain he knew his father was feeling, and to assuage his own sense of guilt, he invited his father and sister to settle in Vienna. "There are many distinguished families here who hesitate to engage a male teacher, but would give handsome terms to a woman."[36] His indecision is quite on the surface: "There is enough for all three of us to live on"; but knowing his economic circumstances, he adds, "Still, I should prefer it if you could hold out for another year."[37]

In the face of these conflicts, Mozart's customary ironic reserve could not hold. Striving to make a living, energetically writing a major opera, Mozart was forced to defend himself against charges of all kinds, made on the basis of information provided to his father by informers and gossips. Stung into fury, he now declared himself impervious to his father's criticisms. "I am sorry to see that you rely more on the gossip and scribblings of other people than you do on me—and that in fact you have no trust in me whatever. But I assure you that all this does not disturb me; people may write themselves blind—and you may believe them as much as you please—but I shall not alter by a hair's breadth." Beyond temporizing, he continued, "I have trouble and worry enough here to support myself, and it therefore does not help me in the very least to read unpleasant letters."[38] Beyond despair, he bursts out that he had asked his father for clothes earlier in the year but they were not sent: "So I had to have some made, as I could not go about Vienna like a tramp. . . . My linen was a pitiful sight. . . . From all your letters I gather that you believe that I do nothing but amuse myself. Well, you are most dreadfully mistaken. I can truthfully say that I have no pleasure—none whatever—save that of being away from Salzburg."[39] Mozart no longer bothered to disguise the equation of "Salzburg" and "father." There was now, in Eibl's phrase, "serious bad blood" between father and son, ironically reinforced by Mozart's customary closing phrase, "your most obedient son."[40]

Mozart had breached the most inviolate family taboos, for which, in accordance with Leopold Mozart's pedagogical code, the child needed to be punished—by reminders of his moral lapses, predictions of failure, and, not least, withholding of paternal regard for his person and his work. Throughout, Leopold Mozart never relinquished the role of guardian of Mozart's moral behavior. Thus, although the issue of a permanent return to Salzburg did not arise again, recriminations spilled over into issues of sexuality, piety, and financial obligation. Leopold complained about Mozart's behavior with women, beginning, belatedly, with an incident that occurred during the Munich carnival in early 1781. "The only association which I had with the person of ill repute was at the ball," Mozart wrote in June, showing his extreme sensitivity about such issues, "and I talked to her long before I knew what she was, and solely because I wanted to be sure of having a partner for the contredanse. Afterwards I could not desert her all at once without giving her the reason; and who would say such a thing to a person's face? But in the end did I not on several occasions leave her in the lurch and dance with others? On this account too I was positively delighted when the carnival was over. Moreover, no one, unless he is a liar, can say that I ever saw her anywhere else, or went to her house."[41] Now he also had to assure his father that he was not romantically involved with Josepha Auernhammer, one of his clavier students.[42] "The young lady is a fright," Mozart contended, "but plays enchantingly, though in cantabile playing she has not got the real delicate singing style." He quoted Fräulein Auernhammer herself: "*I am no beauty—au contraire,* I am ugly. . . . So I prefer to remain as I am and to live by my talent."[43] Despite these assurances, it was not long before he had to confess that his pupil was indeed in love with him and that rumors were circulating "that we are to be married. . . . I know from a certain person that she confirmed the rumor. . . . This enraged me. . . . She is nothing but an amorous fool."[44] Under pressure to demonstrate his chastity, Mozart ends by displaying a streak of sexual nausea and revulsion: "If a painter wanted to portray the devil to the life, he would have to choose her face. She is as fat as a farm-wench, perspires so that you feel inclined to vomit, and goes about so scantily clad that really you can read as plain as print: '*Pray, do look here.*' True, there is enough to see, in fact, quite enough to strike one blind; but—one is thoroughly well punished for the rest of the day if one is unlucky enough to let one's eyes wander in that direction. . . . So loathsome, dirty and horrible!"[45] Clearly, Mozart was inciting his father to apoplexy by such descriptions as well as by further signs of his close connection to his amorous pupil—such as the dedication to her of the Six Violin Sonatas in C, F, F, B-flat, G, and E-flat (K. 296, 376/374d, 377/374e, 378/317d, 379/373a, and 380/374f), published at the end of November 1781 by Artaria & Co. as opus 2, and the joint concert he gave with her on 23 November in the presence of Vienna's elite.

One does not know whether to take Mozart's description of Fräulein Auernhammer at face value (later on, he will encourage his wife to believe that all the women in Dresden are unattractive), for he frequently resorts to sarcasm to fend off his father's wounding thrusts. About his religious observance, he wrote, "Do rest assured that I really hold to my religion; and should I ever have the misfortune (which God forbid!) to fall into evil courses, I shall absolve you, my most beloved father, from all responsibility."[46] Responding to his father's complaint of dizzy spells, he advises, with a straight face, "Get some cart-grease, wrap it in a bit of paper and wear it on your chest. Take the bone of a leg of veal and wrap it up in paper with a kreuzer's worth of leopard's bane and carry it in your pocket. I am sure that this will cure you."[47]

Once again, the issue of Mozart's supposed debt to his father was raised, but it no longer held its old power, for he knew that his salary for the past two years, let alone the fees for various performances and commissions, had been sufficient to liquidate the expenses of the Paris journey. After his return to Salzburg in January 1779, Mozart's salary had been controlled by his father, so that he had to apply to him for pocket money in Munich, and it seems clear that Mozart's earnings from *Idomeneo* in 1781 did not accompany him to Vienna.[48] Accordingly, he was now able to treat the subject with greater equanimity than formerly, turning aside his father's demands for money with repeated promises and a distancing irony. An early letter reminded his father with great directness, "Meanwhile, you are drawing two salaries and have not got to feed me. If I stay here, I can promise you that I shall soon be able to send home some money."[49] Virtually every subsequent letter home alluded to the obligation, and perhaps to some further alleged obligation stemming from his resignation from the archbishop's service: "My duty now is to make good and to replace by my care and industry what you think you have lost by this affair."[50] In June he wrote that he had sent "a small sum"—thirty ducats—by messenger, but subsequent letters show that the messenger somehow departed without the money, that Mozart either had difficulty raising the sum or some resistance to sending it, and that the amount was eventually reduced to twenty ducats. It is even possible that Mozart never actually sent any money, for in September he wrote: "It is certainly not my fault, my dearest father, that you have not yet had any money from me; it is due to the present bad season," adding, in a phrase calculated to infuriate, "Only have patience—I, too, have to cultivate it."[51]

It is doubtful that Mozart inwardly conceded that he owed his father any money, and that may be why his letters managed to avoid describing his Vienna earnings in detail. Perhaps, taking a cue from Leopold's own practice, he didn't want his father to know what he was making from performances in July at the summer residence of Count Cobenzl in the Reisenberg, from salon appearances at the palaces of Countess Maria Wilhelmine Thun-Hohenstein and Archduke Maximilian Franz, from the Auernhammer concert, and from the subscription sales to the opus 2 Violin Sonatas. It was only at the end of December, when he needed to persuade his father that he had a sufficient income to marry, that he disclosed some details of his teaching income—although omitting any mention of income from Auernhammer's lessons—and casually mentioned that he had just received fifty ducats from the emperor for his joint appearance with Muzio Clementi at court on 24 December.

Now, he was in a quandary: to acknowledge that he was doing well raised the question of why he failed to send money to his father; that is why, in the same breath he revealed that he "was sent fifty ducats," he added, "and indeed I need them very badly at the moment."[52] On the other hand, to acknowledge that he was strapped for money was to be found financially unsuited for marriage. Leopold had thereby been handed a powerful lever with which to command Mozart's attention: the withholding of his consent to his son's marriage to Constanze Weber. To be rejected by Mozart's family would cast her in a poor light, as socially or morally unacceptable. And he played this gambit, with exquisite finesse, up until, and even beyond, the very moment Mozart married without his permission.

16

....

CONSTANZE

Leopold Mozart understood instinctively that the pull of a beloved third person on Mozart would endanger his own privileged position. Surely, that is one reason why he adamantly opposed and undermined Mozart's serious love interests: if Mozart were to marry, the game would be up. And Mozart knew that his independence would not be established simply by leaving Salzburg; the true sign of his emergence as a separate individual would be his marriage and fatherhood. Only as a husband and father could he meet his father on an equal plane.

On the first or second of May 1781 Mozart took a room at the Weber residence at *Zum Augen Gottes* (God's Eye), Am Peter 11, second floor. Fridolin Weber had died and the family had moved from Mannheim to Vienna. There his widow supported her three remaining unmarried daughters—Josepha, Constanze, and Sophie—by taking in lodgers. On 9 May Mozart broke with the archbishop, and he handed in his resignation on the following day. He might insist that these events were unrelated, but Leopold Mozart for one would never believe it. By July, Mozart was loquaciously indignant at the gossipmongers who suspected him of harboring a matrimonial intent:

> Because I am living with them, therefore I am going to marry the daughter. There has been no talk of our being in love. They have skipped that stage. No, I just take rooms in the house and *marry*. If ever there was a time when I thought less of getting married, it is most certainly now! For (although the last thing I want is a rich wife) even if I could now make my

Constanze Mozart, ca. 1782. Oil portrait by Joseph Lange.
Hunterian Art Gallery, University of Glasgow.

fortune by a marriage, I could not possibly pay court to anyone, for my mind is running on very different matters. God has not given me my talent that I might attach it to a wife and waste my youth in idleness. I am just beginning to live, and am I to embitter my own life? To be sure, I have nothing against matrimony, but at the moment it would be a misfortune for me.[1]

He acknowledged that Frau Weber had advised him to take rooms elsewhere because he seemed to be paying court to one of her daughters, as yet unspecified. "I am not in love with her," he insisted. "I fool about and have fun with her when time permits . . . and—that is all. If I had to marry all those with whom I have jested, I should have two hundred wives at least."[2] Mozart's tender, playful feelings toward the Weber sisters are betokened by his weaving the names "Sophie" and "Constanze" over an entreating figure into the development section of a fragmentary Allegro for

Example 16.1. Sonata movement in B-flat for clavier, K. 400/372a.
Allegro, mm. 70–73.

clavier, K. 400/372a, written in 1782 (Example 16.1). And surely dating from their courtship period are a few teasing lines in the form of a riddle, inscribed by Mozart in Constanze Weber's prayer book. The riddler asks the identity of the flatterer who hopes "to receive a keepsake," and he answers in Mozart's characteristic backward style:

Trazom—and from whom does he hope to receive it?
From *Znatsnoc.*
Don't be wholly too devout. Good night.[3]

Even after Mozart moved out, he continued to have his mail delivered to the Webers' address, and his letters—to his cousin in Augsburg, to his sister, and even to his father—circuitously hint that he is considering matrimony, perhaps trying thereby to soften the blow. On 15 December he at last frankly disclosed his marriage plans, carefully marshaling the arguments in favor of his taking a wife—namely, his physical needs, his desire for orderly domesticity, and his being in love. "You are horrified at the idea?" he asks, as though he did not already know the answer:

> You must, therefore, allow me to disclose to you my reasons, which, moreover, are very well founded. The voice of nature speaks as loud in me as in others, louder, perhaps, than in many a big strong lout of a fellow. I simply cannot live as most young men do in these days. In the first place, I have too much religion; in the second place, I have too great a love of my neighbor and too high a feeling of honor to seduce an innocent girl; and, in the third place, I have too much horror and disgust, too much dread and fear of diseases and too much care for my health to fool about with whores. So I can swear that I have never had relations of that sort with any woman. Besides, if such a thing had occurred, I should not have concealed it from you; for, after all, to err is natural enough in a man, and to err *once* would be mere weakness. . . . But owing to my disposition, which is more inclined to a peaceful and domesticated existence than to revelry, I who from my youth have never been accustomed to look after my own belongings, linen, clothes, and so forth, cannot think of anything more necessary to me than a wife.[4]

Whether Mozart was literally telling the truth about his chastity has been much debated, but there is no reason to doubt the strength of his hunger for sexual expression. He then reveals that of Frau Weber's three daughters he has fallen in love with Constanze, whom he describes as "the martyr of the family, [who] probably for that very reason, is the kindest-hearted, the cleverest and, in short, the best of them all." He goes on to picture her as a rather plain Cinderella who is exploited precisely because she is so good-natured, and who awaits deliverance by a loving suitor:

> She makes herself responsible for the whole household and yet in their opinion she does nothing right. Oh, my most beloved father, I could fill whole sheets with description of all the scenes that I have witnessed in that house. . . . She is not ugly, but at the same time far from beautiful. Her whole beauty consists in two little black eyes and a pretty figure. She has no wit, but she has enough common sense to enable her to fulfill her duties as a wife and mother. It is a downright lie that she is inclined to be extravagant. On the contrary, she is accustomed to be shabbily dressed, for the little that her mother has been able to do for her children, she has done for the two others, but never for Constanze. . . . Moreover, she understands housekeeping and has the kindest heart in the world. I love her and she loves me with all her heart. Tell me whether I could wish myself a better wife?[5]

One can, if one wishes, find signs here of a profound identification, for Mozart could well be describing himself—the unprepossessing, hardworking, unappreciated mainstay of the family. But the rescue motif may be even more fundamental, and it is powerfully reinforced in this and subsequent letters: "I shall never cease entreating you to allow me to save this poor girl"; "I must rescue her as soon as possible"; "I am longing to be able to set her free and to rescue her as soon as possible."[6] The ramifications of Mozart's rescue fantasy are not altogether clear, but surely he identifies with Constanze precisely because she is mistreated, so that in saving her he may rescue himself. At the same time, inasmuch as she has attributes of his mother and will become the mother of his children, the rescue may be a way of re-finding his mother, even of restoring her to life. In 1778, when he first met the Webers, Mozart had merged the images of Fridolin Weber and Leopold Mozart and voiced his desire to rescue the entire Weber family ("If only I could help them!").[7] Apparently, Mozart's ancient injunction to devote himself to the preservation of his own family needed to find new outlets. Moreover, in Constanze Mozart found a woman who combined in her person features of the opposed sides of his erotic nature: one who, like Aloysia, he could nurture and protect, and one who, like the Bäsle, shared the freer aspects of his sexuality. Constanze conformed so fully to his secret ideal pattern of femininity that he experienced his marriage to her as the rarest fulfillment, a fusion perfectly symbolized by the biblical motto that he appended to a letter written shortly after his marriage, "Man and wife are one body" ("*Mann und Weib ist ein Leib*").[8]

Constanze Weber was born on 5 January 1762 at Zell im Wiesental in southwestern Germany.[9] Her mother was Maria Cäcilia Weber, née Stamm (1727–93), from Mannheim. Her father, Fridolin Weber (1733–79), of Zell, was an uncle of Carl Maria von Weber. He left Zell in 1762 in the wake of a charge of embezzlement and moved to Mannheim, where he worked as a prompter and bass singer at the court theater and earned something as a copyist. His four daughters were well-trained musicians and all of them married musicians or theater people. Aloysia married the eminent actor Joseph Lange; Josepha, first a violinist and then an actor; Sophie and Constanze, composers. After Aloysia received her appointment as court singer at the Munich Opera in 1778, her family accompanied her there and, in September 1779, to Vienna, where she was engaged at the Court Opera. The father's death shortly thereafter left the family reliant on income from boarders to supplement an annual stipend of 700 florins paid to Frau Weber by Aloysia's husband in accordance with a marriage contract.[10] Valentin thinks it almost certain that Constanze attended the Congregation beatae Mariae virginis (Congregation of Notre Dame) in Mannheim, founded in 1720, a school supported by electoral subvention where Catholic girls were taught reading, writing, and religion, as well as other "respectable subjects for young people."[11] She was nineteen when Mozart became a boarder in their Vienna home in May 1781, but the courtship may have begun even earlier, perhaps very soon after Mozart's arrival in Vienna.

The path to their marriage was not a smooth one. The more fervently Mozart sought his father's consent the more intransigent was Leopold's reaction. He was not tempted by Mozart's offer to let him have "one half of *my fixed income*" (an indeterminate amount in any event, for Mozart as yet had no fixed position).[12] Nor was he moved by Mozart's appeal, "Please take pity on your son! I kiss your hands a thousand times."[13] He was not to be bribed or softened up; having undergone a narcissistic catastrophe at the hands of his son, he welcomed the chance to square accounts. Moreover, Mozart's impending marriage summoned up old demons from his own past life; deep within him, by a strange algebra whose fallacies completely eluded him, he may have calculated that if he could prevent Mozart's wedding he could somehow thereby repair the consequences of an earlier wedding, one that had led to a rending estrangement between him and his mother. Conversely, a failure to block the present wedding must inevitably lead to a repetition of that break, but now between him and his son. And indeed, things turned out precisely as he had predicted, confirming the ineluctability of his logic.

If Leopold Mozart's motives were hidden, from himself as well as from Mozart, his aim was clear: to prevent Mozart from marrying Constanze Weber. His arguments were fairly simple: Mozart did not yet have an adequate income and Frau Weber was the incarnation of feminine evil. In addition, he tried to provoke Mozart by repeating ugly remarks allegedly relayed to him by the composer Peter Winter, who was reported to have called Constanze a slut (*ein Luder*).[14] But Mozart, although filled with "rage and fury" at these "disgraceful lies,"[15] was not to be goaded: "Surely you cannot be vexed with me for wishing to marry? . . . Oh, I could say a great deal more in reply to your last letter and make many remonstrances, but my maxim is: what does not affect me I do not consider it worthwhile to discuss."[16]

Meanwhile, Constanze's guardian, Johann Thorwart, an economist who was a financial administrator of the Hoftheater and Nationaltheater,[17] expressed misgivings that Mozart was "far too intimate" with Constanze and might "jilt her." Thorwart and Frau Weber had reason to be alarmed, for Constanze had apparently fled from her home in November and lived for a month with Baroness Martha Elisabeth Waldstätten, who championed the couple and provided them with a lovers' refuge. Mozart was accordingly to be barred from seeing Constanze unless he proved his good faith by entering into a formal contract. "So I drew up a document to the effect *that I bound myself to marry Mlle Constanze Weber within the space of three years and that if it should prove impossible for me to do so owing to my changing my mind, she should be entitled to claim from me three hundred florins a year.*"[18] Constanze, however, took the document from her mother and tore it up, saying: "*Dear Mozart! I need no written assurance from you. I believe what you say.*"[19] If further proof were needed that she was not impelled by mercenary motives, it would be supplied by her breaking off the relationship for a time over an issue of principle, as can be inferred from one of Mozart's letters: "Surely you do not hate me so much that I may be your friend no longer and you—no longer mine?" he asked her in April 1782. "In spite of all my entreaties you have thrown me over three times and told me to my face that you intend to have nothing more to do with me."[20] The cause of the rupture was that Constanze had permitted a young man to measure the calves of her legs in a parlor game. "No woman who cares for her honor can do such a thing," Mozart insisted; "Why in the name of heaven did you not take the ribbon and measure your own calves *yourself.* . . ? Still less, then, should you have allowed it to be done to you by a stranger—with whom I have nothing to do."[21] Constanze had broken off with Mozart because he asked her for an acknowledgment of error—but the engagement was resumed when he offered to take her back unconditionally. "If you will not make a grievance of it, dearest friend, everything will still be all right," he wrote.[22]

Naturally, however, Leopold saw the nuptial agreement as clear evidence of a conspiracy to entrap his helpless child, and he recommended that Frau Weber and Thorwart "should be put in chains, made to sweep streets and have boards hung round their necks bearing the words '*seducers of youth.*'"[23] Again, Mozart tried calmly to turn away his father's virulent charges, thanking him for "your kind and affectionate letter," and remarking, "And even if what you say were true, that in order to catch me she opened her house, let me have the run of it, gave me every opportunity, etc., even so the punishment would be rather severe."[24] He sought to show his respect and ongoing affection by sending home small gifts: a snuffbox, some watch ribbons, and, for his sister, some caps "in the latest Viennese mode" made by Constanze, as well as a crucifix decorated with a "little heart pierced by an arrow."[25] But Leopold Mozart was not to be moved by such transparent appeals to sentiment. Unable to shake his son's determination, he tried to freeze him out as a way of showing the extent of his displeasure. He wrote three letters in March and April, but then, for almost three months beginning 30 April, stopped writing altogether, leaving unanswered four letters written in May—three by Mozart and one by Constanze. It was only after mid-July, when he was asked by Salzburg's Haffner family to approach Mozart to compose a symphony to celebrate Sigmund Haffner's elevation to the nobility that he finally broke his chilly silence. Working at breakneck speed, Mozart spent the next weeks composing the symphony, writing a serenade for winds (probably K. 375), and preparing for his marriage, which took place on 4 August. All this in little more than a fortnight following the most important career event of Mozart's early Vienna years—the premiere of *Die Entführung aus dem Serail* on 16 July 1782, at the Burgtheater.

Mozart accepted the symphony commission to show his spirit of cooperation and to renew his request for his father's consent. "Dearest, most beloved father," he wrote, "I implore you by all you hold dear in the world to give your consent to my marriage with my dear Constanze. . . . My heart is restless and my head confused; in such a condition how can one think and work to any good purpose?"[26] But Leopold nevertheless continued to shut Mozart out, responding coldly to his son's description of his first Viennese operatic triumph and altogether withholding comment on the opera itself, the original score of which Mozart had sent on 20 July. On 31 July Mozart wrote, "I received today your letter of the 26th, but a cold, indifferent letter, such as I could never have expected in reply to my news of the good reception of my opera. I thought (judging by my own feelings) that you would hardly be able to open the parcel for excitement and eagerness to see your son's work, which, far from merely pleasing, is making such a sensation in Vienna that people refuse to hear anything else, so that the theater is always packed. It was given yesterday for the fourth time and is to be repeated on Friday. But you—have not had the time."[27] Mozart appears to have been crushed by his father's coolness toward his success, but he really ought not to have expected anything else. Why should his father be delighted at having been rendered useless? For every fresh triumph was devastating proof of Leopold's superfluity, evidence that Mozart's estimate of his excellent opportunities in Vienna had been correct, and a confirmation that Mozart had neither motivation nor need to return to a modest haven in provincial Salzburg.

Events on the marriage front now moved rapidly. On 29 July, Thorwart applied to the senior court marshal's office to grant permission for Constanze to marry Mozart. On 30 July Mozart made a final appeal to his father, broadly hinting that, as a man of honor, he must marry Constanze because he has compromised her, and expressing his determination to wed her, whether or not he received permission. "You can have no objection whatever to raise—and indeed you do not raise any. . . . All that you have written and may possibly write to me on the subject—can only be *well-meaning advice* which, however fine and good it may be, is no longer applicable to a man who has gone so far with a girl. In such a case nothing can be postponed. It is better for him to put his affairs in order and act like an honest fellow! God will ever reward that. I mean to have nothing with which to reproach myself."[28] Mozart could wait no longer for parental consent, because Constanze was once again staying at the Baroness Waldstätten's and Frau Weber was threatening to "have her fetched by the police."[29] He wrote to the baroness, begging her "to assist us poor creatures," and he proposed immediate action: "The best plan I can think of is to marry Constanze tomorrow morning—or even today, if that is possible."[30]

On 2 August, Mozart and Constanze went to confession and received Communion; on the following day the marriage contract was signed and witnessed; and on 4 August the couple was married in St. Stephen's Cathe-

St. Stephen's Cathedral, Vienna, ca. 1780–90. Color lithograph by Karl Schütz and Johann Ziegler. The British Library: Map Library—Maps 183.s1., pl.9.

dral by Curate Ferdinand Wolf. Present were Frau Weber, Sophie Weber, Johann Thorwart, Johann Carl Cetto Kronstorff (an official from Lower Austria), and Mozart's best man, the surgeon Franz Xaver Wenzel Gilowsky. "When we had been joined together," Mozart wrote, "both my wife and I began to weep. All present, even the priest, were deeply touched and all wept to see how much our hearts were moved."[31] A wedding supper, "more princely than baronial," was given that night by Baroness Waldstätten, and Mozart wrote feelingly to his father: "My dear Constanze—now, thank God, at last my true wife."[32]

Leopold Mozart's consent—if such it can be called—did not arrive until the day after the wedding had taken place and was accompanied by a second, acrimonious letter in which he tried for the last time to deter his son from marrying. These letters have not survived, but from Mozart's response (and a later letter of Leopold's to Baroness Waldstätten) Jahn concluded that Leopold acknowledged "that he could no longer expect Wolfgang to assist in extricating him from the debts he had incurred on his son's behalf; on the other hand, Wolfgang must neither now nor at any future time reckon upon him for support; and he begged him to make his bride fully aware of this circumstance."[33] Mozart was thereby given to understand that if he married he could expect nothing from his father either now as a wedding dowry or later on as a legacy and he was asked to inform his bride that she should be under no illusions as to her lover's future economic prospects. Leopold Mozart's letter evidently suggested that Mozart was leading Constanze to believe otherwise. Mozart responded: "You are very much mistaken in your son if you can suppose him capable of acting dishonestly. My dear Constanze . . . knew my circumstances and heard from me long ago all that I had to expect from you. But her affection and her love for me were so great that she willingly and joyfully sacrificed her whole future to share my fate."[34] Mozart grimly gave thanks "for your kind consent and fatherly blessing," ironically avowed that he married because he knew in his mind that he could "safely rely on" receiving the consent, and corrosively begged "forgiveness for my too hasty trust in your fatherly love."[35]

In his letter to Baroness Waldstätten of 23 August 1782, Leopold Mozart confirmed that he was resigned to accepting the moral and material "degradations" that Mozart had brought upon his own father and that he now absolved himself of all responsibility: "All that I can now do is to leave him to his own resources (as he evidently wishes)."[36] Thus, Leopold Mozart, conceding under duress the inevitability of his son's marriage, which followed hard upon his removal from Salzburg, took a long step toward disinheriting him, just as his mother had done when he himself married in 1747. The final scene in the replaying of this archaic family scenario would have to await the death of Leopold Mozart and the division of property among his heirs.

17

....

TWO FAMILIES

Although their mutual bitterness was never far from the surface, Mozart and his father kept the shreds of civility alive between them, striving somehow to keep the dialogue going, for neither of them could ever bring himself to break relations altogether. Sometimes Mozart's way of maintaining contact with his father was to suggest an imprudent course of action (like wanting to leave Vienna for Paris in 1782) or to exaggerate his prospects (such as his expectation that he would be chosen as music master to Princess Württemberg) so that Leopold might exercise his rational powers to straighten him out. Mozart would then confess his error and pay homage to his father's superior good sense, thereby acknowledging how essential it was to receive paternal advice. This would do something to relieve Leopold's concern that he was no longer essential to his son's career. In addition to making an aging father feel useful, Mozart would throw some business his way. He persuaded Baroness Waldstätten to order a fortepiano through his father's agency, asking him to send in return some "Salzburg tongues" or other local delicacy as a present for the baroness.[1] Although music copying was readily available in Vienna, he engaged Leopold to supervise the making of copies of his scores, for example, to have *Die Entführung aus dem Serail* copied in Salzburg for possible performance at the Berlin court, and he sent Leopold quires of Viennese music paper for the purpose, thereby complicating the lives of future students of Mozart's paper types and their geographical distribution. Mozart also tried to involve his father in his work more directly; perhaps in an attempt to

"Leopold Mozart reads the libretto of his son's opera *Idomeneo, rè di Creta*" (apocryphal). Painted silhouette. Reproduced from Heinz Schuler, *Mozart und die Freimaurerei*.

Maria Cäcilia Weber. Anonymous silhouette. Mozart-Museum der Internationalen Stiftung Mozarteum, Salzburg. © Mozarts Geburtshaus, Salzburg.

revive the spirit of their collaboration on the libretto of *Idomeneo*, he selected its author, the Salzburger Abbate Gianbattista Varesco, as librettist for *L'oca del Cairo (The Goose of Cairo)*.

Naturally, he repaid his father for the copying costs, and in early 1783 he even sent some additional money home to be applied against the old putative debt. "I only hope that the balance may be of some use to you," he wrote in April. "I cannot spare any more at present, as I foresee many expenses in connection with my wife's confinement, which will probably take place towards the end of May or the beginning of June."[2] Ten days later, responding to his father's expression of thanks, he added, "I rejoice with my whole heart that the small sum which I was able to send has been so useful to you."[3]

Whatever his good intentions, however, he could not refrain from hurting his father. He waited almost until his first child was born before asking Leopold Mozart to serve as godfather: "I kept on postponing going down on my knees, folding my hands and entreating you most submissively, my dearest father, to be godfather! As there is still time, I am doing so now. Meanwhile . . . I have already arranged . . . that someone shall present the child in your name, whether is it *generis masculini* or *feminini*! So we are going to call it Leopold or Leopoldine."[4] But when the baby was born, ten days later, on 17 June 1783, Mozart reneged on his promise:

> *Now for the godfather question.* Let me tell you what has happened. After my wife's safe delivery I immediately sent a message to Baron [Raimund] Wetzlar, who is a good and true friend of mine. He came to see us at once and offered to stand godfather. I could not refuse him and thought to myself: "After all, my boy can still be called Leopold." But while I was turning this round in my mind, the Baron said very cheerfully: "Ah, now you have a little Raimund"—and kissed the child. What was I to do? Well, I have had the child christened Raimund Leopold. I must frankly confess that if you had not sent me in a letter your opinion on the matter, I should have been very much embarrassed, and I am not at all sure that I should not have refused his offer! But your letter comforted me with the assurance that you will not disapprove of my action! After all, Leopold is one of his names.[5]

Perhaps Mozart changed his plan because Leopold Mozart's response to the offer had not been altogether enthusiastic. But it is equally likely that, beyond Baron Wetzlar's pressure, Mozart had some inner resistance to naming his child Leopold. And surely Constanze could not have been overjoyed at the idea of naming her first-born after the man who refused to accept her into his family. Perhaps, in the last analysis, Mozart had enough trouble with his father's perpetual psychological presence without having his revenant toddling around the house. Mozart and Constanze's second child was named Karl Thomas (1784–1858), and their third child, born in October 1786, who survived for only a month, was dubbed Johann Thomas Leopold. After Leopold Mozart's death the couple had three more children, none of whom was named after the paternal grandfather: Theresia Constanzia Adelheid Friederike Maria Anna (1787–88); Anna Maria (born and died on 16 November 1789), and Franz Xaver Wolfgang (1791–1844). Two of them, however, bore the names of Mozart's mother.

Leopold complained bitterly about Mozart's constant postponements of his promised visit to Salzburg. At first these seemed fairly reasonable, in light of Constanze's pregnancy and Mozart's busy schedule. In April he sent assurances of "our most ardent wish to embrace you, most beloved father, and my dearest sister," but at the same time he put off the visit until July.[6] When July arrived, however, he revealed apprehensiveness about what might happen if he set foot in Salzburg: "The Archbishop may have me arrested. . . . What chiefly makes me dread this is the fact that I have not yet received my formal dismissal. Perhaps he has purposely held it back, in order to catch me later."[7] He quoted friends who advised him to meet his father and sister elsewhere: "*Well, you will see, you will never get away again. You have no idea of what that wicked malevolent Prince is capable of! And you cannot conceive what low tricks are resorted to in affairs of this kind.*"[8] In a letter of early July, Leopold called his son's fear "humbug" and frankly suggested that Mozart was making up excuses in order to avoid the visit. Although Mozart immediately protested the imputation—"Have I ever given you the impression that I had no desire or longing to see you? Most certainly never!"—he nevertheless tried yet again to postpone their arrival until "August, or certainly in September at the latest."[9] Mozart's anger against Salzburg and all that it represented burst out once more: "I suppose I need not repeat that I care very little for Salzburg and not at all for the Archbishop, that I shit on both of them and that it would never enter my head voluntarily to make a journey thither, were it not that you and my sister lived there."[10] But under pressure he at last yielded, and Constanze wrote to Marianne on the nineteenth of July confirming that they would start on their way in short order.

Mozart had left his hometown, but the depth of his resentment of Salzburg was undiminished. Remorselessly, he continued to disparage the city of his birth, and to discredit not only its rulers but its ordinary inhabitants and its culture. This is surely not just a matter of his inwardly identifying Salzburg with his father. Perhaps Mozart tried to lessen the pain of leaving home by denying the strength of his ancient attachments, by refusing to acknowledge, even to himself, the immensity of his losses—of fam-

ily, friends, streets, shared memories, and the quotidian objects that collectively add up to an image of home.[11] Perhaps Mozart maintained a powerful aversion to Salzburg in order to keep a flood of yearnings at bay, feelings
that drew him back to childhood and its accompanying dependencies. He
may also have needed to justify leaving so as to ameliorate the sense of guilt
for having abandoned those who loved him and who now resented and
envied his departure, which was experienced as an abandonment. From
this need for justification may have come his inner sense of being unwelcome or persecuted in Salzburg. The clearest sign of his anxieties is his fear
that he would be arrested by the authorities upon his return.

Despite Mozart's feelings about Salzburg, he and his wife spent three
months—from the end of July until late October 1783—visiting the city of
his birth. Clearly, the archbishop's court (and perhaps the leading citizens as
well) maintained a cool reserve toward the former favorite during his visit.
Or perhaps Mozart himself preferred to keep his distance from his old
employers and patrons. Whatever the reasons, there were no gala welcoming parties, grand concerts, or court appearances of any kind. Marianne's
diary soberly records the presence of her brother and his wife in the usual
rounds of churchgoing, visiting, cardplaying, and music making, but it was
an uneventful sojourn with only a few noteworthy signposts—a visit to
Maria Plain pilgrimage church and a meeting with the blind pianist Maria
Theresia Paradies on 28 September.

Reconciliation was the plain purpose of Mozart's journey to Salzburg.
To judge from his subsequent letters, he tried while there to conjure up an
older time when comic, or even mildly bawdy, exchanges were an approximate substitute for love-play between an affectionate brother and sister. But
the atmosphere had become so thoroughly contaminated that Leopold
would not allow Constanze to select as a memento even one of the many
gifts Mozart had received on his early journeys.[12] Leopold well knew that
Mozart could not tolerate the continued grievous rejection of Constanze;
for a year he had been receiving his son's letters, signed "W. & C. Mozart"
as pointed reminders that this man and wife were inseparable, indeed were
"one body."[13] But, far from being able to love or accept her, Leopold
Mozart was unable to restrain his hostility toward the woman who had
taken his son from him. As for Marianne, when in 1782 Mozart announced
his intentions to marry Constanze, she adopted her father's view that her
brother was forsaking his family obligations for an unworthy female inter-
loper and she too refused to bless the marriage, turning aside Constanze's
friendly overtures.

Prior to the wedding, Constanze had sent affectionate regards to Marianne and asked for her friendship in return: "Without undue pride I may
say that I partly deserve it and shall endeavor to do so wholly! May I in

exchange offer you mine, which, indeed, has long been yours in the secrecy of my heart?"[14] The coolness of Marianne's responses to such sisterly appeals became a source of great pain to Mozart, and Constanze grew increasingly irate that she was not accepted by Mozart's family. When on 24 July 1782, a week before the wedding, she sent Marianne greetings on her name day, she did not conceal her hurt feelings: "Forgive me for . . . worrying you again with my scrawl. . . . And if my good wishes are a nuisance to you, as all congratulations are, my consolation must be that already I am not the only one who is bothering you in this way. All that I deserve is that for the love of God you should suffer me as you do all the others."[15] During the Salzburg visit Marianne remained unyielding in her attitude toward her sister-in-law. Later in life Constanze recalled the constrained atmosphere there and related how "the behavior towards him and his wife gave [Mozart] the feeling that he had been wronged."[16] He was indeed deeply troubled, for he wanted nothing more than to bring about a loving reconciliation. More than forty years after the visit, Constanze told Mary Novello, who with her husband, the musician and publisher Vincent Novello, came to Salzburg in 1829 to interview Mozart's survivors, that as the family was singing the Quartet "Andró ramingo e solo," from *Idomeneo*, with its rending depiction of a father, a son, and two women torn by conflicting desires, Mozart "was so overcome that he burst into tears and quitted the chamber and it was some time before she could console him."[17]

In Salzburg the Mozarts learned of the death of their baby, who had been left in Vienna in the care of a nursemaid. Mozart had been euphoric about becoming a father. "The child too is quite strong and healthy and has a tremendous number of things to do, I mean, drinking, sleeping, yelling, pissing, shitting, dribbling and so forth."[18] He was thrilled to be told that the child looked like him: "Little Raimund is so like me that everyone immediately remarks it. It is just as if my face had been copied. My dear little wife is absolutely delighted, as this is what she had always desired."[19] But the infant died on 19 August, casting an additional shadow upon their visit to Salzburg. Four months later, Mozart wrote simply, "We are both very sad about our poor, bonny, fat, darling little boy."[20]

It is hard to ascertain precisely what Mozart composed in Salzburg; he is thought to have worked on the operas *L'oca del Cairo* and *Lo sposo deluso* (both of which remained unfinished) there, and it is conceivable that the Piano Sonatas in C, K. 330/300h, A, K. 331/300i, and F, K. 332/300k, were written during the visit, either as teaching material for his Vienna pupils or, it would be nice to believe, as a precious gift to his sister.[21] It was later reported more reliably by two of Michael Haydn's former pupils that as a friendly favor to their teacher, who was unable because of illness to complete a commission from Archbishop Colloredo for a set of six duos for violin and viola, Mozart composed the Duos in G, K. 423, and in B-flat, K. 424, in the summer of 1783.[22] Thus, if we wish, we can imagine Mozart's amusement at the thought of the archbishop unwittingly enjoying the music of his former concertmaster.

The creative highlight of those months was the performance of the Mass in C minor, K. 427/417a, on 26 October, a significant premiere of one of Mozart's supreme works, and a work that in important ways symbolized both the hopes and the disappointments of the family reunion. The C-minor Mass remains, like the Requiem, an unfinished work, consisting of the Kyrie and Gloria, the Credo up to the Et incarnatus, and incomplete drafts of the Sanctus and Benedictus. Begun at the end of 1782, it is unusual in several respects, being Mozart's only major church composition of the decade as well as one of his few works written without an economic motive. In the main, Mozart composed music in order to make a living or to advance his position in his profession—usually in fulfillment of commissions or in anticipation of performance or publication opportunities. For example, the clavier music was written mainly for performance or for teaching purposes; the operas were written in response to specific commissions or occasionally in the hope of a production; the symphonies, for a variety of uses, including, in later years, as showpieces of his capabilities; the orchestral dances, to fulfill his obligations as imperial chamber composer and to earn publication fees; the Salzburg church music, in connection with his responsibilities to the court; the Requiem, to Count Walsegg's order; and the wind instrument concertos, for specific virtuoso players. Occasionally, however, Mozart composed a work in a spirit of inquiry, as an affirmation of his beliefs, or as a gift of love or friendship. The several accounts of its origin indicate that the C-minor Mass arose from a fusion of all three of these motivations.

The C-minor Mass is first mentioned at New Year's 1783, when Leopold Mozart reminded his son of his pledge to visit Salzburg. Mozart responded on 3 January:

> It is quite true about my moral obligation and indeed I let the word flow from my pen on purpose. I made the promise in my heart of hearts and hope to be able to keep it. When I made it, my wife was not yet married; yet as I was absolutely determined to marry her after her recovery, it was easy for me to make it—but, as you yourself are aware, time and other circumstances made our journey impossible. The score of half of a mass, which is still lying here waiting to be finished, is the best proof that I really made the promise.[23]

Constanze's own account adds another dimension: she told the Novellos that the mass was written "in consequence of a vow that he had made to do so, on her safe recovery after the birth of their first child—relative to whom he had been particularly anxious."[24] Nissen offers a very similar account, in which Constanze made sure to stress her role in the work's performance as well as composition: "And this man, how did he use the short time in Salzburg?—He finished the mass, which he had solemnly promised for his wife when her confinement was happily over, and which he had already half completed in January. This mass was rehearsed on 23 August [recte October] in the Chapel and performed on the 25th [recte 26th] in St. Peter's Church, where his wife sang the solos."[25] The reference to finishing the mass in Salzburg may not be entirely in error, because for the performance Mozart is thought to have filled out the missing movements with appropriate sections from his earlier masses.

This mass, then, can be seen to embody a number of complementary motives: It is a peace offering, which aims to demonstrate Mozart's piety and to heal the family rift, thus to achieve reconciliation with his father and sister. At the same time it is a token of his marriage to Constanze, his gift of love to her, the expression of his gratitude to God for having

Autograph manuscript, Mass in C minor, K. 427/417a, Kyrie. Staatsbibliothek Preussischer Kulturbesitz, Berlin, Music Division and Mendelssohn Archive.

granted him this sacred union and blessed it with a child. It is written to glorify Constanze: it is her Magnificat. An autonomous expression of his creativity, it is the greatest gift that he can render. When set alongside Bach's *Anna Magdalena Book,* Beethoven's *An die ferne Geliebte,* and Berg's *Lyric Suite,* it surely stands as one of the most sublime compositions ever written as a gift to a beloved person.

The mass also conveys implications of a quite different kind. By its florid style, bravura solos, and great length, it explicitly goes counter to attitudes toward and restrictions upon church music current in the Vienna of Emperor Joseph II, which limited the performance of instrumentally accompanied church music to the court chapel and St. Stephen's Cathedral. Similarly, it could not have been expected to please Salzburg authorities, whose archbishop held official views on church music very similar to those of Joseph II. In an archiepiscopal letter of 19 June 1780 Colloredo had called for the elimination of complex forms of church music and the substitution of German congregational singing. A pastoral letter of 1782 was directed, Eisen notes, "against the liturgy and the excessive ornateness and ostentation of parish churches," and accompanied sacred vocal music was greatly discouraged.[26] Mozart's mass in no way reflected the official new Salzburg style, which limited duration to forty-five minutes and abolished solo singing and fugues. Clearly, he had no intention of compromising his effort to create a dramatically expressive, elevated church music style that transcended the Austrian mass tradition at the same time as it drew freely upon Italian sources as well as on Bach and Handel—made aware of the latter through his close association in Vienna with Baron Gottfried van Swieten, who promoted their music in private concerts there.

Mozart did not finish the Mass in C minor; it remains a failed action, a torso, an unrealized masterpiece, indeed one that was effectively dismantled several years later by the use of its music in an inferior cantata, *Davidde penitente,* K. 469. Perhaps the work's incompleteness appropriately symbolizes the failure of its main underlying purposes: to express filial piety, to evidence devotion to religious music in an age of reform, and especially to serve as an emblem of Mozart's reconciliation with his father and sister, conditioned upon their acceptance of his wife, whose supreme worthiness to be his bride is betokened by the sublimity of the mass itself.

If it failed to achieve its composer's most coveted goal, the reconciliation of the family to his wife, the C-minor Mass surely succeeded as a declaration of faith, an act of devotion, an expression of Mozart's love for his wife, and a prayer of thanksgiving for the gift of family. And these were surely sufficient warrant for having burdened a work of art with almost miraculous powers and purposes.

★   ★   ★

Mozart and his wife left Salzburg at 9:30 A.M. on 27 October, the day following the performance of the mass in St. Peter's Abbey Church. Marianne's diary succinctly mentions the rehearsal several days earlier: "On the
23rd, at eight o'clock at Mass in the chapel at the rehearsal of my brother's
mass, in which my sister-in-law sang the solo."[27] The performance itself
and the young pair's departure (the last time Mozart and his sister ever saw
each other) get equally laconic treatment, as though to emphasize the lev-
eling of all events in the ebb and flow of Salzburg quotidian life: "On the
27th, Ceccarelli, Wegscheider, Hagenauer visited us. Varesco. At 9:30 my
brother and sister-in-law departed. Afternoon, papa, I, Gretl, and Henry
ate bologna at Bird Inn in Gnigl. In between we went home. We saw a
comedy. A beautiful day."[28] Three days later, on 30 October, Mozart and
Constanze arrived in Linz, where they stayed with Count Johann Joseph
Anton Thun-Hohenstein, the father-in-law of Vienna's Countess Thun.
On 4 November Mozart gave a full-scale concert at the Linz Theater,
which featured the premiere of a new Symphony in C, K. 425 ("Linz"),
which had been written at "breakneck speed" in the space of four or five
days because he had neglected to bring a symphony with him.[29] It is now
considered likely that the Piano Sonata in B-flat, K. 333/315c, was largely
written in Linz.[30] The couple remained there until about the end of
November. The exact date of their arrival in Vienna is not precisely
known, but on 6 December Mozart wrote to his father from there, telling
him of his work on the opera *L'oca del Cairo*, K. 422, and of his plans for a
revision of *Idomeneo* and for six subscription concerts during Lent.[31]

Instead of reconciling the families, the Salzburg sojourn only deepened,
confirmed, and made irrevocable the rift between them—a splintering that
left a residue of sadness and pain on both sides. Ironically, Mozart had now
fully gained the freedom from an infantilizing thralldom for which he had
struggled; though liberated, however, he was cut adrift. In achieving separateness he had opened a vein of isolation and disconnectedness, and even a
glimpse of the void. He was caught in the predicament of those who can
neither "accept their own yearning for a symbiotic union nor endure a
separate individuality," those who are torn between wanting to return to
the engulfing safety of the symbiotic state and the need to be a separate,
autonomous person.[32] In partial compensation for Mozart's deepened
estrangement from his father and sister, however, he now found in his
wife's family, the Webers, a full measure of shelter, love, and comfort as
well as an outlet for his desire to help others.[33] If I have understood the letters and memoirs correctly, it was among the Webers, for the first time
since his mother had died, that he found acceptance as a plain human
being; a place where he could express his fears, his sadness, and his need to

have his wounds bound up; a family in which he was lovingly looked after and to which he could give freely in return, without compulsion.

It was not diplomatic for Mozart to disclose his attachment to the Webers, because this family of all families had from the start been condemned and prohibited by his father, who had viewed Fridolin Weber as a usurper and later named Cäcilia Weber a "seducer of youth," charging that she wove webs to ensnare young men, using her compliant daughters as bait. The bitterness of Leopold Mozart's view of the Webers went far beyond simple explanations; perhaps he saw Frau Weber as a new version of his own mother, plotting to tear his son from him, to separate him from both his flesh and his purse. The hard fact was that he was unwilling to "share" his son with any other person, particularly a woman. (One comes at last to glimpse the force and thoroughness with which Leopold Mozart preempted so many aspects of the mother's role within his family.) At first, failing to observe the sensitivity of this issue and perhaps thinking that his father would be pleased to have him comfortably settled in a good home, Mozart did not conceal his liking for Frau Weber. Soon after his arrival in Vienna, he wrote, "Old Madame Weber has been good enough to take me into her house, where I have a pretty room. Moreover, I am living with people who are obliging and who supply me with all the things which one often requires in a hurry and which one cannot have when one is living alone."[34] He was delighted to be taken care of and he wanted to respond in kind. "Believe me when I say that old Madame Weber is a very obliging woman and that I cannot do enough for her in return for her kindness, though unfortunately I have no time to do so."[35] So powerfully was he drawn to the Weber family that he fell in love with at least two of its four daughters and, after marrying one, adopted the others as his dear sisters.

When gossip about his courtship of Constanze made it necessary for him to seek other quarters, his reluctance to leave was apparent: "Were it not for these rumors, I should hardly think of leaving, for, although I could easily get a nicer room, I could hardly find such comfort and such friendly and obliging people."[36] Having felt the intensity of his father's reaction, however, he abandoned his defense of Frau Weber and let it be known that he was now on his guard against her "designs," pledging that both he and Constanze would in future avoid her influence and in particular would never consent to live with her: "That is out of the question, for on no account would I consent to it, and my Constanze still less. Au contraire, she intends to see very little of her mother and I shall do my best to stop it altogether, for we know her too well."[37] Leopold sought and received assurances from Baroness Waldstätten and from Mozart on this score. "I cannot understand how you got the idea that my highly honored mother-in-law is living here too," wrote Mozart. "Since our marriage we have paid her two visits, but on the second occasion quarreling and wrangling began again, so that my poor wife started to cry. I put a stop to the bickering at once by saying to Constanze that it was time for us to go. We have not been there since and do not intend to go until we have to celebrate the birthday or name day of the mother or of one of the two sisters."[38]

Mozart may well have been stretching the point to avoid aggravating his father. In any event, after Constanze's first confinement, in 1783, the couple and Frau Weber became and remained extremely close. When the delivery was imminent, "At four o'clock I sent for my mother-in-law—and then for the midwife. . . . My mother-in-law by her great kindness to her daughter has made full amends for all the harm she did *before her marriage*. She spends the whole day with her."[39] Two years later, in 1785, when Leopold Mozart visited Vienna, he was feted by Frau Weber in the hope of establishing harmony between the two aged parents. But although Mozart's father had many good things to say about the roast pheasant and its preparation, there is no sign that he was about to fall into Frau Weber's embrace. He left Vienna knowing that his son had, by then, become a loving son-in-law of Frau Weber's and an integral member of her extended family. Constanze's youngest sister, Sophie, recalled, "Well, Mozart became fonder and fonder of our dear departed mother and she of him. Indeed he often came running along in great haste to the Wieden (where she and I were lodging at the Golden Plough), carrying under his arm a little bag containing coffee and sugar, which he would hand to our good mother, saying, 'Here, mother dear, now you can have a little *Jause* [afternoon coffee].' She used to be as delighted as a child. He did this very often."[40] Constanze remembered how concerned her mother was that "because of his manner of living he had weakened his health," and how he replied, "Ah, mama, I can't change my nature."[41] In later years, during Constanze's long period of illness, Frau Weber came to live in the Mozarts' apartment, to be there in case of need, and when Mozart once accidentally suffered a knife-wound in the thigh, it was his mother-in-law who bound him up, put a soothing oil on the wound, and succeeded in healing him.[42] Upon his arrival in Prague in January 1787, Mozart did not neglect to begin a letter to Frau Weber, leaving its completion to Constanze and one of his brothers-in-law.[43] In his last letters, he simply called her Mama.

Mozart needed a mother. In return, he would be a good and loving son, who would devote himself to the family welfare—a not unfamiliar role for him. His close associations with all the Weber daughters continued throughout his life. Aloysia Lange, whom he had once courted, regularly appeared in his concerts and frequently sang his arias, some of which he composed specifically for her. "Indeed I loved her truly," he wrote his father in 1781, "and even now I feel that she is not a matter of indifference to me."[44] In his last year of life he crafted the role of the Queen of the Night for Josepha, who from late 1790 had a contract with the Freihaustheater (run by Emanuel Schikaneder, the flamboyant impresario who later authored the libretto of *Die Zauberflöte*). In Mannheim days Mozart had contemplated traveling to Italy with Aloysia and Josepha; later, in the early Vienna years, he fed his father's prejudices by describing Josepha as "a lazy, gross perfidious woman, and as cunning as a fox."[45] At the end, though, she was his sister, whose name, according to one report, was on his lips when he died. In July 1788 she married the orchestral violinist Franz de Paula Hofer, who even earlier had become Mozart's close companion, accompanying him to Prague in 1787. He also traveled with Mozart to Frankfurt in 1789, where he participated in Mozart's concert and where, according to one report, he and Mozart spent time in the cafés "indulging in the joys of the wine god."[46] Mozart and his other brother-in-law, the renowned actor Joseph Lange, became companions as they moved with assurance among Vienna's cultured elite. A talented artist who painted one of the most characteristic of Mozart's portraits and the best of Constanze's portraits, Lange is mentioned as frequenting Mozart's home concerts and social gatherings. In a masquerade presented at carnival in 1783, he played Pierrot to Aloysia's Columbine and Mozart's Harlequin. The youngest of the daughters, Sophie, who wrote a loving account of Mozart's last days, remained unmarried until 1806; during Mozart's Vienna years she lived with her mother and together they comforted Constanze in her troubles and, it may be, did their best to keep a fragile marriage together.

The sum of all these threads is that the Weber family, which had long ago reminded him so strikingly of his own, indeed became Mozart's family, fulfilling the wishful fantasy that had welled up in him at the moment he first encountered them in Mannheim: "I have become so fond of this unfortunate family that my dearest wish is to make them happy; and perhaps I may be able to do so."[47] Just as he needed them, he felt sure that he too was needed, for in him constantly there stirred the craving to belong to a new family entity.

Petition to the Marriage Bureau for Constanze Weber to marry Wolfgang
Adam Mozart, 29 July 1782. Reproduced from Selma Krasa et al.,
Zaubertöne: Mozart's Wien (Vienna, 1991).

18

ADAM

The reader of Mozart's letters must soon grow accustomed to the numerous permutations to which the composer, who was baptized Joannes Chrysostomus Wolfgangus Theophilus Mozart, subjected his own name, apparently just for the fun of it. Thus, we are not surprised to find such variations on the surname as "De Mozartini," "Mozartus," or "Mozarty," though we may be momentarily startled by such anagrammatical variants as "Trazom" or "Romatz." The name Wolfgang, though occasionally Latinized as "Wolfgangus," Italianized as "Wolfgango," or read backward as "Gnagflow," underwent comparatively few transformations. It is the last of Mozart's forenames, Theophilus, that was subjected to the greatest variety of metamorphoses. Writing to his Augsburg publisher shortly after the birth, on 27 January 1756, of his son, Leopold Mozart noted, "The boy is called *Joannes Chrisostomos, Wolfgang, Gottlieb*,"[1] thus translating the Greek Theophilus into the German Gottlieb, a form that was preserved—as "J. G. Wolfgang Mozart"—on the earliest of the child's published works to bear opus numbers.[2] From about 1770 on, Mozart several times referred to himself as "Wolfgango Amadeo Mozart," but by 1778 he had adopted his favorite—and almost invariable—form of the name, Amadè or Amadé, with occasional ventures into Amadi or the Latinized Amadeus, the latter having originated as early as 1774 in a typically jesting message to his sister.[3] (The almost universal adoption of the form Amadeus is a posthumous process, propelled in large part, I believe, by the wide circulation of Breitkopf & Härtel's *Oeuvres Complèttes de Wolfgang Amadeus Mozart* 1798–1806.)

In all of these substitutes for Theophilus, the meaning of the Greek name is retained in translation, but the most interesting and unusual of these variants is not a translation and it calls for other explanations. Toward the end of July 1782 it became necessary for Mozart and Constanze Weber to obtain from the appropriate authorities several official documents in connection with their marriage. First, Mozart applied to the Vienna Police Administration for a waiver—which he received on 29 July—of the requirement that he produce his baptismal certificate, which, apparently, he had neglected to bring to Vienna from Salzburg. Also on 29 July, Constanze Weber's guardian, Johann Thorwart, successfully petitioned the senior court marshal's office to grant permission for her to marry Mozart. Then, on 1 August, Mozart applied to the Prince-Archbishop's Court (*Fürsterzbischöfliche Konsistorium*) of Lower Austria to allow his marriage at Vienna's St. Stephen's Cathedral even though his residence in Vienna was not officially within the jurisdiction of the cathedral parish.[4]

While the marriage contract itself, dated 3 August 1782, refers to "the well and nobly born Herr Wolfgang Mozart" and was duly signed by "Wolfgang Amade Mozart," in all of these other marriage documents Mozart's name was given as "Wolfgang *Adam* Mozart." Most striking, the marriage register at St. Stephen's Cathedral, dated 4 August 1782, lists "Der Wohledle Herr Wolfgang Adam Mozart, ein Kapellmeister, ledig" ("The noble Mr. Wolfgang Adam Mozart, a kapellmeister, bachelor") as the groom.[5]

Most biographers have ignored these uses of the name Adam, in accordance with the understandable desire to pass over troublesome or opaque issues. To be sure, because Jahn's transcription of the marriage register, which is based not on the register itself but on an 1847 testimonial from a church official, silently corrected the name from Adam to Amadè, scholars were altogether unaware of the issue until Alexander Hajdecki rediscovered the original document at St. Stephen's Cathedral in the early twentieth century.[6] Afterward, Deutsch elected to regard the matter as stemming from a simple "mistake" on the part of Thorwart, Constanze's guardian, but he omitted to discuss the Vienna police document written in response to Mozart's, not Thorwart's, communication, and he did not pause to wonder why Mozart would permit an incorrect entry of his name upon the marriage register.[7] Hajdecki observed that "the decision of the Police Administration [*Polizeidirektion*] indicates indisputably that Mozart signed this petition with the name Wolfgang Adam, just as he also used these given names before the church authorities upon the occasion of the entry in the church registers."[8] Naturally, there is no need to quarrel with those who take a commonsense approach to such matters, those for whom Mozart's temporary adoption of the name Adam is merely a mistake or a trivial jest, another example of his penchant for mystification, which often took such literary forms as wordplay, ciphers, codes, and riddles.[9] But they ought in turn to be tolerant of those who want to speculate about the implications of such things in the belief that there is often a serious substratum to such "errors" and to the comic in general, and that deeper motives may also have been at work here.

At issue is the power of names. As the anthropologists showed long ago, in every premodern society the name is considered equivalent to the individual who bears it. Frazer noted how, in such societies, one "commonly fancies that the link between a name and the person or thing denominated by it is not a mere arbitrary and ideal association, but a real and substantial bond which unites the two."[10] In early societies the widespread, obsessive concealment of names—of individuals, kings, deities, even cities—was intended to offer protection from harm. Thus, the Egyptians and Brahmans gave their children two names, one of which was kept secret and to be used only at ceremonies such as marriage. Frazer notes, "The custom is intended to protect the person against magic, since a charm only becomes effectual in combination with the real name."[11] Name changes often accompanied marriages and ritual initiations. "The savage boy receives a new name at puberty and gives up his old one," Crawley wrote, "just as does the Catholic novice and the Catholic priest and nun: It is part of the very widely-spread human impulse to change one's identity. . . . As the infant at baptism was rescued from Satan, and became by the washing away of the 'old Adam' a new creature, receiving a name [is] the symbol of its new life."[12] Thus, purified, initiated, renamed, we are offered a fresh start.

Freud took the inevitable next step in these interpretations; he observed that our own inner beliefs and superstitions are not very far removed from those of the primitives and the ancients, and held that we are far from immune to the belief that to denote something is to control or even to master it.[13] Later on, Otto Fenichel summarized the psychoanalytic view of the matter:

Words and worded concepts are shadows of things, constructed for the purpose of bringing order through trial action into the chaos of real things. The macrocosm of real things outside is reflected in the microcosm of thing representatives inside. The thing representatives . . . are "possessions"; that is, they are mastered by the ego; they are an attempt to endow the things with "ego quality" for the purpose of achieving mastery over them.

Fenichel concluded, echoing Freud: "He who knows a word for a thing, masters the thing, that is the core of the 'magic of names.'"[14] Of course the power of names was already known to Mozart's contemporaries, such as the early Romantic writer Wilhelm Heinrich Wackenroder, who wrote in 1797: "By means of words we have dominion over all of nature; by means of words we acquire with ease all the treasures of the earth ... We gain power over worldly things by naming them."[15]

In the beginning, naming was the prerogative of the gods. But there was a notable instance where this power was assigned to a surrogate. After God had created all living things, he brought them to one whom he had named "Adam," that being the Hebrew generic name for "man": "And whatsoever Adam called every living creature that was the name thereof" (Genesis 2:19). He who had been the first named thereby became the first namer. Thus it was particularly appropriate that Mozart dubbed himself Adam, for he delighted in naming and in playing with names, both his own and those of others. For example, in a letter of 1787 to his friend Gottfried von Jacquin, Mozart detailed how "we all invented names for ourselves on the journey [to Prague]. Here they are. I am Punkititi. My wife is Schable Pumfa. Hofer is Rozka-Pumpa. Stadler is Natchibinitschibi. My servant Joseph is Sagadarata. My dog Gauckerl is Schamanuzky. Madam Quallenberg is Runzifunzi. Mlle Crux is Ramlo Schurimuri. Freistädtler is Gaulimauli."[16] Although the giving of pet names was clearly part of Mozart's addiction to the play-impulse, it may also have been a means by which he tried to confront issues of identity. True, Mozart is playing. But he is also about to enter a new kingdom, which therefore will need new subjects and new names. In such a land, naturally, everyone is permitted—even required—to take on a new identity, that is, to start over. The initiatory implications are quite clear.[17]

Mozart's choice of the name Adam may well have originated as a conscious, jesting anagram for "Amad[é]." But "Adam" is different in quality and kind from any other anagram for "Amadé" in that it constitutes a multilayered sign with a network of familiar meanings. It is, therefore, plausible that the private meanings of the name for Mozart may overlap its more universal implications.

In renaming himself Adam on a ritual occasion in the summer of 1782, Mozart arrogated to himself a great power. To be Adam is to be mighty, to be the progenitor of mankind, favorite of God, before whom all the angels, save only Satan, kneeled down. To be Adam is to be the first born, shaped from the red clay, sole human tenant of the earthly Paradise. To become Adam is to be reborn in Eden and to gain the promise of immortality. Through the magic of naming, Mozart authorized himself to wipe the slate clean, to liberate himself from the past. Through the word he affirmed that he came pure to his marriage with Constanze; together they were to be Adam and Eve in their own Eden. Through the word, Mozart became his own father's Father and dubbed himself the son of God rather than of the deputy court kapellmeister whose name he bore. The child Mozart was fond of saying, in an apparent ritual of obedience, "First comes God, then Papa." Perhaps he meant this more literally than we have suspected.

There is, however, a tragic substratum to Adam's story: the price of power, favor, and immortality is perpetual innocence and unquestioning obedience, a price neither Adam nor Mozart could afford to pay. For though each was a favorite son, he was simultaneously a rebel willing—perhaps eager—to accept expulsion from Eden in order to gain sexual knowledge and creative freedom. Each preferred liberty to safety. Each married in defiance of his creator's injunction, painfully choosing heresy as the means to achieve distance from an intolerable domination. That may be why the adoption of the name Adam also has the ancillary effect of canceling God's direct presence—Theophilus and its translations—in Mozart's name.

Mozart is not the only creative artist to adopt or to experiment with a new name at a pivotal moment of his life. Renaming is a step toward self-creation by fictive means; it comes naturally to artists and others who are discontented, who are impelled to reshape the nature of things. Picasso takes his mother's name; Mary Ann Evans dubs herself "George Eliot"; Walter Whitman becomes "Walt Whitman"; David Henry Thoreau rearranges his name as "Henry David Thoreau"; Alexey Maximovich Peshkov selects the name "Gorky" ("bitter") "at random" for his first printed story; for a while, twentieth-century totalitarian politics were dominated by individuals who set aside their ancestral names in favor of resonant, mythic ones. By temporarily using a name that had not been assigned to him at birth, an *unauthorized* name, Mozart symbolically canceled a vested paternal privilege and took control of his own life. This at the critical juncture of his unauthorized marriage, and in the aftermath of his flight from Salzburg to Vienna, where he hoped to fulfill his creative mission. The use of a new name may, therefore, be an act of metaphoric aggression, an appropriation, even a theft, even a sign of a rebellious desire to overthrow the existent state of affairs.

The issues are familiar ones: birth and ancestry, gratitude and guilt, self and destiny. That may be why, on the same occasion that Mozart equated himself with Adam, he found himself unable to produce his baptismal certificate, so that he needed a waiver from the authorities. The matter became urgent when he wanted to apply for membership in the Tonkün-stler-Societät (Musicians' Society) to assure that his family would be eligible for death and pension benefits, for the musicians' organization strictly enforced its rule that a baptismal certificate be submitted. In February 1784 Mozart wrote his father, asking for the certificate but lying about the reason he needed it: "Would it be possible to let me have a copy of my certificate of baptism? They all swear here that the first time I came to Vienna I must have been at least ten years old. . . . If I showed them my certificate of baptism I could shut them all up at one go."[18] A year elapsed and the certificate had not been sent. On 11 February 1785 Mozart formally applied for membership, but no waiver was granted, despite his numerous services for the Society. His petition remained "*in suspenso* partly because of the lack of the baptismal certificate and further until the settlement of general Society disputes," the nature of which were not specified.[19] After performances of *Davidde penitente* at Society benefit concerts on 13 and 15 March 1785, Mozart renewed his petition, promising that "as soon as he received the necessary baptismal certificate he would supply it," but the response, dated 24 August, stated: "A further decision will follow when the baptismal certificate has been supplied."[20]

Mozart never furnished the baptismal certificate. Clearly, in the face of his father's unwillingness to send it, he himself had some resistance to procuring the document, a copy of which could readily have been obtained from the Salzburg Cathedral register through the mails or by application in person by any of his Salzburg friends. Perhaps it uncomfortably reminded him of his father's claim upon him, or perhaps he felt he had no right to pursue the matter without his father's consent. Vaguely we can also sense here—and in the renaming as "Adam" itself—the glimmerings of what Otto Rank and Sigmund Freud called a "family romance" fantasy, a fantasy that one comes from a different family than the family one was apparently born into. For the birth certificate was the best evidence that he was a Mozart, at a time when his full membership in that family had become precarious, to say the least. Somehow, the material evidence of Mozart's birth and ancestry had now fallen under some kind of taboo.

All of the indications of Mozart's devotion to the carnivalesque masquerade—his preoccupation with every kind of metamorphosis, his posing of riddles, his playing with names and signs, his "concealment" of his baptismal certificate—circle around issues of identity; all of these implicitly pose the same simple question: "Who am I?" An appeal is also implied: "I myself do not know who I am. Can you help me to find out?" Mozart's constant alterations of his name are his way of experimenting with different identities, trying to tune them to his satisfaction. At the same time the adoption of a new name also signified an abandonment of identity, a yielding to the "family romance." Mozart walks away from his primal, totalitarian family in order to form a new, utopian family of his own.

Mozart, as usual reluctant to confront the most painful issues head on, attempted instead a variety of distancing strategies—deception, flight, concealment, and symbolic or even magical metamorphoses, many of which are crystallized in his experimentation with the name Adam. The renaming has the double character of a masking and an exorcism: a new persona is adopted and a bothersome spirit is laid to rest. But, just as the annual carnival has a finite term followed by a restoration of the status quo ante, both the masquerade and the exorcism were partial. It was not long before the contending forces canceled each other out and the name "Adam" was heard no more. (Or had it gone underground, become Mozart's "secret"? At the Masonic funeral oration in his honor, he was thrice designated "A***" by the eulogist.[21]) Within a few days Mozart reverted to his "given" name; and the tragic cycle of entanglement and disentanglement recommenced, continuing until Leopold Mozart's death a half-decade later—and beyond. Still, the renaming had served its main purpose: by verbal prestidigitation and symbolic metamorphosis to widen the space between Mozart and his father sufficiently to permit the marriage to take place, even without the much-requested but denied blessing from Salzburg.

Mozart. Silhouette by Hieronymus Löschenkohl,
published in *Österreichischer Nationalkalender*, 1785.

19

···

THE IMPRESARIO

From the moment of his arrival in Vienna Mozart explored every possible way to make a living and to fulfill his ambitions as a composer. At last he had the opportunity to demonstrate his powers, unhampered by old family agendas, unrestricted by parochial attitudes. If he were to succeed, he would have to prove himself capable of competing in a major center of the European music world, and now as a mature composer and performer rather than as an erstwhile child prodigy. Mozart unhesitatingly took up the challenge and plunged into an enormous range of activities, stunning in their variety, including not only compositions, performances, and publications of every kind, but several business ventures as well. Although he still hoped for an imperial post, he was not seeking only to find a secure, limited niche for himself: he aimed to make his mark in every conceivable sphere of Viennese musical life. And, indeed, within the space of a few short years, he would succeed in reaching broad segments of the populace, far broader, perhaps, than did either Haydn or Beethoven, for he gained favor with the imperial court, including Emperor Joseph II and Archduke Maximilian Franz, in addition to the connoisseur aristocracy and the corps of visiting princes and diplomats. On occasion, his tunes from *Die Entführung aus dem Serail, Le nozze di Figaro,* and *Die Zauberflöte* and his dances for the Redoutensaal even caught the ear of ordinary Viennese citizens. These successes did not, however, come automatically or all at once.

Because his career centered at first on personal performances and teaching, it was to be a while before he achieved any remarkable productivity as a free-lance composer. His major Viennese work of 1781 was the completion of the set of Six Violin Sonatas, K. 296 and K. 376–80, four of them newly written, that he dedicated to Josepha Auernhammer, for whom, in September, he also composed the Sonata in D for two pianos, K. 448/375a. Similarly written for his pupils were three or more sets of variations on fashionable French melodies, including Twelve Variations for piano and violin on "La Bergère Célimène," K. 359/374a, Six Variations for piano and violin on "Hélas, j'ai perdu mon amant," K. 360/374b, and Eight Variations for piano on Grétry's "Dieu d'amour," K. 352/374c. (The two sets of piano variations, K. 265/300e and K. 353/300f, also date from 1781 or a bit later.) The Serenade in E-flat, K. 375, rounds out Mozart's completed works for the year, which also saw progress on act one of *Die Entführung aus dem Serail* at the end of July.

As his career gathered momentum, Mozart's letters home increasingly came to be filled with references to works being composed, performed, copied, and published; to performances given or contemplated; to subscription concerts and salon appearances. His father's good student, Mozart carefully analyzed the economics of the music world; in particular he realized that Vienna did not constitute a monolithic audience but contained a multiplicity of audiences with appetites for various kinds of music. He now sought to appeal to each of these audiences, to cultivate patronage wherever he could find it—at the imperial court, in aristocratic salons and musical societies, among professional performers, amateur musicians of every capability, concertgoers of every class, and devotees of theater and opera, and not neglecting the denizens of the ballrooms. To reach these diverse audiences Mozart wrote in a full spectrum of styles and genres, from every kind of solo and duo keyboard music to piano concertos, from sonatas and trios to string quartets and quintets, from songs and arias to operas, from music for wind ensemble to full-scale symphonies. In the four years from 1782 to 1785 he wrote more than one hundred and fifty separate compositions.

It was a while before a purposeful compositional pattern began to emerge. For the first nine months of 1782 Mozart's compositions continued the fairly haphazard pattern of 1781, with two soprano arias, "Der Liebe himmlisches Gefühl," K. 119/382h, and "Nehmt meinen Dank, ihr holden Gönner!" K. 383; a Minuet in C for orchestra, K. 409/383f; several mainly risqué Canons, K. 382a–g, written purely for fun; and a number of miscellaneous pieces and fragments for piano, probably including the Fantasia in D minor, K. 397/385g.[1] The only large-scale orchestral works were the Symphony in D, K. 385 ("Haffner"), composed, as we have seen, for a Salzburg celebration, and the Serenade in C minor, K. 388/384a, for a local celebration. True, he was much occupied during these months with the completion of *Die Entführung aus dem Serail* and pinned his main hopes for recognition upon its production.

Although many of these are fine works, the quality of his output as a whole in the eighteen months after his arrival did not represent an advance over his achievements in Paris in 1778, in Salzburg in 1779–80, or in Munich in 1780–81. He seemed to be responding to compositional opportunities rather than creating them, and in the absence of important commissions for major works he was writing relatively small-scale pieces for himself, students, and singers. Many works were begun but remained unfinished, perhaps reflecting the uncertainties of his patronage situation or, as Robert L. Marshall has suggested, the effects of "physical and emotional stress."[2] Perhaps the strains of the move to Vienna and of his turbulent courtship and marriage affected his creativity more than has previously been thought. It is also possible that, now finally on his own, he was not quite certain how to proceed. Whatever the reasons, he appears to have held himself somewhat in check during this transitional period, relying cautiously upon his ability to write in the prevailing styles and for the most part avoiding challenging musical issues. But it was precisely timidity that would not succeed for him in Vienna, for it was here that imagination, new experiences, and deep feeling were wanted by many of the music-lovers who were his potential audience.

As early as his first year in Vienna Mozart had already won over important members of the aristocracy, with performances at the residences of Countess Thun, Count Cobenzl, Prince Galitzin, and Archduke Maximilian Franz, plus the notable joint appearance—a competition, really—with Muzio Clementi at the court, at which he acquitted himself very well. When, in late 1781, his father retailed to him a malicious report that Mozart was not favored by the Viennese elite, he responded confidently, "If you really believe that I am detested at Court and by the old and new aristocracy, just write to Herr von Strack, Countess Thun, Countess Rumbeck, Baroness Waldstätten, Herr von Sonnenfels, Frau von Trattner, *enfin,* to anyone you choose. Meanwhile let me tell you that at table the other day the Emperor gave me the very highest praise, accompanied by the words: '*C'est un talent, décidé!*'"[3] In 1782 he improved his position still further (and doubled his income) with his first "academy" (a concert in a major theater for his own benefit) on 3 March 1782 and with the presentation of *Die Entführung aus dem Serail* in July, which received twelve performances before the year was out and soon became an international success, achieving productions in fifteen German-speaking cities.[4] The Vienna correspondent of a leading German musical journal called it "full of beauties . . . It surpassed the public's expectation, and the author's taste and new ideas, which were entrancing, received the loudest and most general applause."[5] Despite the opera's signal success, however, Mozart only earned the normal flat fee of 100 ducats and perhaps also the proceeds from one of the later performances, plus something for his surreptitious sale in later 1782 of a copy of the score to the Prussian court through ambassador Baron Johann Riedesel.

Indeed, although he was making a reasonable living at the time, Mozart was uncertain during much of 1782 whether he would achieve a breakthrough. For a while he pinned his hopes upon receiving an imperial post. "I have it from a very good source that he [the Emperor] was extremely pleased with me," he wrote in January 1782. "He was very gracious, said a great deal to me privately, and even mentioned my marriage. Who knows? Perhaps—what do you think? At any rate I might make the attempt."[6] Similarly, he wrote that "the manner in which the Emperor has spoken to me has given me some hope."[7] A few months later he reported, with an obvious mixture of exultation and anxiety, that "the whole town is ringing" with talk that Emperor Joseph intended to take him into his service:

> A number of people have already congratulated me. I am quite ready to believe that it has been discussed with the Emperor and that perhaps he is contemplating it. But up to this moment I have no definite information. . . . If things have gone so far without any effort on my part, they can now proceed to their conclusion in the same way. For if one makes any move oneself, one immediately receives less pay, because, as it is, the Emperor is a skinflint. If he wants me he must pay me, for the honor alone of serving him is not enough. Indeed, if he were to offer me 1,000 florins but some Count offered 2,000, I would send my compliments to the Emperor and go with the Count.[8]

As it turned out, Mozart was not given an opportunity to reject an inadequate offer, for none was forthcoming.

The matter became more serious after his marriage, especially when it became apparent that *Die Entführung aus dem Serail* would not provide real security for him and his wife. He began to speak of leaving Vienna, reporting in August that various high nobles "are all very much displeased with the Emperor, because he does not value men of talent more, and allows them to leave his dominions. Kaunitz said the other day to the Archduke Maximilian, when the conversation turned on myself, that '*such people only come into the world once in a hundred years and must not be driven out of Germany, particularly when we are fortunate enough to have them in the capital.*'"[9] He wrote bitterly of quitting Vienna:

> The Viennese gentry, and in particular the Emperor, must not imagine that I am on this earth solely for the sake of Vienna. There is no monarch

in the world whom I should be more glad to serve than the Emperor, but I refuse to beg for any post. I believe that I am capable of doing credit to any court. If Germany, my beloved fatherland, of which, as you know, I am proud, will not accept me, then in God's name let France or England become the richer by another talented German, to the disgrace of the German nation.[10]

Mozart's best patrons were alarmed when he spoke of going to Paris and London and even more when he began to study English and take daily lessons to polish his French. He reported that Countess Thun and Baron van Swieten were making great efforts "to keep me here. But I cannot afford to wait indefinitely, and indeed I refuse to remain hanging on here at their mercy."[11] Anomalously, Mozart's father now found himself having to urge his son not to leave Vienna: "Who will prevent him from pursuing his present career in Vienna if he only has a little patience?" he wrote to Baroness Waldstätten, suggesting that Mozart would do well patiently to await the deaths of Court Kapellmeister Bonno and Court Chamber Composer Gluck.[12]

By the following week, however, Mozart's enthusiasm for departure had diminished (or his mood had shifted): "You are perfectly right about France and England! It is a step which I can always take, and it is better for me to remain in Vienna a little longer."[13] By October, when he was passed over by the emperor for the post of music master to the Princess of Württemberg, he accepted the news with equanimity, probably because he was encouraged by a wealth of engagements, including performances at the residences of Countess Thun and Prince Galitzin, plus a major appearance at Josepha Auernhammer's academy on 3 November. "I am engaged for all [Prince Galitzin's] concerts. I am always fetched in his coach and brought to his house and treated there most magnificiently."[14] In addition, Mozart directed a performance of *Die Entführung aus dem Serail* on 8 October that was attended by Grand Duke Paul of Russia and his wife. He had by this time achieved great celebrity and was formulating a variety of plans to make money. In January, he and Constanze gave a ball in their own apartment, at two florins per head: "We began at six o'clock in the evening and kept on until . . . seven o'clock next morning."[15] The party was attended by Baroness Waldstätten, Herr von Edelbach, Franz Gilowsky, the Stephanies (father and son), the singers Johann Valentin and his wife Maria Anna Adamberger, Joseph and Aloysia Lange—"It would be impossible to name them all." Clearly, Mozart was ever on the alert for strategies to make money. He even considered arranging to print his own music instead of granting rights to publishers, and wrote to his father for advice: "If I have some work printed or engraved at my own expense, how can I protect myself from being cheated by the engraver? For surely he can print off as many copies as he likes and therefore swindle me. . . . Why, I almost feel inclined not to sell any more of my compositions to any engraver, but to have them printed or engraved by subscription at my own expense, as most people do and in this way make good profits."[16]

Mozart had counted his takings from *Die Entführung aus dem Serail* and pondered how he could gain a more equitable share in the product of his creativity; his ruminations centered on the possibilities of acting as his own impresario: "I am willing to write an opera, but not to look on with a hundred ducats in my pocket and see the theater making four times as much in a fortnight. I intend to produce my opera at my own expense, I shall clear at least 1,200 florins by three performances and then the management may have it for fifty ducats. If they refuse to take it, I shall have made some money and can produce the opera anywhere."[17] Because opera production was securely in the hands of the imperial theater management and its lessees, however, it no longer appeared obvious that writing operas was the best way to make large sums of money. What he needed was to find some way to become his own impresario, to take the risks of production and enjoy the full profits instead of settling for standard free-lance fees.

At first it may not have been clear to Mozart how he was to accomplish this goal. After all, to take risks one must have capital, a resource with which Mozart was not well supplied. That is probably why he went into partnership with the concert producer Philipp Jakob Martin to present a series of twelve open-air Sunday summer concerts in the Augarten, plus "four grand serenades" in other public places. "The subscription for the whole summer is two ducats," he wrote, "so you can imagine that we shall have plenty of subscribers, the more so as I am taking an interest in it and am associated with it."[18] He calculated the takings in advance: "Assuming that we get only a hundred subscribers, then each of us will have a profit of three hundred florins (even if the costs amount to two hundred florins)."[19] Although Mozart's letters do not provide a detailed report, the concerts, which began on 26 May, seem to have been well subscribed by an audience that included Archduke Maximilian Franz and other members of the Viennese nobility.

Serendipitously, it may have been Mozart's academy of 3 March 1782 that showed him new possibilities for becoming an impresario. At that concert Mozart played the Piano Concerto in D, K. 175, with a newly composed rondo finale, K. 382, and the performance aroused great enthusiasm. He wrote home, "I am sending you . . . *the last rondo* which I composed for my concerto in D major and which is making such a furore in Vienna. But I beg you to guard it like a *jewel*—and not to give it to a soul to play. . . . I composed it *specially* for myself."[20] Sensing the unusual response to his performances of his own concertos, he now sought to turn the enthusiasm for them to his purpose. He completed three new concertos by early 1783—in A, K. 414/385p, in F, K. 413/387a, and in C, K. 415/387b—and offered manuscript copies of them for sale by subscription in January and played them at academies for himself, Aloysia Lange, and Therese Teyber during March 1783. The manuscript subscription was not a success and Mozart had the takings from only one of the academies, but he now saw clearly that what was required was to increase the number of public concerts featuring himself as composer and soloist; in that way, he could entirely control the production and thereby reap the maximum profits. Because of intense competition and limited availability, however, he could only expect to obtain the use of one of the court theaters for a single major academy for his own benefit per year, and although these remained climactic and lucrative events through 1786, one such annual concert was far from sufficient to fill his purse or satisfy his ambitions. And so he hit upon the idea of presenting multiple subscription concerts for solo piano and small orchestra in unconventional venues, such as the Trattnerhof and the Mehlgrube. The Trattnerhof was a large residential building on the Graben named after its owner, Johann Thomas Trattner, and it contained a large room that could serve as a concert hall. The Mehlgrube was a restaurant-inn with an adjoining ballroom.[21] At the Trattnerhof in 1784 he presented a series of three concerts and at the Mehlgrube in 1785 a series of six concerts. All in all, he gave four subscription concerts in 1784, ten in 1785, and four in 1786; in addition he performed privately in aristocratic salons a minimum of eighteen times in 1784, and five times in 1785.

For a performer-composer to present so many public concerts in Vienna was almost unprecedented; rarely had anyone given more than one concert in a season.[22] The first climax of this enterprise was described in a letter of 4 March 1784, in which Mozart listed twenty-two events, including the three concerts at the Trattnerhof and two projected academies at the Burgtheater (one of which did not materialize). "You must forgive me if I don't write very much," he excitedly advised his father, "but it is impossible to find time to do so, as I am giving three subscription concerts in Trattner's room on the last three Wednesdays of Lent, beginning on March 17th. I have a hundred subscribers already and shall easily get another thirty. The price for the three concerts is six florins. I shall probably give two concerts in the theater this year. Well, as you may imagine, I must play some new works—and therefore I must compose. The whole morning is taken up with pupils and almost every evening I have to play. . . . Well," he concluded with evident pride, "haven't I enough to do? I don't think that in this way I can possibly get out of practice."[23] Two weeks later he forwarded the full list of his subscribers, whose number had now risen to 176 and constituted a roll call of the higher nobility, with room left over for luminaries of the lesser nobility and state bureaucracy and Vienna's most distinguished cultural figures.[24] Like the subscribers to Beethoven's Trios, op. 1, a decade later, the connoisseur aristocracy had collectively recognized and paid homage to greatness in its midst. "The first concert on March 17 went off very well. The hall was full to overflowing; and the new concerto [probably K. 449] I played won extraordinary applause. Everywhere I go I hear praises of that concert."[25] After the Burgtheater concert on 1 April he wrote, "I have done myself great credit with my three subscription concerts, and the concert I gave in the theater was most successful. I composed two grand concertos [K. 450 and K. 451] and then a quintet [K. 452 for winds and piano], which called forth the very greatest applause: I myself consider it to be the best work I have ever composed. . . . How I wish you could have heard it! And how beautifully it was performed! Well, to tell the truth I was really worn out in the end after playing so much—and it is greatly to my credit that my listeners never got tired."[26]

In the euphoria of his success as a performer-impresario, Mozart once again sought to become a concert promoter for other artists. Jointly with another popular pianist, Georg Friedrich Richter, he took an option on the Trattnerhof hall for a six-month period, or even leased it for that time (with an escape clause), and between them he and Richter scheduled as many as nine concerts, intending to lease the remaining dates. The hall rental per diem was only about 13 florins, so the profit potential was considerable, but the six-month rental was 550 florins, and apparently the complexity of the project (or Trattner's plan to install a casino in his building) soon led them to abandon it. We know of this inconclusive business venture from an entry in Trattner's rent book, probably for April 1784: "20th do., Wolfgang Amadeus Mozart, for 3 musical concerts likewise held during this Lent, 9 Austrian ducats, id est 38 florins, 42 Kreuzer; the rent for the remaining period to be canceled, 433 fl. 54 kr."[27] The entry shows that Trattner, who with his wife, Maria Theresia, stood godparents for four of Mozart's children, charged only for the nine scheduled dates.[28]

Mozart was now holding the reins of the family enterprise. Taking up where his father had left off, he had become his own impresario, driving himself to the limit but, as always, showing an infinite capacity for creative work. The main vehicle of his success was the piano concerto, conceived to display the full range of his keyboard capabilities, to express a range of hitherto unplumbed affects, and to exploit new technical and dramatic potentialities of the classical style. He understood that novelties of expression and form were required, not only to please his listeners but to keep them returning to successive concerts. Thus, he wrote three or four con-

certos for each of the four seasons from 1782–83 to 1785–86 and renovated several earlier concertos for present use. It was a genre that temporarily united several different audiences into a unique, amalgamated one. And
here his greatest feat was to bridge the gap in aesthetic sensibility between
Viennese musical connoisseurs (many of them members of the aristocracy)
and the less adventurous or rarefied court audience, which primarily
sought comfortable rather than edifying musical experiences or which
wanted its composers to hold up gleaming mirrors in which princes might
behold their reflections. Mozart understood the delicate balances that
momentarily seemed to join such diverse audiences, reporting to his father:
"These concertos [K. 413/387a, K. 414/385p, and K. 415/387b] are a
happy medium between what is too easy and too difficult; they are very
brilliant, pleasing to the ear, and natural, without being vapid. There are
passages here and there from which the connoisseurs alone can derive satisfaction; but these passages are written in such a way that the less learned
cannot fail to be pleased, though without knowing why."[29] Here, Mozart
was taking the chance of trying to forge a new audience rather than
responding to an existing one. For the present he had calibrated perfectly,
creating a harmonious connection between an eager composer-performer
and a delighted audience, which was given the opportunity of witnessing
the transformation and perfection of a major musical genre.

From the winter of 1782–83 to the Burgtheater academy of 7 April 1786,
piano concertos were the primary focus of Mozart's compositional productivity and the main source of his income, and their sheer quantity—fourteen in all during that period, plus several separate concerto-finale movements—overshadowed his work in other genres, with the sole exception of
the string quartet. In contrast to the concertos, which were written in concentrated bursts for specific performance opportunities, Mozart worked in
a leisurely fashion on the set of Six String Quartets—in G, K. 387; D
minor, K. 421/417b; E-flat, K. 428/421b; B-flat, K. 458; A, K. 464; and
C, K. 465—that he eventually dedicated to Haydn, completing one at the
end of 1782, two in mid-1783, taking them up again only in the fall of
1784 and completing the last by 14 January 1785. It was as though in order
to press at the boundaries of his art he needed to be free both of deadlines
and of any pecuniary motive. Thus, one might want to see the string quartets as the emblem of Mozart's economic independence, as a sign that he
could devote himself to pure music apart from commercial considerations
or even performance opportunities.

It is doubtful that Mozart could have imagined at the outset that the
quartets, despite their experimental style and the difficulties they presented
to most performers, might also prove a valuable commodity in the publish-

The Graben, Vienna (1781), with Trattnerhof in the right foreground.
Engraving by Karl Schütz.

ing market, but the fact that the final three of the set were completed more
rapidly, during a two-month period, suggests that he had by then entered
into an agreement for their publication. Because it was possible to make a
profit on sales of only 100 copies (the usual size of an edition), publishers
were encouraged to appeal to specialized groups of performers. Engraved
editions of Mozart's music and offerings of manuscript copies of his scores
included "learned" works as well as overtly popular pieces and aimed at
performers and music-lovers of every capability, whether professional musicians, competent dilettantes, or beginners. Apparently his music had a
ready market, for many of his Vienna publications went through two or
three editions (reprints were usually 20 to 30 copies), while those of some
of his German dances and minuets reached as many as five editions. Thus,
the engraving rights to Mozart's most advanced instrumental works of the
early Vienna years, the six "Haydn" String Quartets, were acquired by
Artaria & Co. (and published by them in October 1785) for the munificent
sum of 450 florins, equivalent to the usual composer's fee for an opera.

Apart from the string quartets, Mozart did not systematically cultivate
chamber music composition during these years. Between the Quintet in
E-flat for horn and strings, K. 407/386c, written at the end of 1782 and
the Quintet in E-flat for piano and winds, K. 452, dated 30 March 1784,
he wrote only the two Duos for violin and viola in G, K. 423, and in
B-flat, K. 424. The Violin Sonata in B-flat, K. 454, written for the virtuoso Regina Strinasacchi, is dated 21 April 1784 and was published later

that year by Torricella as part of a set that also included the Piano Sonatas in D, K. 284/205b, and in B-flat, K. 333/315c. In 1785 he wrote two chamber-music works, the Piano Quartet in G minor, K. 478, dated 16 October 1785, and the Violin Sonata in E-flat, K. 481, dated 12 December 1785. The piano quartet was immediately published by Hoffmeister, who, contrary to legend, was so little discouraged by the reception of this his first Mozart publication that he issued eleven others of his works over the next three or four years. These included several of Mozart's more uncompromising compositions, such as the String Quartet in D, K. 499 ("Hoffmeister"), the Fugue in C minor for two pianos, K. 426, and the Sonata in C for piano duet, K. 521.[30]

For solo piano Mozart also wrote several sets of variations: Six Variations in F on "Salve tu, Domine," K. 398/416e; Eight Variations in A on "Come un agnello," K. 460/454a; and Ten Variations in G, on "Unser dummer Pöbel meint," K. 455, the latter dated 25 August 1784 in Mozart's thematic catalog. In the C-minor Fugue, K. 426, of 1783 (arranged by Mozart for strings in 1788 as K. 546) Mozart continued his efforts in counterpoint that had begun the previous year. A comic "Marche funebre del Sigr Maestro Contrapunto," K. 453a, probably belongs to 1784. The Fantasy in C minor, K. 475, and Sonata in C minor, K. 457, were composed in 1785 and published in that same year by Artaria & Co. as a single work. Were it not for the researches of Plath and Tyson, that work would still be thought to be Mozart's sole contribution to the sonata literature from these years, but, as we have already mentioned, we now can safely assign the Sonata in B-flat, K. 333/315c, to late 1783 and tentatively place the Sonatas in C, K. 330/300h, in A, K. 331/300i, and in F, K. 332/300k, in August–November 1783. Here, we may want to observe that Artaria & Co. published the three sonatas only months after the Mozarts' return from Salzburg.

There was little demand for Mozart to add to his orchestral repertory between 1783 and 1785: the Symphony in C, K. 425 ("Linz"), was composed in late fall of 1783, on the way home from Salzburg, and apart from the piano concertos there is only one other concerto, the Horn Concerto no. 2 in E-flat, K. 417, dated 27 May 1783. The Horn Concerto no. 3 in E-flat, K. 447, previously thought to date from 1783, probably was completed in 1787 or 1788, although the Romance movement may have been written earlier.[31] An Andante for a violin concerto, K. 470, dated 1 April 1785, is lost.

He did write a fair number of individual operatic arias during these years, almost all of them in 1783. Several of these, including the Soprano Arias "Vorrei spiegarvi, oh Dio," K. 418, and "No, no che non sei capace," K. 419, along with the Tenor Aria "Per pietà, non ricercate," K. 420, were written in mid-1783 for use by Aloysia Lange and Johann Valentin Adamberger as replacement arias in Anfossi's opera *Il curioso indiscreto*. A brilliant Scene, "Mia speranza adorata"—"Ah, non sai, qual pena," K. 416, was

performed by Lange in her own concert on 11 January and then at Mozart's
academy on 23 March. Closing out the year was a Bass Recitative and Aria,
"Così dunque tradisci"—"Aspri rimorsi atroci," K. 432/421a, written for
Ludwig Fischer, who played Osmin in *Die Entführung aus dem Serail,* and a
Tenor Recitative and Aria, "Misero! o sogno!"—"Aura, che intorno," K.
431/425b. Two years later, Mozart composed two works as insertion
ensembles for a performance of Bianchi's *La villanella rapita* at the Burgtheater on 28 November 1785: a vocal Quartet, "Dite almeno in che mancai,"
K. 479, and a Trio for soprano, tenor, bass, "Mandina amabile," K. 480. A
dozen or so lieder, an equal number of orchestral dances, five insubstantial
Divertimentos for two basset horns or clarinets and bassoon or for three
basset horns, K. 439b, two Adagios for similar instrumentation, K. 411/484a
and K. 410/484d, and a great deal of Masonic music dating from 1785 round
out Mozart's production for these years.

  With due allowance for the masterpieces in other genres on this
extremely diverse list, it may fairly be said that Mozart's supreme achievements between his arrival in Vienna and the premiere of *Le nozze di Figaro*
in May 1786 are to be found in the piano concertos, the "Haydn" Quartets, and the C-minor Mass. In the absence of a strong prevailing tradition,
Mozart essentially invented the classical piano concerto and then elaborated
the concerto's potentialities of form and expression in a series of highly
individual masterpieces. He unveiled a universe and then devoted himself
to populating it with the most diverse creations. Then, noting the example
of Haydn's opus 33 String Quartets, but uninterested in imitating them or
merely extending their implications, Mozart was determined to write six
highly differentiated quartets of his own; the resultant works permanently
transfigured the genre and imbued it with a degree of subjectivity and
intensity of feeling that was not again reached until Beethoven's "Razumovsky" Quartets two decades later. Finally, Mozart was not moved by
appeals to liturgical reform by Emperor Joseph and Archbishop Colloredo,
and his C-minor Mass uses baroque, classical, Salzburg, Viennese, and Italian materials as the alphabet of a hitherto undiscovered language. What
may be most extraordinary, and has not been sufficiently emphasized, is the
concurrent origination in the closing months—or even closing weeks—of
1782 of Mozart's works in these three genres: the great line of piano concertos, the "Haydn" Quartets, and the C-minor Mass. He was simultaneously at work on the first three of his Vienna piano concertos, in A, K.
414/385p, in F, K. 413/387a, and in C, K. 415/387b, and had completed
one of them (probably the A-major) by 28 December 1782; the autograph of
the G-major String Quartet is dated three days later, 31 December 1782;
and the first mention of the recently begun C-minor Mass is in Mozart's
letter to his father of 4 January 1783. Clearly, Mozart was undergoing a

moment of supreme, protean inspiration, one that was to transform not only his career but the entire art of music. In the martial opening strains of the C-major Concerto, K. 415/387b, where the military style boldly moves to annex Viennese classicism as part of its theater of operations; in his dedicatory preface to the string quartets—"They are, indeed, the fruit of a long and laborious toil"—where he publicly affirms the momentousness of his purpose; and in his disdain—even defiance—of the church-music reforms, Mozart proclaims his intention to be an original composer and his refusal to accept any restraints upon the expression of his creative impulse. After eighteen months of relative timidity, Mozart had absorbed the shocks attendant on his liberation from Salzburg and was ready to renounce the limitations of his father's neoclassicist aesthetic. Freed from prohibitions both external and internal, he had embarked upon a voyage "through strange seas of thought, alone" (Wordsworth). We seem to be in the presence of the reshaping and mature crystallization of Mozart's composer's voice, a great, multifarious eruption of the imagination whose fallout will take years to settle to earth.

It was not long before Mozart began to earn a good living in Vienna (see Table 1). Even in 1781, his first year in the capital, he earned almost 1,000 florins from teaching and performances, more than double his Salzburg salary. This was not yet a large sum, for life in Vienna was much more

Table 1. Summary of Mozart's Vienna Earnings, By Year★

Year	Estimated earnings (in florins)
1781	1,084 to 1,284
1782	2,174 to 3,074
1783	1,892 to 2,408
1784	3,720
1785	2,959
1786	2,604 to 3,704
1787	3,321
1788	1,385 to 2,060
1789	1,483 to 2,158
1790	1,850 to 3,225
1791	3,672 to 5,672
Total, 1781–91	26,144 to 33,585
Total, 1786–91	14,315 to 20,140

★ *See Appendix for details.*

expensive than in Salzburg. He wrote: "With [1,200 florins] a man and his wife can manage in Vienna if they live quietly and in the retired way which we desire; but, of course, if I were to fall ill, we should not make a kreuzer."[32] In 1782 and 1783, primarily as a result of income from personal appearances, he earned more than 2,000 florins per year, and during the years 1784 and 1785 his income was elevated to levels normally reached only by well-to-do Viennese, averaging something more than 3,000 florins. Calculating the profits on Mozart's concerts in February and March 1785, Leopold Mozart wrote, "If my son has no debts to pay, I think that he can now lodge two thousand florins in the bank. Certainly the money is there, and so far as eating and drinking is concerned, the housekeeping is extremely economical."[33]

These calculations went awry, however, and Mozart seriously needed money to supplement his earnings.[34] Somehow, his extraordinarily large earnings had been dissipated. It seems quite clear that he had begun to live well beyond his income from as early as October 1784, when he moved from his "decent quarters" in the Trattnerhof—where his rent was 150 florins per year—to the very expensive apartment at 846 Schulerstrasse in the center of the city: "That your brother has very fine quarters with all the necessary furniture you may gather from the fact that his rent is 460 florins."[35] By way of comparison, Leopold Mozart's own rent for seven rooms and a large salon in Salzburg's Tanzmeisterhaus was only 90 florins per year.[36] Around this time, Mozart also made several substantial purchases, of a fortepiano with a specially constructed pedal attachment at a cost of perhaps 900 florins, and a billiard table for about 300 florins. He owned a variety of other musical instruments.[37] He had his own carriage, and enjoyed the luxury of keeping a horse for recreation. As for food and clothing, his European journeys had taught Mozart the need to demonstrate that one might associate with aristocratic patrons on a level of nonchalant equality, and Mozart had no difficulty in learning this lesson; soon after his arrival in Vienna he wrote, "One must not make oneself cheap here—that is a cardinal point—or else one is done. Whoever is *most impertinent* has the best chance."[38]

We do not know whether Mozart spent his money in more dramatic ways—on gambling or women, for example. In a challenging article published in 1976, Uwe Kraemer proposed that Mozart was a compulsive gambler, who wasted huge sums at billiards and cards.[39] But the evidence he adduced simply confirmed that Mozart frequently played billiards and cards, not that he gambled heavily, let alone squandered fortunes in the process. It is true that gambling was prevalent in his society at every level, from the aristocracy and bureaucracy to intellectuals and ordinary citizens. "By the end of the century everyone indulges in it freely, the young Romantics even more than the rest," wrote the historian Brunschwig about Prussia;[40] closer to home, at Philipp Jakob Martin's Friday night "Liebhaber" ("music-lover") concerts in the Mehlgrube during the winter of 1781–82, it was announced that "card tables will be placed in the ante-rooms, and money for play provided at discretion; the company will also be provided with every kind of refreshment."[41] Lotteries were used by rulers everywhere to balance their budgets and pay their armies. But Johann Pezzl, in his guidebook to Vienna published while Mozart was still alive, wrote that the "passion for gambling" there had subsided somewhat by the later 1780s; punishments for playing games of chance were "meted out with severity" and "the more intelligent members of society" turned to "honorable and intellectual pursuits—household theater, music recitals, friendly conversation."[42] All in all, it does not seem improbable that Mozart played cards or billiards for money. But his known extravagances in dress, lifestyle, and lodgings, along with occasional unsuccessful financial ventures, more readily account for the disappearance of his earnings.

Mozart should have known better. Indeed, he did know better. In a famous letter to his father of June 1781 he had approvingly quoted Count Arco's warning to beware the transitoriness of Viennese acclaim: "You allow yourself to be far too easily dazzled in Vienna," Arco told him. "At first, it is true, you are overwhelmed with praises and make a great deal of money into the bargain—but how long does that last? After a few months the Viennese want something new."[43] To this Mozart countered: "It is perfectly true that the Viennese are apt to change their affections, *but only in the theater;* and my special line is too popular not to enable me to support myself. Vienna is certainly the land of the clavier! And even granted that they do get tired of me, they will not do so for a few years, certainly not before then. In the meantime I shall have gained both honor and money."[44]

Flush with his enormous success, however, Mozart had not thought it necessary to put money aside for future contingencies. Jahn's Victorian appraisal still stands: "He was not by any means a thoughtless, dissipated spendthrift. But a spendthrift he was, if the word be taken to signify one who fails to control his wants and luxuries, so that they may be in proportion to the actual state of his finances."[45] Perhaps his high income had fostered feelings—fed by his fabled earlier success as a young prodigy—that he was the perennial beneficiary of an infinite largesse, a fortunate child who could spend as much as he liked because his supplies would always be replenished.

Although he was probably not a compulsive gambler, Mozart may have had a gambler's mentality, may have been caught within an endless loop of aggression and self-punishment, between wanting to win and to lose. Desire for what is prohibited drives a gambler to great risks, but his "psy-

chic equilibrium . . . depends upon his losing, so that the inner books may
be balanced."[46] The significance of "winning" may not have been altogether transparent to Mozart. To earn and accumulate money was somehow to accept his father's cash-oriented values. To waste money, on the
other hand, held out more interesting possibilities, for it opened a way to
challenge Leopold Mozart—to cast away what Leopold appeared to hold
precious, and to repudiate the accumulation of wealth as an end in itself.
After all, the achievement of considerable material success had not gained
Mozart his father's approval; indeed, in some way, it seemed only to have
further irritated Leopold Mozart that his son had attained success so readily
on his own. Therefore, if money cannot bring love and respect, why not
waste it? Why not use it up? Why not enjoy it? In the end, however, defiance has its own price tag; it is followed by punishment both internal and
external, including the loss of money that Mozart and his family needed
for its subsistence.

The popularity of Mozart's concerts continued strong into 1785. In February and March he presented his six concerts at the Mehlgrube, gave a
major academy at the Burgtheater on 10 March featuring the Concerto in
C major, K. 467, and participated in academies by Auernhammer, the
prima donna Franziska Lebrun and her husband the oboist Ludwig August
Lebrun, the English soprano Anna (Nancy) Storace, and the singer Elisabeth Distler (he played his Concerto in D minor, K. 466, at the latter's
concert on 15 February). In addition, he played at the residences of Count
Zichy and Prince Kaunitz and still found time, on 12 February, to mount a
private performance of the last three of the "Haydn" Quartets. The older
composer was present on that occasion, as was Leopold Mozart—overwhelmed by the bustle of activity and by the high praise for his son from
every quarter, including Haydn and the emperor. Mozart was at the apogee
of his career.

With the Lenten season of 1786, however, the triumphal series of public concerts entered its final stage (most concerts were held during Advent
and Lent). Mozart gave his annual academy at the Burgtheater on 7 April,
featuring the just-completed Concerto in C minor, K. 491, but for the first
time since 1783 there were no scheduled subscription concerts. Not coin-
cidentally, this drastic downturn coincided with the resumption of his
career as an opera composer after a hiatus of three and a half years.

After the premiere of *Die Entführung aus dem Serail* in July 1782, Mozart
had set aside his ambitions to be an opera composer, with only two fragmentary opera projects, *Lo sposo deluso* and *L'oca del Cairo,* of 1783–84, to show for
the years since then. On 9 February 1784 he frankly stated why Varesco's
L'oca del Cairo was deliberately put on the back burner: "At present I

haven't the slightest intention of producing it. I have works to compose which *at the moment* are bringing in money, but will not do so later."[47] The "works to compose" were primarily the piano concertos—in E-flat, K. 449; B-flat, K. 450; D major, K. 451; and G major, K. 453—which Mozart completed between 9 February and 10 April 1784 because he needed to supply fresh material for his public concerts and for those of the pianist Barbara Ployer as well. Starting in September 1784 he wrote four more concertos—in B-flat, K. 456; F, K. 459; D minor, K. 466; and C, K. 467—to prepare for the 1785 Lenten season. In 1786, however, opera once again supplanted the piano concerto as Mozart's main medium. The reasons for this are not altogether clear. We know of his passion for the theater, his overriding desire to be an opera composer; we know, too, that he resented being regarded as a performer, a *Musikus* as opposed to a *Komponist* or *Kapellmeister,* that he was impatient with concert audiences, and that he wanted to free himself from the imperative to "perform" that had been impressed upon him so long ago. Mozart wanted to be regarded as a composer rather than a performer. Perhaps, too, he had for the time being exhausted the potentialities of the concerto as a vehicle of his musical thought. But it seems equally possible that the audience for his subscription concerts was starting to fade, and he was acute enough to sense that it was time to change his plans. He knew that sooner or later he would saturate the market for his concert performances; moreover, if programmatic novelty were required, it would not be easy to make further developments in the piano concerto genre. It would be best, then, to make the transition to another viable sphere of composition before the market dried up.

A chance comment by Beethoven's nephew in early 1824 offers other food for speculation regarding Mozart's shift away from a piano virtuoso's career, which had been the foundation of his popularity as well as of his most lucrative endeavors, both in public halls and aristocratic salons: "Mozart's fingers were so bent by the constant playing," wrote Karl van Beethoven in the deaf composer's conversation book, "that he couldn't even cut his meat."[48] The most startling aspect of the story—Mozart's awkwardness in using his hands—is apparently confirmed by Nissen, who wrote: "One knows that apart from clavier playing he was very clumsy in the use of his hands, that he couldn't cut meat and so forth and that his wife had to cut his meat as though he were a child."[49] Schlichtegroll had already told the story somewhat differently, emphasizing Mozart's fear of cutting his fingers.[50]

One possible inference to be drawn from these reports is that Mozart was suffering from a painful condition in his hands that might have adversely affected or threatened to affect his pianistic abilities and compelled him to think about alternative ways of making a living. Such a condition is consistent with Mozart's repeated bouts of rheumatic fever—in 1762, 1766, 1784, and perhaps 1787—a disease that can be cumulative in its effects and that probably was the main cause of his death. Arthritis is the most common clinical manifestation of rheumatic fever; typically, the affected joints become painful and tender, and may also become inflamed and swollen. We know from Leopold Mozart that when Mozart was a child, his joints were so severely affected after the early bouts that "he could not stand on his feet or move his toes or knees."[51] The joints affected are usually the ankles, knees, elbows, or wrists, but in the days before anti-inflammatory therapy, migration of the arthritic condition to the shoulders, hips, and the small joints of the extremities, including the fingers and toes, frequently resulted. If this speculation has any merit—for there is no con-temporary report that his virtuoso powers were affected—Mozart's condi-tion naturally was not to be advertised, because he would not have wanted to abandon piano-playing after 1786. And he did continue to perform occasionally, although such performances as he gave were either in foreign cities—his playing was highly praised in both Prague and Dresden—or in the privacy of his own home rather than in the major arenas where his capacities were well known. Additional arguments against this speculation are the consistently fine calligraphy of his scores and his reported skill at billiards. In the end, this story of a grown man unable to cut his food may turn out to be just another aspect of the myth of the eternal child.

Mozart surely hoped for a seamless transition from his concerto phase to his opera phase, for he began to write *Le nozze di Figaro* as early as October 1785, even as he made plans for three subscription concerts in late Decem-ber; he also wrote three new piano concertos—in E-flat, K. 482; A, K. 488; and C minor, K. 491—between mid-December and the following March. Perhaps he did not have enough time to prepare subscription con-certs for the 1786 Lenten season: even as he was composing *Figaro,* he accepted two other operatic commissions. One was *Der Schauspieldirektor* ("The Impresario"), a one-act singspiel that he wrote between 18 January and 3 February to a libretto by the younger Stephanie; the other was a revision of *Idomeneo,* with several new numbers (a Duet for soprano and tenor, "Spiegarti non poss'io," K. 489, and a Tenor Scene with Rondo, "Non più, tutto ascoltai"—"Non temer, amato bene," K. 490) for perfor-mance at the palace of Prince Johann Adam Auersperg on 13 March.

Mozart had great expectations for *Le nozze di Figaro,* which was his most ambitious opera buffa until then, intended to rival the great works in the genre and to move him into the front rank of Italian opera composers. Clearly he hoped to emulate the great success of Paisiello's *Il barbiere di Siviglia,* which premiered on 13 August 1783 (just after *Die Entführung aus dem Serail*) and enjoyed sixty performances by 1791, becoming the most popular Vienna opera of its time.[52]

Even before its premiere, there were signs that *Figaro*'s reception might be problematical. A year earlier, a German translation of Beaumarchais's comedy *La folle journée ou Le mariage de Figaro* encountered difficulties with the censor. Emperor Joseph expressed his recommendations to Count Pergen:

> I hear that the well-known comedy *Le Mariage de Figaro* is said to have been proposed for the Kärntnertor Theater in a German translation; since this piece contains much that is objectionable, I therefore expect that the Censor shall either reject it altogether, or at any rate have such alterations made in it that he shall be responsible for the performance of this play and for the impression it may make.[53]

The German translation, by Johann Rautenstrauch, was eventually approved by the censor, but only for publication and not for public performance, which had been announced for 3 February 1785 by Schikaneder, who held the directorship of the Kärntnertor Theater for a few months beginning in November 1784. In light of this history, it seems reasonably clear that Mozart was taking something of a risk to set the play to music, using a libretto by Lorenzo Da Ponte. That may be why Da Ponte in his preface to the libretto referred to some of the changes he had made as motivated by "prudent considerations and exigencies imposed by morality, place, and audience."[54]

Leopold Mozart had his own reasons for fearing that the opera might not prevail. On the eve of the premiere he wrote to his daughter:

> It will be surprising if it is a success, for I know that very powerful cabals have ranged themselves against your brother. Salieri and all his supporters will again try to move heaven and earth to down his opera. Herr & Mme. Duschek told me recently that it is on account of the very great reputation which your brother's exceptional talent and ability have won for him that so many people are plotting against him.[55]

On 1 May 1786 *Le nozze di Figaro,* billed as "An Italian Singspiel in four acts," had its premiere at the Burgtheater, with Mozart leading the first two performances from the keyboard. The opera was given nine times before the end of the year and achieved thirty-eight performances in Vienna by 1791. It has long been debated whether *Le nozze di Figaro* was initially a success or a failure, but the issue cannot be framed quite so simply. To judge from the applause, calls for encores, and contemporary reviews, there were already numerous indications of its sweeping future popularity. So many pieces were encored—almost doubling the length of each performance—that Emperor Joseph was moved to issue an order on 9 May proclaiming that "to prevent the excessive duration of the operas . . . no piece for more than a single voice is to be repeated."[56]

Fears of censorship proved unfounded. Reviewing the premiere, the *Wiener Realzeitung* reported, " 'What is *not allowed* to be said these days, is sung,' one may say with *Figaro*. This piece, which was *prohibited* in Paris and not allowed to be performed here as a *comedy* either in a bad or in a good translation, we have at last had the felicity to see represented as an *opera*."[57] Unfortunately, along with the bravos there was some hissing from the balconies, and opinion remained divided. "The public . . . did not really know on the first day where it stood," declared the reviewer in the *Realzeitung*. The end result was that the opera was both a triumph and a disappointment. To look at it in terms which very much preoccupied Mozart at that time, the Vienna production of *Le nozze di Figaro* did not earn him a great deal of money.

Mozart received 225 florins for *Der Schauspieldirektor* and probably an equal amount from Prince Auersperg for *Idomeneo*. Thus, with the 450 florins fee for *Figaro* his three operatic ventures brought in some 900 florins in 1786, which partially offset the shortfall of 1,500 florins in income from his 1786 subscription concerts as compared to 1785. With the approximately 600 florins that he probably earned at the end of 1786 from his very last subscription concerts, and perhaps some additional compensating income, he had not done too badly. Even so, prospects were not bright: apart from the close of his subscription concert enterprise, Mozart was to give no further academies in Vienna during his lifetime, which further reduced his annual income by at least 600 florins. The Piano Concerto in C, K. 503, completed on 4 December 1786, was his last work in that genre for a considerable time. Probably it was intended for performance at one of four planned Advent concerts at the Trattner Casino, but there is no documentary evidence that those concerts actually took place.[58]

For three or four years Mozart had tasted the freedom of being his own master, of being a concert promoter who reaped the profits of successful ventures. Now, once again, he was at the mercy of the concert promoters and theater managements who controlled the avenues through which music reached audiences in Vienna. Once again, he was compelled to rely for his living primarily on fees from producers, publishers, and patrons. Although he did not yet know it, Mozart's impresario period had come to a close.

By 1786 Mozart was ready to furnish whatever music might be ordered from him. In the summer, he offered to provide new compositions for the Prince von Fürstenberg. During the second half of the year he wrote numerous works in a variety of genres for an assortment of clients, including the Piano Quartet in E-flat, K. 493; the String Quartet in D, K. 499 ("Hoffmeister"); two Piano Trios, in G, K. 496, and in B-flat, K. 502; a Trio in E-flat for piano, clarinet, and viola, K. 498; a dozen Duos for horn, K. 487/496a; Twelve Piano Variations in B-flat, K. 500; a Sonata in F for piano four hands, K. 497; the Rondo in F, K. 494, that he published in 1788 as the finale of the Piano Sonata, K. 533; and Five Variations on an Original Andante in G, for piano four hands, K. 501. A Soprano Scene with Rondo, "Ch'io mi scordi di te"—"Non temer, amato bene," K. 505, for orchestra with piano obbligato was written for Nancy Storace just before her departure from Vienna. The Horn Concerto no. 4 in E-flat, K. 495, was, like all Mozart's works in this genre, written for his friend Joseph Leutgeb, formerly of Salzburg. Despite his productivity, however, he needed to find other sources of income.

In November, Leopold wrote to his daughter, reporting that Mozart "was proposing to undertake a journey through Germany to England in the middle of next carnival."[59] That journey was set aside in favor of plans for another trip, for which by 6 December he composed the Symphony in D, K. 504, now known as the "Prague" (but probably intended to serve double duty at an Advent concert in Vienna). Mozart had decided that the Bohemian capital held important prospects for him.

Mozart, 1788. Boxwood medallion by Leonard Posch. Location
unknown. Formerly, Mozart-Museum der Internationalen
Stiftung Mozarteum, Salzburg.

20

·······················

PORTRAIT OF A COMPOSER

Writing in the mid-1820s, the tenor Michael Kelly recalled Mozart as "a remarkable small man, very thin and pale, with a profusion of fine, fair hair, of which he was rather vain."[1] Evidently, Kelly needed to reinforce his memory, and perhaps he consulted Schlichtegroll's obituary notice, where Mozart's sister used almost identical language to describe her brother: "small, thin, pale in color."[2] We know that Mozart indeed was small of stature and unprepossessing in appearance, his face somewhat disfigured by smallpox marks. "There was nothing special about [his] physique. . . . He was small and his countenance, except for his large intense eyes, gave no signs of his genius," wrote Niemetschek, who stressed his "ungainly exterior."[3] As Paul Nettl once observed, tradition holds that Mozart was "often mistaken for some underling until the embarrassing discovery is made that this indifferent little man is the great master Mozart."[4] Such reports became almost a biographical trope: the composer Johann Nepomuk Hummel's widow told Jahn in 1855 of a Berlin concert that her husband gave, "without being aware of Mozart's presence"; afterward they embraced with the "tenderest expressions of joy."[5] The Romantic writer Ludwig Tieck's memoirs described his 1789 encounter in a Berlin opera house with "an unprepossessing figure in a gray overcoat" who turned out to be Mozart.[6] The actor Wilhelm Backhaus recalled a very similar story in connection with Mozart's visit to a Mannheim theater in 1790: "I took him for a little journeyman tailor, and refused to let him in. 'You will surely allow Kapellmeister Mozart to hear the rehearsal?'"[7]

There is no particular reason to believe these stories, for it can be seen from his letters and several of his portraits that Mozart passionately liked fine clothing; he would scarcely have been found wearing a drab overcoat. Nissen wrote on good authority of Mozart's fondness for "beautiful clothing, lace, and watch-chains."[8] Kelly remembered that at the first full orchestral rehearsal of *Le nozze di Figaro,* "Mozart was on the stage with his crimson pelisse and gold-laced cocked hat, giving the time of the music to the orchestra."[9] His appearance was so elegant that on the occasion of their joint imperial performance in 1781 Clementi took him "for one of the Emperor's chamberlains."[10]

It is often difficult to resolve contradictory descriptions of Mozart: Niemetschek wrote of Mozart's "small, beautiful hands," but the physician Joseph Frank, who had a dozen piano lessons from Mozart, remembered his "fleshy hands."[11] Unfortunately, Constanze left no adequate description of her husband, except to say, "His voice was a tenor, rather soft in speaking and delicate in singing, but when anything excited him, or it became necessary to exert it, it was both powerful and energetic."[12] A British visitor penned a vivid sketch of him in the summer of 1785:

> It was a hot day but Mozart was quite formally dressed. He had been hard at work on some compositions for string quartet but seemed not at all put out at being interrupted. . . . I was surprised when he rose to find him of not more than about five feet and four inches in height and of very slight build. His hand was cold but his grip was firm. His face was not particularly striking, rather melancholy until he spoke, when his expression became animated and amused and his eyes . . . were full of kind concern in our doings about which he inquired with obvious interest.[13]

Another Englishman, Thomas Attwood, who was Mozart's composition student between 1785 and 1787, remembered him as being "of cheerful habit," though his "health [was not] very strong," and he recalled that "in consequence of being so much over the table when composing, he was obliged to have an upright Desk and stand when he wrote."[14]

The most succinct description of him is his own: "Mozart magnus, corpore parvus"—"Mozart the great, small in size."[15] After his marriage he began to eat better, merrily dubbing himself the pregnant Constanze's "little husband, who is not pregnant, but fat and flourishing."[16] His tastes in food improved with his social standing. Whereas in Milan in former times he had asked for liver dumplings and sauerkraut, in Vienna he had become accustomed to a more refined cuisine: his father described meals served for them in February 1785 that included roast pheasant, rare meats, oyster, glacé fruits, and "several bottles of champagne."[17] Later on, Mozart reported home from Regensburg about the "angelic cooking" and the "glorious Moselle wine."[18]

During his early years in Vienna, Mozart would customarily arise at six o'clock, be at his desk by seven, and compose until nine or ten, when he would make the rounds of his pupils, giving lessons until one o'clock. "Then I lunch," he reported to his sister, "unless I am invited to some house where they lunch at two or even three o'clock. . . . I can never work before five or six o'clock in the evening, and even then I am often prevented by a concert. If I am not prevented, I compose until nine."[19] Returning to his room after several hours of social visits, he would again compose for an hour or two: "I often go on writing until one—and am up again at six."[20] He slept five or six hours, though he would have preferred seven. With variations, that was Mozart's daily routine as he described it in his letters home, perhaps somewhat idealized to impress his father and sister with his diligence but borne out in the main by the objective records of his productivity. After 1784 he gave lessons only in the afternoon, "in order to keep the morning free for composing."[21] Sometimes he was so busy writing that he did not even dress or have his hair done (a friseur woke him each morning); other days the only time he had for composing was in the evenings, "and of that I can never be sure, as I am often asked to perform at concerts," in other words, he was in demand as a free-lance accompanist or guest artist.[22] "Every minute is precious," he wrote on one occasion; "I have so much to do that often I do not know whether I am on my head or my heels," he wrote again, echoing one of his mother's stock expressions.[23] He described his enthusiasm while composing *Die Entführung aus dem Serail:* "I rush to my desk with the greatest eagerness and remain seated there with the greatest delight."[24] "I have so much to compose and not a minute must be lost," he wrote; "you know that usually I go on composing until I am hungry."[25] His wife came to believe that he "killed himself with overexertion," recalling that he "frequently sat up composing until two and rose at four, an exertion which assisted to destroy him."[26]

Although stories of the colossal pace at which he was able to compose have passed into the realm of the legendary, there is no question but that he ordinarily worked at an extremely fast rate. He wrote the violin part of the Sonata in G, K. 379/373a, in an hour on the night before the performance—"but in order to be able to finish it, I only wrote out the accompaniment for Brunetti and retained my own part in my head."[27] He wrote three numbers of *Die Entführung aus dem Serail* in one day, the "Haffner" Symphony in about two weeks, and, as we have seen, the "Linz" Symphony in five days at most. He was undaunted by deadlines; his father described how the D-minor Concerto, K. 466, was still being copied when he arrived on the day of its premiere, and "your brother did not even have time to play through [the rondo], as he had to supervise the copying."[28] To keep track of his very numerous compositions, Mozart commenced in February 1784 to keep a thematic catalog "of all my works" (called *Verzeichnis aller meiner Werke*) of his completed compositions, which he scrupulously maintained with only minor omissions until just before his death.[29]

To try to keep ahead of his commissions, as well as to jot down ideas as they occurred to him, he would compose portions of some works in the expectation of completing them later on: some of the numerous Mozart fragments (150 of them survive, for a ratio of 1 to every 4 finished works)[30] thus represent not only rejected or abandoned pieces but also "work in progress," as Tyson puts it, and he also points out that not only string quartets but several piano concertos as well were composed over fairly extended time spans, the thematic catalog giving only the completion dates.[31] Christoph Wolff was perhaps the first to observe that certain of "the fragments may be understood as incipits of partially, if not fully composed pieces. This means that Mozart, while preserving fragments 'on file,' actually kept thereby the mnemo-technical records of whole conceptualized compositions."[32] Still, this compositional procedure may suggest a more methodical way of scheduling his time than was actually the case: the thematic catalog shows dozens of works that were completed only weeks or even days before their intended performances.

Contrary to legend, in the preliminary stages of composition Mozart used sketches and drafts, of which relatively few have survived, perhaps because he periodically discarded them. We also know that his widow "destroyed many" of them because of what she termed their "utter unusability," while retaining the fragments, which she hoped to have completed by other composers.[33] Nevertheless, we have learned from Ulrich Konrad that some 320 sketches and drafts survive, and that sketch material still exists for 10 percent of Mozart's works.[34] Some sketches are simple notations of usable ideas whereas others have to do with knotty compositional problems, usually of a contrapuntal or chromatic nature. There are few surviving "continuity sketches," such as those Beethoven used, but Mozart often outlined substantial sections of major works in his usual manner—notating the main (top) line and the bass part, leaving the remainder to be filled in later on. Whereas in his earlier works he often completed the scoring of each section and then moved on to draft the next, in Vienna he developed the practice of fixing the outer voices of an entire movement before returning to fill in the inner voices.[35]

Despite Mozart's immense productivity and devotion to his work he was not isolated from the world, and the richness and variety of his social contacts and friendships is extraordinary to contemplate. His early letters from Vienna describe a large cast of characters—aristocrats, music patrons, musicians, pupils, fellow countrymen from Salzburg, and numerous friends and acquaintances. Some, such as the Mesmers, Bonnos, and Fischers, were known to him from his prior visits to the capital. He moved simultaneously among a number of different, sometimes overlapping circles in Vienna, equally at ease in the palaces of the Habsburg high nobility and the salons and homes of the financial aristocracy, lesser nobility, and official bureaucracy. Apart from leading nobles like Archduke Maximilian Franz ("I can say that he thinks the world of me"),[36] Counts Cobenzl and Thun, Countess Thun, the Princes Lichnowsky, Galitzin, and Kaunitz, and others too numerous to list and too important merely to be listed, he had many close ties to Vienna's cultured elite, including Gottfried van Swieten, the prominent government official and musical connoisseur; Joseph von Sonnenfels, a central figure of the Austrian Enlightenment's reform movement; and Ignaz von Born, a scientist and leader of the rationalist wing of the Freemasons. As we shall see, after 1784 Mozart himself was centrally involved with Freemasonry, and many of his closest associations were with lodge brothers, among whose ranks could be found most of the intellectuals of the day.

Naturally, Mozart, as a central figure in the vast profession of music-making in Vienna, was intimate with performing musicians as well as celebrated composers and generously appeared at academies given by other virtuosos or singers who were his friends. Moreover, he was an inveterate opera- and theatergoer; he not only attended the theater on every possible occasion but also often was to be found in the company of the actors, singers, playwrights, and impresarios who populated that world, such as the actor (and Mozart's brother-in-law) Joseph Lange, the playwright Johann Gottlieb Stephanie the younger, and the librettist Lorenzo Da Ponte, who arrived in Vienna in the same year as Mozart (they met at the home of Baron Raimund Wetzlar, the godfather of the Mozarts' first child). The Mozarts were central figures in the Viennese *beau monde,* part of the social whirl. Glittering all-night parties were held at their apartment; they were to be seen at the masked balls and carnival festivities; musicians and actors serenaded Mozart on special occasions.

Obviously, the possibility of a hidden existential loneliness is not to be excluded, but it must be considered in the context of this richly textured social life with its network of friends, patrons, and associates. On the evidence of the surviving letters, it seems that Mozart's closest male friends were Gottfried Jacquin, Count August Hatzfeld, and Sigmund Barisani, men of his own age or younger who shared with him a dedication to beauty, a devotion to rationality, a disdain for superstition, a passion for justice, and—not least—a common love of amusement. Of these he was perhaps closest to young Gottfried von Jacquin (1767–92), the son of the famous botanist Nikolaus von Jacquin. He was much beloved of Mozart and, together with his sister, Franziska, who was a singer and a pupil of Mozart, they formed the nucleus of a group that gathered weekly for "discussions, games, and music-making" at the Jacquin residence.[37] Between 1783 and 1788 Mozart wrote a considerable amount of music for the Jacquin household, including six vocal ensembles, K. 436–39, K. 346/439a, and K. 549, the Terzett, "Liebes Mandel, wo is's Bandel?" K. 441, and the Bass Aria, "Mentre ti lascio, o figlia," K. 513, written 23 March 1787 as a gift for Jacquin, who was a good bass singer. Another Bass Aria, "Io ti lascio," K. Anh. 78/621a, was thought by Mozart's widow to have been jointly written by Mozart and Jacquin. The "Kegelstatt" Trio in E-flat, K. 498, the Sonatas for piano four hands in F, K. 497, and in C, K. 521, and the Flute Quartet in A, K. 298, very likely were written for members of the family or at least for performance at the Jacquin home.[38]

Mozart even wrote love songs for Jacquin to use in courtship, and several of these, "Als Luise die Briefe ihres ungetreuen Liebhabers verbrannte," K. 520, and "Das Traumbild," K. 530, were published under Jacquin's name, surely with Mozart's permission, in March 1791. When Mozart sent his friend the latter song in November 1787, he wrote: "If the song in question is necessary to prove my friendship for you, you have no further cause to doubt it, for here it is. But I trust that even *without this song* you are convinced of my true friendship."[39] So central were the Jacquins to Mozart's musical amusements of this period, that I think it is conceivable that several works for which we possess no provenance, such as *Ein musikalischer Spass,* K. 522, and *Eine kleine Nachtmusik,* K. 525, may have been written for their circle. That Mozart and Jacquin were able unabashedly to express their affection for each other is clear from Jacquin's entry in Mozart's souvenir album dated 11 April 1787: "True genius without heart is a thing of naught—for not great understanding alone, not imagination alone, nor both together, make genius—Love! Love! Love! that is the soul of genius."[40] On his side, Mozart addressed Jacquin as his "dearest friend," writing from Prague: "I must frankly admit that, although I meet with all possible courtesies and honors here and although Prague is indeed a very beautiful and pleasant place, I long most ardently to be back in Vienna; and believe me, the chief cause of this homesickness is certainly *your* family."[41] That same letter closes: "Farewell, beloved friend. Keep me in your precious friendship."[42]

Mozart traveled with a convivial, pleasure-loving crowd, moving readily among individuals with liberated moral attitudes. This is amply clear from his relationship with Baroness Martha Elisabeth Waldstätten, née Schäfer (1744–1811), who had been a champion of the pre- and postnuptial Mozarts.[43] She freely lent Mozart money, gave the couple gifts, and provided their wedding dinner. She was generous and affectionate to Mozart;

on his name day in 1781 she invited him to her home in Leopoldstadt, where he was treated to a serenade by the musicians, who placed themselves "in the center of the courtyard, surprised me, just as I was about to undress, in the most pleasant fashion imaginable with the first chord in E-flat."[44] In turn, he wrote high-spirited, comic letters to her, replete with puns, word-play, and racy innuendo. She was separated from her husband and, in Mozart's phrase, was "inclined to be promiscuous with her favors."[45] He also reported that she had a succession of love affairs of fairly short duration: "You may put whatever construction you like on this," he wrote his father. "Suffice it to say that the result . . . is that people speak very lightly about her. She is weak. . . . I have received a great many kindnesses from her and so it is my duty to defend her so far as possible, or at least to say nothing."[46]

Mozart maintained ties with several transplanted Salzburgers, including Franz Xaver Wenzel Gilowsky, who was the witness at his wedding; Franz Xaver Gerl, a bass who played Sarastro in the first production of *Die Zauberflöte,* and had been a pupil of Leopold Mozart's; and his cherished personal physician, Sigmund Barisani, who wrote in the composer's souvenir album:

> Do not forget thy friend, whose happiness
> And pride it is to know he served thee twice
> To save thee for the world's delight.47

Mozart wrote all of his horn concertos and the Quintet in E-flat, K. 407/386c, for the Salzburg-born horn player Joseph Leutgeb (who had set-tled in Vienna as a cheesemonger) and made him the butt of a strange kind of insulting humor. It is said that Mozart would throw "all the parts of his concertos and symphonies about the room, and Leutgeb had to collect them on all fours and put them in order."[48] On another occasion Leutgeb was forced "to kneel down behind the stove" while the composer was at work.[49] On the autograph of the Horn Concerto in E-flat, K. 417, is the notation: "Wolfgang Amadé Mozart takes pity on Leutgeb, ass, ox, and simpleton, at Vienna, 27 March 1783." By his own admission, Mozart was much given to practical jokes with a slightly unkind edge: "I can never resist making a fool of someone," he wrote.[50] It is almost as though Leut-geb, who was a generation older than Mozart, served him as willing buf-foon or court jester.

A friendship of a quite different kind was that of Mozart with Joseph Haydn. So far as we know, theirs was neither an intimate nor a convivial relationship. They did not meet frequently (Haydn's occasional visits to Vienna from Hungary, where he was Kapellmeister to Prince Paul Anton Esterházy, were brief and he was much occupied with his own professional obligations) and Haydn is mentioned only a few times in the Mozart correspondence. They had many friends in common within the music world, including the visiting British musicians Anna and Stephen Storace, Thomas Attwood, and Michael Kelly, the violinist Regina Strinasacchi, the Italian composers Giovanni Paisiello and Giuseppe Sarti, and the publishers Franz Anton Hoffmeister and Artaria & Co. Both composers frequented the salons of Countess Thun (she had been Haydn's pupil) and Franz Sales von Greiner, as well as the musicales organized by Baron van Swieten, a devoted advocate and friend of both composers. Mozart and Haydn became Freemasons almost simultaneously: Haydn applied for admission to "True Concord" ("Zur wahren Eintracht") Lodge by letter of 29 December 1784, about two weeks after Mozart was admitted as an Apprentice to the "Beneficence" ("Zur Wohltätigkeit") Lodge. Over the next weeks, Haydn, now Mozart's Masonic "brother," twice visited the latter's home to hear the six string quartets that were to be dedicated to him; as late as 1789, he was invited to a rehearsal of *Così fan tutte*.

These highlights of their contacts are significant enough. On a more important level, however, Mozart found in Haydn a master composer who not only recognized his genius but voiced appreciation of the younger man's greatness directly, unhesitatingly, and with rare generosity. On the occasion of hearing the last three of Mozart's "Haydn" String Quartets, he said to Leopold Mozart (who reported it to his daughter): "Before God and as an honest man I tell you that your son is the greatest composer known to me either in person or by name. He has taste and, what is more, the most profound knowledge of composition."[51] Even with due allowance for the occasion on which it was made and the fact that it survives only in a private letter, it was an extraordinary remark that has few parallels. There is in it no hint of the dismay that Hasse, for example, displayed when he commented that Mozart's genius would consign other composers to oblivion, or of the later resistance to Mozart's innovative style by such composers as Naumann and Dittersdorf. It is, as we know, a remark that Haydn never even came close to making about Beethoven, who waited in vain for his teacher's acknowledgment. Gluck was loud in his praise of the "Paris" Symphony in 1783; Sarti told Mozart he was exceedingly pleased by the set of variations, K. 460/454a, that Mozart wrote on his "Como un agnello"; and, later on, Salieri would be unstinting in his praise for *Die Zauberflöte*. But these do not even approach Haydn's unqualified encomium. When Mozart fell into financial difficulties, Haydn expressed his indignation that so great an artist was "not yet engaged by some imperial or royal court!"[52] This is not to say that either man was free of ambivalent feelings toward the other: Haydn was said to have distanced himself from the radical opening of the "Dissonance" Quartet, and there is a report of his perturbation when he was told by some talebearer that Mozart had disparaged him.[53] But in his intimate letters to his friend Frau Maria Anna von Genzinger, we see how deeply Mozart's music reached him, how he wanted to hear her "play Mozart's masterpieces, and to kiss your hands for so many beautiful things."[54] Mozart even appears in one of Haydn's dreams—or nightmares, perhaps: "I could sleep little, even my dreams pursued me; then, as I was fairly hearing the opera *Le nozze di Figaro* in my dreams, the horrid North wind woke me up and nearly blew my nightcap off my head."[55] For Mozart, Haydn was "his dear friend," and there is a touching though perhaps apocryphal report that on Haydn's departure for London in December 1790, Mozart said, with tears in his eyes, "I fear, my father, that this is the last time we shall see each other."[56]

According to Niemetschek, Mozart "often called [Haydn] his teacher,"[57] and there are several unreliable anecdotes floated by Friedrich Rochlitz in which he claimed that Mozart had high praise for the Esterházy master.[58] The dedicatory letter published in the first edition of the six "Haydn" String Quartets, however, is by itself sufficient to indicate the extent of Mozart's veneration of Haydn as well as his desire to take his place squarely alongside him, for by the salutation "Al mio caro Amico Haydn" Mozart put himself on an equal plane with the much admired older composer:

> To my dear friend Haydn.
>   A father who had decided to send out his sons into the great world, thought it his duty to entrust them to the protection and guidance of a man who was very celebrated at the time and who, moreover, happened to be his best friend.
>   In like manner I send my six sons to you, most celebrated and very dear friend. They are, indeed, the fruit of a long and laborious toil; but the hope which many friends have given me that this toil will be in some degree rewarded, encourages me and flatters me with the thought that these children may one day prove a source of consolation to me. . . .[59]

Mark Evan Bonds amply demonstrates that this document draws on conventional strategies of "dedicatory rhetoric," and he rightly warns that acceptance of the letter entirely at face value tends to perpetuate "an exaggeratedly idealistic view" of the relationship between Mozart and Haydn. But it does not necessarily follow either from Mozart's use of commonplace rhetorical "ritualistic formulations" or from Artaria & Co.'s patently commercial motive in linking the set to Haydn that the positive implications of the letter do not hold.[60] Rather, the imagery seems to resonate with Mozart's very personal yearning for an ideal paternal/filial harmony, for a vigorous, creative, and accepting musical father. For it is not only Mozart's

> ## Al mio caro Amico Haydn
>
> Un Padre, avendo risolto di mandare i suoi figlj nel gran Mondo, stimò doverli affidare alla protezione, e condotta d'un Uomo molto celebre in allora, il quale per buona sorte, era di più il suo migliore Amico. — Eccoti dunque del pari, Uom celebre, ed Amico mio carissimo i sei miei figlj. — Essi sono, è vero il frutto di una lunga, e laboriosa fatica, pur la speranza fattami da più Amici di vederla almeno in parte compensata, m'incoraggisce, e mi lusinga, che questi parti siano per essermi un giorno di qualche consolazione. — Tu stesso Amico carissimo, nell'ultimo tuo Soggiorno in questa Capitale, me ne dimostrasti la tua soddisfazione. — Questo tuo suffragio mi anima sopra tutto, perché io te li raccomandi, e mi fa sperare, che non ti sembreranno del tutto indegni del tuo favore. — Piacciati dunque accoglierli benignamente, ed esser loro Padre, Guida, ed Amico! Da questo momento, io ti cedo i miei diritti sopra di essi: ti supplico però di guardare con indulgenza i difetti, che l'occhio parziale di Padre mi può aver celati, e di continuar loro malgrado, la generosa tua Amicizia a chi tanto l'apprezza, mentre sono di tutto Cuore.
>
> Amico Carissimo   il tuo sincerissimo Amico
> Vienna il p.mo Settembre 1785.
>   W.A. Mozart

Mozart's dedication to Haydn of the six "Haydn" Quartets, 1 September 1785. Reproduced from first edition published by Artaria & Co. Private collection.

"sons" but himself whom he entrusts to Haydn's care. In consigning his musical children to his friend (and Masonic brother) Mozart conscripted Haydn to become his father, while at the same time he validated his own claims to creative fatherhood. Mozart once saw in the Bäsle a fusion of all the primal feminine figures of his existence; what gives the dedication of the "Haydn" String Quartets its poignancy is its fusion—even confusion—of the primal masculine figures, its public avowal that, for Mozart, Haydn is simultaneously his best friend, good brother, and caring father.

Mozart's exalted opinion of Haydn does not appear directly in his letters home, nor does Leopold Mozart have very much to say about Haydn. One begins to wonder if Mozart might have been reluctant to reveal to his father his feelings about Haydn, either as composer or as father surrogate.

But this must be considered in context: only rarely in his letters from Vienna did Mozart have an enthusiastic word for contemporary composers. He has mild praise for men like Benda, Cannabich, Jomelli, and Mysliveček, but he disparages Righini, Umlauf, Eberlin, and Naumann; he calls Clementi "a mere mechanicus" and a "*ciarlatano,* like all Italians";[61] and he has harsh words for an opera by Johann Mederitsch(-Gallus), for Gassmann's *La notte critica* and Umlauf's *Welche ist die beste Nation?*[62] It is probably true that much of this music, and more, is mediocre or wretched, though the references to Clementi seem ungenerous, but the letters home are also oddly free of enthusiasm or high praise for the more important composers. Although Mozart attends a gala performance of Gluck's *Alceste* at Schönbrunn Palace on 25 November 1781, he does not offer his opinion of the opera. He is similarly noncommittal about music by Paisiello, Cimarosa, Martín y Soler, Dittersdorf, Sarti, and Salieri. And there is not a word about any composition by Joseph Haydn. Whereas on his journey to Mannheim he had found Holzbauer's music "very beautiful" and filled with "fire," his sole words of praise now are for his beloved J. C. Bach, who had just died ("What a loss to the musical world!").[63] Only Haydn's pupil Ignaz Pleyel gets relatively high marks, for his newly published string quartets, which Mozart sends home with a caveat about their imitativeness: "You will find them worth the trouble. They are very well written and most pleasing to listen to. You will also see at once who was his master. Well, it will be a lucky day for music if later on Pleyel should be able to replace Haydn."[64]

Of course, it may simply be that Mozart took the greatness of a Haydn or a Gluck so much for granted that he felt no need to communicate his feelings about their music. Perhaps, however, all this connects in some way with Leopold Mozart's customarily uncharitable attitude toward fellow composers, and not only his rivals at Salzburg, but those who had achieved great reputations in Europe. It is difficult to explain why he warned Mozart, when he was en route to Paris, not to associate with the leading composers: "If Gluck and Piccinni are there, you will avoid their company as much as possible; and you must not form a close friendship with Grétry."[65] Possibly he feared that his son would fall under their influence. In any event, it begins to appear as though Mozart understood his father's sensitivity about other composers, especially innovative ones, and by his silence concerning the composers he admired and his unsparing remarks about those he considered wretched, avoided roiling the waters.

A fair-sized body of anecdotes bears on the more informal side of Mozart's family life in Vienna. There are tales of Mozart and Constanze dancing to keep warm in an unheated apartment. And Constanze never forgot that when she was in labor with their first child, Mozart, who was working in the same room, would console her during each contraction and then resume his work on the Minuet and Trio of the D-minor String Quartet, K. 421.[66] A famous anecdote relates that while walking one day in the Augarten with their dog, Mozart and his wife engaged in a mock battle and this caused Emperor Joseph, who was passing by, to chide them: "My, my, married only three weeks and already fighting?"[67] So easygoing was Mozart's relationship with the emperor at this time that the latter fell into a reminiscent mood, asking if Mozart recalled details of his visit to Vienna in December 1762 as a boy of six: "Do you still remember the story about Wagenseil? and how I played violin and you were listening in the anteroom, calling out, 'Pfooey, that was out of tune,' and then 'Bravo!'"[68]

The numerous tales about Mozart's generosity constitute a suspect genre that usually merges into sermons about his impecuniousness. Rochlitz "recalled" an exchange between Mozart and an "old honored piano tuner" in Leipzig:

> "Dear old man," said Mozart, "what do I owe you for your efforts? Tomorrow I leave here."
>
> The old man, who was constantly embarrassed whenever he spoke with anyone, stuttered: "Your imperial majesty—I'd like to say—Your imperial majesty, Sir Kapellmeister—I have indeed been here on several different occasions—I ask nevertheless—one Thaler—"
>
> "One Thaler? That is not enough to pay such a good man, even for only one visit." And thereupon he pressed into his hand several ducats.[69]

Rochlitz became quite indignant that Mozart sometimes wasted his generosity on unworthy recipients: "How much he worked out of pure kindness for mere acquaintances! How much more for his friends! How often did he sacrifice himself for poor traveling virtuosos! How often did he write concertos, of which he retained no copy, so that they would get a good reception and could find assistance! How often did he share bed and board etc. with them, if they came without money and acquaintances to Vienna."[70]

Mozart was less charitable to a young parlor-maid from Salzburg whom he and Constanze had taken into their employ in Vienna. Perhaps wondering whether young Lisa Schwemmer might be tattling about their private life, Mozart opened and read a letter she had written to her mother and reported the contents to his father:

> She complains that she gets to bed too late and has to get up too early—though I should have thought that one would get enough sleep between eleven and six, which is after all seven hours! . . . Then she complains about the food and that too in the most impertinent fashion. She says she

has to starve and that the four of us, that is, my wife, myself, the cook, and she do not get as much to eat as she and her mother used to have between the two of them. You know that I took this girl at the time purely out of pity. . . . We promised her twelve florins a year, and she was quite satisfied, though in her letter she complains about this. And what has she to do? To clear the table, hand round the dishes and take them away and help my wife to dress and undress. . . . She cannot even light a fire, let alone make coffee. . . . We gave her a florin and the very next day she was asking for more money.[71]

After enumerating Fräulein Schwemmer's failings in further detail, he declared his decision to fire her and asked his father to notify her mother accordingly: "Were it not that I hate to make people unhappy I should get rid of her on the spot."[72] Probably, while providing a surfeit of documentation about Schwemmer's trivial transgressions, Mozart left much more unsaid—especially his discomfort with the notion that his family's private affairs were being broadcast to Salzburg by their maid. But of course he knew that his father could easily grasp the subtext of the story.

In his hunger to be in the world in every possible way, Mozart had a fondness for the small commonplaces of existence, for the comforting trivialities of daily life, for a new watch, a red coat with gold buttons, for a daily walk in the Augarten, a day in the country, an evening at whist, a game of billiards, a bawdy canon, a tough riddle, a good joke, a glass of champagne, and a household pet. A Mozart bestiary would include not only the dog Wimperl, whom Emperor Joseph met that day in the Augarten, but also a caged canary, a pet starling, and the horse (the *Kleper,* or "nag") that he rode for pleasure until his last year. The starling has been immortalized because it was talented enough to learn the tune that Mozart used as the theme for the closing variations of the Piano Concerto in G, K. 453. The bird didn't quite get it right, as we know from an entry in Mozart's cash book for 27 May 1784 (Example 20.1).

Example 20.1. From Mozart's cashbook, 27 May 1784.

Forgiving his pet for adding an unwanted sharp, Mozart appended to this the words, "Das war schön."[73]

Initiation of an Apprentice at a Viennese Masonic lodge.
Unsigned oil painting, ca. 1790. Historisches Museum
der Stadt Wien, inv. no. 47.927.

21

....

FREEMASONRY

Toward the close of 1784 Mozart was proposed for membership in the "Beneficence" ("Zur Wohltätigkeit") Lodge of the order of Freemasons, and was admitted as an Apprentice Mason on 14 December 1784. The speaker at his induction ceremony addressed him as follows:

> Favorite of a guardian angel. Friend of the sweetest muse. Chosen by benevolent Nature to move our hearts through rare magical powers, and to pour consolation and comfort into our souls.—You shall be embraced by all the warm feelings of mankind, which you so wonderfully express through your fingers, through which stream all the magnificent works of your ardent imagination![1]

He was promoted to Journeyman on 7 January 1785, and shortly thereafter, he achieved the highest rank, that of Master Mason.[2]

From the start he was an active and loyal participant of the order, attending meetings not only of his own lodge but also of the more prestigious "True Concord" ("Zur wahren Eintracht"), lending his talents at lodge functions and benefit concerts, and composing a considerable amount of Masonic music. In late March 1785 he wrote a lied, "Gesellenreise," K. 468, for use at the installation of new journeymen; his cantata *Die Maurerfreude* ("The Mason's Joy"), for tenor and male chorus, K. 471, which was performed 24 April 1785 in his father's presence, was written to honor Ignaz von Born, Grand Secretary of the Austrian lodges and Master of the "True Concord" Lodge; the orchestral *Maurerische Trauermusik*

(Masonic Funeral Music), K. 477/479a, was composed no later than November 1785 for memorial services at "Crowned Hope" Lodge for two noble lodge brothers, Duke Georg August von Mecklenburg and Count Franz Esterházy von Galántha. A fragment of a cantata, *Dir, Seele des Weltalls*, K. 429/468a, probably also dates from 1785 and may have been conceived for a Masonic event, and two additional Masonic songs (the music to which is no longer extant) by Mozart were performed at "True Concord" on 12 August 1785.[3] Through his fame and his devotion to the order, Mozart soon came to be regarded as one of the outstanding Masons of the time, welcomed in the lodges, in Deutsch's description, "as the best of the musical 'Brothers.'"[4] At his death he was eulogized at "New Crowned Hope" ("Zur Neugekrönten Hoffnung") Lodge: "Half Europe revered him, the great called him their darling, and we—we called him our Brother," said the orator, describing Mozart as "a diligent member of our Order: brotherly love, a peaceable disposition, advocacy of a good cause, beneficence, a true, sincere sense of pleasure whenever he could help one of his Brethren with his talents: these were the chief characteristics of his nature."[5]

During the first years of his reign Emperor Joseph II enlisted the Freemasons as part of his advance guard, as capable propagandists for his program who supported his attempts at a thoroughgoing reformation of church and state. Soon, however, schisms within the movement, the spread of irrationalist doctrines, and the susceptibility of some of the members to ideological and religious heresies, caused him to worry that Freemasonry would go into opposition. By means of the *Freimaurerpatent* (Masonic Decree) of 11 December 1785 the lodges within the Habsburg domains were brought under stricter government supervision, the eight Viennese lodges were consolidated into two new ones ("New Crowned Hope" and "Truth" ["Wahrheit"]), and new masters were appointed by Grand Master Prince Johann Baptist Carl Dietrichstein. In addition, the total number of Masons was to be curtailed and membership lists provided to the authorities. As a result of the reform, membership, which had been burgeoning, soon declined from 706 to 547.

One of the regime's stated goals was to curb the influence of the secret order of the Rosicrucians (including the Rosicrucian offshoot, the Asiatic Brethren), and to limit the diversity of proliferating Masonic sects. By so doing, the Josephinian government took its stand on the side of the enlightened and rationalist Masons as against the adherents of unorthodox and occult tendencies. The decree referred disdainfully and provocatively to Masonic "mysteries" (*Geheimnisse*) and "impostures" (*Gaukeleien*).[6] Because they sympathized with the alleged aim of purging Masonic ranks of Rosicrucian, alchemist, and other mystical tendencies, leaders of the rationalist wing of Freemasonry helped to promote and afterward saluted the imperial decree.

It was not long, however, before the decree was turned against them as well, and it seems possible that this may have been one of the primary imperial aims from the beginning. In particular, a result of the *Freimaurerpatent* was restriction of the influence of still another group—the enlightened, anticlerical Order of Illuminati, which carried on its work and exercised a powerful influence within the Masonic lodges, numbering among its members many of the most powerful Freemasons of the period.[7] Earlier in 1785, the Illuminati had been banned in Bavaria, where the order was founded in 1776, and extravagant reports of its subversive capabilities were widely circulated. Furthermore, because the leading Viennese Illuminists were revered in intellectual and Masonic circles, had earned widespread respect as allies of Emperor Joseph, and occupied positions of power in every sphere of Habsburg life, the order—and the rationalist wing of Freemasonry in general—was perceived as a potential alternative center of power, or even as a state within the state.[8] The net effect of the edict was the transformation of the Masonic lodges into quasi-official imperial lodges, a contradiction in terms for a movement dedicated to freedom of thought, let alone for a secret society. Of course it was equally a contradiction in terms for the imperial government, however enlightened, permanently to tolerate within its midst secret organizations with suspected conspiratorial capabilities.

As a consequence of the decree of December 1785 many Masons resigned from the ranks, some because of the limitations on membership, others in protest or out of timidity. As an organization, the Order of Illuminati ceased to function in Vienna, and many of the most prominent Illuminists quit the lodges in 1786 and 1787, including Born, Joseph von Sonnenfels, and Otto von Gemmingen, who had been the master of Mozart's "Beneficence" Lodge. One of the two combined lodges, "Truth," which was headed by Born, lost thirty-seven lodge brothers in the course of 1786, of whom thirty-three were former members of "True Concord"; "Truth" suspended its activities altogether in mid-1787 and was officially closed down in 1789. Splits developed between former comrades, leaving the Illuminati in disarray: Sonnenfels continued to support the Masonic reform, whereas Born became disillusioned with it.[9] In a letter of August 1786, a Freemason wrote: "Of the Illuminati there has long been neither any further talk or inquiry. The Order has completely ceased here."[10] Thus, the Illuminati and other enlightened Freemasons had discovered to their dismay that the decrees had more far-reaching aims than the limitation of superstitious trends in the lodges. Without directly moving against the Illuminati as had the elector of Bavaria, the emperor had effectively eliminated them as a force in Habsburg affairs. Ironically, it was the Rosicrucians and other adherents of hermetic trends within Freemasonry who came through relatively unscathed.

★ ★ ★

Mozart unreservedly supported Habsburg Masonic policies, publicly, at least: the text of his *Maurerfreude* expresses unabashed reverence for the emperor: "Take, beloved, this crown from the hands of our eldest son, from Joseph. This is the jubilee of the Masons, this is the triumph of the Masons."[11] In the wake of the *Freimaurerpatent,* Mozart wrote two lieder for tenor, male choir, and organ, K. 483 and K. 484, to celebrate the opening on 14 January 1786 of his new lodge, "New Crowned Hope," which had been formed by combining three lodges (including his own, "Benefi-cence"). The first of these lieder, designated "For the Opening of the Lodge," was entitled "Zerfliesset heut', geliebte Brüder" and was composed to a text in praise of Joseph II's restructuring of Viennese Freemasonry:

> Today, beloved brothers, break
> into songs of rapture and jubilation,
> Joseph's beneficence
> Has crowned anew our hope
> And in our hearts
> a threefold flame now burns.[12]

Mozart's attitude was fully consonant with that of the orthodox Josephinians and their rationalist partisans among the Illuminati, who at first greeted the *Freimaurerpatent* with enthusiasm. For example, the Illu-minist (and subsequent Jacobin) Aloys Blumauer wrote an even more syco-phantic poem, "Joseph der Zweyte, Beschützer des Freymaurerordens" ("Joseph II, Guardian of the Masonic Order"), in defense of the repressive decree.[13] But Mozart remained a lodge member even after the exodus of the Illuminists from the lodges. His letters to fellow Masons Puchberg and Hofdemel between 1788 and 1791 contain open Masonic references, and in his entry in Johann Georg Kronauer's souvenir album he proudly signs himself "Member of the very hon. [lodge] of The New-crowned Hope in the Orient of Vienna."[14] He was still a member of that lodge as late as 1790 and 1791.[15] It is curious, though, that he wrote little additional music for the lodges until 1791, the year in which he produced his second sheaf of Masonic compositions. In fact, pleading indisposition, Mozart didn't attend the celebratory opening of "New Crowned Hope" in January 1786, and there is little evidence that he took an active part in lodge functions during the next few years.

Though he remained a Mason even after the twilight of the Illuminist movement, the preponderance of the evidence suggests that Mozart belonged to the rationalist, Illuminati-dominated wing of Viennese Freemasonry. The membership of his home lodge, "Beneficence," and its

Speech at the induction of Mozart into the "Beneficence"
("Wohltätigkeit") Lodge, 14 December 1784. From *Friedrich Hegrads vermischte Schriften* (Frankfurt and Leipzig, 1785), vol. 2.

sister lodge "True Concord," which he frequented, was almost wholly
made up of adherents of enlightened reform.[16] Born, a revered scholar and
scientist who advocated the suppression of the monastic orders, had specifically shaped the intellectually elite "True Concord" Lodge to combat mystical and superstitious tendencies in Freemasonry, hoping to establish the
lodge as a sort of "Masonic Academy of Science."[17] In his obituary of Born,
Schlichtegroll wrote of "True Concord": "It was a learned society; most of
the writers and friends of literature of the Imperial city gathered in it.
Templar doctrines, Catholicism, and Alchemical fanaticism had no entrée
to it; it was a temple of truth, of wisdom, and of free inquiry into science
and also into such matters about which the hierarchy had forbidden
thought and speech."[18] Georg Forster, the noted German writer and subsequent Jacobin who visited the Viennese lodges in 1784, was much
impressed by "True Concord," because "the best minds of Vienna among

the scholars and the best poets are members there."[19] Mozart's home lodge, "Beneficence," was a twin lodge of "True Concord," ideologically indistinguishable from it, though less elite in its membership.

It is also certain that, like the young Beethoven in Bonn at this same time, Mozart was closely associated with many of the Illuminati. In Vienna, these included Gemmingen, who had befriended him at Mannheim and who may have recruited him into the "Beneficence" Lodge; Born, whom an uncertain tradition holds to have been the model for Sarastro in *Die Zauberflöte;* and Sonnenfels, who was a prominent member of the imperial government and a leading advocate of human rights, whose collected works in ten volumes were in Mozart's library.[20] The principal offices of both "Beneficence" and "True Concord" were firmly under the control of the Illuminati and their partisans.[21] Of eighty-three members of "True Concord" in 1783, thirty-six were identified as Illuminati, and the percentage of Illuminati in "Beneficence" was also very high.[22] Thus, prior to the *Freimaurerpatent,* Mozart joined a lodge controlled by the Order of Illuminati and was a frequent and welcome guest at a second controlled by the same order. Several of his closest friends and associates were closely linked to the Illuminati. His "dearest and most beloved friend," as he called Count August von Hatzfeld (1754–87),[23] was an Illuminist: the obituary of him in Cramer's *Magazin der Musik* by the Illuminist leader (and Beethoven's teacher) Christian Gottlob Neefe related how he received the last rites from "an upright, enlightened, unprejudiced secular priest."[24] Mozart's influential friend, Baron Gottfried van Swieten, was also reportedly an Illuminist, though there is no proof of this.[25] Mozart's disproportionately numerous contacts with members of the Illuminati, almost all of whom also belonged to Masonic lodges, went back to Munich, Mannheim, and Salzburg as well, and included a broad range of his patrons, friends, and fellow musicians in those cities, men such as Count Seeau, Count Johann Philipp Cobenzl, Count Starhemberg, Christian Cannabich, and Salzburg canon Count Friedrich Spaur.[26]

All of these lines of convergence suggest at the least Mozart's ideological compatibility with or even sympathy for the goals of the Illuminati. It is, however, highly improbable that Mozart was an actual member of the order itself; certainly his name does not appear on any membership lists. A report published in 1911 alleges that both Mozart and his father were closely associated with the eclectic Illuminati-influenced lodge "Prudence" ("Fürsicht") in Salzburg, and even that Mozart participated in secret nocturnal meetings with Illuminati in the grotto in Aigen near Salzburg, but it lacks documentary support and seems demonstrably unreliable.[27] Nor can we be confident that Mozart knew that his Viennese friends belonged to the Illuminati, for its cadres within the Masonic lodges identified themselves only to those whom they found worthy of recruiting: "We shall regard this as our nursery," wrote the founder of the order, Adam Weishaupt, using his code name Spartacus. "To some of these Masons we shall not even disclose that we have something more than the Masons have. . . . All those not suited to the work shall remain in the Masonic Lodge and advance there without knowing anything of the further system."[28]

Some historians would like to read Mozart as a premature Jacobin devoted to political reform, but others have suggested that he was a secret adherent of the Asiatic Brethren, the Rosicrucians, or of one or another of the esoteric, occult, cabbalistic, and alchemical trends that flourished under the umbrella of Freemasonry.[29] They can point to Asiatic Brethren affiliations of several members of "Beneficence," to the anomaly that Gemmingen and Prince Dietrichstein belonged to both the Asiatic Brethren and the Order of Illuminati,[30] and to Mozart's visit to the Prussian court in 1789, where Friedrich Wilhelm II was himself a Rosicrucian. To counterbalance the many rationalist and enlightened books in Mozart's personal library, they might want to make something of his ownership of *Die Metaphysik in Connexion mit der Chemie* (Schwäbisch-Hall, 1770) by Friedrich Christoph Oetinger, who corresponded with Swedenborg and was a follower of the mystic Jakob Böhme.[31] They might also stress that Mozart's *Maurerische Trauermusik* was first performed at "Crowned Hope" Lodge, which numbered many prominent Rosicrucians among its members. And of course it can be asserted that the Rosicrucians could not to be expected to identify themselves: one of their mottos was, "Learn to know all, but keep thyself unknown."[32] As Frances Yates observed, "The normal practice of Rosicrucian writers is to say that they are not themselves Rosicrucians, nor have they ever seen one."[33] Nevertheless, the fact is that the Rosicrucian lodges were clearly known: like other members of the various Masonic sects the Rosicrucians tended to cluster together in their own lodges, wanting to associate with like-minded brethren. Prior to the *Freimaurerpatent,* the Rosicrucians and Asiatic Brethren dominated or strongly influenced several lodges, including not only "Crowned Hope," but "Steadfastness" ("Zur Beständigkeit"), "Three Fires" ("Zu den drei Feuern"), and "Saint Joseph" ("Zum heiligen Joseph") as well.[34]

We will do well to remember, however, that Mozart was firmly associated with rationalist and Illuminist lodges rather than with those of the Rosicrucians or Asiatic Brethren, that his close Masonic brothers were anticlerical and believers in natural law, and that he nowhere expressed even veiled sympathy for occult or pseudo-scientific currents. On the latter point *vide* his spoof of Mesmerism in *Così fan tutte* and, perhaps, as Eibl suggests, his reference to the Count Franz Joseph Thun-Hohenstein—who was well known for his esoteric and Mesmerist interests—as a "peculiar but well-meaning" gentleman.[35] Moreover, it is amply clear that Gemmingen was playing some sort of double game, and, as we shall see, Mozart was not welcomed as a Masonic brother at the Prussian court in 1789. It has not yet been suggested that Mozart infiltrated the lodges of the rationalists to work on behalf of the Asiatic Brethren. Nevertheless, there will be no end to the spinning of conspiracy theories about Mozart and the Masons, because Freemasonry, by virtue of its secrecy, its exoticism, and ceremonial trappings, provides a fertile ground for unanswerable questions and fantastic scenarios.

Mozart's Freemasonry had a long incubation period. Apart from his youthful personal contacts with Freemasons, he was receptive to Masonic texts well before his Vienna years: *Thamos, König in Ägypten,* for which he composed incidental music in 1773, is a quasi-Masonic play, and in 1778 he considered writing a melodrama to Gemmingen's Masonic libretto *Semiramis.* The lied "O heiliges Band," K. 148/125h (composed toward the mid-1770s) was marked "Hymn of Praise for Festivities at the St. John Lodge":[36]

> Up, Masons, and sing; today, let the entire globe hear,
> This is the day which this song consecrates,
> A glorious, great day of honor,
> A high feast of devotion and unity.

When Mozart traveled to Paris in 1778 he carried letters of recommendation from Gemmingen and Christian Cannabich, both Illuminists; Chailley speculates that Gemmingen's recommendation was directed to the Parisian Masons who were associated with the Loge Olympique and the Concert Spirituel, the latter directed by Joseph Legros, who was himself a Mason.[37] Moreover, Leopold Mozart's rationalism and anticlericalism (recall the Egglstainer affair of 1756) early descended to his son, who was equally disdainful of the priesthood—"for a priest is capable of anything," exclaimed Mozart in 1783.[38] He probably also shared his father's animosity toward the monastic orders, his approval of the expropriation of the Jesuit monasteries in 1773, and his advocacy of the dissolution of the convents in 1775.[39] Opposition to the Jesuits was a central issue for many of the Masonic subgroupings; the Rosicrucians had arisen "almost as a mirror image of the Jesuit Order";[40] and Adam Weishaupt had conceived the Order of Illuminati as an anti-Jesuit organization modeled upon Jesuitical methods and organizational forms. The Jesuits responded in kind: it was widely believed that the suppression of the Illuminati in Bavaria was instigated by them.

★ ★ ★

After a hiatus of five years, Mozart resumed the composition of Masonic music in 1791, with a cantata for tenor and piano, *Die ihr des unermesslichen Weltalls Schöpfer ehrt,* K. 619, to a text by Franz Heinrich Ziegenhagen (a disciple of Rousseau who was an advocate of back-to-the-soil utopian communes),[41] and the *Kleine Freimaurer-Kantate* ("Little Masonic Cantata"), *Laut verkünde unsre Freude,* K. 623, for soloists, male chorus, and orchestra. The text of the former has powerful polytheistic overtones characteristic of Masonic ritual and exhorts mankind to usher in an age of peace ("create the Garden of Eden from the desert") through love and fraternity. Completed on 15 November 1791 and performed on 18 November under the composer's own direction, it was the last composition entered in Mozart's thematic catalog. It was written for the inauguration of a new temple of "New Crowned Hope" to an unsigned text—often mistakenly attributed to Schikaneder—by a member of that lodge:

> Today, by the golden chain of brotherhood
> and the true union of hearts,
> we consecrate this place
> as our temple.[42]

After Mozart's death, the Masons sponsored the publication of the *Kleine Freimaurer-Kantate* for the benefit of his "distressed widow and orphans."[43] That was only one sign of the great affection and pride the Masons had for their most eminent musical brother.

Freemasonry evidently satisfied a wide variety of Mozart's needs and longings. On the simplest level, it served to fulfill his yearnings for friendship and social fellowship. Many of his Viennese friends and associates were Masons, from intimates like Hatzfeld and Lange to fellow musicians like Haydn, Paul Wranitzky, Stadler, and Valentin Adamberger to writers, theater people, and enlightened aristocrats. Thus, the convivial side of Mozart's personality found a congenial outlet in Freemasonry: according to the composer Ignaz Seyfried, Mozart frequented the so-called "eating lodges" during his last years, where "the brethren busied themselves . . . with games, music & the many pleasures of a well-covered table."[44] But Mozart's passion for skittles, cards, and billiards could of course have been gratified elsewhere. It may also be thought that Mozart aimed to advance his career through Masonic membership, and it was frequently charged that the lodges were populated by such opportunists.[45] Certainly, then as later, belonging to a lodge had favorable implications for advancement in one's profession; during the heyday of Viennese Freemasonry it was fashionable to become a Mason, and Masons were to be found within the highest circles of society and government. Many aristocrats were Masons, making up almost half the membership of "True Concord" and more than half the membership of "Crowned Hope," although the membership of the "Beneficence" and "New Crowned Hope" lodges came primarily from the lesser nobility, government bureaucracy, merchant, and professional classes. In 1785, only seven of the forty-four members of Mozart's lodge, "Beneficence," were aristocrats, with officials constituting the largest group, followed by artists and teachers.[46] Many leading patrons of music were Masons, including the Thuns, Esterházys, Prince Karl Lichnowsky, Count Anton Georg Apponyi, Dietrichstein, and Count Joseph Pálffy. Mozart also had frequent business dealings with fellow Masons; virtually all of his Viennese publishers seem to have been Masons, including Pasquale Artaria of Artaria & Co., Christoph Torricella, and Franz Anton Hoffmeister. The Sonatas, op. 7 (including the Piano Sonatas, K. 333/315c and K. 284/205b, and the Violin Sonata, K. 454) were published in a subscription edition by Torricella in August 1784 with a border of Masonic emblems decorating the title page.

Surely, though, Mozart did not become a Mason primarily in order to advance his career: he joined only in December 1784, close to four years after his arrival in Vienna, and long after he had already achieved signal successes there. Membership may have helped him at the outset, because the Masons, charitable toward others, also practiced mutual aid, and as members of an internationalist movement they could count on fraternal hospitality and even financial assistance when abroad: during Mozart's travels between 1787 and 1791 he was apparently welcomed and befriended by Masons in Prague and perhaps other cities. It seems, however, that after the decrees of December 1785 ongoing membership could also have had a negative effect on his career, but his continuing membership clearly did not make him *persona non grata* with the imperial court, which appointed him imperial chamber composer in December 1787 and granted him major operatic commissions in his last years. Fellow Masons did play a crucial role in helping Mozart financially: lodge brothers—Lichnowsky, Franz Hofdemel, Michael Puchberg—were among the most important sources of loans to him. And he helped others in turn, making loans to Masons Anton Stadler and Franz Anton Gilowsky, and performing at a lodge benefit concert on 20 October 1785 to raise money for two visiting horn players, Anton David and Vincent Springer, who were down on their luck.

Mozart's attachment to Freemasonry extended far beyond commonplace economic and recreational motivations. There was a powerful appeal in Freemasonry's idealism, its undogmatic approach to religion, its teachings on self-development and spiritual uplift. It surely exercised a powerful ideological pull upon Mozart that stemmed from its humanitarian and enlightened aspirations, its ideals of equality, liberty, tolerance, and fraternity, and its vision of salvation through love and reason. Freemasonry was not a separate sphere that Mozart occasionally entered as a man seeking a formalized respite from his daily life and activities, or as a professional musician seeking patronage, or a borrower seeking sources of cash. It engaged deeper levels of Mozart's personality, even going beyond simple beliefs in humanitarian ideals. Freemasonry gratified his play impulse through its initiatory practices, tests, and ordeals; it touched his religious yearnings through its fusion of contemporary enlightened teachings with ancient traditions, and through its polytheistic eclecticism, which combined Christian, classical, and exotic religions into a heady blend—witness the opening lines of Mozart's cantata, K. 619, with its undogmatic acceptance of every deity:

> You who revere the
> Creator of the boundless universe,
> call Him Jehova or God,
> call him Fu, or Brahma.
> Hark! Hark to the words
> of the Almighty's trumpet call!
> Ringing out through earth, moon, sun,
> its sound is everlasting.[47]

Masonic ceremonies, and especially those depicting symbolic death followed by resurrection, touch fundamental longings to partake of archaic, universal patterns of experience, and many have observed the clear correlation between primitive rites of passage and rituals for initiation into secret societies. "What . . . is original and fundamental in the phenomenon of secret societies," wrote Mircea Eliade, "is the need for a fuller participation in the sacred, the desire to live as intensely as possible the sacrality peculiar to each of the two sexes. This is the reason why initiation into secret societies so much resembles the initiatory rites of puberty. We find the same ordeals, the same symbols of death and resurrection, the same revelation of a traditional and secret doctrine."[48]

The basic tenets of Masonic belief—idealism, mutual aid, sacrifice, benevolence—gave it the character of an extended, ideal patriarchal family, and we can readily imagine that in some way this compensated for the rupture of Mozart's tie to his father. Perhaps in an attempt at reparation, and surely as a symbol of a desired reunion, Mozart brought his father into the order as an honorary member toward the end of the latter's 1785 visit to Vienna: Leopold Mozart was admitted to "Beneficence" Lodge on 6 April 1785, passed to the second degree 16 April 1785, and raised to the third degree on 22 April 1785, three days before his return to Salzburg.[49]

To move from the familial to the universal, Freemasonry symbolically fulfills fantasies of ideal brotherhoods guided by benevolent priests who have access to hermetic doctrine and utilize their quasi-magical powers to preserve virtue and promote happiness. The orator who spoke on the occasion of Haydn's acceptance as a journeyman into "True Concord," on 11 February 1785, sounded several of these chords:

> I know of no more dignified concept, no more delightful concept, none wherein the upright man can find true happiness and real joy, than a society of noble human beings, each driven by the same thirst to drink from the spring of wisdom; who seek not to be parsimonious with the knowledge that is given them in the Temple of Truth, but on the contrary seek to share it with the others for the common good; a society . . . where the manly handclasp is the sign of a heart expanded to much greatness, not the mask of a false friendship; where the clear-eyed lead the mistaken to the truth without rancor; where man may open his heart to man without having to fear prejudice, hate, or intrigue; a society in which the meetings represent a day of joy for each member, a day to which one looks forward with impatient delight, and which one leaves with the deep pleasure gained from good deeds accomplished and with the joy of an intellect satisfied.[50]

This is a statement of Freemasonry's genuine ideals, but it is surely too roseate a view of the order, a movement that had its oppressive side as well. To belong to the Masonic lodges during an age of suspicion, to belong to a secret society in a pre-revolutionary period, was to enter an ominous shadow world. Freemasonry was an order riven by splits along doctrinal lines, a confederation of warring sects dedicated to each other's destruction, for each claimed to be the sole guardian of the true way. Secrecy made it vulnerable to penetration, and its ranks were infiltrated from several simultaneous directions—by agents of the imperial secret police; by informers and turncoats currying favor with the authorities; by Illuminati who gained control of many leading posts and used the lodges as recruiting outposts; by Jesuits and Rosicrucians seeking to counteract and undermine each other. One Freemason wrote: "I say to you that the brothers themselves hate and persecute one another and that some lodges are embittered against one another like Prussia against Austria."[51] And because the existence of secret societies with esoteric rituals feeds a paranoid strain in police regimes, the authorities came to regard the societies as aspiring to overthrow the social order. Thus were ordinary citizens deemed conspirators, and Freemasons came to distrust their fellows, to see evil and possibilities of betrayal everywhere. Things were not what they seemed: apparent

Freemasons are actually (or perhaps not) secret Rosicrucians, Asiatic Brethren, or Illuminati seeking to seize control of the lodges. Even those who pledge allegiance to the emperor and his policies could be suspected of treachery, for public statements are not necessarily to be believed. Everything can be shown to mean something other than what it appears to mean; subjected to numerological analysis, its hermetic significance emerges, and even a variety of different hermetic meanings can be uncovered, depending on the methods of the investigator.

Even while he remained a member of "New Crowned Hope," Mozart himself planned to start his own secret society in company with several of his friends. "You know that my husband was a Freemason," wrote Constanze Mozart in 1799 to the publisher Breitkopf & Härtel, in the course of furnishing information in connection with a projected biography of Mozart. "He also wanted to found a society to be called *Die Grotte* [The Grotto]. I have found only a fragment of his essay about it and gave it to someone who perhaps was in a position to complete it, because he took part in it."[52] Six months later, she forwarded the essay, unfortunately now

"Triumph of Emperor Joseph's Liberal Idea." Engraving by C. J. Mettenleiter after Johann Ernst Mansfeld. Historisches Museum der Stadt Wien, inv. no. 47.927.

lost, which had been completed by Mozart's friend and fellow Mason, the clarinetist Anton Stadler: "I am herewith lending you for use in the biography . . . an essay, largely in my husband's own handwriting, about an order or a society which he wanted to found, called 'The Grotto.' I cannot furnish any more information about it. The elder Stadler, presently court clarinetist, wrote the rest of the essay and could probably explain it. But he is reluctant to admit what he knows about it because secret orders and societies are so much hated."[53]

It is intriguing to speculate on why Mozart wanted to start his own secret society. Perhaps, after all, he did have unvoiced reservations about imperial control of Freemasonry; perhaps he felt constricted by the increasing network of regulations that hampered the Viennese Masonic lodges in his last years; perhaps he did not feel a close kinship with the large number of Rosicrucians and Asiatic Brethren who had registered as members of "New Crowned Hope" after the *Freimaurerpatent*. Surely "The Grotto" was intended to be something more than a social club, for if it were only that Stadler need not have been overly concerned about political reprisals. Or, perhaps, like so many reading societies, fraternal orders, and cultural associations that proliferated under repressive Habsburg regimes, "The Grotto" would have been committed to activities not welcomed by the authorities, even if these were simply the voicing of independent opinions. One would like to imagine that Mozart's secret society would have avoided the elitism and exclusively male character of the Masonic lodges, which drastically curtailed Freemasonry's claims to speak on behalf of egalitarian ideals; as the poet Wieland wrote, "As far as women were concerned, Freemasons were willing to open their hearts but not their lodges."[54] What seems clearest is that Mozart's hankering for secret societies, which is traceable to his early childhood, when he presided over his "Kingdom of Back," was not wholly satisfied by Freemasonry in its late Habsburg form, especially in the years just prior to its total suppression by the successors to Emperor Joseph II.

These are speculations, and ultimately we are groping in the dark. In founding "The Grotto" Mozart would have become a leader of a secret society working within another secret society, perhaps for the purpose of furthering the aims of the former, which was designed to be more deeply "secret" than the official Masonic lodge. Ignorant of the intended nature of Mozart's "Grotto," we oscillate between a variety of explanations for Mozart's actions, wondering what his "real" beliefs and purposes might have been.

But in the end we probably will not go far wrong if we view Freemasonry as touching many of Mozart's desires and aspirations, from his attraction to mystery to his pull toward illumination, from his search for knowledge to his quest for beauty, from his love of make-believe and fantasy to his yearnings for an unrancorous brotherhood and a benevolent father-hood. No less than the Rosicrucians, the rationalists and Illuminati among the Masons believed in miracles—in their case, however, in the miracle of possible social transformation and the return of humanity from a state of alienation to a state of innocence and grace. A young composer's fascina-tion with *The Arabian Nights,* with Fénelon's rationalist utopian novel, *Les Aventures de Télémaque,* and with every variety of literary and musical ori-entalism converge in the Masonic Temple, creating in its consecrated premises a miniature simulacrum of a fantastic illuminated city, casting an anticipatory beam of light from a desired future into a shadowed present. We are left without certainty, but perhaps with some room for mystery and the miraculous.

Masked ball in the Redoutensaal, ca. 1780. Unsigned pen-and-brush drawing. Historisches Museum der Stadt Wien, inv. no. 141.923.

22

··

THE ZOROASTRAN RIDDLES

On 19 February 1786, during the Viennese carnival, a masquerader cloaked in the robes of an Oriental philosopher proceeded to the Redoutensaal of the Hofburg, where festivities were in progress. There he passed out copies of a broadside sheet containing eight riddles and fourteen proverbs, entitled "Excerpts from the Fragments of Zoroaster" and printed for "the edification of the masked ball." The masquerader and author was Mozart. Copies of the broadside have not survived, but Mozart sent one to his father, who found many of its thoughts commendable; he, in turn, forwarded it to his daughter, Marianne:

> Your brother sent this printed enclosure to me. The first seven riddles were immediately solved on sight. The eighth is more difficult. The *Fragments* [i.e., the proverbs] are really *good* and *true* from *first* to last and should really be taken to heart. . . . Please return the sheet to me.[1]

However strained the relationship between father and son may have been at this time, Leopold Mozart was unable to conceal delight in his son's creative accomplishments, and that is how one of the riddles and seven of the proverbs were preserved: Leopold Mozart placed them at the disposal of Lorenz Hübner, editor of the Salzburg *Oberdeutsche Staats-Zeitung*, who published them in the issue of 23 March 1786 though without mentioning Mozart's name, for Hübner did not regard the materials to be quite as edifying as did Mozart's father.[2]

The proverbs are Mozart's own formulations of standard European and classical proverbs on matters of behavior and morality, concentrating on such familiar dualities as vice/virtue, poverty/riches, hypocrisy/honesty, and diligence/laziness:

1. Say much—speak evil; but in the end it goes without saying that all eyes and ears will be upon you.
4. I prefer open vice to ambiguous virtue; at least I know where I stand.
5. A hypocrite imitating virtue can do so only in watercolors.
10. It won't do for everyone to be modest; only great men can be so.
11. If you are poor but clever, arm yourself with patience: work. If you don't grow rich, you will at least remain a clever man.—If you are an ass but rich, then use your prerogatives: be lazy. If you don't become poor, you will at least remain an ass.
12. The most reliable and tender way to please a lady is to speak evil of her rivals. How many men are not women in this respect?
14. If you are a poor blockhead, become a c---[cleric?]. If you are a rich blockhead, become a leaseholder. If you are a noble but poor block-head, become what you can, to make a living. But if you are a rich, noble blockhead, become what you want; just not, a man of sense—that I won't have.[3]

Leopold Mozart was pleased by such sentiments, which harmonized with his own outlook on life. "The riddles are only for fun," he wrote to Marianne on 28 March, but the proverbs "are really for the improvement of morality."[4] He especially liked his son's apparent devotion to the performance principle: "Every sensible person must work, so long as he lives," he wrote to his daughter, a sentiment he had often tried to impress on his son.

The *Oberdeutsche Staats-Zeitung* printed only one of the riddles, followed by the solution contained in an anagram that Mozart set beneath it:

> One can possess me without seeing me.
> One can carry me without feeling me.
> One can give me without having me.
> "Horns" (*D.e.e.h.i.n.ö.r.r., i.e., Die Hörner*)

In the absence of the other riddles, this solution seemed innocuous enough. But the recent discovery of the remainder of Mozart's Zoroastran riddles indicates that the entire matter was considerably richer in its implications than it had seemed to the composer's father at the time.

A quarto sheet in Mozart's hand (see illustrations on pages 340–41), currently in the Berlin Staatsbibliothek Preussischer Kulturbesitz (collection

Hermann Härtel), contains drafts of the other seven riddles, two of which have been rendered quite illegible, evidently by Georg Nissen, Constanze Mozart's second husband, who also defaced parts of Mozart's correspondence that he considered objectionable.[5]

[1.] We are many sisters; it is painful for us to unite as well as to separate. We live in a palace, yet we could rather call it a prison, for we live securely locked up and must work for the sustenance of men. The most remarkable thing is that the doors are opened for us quite often, both day and night, and still we do not come out, except when one pulls us out by force.

[2.] I am an altogether patient thing, I let myself be used by everyone. Through me the truth, the lie, erudition, and stupidity are proclaimed to the world. He who wants to know everything need only come and ask me, for I know everything. Since everybody needs me I am told everything. Money changers can well use me; I also serve barbers sometimes. I am inevitably necessary to the [illegible word] and [illegible word]. Through me are the most important affairs of state arranged, wars conducted, and lands conquered. Through my endurance the sick receive health, also frequently death. In brief, happiness, unhappiness, life, and death often depend upon me. One would imagine that so many superior qualities would make me happy; O no! My death is generally terrifying— painful, and when it happens gently, base and contemptible. Nevertheless, should I die in the last manner at the hand of a beautiful woman, so shall I take that consolation with me to the grave, that I have seen some things which not everyone gets to see.

[3.] I am an unusual thing [ein sonderbares Ding]; I have no soul and no body; one cannot see me but can hear me; I do not exist for myself: only a human being can give me life, as often as he wishes; and my life is only of short duration, for I die almost at the moment in which I am born. And so, in accordance with men's caprice, I may live and die untold times a day. To those who give me life I do nothing—but those on whose account I am born I leave with painful sensations for the short duration of my life until I depart. Whatever passions a man finds himself in at the time when he grants me life I will surely bring those along into the world. For the most part, women produce me gently and amiably; many have modestly confessed their love in this way. Many have also saved their virtue through me; in these cases, however, my life can scarcely endure a quarter of an hour. I must come into the world by a singular stroke of fortune: otherwise there is no outlet—the man is deformed.

[4.] I serve many as an ornament, many as a mutilation. However, I am highly necessary to everyone. Sometimes it would be better if I were not there; sometimes, on the other hand, it is a blessing [*Wohltat*] that I am there. Frequently even entire [illegible word] are uncovered through me. Frequently many men are even freed of [illegible word] insults through me. Men regard me as a good recommendation to women. I serve old people also, beyond my obligations; on that account [two illegible words] people who become old [illegible word] take care of me, so that I am not spoiled, let alone die before my time.

[5.] We are created for man's pleasures. How can we help it if an accident befalls by which we become the opposite of them? If he is lacking one of us, then he is—defective.

Mozart. Zoroastran riddles, page 1. Staatsbibliothek Preussischer Kulturbesitz Berlin, collection Hermann Härtel.

Mozart's Zoroastran riddles, page 2. Staatsbibliothek Preussischer
Kulturbesitz Berlin, collection Hermann Härtel.

My main concern here is less with the solutions of the riddles than
with some of their possible biographical implications. For, although a riddle's symbolic import can be unraveled, its mystery does not disappear
when the decoding has been accomplished. Paul Ricoeur notes that the
dream and its analogues, such as the riddle, are "set within a region of language that presents itself as the locus of complex significations where
another meaning is both given and hidden in an immediate meaning," and
that the making of a riddle "does not block understanding but provokes it,"
for it calls attention to "double meaning, the intending of the second
meaning in and through the first."[6]

Riddling involves a game of wits. The riddler's strategy is to offer a
"roundabout description of an unnamed object,"[7] so worded as to lead us
to draw inferences that will finally be shown to be false.[8] Aristotle placed
the riddle under the rubric of metaphor, stressing its use of deception,

which arouses a "sense of surprise at the way in which the sentence ends and the soul seems to say, 'Quite true, and I had missed the point.'"[9] By way of example, Mozart's "Horns" riddle combines several commonplace traditional riddles. The experienced riddler will anticipate the usual solutions, such as "a name," or "your word" for all three lines, or "your heart," "a thought," "death," or "blood" for one or more of them. Mozart's "Horns" solution defeats the reader's expectations by a novel yet appropriate answer that strikes a comic, slightly absurd note, thus evoking the delight and surprise—mixed with chagrin—of a successfully wrought jest.

The pleasure is heightened by the more than faint—and less than accidental—phallic implications of Mozart's solution, which is resonant of Falstaff's remark: "Well, he may sleep in security, for he hath the horn of abundance, and the lightness of his wife shines through it."[10] It is also reminiscent of the riddle that Mozart once posed to his Augsburg cousin, in which she was to have a choice between two phallic objects, the one "fair, straight and serious," the other "untidy, crooked and jolly."[11] The phallic connotation of the "Horns" riddle collides with the other main implication, the horns of cuckoldry, a contradiction that cannot be fully resolved, because the word "horns" can symbolize power or inadequacy, honor or disgrace, and even—as in the horns of Moses and Lucifer—extremes of good and evil.[12] We quickly come to realize that the unmasking of the riddle's double meaning by a strategy of symbolic interpretation does not exhaust all possibilities. Indeed, Mozart's double meaning in turn has a double meaning.

Another example: The intended solution of the riddle about the many sisters who live in a palace/prison and cannot go out unless one of them is pulled out by force is "Teeth." It is common in riddles to personify the teeth as sisters or maidens, for example the Westphalian riddle about "Thirty-two maidens dressed in white," or the Javanese, "The front teeth are six sisters."[13] Here, Mozart's strategy is to suggest erotic activity, perhaps in a brothel from which the occupants cannot escape. The unambiguously correct, "innocent" solution then frustrates these vaguely formed inferences. Thus, for a moment the riddle temporarily suspends moral inhibition, leading to the discharge of repressed psychic energy, and then restores the balance by denying that any moral infraction has taken place.[14]

This double-edged character survives the riddle's solution, however, for, as in the "Horns" riddle, we again have an "innocent" answer that, closely examined, revives the bawdy overtones of the imagery: in German slang, "to pull out a tooth" (*sich einen Zahn ausreissen*) strongly suggests a sexual act, and a *Zahn* may signify a "bride" or "bed partner."

Thus, Mozart's riddles belong to the tradition of salacious or obscene riddling, which, originating in primitive rites, took on new life in the

Renaissance, when practitioners of the rarefied literary riddle became extraordinarily proficient at constructing indecent riddles while simultaneously protesting their innocence. *Honi soit qui mal y pense* was the motto of such riddlers, many of whose works nevertheless ended up on the *Index librorum prohibitorum*.[15] So far as we know, Mozart's interest in riddling centered on its role as social recreation and entertainment. In this, he was far from unusual: Goethe, Schiller, Voltaire, and Rousseau—to name only a few of his contemporaries—all wrote riddles for entertainment, and riddling burgeoned in popularity in Europe particularly during the 1780s. Only a few collections of German riddles had appeared in the preceding thirty years, but the decade commencing in 1779 saw a spate of such publications, with more than twenty separate books of riddles issued in German and Austrian cities.[16]

Although the plain motivation of Mozart's Zoroastran riddles surely was to amuse and confound his friends, the underlying connection to the archaic levels of riddling—to the mythic, the sacred, and the dangerous—is not wholly lost in them. One such link is provided by the festival of carnival, the winter celebration that precedes Lent in Catholic countries. On the surface, carnival was a time to have fun, to adopt a new persona, to startle, frighten, and amuse. "When the carnival was on, did you have some good fun?" Mozart asked his beloved cousin. "One can have far more fun at this time in Augsburg than here [in Mannheim]."[17] The observance of carnival goes far back in Mozart's life and music.[18] At an early age, we find him attending carnivals in major cities of Austria, Germany, and Italy, and as many as five of his operas, including *Mitridate, rè di Ponto, Lucio Silla,* and *Idomeneo,* were specifically written for carnival seasons, in Milan, Munich, or Vienna. Furthermore, for Mozart the virtuoso keyboard artist, the pre-Lenten concert season was the most active of the year, making carnival a time to exercise his creativity as well as to participate in the festivities.

On a personal level, carnival recalled the many times when the Mozarts participated together in festivities, Leopold wearing his Harlequin costume, Mozart in a variety of masks, Marianne once appearing in Munich as an Amazon. And carnival brought to mind warm memories of all the good occasions during their travels when a benevolent father and a gifted son donned their costumes, watched the processions, participated in the festivities, and danced at the masked balls in Milan, Venice, Vienna, Munich, Salzburg, and Paris. Leopold once tried to tempt Mozart to return to Salzburg with promises of carnival fun, and once, from Vienna, Mozart asked to borrow his father's Harlequin costume for a pantomime at the carnival in 1783. "You are doubtless aware that this is carnival time and that there is as much dancing here as in Salzburg and Munich. Well, I should very much like to go as Harlequin (but not a soul must know about it)—because here there are so many—indeed nothing but—silly asses at the Redoutes. So I should like you to send me your Harlequin costume."[19] Thus Mozart may have tried to arrange that his father could be symbolically present at the carnival pantomime.

More fundamentally, the modern carnival retains the imprint of the ancient seasonal festivals (the Roman Saturnalia, the French Feast of Fools, the English Lords of Misrule) of which it is a survival. Sir James Frazer explained the festivals as "an annual period of license, when the customary restraints of law and morality are thrown aside, when the whole population give themselves up to extravagant mirth and jollity, and when the darker passions find a vent."[20] ("It is just as if everyone here were going mad," wrote Leopold Mozart from Milan.[21]) The characteristic verbal and literary mode of the festivals is satire—mockery, ridicule, burlesque. It is a time of derision and profanation, when things are turned topsy-turvy and inside out, when lower and higher are interchanged. Obscenity, sexual wordplay, and double meaning are the natural language of carnival, in the *Fastnacht-spiele* (traditional carnival plays) as in Mozart's riddles.[22] Thus, it is a time when Mozart's propensities for the bawdy, the riotous, and the scatological could be revealed to society at large.[23]

It is at *Fastnacht* (Shrove Tuesday) that the performance principle is momentarily set aside and the *Spieltrieb* ("play impulse") holds sway. In modern carnivals the original festive element has been narrowed down, but it has not disappeared. Carnival remains a time of defiance and reversal, when beggars become princes and scapegoats kings. In Bakhtin's words, "It is a temporary transfer to the utopian world."[24] It is a holiday from conformity. And it is also what Kris calls "a holiday from the superego."[25]

That may be why we sense that many of Mozart's long-standing preoccupations merge to create the carnival riddles of 1786. We know of his fondness for codes and ciphers and his love for secret tongues: in 1772, he even learned the sign language of the deaf. Then there was his attachment to secret societies and orders—to the imaginary "Kingdom of Back" of his childhood, to the Masonic lodges, and to "The Grotto," about which his wife reported so reticently after his death. Mozart's attraction to a Zoroastran orientalism is in the tradition of the Masonic lodges and reading societies, which were hotbeds of interest in the exotic, the oriental, and the miraculous. (Zoroaster may be later reincarnated as Sarastro in Mozart's mythic-Masonic opera, *Die Zauberflöte*.) Mozart loved wordplay of every kind, including neologisms, transpositions, reversals, puns, rhymes, wordsalads, and the like. If *Fastnacht* derives from "faseln"—to talk nonsense—it was a holiday season designed for Mozart, for this was the mother tongue of his Kingdom of Back. The riddles display Mozart's antic disposition as clearly as do his bawdy letters to the Bäsle, his outrageous first-person entries in his sister's personal diary, and his obscene canons of the 1780s.

What these tendencies and preoccupations have in common, of course, is the play principle and, beyond that, a longing for the secret and the forbidden. In the Vienna carnival of 1786, Mozart did publicly what he dared not attempt in private: he violated taboos without conscious expectation of punishment. For carnival is precisely the time when ritual laughter can be directed against the gods, when the overthrow of the primal fathers is licensed. During the "fire festival" that marked the climax of the Roman carnival, shouts of "Death to you!" were heard everywhere, as each person contended with stranger and friend alike to blow out his lighted candle, the symbol of flesh and mortality. Goethe was particularly entranced to see a young boy blow out his father's candle, crying "Sia ammazzato, il signor Padre!"—Death to you, Sir Father![26] Mozart, as the carnivalesque son, takes the place of the father by donning the robes of a powerful, exotic lawgiver and by formulating apodictic proverbs and obscure, grandiose riddles. He has seized the trappings of divinity and wisdom, has fashioned himself as an oracle, as one who can penetrate ultimate mysteries. He has transformed himself from the supplicant Oedipus into the all-knowing Sphinx, the maker of riddles. More, he has taken both roles—simultaneously posing riddles and offering their solutions. The mythic hero addresses questions to destiny; Mozart addresses questions to himself as well.

Mozart addressed his riddles not only to himself and to fate, however, but to at least one other person. He sent them to his father and, in effect, dared him to solve them. His riddling thereby became a heavy wager, a critical test risking a grave forfeit.

Neither distance nor the passage of time had lessened the overwhelming intensity of the entanglement between Mozart and his father. The matter reached perhaps its most poignant expression one year before the composition of the riddles, at carnival time 1785, with Leopold Mozart's arrival on 11 February for a stay of two and a half months. There he was subjected to a vivid and unrelenting demonstration of his son's triumphs as a performer, composer, and impresario at the pinnacle of his career. Within a space of only six weeks, Mozart gave numerous concerts, including some half dozen academies and subscription concerts; at the singer Luisa Laschi's academy at the Burgtheater on 13 February he played a piano concerto (probably the B-flat, K. 456) in the presence of the emperor, who "waved his hat and called out, 'Bravo, Mozart!'"[27] Leopold Mozart was ecstatic in his descriptions of these events in his letters to his daughter and he had nothing but the highest praise for his son's music, calling one concerto "very fine," another "glorious," and one full concert "magnificent." So moved was he by Mozart's performance on one occasion that "for sheer delight tears came into my eyes." In addition, he was daily witness to his son's warm acceptance by members of the highest strata of Viennese society, attending parties, balls, and banquets as part of Mozart's entourage, visiting the Masonic "Beneficence" Lodge and securing membership there under his son's sponsorship. Nor were Mozart's triumphs limited to the professional sphere. Leopold was also much taken by the elegance of Mozart's quarters, by the "perfection" of a meal served by Constanze's mother, by another extraordinary luncheon at the home of the younger Stephanie, with food "fit for a prince." And he found his grandson Karl to be not only the picture of his father, but "charming, for he is extremely friendly and laughs when spoken to."

Perhaps the high point of all this was reached the day after his arrival, following a private run-through, at Mozart's apartment, by Mozart, his father, and Anton and Bartholomäus Tinti of the "Haydn" String Quartets, K. 458, K. 464, and K. 465 in the presence of their dedicatee. It was on that occasion that Joseph Haydn told Leopold Mozart what any father, and especially one who was himself a composer and court musician, would have longed to hear—that he regarded Mozart as "the greatest composer" of the age.[28]

It was against this whirling, carnivalesque backdrop that Leopold's ability to bear his son's limitless triumph finally gave way. In a letter to Marianne of 12 March, he wrote, "We never get to sleep before one o'clock in the morning, we never get up before 9 o'clock, and we eat at 2 or half-past 2. Horrible weather!"[29] These were reasonable complaints for an elderly man, one who was moreover coming down with a bad cold. But his next words indicated that he was more than just physically weary of the constant round of events. "Daily academies, constant lessons, music, composing, etc. How shall I bear it! If only the concerts were over: it is impossible to describe the constant vexation and restlessness (*Schererey und Unruh*)."[30] By the beginning of April he frankly confessed: "I am really ill-tempered, since I would gladly be away from Vienna, and the weather so cold and detestable as though it were February."[31]

Leopold Mozart left Vienna on 25 April 1785. It may have been during this visit that Mozart came to understand the extent and nature of his father's competition with him. He may now even have realized that his father's rejection of him went beyond alleged character flaws and a perceived abandonment, but extended to his creativity as well. It was surely inevitable that, with each new evidence of Mozart's musical genius, Leopold would come to feel that the gulf between them had widened, intensifying his sense of being unneeded. Mozart's creativity itself became a hallmark of their estrangement and of his own impotence, even as it thrilled him to consider that he had fathered, shaped, and nurtured so miraculous a being. Each of Mozart's grand successes—imperial salutes, Haydn's encomium, popular acclaim, financial rewards—demonstrated once and for all that Leopold's parochial cautions had been far off the mark. (No one needed to be reminded that if Mozart had heeded Leopold's advice, he would still be court organist and composer in the service of the Salzburg archbishop, and the operas and piano concertos that arose in response to opportunities in Vienna would never have been written.)

Thus, intentionally or not, Mozart gave his father a series of object lessons, even compelling him to acknowledge that Constanze's household management was both splendid and economical, and that the despised Frau Weber was an elegant hostess and a good cook. Primarily, it was proved beyond question that Mozart himself, far from being an eternal child, was a conspicuously successful entrepreneur who was earning large sums of money and who was beloved of Haydn, the emperor, the people, and the haut-monde. In brief, the visit had pulled down the entire family mythology, root and branch.

It had not, however, resolved the issue between father and son, for a curious and painful fact now became transparent: fulfilling his father's stated goals did not bring parental approval; his father's discontent seemed to increase in direct proportion to his son's accomplishments. Now Mozart could no longer ignore the likelihood that an unspoken grievance against him was that he had surpassed his father's expectations. And if that were so, then he could never hope to obtain his father's approval or forgiveness, or even to demonstrate retroactively that he had been in the right. Thus, he was involved in a contest from which he could never emerge victorious. He could neither be loved for his person nor praised for his achievements. His only hope was to settle the score. Unwinnable contests evoke desperate remedies. In the present contest, Mozart proved the more subtle, and even the more deadly, antagonist.

That Mozart worked assiduously to bring his father's resentments to the surface is quite clear. Mozart put on a demonstration of his success, affluence, and musical achievements sufficient to arouse the envy even of Saint Cecilia, patron saint of music. Heedless of his father's advanced age and weakened physical condition, he arranged for his presence at every concert and festivity: it was as though he had staged this triumphant panorama—this Mozart carnival—for the purpose of finally putting his father's reproaches to rest. And—let it be said plainly—of demonstrating his own superiority and vitality at the expense of a lonely old widower.

This may help explain why a striking cluster of images in Mozart's Zoroastran riddles, written in the aftermath of and on the first anniversary of Leopold Mozart's Vienna visit, center on themes of deformity and mutilation. Multiple references indicate the central preoccupations of the riddles: "the man is deformed" (Riddle 3); "I serve many as an ornament, many as a mutilation" (Riddle 4); "people who become old take care of me, so that I am not spoiled" (Riddle 4); "if an accident befalls . . . and [a man] is lacking one of us, then he is—defective" (Riddle 5). Even the "Teeth" riddle carries similar overtones, with its fusion of aggressive orality and implied dangerous sexuality; further, in Karl Abraham's experience, the loss of a tooth in dreams is a "symbolic occurrence which typified both fear of castration and of an object-loss."[32]

The imagery of bodily mutilation mingles with the imagery of death. In Riddle 2, the grandiose oracle claims to be an ambassador of death; he tells us that "life and death" depend on him and he describes his own death as "generally terrifying" and "painful"; the remarkably insubstantial and soulless being of Riddle 3 dies "untold times a day" and lives for only the shortest period of time: "I die almost at the moment in which I am born"; the narrator of Riddle 4 fears that he will "die before [his] time." Of

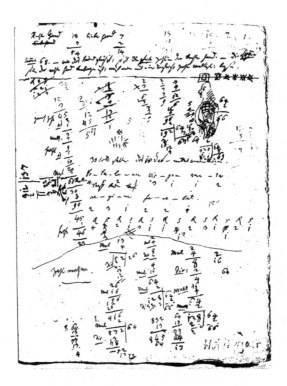

Caricature and notations from card games on verso of Zoroastran riddles.
Staatsbibliothek Preussischer Kulturbesitz Berlin,
collection Hermann Härtel.

course, in the language of venery, the verb "to die" is also a metaphor for various sexual and bodily processes.[33] Mozart's "should I die . . . at the hand of a beautiful woman" is the closest kin to Benedict's words to Beatrice: "I will live in thy heart, die in thy lap, and be buried in thy eyes."[34]

With a few swift strokes, the riddles plunge from a comic, ironic surface to a center where fear of death and castration dominate. While seeking to assuage anxiety, the comic impulse has inadvertently brought it into being.[35] Seeking to establish superiority over his father, Mozart succeeds in quickening his own sense of dread. The riddles are the hieroglyphics of a secret discourse, a deadly play between a father and his son. But this is no abstract contest for supremacy. The surface is comic, the undercurrent is terror, the "answers" are mostly phallic, but the subject may well be Mozart's mother, Leopold's wife, as an emblem of the feminine. She is the prize for whom the contest is waged; she herself is a riddle whose secret is to be solved at all costs. In life, she had been Mozart's shield against punishment, mutilation, and death; in death, she became the focus of Mozart's guilt, heightened when his father charged him with causing her death by his negligence. Because the stakes are so high, the feminine becomes a zone of danger: In the first riddle, she is the fanged temptress, *vagina dentata;* in the "horns" riddle, she betrays her husband. A masquerading virility continues in Riddle 2, where the lover is quite ready to "die at the hands of a beautiful woman," content to know that his flesh has seen something "which not everyone gets to see." In Riddle 3, the woman temporarily preserves her chastity by surrounding herself with noxious odors. The misogyny is only partly feigned, for Mozart could not remain altogether immune to his father's cautions against the dangers of sexuality, both conjugal and illicit. In the riddles' equations of pleasure and mutilation, sex and death, orgasm and annihilation, we have echoes of Leopold Mozart's warnings against what he viewed as the ensnaring, labyrinthine, contaminating woman, warnings by which he unconsciously aimed both to separate Mozart from his mother and to keep Mozart for himself.

Still, it is—or ought to be—an essential principle of reading a text that its plainest meaning should not be overlooked. That, at any rate, was the lesson of Poe's "Purloined Letter." Here, too, the most obvious fact about Mozart's riddles may be the most difficult to perceive: all of them are written in the first person, singular or plural. To write and distribute the riddles was not only to ask questions but to make a statement. To send them to Leopold Mozart was to write him a coded letter, just as in the old days. Beneath the witty surface, beneath the literary convention, beneath the aggressive implications and the taunting double entendres, Mozart may have sent home to Salzburg a plain confession and a call for help. The first riddle conveys his feeling of captivity in a palace that is really a prison, where he must work for the benefit of others rather than for his own gratification or fulfillment. The second tells of his genius, his sense of greatness: "One would imagine that so many superior qualities would make me happy; O no! My death is generally terrifying [and] painful." In the third riddle, an uncanny sense of dissociation overcomes the narrator: "I have no soul and no body. One cannot see me but can hear me." (We may now acknowledge the musical implications of this phrase: incorporeal, the narrator/composer exists only in the sounds he produces.) His very being is in question: "I do not exist for myself." He owes his life to another: "Only a human being can give me life, as often as he wishes"; he has a foretaste of doom: "my life is only of short duration" and depends wholly upon "the caprice of men." He is overcome with guilt: "To those who give me life I do nothing—but those on whose account I am born I leave with painful sensations for the short duration of my life."

Similar themes echo through the fourth riddle: "I serve many as an ornament, many as a mutilation. . . . Sometimes it would be better if I were not there, sometimes . . . it is a blessing that I am there." He knows of his power to discover and to heal, but his pathetic wish is to be of service to others in the hope that they may reciprocate with kindness: "I serve old people also, beyond my obligations; on that account, people who become old take care of me, so that I am not spoiled, let alone die before my time." This glimmer of hope dissolves in Riddle 5, the most despairing and aggressive of the set: We are "created for man's pleasures. How can we help it if an accident befalls by which we become the opposite? If he is lacking one of us, then he is—defective."

Mozart's riddles oscillate between concealing and revealing, between mystery and clarity, between asking and waiting for an answer. This is not only in the nature of riddling; it is in the nature of Mozart's needs. Though he cannot overcome the anxiety aroused by his father's imperatives, he will not submit; he cannot restore the old relationship of domination/humiliation without undermining his creativity. He turns aside the homosexual blandishment of a perpetual childhood under the protection of a compassionate and omnipotent father. Fearing punishment, he becomes a masquerader; to avoid discovery, one can flee or one can hide. But the phallic pretense of the maimed clown is insufficient to neutralize his fear or to delude the punishing superego. So he plainly needs to confess the extent of his woundedness. He needs Leopold Mozart's help but cannot openly ask for it.

And so the real riddle is posed: Who is it that is deserving both of your punishment and of your forgiveness? Unfortunately, Leopold Mozart had insufficient patience with his son's studied obscurity of expression. Almost ten years earlier, Mozart had playfully teased his father: "In my next letter I may perhaps be able to tell you something *very good* for you, but only *good* for me, or something *very bad* in your eyes, but *tolerable* in mine; or it may be something *tolerable* for you, but *good, precious and valuable* for me!"[36] Mozart insisted that though this might be "obscure," and even "rather in the style of an oracle," yet it was "intelligible." His father disagreed strongly. "*Blast your oracular utterances!*"[37] he wrote, asking for a plainer explanation.

At carnival 1786, the oracle-harlequin once again asked Leopold Mozart to investigate; but the eighteenth-century deputy kapellmeister, secure in his rationality and righteousness, failed to perceive a mystery.

Mozart's Zoroastran riddles may help us understand something about Mozart's personality—and even, perhaps, his creativity, for raw materials such as these are better suited for psychological analysis than are structured works of art. In artistic creativity, the process of sublimation retains its etymological meaning—to refine, to elevate, to purify, i.e., to convert into a higher form. Thus, the artist's personal motivations, experiences, and drives may be so thoroughly absorbed—or objectified—in a successful creation that the retrieval of autobiographical implications can scarcely be accomplished without his close cooperation, if at all. In his work, the artist finds ways symbolically to repair psychic injuries and object losses, to neutralize anxieties. But he does this by means of socially developed techniques and forms of art, so that what had been private and opaque becomes a shared communication. The artist, remarked Freud in a famous passage, "understands how to elaborate his day-dreams, so that they lose that personal note which grates upon strange ears. . . . He knows too how to modify them sufficiently so that their origin in prohibited sources is not easily detected."[38]

To put this somewhat differently: the work of art mediates between an archaeology and a teleology. The productive imagination brings into being objects that have sources in current and archaic materials but that nonetheless have never previously existed in these individual forms. In Paul Ricoeur's splendid formulation, we can say that "the work of art goes ahead of the artist; it is a prospective symbol of his personal synthesis and of man's future, rather than a regressive symbol of his unresolved conflicts."[39] If the sublimated transformations and symbolic disguises that lie near the core of artistic creativity are not sufficient to daunt the investigator of links between biography and art, consider the additional difficulty for the music historian, who deals with materials that are largely nonverbal and even preverbal. I have no doubt that, in the process of creation, the originating impulses are preserved precisely at the same time that they are mastered. Something of a composer's personality and experience flows into his works and perhaps even constitutes an important ingredient of his artistic individuality, his style. The difficulty lies in reading the runes.

It is less difficult to read Mozart's riddles, for, apart from their being verbal rather than musical productions, they are incomplete, even unsuccessful sublimations. And it is precisely failed actions, whether those of daily life or works of art and science, that give us a glimpse of the interior. Here, the original libidinal impulse has not been wholly transmuted, let alone mastered in form. In his riddles, Mozart lets his guard down, unaware that the riddles are anything other than literary exercises written purely for the fun of it. He believes that his riddles convey a clear set of objective signals that only require rational decoding for their significance to be grasped and enjoyed. He is unaware that the riddles are also free-associational products of his imagination, symbols to which are bonded fragments of a hidden life.

23

·······································

THE CARNIVALESQUE
DIMENSION

We have already encountered in Mozart some classic characteristics of a radical, a heretic, or even a revolutionary. Altruistic to the bone, he is consumed by a rage for fairness and a white-hot anger against those who misuse power. He sympathizes with the victims of injustice and he rails against those who have slighted or maltreated others. Embedded in Mozart's letters are many signs of his impulse to take heroic action and thereby gain revenge for indignity. From Munich, he told of the singer Marchesi, who, because he had betrayed his mistress, was supposedly offered a choice by a group of thugs—to drink poison or be murdered. "He chose the former," wrote Mozart, absorbed in this sensational tale: "Had it been myself and had it been absolutely necessary for me to die, I should have taken at least a couple of them with me into the next world."[1] Later, following Count Arco's kick, Mozart related to his father "a shocking story" about a Herr von Wibmer who was beaten and insulted in Innsbruck by a certain Baron Buffa. When he brought his case before the authorities, it was Wibmer who was arrested and "condemned to receive twenty-five [later raised to fifty] lashes on his behind" for having struck a nobleman. Wibmer was now in Vienna appealing to the emperor for justice: "Nothing else is being talked of," wrote Mozart, deeply moved by empathy for a wronged individual, asking, "How can this man ever obtain adequate compensation? The lashes must always remain," and he avowed that, in similar circum-

"Der Guckkastenmann" ("The Peep Show Man"). Etching by
F. A. Maulpertsch, 1785. Graphische Sammlung Albertina, Vienna.

stances, "I would run my sword through his heart."[2] Mozart harbors fantasies of revenge for his treatment by Arco, even if he has "to wait twenty years for it,"[3] and he writes, "I shall feel bound to assure him in writing that he may confidently expect from me a kick on his behind and a few boxes on the ear in addition. For when I am insulted, I must have my revenge."[4] Mozart was no stranger to the blend of rage and ironic insolence that gave rise to Figaro's revenge fantasy in "Se vuol ballare": Mozart, too, will make the count dance.

Beyond his fantasies of retribution, Mozart has scant deference for rank or position, whether in the secular or the religious spheres: archdukes, archbishops, emperors, and empresses alike are the subject of his scorn. He is skeptical of all authority, whether princes, kings, priests, or legislators. He cannot be taken in, as Beethoven was, by benevolent emperors and first consuls, perhaps because he knew these men at first hand in a way that Beethoven did not. "Stupidity oozes out of his eyes," writes Mozart of his admiring patron, Archduke Maximilian Franz. "He talks and holds forth incessantly and always in falsetto—and he has started a goiter."[5] Hearing of Empress Maria Theresia's mortal illness, he is irked that he would have to feign grief: "Next week everyone will be in mourning—and I, who have always to be about, *must also weep* with the others."[6] He is, we know, particularly sensitive to issues of economic exploitation: "No man ought to be mean, but neither ought he to be such a simpleton as to let other people take the profits from his work, which has cost him so much study and labor, by renouncing all further claims upon it."[7] With heavy irony, he writes, "You know well how services are generally rewarded by great lords."[8] Even Emperor Joseph II, whom he admired and wished to serve, did not escape Mozart's scalpel: he was characterized as "a skinflint" who "was well aware of his own meanness."[9] For Mozart, the movers and shakers of society are fallible human beings rather than objects of veneration. He reports that the emperor has a sexual interest in Elisabeth Wilhelmine Louise, the teenage princess of Württemberg: "This affair is an open secret in Vienna, but no one knows whether she is going to be a morsel for himself or for some Tuscan prince. Probably the latter. . . . I am really astonished, because she is, you might say, still a child."[10]

Because there exist in him tensions between rage and restraint, arrogance and submission, destruction and decorum, Mozart's radical impulses do not take commonplace, vulgar, or predictable pathways. Skeptical, wary of easy solutions, doubtful of men's motives, disdainful of panaceas—in these respects, wholly his father's son—he does not uncritically attach himself to charismatic political leaders or their reform programs, which had so strong an attraction for young idealists. Nor does he turn to esoteric doctrines or hermetic movements in reaction against a watered-down Enlightened rationalism. His radical energies instead come under the sway of the play impulse, of art, of language, of ritual, indeed of every variety of the imaginative, thereby opening channels for the expression of his altruism, outlets for his fury, and alternatives to a discontented world. It is Mozart's transformative, metamorphosing impulse that is the common matrix of many of his idiosyncratic concerns and enthusiasms, linking together his penchant for unorthodox and bawdy language, his deep commitment to Freemasonry, and his passion for carnival.

Carnival repeals actuality, suspends time. Removed to an alternative plane of experience, swept onward in processions of dancing and chanting masqueraders, the carnivalesque actor, disguised, cloaked, and masked, ascends a stage where a festive drama is under way, riotous, tumultuous, seemingly chaotic, but with its own insistent logic: on that stage, but only during the interval of the pre-Lenten abrogation of the temporal order, what was prohibited must now be privileged. Thus, Mozart's obscene riddles, his penchant for the bawdy in general, emerge within the space formed by the carnival's multiple nullifications—of time, actuality, rationality, law, and logic. Carnival overthrows the rationalist-theological preference for spirit over body, the relegation of sexuality and the ordinary functions of the human body to the "animal" sphere, the condemnation of fleshly pleasures and pursuits, the elevation of high seriousness over enjoyment. The carnivalesque opposes all official, hierarchical, dilutely spiritualized views of mankind; it demystifies the body and its processes in order that the disembodied may be reembodied. In Bakhtin's formulation, "the drama of bodily life," that is, "copulation, birth, growth, eating, drinking, defecation," provides a temporary entry into a utopian realm that accepts the natural cycle of birth, death, and rebirth. Through death and defecation the dying world gives birth to the new and this "is represented in the images of the material bodily lower stratum; everything descends into the earth and the bodily grave in order to die and to be reborn."[11] This is a stratum that resounds with a laughter that has overcome fear by refusing to locate the fearsome either in death or in the recesses of the human body: "There can be nothing terrifying on earth, just as there can be nothing frightening in a mother's body, with the nipples that are made to suckle, with the genital organ and the warm blood."[12]

Mozart's wit acknowledges no inhibitions, no limitations, rejoices in the merely human and in the sensuous materiality of the quotidian: "With your ladyship's permission," he writes Baroness Waldstätten on the occasion of a forthcoming visit by himself and his wife, "we shall both have the honor to wait upon your Ladyship . . . and to give Fräulein Auernhammer an enema, if she won't keep the door to her room more firmly shut."[13] As early as the Italian journeys, in a letter to his sister from the town of Bozen (Bolzano), he outrageously expressed his fearlessness about naming the openings of the body:

> Bozen, this sow's hole. . . .
> Rather than come again to Bozen,
> I'd prefer to whack myself in the cunt.[14]

Nor does he shrink even from offering what appears to be a prose description of a farcical sexual encounter as a narrative approximation of a musical composition, interlineated in the autograph of the Rondo of the Horn Concerto in D, K. 412 + 514/386b, where the text corresponds roughly to actual musical events in the score:

> For you, Mr. Donkey—Come on—quick—get on with it—like a good fellow—be brave—Are you finished yet?—for you—beast—oh what a dissonance—Oh!—Woe is me!!—Well done, poor chap—oh, pain in the balls!—Oh God, how fast!—you make me laugh—help—take a breather—go on, go on—that's a little better—still not finished?—you awful swine!—how charming you are!—dear one!—little donkey!—ha, ha, ha—take a breath!—But do play at least one note, you prick!—Aha! Bravo, bravo, hurrah!—You're going to torture me [seccarmi] for the fourth time, and thank God it's the last—Oh finish now, I beg of you!—Confound it—also bravura?—Bravo!—oh, a sheep bleating—you're finished?—Thank heavens!—Enough, enough!

Approximately, then, Mozart's bawdy celebration of the body and its physical functions can be seen to represent his instinctive repudiation of a brittle rationalism that elevates mind over life, which is to say, a rejection of fathers and archbishops, emperors and popes, of all reified divisions of society, of every pious scourging of the flesh. We have already seen how, using the language of the lower bodily stratum, Mozart gets "Blow into my ass, blow into my ass" ("Pfeif mir im Arsch, pfeif mir im Arsch") to equal "Papa."[15] Similarly, the enlightened, reform-minded, but *stingy* Archbishop Colloredo becomes a grotesque participant in a Hieronymus Bosch phantasmagoria, his name being spelled out by the initials of certain key words in one of Mozart's letters: "If only the *a*ss who smashes a *r*ing, and by so doing *c*uts himself a *h*iatus in his *b*ehind so that *I* hear him *s*hit like a castrato with *h*orns, and with his long ear *o*ffers to caress the fox's *p*osterior, were not so."[16] Although the riddler in the end pleads innocence ("Just kidding!"), the imprint of his obscene message is not readily scrubbed from consciousness.[17]

Mozart's bawdiness rises primarily, though not exclusively, within an excremental zone, but not one that is withholding, willful, pedantic, classifying, collecting, controlling, constipated, parsimonious, or cheap: those traits belong to the fathers. His excremental universe is copious, free-flowing, generative, playful. "Oui, par ma foi. I shit on your nose and it will run down your chin," he writes to his cousin, the secret sharer of this backwards kingdom.[18] It takes in and gives back, withholding nothing: "We are lunching this very moment, so that after that we may shit again, however that may be."[19] It is a realm of delight: "Oh, oh, when you've emptied yourself, life is far more worth living."[20] It is an affectionate zone as well, for to accept the excremental without fear or disgust is to be capable of loving the body's apertures of love and procreation: "Blow into my ass";[21] "Ah, muck! Sweet word! Muck! taste! That too is fine. Muck, taste!—muck!—lick!—o charmante!"[22] Through excremental generosity, Mozart also returns to his mother, offers her his body, unashamed, needy, and vulnerable, for loving, caring, and licking. Nutrition and excretion, sucking and cleansing are insignia of maternal-infant fusion: Mozart's easy interchanges with his mother about his bowel functions were expressions of their intimacy, a regular feature of their verbal discourse. In 1778, while traveling with the Webers, he wrote to her in Mannheim:

At night of farts there is no lack,
Which are let off, forsooth, with a powerful crack,
The king of farts came yesterday
Whose farts smelt sweeter than the may. . . .
Well, now we've been over a week away
And we've been shitting much muck every day. . . .
on Monday I'll have the honor, egad,
To embrace you and kiss your hands so fair.
But first in my pants I'll shit, I swear.
Your faithful child[23]

Elsewhere he promises to keep his ass clean. A good boy makes his mother happy by shitting and cleaning.

However, the carnivalesque excremental is equally an outlet for Mozart's rage and defiance. "Lick my ass," "Lick my ass nice and clean," "May the one who does not want me lick my ass" are Burma-Shave signposts on Mozart's private highway, turning up in canons, correspondence, and conversation as verbal emblems of resistance and refusal: rejected, insulted, humiliated, Mozart departs for new realms by turning his hindquarters to the old. Donning his antic mask, playing the harlequin, hairdresser's boy, dandy, or peasant bridegroom, Mozart achieves carnivalesque equalizations, brings down the mighty, gains revenge for a kick in the behind. Mozart's bawdy is a strategy of carnivalesque uncrowning, a humorous debasement of hegemony and hierarchy, of power and pomp, a parody of rationality, cleanliness, and order. It sets up barriers against every form of intimidation or recrimination, threat or prohibition. As Middleton Murry understood, nonsense and comedy have constructive powers, shaping new worlds even as they dismantle old ones: "For the comic spirit, any cosmos is an illusion to be shattered; but—this is the point—to be shattered gaily, not desperately, with an exuberance of high spirits, and almost with the suggestion that the same force of genius which destroys the existing cosmos might easily create another and a better."[24] Mozart's bawdy brings kindling to what Bakhtin calls "the gay carnival bonfire in which the old world is burned."[25]

Even with his evocation of the carnivalesque, however, Mozart cannot forever evade tragic modalities. In the years of his Vienna "exile," the Zoroastran riddles showed us, Mozart's bawdy comes to be penetrated by his sense of mutilation; the transformative power of nonsense can no longer anesthetize his pain. With the attainment of forbidden goals—separation from his father, creative triumph, economic success, and marriage—the bawdy somehow lost much of its joyous force. Now it speaks of castration, death, mutilation, old age, and isolation. Mozart's pen has not lost its point, but he has lessened his reliance on the excremental and scatological zones in favor of a lonely phallic wit, as also in his later, loving, melancholy letters to Constanze. For Mozart, the comic no longer consistently resonates with hope of rejuvenation and rebirth: crippled, deformed, locked within the grinding jaws of the thirty-two sisters, still bound by the imperative to care for his aged father, increasingly despairing and death-haunted, Mozart cannot locate the apertures of paradise.

Thus we learn what we should have known to begin with: that all strategies to defeat mortality and power are partial, imperfect, and sooner or later terminate in disillusionment. That is why such strategies need revision, with new ones formulated as old ones lose their imagined force. In Freemasonry Mozart found another such ideal mock universe, an alternative reality. Like the participant in carnival, the Masonic initiate slips from the everyday world into a parallel society with a peculiar set of rules. In a sense, though, these are opposite ways, for Freemasonry claims to exalt sobriety, high seriousness, rationality, and order, whereas carnival is ludic, unpredictable, profane, topsy-turvy. What connects them is that both suspend the natural hierarchical order of the "real" world: all come equal to Freemasonry and, at least in theory, each may rise within its ranks in accordance with his abilities and his dedication to the craft rather than in accordance with his position in ordinary social and class structures. A speaker at

Illustration for title page, *Ein musikalischer Spass*, K. 522. Published
by Johann Anton André, 1802. Private collection.

Haydn's ceremonial acceptance into a Masonic lodge called it "a society in
which neither the smile of fortune nor the chance of birth reign, but in
which the wisest and best are given the leadership."[26] In *Die Zauberflöte*, the
first priest says of Tamino, "Consider well. He is a prince!" But Sarastro's
volcanic reply comes from the depth of Masonic doctrine: "More! He is a
man!" As a Mason, Mozart repairs external indignities by participating in a
"society" of equals whose regard for him formally has nothing to do with
issues of birth, power, or money.

Freemasonry and the carnivalesque are also connected at the level of
radical rejection, with both providing outlets for Mozart's sense of woundedness, his rage, his desire to overthrow the existent, his patricidal impulses,
his contempt for authority. But they are also profoundly different: in the
Masonic sphere, fathers and sons and their surrogates meet on a level of
absolute equality, love, and common participation in good works or mutual
aid, whereas the carnivalesque world is a vengeful one, in which sons top-
ple or cuckold primal fathers, usurp power, and overthrow the "natural"
order of social and familial relationships. The one seeks self-development,
harmony, and spiritual elevation in a sacral mode, whereas the other
encourages discharge of sexual and patricidal impulses in a ludic mode.

Despite their radical and utopian perspectives of transformation, however, neither Freemasonry nor carnival can escape complicity in the social
order: Freemasonry by reason of its rigid internal hierarchy, which mirrors

the patriarchal order, and carnival by providing an escape valve for suppressed energy and pacifying discontent through a symbolic, licensed rebellion that ends at dawn on Ash Wednesday, after which there is a return— exultant, meek, sullen, or shamefaced—to the status quo ante. Both are readily appropriated to the purposes of the state. Both are permeated by utopian fallacies—Freemasonry by the illusion of a benevolent order and carnival by the belief that symbolic action alone can permanently alter a recalcitrant reality. Still, Mozart found, these are nevertheless worthwhile fallacies, fallacies to live by.

Of course, Mozart's music was his primary means of creating alternative universes, discharging suppressed feelings, giving material form to his imaginings, recalling times of loving fusion, and repairing an unhappy reality. But it is not surprising that he was driven to seek still other outlets for his productive imagination, for his was a metamorphosing nature, restlessly imbued with a drive to play with—and thereby to transform—every conceivable form of reality. Art is everything, the life of Mozart tells us, but it is not sufficient. The drive to reconstruct reality was so powerful in him that it spilled over from the aesthetic sphere, into carnival, unorthodox language, and Freemasonry, all of which provided him with singular surrogates for reality, materializations of his innermost fantasies. Exuberantly, Mozart wore the comic mask, danced in the carnivalesque procession, pondered the Masonic mysteries of Isis and Osiris, devoutly affirming the healing power of the imaginative, even as the shadows of mortality, doubt, pain, and tyranny descended around him: "Do go on loving me," he had written to his cousin in 1777, using carnivalesque speech that has been liberated from the shackles of common sense, "as I love you, then we shall never cease loving one another, though the lion hovers round the walls, though doubt's hard victory has not been weighed and the tyrant's frenzy has crept to decay; yet Codrus, the wise philosopher, often eats soot instead of porridge, and the Romans, the props of my ass, have always been and ever will be—half-castes."[27]

Autograph manuscript, Piano Concerto in C, K. 467, Andante.
The Pierpont Morgan Library, Dannie and Hettie Heineman Collection.

24

....

FEARFUL SYMMETRIES

Mozart's mature instrumental music represents our civilization's sign for the beautiful. We cannot think of him without thinking of beauty; we cannot refer to beauty without recalling his music. I believe this is so, not necessarily because his works are more beautiful than those of other composers, though this may well be true, but because he created—or, at least, brought into the forefront of aesthetic consciousness—a special kind of musical beauty, one that thenceforth came to exemplify the idea of superlative beauty itself. There are many beauties in Mozart's earlier works as well, but with a few exceptions (like the opening of the A-major Symphony, K. 201/186a) they are missing the excruciating, surplus quality that transforms loveliness into ecstasy, grace into sublimity, pleasure into rapture (Example 24.1).

Example 24.1. Divertimento in D, K. 334/320b. Menuetto, mm. 1–8.

There are rare beauties especially in those Salzburg compositions deriv-
ing from Mozart's serenade style. In those works, which inhabit a world of
plenitude, beauty is everywhere for the mere taking. Thus, in Mozart's last
three violin concertos, the beauties succeed each other with a breathtaking
rapidity, their outpouring of episodic interpolations suggesting that we
need not linger over any single moment of beauty, for beauty is abundant,
it is to be found "here, too," and "there, as well" (Example 24.2a-c). Such

Example 24.2a. Violin Concerto in D, K. 218. Andante cantabile, mm. 11–14.

Example 24.2b. Violin Concerto in D, K. 218. Andante cantabile, mm. 21–24.

Example 24.2c. Violin Concerto in D, K. 218. Andante cantabile, mm. 30–34.

beauties convey a sense of discovery, revealing that which we have not previously seen, and the element of surprise is accompanied by a leap in
understanding, an expansion of sensibility: The "oh" in our reaction to this
kind of beauty is the "oh" of wonder, the discovery of something beyond
what we thought existed. The intake of breath says that we have taken into
ourselves something extraordinary, which we are loath to let go until
silence has restored us to the ordinary world. The beautiful in the serenade
style operates in accordance with the pleasure principle, or perhaps is heedless of the imperatives of the reality principle, because reality is excluded
from the affective geography of the pastoral, which, in Allanbrook's poetic
formulation, is "dreamlike, halcyon, with no limits or consequences, innocent of shame and heedless of the world."[1] Despite powerful undercurrents
of sadness (after all, beauty is the image of transience, the symbol of loss as
well as of desire), such beauty is not seriously tinged with pessimism;
rather, the *amoroso* style, if it does not bespeak fulfillment, always tells of
hope and expectation.

With Mozart's Paris sonatas and his Sinfonia Concertante, K. 364/320d,
of 1779 there is a shift toward quite unexpected conceptions of beauty,
which now embody a sense of restlessness and instability, and even of the
dangerous or uncanny. In the post-Paris works, a specifically Mozartean
array of beauties emerges—death-tinged, melancholy, painful, containing a
mixture of resignation and affirmation. In seeking release from pain, they
consider release from life as one solution to the dilemma of existence.
Now, extreme beauties embrace endangered stabilities as Mozart traverses
many paths that lead from fragmentation to restoration. Finally, in his late
works, there is a beauty that can only be defined not by single qualities or
conformity to universal formal laws, but by the sum of its unique examples, each of which is incommensurable with any of the others. It is a
beauty that rises from remaking the rules rather than from exemplifying
them, informing us of things that have never been named, for these beauties express the nameless feelings, those that are elusive, fused, ambivalent,
fantastic.

It is easier to say these things than to demonstrate what is "new" in
Mozart's conception of beauty. All we can do is to offer a few examples
from his portfolio of the beautiful, starting with the Andante of the Sinfonia Concertante, K. 364/320d, actually a double concerto for violin,
viola, and orchestra (Example 24.3). Against a murmuring *amoroso* figure
in the divided violas a tender questioning figure is offered three times by
the violins, which twice confidingly reply to the queries. But instead of
the expected reply in measure 6 to prepare for a symmetrical close, a

Example 24.3. Sinfonia Concertante in E-flat, K. 364/320d.
Andante, mm. 1–11.

sforzando on the downbeat springs a hinge, breaking off the flow of thought and exposing a suppressed undercurrent of feeling, compounded of anxiety and longing. The *sforzando* in turn triggers a syncopated *sforzando* in the violas a sixteenth note later, confirming the short-circuiting that has occurred, a disconnection that cannot be quite sealed over by the long yearning phrases in measures 6 and 7, which serve to prepare for a revised effort. We note the pungent cross-relation of F-sharp and F-natural in measure 7 that issues in the sweeping descent in the strings and the entrance of the violin soloist; soon we will also note the overlapping structure of the two solo parts, the loving implications of their melodic intertwinings, the way they imply an unwillingness to yield to premature or unsatisfactory closure. The initial eight-measure statement in the violins, played in octaves to augment its sense of austere melancholy, now is shown to have contained only a restrained outline of the theme, which is filled in by the solo violin, who is authorized to tell us through swelling ornamentations what had been locked within the orchestra's heart, somehow thereby to overcome the sense of uneasiness that had so quickly penetrated a simple moment of bliss.

The subversion of bliss also informs the opening of the String Quintet in G minor, K. 516 (Example 24.4). Again, a question and an answer: An

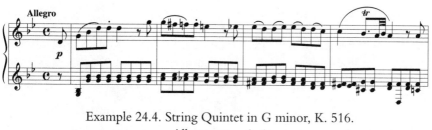

Example 24.4. String Quintet in G minor, K. 516.
Allegro, mm. 1–4.

arpeggiated ascending tonic triad contrasts with a descending chromatic figure—a juxtaposition of musical signs for yearning and lament—followed by a repeated sighing motif that issues in a half close. But the traditional descending *lamento* sequence is here crowded into the smallest possible chromatic compass and succeeds in reaching no lower than the sixth degree of the scale, where it is left incomplete, in a state of suspense, signifying, as Lewis Lockwood suggests, that "the yearning is in the lament as well."[2] In the Adagio ma non troppo of the quintet, Mozart pushes his exploration of the disjunctive even further, stringing together a succession of beautiful fragments—stuttering, halting, inconclusive—beautiful precisely because they are incapable of articulation. Somehow, they will be joined together by the end of this movement (Example 24.5).

Example 24.5 String Quintet in G minor, K. 516. Adagio ma non troppo, mm. 1–6.

In the Andante of the Piano Concerto in C, K. 467, an enormously long line of slowly generating melody sustains itself in a floating world far removed from reality, until at last it subsides into repose (Example 24.6). C. M. Girdlestone was the first to emphasize that the subtle placidity of this piece conceals inner agitation, "perpetual instability," and even "morbid disquiet," evidenced by the constant modulations and sudden chromatic outbreaks that hint at the existence of a troubled subterranean layer beneath the gossamer surface.[3] The pulsating triplet accompaniment is gently disrupted by the sixteenth-note upbeat in measure 24, by the four against three on the last beat of measure 25, the two against three of measure 28, and by a cadence at measure 36 that prepares us to leave F major and that lingers for half a breath on time's abyss before continuing its incessant gliding progression. The floating, soaring character of the melodic line is dramatically sabotaged by the extravagant downward leap of three octaves and a third from a high C to a low A in measure 30, as though to symbolize immeasurable longing.

In this movement, Mozart essays an entire movement of unrelieved, time-stopping beauty, blending chromatic pathos and measured tranquillity,

Example 24.6. Piano Concerto in C, K. 467. Andante, mm. 23–36.

sustaining a line of overarching beauty until the distant double-bar, which
is to say, for something just short of eternity. (The finale will have to provide quick relief from an overpowering experience, for it is no small feat to
have rescued beauty from the ravages of time.) Frequently, however, in
mature Mozart the greatest beauties exist in brief compass, concentrated in
fleeting, self-contained passages whose overwhelming effect is magnified by
their unexpected emergence from and subsidence into a less rapturous context; we await their reemergence with the impatience of a lover seeking a
glimpse of the beloved, wondering if what was felt can really be true
(Examples 24.7, 24.8).

Example 24.7. Symphony No. 39 in E-flat, K. 543. Andante
con moto, mm. 53–60.

Such moments wait to be discovered: they are transitional, passing references to pure beauty, captured for an instant before they sink back into
the relatively quotidian. A more explicit variant of this archetype of transience is in the Andante of the G-major Piano Concerto, K. 453. Here,
Mozart opens with a five-measure theme, or "motto," that strives hero-
ically to lift its own enormous weight and then succumbs to the imperatives of a premature modulation to the dominant (Example 24.9). Translated into our inexact metaphoric vocabulary, this "motto" theme may be
taken to represent a brief moment of surpassing beauty (a symbiotic
moment), whose implications are premature and whose full meaning cannot be grasped until it has been repeatedly lost, forgotten, submerged, and

Example 24.8. Piano Concerto in C, K. 503, Allegro Maestoso, mm. 50–58.

Example 24.9. Piano Concerto in G, K. 453. Andante, mm. 1–5.

then remembered. If this is so, the rest of the movement may be read as an extended, strife-ridden quest to re-find the opening theme.[4] It is a melancholy but valiant attempt to overcome transience.

In a distinguished and influential paper, Edward E. Lowinsky uncovered a surprising feature of Mozart's classicism, disclosing that much of his greater music is constructed from an array of studied irregularities and asymmetries—of thematic construction, phrase grouping, harmonic movement, and rhythmic motion. These irregularities give rise to intensifications, disequilibriums, and accumulations of tension that require resolution, rebalancing, and clarification. A "dynamic asymmetry" seeks a "symmetrical answer"; a "seeming disorder" drives the music "to return to symmetric regularity."[5] Thus, a presumed classical "clarity and lucidity are only one side of Mozart's genius," and his procedures are radically different from the uniform compositional processes and "mechanical symmetry" of his lesser contemporaries.[6]

One could perfectly well turn Lowinsky's insights into an argument for yielding the later Mozart to romanticism, although Lowinsky—and those whom he has influenced—is not prepared for so drastic a step, holding that a "symmetrical answer" is inevitably reached, positing an almost Nietzschean "desire for lucidity," an "inner force operating in Mozart's mind that immediately restores the disturbed equilibrium."[7] For example, in the first movement of Mozart's last string quartet, the irregularity of the opening three-measure theme is magnified by the sudden *forte* at measure 2 and "by the curious breaking off on an unaccented beat after an impetuous run."[8] Nevertheless, Lowinsky argues, the symmetrical answer in measures 4–5 restores the equilibrium almost before we have absorbed the sense of disruption (Example 24.10).

Example 24.10. String Quartet in F, K. 590. Allegro moderato, mm. 1–6.

It can also be held, however, that Mozart's music exemplifies a delicately balanced tension between form and disorder, a precarious negotiation of the fragile borders that separate the familiar from the alien. And it is this tension, this precariousness, these calculated imperfections of proportion, these fearful symmetries, that add a tinge of strangeness to the beautiful in Mozart's mature works.

Mozart's conception of the beautiful is no longer that of the ancients, who considered perfection to be its invariant characteristic. Plato named simple geometrical shapes, primary colors, and unaccompanied melodies as objects that are inherently and absolutely beautiful because they are lucid, rational, precise, perfected, and therefore free of those base qualities, such as an "admixture of pain," that undermine rationality and distort judgment: "When sounds are smooth and clear, and utter a single pure melody, then I mean to say that they are not relatively but absolutely beautiful, and have a natural pleasure associated with them."[9] This tradition had not lost its power in Mozart's time; the classical scholar Johann Winckelmann's ideals of the beautiful remain those of repose, simplicity, and the absence of pain and disorder: "The idea of the highest beauty may seem to be the simplest and easiest thing, demanding no inquiry into the passions and their expression."[10]

Of course, there has long been a counter tradition that was dissatisfied with the classical equation of beauty with perfected forms possessing symmetrical, even geometrical properties. Plotinus asked: "Why are the most living portraits the most beautiful, even though the others happen to be more symmetric?" and suggested that "beauty is that which irradiates symmetry rather than symmetry itself."[11] But it was Francis Bacon who seems to have been the first to observe two salient characteristics of beauty that the ancients had overlooked—transience and strangeness: "Beauty is as summer fruits, which are easy to corrupt, and cannot last"; and in an aphorism that was taken up by Romantic aesthetes from Poe to Pater, he proposed that beauty is somehow bound up with a special kind of imperfection: "There is no excellent beauty that hath not some strangeness in the proportion."[12] Poe's hero, first quoting and then endeavoring to confirm Bacon's observation, examined every feature of his beloved's face, trying "in vain to detect the irregularity and to trace home my own perception of 'the strange,'" and it was only when he gazed into Ligeia's eyes that he fully understood the truth—and the terror—of Bacon's insight. Subsequently, Baudelaire refined the conception so that it would not be limited only to the unnatural or abnormal. *"The Beautiful is always strange,"* he underscored:

I do not mean that it is coldly, deliberately strange, for in that case it would be a monstrosity that had jumped the rails of life. I mean that it always contains a touch of strangeness, of simple, unpremeditated and unconscious strangeness, and that it is this touch of strangeness that gives it its particular quality as Beauty. It is its endorsement, so to speak—its mathematical characteristic. Reverse the proposition, and try to imagine a *commonplace Beauty!*[13]

Mozart's conception belongs to the emergent idea of what Mario Praz called "a beauty imperiled and contaminated."[14] Unlike Poe and Baudelaire, however, his aesthetic sensibility does not go so far as to entangle beauty and corruption. Rather, it is closer kin to Shelley's "tempestuous loveliness of terror" ("On the Medusa of Leonard da Vinci in the Florentine Gallery") or to his "Our sweetest songs are those that tell of saddest thought" ("To a Skylark").

But beyond strangeness and melancholy there is an extensive constellation of feelings that connect beauty to issues associated with mortality. Beauty is death's close neighbor, companion, twin, or sibling, as the German classical poets would have it. Herder visualized death not as a "horrifying specter" but as "the lovely youth who puts out the torch and imposes calm on the billowing sea."[15] Goethe, delighted by the idea of death as the brother of sleep, remarked, "In this theme we could now really celebrate the triumph of beauty in lofty terms."[16] So there was ample precedent among Mozart's contemporaries for a constellation of ideas that later became the theme of Victor Hugo's sonnet on beauty and death: "Deux soeurs également terribles et fécondes/Ayant la même énigme et le même secret." The strange, the uncanny, the alien, and the unfamiliar are groping responses to death, cloaked in beauty to counteract its fearsomeness. Beauty's promise of bliss diminishes the dominion of death. But it is an unstable promise, for beauty, suspended in art's frozen, translucent alembic, remains always the image of that which passes, insensible of every Faustian plea to "Tarry awhile, thou art so fair." That is why beauty and sadness are inseparable: "Death brings with it the striving after permanence, stability, immobility," wrote the psychoanalyst Hanns Sachs, suggesting that "the presence of death makes itself felt in the sadness of beauty."[17] Or, in Herbert Marcuse's formulation, "The moment embodies the bitterness of its disappearance," and "The beautiful moment must be eternalized in order to make possible anything like happiness."[18] The beautiful kindles a utopian fantasy of fulfillment, modeled on (remembered from) an ineffable early state of loving fusion, which is felt in the here-and-now as a quasi-reality, evoking feelings of ecstasy that are, however, interwoven with other, afflictive memories—of parting, abandonment, and loss, which is to say, of every leave-taking that is a potential reminder of a fearsome finality.

We have touched on beauties in Mozart that are constructed out of odd compounds and asymmetries and, therefore, have in them both a touch of the marvelous and the abnormal. Of course, not all beauties in later Mozart partake of these qualities. Works such as the horn concertos, *Eine kleine Nachtmusik,* and the "Linz" and "Haffner" symphonies contain moments of great beauty, but these do not convey traces of anxiety, let alone of more disturbing affects. They may display beauties that are celebrations of sheer joy, expressions of mirth that revel in the pleasures of creation, that deliberately eschew conflict, that are embodiments of grace, decorum, and other "classical" virtues, that have achieved freedom from the imperatives of mortality, set aside modalities of struggle and rediscovered the harmonious repose—touched with poignancy, longing, and sweet melancholy—that had once come so naturally in Mozart's Salzburg music. And there are still other superlative beauties in his music that do not directly or immediately partake of strangeness or of the unstable, the restless, and the disruptive. Indeed, what may be most unusual about them is their wholeness, their encapsulated sense of completion, their inherent resistance to forward motion because they have already approached a state of perfection from which are absent those instabilities that would stimulate continuation and delay premature closure. It is not surprising that the classical criteria of the beautiful—purity, proportion, simplicity, wholeness, symmetry, perfection, regularity, evenness, measure, and harmony—should serve as the ideal images of life, health, plenitude. But it seems possible that the features of perfected, classic beauty also have the capability of representing depletion, disorder, and death.

We know that the idea of death can be approximately conveyed in music through the rhetoric of grief, lament, and sorrow, through the conventional tonal vocabularies of mourning and consolation. We sense the evocation of death when music deals with emotions of dread, fear, and terror. We associate death with musical representations of heroism and struggle, for death is implicated in all serious combats. Now the additional possibility arises that music, through its juxtapositions of formal materials rather than solely through its rhetoric, is capable of representing mortal contests, in particular of symbolizing clashes between generative and disintegrative forces.

In the opening movement of the Piano Concerto in B-flat, K. 595, a singing melody emerges from a tensionless preparatory measure of rocking accompaniment on the tonic, moves upward in a yearning pattern and

peacefully returns to its point of departure, having apparently found closure
in measure 5 after a brief circuitous journey (Example 24.11). There is no

Example 24.11. Piano Concerto in B-flat, K. 595. Allegro, mm. 1–10.

inherent need to continue, for on its face this seems to be a completed
phrase rather than an asymmetrical motive capable of generating further
activity out of latent energy stored within itself. However, the abrupt
rhythm of the cadence—emerging so unpredictably—creates an expectation at the very moment of its arrival. And now a unison horn call in the
winds (a Mozartean trope that is put to similar purposes in the opening of
the "Jupiter" Symphony) disrupts this momentary state of an expectant
inertia, arousing the music from inwardness, impelling it toward wakeful-
ness. The ensuing second strain of the melody is a quiet elaboration of
unsuspected potentiality, one whose own disposition toward closure is less
powerful than that of the opening phrase; but though it succeeds in reaching a nominal state of disequilibrium that bids to defeat inertia, a second
horn call at measures 9–10 is required to buttress its forward motion. With
the close of the third strain and the ensuing, triumphant trumpet call and

flourish in the strings, a process of creation is safely under way, although the possibility of untimely closure remains always in view, lending an undercurrent of unease to the gathering sense of exultant arrival and unstoppable motion.

Henceforth, the music keeps itself alive by the constant introduction of instabilities, tensions, and disequilibriums that cause postponements even as they require resolutions; by constantly posing questions—harmonic, rhetorical, structural—that require answers; by inconclusive or deceptive cadences and overlapping phrases; and by disturbances of symmetry that are imperative signals for prolongation. More simply, the music stays alive by inventive continuation—still another thought occurs to Mozart—for so long as there are new possibilities of motion and metamorphosis there can be no ceasing to be.

There is now little danger of slipping back into a state of equilibrium. Mozart even allows himself touches of playfulness and wit, sure signs of the mastery of dangerous materials. By the close of the exposition, a certain wholeness has been achieved, even though the music carries an ever-abiding sense of weariness. The development, testing the durability of this achievement, engages in a risky process of fragmentation and restoration. The wholeness appears now only as a memory, replaced by anxiety, grief, and longing. The passage in F minor hints at further possibilities of loss or vulnerability, but by this time the issue of bare survival no longer pertains: free will has overcome the pull toward stasis.

The recapitulation begins to guide us home, an arrival leavened by the realization that the final double-bar is both a yielding to inertia as well as a triumph over it. Mozart's cadenza reawakens an intimation of unrest— the possibility of falling into immobility is everywhere transparent, closure is at hand in the endings of each phrase or flourish—but the certainty of continuation is confidently placed in the hands of the creator and his soloist surrogate. The closing measures suggest that the music can now end of its own volition, can die in its own way, after having run its life course.

We have been looking at the first movement of Mozart's last concerto in terms of metaphors drawn from one of Freud's metapsychological speculations. In *Beyond the Pleasure Principle,* Freud proposed that there may be in all organic life a tendency or instinct "impelling it towards the reinstatement of an earlier condition."[19] This tendency reveals itself in a compulsion to repeat earlier experiences, including painful ones, in order thereby to gain mastery over those experiences, and to transform pain into pleasure. The repetition-compulsion, as he called it, is "the manifestation of inertia in organic life,"[20] and he concluded that, alongside "the instinct to preserve living substance and to join it into ever larger units, there must exist another, contrary instinct seeking to dissolve those units and to bring them back to their primeval, inorganic state."[21] The unprovable premise of the present discussion is that musical form is capable of symbolizing the process by which creativity resists the natural tendency of all things to go out of existence, that a composition can stand for a discrete and rounded universe of experience carved out of a surrounding field of tonal disorder and silence. Musical form may be an amalgam of sequential and simultaneous liquid images, written in the invisible fluid of sound, serving as referential moments in an unuttered, implicit narrative. In such a reading, musical form may serve as a bulwark against extinction, warding off mortality by creating alternative universes in which the powers of inertia are challenged, thwarted, and symbolically fought to a standstill by the architectural powers of the creative imagination.

If we want to take this notion further, to explore how certain of Mozart's works, whatever their other implications, also evoke images lying beyond the pleasure principle, we will need to develop a vocabulary that can describe the process by which music constantly defeats the tendencies for it to come to rest, thereby serving as an exemplary model of creative affirmation in the face of inevitable mortality. We will need to describe the strategies by which Mozart keeps his music from succumbing to a longing for inanition. We will need to understand how musical repetition, whatever else it may represent—whether simulacrums of the patterns of thought, the processes of nature, or the actions of the play impulse—also may serve to counter painful experiences and to reexperience pleasurable ones, as the child does with his endless game of "Fort" ("Gone") and "Da" ("Here"), causing an object to disappear and reappear. And just as the child who plays "Fort" and "Da" practices reparation, music embodies what Ricoeur calls a "nonpathological aspect of the death instinct," consisting in the mastery "over the negative, over absence and loss, implied in one's recourse to symbols and play."[22] Confronting the tendency of things to go out of existence, Mozart opts for a position like that of Spinoza, who wrote: "Everything, so far as it can, endeavors to persevere in its being."[23] Amid the welter of conflicting tendencies from which it issues, beauty is, in the end, a mastery rather than a yielding. Beauty heals, comforts, transforms, preserves, remembers, promises, buries the dead and raises them once again, reminds us not only of what we have lost but of what may be ours once again, even if only as a symbol. The beauty of Mozart's music is in its refusal to remain quiescent until it has exhausted all its possibilities, or at least until it has shown, by example, that those possibilities are manifold and endless.

I will not try to defend Freud's biological or psychological assumptions or my own aesthetic premises, which are only metaphoric approximations of a particular way of listening to Mozart's music and viewing his conception of beauty. At the very end of *Beyond the Pleasure Principle,* Freud himself prepared a useful line of retreat, drawing back from total commitment to his hypotheses: "I do not know how far I believe in them. . . . One may surely give oneself up to a line of thought, and follow it up as far as it leads . . . without, however, making a pact with the devil about it."[24] But even if we are unwilling to enter into a Faustian wager about ways that music mediates between beauty and death, it is worth reminding ourselves of Mozart's own equation of death and bliss, his image of death as a beautiful consolation purged of terror, indeed as a doorway to happiness. In April 1787 he wrote to his father: "As death, when we come to consider it closely, is the true goal of our existence, I have formed during the last few years such close relations with this best and truest friend of mankind, that his image is not only no longer terrifying to me, but is indeed very soothing and consoling! And I thank my God for graciously granting me the opportunity (you know what I mean) of learning that death is the *key* which unlocks the door to our true happiness."[25] Just less than a decade before that letter, we recall that Mozart held fast to the promise of a beautiful reunion with his mother in death, cleaving to the expectation "that she is not lost to us forever—that we shall see her again—that we shall live together far more happily and blissfully than ever in this world. We do not yet know when it will be—but that does not disturb me; when God wills it, I am ready."[26] In Mozart's thoughts, beauty and death were consciously joined.

As we probe the nature of beauty in Mozart, many apparently disparate themes converge and blend. Classical and neoclassical formulas dissolve—notions of proportion, symmetry, order, and decorum are suffused with their opposites. We gaze at consolation and find terror; we examine grief and find love; we cannot think of bliss without awakening fears of abandonment; a commonplace musical figure with martial connotations reveals, through the flattening of the third degree of the scale, a rare and strange kind of beauty; a perfectly regular periodic phrase turns out to be a potent symbol of a pull to inertia that will require heroic efforts to overcome. The chaste, sublimated surface of Mozart's music conceals turbulent, potentially eruptive currents of feeling. The strange, the terrible, the uncanny, and the deadly aspects of beauty (Henry James once referred to "the fatal gift of beauty")[27] are interwoven with its erotic implications. It may be worth observing that, owing to the circumstances of his upbringing, where sexual expression was surrounded by prohibitions, Mozart had good reason to associate punishment, destructiveness, disease, and death with the pursuit of beauty and pleasure. Kierkegaard was the first to essay an erotics of Mozart's music, a topic that has briefly but eloquently been elaborated by Rosen, who wrote: "Perhaps no composer used the seductive physical power of music with the intensity and the range of Mozart. . . . What is most extraordinary about Mozart's style is the combination of physical delight—a sensuous play of sonority, an indulgence in the most luscious harmonic sequences—with a purity and economy of line and form that render the seduction all the more efficient."[28] He added: "In all of Mozart's supreme expressions of suffering and terror . . . there is something shockingly voluptuous. . . . The grief and the sensuality strengthen each other, and end by becoming indivisible. . . . In his corruption of sentimental values, Mozart is a subversive artist."[29]

In a profoundly unsettling series of lectures in 1960, the art historian Edgar Wind observed that in our time, "The dreaded demon of the imagination, which [Plato] had tried in vain to exorcise, has finally lost the power to hurt us. . . . However wildly our lions and leopards may jump, we know they are tame, and their antics will not frighten us."[30] The possibility that we might become largely immune to the dangers of beauty was not foreseen by Plato or those later guardians of the social order who understood viscerally that beauty, as Marcuse once wrote, "contains a dangerous violence that threatens the given form of existence" simply because the "immediate sensuousness of beauty immediately suggests sensual happiness."[31] There is a long-standing tradition that sees in Mozart's music the embodiment of grace, nobility, and decorum, regarding it as the classic exemplar of disinterested beauty, beauty disengaged from the terrors and brutalities of history, the anxieties and fears of individual existence. For example, according to Rosen, Robert Schumann saw in the G-minor Symphony, K. 550, "nothing but lightness, grace, and charm"—which Rosen himself described as "a work of passion, violence, and grief." He warned that Schumann's "attitude to Mozart ends by destroying his vitality as it canonizes him. It is only through recognizing the violence and the sensuality at the center of Mozart's work that we can make a start."[32] In this view, to be true to Mozart is to rediscover the underlying strangeness, the pain, the sense of danger in his art.

Naturally, there is something within each of us that wants to limit the power of the imaginative to touch us, for that may open us to our deepest fears and most regressive yearnings. But no one ever claimed that giving ourselves to great art was wholly free of risk; it perhaps is only when we feel the power of Mozart's music to bruise us that we can discover its enchanted healing power as well. Schumann surely had earned the right to feel that anodyne, consolatory power, as had Schubert, who in a passage quoted in the prologue to this book found in Mozart "comforting perceptions of a brighter and better life." Then we, too, may celebrate Mozart's sublimated surface, which is emblematic of every kind of wholeness, symbolic of the restoration of splintered experience. We may revel in the coruscating commedia dell'arte theatricality of his allegros and rondos. We may follow the joyous path pursued by Mozart's play impulse, delighting in his antic disposition, marveling at his capacity for turning things inside out, for finding carnivalesque juxtapositions and endless possibilities, at every turn affirming the sheer vitality that inhabits the universes of sound inscribed on a slate of silence that he brought into being.

Toward the end of his life, in 1891, exactly one century after the death of Mozart, Brahms posed the question of how to pay homage to Mozart without surrendering one's own individuality. He selected a genre—the clarinet quintet—that belonged to Mozart. The opening theme of Brahms's slow movement yearns for Mozart, and though unable to find him, does not cease its longing (Example 24.12). It is the image of a restless

Example 24.12. Brahms, Clarinet Quintet in B minor. Adagio, mm. 1–4.

romanticism questing for what has now become a classical ideal. Brahms's theme appropriates the opening three notes of Mozart's Clarinet Quintet, blocking the theme, and refusing to allow it to continue, let alone to come to rest. In the end, Brahms knew, we cannot reach Mozart, we can only hope to come nearer to him.

It remains to let the theme continue, as Mozart did (Example 24.13).

Example 24.13. Clarinet Quintet in A, K. 581. Allegro, mm. 1–7.

"Parnassus" (detail), by Raphael. From frescoes for the
Stanze della Segnatura, Vatican.

ENDINGS

Benedictine Abbey of St. Peter's, Salzburg. Engraving by Karl Remshard after a drawing by Franz Anton Danreiter, eighteenth century.

25

....

LITTLE LEOPOLD

When Leopold and Marianne Mozart left Munich on 13 March 1781, after their lengthy reunion with Mozart in connection with the premiere of *Idomeneo,* and headed for Salzburg, traveling with them was eleven-year-old Heinrich Marchand (born 1769), the son of Theobald Marchand, a theater manager whose family had befriended the Mozarts in Munich. Heinrich was going to study violin, clavier, and composition under Leopold Mozart's expert tutelage while boarding in his home in the Tanzmeisterhaus. A year later he was joined by his sister Maria Margarethe (1768–1800), a talented singer, and early in 1783, after another carnival visit to Munich, Leopold brought back from there yet a third pupil, eight-year-old Maria Johanna Brochard, whose parents were the dancer Georg Paul Brochard and the actress Eva Brochard.

Although Leopold Mozart had often in his letters to Mozart expressed his distaste for what he called "the *wearisome task* of giving lessons" and had complained that "one has to talk oneself hoarse if one is *to make even a pittance,*"[1] he now turned to teaching with a will, for he had a high purpose in mind, one that he connected with his son's defection. "My son is in Vienna and is remaining there," he wrote to the publisher Breitkopf in 1782. "Meanwhile I am keeping two pupils, the twelve-year-old son and the fourteen-year-old daughter of Herr Marchand. . . . I hope to make a great violinist and clavier-player out of the boy and a good singer and excellent clavier-player out of the girl."[2] The project could not have been more transparent: Leopold Mozart was aiming to recapture the past, to re-create the years of his great triumphs, but with a different cast of characters. Having "lost" the son whom he had raised to be a great musician, he was, I believe, trying to start over, hoping to demonstrate that his guidance and instruction could again bring genius into existence, and, by implication, to show that it was he who was to be credited for the flowering of Mozart's talents. At the same time, of course, he was trying to fill the void left by Mozart's departure.

Mozart knew his father's motives, and he seems not to have been happy at the prospect of being "replaced" by the Marchand children, whom he had met in Munich. In July 1781, in all apparent innocence, Mozart retailed some horrid gossip about the Marchands, father and sons. Marchand *père* was allegedly involved with a woman lodger; Heinrich's younger brother Daniel responded to parental criticism by threatening to amputate his finger; both boys were disrespectful of their father; and Heinrich made improper advances to a little girl. Finally, in a particularly malicious touch, Mozart warned: "In Mannheim no one ever allowed their boys to go where the Marchands were. For they [Heinrich and Daniel] were caught—helping one another."[3] Mozart concluded on an apparently guileless note calculated to infuriate his father: "Well, it is a great pity for the lad himself; but you, my father, will be able to reform him completely, of that I am quite sure."[4] Following his visit to Salzburg in 1783, Mozart was not above offering some unsolicited advice to Heinrich and Margarethe (Greta), as though to supplement his father's instruction. He wrote his father: "Please give a special message to little Greta, and tell her that when she sings she must not be so arch and coy. . . . Only silly asses are taken in by such devices. I for one would rather have a country lout, who does not hesitate to shit and piss in my presence, than let myself be humbugged by such false toadyings, which after all are so exaggerated that anyone can easily see through them."[5]

A strong bond developed between Leopold Mozart and his pupils, and he was particularly fond of Heinrich, whose education he supervised. In a letter to Sebastian Winter he described him as "*an excellent violinist* and *performer on the clavier* and also he has come very far as a *composer.* At the same time he has not neglected his Latin, although as his chief sideline he has been learning Italian and French, in which he has made good progress."[6] Although the three children were returned to their parents at the end of August 1784, Leopold Mozart continued to take a paternal interest in their subsequent careers: he took Heinrich with him to Vienna in 1785, guided him in his successful pursuit of a position as solo violinist in Salzburg, and reported glowingly to Marianne on the success of his concerts there. "Heinrich is now first violin at the court," he wrote proudly.[7] His hope that his pupil would make a great career apparently ended, however, with Heinrich's two poorly attended concerts at Vienna's Burgtheater on 2 and

14 March 1785, in his eager teacher's presence.[8] Brochard, too, became a professional artist, joining the Munich court theater in 1790. Of Margarethe's early difficulties in getting established, Leopold Mozart wrote to his daughter: "Just wait a little while, until our ship comes in from America, then we will form our own orchestra."[9] During Heinrich's stay in Salzburg in 1786–87, the young man and his mentor were often in each other's company.

Although they all became professional musicians, none of Leopold Mozart's three pupils achieved the greatness that he had hoped for. Pondering the situation, he may have concluded that another ingredient was needed to accomplish his purpose—his own biological inheritance. An opportunity to test this hypothesis soon arose. In July 1785 Marianne Mozart, now Frau Berchtold zu Sonnenberg (she married on 23 August 1784), traveled from her home in St. Gilgen to Salzburg, where, on the twenty-seventh of July she gave birth to her first child, whom she named Leopold Alois Pantaleon after her father, who was the baby's godfather. At the end of August she returned to her husband and five stepchildren in St. Gilgen, but little Leopold ("Leopoldl") remained in her sixty-five-year-old father's home in the care of a nursemaid, Nandl, Marianne's maid, Monica, and the cook, Lena.

A carefully worded letter from her father awaited her in St. Gilgen; its purpose was to persuade her husband to ratify a decision apparently already reached. "You know how much I love the child," Leopold Mozart assured Berchtold, whom he called "Herr Sohn" ("Mr. Son"), and assured him that there was no need to be "anxious," for the infant was in a state of perfect contentment.[10] "Today he was even more friendly and livelier than yesterday. . . . Today after noon he again had clear eyes and he slept sweetly and quietly." After this preamble he stated his purpose, which was to suggest that the parents leave the newborn infant with its grandfather for a period of nine months; such an arrangement would be in everyone's best interests. "You have five children there—and the sixth is well provided for here until you make a decision," he wrote, assuring them of his servants' competence to care for the baby. Having argued his case, he left the decision in his son-in-law's hands: "If Herr Sohn will leave Leopoldl here, it would be a pleasure for me to care for him and you will get the child—if God preserves it—nicely *dried out,* as people say, when he is already three quarters of a year old. Nandl will remain at my house and I must say that with her the child is magnificently cared for. That I will do all this with delight and at my own expense, is self-evident." He added, "I must ask you, if you want Leopold to leave, to give me time to relinquish him."

Leopold asked for the child in the most matter-of-fact way, as though it were quite routine for an elderly widower to take the place of an infant's natural parents. He did not specify his motives; indeed he suggested that he was doing this as a favor, at his cost, as though to relieve the couple of a burden. Clearly, however, they did not object to his request, or if they did their reluctance is not reflected in Leopold's subsequent letters. One may surmise that Marianne wished to provide her father with solace, delight, and purpose in his lonely old age; or perhaps she could not deny him any request. As for Berchtold, all we know is that he voiced no objection.[11] Or perhaps the couple was persuaded of the pedagogical soundness of the plan, viewing Leopold Mozart according to his own evaluation as a specialist in child-rearing: "You know I understand what youth is, I have studied children and young people."[12]

Before any decision was arrived at, the child came down with a severe case of thrush, with attendant mouth-sores and fungus growths; he was unable to sleep from the pain and fever. Leopold quickly used the illness as a further argument against returning the child. "You know me, the way I think, and you know what kind of heart I have. It seems to me impossible to let six children stay one next to the other, where one of them is a six-week-old child, and Karl is at the age when one must not only be concerned that he doesn't get a hole in his head or doesn't break his arms or legs, etc."[13] Little Leopold temporarily recovered by the fifteenth of September, but a week later the grandfather had to prepare the parents for the possible death of their infant, while asking them not to abandon hope: "I am very sad. We had believed that the thrush was on the wane, but now it has broken out again. . . . I cannot describe all the stupefaction and fear. . . . Now we must await the will of God. . . . Don't think that things are worse than I have reported. No! There is more hope for improvement. . . . Birth is already halfway to death. Therefore have patience!"[14] A week later, he exulted, "God be praised. It is a great miracle *that the child is again so well* that nobody would have believed it, if they hadn't seen it."[15] Thereafter, all news was good news and a leitmotif of each of Leopold Mozart's subsequent letters to his daughter was, with variations in wording, "Little Leopold is, God be praised, healthy" (*"Der Leopoldl ist, Gott Lob, gesund!"*).[16]

Marianne Berchtold's biographers are at a loss to explain why she permitted her son to be raised by her father. Some, following Leopold Mozart's suggestion, would like to think that it was because she was too occupied with her stepchildren to care for her own first-born, and Deutsch and Paumgartner mistakenly claim that Leopoldl was, at first, too sick to be moved. But in fact, the child became sick only after the transaction had been finalized, and it is amply clear that the entire impetus for the arrangement originated with the grandfather. In a rare departure from his scrupulous adherence to demonstrable facts, Jahn explains, "As [his daughter's] health long remained delicate, L. Mozart kept his little grandson."[17]

By the time the child had recovered, there was no further talk about returning him to St. Gilgen at the end of nine months; an undated letter from Munich in early 1786 acknowledges, "Consequently you know my whole intention, and thus I say to you that I will keep Leopold with me so long as I live; this is and was already my resolve from the beginning. In the summer I will bring him with Nandl for a while; but I also will take him back with me."[18] Shortly thereafter, as though to make a sacred compact, he again avowed that little Leopold would remain in his charge indefinitely: "Leopold will stay with me so long as I have the capacity to maintain him. God sees into my good heart, the rest He knows how to arrange, the fate of all men is in His hands."[19]

Soon the child had settled in, and a steady flow of reports about him, his health, development, and activities went to his parents. Monica was replaced by Tresel, who helped Nandl with the feedings, did all the heavy work, and "sings and plays with the child until they die laughing."[20] Marianne's former suitor, Franz d'Ippold, visited the baby: "I cannot describe what a delightful conversation he had with Leopoldl; he remained over an hour with the child, joked, laughed and played with him; and although he was a stranger to the child, it was very remarkable how he laughed and made all kinds of faces and mouths."[21] At the celebration of Leopold Mozart's (and little Leopold's) name day, they went to see fireworks and a balloon ascent. The grandfather was delighted with the progress of his charge, writing, "Leopoldl is merry and well, not only in his *face,* his *head,* his *ears* and . . . *fingers,* but also in his *ass.* He shits and pisses mostly while sitting on a pretty earthenware chamber pot."[22] He also reported encouragingly on the child's precocity. "He clearly says a and b, and thus I am jokingly teaching him to speak the alphabet, not in strict order, but rather I try to teach him those letters which are easiest to speak."[23] He also noted approvingly that the child was learning lessons in compliance: "Leopoldl is healthy and obedient, if only he hears my name."[24]

Above all, the grandfather watched for, and reported on, the slightest sign of musical aptitude in little Leopold. When the child was only three months old, Leopold Mozart wrote to his daughter, "I can never look at the child's right hand without being moved. The most skilled pianist cannot place his hand so beautifully on the keyboard as he customarily holds his hand; often he doesn't move the fingers; often the fingers are placed with curved hand in the playing position, and when he sleeps his hands lie in such a way as though the fingers were really touching the clavier, as well as with the most proportional relaxation and curvature of the fingers. In brief! one could not see anything more beautiful.—I am often truly saddened when I see this, for I wish he were already just three years old . . . so that he would already be able to play."[25] Two months later, he told of an experiment that confirmed his belief in the infant's unusual abilities: "I haven't yet let him hear a *violin*. I performed a safe test with a *brass candle-stick*, where I alternately played *pianissimo* and then *forte* with a small key on the *rim* and sang along with it. At that moment he became so motionlessly attentive that he could not take his eyes off me; he didn't move his feet or hands, not so much as a finger, although usually he would be constantly in motion. . . . People could say what they wanted to him, it wouldn't matter, he wouldn't pay the least attention to it. In brief! he remained motionless looking at me and the candlestick."[26]

Marianne was happy to hear every detail about her son, but although she sent him shirts and linens, she saw him only rarely. Leopold took the child to see her in St. Gilgen in early summer of 1786 and she visited Salzburg for a month in early fall of the same year. Clearly, she was not an essential ingredient in her father's plans for little Leopold.

Leopold Mozart's health began to trouble him in the fall of 1786. He complained of humming noises in his head: "Sometimes it lasts the whole day. I never have it in the morning when I get up. Who can tell where it comes from? It isn't in the blood; perhaps it is wind; perhaps it comes from the digestion? Or a weakness of the nerves. Or from the humors. I have no pains."[27] In January he wrote, "My health is not yet what I would like. I hope that the warm weather will be favorable to me."[28] He had reason to feel seriously concerned, writing, "I only hope that God will still lend me enough life that I may be useful to Him through energetic instruction. Amen!"[29] Nevertheless, he retained his equanimity and his sense of humor. "Old people no longer become young!" (*Alte Menschen werden nicht mehr jung!*)[30] and again: "With an old man there can no longer be any talk of perfect health, because something is always lacking and an old man takes away what a young one takes on. In brief! One must patch so long as one can patch."[31] In mid-February he made his last journey to Munich, traveling with Heinrich Marchand, with whose family he stayed during an abbrevi-ated visit of ten days. While there he visited his old friend Bullinger, who was now working as a tutor, and heard Margarethe Marchand sing a lead-ing role in a new opera by Georg Joseph Vogler.

On 16 March 1787, he reverted to his complaints about his son, but now he used Mozart's given name, something he almost never permitted himself to do, for he had been using the phrase "your brother" almost exclusively in his letters to Marianne: "From Wolfgang Mozart I have had not a single letter of the alphabet, although I immediately wrote to him in Vienna."[32] There is a two-month hiatus in the correspondence with his daughter, because his condition had worsened and she had come to Salzburg to care for him. After Dr. Joseph Barisani diagnosed "blockage of the spleen" in May, Leopold asked Heinrich to inform Theobald Marchand that he was dying, and Marchand expressed his distress "that you fear that you will hardly survive the summer."[33] He was less resigned in his final letter to his daughter, written on 10–11 May 1787: "I find myself not worse, praise God, and I place my hopes upon fair weather, so that I can get some fresh air." He asked her not to be anxious ("If I become worse, I will immediately advise you") and he assured her that "Leopoldl is healthy, kisses you, and I am happy that he now is such an extraordinarily good friend with Lisel,"[34] the latest maidservant to join the household. This same letter contains his last reference to Mozart; characteristically, he continues to look for evidence that his son remained incapable of caring for himself and that his wastefulness has brought him into financial straits: referring to the less expensive apartment to which Mozart and Constanze had just moved, he noted, "Your brother now lives on the Landstrasse, No. 224. He writes, however, no reasons for that. Nothing! Unfortunately I can guess the reason."[35]

And so, at the end of Leopold Mozart's life, we find him combating his isolation, his widowerhood, his embitterment, his physical decline, and the disintegration of his status by a variety of effective strategies. He continued to do business, selling keyboard instruments and books, lending money, and negotiating with dealers to dispose of jewelry and other valuable objects on behalf of his son-in-law. He kept up his correspondence, not only with Marianne and Mozart (none of his letters to Mozart from these years survive) but also with friends and contacts in many cities. He observed Salzburg life and chronicled its events—from the deaths of humble citizens to a bishop's winnings at faro—with a historian's sense of high purpose and a gossip's ironic sense of humor. However tormented he may have been, he does not permit himself wholly to give way to the melancholy that had always afflicted him: he often attends the theater and views every production with a theatergoer's enthusiasm combined with an impresario's belief that he could have improved on the production; every winter he travels to Munich to attend the carnival festivities there in company with old cronies, donning harlequin guises, attending masked balls, and above all, listening to music. And he holds fast to the remaining threads of kinship—to his daughter, to her husband, to the Marchand children, and especially to Leopoldl, in whom he sees the prospect of immortality and whose new life he nurtures as devotedly as any mother her infant child.

Mozart's letters were less frequent, on average one per month, and, to Leopold Mozart's chagrin, were shorter than previously.[36] Even when Mozart did not choose to enlighten him about his doings, Leopold, through his contacts, made it his business to know things about his son—his whereabouts, publications, performances, the fluctuations of his fortunes. Thus Leopold remained wholly in and of the world until the very end.

Following Leopold Mozart's death, on 28 May 1787, Leopoldl returned to his parents' house, where he was cared for mostly by his older half-sister Marianne until 1794–95. Then, after lodging briefly with his uncle Franz Anton Berchtold, he attended gymnasium in Salzburg, became a soldier in 1806, was discharged with the rank of lieutenant, and served as a customs officer at various posts in Austria and Bavaria. He became joint heir of his father's estate in 1813, married in 1816 in Bregenz, moved to Innsbruck in 1830, and died there in 1840 after a career in government service as a worthy servant of the state, an auditor in the imperial revenue administration. He played the piano a bit in his youth, but was otherwise unremarkable, except that he became known as a collector of old weapons and privy seals. Marianne's biographer, Walter Hummel, misses the point when he remarks that Leopold Mozart "was spared the disillusionment that in later life his grandson turned out to be wholly unmusical."[37] For Leopold Mozart held with the horticultural view, that the seed of a genius could only flower through dedicated and skilled cultivation; for him, musical genius was the product of a partnership between a compliant subject and an enlightened master musician/pedagogue. Therefore, genius did not altogether reside in the subject who possessed it nor was it the exclusive property of that individual. In the instance of genius best known to him, it might be said to be a family affair.

The story of little Leopold was to be kept secret from Mozart, who was not meant to learn that his father was raising Marianne's baby. This is surely the strongest confirmation that the infant was a surrogate for Mozart and that he was somehow intended to become an instrument to rebuild the family structure that Mozart had demolished. In November 1786, when the baby was almost sixteen months old, Leopold Mozart was upset to find that Mozart had managed to learn the secret: "Herr Müller, that good and honest maker of silhouettes, had said a lot of nice things about little Leopold to your brother, who heard in this way that the child is living with me. I had never told your brother."[38] A few days later he added, "That I didn't write to your brother about the way in which the child came to be staying with me, you will readily understand; however, what I wrote to him, and how, is really too copious a matter, so I must someday tell you about it verbally."[39] Although Mozart did not himself openly refer to little Leopold, several of his actions suggest that he had indeed already discovered his father's—and sister's—secret. As always, his reactions are a blend of competitiveness and compliance.

Beginning probably in early 1786, about six months after the birth of little Leopold, Mozart himself took a small boy—Johann Nepomuk Hummel—as his student.[40] Hummel, who was born in November 1778, was taught gratis and lived with the Mozarts from his seventh to his ninth year, as he later recalled, and emerged as one of the great keyboard virtuosos of the classic period, rivaling and sometimes besting both Mozart and Beethoven in reputation.[41] The four-year tour of Europe that he and his family undertook between 1788 and 1792 was closely modeled on Mozart's own early journeys, and his promotional announcements featured his connection to Mozart: "He is a pupil of the famous Herr *Mozart* and surpasses in dexterity, accuracy and delicacy all expectation."[42] At a time when Leopold Mozart was still anxiously watching the curve of little Leopold's fingers, Mozart was preparing his own pupil to launch an epochal virtuoso career. And if circumstances had been slightly different he could have been the young Beethoven's teacher as well, for in Bonn Beethoven was being groomed to be Mozart's successor by such Mozart admirers as Neefe, Count Ferdinand Waldstein, the Hatzfelds, and Elector Maximilian Franz, who sent him to Vienna in April 1787 to advance that purpose. The sixteen-year-old Beethoven, however, was not yet ready to be on his own. At his father's urging, the young virtuoso left Vienna after only two weeks and returned home in a state of despondency over his mother's consumptive condition—and perhaps over a rejection by Mozart, who was preoccupied with his own affairs, including his worrisome financial condition, and may not have been able seriously to consider taking on another pupil, even one of great talent and backed by eminent patrons. Furthermore, Beethoven arrived when news of Leopold Mozart's imminent death had probably already reached Mozart, and at a time when Mozart was preparing for his second journey to Prague, planning if not already beginning to work on *Don Giovanni,* and writing a vast amount of other music. It is noteworthy that Beethoven remained in Bonn after his mother died later in that year, returning to Vienna only after Mozart's death.

Mozart's emotional turmoil over the issue of little Leopold showed itself in more poignant ways than competitiveness.[43] In what seems to have been a gesture of conciliation, or even submissiveness, and almost surely against his wife's wishes, he named his son, born on 18 October 1786, Johann Thomas Leopold, thereby matching Marianne's filial offering. Now there were two little Leopolds. And then he took a seemingly impossible step: He asked his father if he would board both of his sons while he and Constanze went on a professional journey across the continent. We know of this from Leopold Mozart's indignant report to his daughter in November: "Your brother actually suggested that I should take charge of his two children, because he was proposing to undertake a journey through Germany to England in the middle of next carnival."[44] Mozart's offer was an act of profound deference, if not utter abasement, suggesting that, at that moment, he was again willing to return to the most painful patterns of submission. Perhaps he was stirred to the depths by the evidence of his father's neediness and of Marianne's infinite devotion, or perhaps he could not bear the attempt to replace him. It is within the context of these powerfully contradictory emotional pulls that the Zoroastran riddles, with their sardonic images of mutilation and annihilation, their residues of desperation and rage, were written in February 1786. The riddles came into existence at the very time that a series of events was playing out in Salzburg, with implications that struck to the very bone, for Mozart was given sufficient reason to believe that he was being repudiated and even replaced by his father.

Leopold was unwilling to accept—or was no longer capable of recognizing—even so abject a surrender, seeing his son's request instead only as a crass attempt to subvert the master plan to raise Marianne's little Leopold as Mozart's replacement. He sensed hostile motives behind the surprising isomorphism of Mozart's offer; he suspected that something was wanted of him rather than offered to him. And he had no doubt that it was because Mozart had discovered the secret of little Leopold that, as he exclaimed in righteous anger, "the brilliant idea occurred to him or perhaps to his wife. Not at all a bad arrangement! They could go off and travel—they might even die—or remain in England—and I should have to run off after them with the children. As for the payment which he offers me for the children and for maids to look after them, well—Basta! If he cares to do so, he will find my excuse powerful and instructive."[45] His extravagant speculations—that Mozart and Constanze might die or emigrate, abandoning their children—show the morbid, disordered direction of his thoughts as he entered the final months of his life.

Clearly, Leopold Mozart understood well how to "reach" his son, how to play upon his desire to be "good," his yearning to restore the old family structure, however burdensome or oppressive. He knew Mozart's vulnerabilities and, especially, he knew how to punish him for his transgression against the family compact. To reject Mozart's children, especially at the very moment when he was raising Marianne's infant as his own, was an afflicting action. Mozart's wife had been rebuffed, permanently excluded from the family; now, with the scornful turning aside of Mozart's overture, their progeny were rejected as well. The disowning of Mozart's family was effectively complete. The ongoing process of disowning Mozart himself had passed into its penultimate stage.

Leopold Mozart would not have been surprised if Mozart had retaliated; on the twenty-ninth of November he wrote, without a trace of a bad conscience: "I have had no letter from your brother since my last and do not expect one any too soon, although I explained everything to him in the most benevolent way."[46] He knew that Mozart would react, but his prediction was inexact: for the remaining six months of his father's life, Mozart continued to write a few lines once a month, just as he had previously done, but he kept his father minimally informed, so that Leopold continued to rely on other sources for information about him. ("As for your brother I hear that he is back in Vienna. I had no reply to the letter I sent to him at Prague.")[47] More fatefully, he deliberately did not inform his father about an event that magnified the effect of Leopold's blunt refusal: one of the children—the infant Johann Thomas Leopold—died 15 November, in the brief interval between Mozart's request and his father's response. It was not until the beginning of March that Leopold learned of the death of his grandchild, and he learned it, not from Mozart, but from a group of his British friends from Vienna who were passing through Salzburg on their way home: "The English company told me . . . that little Leopold, his last boy, has died, and that, as I had gathered, he wants to travel to England."[48] Ignoring the death, voicing no word of sympathy or regret, Leopold instead recalls "a fatherly letter," in which he warned Mozart against his injudicious planning for such a journey. But he could not have been insensible to one clear implication: if he could keep secrets, so could his son, who by his silence signaled that Leopold Mozart no longer had the right to know of his son's sorrows, not even to learn that his own namesake had died. Of course, that was not Mozart's sole purpose: in the aftermath of his offer and its rejection, he tried to close down the lines of affective communication that made him so vulnerable to his father's actions. He had done this often before; it was his way of adapting, of defending himself against intolerable feelings, but it is doubtful that it significantly, let alone permanently, eased his pain.

Leopold Mozart did not want his son to know that he intended to mold a tiny bit of flesh into a new and malleable object, one through which he could again find fulfillment and glory. However, the story of little Leopold had to be kept from Mozart for other reasons as well: Leopold Mozart knew that Mozart would have seen this pedagogical project as a chimera, a will-o'-the-wisp, a hallucination, a pathetic fantasy. And he knew that Mozart would have regarded it as the latest and perhaps most extreme instance of a familiar, coercive paternalism. Beyond these, it was the darkly pathological substratum of it all that needed to be concealed. For, to put it simply, Leopold Mozart, by some strange *droit de seigneur*, had taken his daughter's first-born son from her, and she, in accordance with a long-established pattern of submissive acquiescence, had surrendered her son to him without demur, thereby giving her father a baby. That the two of them were also playing out a barely veiled incest scenario was perhaps not something that Mozart or any of the other participants in this bizarre episode would have permitted themselves to acknowledge.

They would surely have sensed, however, what may have been the deepest underlying motivation of Leopold Mozart's appropriation of little Leopold—an old man's desperate strategy to extend his life by setting himself a task, the raising and education of a child, that would take many years to complete. Even in his very first letter to Marianne and Berchtold he admitted that he wanted the child for more than the first months of its life, and saw him as a source of renewed youth: "I . . . want to have him for so long, until I can bring him by the hand to you in St. Gilgen, for which I must, I confess, still live about ten years, and consequently little Leopold will have to lead me and not I him."[49] To an old man, ten years may be shorthand for immortality. It was clear to the enlightened deputy kapellmeister that he had once again been called upon to transform "a poor inch of nature" into a miraculous child, whose wonders would in due course be revealed to an amazed mankind. Once again Leopold Mozart had made his calculations; unfortunately, there was not enough time for God to ratify them.

26

·····································

"CARISSIMA SORELLA MIA"

In early years, Mozart and his sister, Marianne, were as one flesh, one spirit. They were "the Mozart children," living and working together for common goals within the family enterprise, studying, traveling, and performing as symbiotic members of a single organism, sharing every life experience, from triumphal events to watching each other hover on the brink of death. At three, Mozart was inspired to study music by observing his father's instruction of Marianne: he wanted to be like her. As children, they shared a secret language, were together the leading citizens of their jointly invented fantasy "Kingdom of Back," he its king, she his queen. In his hilarious mock entries in Marianne's personal diary, Mozart sometimes actually became his sister, assumed her personality, thought her thoughts, and wrote them down as if they were her own. The bantering intimacy of their earliest surviving letters, during Mozart's Italian journeys, at once masks and reveals the depth of their attachment. He sends her "a hundred kisses or smacks on your marvelous horseface,"[1] conveys outrageous greetings to her "from Catch-me-quick-and-then-you-have-me and from Don Cacarella, especially from behind."[2] He continues to play the mock king to her queen: "I hope, my queen, that you are enjoying the highest degree of health and that now and then . . . you will sacrifice for my benefit some of your important and intimate thoughts, which ever proceed from that very fine and clear reasoning power, which in addition to your beauty, and although from a woman, and particularly from one of such tender years, almost nothing of the kind is ever expected, you possess, O queen, so abundantly as to put men and even graybeards to shame."[3] On occasion he

Marianne Mozart, Salzburg 1763. Unsigned oil portrait attributed to Pietro Antonio Lorenzoni. Mozart-Museum der Internationalen Stiftung Mozarteum, Salzburg. © Mozarts Geburtshaus, Salzburg.

plays papa as well—"Tell me little girl, where have you been, eh?"—sometimes to both sister and mother—"Addio. Farewell, my children."[4] His
adolescent letters to her are replete with references to amatory matters, she
acting as his intermediary with several of his Salzburg crushes and he chiding her on breaking hearts: "One thing distresses me, and that is that you
have made Herr von Mölk sigh and suffer so frightfully and that you did
not go sleigh-driving with him. . . . How many handkerchiefs will he not
have used that day, weeping on your account. No doubt he will have previously taken an ounce of tartar, which will have purged his wretchedly
dirty body."[5] Often he sounds a salacious note, once charging Marianne to
ask a certain court baritone "whether he has again made the mistake of
thinking that I was in bed instead of you,"[6] and sternly insisting that she
carry out her brother's orders—"Otherwise I shall give you a whipping.
Quel plaisir!"[7] In her infrequent letters (mostly postscripts to her father's
letters) she responds in kind, evidently delighting in the sexual banter, calling him "my brother, that blackguard," writing, "to you, you rascal! you
villain! I give a juicy kiss."[8]

Throughout, there is the sense of their mutual caring and love, magnified by the belief that their relationship, like the fabulous childhood in
which it flowered, would endure forever. He expresses his hope that "God
will always grant you good health and will let you live another hundred
years and will let you die when you have reached a thousand."[9] Repeatedly
he assures her of his own love and asks her, in return, to "aimez-moi tou-
jours."[10] He addresses her as "Carissima sorella mia" or as "allerliebste
Schwester," and multiplies his kisses until they reach the millions and tril-
lions.[11]

As they matured, the teasing tone was more often set aside to reveal
their underlying profound feelings. On 20 July 1778, following their
mother's death, he sent her belated greetings from Paris on her name day:
"Let us hope that the happy future is not far off when a brother and sister,
so united and affectionate, will be able to talk to one another and tell one
another all their most intimate thoughts and feelings. Meanwhile farewell—
and love me, as I do you. I embrace you with all my heart, with all my
soul, and ever remain your sincere—your true brother."[12] A few days later
he wrote again, trying to console her on her sorrow: "Adieu, farewell. I
will not awaken sad memories. Resign yourself to the will of God and trust
in Him. Remember that you have a brother, who loves you with all his
heart."[13]

Somewhere along the way they began to lose each other. At first it
may have been the normal divergence of a brother and sister who continue
to cherish memories of shared early experience despite the awkward sense
that they have grown apart. By the end, however, there was a break

between Mozart and his sister so total that when she furnished biographical data for Schlichtegroll's obituary in mid-1792 she claimed complete ignorance of the most basic information about her brother during his last years, including "who his wife was, how many children they had of their union, how many of them are still alive etc."[14] Marianne not only didn't personally inform Mozart that their father had died, but didn't even let him know he was dying. "I was not at all surprised," he wrote her, "as I could easily guess the reason, that you yourself did not inform me of the sad death of our most dear father, which to me was quite unexpected."[15] Even earlier, though, communication between them had slowed to a trickle by the mid-1780s. She did not attend his wedding, nor he, hers, and neither of them ever saw the other's children. During the last three years of his life a heavy curtain of silence fell between them, and at his death no word was exchanged between his sister and his widow.

The correspondence sheds little light on the early sources of the bitter and hostile state into which their relationship eventually descended. One finds there no outward indication that Marianne resented his having come to absorb so much of their parents' attention or that she envied Mozart's success, fame, and adulation, which far overshadowed her own accomplishments. Although she was highly praised for the accuracy of her playing, she essentially ended her public career as a wunderkind in 1768, with very occasional performances as Mozart's collaborator in later years, and only a handful of appearances as a soloist and accompanist in Salzburg.[16] By the time she passed her eighteenth birthday she came to be judged by a different standard than that applied to her as a child; thereafter, she stayed at home giving piano lessons whereas Mozart continued to make his mark in the capitals of Europe. While Leopold and Mozart spent the better part of the next four years soaking up the splendors of Italy and hobnobbing with princes and popes, she and her mother languished in Salzburg, silently resenting though outwardly accepting Leopold's repeated explanations that he could not afford to let them travel, even for a short time. Perhaps there was no possibility of expressing rivalrous feelings so long as Mozart remained a faithful component of the family enterprise. Or perhaps Marianne's natural resentments against her brother were kept in check because of his centrality to the family's welfare.

Marianne Mozart had an apparently unlimited capacity for compliance: she was her father's daughter, obedient, subservient, self-sacrificing. Yet, if she could not express her feeling of despair when her mother and brother left Salzburg in September 1777 on their extended journey, her body spoke for her. "The day of their departure I spent mostly in bed, I vomited and had an extraordinary headache, that was the 23rd of September," she recorded without affect in her diary.[17] Leopold described her reaction in richer detail: "Nannerl wept bitterly and I had to use every effort to console her. She complained of a headache and a sick stomach and in the end she retched and vomited; and putting a cloth round her head she went off to bed and had the shutters closed."[18] Her fear of abandonment was quite on the surface: "I kiss Mamma's hands and I beg you not to forget me," she wrote on 4 October.[19] A few weeks later she wrote: "When things fare well or badly with you, think of us, who are obliged to live sadly here, separated from you both."[20] It was four months later that Frau Mozart, now about to leave for Paris, at last set down the words, "I shan't forget Nannerl."[21] She loved her Marianne and thought their connection absolutely secure, and so, preoccupied with her son's affairs and her husband's anxieties, she did not fully register her daughter's signals. During the last ten months of her life she never wrote a separate letter to Marianne, confining herself to wishing her well, sending her greetings, and alluding brightly to Mannheim and Paris fashions that might interest her.[22] Soon, Marianne's letters give the impression that all was indeed well with her, as she reported blandly and cheerily on the weekly shooting contests and other miscellaneous Salzburg events. For it was her role to present an uncomplaining face to the world while she pursued her primary duty: to attend upon her father, and to keep him from falling into a melancholy temper.[23]

For his part, despite abundant laments about himself, Leopold neither looked for nor perceived any signs that his daughter might be troubled: "I must tell you that in everything which has to do with the house Nannerl is extraordinarily industrious, hard-working and amazingly attentive; besides which she plays as much as she can and is an excellent accompanist. Every evening we practice for two or two and a half hours at least."[24] Obviously pleased at her talents as a housekeeper and companion, it was not in his interest to observe that his daughter, beneath her surface tractability, was discontented.

Mozart, during the early months of the journey to Paris, also failed to pay his sister sufficient attention. She wrote, "Since you have now become so distinguished and your time is so much taken up that you cannot write to me, probably you will have no time to read a few lines from me either."[25] But Mozart was aware of her malaise, for she confided to him things that she could not tell her parents. To him she revealed that she, too, wanted to leave what she called "this dull Salzburg,"[26] emphasizing that she "should like to have the pleasure of seeing you soon again, provided it is not in Salzburg."[27] A much more painful issue, however, was her father's reluctance to let her marry. Repeatedly he turned away her suitors on transparent pretexts. Nothing seems to have come of her flirtation with young Franz von Mölk, whose name Mozart teasingly invoked as early as

1770. In 1778, when she was already twenty-seven years old, she was courted by a widower named Johann Joseph Adam, who proclaimed his love for her from the housetops—to no avail. Leopold described to Mozart how he had handled this effrontery: "The court valet *Adam,* now Lord High Steward, sought to make your sister's acquaintance. Once he took us by surprise but from that time on we were never any longer at home, and finally, since he often spoke about his love to our maid Tresel, I ordered her to tell him that we would be honored to receive him and his wife should be marry someday, but as long as he is a widower we must prohibit him from visiting us, inasmuch as my daughter does not want to be the talk of the town."[28] It is not given whether Marianne returned Adam's affections or those of other suitors whose names may not have survived, but it seems sure that she was in love with Captain Franz Armand d'Ippold (ca. 1730–90), an older man of moderate means.[29] The matter had progressed so far by the summer of 1781 that he and Marianne hoped to marry, if only they could be assured of supporting themselves and obtaining Leopold's consent. But Leopold had by then apparently raised objections to the marriage and Marianne had fallen ill, her frequent reaction to disappointment or inner conflict.

From afar, Mozart strongly supported the match and exchanged letters with both d'Ippold and his sister about it: "I should very much like to know how things are progressing between you and a certain good friend, you know whom I mean. Do write to me about this! Or have I lost your confidence in this matter."[30] Things had reached a critical point in September, when Mozart wrote:

> I am going to be quite frank with you about your constantly recurring indispositions. Believe me, dearest sister, that I am quite serious when I say that the best cure for you would be a husband—and if only because marriage would have such a profound influence on your health, I wish with all my heart that you could marry soon. . . . For you and d'Yppold there are scarcely any—indeed, I may say with certainty—no prospects in Salzburg. But could not d'Yppold manage to get something *here?* I suppose he is not *absolutely* penniless? Ask him about it—and if he thinks the project at all practicable, he has only to tell me what steps to take, and I will certainly do my utmost, for I take the greatest interest in this affair. If this were accomplished, you could certainly marry; for, believe me, you could earn a great deal of money in Vienna for example, by playing at private concerts and by giving lessons. You would be very much in demand—and you would be well paid. In that case my father would have to resign his post and come too—and we could live very happily together again. I see no other solution—and even before I knew that your affair with d'Yppold was serious, I

had something like this in mind for you. Our dear father was the only difficulty, for I wanted him to enjoy his rest and not to have to worry and torment himself. But I think that in this way it might be arranged. For with
your husband's earnings, your own and mine, we can easily manage, and
enable our father to live in peace and comfort.[31]

Whether or not Leopold learned of Mozart's attempt to help Marianne
does not appear; what is known is that her possibly surreptitious correspondence with Mozart on this matter suddenly came to an end. Her illness
worsened, so that only a few days after his fraternal proposal Mozart was
writing to his father, "You gave me rather a fright about my sister, because
it was so unexpected. I do hope that she is better now. I kiss her a thousand
times and kiss your hands a hundred times and am ever your most obedient
son."[32] Concern about her condition did not abate for several months, but
by then there was no further prospect of marriage. Presumably Leopold, not
yet ready to yield his daughter to another man or desirous of a match with
someone of higher social standing, had terminated the affair: at least, that is
the consensus of Marianne's biographers.[33] Hummel writes that she now
showed "renewed courage in the fulfillment of the duty which she had
undertaken, to fashion a peaceful, quiet existence for her aging father."[34]
Within the confines of that quiet existence, Marianne Mozart
reflected upon the depth of her loss and considered what might have
been. Perhaps she measured her state against that of her brother, who
had delivered himself from stultifying Salzburg and established a separate
career in the glamorous capital. Now, he was about to marry a woman
whom he loved, thereby putting a full stop to his family obligations. Her
brother's emergence coincided with her unsuccessful love affair. In a few
years she was married off to Johann Baptist Berchtold zu Sonnenburg—
an elderly and ill-tempered widower with five youngsters—chosen by
her father for his wealth and social standing.[35] Shortly thereafter she left
her first-born with her father—without caveat, blindly, automatically—
either unaware of the depth of her sacrifice or wholly anesthetized to
her own pain. Mozart alone had tried to save her, had encouraged her to
marry a man she loved and to make her own living as a creative musician. In retrospect, though, it seems inevitable that she would be unable
to take these steps, which must have seemed so extreme to her. In the
end, the risks were too great: she had neither the stomach nor the temperament to enter into a mortal contest with her father. One cannot say
which of the Mozart children carried a heavier burden, the young
woman who was asked to give up her lover and her first-born or the
young man who was asked to curtail his vital forces and remain the eternal family provider.

★　★　★

In some way, the manifest ideal of the Mozart family had always been that of self-sacrifice: each member of the family was enjoined to sacrifice himself or herself for the others and sacrifice was seen both as an absolute good and as an absolute obligation. This ideal had overtones of Christian martyrdom, and Leopold Mozart more than once referred to his own crucifixion, as when he wrote of the "Salzburg cross, on which I am still hanging."[36] In the course of time Mozart came to renounce the sacrificial compulsion, but because it played upon deep altruistic and familial currents within him it nevertheless continued to exercise a powerful hold on him. What he could never fully grasp was that it is the logic of such fanaticism that those who will not conform to it are expelled from the kinship group, regarded as apostates and sinners against the sacred alliance. That is why Mozart's resistance to Leopold's absolutist demands in effect made him a culprit to his own family, one whose punishment was to be sent to Coventry. In contrast, Marianne, like a soldier of the Cross or a dedicated sister of mercy, could never consider placing her own interests above those of the family and especially those of her father, who represented the family incarnate.

Even as she was drawn ever closer to her father, she was held up to Mozart as a paragon of filial piety—and even as her brother's replacement:

> Your sister alone is now my support, and I try to banish the cares which seem to overwhelm me by a very quiet form of entertainment, which is, to play through on the violin from six to eight every evening, arias, symphonies, masses, vespers, and so forth, while your sister plays the figured bass and gets practice in accompanying. . . . She extemporizes so successfully that you would be astounded. And do you know what has inspired her with this determination and terrific industry? *My death!* She realizes and foresees the misery into which she would be plunged, were I suddenly to breathe my last.[37]

And so Marianne Mozart remained a dutiful daughter, agreeing with her father's every judgment and sharing his every prejudice. Her attitude toward her brother became indistinguishable from that of her father, for whom she acted as both surrogate and apologist: in later years, when she was asked by a biographer to explain how it came about that Mozart "took his already old mother with him" on the journey to Paris, she responded to this sensitive question by invoking the eternal-child myth:[38]

> Concerning his faults, I can attribute only one to him, which consisted of his having had too good a heart, that he didn't know how to manage money, that whoever flattered him could obtain everything from him. So

long as he remained with his father he was provided with all the necessities; since he was always busy he thought nothing about how he would some day have to manage money; and because he knew that he himself was not in a position to manage things this was also the reason that his mother was sent with him to Paris, inasmuch as our father was unable to accompany him because of his duties.[39]

Trembling with guilt and doubt over his defiance of his father, Mozart had waited vainly for any sign of encouragement, sympathy, or understanding from his older sister. Instead, she did not protest when Leopold, knowing Mozart's vulnerability on the issue, repeatedly invoked sister against brother, charging that Mozart's departure from Salzburg would lead to her impoverishment. He pictured her as distraught over Mozart's plan to tour Italy with the Webers. "Nannerl has wept her full share during these last two days," he wrote in February 1778.[40] And when Mozart shot back, "Tell her she must not cry over every silly trifle, or I shall never go home again,"[41] he only succeeded in arousing his father's wrath. In a heated response Leopold told how Marianne had come to fear that after his death she would be forced into domestic service, despite which she was willing to tender her own savings as security to help an unfeeling and profligate brother: "So your sister was not crying over a silly trifle, when she wept over your letter."[42]

Clearly, Mozart needed an ally, but, to judge from the correspondence, Marianne during this period never dissociated herself from her father's views. Instead, she reinforced the mythology that her brother was destined to be the instrument of the family's security and of her personal deliverance: "We are both longing for you to make your fortune, for that, I know for certain, will mean happiness to us all."[43] Eventually, it became clear to Mozart that he would never again receive comfort from his sister.

Having failed to gain acceptance for Constanze during the 1783 visit to Salzburg, Mozart continued from Vienna to try to jolly his sister into showing the old affection, writing her, with perhaps just a trace of hostility:

We both send Nannerl
   (1) a couple of boxes on the ear
   (2) a couple of slaps on the face
   (3) a couple of raps on the cheek
   (4) a couple of whacks on the jaw
   (5) a couple of smacks on the jowl
   (6) a couple of cuffs on the mug.[44]

Similarly, in 1784 he warmly congratulated her on her marriage, expressed

his regret at not attending the wedding, and offered instead a merry dog-
gerel verse to alert her to her forthcoming conjugal responsibilities.

> Wedlock will show you many things
> Which still a mystery remain;
> Experience soon will teach to you
> What Eve herself once had to do
> Before she could give birth to Cain.
> But all these duties are so light
> You will perform them with delight.[45]

But by this time their connection had been thoroughly undermined.
Although Mozart wrote to her again in November (the letter does not survive), their correspondence effectively came to a halt for the next three
years. From Vienna during his 1785 visit, Leopold Mozart cautioned her
to be careful to "write a letter *that your brother also can read,*" suggesting that
her letters to him could be construed as unfriendly to Mozart.[46] During
those three years Marianne relied on her father for news of Mozart—
births, concerts, journeys, compositions, publications, and changes of lodgings—that he gleaned from his son's letters home. On one or two occasions
she seems to have tried to initiate a friendly exchange, but without success.
In early November 1785, Mozart failed to acknowledge her congratulations on his name day (31 October) and instead sent his regrets and regards
to her through their father, who wrote to her that Mozart "hasn't time to
answer your letter at once."[47] Mozart and his sister, too, had once been one
flesh, but that time was gone. In the aftermath of the Salzburg visit and the
rejection of his bride, Mozart gave up his sister. In the depths of her bitterness she gave up her brother.

In some way that she could never specify, Mozart had spoiled Marianne's chances for happiness. Somehow, she had been denied the blessings
of fortune because her brother had seized his own opportunity to make a
life for himself, for it was clearly inconceivable that both of them could
forsake their father. And, of course, in showing Marianne the very possibility of fulfillment Mozart could only cause her additional pain. Unfortunately, she never gave any indication that she felt her brother's pain or that
she understood the price he had paid for his "freedom." She had become
the vessel into which Leopold's rancor and discontent overflowed, and
once Mozart had irrevocably broken with the family enterprise, she was
not only at last able to express pent-up hostility toward him, but to do so
with the encouragement and approval of her father. What she could never
understand was that her bitterness of spirit was discharged against the
wrong object, for it was not Mozart who had crippled her life, conscripted

Marianne von Berchtold zu Sonnenburg, c. 1785. Unsigned oil portrait.
Mozart-Museum der Internationalen Stiftung Mozarteum,
Salzburg. © Mozarts Geburtshaus, Salzburg.

her as a surrogate wife and servant, turned away her suitors, and married
her to Berchtold.

But in compensation for her misfortunes—not least of which was the
loss of her brother—she gained her father's attention, gratitude, and love.

Now it was she who became Leopold's consolation, his main correspondent, for whom he penned an epistolary chronicle of Salzburg daily life between 1784 and 1787. Now, father and daughter achieved a harmonious interchange and understanding, free of complaint, marked by deep mutual caring. "Deeds and not wishes are the indications of true friendship and tender fatherly love," he wrote her on her name day in July 1786. "Of this you are convinced, I know that; and that pleases me. I wish you continued health and—everything else you might wish for yourself."[48] On balance, she had not done too badly, and she had the deep satisfaction of knowing that she had been faithful to the principles of family solidarity to which the Mozarts had been pledged and by which they had made their lasting mark on eighteenth-century musical life. If, in the process, a brother and sister lost one another, that had to be accepted as the natural consequence of an unavoidable moral imperative.

The hostility and resentment, so long held in check, poured out of them when their father died in the spring of 1787. It was not that he was no longer there to mediate between two warring siblings, for he had not previously hesitated to set them against each other. Rather, by his disposition of his estate Leopold Mozart finally arranged things precisely so as to make the break inevitable and wounding.

Mozart was informed of his father's death by Marianne's old suitor, Franz d'Ippold, in a letter of 28 May 1787 that also disclosed testamentary matters. Mozart revealed the fullness of his grief in two economical lines to his closest friend, Gottfried von Jacquin: "I inform you that on returning home today I received the sad news of my most beloved father's death. You can imagine the state I am in."[49] On 2 June, Mozart wrote to his sister in a guarded tone:

> You can easily imagine, as our loss is equally great, how pained I was by the sad news of the sudden death of our dearest father. Since at the moment it is impossible for me to leave Vienna . . . and since it would be hardly worth my while to do so for the sake of our late father's estate, I must confess that I too am entirely of your opinion about having a public auction. But before it takes place I should like to see the inventory, so as to be able to choose some personal effects. But if, as Herr F. d'Yppold has written to tell me, there is a dispositio paterna inter liberos, then, of course, I must be informed of this dispositio beforehand, so as to be able to make further arrangements;—hence I am now expecting an accurate copy of it and after a rapid perusal of its contents I shall let you have my opinion at once.[50]

In the first line, Mozart claims equality in grief with his sister, affirming that he loved his father as much as she did. Otherwise, beneath his controlled words are sorrow, anger, and disappointment: he will not come to Salzburg because "it would be hardly worth my while"; he quickly turns to matters of business. Clearly, he was not pleased with what he had learned from d'Ippold concerning Leopold's division of his estate. Neither the "dispositio paterna inter liberos," a testamentary order that regulates the division of an estate among heirs, nor the full inventory of the estate has survived, but there is sufficient documentary evidence available to conclude with a high degree of probability that Leopold Mozart's entire estate was left to his daughter, except for his personal effects, which were to be auctioned and the proceeds divided between his children. Walter Senn concludes that "Leopold Mozart disposed of a portion of his possessions and thereby did not forget his daughter (even though the writings do not reflect this) [and] that in the instructions concerning the effects (whether by testament or codicil) the individual possessions which were to be divided by the siblings, as legal heirs, were not named." He takes Mozart's failure subsequently to refer to a testament as "a sign that his father had provided only an unsatisfactory portion for him."[51]

Leopold Mozart had never revealed to Mozart the extent of the profits from the Grand Journey and the Italian journeys. On the contrary, in the letters from 1778 onward he always gave the clear impression that the family's economic condition was a precarious one and that he had gone into debt in order to promote his son's interests. Of course, Mozart surely suspected otherwise; he was not blind to the evidence of his father's multiple business activities, fine apartment, and servants. Nor was the effective disinheritance (save only for a portion of the value of personal effects) something that should have surprised him: we need only recall that when he married he had been bluntly warned not to "expect" anything from his father. Now, however, reading his father's will, he experienced with full force the shock of being excluded from his share of funds that were largely the result of his own talents and labor.

As though contemplating what would happen when his father died, Mozart seems to have tried to convert his imagined future anger into comedy and his grief into cynicism. This may underlie his scenario of a farce entitled *Der Salzburger Lump in Wien* (The Salzburg Scoundrel in Vienna), K. 509b, written by him probably in early 1787, where he describes the action in Act I, scene 1: "Herr Stachelschwein [Mr. Porcupine] reads a letter that he has just received from his mother, informing him of the death of his father. He expresses grief over his loss, but at the same time rejoices over his inheritance."[52] In Act II, scene 2, "Herr Stachelschwein tells his friend that he now, through the death of his father, will soon come into better circumstances." Thus did Mozart in fantasy rewrite his father's will.

To compound his sense that he had been treated unfairly, Mozart soon learned that Marianne, repeating her father's similar refusal in 1783, would not let him choose some personal effects for himself, and she even asked him through a third person[53]—she would not write him directly about this—to waive any claim on proceeds from the sale. Only now, in his blunt letter of 16 June, by which time he had received a copy of the testament and the inventory, did he openly express his anger, chiding her for not personally informing him of their father's death and taking issue with her request for a waiver. He wrote: "If you were still unprovided for, all this would be quite unnecessary, for as I have already said and thought a thousand times, I should leave everything to you with the greatest delight. But as the property would really be of no use to you, while, on the contrary, it would be a considerable help to me, I think it my duty to consider my wife and child."[54]

Negotiations now commenced between Mozart and his brother-in-law to permit Marianne to withhold from the auction whatever she wanted for herself in exchange for a flat payment to Mozart. On 1 August, the deal was struck: Mozart was to get 1,000 florins in Viennese currency and he was to regain possession of his own manuscript scores—many of which had been stored in his father's care—for these, too, had become a subject of contention, inasmuch as Leopold had apparently bequeathed all musical scores to his daughter. "Please do not forget about my *scores*," Mozart underlined in his letter.[55] The inventory of Leopold's goods numbered 579 items,[56] but when the auction took place between 25 and 28 September only 314 items were sold, bringing in 1,507 florins, 56 kreuzer. Included in the sale were "court dresses, hunting-gear, linen, kitchen utensils, furniture, jewelry and musical instruments."[57] Mozart received more than half of the proceeds, but Marianne retained many of the most valuable items, including musical instruments (violins and a clavichord among them), paintings, fine clothing, and luxury items. To judge from the auction list, she also retained most of the unique and expensive gifts to Mozart gathered during the early journeys.[58] After some delay, the scores were returned to him toward the end of December 1787, but in keeping with the pettiness of spirit that surfaces in such conflicts, his sister withheld all duplicate copies and performance materials as her own property.[59] Leopold's church music was sent to Holy Cross Monastery at Augsburg, and Marianne kept the family letters for herself.[60]

Because the primary documents concerning Leopold Mozart's estate—including the testament, the inventory, and the records of the negotiations between Mozart and his sister—are no longer extant, the amount of money he left to Marianne, except for 30 florins in loose coins, cannot be fixed (assuming, of course, that the money was formally bequeathed rather than handed to her sub rosa to avoid taxation). But the absence of documentation should not lead us to conclude that Leopold Mozart left no money. By an admittedly approximate estimate, Leopold's earnings from the first European journey (through the end of 1767) equaled more than 10,000 florins, and even after allowing for certain losses during the trip to Vienna in 1768 and the Mannheim/Paris journeys in 1777–78, the bulk of this fortune remained intact thereafter. Indeed, it had doubtless increased substantially in later years from earnings of several thousand florins on the Italian journeys, from interest and investments, and from Leopold's various business enterprises, all conducted while he continued to draw his full salary as deputy court kapellmeister. Whatever the margin for error in these estimates may be, when Leopold's frugality and modest expenses are also taken into account, it is not reasonable to believe that his savings could have evaporated.

Fortunately, we can partially reconstruct Leopold's ultimate cash position by considering some details of his daughter's financial situation, including the data from her own estate. Her marriage portion consisted of a dowry of 500 florins, the interest on which was secured to her as "pocket money," plus an additional 1,000 florins from Berchtold and a further 500 florins to be paid the day after the wedding night as a premium should she prove to be a virgin ("Morgengabe seu in praemium virginitatis").[61] When her husband died, on 26 February 1803, he left her, out of a gross estate of 28,000 florins, sufficient capital to fund a pension of 300 florins per annum, the capital to revert to his children upon her death.[62] It is likely that she was left so little by her husband because he knew that she was already provided for by her father. At best, her dowry and legacy gave her a capital of 1,000 to 2,000 florins; her modest pension was sufficient for subsistence but not enough to generate further savings, even with her tiny income from giving piano lessons (which she resumed after her return to Salzburg in October 1801). Nevertheless, when she died, on 29 October 1829, she left to her sole surviving child bonds in the amount of 6,775 florins, plus cash in the amount of 145 florins.[63] Factoring in the possibility that she used up some capital to cover a portion of her living expenses during her last quarter century, I estimate that she had received from her father in cash somewhere between 6,000 and 10,000 florins. And if, in anticipation of her death, she had already transferred some money to her son in cash, the amount might have been substantially higher.

In his letter of 1 August 1787 Mozart bid his sister "a thousand farewells," his subtle way of telling her that they would greet each other no longer. And in a letter of 19 December he advised her not to expect that he would answer promptly in the future: "Well, good-bye, dear sister. Write to me frequently. If I don't always answer promptly, put it down not to any negligence on my part, but simply to stress of work."[64] There is one final letter, dated 2 August 1788, doubtless written because she had reproached him for neglecting to congratulate her on her name day (26 July): "Dearest sister," he wrote, with a mixture of nonchalance and cruelty, "with my whole heart and soul I wish you all that you believe is most advantageous to yourself. . . . Dear sister! You must realize that I have a great deal to do. Besides, you know very well that I am rather lazy about letter-writing. So do not take it amiss, if I *seldom* write to you. But this must not prevent you from writing very often to *me*."[65] Whether to offset the harshness of these words or to underline them, Mozart sent Marianne some of his latest piano compositions and gave her news about his recent accomplishments: the Prague performances of *Don Giovanni* and his appointment as chamber composer to the emperor the previous December; he made sure to emphasize that he was receiving a salary of only 800 florins. She understood him perfectly and made no further protest, for she knew that her brother was expert at cloaking chilly rejections in expressions of deep sentiment and concern, reinforced by regrets and excuses. There was no point in pretenses of cordiality. And indeed there was no further contact between them; later on, after his death, she was at a loss to explain their ultimate remoteness from one another: "Since on the whole he wasn't fond of writing, I no longer received any letters from him after the year 1788."[66]

During an earlier crisis, in 1778, Mozart had reassured his beloved sister, "Please trust me absolutely and never think that I shall forget you." But even then he warned her—and himself—of the unpredictability of fortune, for he asked her to "remember that things do not always turn out, or at least not always exactly, as one wishes."[67] What eventually turned out was that they were torn apart and then tried to pretend that they were still whole. To judge from her biographical notes and correspondence, it was many years before she could let herself feel the grief of their separation, and she never let herself consider that her brother might have been unfairly treated by their father. But a provision in the codicil to her will, written shortly before she died, suggests that she somehow wanted to make amends or even to repair at least a small portion of an old injustice to which she had been a party. The codicil specified that six items of jewelry were to be willed to her son Leopold during his lifetime, but after his death they were to be given over to the heirs of the Mozart family, "because these derive from the property left by their great-great-grandmother."[68] Included were an antique gold ring with eleven diamonds, a cross with garnets, two gold earrings with blue stones, an enameled pendant, a silver scent box in a wooden case, and "the wall clock in my bedroom." Mozart may not have received his fair share of his father's property, but as she prepared to meet her maker Marianne saw to it that eventually his family would receive what his mother's mother would have wanted him to have. Clearly, even good impulses have their limits: Marianne could not bring herself to will the items directly to her sister-in-law, let alone simply to hand them over to her. However, showing rare tact and understanding, her son—formerly little Leopold—presented the six items to Constanze Mozart in 1830, not long after his mother's death on 29 October 1829.

By the unequal division of his estate Leopold Mozart had prepared the ground for further conflict between his children, raising explosive issues of fairness and favoritism, and guaranteeing that a time that should have been devoted to mourning and healing would be fraught with bitterness and reproach. Clearly, he could not have acted otherwise, for he remained in the grip of a compulsion to resurrect and reenact as literally as possible the scenario of disinheritance that had been played out in Augsburg earlier in the century between himself and his own mother. In the aftermath of her father's death Marianne precipitated the final rupture with Mozart, perhaps in the knowledge that she was carrying out what she understood to be her father's wish to disinherit his son, her brother. She may have felt disinheriting him as an act of piety, for in her grief Marianne may have believed that Mozart caused their father's death, or caused him to die in anguish. At the very least, it was self-evident to her that Mozart had blighted his father's last years by his egoistic elevation of his own interests above those of the family. Thus, Mozart and Marianne's quarrel was not really about money, but about who would possess the father's surviving substance, which is to say, the memory of his love, his protection, his favor. By compelling Mozart to accept an unfair division of the estate, she was impressing upon him that despite his brilliant career, his fame, his wife, and his fancy Viennese existence, it was she who had tangible proof of their father's love, definitive proof that she, rather than Mozart, was Leopold Mozart's favorite child and heir.

Nevertheless, she surely knew that Mozart's bond to his father was somehow more resonant than her own; that whatever his unending complaints against his son, Leopold Mozart never ceased to define his own life by his son's achievements. Even in his last years, when Leopold was railing against Mozart and always suspecting the worst, he was desperate for any word from him, even the briefest letter: "I do hope that I shall have a letter tomorrow, as I have written to him twice. Or perhaps he is going to come [here] himself?"[69] "Perhaps [a letter] will come tomorrow," he wrote in 1787,[70] indicative of a pathetic need that he did not succeed in concealing from his daughter, to whom it may have seemed that her father's letters were filled with a constant stream of reports about Mozart. Nor could he ever conceal his almost trembling excitement about his son's latest compositions: "I forgot to write about the libretto for Figaro," we read in his letter to Marianne of 16 September 1786. "Bring it along—I must have it."[71] Deep as Leopold's affection for his daughter was, and limitless as was her capacity for compliance with his wishes, she knew that she was no match for her brother in the competition for paternal love, that Leopold Mozart's attachment to his son was the supreme passion of his life, so dramatically highlighted, at the end, by his effort to raise little Leopold to be a new Mozart. Perhaps the saddest aspect of this sad story is that Marianne Mozart understood that she could never fill her brother's place in her father's heart.

27

....

PRAGUE AND BEYOND

Mozart's plan to travel to England during the 1787 carnival season was postponed. Instead, on extremely short notice he journeyed to Prague during the first week of the new year, in the aftermath of the production there of *Le nozze di Figaro*. The opera was presented at the National Theater by the company of the Prague impresario Pasquale Bondini in early December 1786 and fueled an enthusiasm for Mozart that has passed into legend, with Prague seen as the good city that supported and understood him at a time when he had allegedly been neglected, even scorned, by Vienna. "All the connoisseurs and artists of our capital were Mozart's staunch admirers, the most ardent ambassadors of his fame," wrote the composer's early biographer, Franz Niemetschek, himself a proud resident of Prague. In Bohemia, Niemetschek claimed, "all his works were recognized and appreciated at their true value."[1] The Italian librettist Lorenzo Da Ponte also marveled at the Prague reception of his three collaborations with Mozart: "It is not easy to depict the enthusiasm of the Bohemians for this music. The numbers which are least admired in other countries are by this people considered divine; and . . . the great beauties of the music . . . were perfectly understood by the Bohemians at the first hearing."[2] Local reviews confirmed the impact of *Le nozze di Figaro* in particular and stressed the superiority of the local production. "No piece (so every one here asserts) has ever caused such a sensation as the Italian opera *Die Hochzeit des Figaro,* which has already been given several times here with unlimited applause," reported the Prague *Oberpostamtszeitung* on 12 December 1786. "Connoisseurs who have seen this opera in Vienna are anxious to declare that it was

Prague seen from Isle of Kampa. Watercolor by Fr. Sandmann.
City Museum, Prague.

done much better here. . . . Our great Mozart must have heard about this himself, for there has been a rumor that he will come here in person to see the piece."[3] Niemetschek wrote that public enthusiasm "was without precedent. . . . Figaro's tunes echoed through the streets and the parks; even the harpist on the alehouse bench had to play 'Non più andrai' if he wanted to attract any attention at all."[4]

The invitation to Mozart, issued by "the orchestra and a company of distinguished connoisseurs and music-lovers," was a generous one, for he arrived in Prague on 11 January 1787 with an entourage that included his wife, a servant, his future brother-in-law, the violinist Franz de Paula Hofer, and the thirteen-year-old violin virtuoso Marianne Crux.[5] The group was comfortably lodged at the palace of Count Johann Joseph Thun-Hohenstein (born 1711), dedicatee of the "Linz" Symphony and patriarch of the Viennese Thun family. That very evening, accompanied by the music patron Count Joseph Emanuel Canal, they attended the so-called Bretfeld ball, where Mozart witnessed for himself the *Figaro* craze: "I looked on . . . with the greatest pleasure," he wrote to Jacquin, "while all these people flew about in sheer delight to the music of my 'Figaro,' arranged for contredanses and German dances. For here they talk about nothing but 'Figaro.' Nothing is played, sung, or whistled but 'Figaro.' No opera is drawing like 'Figaro.' Nothing, nothing but 'Figaro.' Certainly a great honor for me!"[6] It is believed that Mozart was taken up by the local Freemasons, among whom were Count Thun, Count Canal, and the imperial librarian Raphael Ungar, whose collection they viewed at such length that they "almost stared our eyes out."[7] On 12 January at Count Thun's palace Mozart played in one of his piano quartets, and the humorous vocal trio "Liebes Mandel, wo is's Bandel?" K. 441, was sung. On the seventeenth, *Le nozze di Figaro* was performed in Mozart's presence. His main opportunity to earn money came on the nineteenth with an academy at the National Theater at which the Symphony in D, K. 504 ("Prague"), was presented and Mozart played three clavier improvisations, the last on "Non più andrai" from *Le nozze di Figaro*. Niemetschek, who was present, wrote: "We did not, in fact, know what to admire most, whether the extraordinary compositions or his extraordinary playing; together they made such an overwhelming impression on us that we felt we had been bewitched. When Mozart had finished the concert he continued improvising alone on the piano for half an hour."[8] All in all, he recalled, Mozart "counted this day as one of the happiest of his life."[9] The whirlwind of activity ended on the twenty-second, when Mozart himself directed a performance of his opera; on the same day he probably participated in a concert by Marianne Crux at Count Thun's. His enthusiasm evidently bordered on euphoria, and one member of the opera orchestra remembered his giddy habit of "laying aside mere speech in favor of musical recitative, which even in public he would use as a means of making remarks and conveying requests to his circle of friends."[10] When the Mozarts left Prague, probably on 8 February, he had in hand 1,000 florins and a contract from Bondini to compose a new opera for the following fall season at a fee of 100 ducats plus the box-office receipts from one performance.

Despite his success in Prague, Mozart was preoccupied with other plans. "Although I meet with all possible courtesies and honors here and although Prague is indeed a very beautiful and pleasant place, I long most ardently to be back in Vienna," Mozart wrote to Jacquin in January.[11] Mozart still hoped to go to England for an extended stay, perhaps permanently; his letter confirmed what had been reported by the Prague *Oberpostamtszeitung* on the eve of his arrival, that Mozart "is preparing to travel to London in the coming spring, having the most advantageous offers there. He will go by way of Paris."[12] Apparently, however, a definite opera commission or guaranteed subscription concerts did not quickly materialize in England, despite the efforts of his pupil, the composer Thomas Attwood, among others. So Mozart's English lessons could not yet be put to good use, apart from several English-language entries in souvenir albums of friends and fellow Masons.

Back in Vienna, Mozart gave no concerts of his own, his only appearance being his presumed participation in the soprano Anna Storace's farewell concert on 23 February 1787 before her return to England. Between March and August he produced a substantial quantity of instrumental works, including the Rondo for piano in A minor, K. 511, the String Quintets in C, K. 515, and G minor, K. 516, the Piano Sonata for four hands in C, K. 521, *Ein musikalischer Spass* ("A Musical Joke"), K. 522, the Serenade in G, *Eine kleine Nachtmusik*, K. 525, and the Violin Sonata in A, K. 526. The sources of the commissions for these works, or the occasions for their performance, are not known. Several other works were composed for fellow musicians or friends—a Scene, "Alcandro, lo confesso"—"Non sò, d'onde viene," K. 512, for the bass Ludwig Fischer to sing at an academy on 21 March, an aria, "Mentre ti lascio, o figlia," K. 513, for Jacquin, and half a dozen lieder, K. 517–20 and K. 523–24.

But the main work of 1787 was *Don Giovanni*, the second of Mozart's operas to a libretto by Da Ponte, which needed to be completed for performance in Prague in mid-October. Nothing precise is known about when Da Ponte wrote the libretto and Mozart commenced its composition. Indeed, after the death of Leopold Mozart on 28 May 1787, there are very few letters to tell us about Mozart's activities, so that many events of his last Vienna years remain obscure or unknown. Presumably, however, the composition of *Don Giovanni* was Mozart's main occupation for a minimum of three full months; he and Constanze returned to Prague on 4 October, and apparently a good deal of work still remained to be done, for the second finale and overture are written on locally purchased music paper.[13] According to a famous anecdote, Mozart worked through the night, Constanze endeavoring to keep him awake by various strategies, so that he could complete the overture by the morning of the premiere on 29 October (more probably, the morning of the general rehearsal on the twenty-eighth): "The copyists were only just ready in time for the performance" and the orchestra played it at sight. Mozart remarked, "Some of the notes fell under the desks, it is true, but the overture went remarkably well on the whole."[14]

Da Ponte was in Prague from 8 to 15 October, working with Mozart to put the finishing touches on the opera, which was originally scheduled for performance on the fourteenth in honor of the wedding of Archduchess Maria Theresia and Prince Anton Clemens of Saxony. At the last minute *Le nozze di Figaro* was substituted, with Mozart conducting. "The zeal of the musicians and the presence of Mozart, the Master, awakened a general approbation and satisfaction in Their Highnesses,"[15] reported the *Oberpostamtszeitung*. *Don Giovanni* was then rescheduled for the twenty-fourth, but was postponed again owing to the illness of one of the singers. The glowing review of the premiere at the Ständetheater on the twenty-ninth indicated that there were some performance problems: "Connoisseurs and musicians say that Prague had never yet heard the like. Herr Mozard conducted in person; when he entered the orchestra he was received with threefold cheers, which again happened when he left it. The opera is, moreover, extremely difficult to perform, and every one admired the good performance given in spite of this after such a short period of study. . . . The unusually large attendance testifies to a unanimous approbation."[16] Evidently the opera was a financial success, even if we do not accept Nissen's (or Constanze's) claim that "through *Don Giovanni* Mozart saved Bondini";[17] there were three repetitions by 3 November and 116 Prague performances in all during the next ten years.[18] Mozart's "opera for Prague" became, according to Niemetschek, "the favorite opera of the élite of Prague,"[19] subtly implying that ordinary music-lovers may have had some reservations.

His mission completed, Mozart lingered in Prague for several weeks in the company of fellow musicians, music-lovers, and admirers, including especially his dear friends the Duscheks, at whose Villa Bertramka he and Constanze were staying. For Josepha Duschek he wrote the Scene, "Bella mia fiamma"—"Resta, o cara," K. 528, on 3 November, and two lieder, K. 529–30, on 6 November. A glow of good feeling lingered in the wake of his departure, on 12 or 13 November, but though he passed through

Prague briefly on his way to and from Berlin in 1789 he made no further professional appearances there until the summer of 1791. It might be thought that Prague neglected him after the sensational reception in 1787, and this was evidently Haydn's opinion, when he wrote in December 1787 to Franz Rott, an influential local music-lover: "Prague should hold fast to the precious man—but should reward him, too; for without this, the history of great geniuses is sad indeed and gives but little encouragement to posterity to further exertions; and unfortunately this is why so many promising intellects fall by the wayside. It enrages me to think that this incomparable Mozart is not yet engaged by some imperial or royal court!"[20]

It seems clear, however, that Mozart had reasons of his own for not returning to Prague. He wrote to Jacquin on 4 November: "People here are doing their best to persuade me to remain on for a couple of months and write another [opera]. But I cannot accept this proposal, however flattering it may be."[21] This is difficult to understand, for he would have made 1,000 florins at a minimum from the fee and box-office receipts; and it was in 1788 that he urgently needed to supplement his income. Understandably, however, Prague could not figure greatly in his future plans because, in the last analysis, it had a relatively provincial musical establishment, not one capable of supporting a major composer. Indeed, Prague had long been an exporter of musicians and composers, who were unable to make a living at home. Prague's most distinguished patrons maintained local palaces but were seldom resident there; the Prague orchestra was zealous, and reportedly had a good wind section, but was otherwise not strongly

Villa Bertramka. Unsigned drawing. Reproduced from
Walter Hummel, *Mozarts Söhne.*

manned; the new opera house had been established only in 1783 and Bondini's troupe was really a quasi-itinerant one, which alternated seasons in Prague and Leipzig and had no singers of great rank. In 1788 Hummel's father wrote in his diary after hearing performances of *Figaro* and *Don Giovanni* in Prague, "the music is not very well done."[22] Genuinely thrilled as he was by the reception of *Don Giovanni*, Mozart could not have been happy with the reviewer's remark about the roughness of the performance.

Mozart had other commitments in Vienna and other travel plans for 1788, especially the hope of visiting England in the summer. It was around this time that he became music director of the society of ancient music, which called itself the Society of Associated Cavaliers (Gesellschaft der Associierten Cavaliere), a consortium of nobles, headed by Baron van Swieten, that included Princes Schwarzenberg, Lobkowitz, and Dietrichstein, Counts Apponyi, Batthyány, Esterházy, and others who covered the costs of performances of major choral works through a subscription.[23] For the Society's concerts between early 1788 and mid-1791 Mozart reorchestrated and conducted four works by Handel—*Acis and Galatea, K. 566, Messiah, K. 572, Alexander's Feast, K. 591,* and *Ode for Saint Cecilia's Day, K. 592.* His first appearance for the Society was as conductor of C. P. E. Bach's cantata *Die Auferstehung und Himmelfahrt Christi,* in two performances at Count Esterházy's residence on 26 February and 4 March 1788 and another, for the general public, on 7 March at the Burgtheater. As befitted a major event, the Society provided an orchestra of eighty-six and two rehearsals, and a portrait of Bach circulated in the hall. A notice of the first performance commented: "The Princesses and Countesses present and the whole of the brilliant nobility admired the great composer, and there occurred a hearty *vivat* and a threefold, loud round of applause."[24] Later in the year, in November, Mozart directed *Acis and Galatea* in a concert for his own benefit at the hall adjoining Ignaz Jahn's restaurant, with a private repetition on 24 December at Count Esterházy's. The precise amount of Mozart's remuneration is not known, but clearly the Society was now a substantial, regular source of income for him, demonstrating the high level of support he continued to receive—contrary to biographical legend—from illustrious members of the high nobility.

Moreover, shortly after his return to Vienna, on 7 December 1787, Mozart was decreed chamber composer to Emperor Joseph II at an annual salary of 800 florins, succeeding Gluck, who had died on 15 November.[25] The emperor's purpose was twofold: to express the court's homage to a great composer within its midst and to head off Mozart's bruited departure from Vienna. A contemporary almanac reported: "Herr Wolfgang Mozart has been taken into the actual service of His Majesty the Emperor. . . . All lovers of music will doubtless feel the most lively satisfaction at this promotion, this excellent musician having for so long been misjudged and not valued according to his true merits."[26] A private court memorandum written in 1792 confirmed that the emperor did not want to lose Vienna's greatest composer: "The late Hofkompositor Mozart was accepted into Court service expressly to prevent an artist of such outstanding genius from being obliged to seek his subsistence abroad."[27] Mozart had finally achieved a secure imperial post, even if the pay was less than he needed. The salary was honorary, for the duties were undemanding, limited only to providing dances for the annual balls in the Redoutensaal. "As Chamber Composer, the court never gave him a commission," Nissen reported, certainly reflecting a complaint of Constanze's: she told how Mozart reproached the imperial taxation bureau, saying, "Too much for what I do, too little for what I could do."[28] Not without a touch of apparent pride, Mozart informed his sister in August 1788 that the poster for the Vienna production of *Don Giovanni* stated, "The music is by Herr Mozart, duly appointed kapellmeister to His Imperial Majesty."[29] Of course, only Salieri and Giuseppe Bonno were officially entitled to use the title "court kapellmeister," but like his father, who long ago had scratched the word "kapellmeister" onto a Frankfurt windowpane, Mozart needed to fulfill a deeply rooted ambition, to bear the highest official title available to any European musician.[30]

Thus, in late 1787 Mozart once again had hopeful prospects in Vienna, not least among them a production of *Don Giovanni* in the coming spring. Clearly, too, he was still very much in favor in the capital, enjoying both imperial and aristocratic backing and with several stable sources of income, even if his popularity was not translating itself into large amounts of cash. His output became somewhat patchy as he awaited the production of his opera. In January he wrote only an Allegro and Andante for piano in F, K. 533, and a number of dances for orchestra, K. 534–36; the sole work for February was the Piano Concerto in D, K. 537 ("Coronation"). The last of his arias for Aloysia Weber, "Ah se in ciel, benigne stelle," K. 538, was completed on 4 March, and his only other work that month was the Adagio for piano in B minor, K. 540. In April he was much occupied with new music for the Vienna premiere of *Don Giovanni,* including an Aria, "Dalla sua pace," for Don Ottavio, K. 540a, the Duet, "Per queste tue manine," for Zerlina and Leporello, K. 540b, and the Scene for Donna Elvira, "In quali eccessi"—"Mi tradì quell'alma ingrata," K. 540c.

The Viennese reception of *Don Giovanni,* which had its premiere on 7 May in the Burgtheater, left much to be desired. Shortly thereafter, Emperor Joseph II, though he had not yet heard the opera, wrote, "Mozard's music is certainly too difficult to be sung" ("La musique de Mozard est bien trop difficile pour le chant").[31] Though it was performed fifteen times during 1788, it fell out of the repertory in Vienna during the remaining years of Mozart's life. Its reception suggests that Mozart had overestimated the capabilities of Viennese opera audiences to adjust to a new musical aesthetic. Countess de la Lippe found "the music learned, little suited to the voice."[32] Archduchess Elisabeth Wilhelmine wrote to her husband, "In the last few days a new opera composed by Mozart has been given, but I was told that it did not have much success."[33]

There were no reviews of the Vienna production, but later notices indicate the gist of contemporary *Don Giovanni* reception. "Is such magnificent, majestic and powerful song really stuff for ordinary opera-lovers, who only bring their *ears* to the Singspiel and leave their *hearts* at home?" asked one critic, adding, "The beauty, greatness and nobility of the music for *Don Juan* will never appeal anywhere to more than a handful of the elect. It is not music to everyone's taste, merely tickling the ear and letting the heart starve."[34] A critic of a 1790 Berlin production was crudely antagonistic: "That Mozart is an *excellent*, a *great* composer, all the world will admit; but whether nothing *greater* had ever been written before him, or would ever be written after him, than this opera under review, we beg leave to doubt. Pedants and pettifoggers may go on measuring, bar by bar, the progressions of notes and the harmonies necessarily resulting therefrom . . . ; but theatrical music knows no other rule, no other judge, than our hearts, and *whether* and *how* it works upon them is what determines its whole value." In sum, "Whim, caprice, pride, but not the heart created *Don Juan*."[35] The same journal described *Le nozze di Figaro,* too, as overly learned and artificial. After the obligatory obeisances to Mozart's "great genius" it suggested that only a few connoisseurs were capable of grasping his thought: "How interesting for those who understand; how grand, how overwhelming, how enchanting the harmony! Is it also for the general public? That is another question."[36] Even Gerber's authoritative *Historisch-biographisches Lexicon der Tonkünstler,* published in 1790, observed that "an unpracticed ear finds it difficult to follow his works. Even more experienced ones have to hear his things several times."[37] Apparently Mozart came to be considered a difficult or radical composer in the wake of his "Haydn" Quartets and Da Ponte operas; the Dresden composer Johann Gottlieb Naumann reportedly even called him "a musical *sans culotte*."[38]

The enormous initial popularity of *Figaro* also may have been more apparent than real, based as it was on delight in its beguiling melodies rather than on an appreciation of its unprecedented advances in dramatic characterization, musical structure, and social commentary. Certainly the first two Da Ponte operas were enthusiastically greeted by the cognoscenti, but they were insufficiently favored by the majority of operagoers, who preferred the more traditional and less demanding products of the Italian composers. Mozart turns up seventh in a recent tabulation of most frequently performed opera composers in Vienna during his years there, and this was not good enough for either his income or his reputation.[39]

Mozart earned a considerable amount for composing *Don Giovanni*—a fee of 100 ducats in Prague, 50 ducats in Vienna from the Burgtheater management, plus perhaps 600 florins in box-office proceeds from one Prague performance for the composer's benefit, as agreed, for a total of as much as 1,275 florins. Nevertheless, the opera did not improve his long-term financial position, for he did not obtain another opera commission until that for *Così fan tutte* in late 1789. It was now more than two years since Mozart had diverted his main energies from the concert hall to the opera stage, but clearly the turn to opera had not solved his career problems. Moreover, the prospect of a profitable sojourn to England was still uncertain, and his publishing income had dropped drastically, from as much as 900 florins in 1785 to as little as 210 florins in 1788. Now, with assured income only from his imperial post and Swieten's Society of Associated Cavaliers, he had to search for new solutions.

Unfortunately, he appears for a time to have lost his entrepreneurial touch. He was unsuccessful with repeated advertisements seeking subscribers for manuscript copies—"finely and correctly written"—of the String Quintets in C minor, K. 406/516b, C, K. 515, and G minor, K. 516, at a price of 4 ducats. It was an embarrassment, perhaps a humiliation, for Mozart to confess publicly in an advertisement of late June 1788: "As the number of subscribers is still very small, I find myself obliged to postpone the publication of my 3 Quintets until 1 January 1789."[40] Probably in a last-minute attempt to earn something over the summer, he began to write at a furious pace, completing the Trio in E, K. 542, the Symphony in E-flat, K. 543, the Sonata in C, K. 545, the Violin Sonata in F, K. 547, and the Adagio and Fugue for string quartet in C minor, K. 546, within a space of a few weeks in June and early July.

Now he scheduled a series of summer concerts, either in the Trattnerhof or in Philipp Otto's new Casino in the Spiegelgasse. Although Mozart enclosed two tickets to these concerts in a letter of early June, saying that they were to begin "next week," it is not certain that they took place, for they have left no other trace—here again, we suffer from the cessation of the Mozart family correspondence.[41] It seems likely that Mozart's last three symphonies, in E-flat, K. 543, in G minor, K. 550, and in C, K. 551, were written for these planned concerts, or as a "portfolio" for the journey to London, or perhaps to serve both purposes. Probably Mozart was hoping to attract audiences with an ambitious new repertory to replace the piano concertos that had formerly been the main staple of his subscription concerts.

The symphonies are dated, respectively, 26 June, 25 July, and 10 August. He also composed several piano trios at closely parallel times: the one in E, K. 542, was entered in his thematic catalog on 22 June, and that in C, K. 548, on 14 July. Perhaps each concert was meant to feature both a symphony and a piano trio: one of Mozart's trios from 1786, such as the Trio in G, K. 496, or the Trio in B-flat, K. 502, might have served as the third in the series; possibly the Trio in G, K. 564, was set aside until late October because the occasion for its earlier performance had disappeared. (The idea of making a symphony one of the centerpieces of an academy seems first to have occurred to Mozart in late 1786, with the "Prague" Symphony, K. 504, which probably was written, along with the Concerto in C, K. 503, for his planned Advent concert series.) Deutsch observes that after the summer of 1788, Mozart neither announced nor presented any more public concerts of his own music in Vienna, nor did he compose any new symphonies or keyboard concertos, except for the Concerto in B-flat, K. 595, of January 1791, which was presented at an academy for the clarinetist Joseph Beer rather than at one of Mozart's own.[42]

In 1786 and 1787 Mozart's income started to come under great pressure: in 1786 he most likely earned only 2,600 florins or so, a drop of 30 percent from 1784. A similar drop was recorded in 1787 but was offset by the 1,000 florins he received as his share of his father's estate. These declines were considerable but still tolerable, given the possibility of instituting economies in the family's expenditures. Mozart was slow, however, to adjust his expenditures to these new income levels: it was not until April 1787 that his family moved from their expensive apartment in the Schulerstrasse to an inexpensive one in the outskirts—Landstrasse 224—at an annual savings of approximately 175 florins. There was an even more precipitous decline in income over the next two years, in 1788 to less than 2,000 florins, and perhaps to as low as 1,400 florins, its lowest level since 1781, representing a decline of almost 66 percent from his best years. His income in the year 1789 was not much better, somewhere between about 1,500 florins and 2,000 florins. An unexpected downturn in commissions, performance opportunities, and publications had sent his earnings into a dizzying downward spiral, so that further economies alone could not solve his difficulties.[43]

The main signs of Mozart's financial embarrassment start to emerge in 1788: he borrowed money and sought further loans; he pawned valuables and within a few weeks even tried to raise additional money on the pawn tickets themselves;[44] he sought to obtain advances from the publisher Franz Anton Hoffmeister and to embark on various speculative ventures. The series of twenty-one letters, starting in June 1788, soliciting loans from a fellow Freemason, the merchant Michael Puchberg, are so dramatic that they have fed a widespread belief that Mozart was actually impoverished in his last years.[45] Indeed, one contemporary wrote, "He is in very straitened circumstances and supports himself by teaching,"[46] and Niemetschek, writing in 1798 from information provided by Constanze Mozart, launched the tenacious legend of Mozart's poverty with the comment, "It is true he had often earned considerable sums, but with an insecure and irregular income, added to the frequent accouchements and lengthy illnesses of his wife in an expensive town like Vienna, Mozart in fact very nearly starved."[47]

Mozart did need money. In the course of his doleful letters to Michael Puchberg, which continued until June 1791, he asked for a total of 4,000 florins and received loans of 1,415, in fifteen piecemeal installments ranging from 10 to 300 florins. According to Puchberg's notations, he sent Mozart 300 florins in 1788, 450 in 1789, 610 in 1790, and 55 in 1791. (When the correspondence began, Mozart still owed Puchberg 36 florins from previous transactions.) Of course, Puchberg was not acting solely out of friendship: he was both a merchant and a banker who lent money for profit and handled banking transactions for others, including Mozart and Haydn.[48] Mozart continually stressed that he did not expect interest-free loans: he asked Puchberg to "assist me for a year or two with one or two thousand florins at a suitable rate of interest";[49] "I shall willingly pay the interest."[50] He even professed unconcern about the rate of interest: "The amount of the sum I shall have to repay is a matter of indifference to me."[51] The loans were reportedly repaid in full, although the circumstances of their repayment remain unclear.[52] Mozart's final letter to Puchberg, asking for "a small sum," and informing him that "in a few days ... you will receive 2,000 florins in my name, from which you can then refund yourself," may imply that in June 1791 the debt was about to be discharged.[53] That might explain why Puchberg's name does not appear on the list of Mozart's creditors after the composer's death.

Mozart borrowed money from others as well, but we have only fragmentary details about these loans. On 2 April 1789 he repaid 100 florins to Franz Hofdemel, who was an official in the Ministry of Justice and was yet another lodge brother who found a profitable sideline as a moneylender.[54] On 1 October 1790 Mozart received a two-year loan from the merchant Heinrich Lackenbacher, in the amount of 1,000 florins, the security to be "all my goods and chattels."[55] Presumably this is the same loan—which Mozart hoped would be for 2,000 florins—mentioned in the letters to his wife from Frankfurt, for which Hoffmeister was to serve as guarantor in exchange for a pledge of rights to Mozart's future publications. (The fact that Hoffmeister would be willing to stand security on so large a sum— 1,000 or 2,000 florins—strongly suggests that Mozart received more substantial income from his publishers than has been suspected.) Lackenbacher, too, does not appear on the list of Mozart's creditors after his death, so he too may have been repaid before then.[56] There are also veiled references to other possible loans, such as "that business which has not been settled" and "my business" in Mozart's letters to Constanze of mid-1791.[57]

The recently discovered minutes of the Lower Austria Court (*Landrecht*) for 9 November 1791 record an execution of a judgment against Mozart for nonpayment of a debt owed to his friend and patron Prince Karl Lichnowsky in the amount of 1,435 florins and 32 kreuzer, along with an order to the imperial court chamber for attachment of half of Mozart's salary as court composer, plus court costs of 24 florins.[58] The nature of the debt is not known, because the main court documents, including the complaint and the testimony, do not survive. Here again, as with Puchberg and Lackenbacher, no claim was made against Mozart's estate, nor was the attachment enforced: the full amount of Mozart's salary for November and December 1791 was paid to his widow. It could be that the judgment was paid by Constanze Mozart out of the proceeds of benefit concerts, the first of which was specifically authorized by the emperor for the purpose of paying her husband's debts.[59] Be that as it may, on the face of it, the Lichnowsky debt seems to represent another loan to Mozart, this time from an aristocratic patron rather than a commercial friend or moneylender.[60] Thus it is amply clear that Mozart had access to a variety of lenders from whom he could, and did, borrow substantial sums.

In addition to trying to make up for the decline in his income, Mozart now had the burden of paying these debts plus substantial amounts of interest. The promissory note to Lackenbacher provided for annual interest of 10 percent, a high rate, but Mozart's letter to Constanze of 8 October 1790 indicated that he was willing to allow the entire two-year interest of 20 percent to be deducted in advance, a standard practice in usury. That he was willing to pay such rates is apparent from a letter to his wife about the Hoffmeister deal. "After deducting interest at the rate of 20%, I shall have 1,600 out of 2,000 florins," he wrote. "I can then pay out 1,000 florins and shall have 600 left. . . . I need never repay the sum, *as I am composing* for Hoffmeister—so everything will be quite in order."[61]

What emerges from the latter transaction is that Mozart was borrowing from Peter to pay Paul. Either he was being pursued for payment by a prior lender or he was trying to replace a loan at an exorbitant rate with one at a more reasonable rate. Naturally, the new lender was not to learn of this, for it would undermine his belief in Mozart's creditworthiness. That is why Mozart explicitly instructed Constanze that in negotiating the loan against Hoffmeister's draft she was not to let the lender know that the money would be used to repay debts: "But you will have to give some other reason; you may say, for example, that I am making some speculation about which you know nothing."[62] With the loan he hoped to pay off a debt of "800 or 1,000 florins" immediately upon his return from Frankfurt.[63] Evidently in Lackenbacher as in Puchberg Mozart had found a lender at a bearable rate of interest, whereas he apparently was forced to pay usurious rates to others because he had little security to offer apart from his fluctuating earning power. That he also was now caught up with pawnbrokers and usurers is evidenced by Constanze Mozart's rueful recollection: "When he wanted to travel to Frankfurt in 1790, and needed money for that purpose, which was tendered to him only at huge interest rates, he suggested to his wife that her silver toilet articles and jewels be pawned."[64] In May of that year he wrote to Puchberg, "As I can find no true friends to help me, I am obliged to resort to money-lenders; but as it takes time to seek out the most Christian among this un-Christian class of people, I am at the moment so destitute that I must beg you . . . to assist me with whatever you can spare."[65] Otto Jahn understood the composer's predicament perfectly, when he wrote that Mozart "had fallen into the hands of usurers, from whom he had striven in vain to free himself by Puchberg's intervention. These facts prove only too clearly that from the time of his marriage Mozart became gradually entangled in a net of embarrassments, without any hope of permanent extrication."[66]

Carl Bär has cautiously estimated Mozart's expenditures for the six years from December 1785 to December 1791 at 11,000 florins.[67] This estimate is surely too low by a substantial margin; it allots far too little for clothing, and altogether omits costs of furniture, keyboard instruments, decorating, moving, entertainment, articles of adornment, a horse and carriage, wine, culinary delicacies, medical expenses, and music copying. Also omitted is the sum of 400 florins per annum for the cost of sending Mozart's son Karl Thomas to a prestigious boarding school.[68] I have estimated Mozart's earnings during those same years at somewhere between 14,315 and 20,140 florins. Assuming Bär's figure to be understated by 50 percent, that would leave Mozart either with a shortfall of some 2,200 florins or a surplus of about 4,600 florins to be applied to his debts and to the cost of accumulated interest, which even at ordinary rates would have placed an extraordinary burden on Mozart's budget. To put this in perspective, the debts eventually could be cleared with 3,000 florins, or so his widow informed Joseph II's successor, Emperor Leopold II, a few weeks after Mozart's death.[69]

Finally, Mozart's economic situation cannot be fully understood without considering the surprising fact that there were occasions when he became a lender instead of a borrower. The balance sheet prepared after his death showed two uncollected loans totaling 800 florins. The first loan, for 300 florins, dated 23 August 1786, was to Franz Anton Gilowsky; the second, for 500 florins, was to the clarinetist Anton Stadler, and probably dates from 1791 (the Clarinet Concerto, K. 622, was written for Stadler in October of that year).[70] We may be sure that this is an incomplete list of loans made by Mozart, for we have managed to learn only about those who defaulted on their loans, not about those who actually repaid them. In light of this, one needs also to consider the possibility that several of the opaque financial allusions in the letters—e.g., those of mid-1791—are actually references to Mozart as a lender rather than borrower.

Mozart's loans to Gilowsky and Stadler have usually been explained away as the foolhardy actions of an innocent soul, as "carelessness," in Braunbehrens's word.[71] "His most dangerous qualities were a good-natured softheartedness, and a spontaneous generosity," wrote Jahn, citing Mozart's loans and assistance to Stadler. "He gave, as it were, involuntarily, from inner necessity . . . All this shows culpable weakness on Mozart's part."[72] Friedrich Rochlitz's influential—and largely invented—"Authentic Anecdotes of Mozart" pictured the composer as negligent in money matters, generous to a fault, a soft touch for friends and musicians in need. Of course, it is true that Mozart often spent money freely: the nonchalance with money that was such a source of friction with his father is mentioned by both Schlichtegroll and Niemetschek, the latter writing, "It is true, he should have been more careful with his money; but is a genius not allowed any weaknesses?"[73] Not surprisingly, Mozart's widow ratified these views—where she was not their source—for she had an interest in exaggerating Mozart's magnanimity, his naïveté about worldly matters, and his insolvency.

Yet it is amply clear that on occasion Mozart himself put his excess funds to work earning interest. This was not altogether unusual in Mozart's family: there are instances of moneylending by Leopold Mozart, by his son-in-law, Berchtold zu Sonnenburg, and even a loan by Constanze Mozart to singer Josepha Duschek of 3,500 florins in 1797, after her fortunes had taken a healthy turn.[74] Clearly Mozart had some capital available in August 1786, when the Gilowsky loan was made, and the loan to Stadler probably signals that by 1791, when his income again exceeded 4,000 florins and he obtained several large sums of money with which to clear many of his own debts, Mozart was once again in a position to become a lender.

Whether as lender or borrower, however, Mozart was always skating on the edge of disaster. Certainly he would continue to wear fine clothing, keep a horse, order multiple pairs of shoes when it suited him, and send his wife to expensive spas and his son to a school for the children of aristocratic and wealthy families. And he would continue to lend money, even when he still owed money to others, and to deal with various shadowy characters whose names were sometimes recorded by the code letters "N.N." for reasons of discretion. When by dint of his prodigious talent and capacity for work he momentarily emerged from debt, there could be no guarantee that he would not slip back into it in relatively short order. He constantly formulated good resolutions. Writing to Constanze from Frankfurt in the autumn of 1790, he made plans to husband their resources, to give concerts, and even to give lessons again: "If I work very hard in Vienna and take pupils, we can live very happily."[75] He had once given similar assurances to his father. Still, despite Mozart's professions of repentance and his promises to devote himself wholly to his work, it seems unlikely that he could ever permanently alter his free-spending and risk-taking nature—for at some level, he was altogether certain that he could always come up with a way of defying the gods and satisfying his creditors.

Mozart's career difficulties and financial embarrassments could not be readily solved as long as Austrian cultural life itself was suffering the consequences of a debilitating and unpopular war against Turkey between early 1788 and 1791. Of course there was at the start the usual rallying around the flag. Mozart himself instantly composed "Ein deutsches Kriegslied" ("A German War Song") with orchestral accompaniment, K. 539, which was sung by the popular actor Friedrich Baumann at the Leopoldstadt Theater on 7 March 1788, a few weeks after the declaration of war. Copies of the score were advertised for sale in the Wiener Zeitung on 19 March 1788 along with a contredanse variously entitled "La Bataille" or "Die Belagerung Belgrads" ("The Siege of Belgrade"), K. 535; the advertisement read: "New Battle-Song ["Neues Kriegslied"] of a German soldier, by Herr Mozart, Kapellmeister in actual service of His Majesty the Emperor."[76] And even as late as the end of 1790 Mozart composed his Adagio and Allegro for mechanical organ, K. 594, in memory of Field Marshal Laudon, a hero of the Turkish War who had died in July.

But the war was not a popular one, and its conclusion in 1791, by Emperor Leopold, was the occasion for considerable relief.[77] The opposition to Joseph II's expansionist adventure was not wholly a matter of principle: the failure to win a decisive early victory was one factor, along with huge war expenditures, bad harvests, and inflation that together threatened the populace with impoverishment. Inevitably these circumstances diminished the expenditures of the wealthy upon luxuries, leading to a drastic curtailment in Vienna's cultural life.[78]

Opera, because of its great cost, was particularly vulnerable; by early February 1788 the German Opera was disbanded, the performances of singspiels at the Kärntnertor Theater were discontinued, and that theater itself was closed until 16 November 1791.[79] Plans to cancel the Italian

Opera as well were sufficiently advanced that most of the performers were given notice in August 1788, but the orders were later rescinded.[80] (The stagnation was far from complete, even in the theater: the Burgtheater remained open and Schikaneder began to present his exotic and comic productions at the suburban Freihaustheater, also called the Theater auf der Wieden, in July 1789.) There was also a precipitous decrease in concert activity in the years 1789 and 1790, both in the concert halls and the private salons (see Table 2, page 434).[81] More generally, the morale of the cultural elite was severely eroded; fears of conscription led many aristocratic families to leave Vienna, and there were widespread feelings of disillusionment with Emperor Joseph, a sense that he had betrayed the promise of his enlightened reform movement. To be sure, the process of disenchantment with Joseph had started several years earlier, with his preemptive strikes against the idealistic wing of his own movement, his institution of harsh criminal penalties, and the aggressiveness of his foreign policy. Now, the sense that Austria's *bon prince* had failed to live up to his own standards as a rational and humane custodian of his people accelerated and began to approach critical mass. To these perceptions was added what was seen as Joseph's failure properly to honor those who pursued the life of the mind. In an acrid pamphlet, the well-known literary figure Joseph Richter wrote in 1787, "The best among our people desire that Emperor Joseph should show more respect for the arts and sciences, because it is humiliating for a nation if its artists have to beg for their bread, and if the writers who have contributed to the enlightenment of the people are suffering deprivation."[82] Like many others, Mozart found himself in the predicament of a beleaguered supporter of Josephinian reform in the declining years of the emperor's reign.

Occasional idyllic moments only served to reinforce the grimness of his situation. On a Sunday afternoon in late August 1788, Constanze's brother-in-law Joseph Lange brought several theater people, including two visiting Danish actors, to see Mozart at home. (According to the tenor Michael Kelly, Mozart had given regular Sunday concerts in earlier years; perhaps he held these now as a way of earning some extra money.) One of the Danes described the visit in his diary:

> There I had the happiest hour of music that has ever fallen to my lot. This small man and great master twice *extemporized* on a *pedal pianoforte,* so wonderfully! so wonderfully! that I quite lost myself. He intertwined the most difficult passages with the most lovely *themes.*—His wife cut quill-pens for the copyist, a pupil composed, a little boy aged four walked about in the garden and sang recitatives—in short, everything that surrounded this splendid man was *musical!* . . . He [now] writes church music in

Table 2. Concerts in Vienna, 1786–91

Year	Public Concerts	Private Concerts	Total
1786	21	13	34
1787	26+	13	39+
1788	24+	13	37+
1789	12	4	16
1790	2	5	7
1791	25	13	38

Source: Mary Sue Morrow, *Concert Life in Haydn's Vienna,*
Appendixes 1 and 2.

Vienna, and as the *Operetta* has closed down, he has nothing to do with the theater [any longer].[83]

Mozart indeed had no current prospects for further work in the theater. The reference to his writing "church music" may have to do with his arrangements of Handel's oratorios for Swieten's Society of Associated Cavaliers, although Tyson observes that several fragmentary mass settings seem to date from 1788 or early 1789 and wonders whether Mozart was perhaps "hoping to obtain an ecclesiastical position."[84] Uncertain as to what route he ought to follow, Mozart was casting about in many directions.

Throughout his life, at critical junctures, Mozart's reaction—engrained, instinctive—was to take to the road. His father had taught him the virtues of being on the move, for a journey was capable of solving everything, of opening up new vistas and opportunities or at least of changing the odds. It was also a way of emerging from restrictions and confinements, of moving from the everyday to the miraculous, of escaping from the drudgery of the familiar into the potential wonders that lay beyond every turning of the road. On the road, Mozart could hope to recapture early glories, to relive the family journeys, to revive in himself the desire to perform, to rediscover somehow the joyous sense of well-being that had once come from belonging to the family organism. Perhaps it was inevitable, then, that any new journey would also be tinged with sadness, especially in the aftermath of his father's death, the "loss" of his sister, and the estrangement from his hometown, Salzburg.

The journeys to Prague in 1787 had left a golden glow in their wake, resonating with a knowledge of fulfilled creativity, new friendships, even a mythologically tinged sense of the conquest of a new city. Furthermore, Mozart had earned more than 2,000 florins there in a single year. Another such journey, and he could simultaneously lift his languishing spirits and keep his family from falling further into debt. Arrangements for a journey to London, where very large sums could be earned, were not yet in place. Meanwhile, there had been talk of another opera commission for Prague; surely it was worth a trip there to confirm that commission. And beyond Prague, Mozart claimed, he now had great prospects in Berlin, and in adjoining Potsdam, where the Prussian court was located.

The Royal Castle in Potsdam. Colored drawing. Reproduced from
Walter Bullert, *Potsdam zur Zeit Friedrichs des Grossen.*

28

....

THE JOURNEY TO BERLIN

On 8 April 1789, the day after he conducted a performance of his arrangement of Handel's *Messiah,* K. 572, at Count Johann Esterházy's palace for Swieten's Society of Associated Cavaliers, Mozart left Vienna for a lengthy journey to Berlin and several neighboring cities in northern Germany, accompanied by his friend, patron, and Masonic brother Prince Karl Lichnowsky. He was to be absent from home for a full two months. It was the first time he and Constanze had been separated since their marriage in August 1782: they had traveled together to Salzburg in 1783 as well as on visits to Prague in January–February 1787 and again in October–November of the same year. From the first post station, he described how he wept as he looked at her portrait: "I write this note with eyes full of tears."[1] The couple had eased the pain of their parting with a collaborative love poem that foretold a joyous reunion; she supplied the closing rhymes, to which Mozart penned the verses, which he entitled, "On the Impending Journey":

> To Berlin I must travel [*Reisen*],
> Hoping there to gain much honor and fame [*Ruhm*].
> But I look down upon all praise [*Preisen*]
> If in its chorus, you, my wife, remain mute [*stumm*].
> When we two meet again, oh, what kissing [*Küssen*],
> Clasping and rapture-filled pleasure [*Lust*]!
> But tears, tears of sorrow are flowing [*fliessen*]
> Now, and sundering both heart and breast [*Brust*].[2]

Traveling by way of Moravian Budweis (Moravské Budějovice), Mozart and Lichnowsky arrived in Prague on the tenth. From there he reported to Constanze on two matters of great import that virtually guaranteed a prosperous outcome to his journey: he had sought out Domenico Guardasoni, who had succeeded Bondini as impresario of the Italian opera in Prague, and had received from him a commitment for a new opera to be presented "next autumn" on most favorable terms—250 ducats (1,125 florins) including travel expenses; it was all "practically arranged," wrote Mozart.[3] Even more exciting, he told her he had received confirmation that King Friedrich Wilhelm II of Prussia not only would welcome him but was anxiously awaiting his arrival in Potsdam. The oboist Friedrich Ramm, who had just come from Berlin, had said to Mozart "that the King had frequently and insistently inquired whether it was certain that I was coming to Berlin, as I had not yet appeared. He had said a second time: 'I fear that he will not come at all.' Ramm became very uneasy and tried to convince him that I really was coming. Judging by this, my affairs ought to be fairly successful."[4] Clearly, Constanze was led to believe, her husband was on the verge of solving all of their problems at a single stroke.

Mozart and Lichnowsky arrived in Dresden on the twelfth, and there Mozart energetically made the usual rounds and spent several productive days. On the thirteenth he gave a private concert at the Hotel de Pologne, featuring his Divertimento in E-flat, K. 563, and arias from *Le nozze di Figaro* and *Don Giovanni* sung by his old friend Josepha Duschek, who happened to be in town at the time. On the fourteenth he performed for Elector Friedrich August III of Saxony and his wife, Amalie, playing the Piano Concerto in D, K. 537 ("Coronation"), and receiving for his efforts "a very handsome snuffbox" that contained 100 ducats.[5] A local newspaper reported, "On 14 April the famous composer Herr *W. A. Mozart* of *Vienna* was heard at the fortepiano by *His Elect. Highness*—furthermore he also played here at *Dresden* in many noble and private houses with boundless success; his agility on the clavier and on the fortepiano is inexpressible— and to this is added an extraordinary ability to read at sight, which truly borders on the incredible. . . . He goes to *Berlin* from here."[6] On the fifteenth Mozart played in an informal competition with the Erfurt organist, Johann Wilhelm Hässler, on the organ of the court church and later on the clavier for the Russian ambassador. But then his pace slowed considerably; he remained in Dresden for three days after his last performance there, departing only on the eighteenth, and then, instead of proceeding the one hundred miles to Potsdam, where the Prussian court was located, he made a seventy-mile detour to Leipzig, which still left him eighty miles from his destination.

He arrived in Leipzig on the twentieth and remained probably until the twenty-third. On 22 April he improvised on the organ at the Thomaskirche in the presence of J. S. Bach's successor, Cantor Friedrich Doles, and the organist Karl Friedrich Görner. A contemporary left an account of this recital:

> On 22 April, without a prior announcement and without payment he permitted everyone to hear him play the organ of the Thomaskirche. For a full hour he played beautifully and artfully for a large audience. The then organist, Görner, and the late Cantor Doles sat alongside him and pulled the stops. I myself saw him, a young modishly dressed man of medium height. Doles was wholly delighted by the performance and declared that . . . the old Sebastian Bach (his teacher) had risen again. With very good grace, and with the greatest agility, Mozart brought to bear all the arts of harmony, improvising magnificently on themes—among others on the chorale, "Jesu meine Zuversicht."[7]

It was probably on this occasion that the choir of the Thomasschule performed Bach's motet, "Singet dem Herrn ein neues Lied," BWV 225, to honor their visitor, and Mozart delightedly examined Bach's autographs, "the parts spread all around him, held in both of his hands, on his knees, and on the adjoining chairs."[8] This is all very good, but it is strange that Mozart would have spent the better part of a week like a gentleman of leisure, extending his stay in Dresden and visiting Leipzig at such a measured pace rather than proceeding to Potsdam, where, as he reported to Constanze, the king of Prussia was looking forward to his visit. And it is all the more puzzling because a court document dated 26 April shows that, far from the king's eagerly awaiting him, Mozart's arrival at court was wholly unexpected:

> One named Motzart (who at his ingress declared himself to be a Kapellmeister from Vienna) reports that he was brought hither in the company of Prince Lichnowsky, that he desired to lay his talents before Your Sovereign Majesty's feet and waited the command whether he may hope that Your Sovereign Majesty will receive him.[9]

The king, supposedly so impatient for Mozart's arrival, did not grant him an audience; instead, he wrote on the document the words, "Directeur du Port," meaning that Mozart was to be referred to the director of chamber music at the Prussian court, the cellist Jean Pierre Duport, for whatever action the latter considered appropriate. On 29 April Mozart completed a set of piano variations on a theme by Duport, K. 573, but, despite this attempt to curry favor, he did not obtain an early royal audience. Mozart claimed to Constanze that he remained in Potsdam for seventeen days, but his activities there are not known.[10] Contrary to his usual practice, he seems to have paid no visits to local musicians, music-lovers, or aristocratic connoisseurs. For almost two weeks following the announcement of Mozart's arrival at court on 26 April, nothing is known about him until his return to Leipzig on 8 May. Indeed, there is nothing to confirm that he actually remained in Potsdam.

Mozart explained to Constanze why he decided to give a public concert in Leipzig after he found himself there in the second week of May. He wrote that he had intended to leave on the very day of his arrival or on the next day: "I was leaving at two o'clock that night; but the insistent requests of my friends persuaded me . . . to give a concert on Tuesday, the 12th."[11] The program of his 12 May concert at the Gewandhaus theater lists several unidentified symphonies, two piano concertos, a piano fantasy (perhaps a free improvisation), and two scenes performed by Mme Duschek.[12] Given on short notice and with inadequate preparation, the concert was poorly attended and many of those who did attend were given free tickets. "From the point of view of applause and glory this concert was absolutely magnificent," wrote Mozart, "but the profits were wretchedly meager."[13] But, if Mozart explained—however feebly—why he presented the Gewandhaus concert once he was in Leipzig, it is hard to fathom why he made this second excursion to that city altogether. He told Constanze, "Lichnowsky alone is to blame for this, for he gave me no peace but insisted on my returning to Leipzig. I shall tell you more about this when we meet."[14] Nor did he adequately explain why, following this financial failure, he did not speed his return to Berlin so that he could recoup his losses but instead remained in Leipzig until 17 May. First he said he didn't want to leave his friends, Johann Leopold Neumann, Frau Neumann, and Mme Duschek, who had come over from Dresden: "The pleasure of being as long as possible in the company of these dear good people . . . has up to the present delayed my journey"; then he said, "I wanted to get away yesterday, but could find no horses. I am having the same difficulty today. For at the present moment everyone is trying to get off and the number of travelers is simply enormous."[15]

On 19 May Mozart returned to Berlin, where he had one last opportunity to vindicate the purposes of the journey. The writer Varnhagen recalled, "In May 1789 he came twice from Leipzig to Berlin. He stayed here at the inn Zur Stadt Paris, in the Brüderstrasse, and played double sonatas with the daughter of the landlady, Dlle. Dacke, later the wife of Privy Councillor Selle."[16] Other reports are less tangible: Mozart may have visited the Berlin music publisher Johann Carl Friedrich Rellstab, who advertised "the complete works of Mozart" in a Berlin newspaper on 9

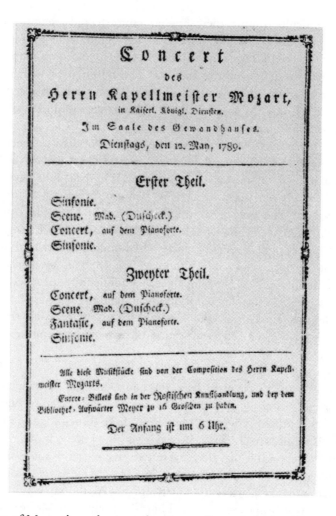

Program of Mozart's academy at the Gewandhaus, Leipzig, 12 May 1789.

May 1789,[17] and, in addition to his rumored presence at a performance of
Die Entführung aus dem Serail on 19 May, he may have attended a concert
by his pupil Hummel on 23 May. But Mozart's aim was not merely to be
seen in public or to play four-hand music with an innkeeper's daughter. He
could scarcely return to Vienna without some tangible confirmation of his
assertion that he had been expected at the Prussian court, and indeed he
now wrote Constanze that he had been summoned to perform for the
Queen on the twenty-sixth, in addition to which he did bring home 100
friedrichs d'or (equivalent to some 800 florins) in cash plus commissions to
write six string quartets for the king and six easy clavier sonatas for
Princess Friederike.

The difficulty is that there are no court records, letters, memoirs, newspaper accounts, or documents of any kind to confirm Mozart's appearance at court, the commissioning of the two sets of works, or the payment to him of any sum of money.[18] The Berlin archivist Ernst Friedlaender, who made a thorough search of the court records a century ago and discovered only the single report of Mozart's arrival in Potsdam on 26 April with its humiliating referral to Duport, commented, "It is astonishing how little concerning Mozart's stay here and in Potsdam has been handed down."[19] The only evidence that Mozart played for the queen is his own statement in a letter written to his wife on 23 April, four days after his arrival, "The Queen wants to hear me play on Tuesday, *but I shan't make much money.*"[20] The only evidence for a payment from the court is his ambiguous reference in the same letter to "the money I shall bring" home. Without specifying its source he writes, "A hundred friedrichs d'or are not nine hundred florins but seven hundred."[21] In 1856 an anonymous memoirist calling himself "an old campaigner" amplified the story, recalling that Mozart received a valuable gold snuffbox containing that sum along with a complimentary letter from the king.[22] Mozart, who would have been delighted to have such solid verification of his statements, makes no mention of either a snuffbox or a letter.

Strictly speaking, Mozart nowhere actually wrote that the hundred friedrichs d'or was a payment from the court, nor did he flatly assert that he had been commissioned to write the sets of quartets and sonatas, merely that he was composing them and hoped to make something from the dedications. Without actually lying, he did give his Masonic brother Puchberg the distinct impression that these were two major commissions from Potsdam: "Meanwhile I am composing six easy clavier sonatas for Princess Friederike and six quartets for the King. . . . At the same time the two dedications will bring me in something."[23] An entry in Mozart's thematic catalog next to the listing of the String Quartet in D, K. 575, reads: "for his Majesty the King of Prussia." But, despite a marked reduction in commissions in 1789 and 1790, it is striking that he abandoned the set by mid-1790 after writing only three of them, K. 575, K. 589, and K. 590, and that, with the possible exception of a G-minor fragment, K. 312/590d, he never even commenced the set of easy sonatas for Princess Friederike. In June 1790 Mozart informed Puchberg: "I have now been forced to give away my quartets (that exhausting labor) for a mere song, simply in order to have cash in hand to meet my present difficulties."[24] When the quartets were published by Artaria a few weeks after Mozart's death, it was without any dedication. Royal commissions were not usually treated so cavalierly.

Unless new documentary evidence emerges, then, it would be prudent to question that Mozart actually performed at the Prussian court or that he received either a substantial sum of money or any commissions from the king. Tyson and Hildesheimer have taught us not to read Mozart's letters—especially those to his father—too literally, but despite such warnings almost everyone has taken the letters he wrote to Constanze from northern Germany at face value. Tyson was worried why the entries in the thematic catalog for the String Quartets, K. 589 and K. 590, made no reference to the King of Prussia, and he suggested that "we must . . . keep an open mind as to whether the King of Prussia had really commissioned six quartets."[25] Now, when we approach these letters with a full measure of suspicion, we see that Tyson's skepticism was warranted. Mozart could scarcely have returned to Vienna empty-handed; he needed the "commissions" to offer some justification for an unnecessary trip to Berlin, to deflect his wife's wrath, and to serve as security for loans from Puchberg. He also needed to borrow a substantial sum of money—say, 100 friedrichs d'or—in order to account for the journey to his wife and creditors. Perhaps Mme Duschek or Lichnowsky, whom he eventually came to owe the sum of 1,400 florins, was good enough to help him out in this pinch. Mozart left Berlin on 28 May; by the thirty-first he was again in Prague, and on 4 June he arrived home. There would be considerable explaining to be done upon his arrival.

At the start of the journey, as was to be expected, Constanze received regular letters from her husband—from Budweis on 8 April, from Prague two days later, from Dresden on the thirteenth and again on the sixteenth of April. His letters are loving, frank, and filled with very detailed descriptions of his activities and encounters and his musical judgments, including his opinions of composers and performers, all related "as minutely as possible."[26] Clearly, he wanted to share his experiences with his wife in a very full way and she expected regular, circumstantial reports from him. Thus, it was all the more disquieting when, following his letter of 16 April, she did not hear from him for a full month. On 16 May, writing to her from Leipzig, Mozart tried to explain what had happened. His explanation was an economical one: he had indeed written to her regularly, but his letters had never been delivered. "God knows what the cause may be!" he exclaimed.[27] He listed four such letters that had somehow gone astray: "I wrote to you from Leipzig on April 22nd, from Potsdam on the 28th, again from Potsdam on May 5th, from Leipzig on the 9th, and now I am writing on the 16th." And he claimed that he in turn did not receive any letters from her between 13 April and 8 May, so that "I spent seventeen days in Potsdam *without any letters*," and was accordingly "very anxious from April 24th until May 8th, and to judge from your letter this was also the time when you were worried."[28] In his letter of 23 May 1789 he again punctiliously listed all the letters he had supposedly sent to her. "Thank God, we shall soon have got over these mischances.

View of the Thomaskirche and Thomasschule, Leipzig. Colored engraving
by Georg Balthasar Probst. Stadtgeschichtliches Museum, Leipzig.

In your arms I shall be able to tell you all, all that I felt at that time. But you
know how I love you."[29]

We do not have any of Constanze Mozart's letters to her husband,
but the improbability that four separate letters, mailed on four different
days from two different cities, could have gone astray, surely did not
escape her, inasmuch as the mails were extremely reliable in those days.
Nor could she have failed to fashion possible scenarios to account for her
husband's silence, his confused explanations, his anomalous journeys to
Leipzig, his extended stays in both Dresden and Leipzig, his failure to
hasten to Potsdam despite the king's supposed keen anticipation of his
arrival, his inability to gain an audience at the Prussian court, his neglect
of concert and other opportunities in Berlin, his failure to account for his
time between 26 April and 8 May, his unnecessary prolongation of his
journey. At best, he had been wildly irresponsible; at worst, he had been
unfaithful to her.

Tradition has linked Mozart with a famous Berlin soprano who was a mis-
tress—though far from the only one—of King Friedrich Wilhelm II of
Prussia. The very first of Rochlitz's "Authentic Anecdotes" describes
Mozart's unheralded appearance at a performance of *Die Entführung aus dem
Serail* (under the title of *Belmont und Constanze*) during his Berlin stay:

Several of the musicians recognized him and the word spread like wildfire through the orchestra and the theater: Mozart is here!—Several of the actors, especially the esteemed singer Madame B, who played "Blonde" (Blondchen), didn't want to come back on stage. This news quickly reached the attention of the music director; in his embarrassment he told Mozart, who had now come up close behind him. In a flash he was in the wings: "Madam," he said to her. "Why do you carry on so? You have sung magnificently, and so that you can do even better another time, I will rehearse the role with you!"[30]

"Madame B" was Henriette Baranius, who took the role of Blonde at that performance and in December 1790 played Zerlina in a Berlin production of *Don Giovanni*.[31] Rochlitz's deadpan hint that she and Mozart became intimate is made explicit decades later by the same anonymous "old campaigner" who had conveniently supplied Mozart with a snuffbox and letter from the king; he reported that when Mozart returned to the theater to apologize for the disturbance and to praise the singers, he became entangled with Madame Baranius, so that it cost his Berlin friends much effort and skill to bring "these hidden and forbidden perfect fifths to a resolution."[32] Jahn believed the story.

However, Mozart did not arrive in Berlin, where Madame Baranius was to be found, until 19 May, the very day of the performance and near the close of his journey—too late to account for the journey's earlier anomalies. Nor does it appear likely that an affair between them could have flamed up at nearby Potsdam in late April or the first week of May, for if that had been the case, he would not then have left the Berlin region on an unnecessary trip to Leipzig—one, moreover, where her presence would have been conspicuous. Thus, chronological discrepancies alone appear to rule out Baranius. Furthermore, inasmuch as Rochlitz was a prolific fabricator of biographical materials about Mozart—and later about Beethoven— there is no certainty that Mozart even attended the performance of *Die Entführung aus dem Serail* in Berlin; he wrote to Constanze from Berlin on the nineteenth and the twenty-third without mentioning any such event, nor was his presence remarked in the review of the 19 May performance in the Weimar *Journal des Luxus und der Moden*.[33]

Baranius can't easily be cast as Mozart's lover, but another famous singer was on hand to fill the bill in the spring of 1789. She is Josepha Duschek (1754–1824), née Hambacher, the wife of Franz Xaver Duschek (1731–99). Formerly her teacher, Duschek was a Prague pianist, teacher, and composer and was twenty-three years her senior. Her name has frequently been romantically linked with Mozart in connection with his visits to Prague.[34] The Duscheks became closely acquainted with the Mozarts in

Salzburg during a visit to Frau Duschek's relatives in 1777—she was the granddaughter of Ignaz Anton von Weiser, the former mayor of Salzburg—and retained close ties to Mozart through the years; they were instrumental in furthering his career in Prague. During her Salzburg visit she participated in a concert at the Tanzmeistersaal at which Mozart and his sister played four-hand music on the harpsichord. As early as September 1777, when Mozart was seeking a post outside Salzburg, the Duscheks offered to help him get established in Prague. "Madame Duschek has replied to my letter," wrote Leopold Mozart to his wife (who was traveling with Mozart), "and tells me that she too has heard of our worries in Salzburg, that they both sympathize very deeply and long to see our merits rewarded and that Wolfgang, who, she supposes, must now be more of a scamp than ever, should come directly or indirectly to Prague, where he will always be given a very warm welcome."[35]

In March 1786 the Duscheks were summoned to Vienna, where she gave several private recitals and an academy at the Burgtheater in the presence of the emperor and the entire nobility; she also appeared at the Hofburg with Mozart, and probably participated in his academy of 7 April.[36] According to Jahn, "She accomplished the most difficult bravura passages with perfect ease, without neglecting the effect of a perfect *portamento;* she united fire and energy with grace and expression—in short, she maintained in every respect her claim to be ranked with the first Italian singers of her time."[37] Leopold Mozart didn't like her vocal style ("She shrieked out an air of [Johann Gottlieb] Naumann's with *exaggerated* expression, just as she used to do, only worse"), her appearance ("She seems to me to show signs of age already; she has rather a fat face, and was very carelessly dressed"), or her morals (he reported that Count Christian Clam was her "declared lover" and "kept her whole establishment").[38] In August 1777 Mozart wrote the Scene "Ah, lo previdi"—"Ah, t'invola agl'occhi, miei," K. 272, for Duschek. Ten years later, during the second journey to Prague, he stayed at the Duscheks' Villa Bertramka in the suburbs, where he finished *Don Giovanni* and composed the Scene "Bella mia fiamma"—"Resta, o cara," K. 528, for her. A Mozart family tradition attaches to the composition of the latter:

> Mozart had promised his friend, Madame Duschek, that he would compose a new concert air for her; as usual, however, he could not be brought to the point of transcribing it. One day she locked him into a summer house on the Weinberg, and declared she would not let him out until he had finished the aria. He set to work at once, but having completed his task, retorted that if she could not sing the song correctly and well at first sight, he would not give it to her.[39]

The paths of Mozart and Duschek were to converge in an extraordinary way during the spring of 1789. Headed north from Vienna, he passed through Prague on 10 April and there, as if by chance, he visited Herr Duschek and discovered, to his great surprise, that Frau Duschek was also on her way to northern Germany: "As my drive took me past the Duscheks', I called there first and was told that Madame had left yesterday for Dresden! So I shall meet her there."[40] Two days later he arrived in Dresden and went directly to the home of Johann Leopold Neumann, a privy councillor of the War Office, with whose family Frau Duschek was staying, "in order to deliver her husband's letter."[41] Mozart described their mutual delight and the accompanying badinage at this unexpected reunion in an out-of-the-way place:

> Her room is on the third floor beside the corridor and from it you can see anyone who is coming to the house. When I arrived at the door, Herr Neumann was already there and asked me to whom he had the honor to speak. "That I shall tell you in a moment," I replied, "but please be so kind as to call Madame Duschek, so that my joke may not be spoilt." But at the same moment Madame Duschek stood before me, for she had recognized me from the window and had said at once: "Why here comes someone who is very like Mozart." Well, we were all delighted.[42]

Mozart thereafter spent much of his time in Dresden with the Neumanns and Madame Duschek—at lunch, at an impromptu private concert at the Hotel de Pologne, and at court where they gave a joint concert for the elector.

Thus, as Mozart tells it, it was merely a fortunate series of chance events that had brought them together. He had happened to pass the Duscheks' house in Prague. There he had learned to his surprise that Frau Duschek was absent, indeed was in Dresden, and it was only natural that he should offer to carry a letter to her there from her husband. And, despite being convinced that the Prussian king was fretfully awaiting him, Mozart had instead decided—without informing his wife—to go to Dresden to visit the elector of Saxony, who was not expecting him and with whom it was notoriously difficult to gain an audience.

Unless Mme Duschek accompanied Mozart on his visits to Leipzig and/or Potsdam, they didn't meet again until early May, in Leipzig; the precise date cannot be ascertained, for he may have left Potsdam to return to Dresden or Leipzig as early as 27 April or as late as 6 May.[43] Certainly he arrived in Leipzig no later than 8 May, in sufficient time to arrange for his 12 May concert at the Gewandhaus, where the noted singer joined him once again. "Madame Duschek, who happens to be in Leipzig, sang" at the concert, he wrote, describing this stroke of good luck.[44] Whether the Neumanns had also come over from Dresden, as Mozart claimed, cannot be confirmed. As we have seen, Mozart then spent an additional four or five days in Leipzig, first because, as he said, he could not bear to be parted from "these dear good people" and then because of the shortage of coach horses.

When he left Berlin on 28 May, Mozart was beset by urgent longings to be reunited with Constanze. Naturally, any extended trip requires stopovers on the way, and since Dresden and Prague are in a direct line between Berlin and Vienna, it is not surprising that he stopped in those cities—the first where Duschek was staying, the second her home. He told Constanze of his intention to stop both in Dresden ("where I shall spend the night") and Prague, which was a hub for travelers to every point of the compass. He asked her to address her letters care of Herr Duschek and

Josepha Duschek, 1796. Engraving by August Claar after a lost oil portrait by Haake. Mozart-Museum der Internationalen Stiftung Mozarteum, Salzburg. © Mozarts Geburtshaus, Salzburg.

wrote, "On June 1st I intend to sleep in Prague."[45] He apparently had some hesitation to tell her that the schedule called for his arrival on 31 May, so that he would actually spend two nights there before taking the carriage to Vienna on 2 June. We do not know whether Josepha Duschek accompanied Mozart on the journey from Dresden to Prague.

All of this, beginning with the tale of the fretful, impatient king—a convenient fable to justify the journey in the first place—suggests that Mozart wanted to leave Vienna in the spring of 1789 to pursue some private agenda. Nevertheless, it is not certain that Mozart was unfaithful to his wife on this occasion. The opacities, lies, coincidences, evasions, disappearances, and mysteries of the Berlin journey may ultimately yield to other explanations—a breakdown, a conflict about returning to Vienna, a momentary impulse to leave Constanze—although these may not be inconsistent with a romantic adventure. We can construct one plausible scenario according to which Mozart, distressed by both family and career circumstances, invented tales of opera commissions from Guardasoni and invitations from the king in order to justify a furlough from Vienna. After his rebuff at Potsdam, however, he found himself unable to deal with the consequences of his prevarications and fell silent instead. He then improvised a Leipzig concert in the vain hope of improving his situation, and eventually decided that the best way out was to fabricate a story of a successful reception at court and to bring home borrowed money as evidence of royal commissions. If this scenario approximates the truth, and even if he was innocent of any infidelity, his actions could surely have given rise to the perception that he had been unfaithful, and that is why the reverberations of his wife's fear that she had indeed been betrayed are not difficult to locate.

If one reads Mozart's letters to Constanze with this in mind, one begins to understand why he so frequently tries to reassure her, not only of his undying affection, but of his ongoing fidelity. He penned a heart-tugging scene of himself alone in his hotel room: "Please remember that every night before going to bed I talk to your portrait for a good half hour and do the same when I awake."[46] From Berlin he chided her for believing that he is neglecting her and he told her of his unquenchable desire for her: "Oh, how glad I shall be to be with you again, my darling! But the first thing I shall do is to take you by your front curls; for how on earth could you think, or even imagine, that I had forgotten you? How could I possibly do so? for even *supposing* such a thing, you will get on the very first night a thorough spanking on your dear little kissable ass, and this you may count upon."[47] A week later, from Berlin, he reassured her that he was leading a solitary existence: "Well, where do you think I am writing this letter? In

my room at the inn? Not at all. In a restaurant in the Tiergarten (in a sum-
mer-house with a lovely view) where I lunched today *all by myself,* in order
to devote myself wholly to you."[48] And then, in a now famous passage, he
described how his body was yearning for her: "I intend to sleep . . . on the
4th—the 4th—with my darling little wife. Arrange your dear sweet nest
very daintily, for my little fellow deserves it indeed, he has really behaved
himself very well and is only longing to possess your sweetest [word oblit-
erated]. Just picture to yourself that rascal; as I write he crawls on to the
table and looks at me questioningly. I, however, box his ears properly—but
the rogue is simply [word obliterated] and now the knave burns only more
fiercely and can hardly be restrained."[49] Sometimes Mozart teased Constanze to allay her concerns about other women; from Dresden he
reported, "There was a large party, consisting entirely of ugly women, who
by their charm, however, made up for their lack of beauty."[50]

Constanze was not reassured, however. In the wake of Mozart's return
from the Berlin journey, she, who had been pregnant since the middle of
February, took ill. His letters to Puchberg in July suggest that he actually
feared she might succumb to illness: "At the moment she is easier, and if
she had not contracted bed-sores, which make her condition most wretched,
she would be able to sleep. The only fear is that the bone may be affected.
She is extraordinarily resigned and awaits recovery or death with true
philosophic calm. My tears flow as I write."[51] In August, on the recommendation of the physician Dr. Thomas Franz Closset, she took the cure at
Baden, and Mozart, in his letters to her from Vienna, expressed his deep
solicitude about her health, mingled with warnings against unseemly conduct on her part. She was unhappy; she doubted his love; she had the
impulse to retaliate against him.

> Dear little wife! I want to talk to you quite frankly. You have no reason
> whatever to be unhappy. You have a husband who loves you and does all
> he possibly can for you. As for your foot, you must just be patient and it
> will surely get well again. I am glad indeed when you have fun—of course
> I am—but I do wish that you would not sometimes make yourself so
> cheap. In my opinion you are too free and easy with N.N. and it was the
> same with N.N., when he was still at Baden. Now please remember that
> N.N. are not half so familiar with other women, whom they perhaps
> know more intimately, as they are with you. Why, N.N., who is usually a
> well-conducted fellow and particularly respectful to women, must have
> been misled by your behavior into writing the most disgusting and most
> impertinent sottises which he put into his letter. A woman must always
> make herself respected, or else people will begin to talk about her. My
> love! Forgive me for being so frank, but my peace of mind demands it as

well as our mutual happiness. Remember that you yourself once admitted to me that you were inclined to *comply too easily*. You know the consequences of that. Remember too the promise you gave to me. Oh, God, do try, my love![52]

Mainly, however, he pleaded with her to put an end to her anguished thoughts about his infidelity: "Be merry and happy and charming to me. Do not torment yourself and me with unnecessary jealousy—have confidence in my love, for surely you have proofs of it."[53] He hoped that by constant reassurance she would be persuaded of his love. Or at least that she would forgive him.

Soon after Mozart's death the press began to circulate intimations of his alleged promiscuity. Scandal sheets like *Der heimliche Botschafter* (*The Secret Messenger*) wrote that "Mozart unfortunately had that indifference to his family circumstances which so often attaches to great minds."[54] Sensational reports guilefully linked notices of Mozart's death with the attempted murder, on the day of Mozart's burial, of Magdalena Hofdemel and the suicide of her jealous husband, his friend and creditor Franz Hofdemel, so that the existence of an affair between Mozart and Frau Hofdemel (who is thought to have been his pupil) was widely believed.[55] There is no reason uncritically to accept journalistic gossip: contemporary newspapers also inflated Mozart's debts to 30,000 florins, many times the true figure. Surprisingly, however, Mozart's family and the authentic biographers who spoke for them confirmed the essence of the reports about Mozart's infidelities. In his careful obituary article, Schlichtegroll was absolutely straightforward: "In Vienna he married Constanza Weber and found in her a good mother for their two children and a worthy wife, who tried to deter him from many follies and debaucheries [*Thorheiten und Ausschweifungen*]," he wrote, adding a blunt reference to Mozart's "overwhelming sensuality and domestic disorder [*überwiegende Sinnlichkeit und häusliche Unordnung*]."[56] The same subject surfaced in Niemetschek's biography, which was written with Constanze's cooperation and represented her standpoint throughout. To establish his bona fides, Niemetschek took strong issue with "malicious stories about the confusion of [Mozart's] financial affairs, his extravagance and such-like defamation of character," and decried "the tainted sources from which flowed so many ugly tales of his frivolity and extravagance."[57] But having thus disassociated himself from Mozart's enemies, he went on to acknowledge that "Mozart was a man, therefore as liable to human failings as anyone else. The very characteristics and strength which were needed for his great talent were also the origin and cause of many a blunder. They brought out inclinations which are not found in ordinary persons."[58] He was the first to say that Constanze forgave her husband: "Mozart was happy in his marriage to Constanze Weber. He found in her a good and loving wife. . . . He loved her dearly, confided everything to her, even his petty sins—and she forgave him with loving kindness and tenderness."[59] Nissen—which is to say, Constanze's surrogate—approvingly used this passage verbatim (although without crediting Niemetschek), adding that she would always say, "One must forgive him, one must make things good for him, because he was so good."[60] Nissen also wrote: "As a man he may have had many weaknesses. . . . He was high-spirited [*Lebenslustig*] and pleasure-seeking, even in his youth."[61]

Less reliable biographers spread similar reports: in 1801 Rochlitz wrote about the "vulgar, disordered and (why not say it outright?) foolish [*Läppische*] aspects of his behavior."[62] Three years later (1804), Suard wrote, "Mozart was tenderly attached to [Constanze]; but that did not prevent him from conceiving a fancy for other women, and his fancies had such a hold over him that he could not resist them."[63] Arnold, in *Mozarts Geist* (1803), a book that Nissen regarded highly but that is primarily an embellished compendium of previously published reports, summed up the general opinion: "He was a husband, brought up two children, . . . and had many intrigues with lively actresses and other women, which his wife good-naturedly overlooked."[64] Clearly, in the absence of fresh material, biographers had taken to copying from one another.

Later writers attached specific names to these reports, in such profusion that, as Jahn rightly observed, Mozart "was credited with intrigues with every pupil he had, and every singer for whom he wrote a song."[65] Joseph Henikstein, a Viennese banker and music-lover whose sister had some lessons from Mozart, told the Novellos, who were gathering information for a projected biography of the composer, "Mozart would not take pains in giving Lessons to any Ladies but those he was in love with."[66] Then there were those rumors of romantic entanglements with such pupils as Josepha Auernhammer and Magdalena Hofdemel. Baranius and Duschek are only two of a long list of singers mentioned in this connection. Such a list must also include a certain Mlle Kaiser, a singer whom he met in Munich in 1777;[67] Anna Storace, the outstanding English soprano who was in Vienna between 1783 and 1786 and for whom Mozart wrote the aria "Ch'io mi scordi di te"—"Non temer, amato bene," K. 505;[68] an unknown singer in Mainz in 1790, for whom he supposedly composed the song "Io ti lascio," K. Anh. 245/621a, even though that song had in reality been composed by Gottfried von Jacquin; Anna Gottlieb, who played Barbarina in *Le nozze di Figaro* in 1786 and became the first Pamina in Mozart's *Zauberflöte* in 1791; Barbara Gerl, née Reisinger, a singer at Schikaneder's Freihaustheater, who played Papagena in the premiere of *Die Zauberflöte*.

And of course Aloysia Lange is never far from center stage. In 1781, upon his arrival in Vienna, Mozart wrote home, "Indeed I loved her truly, and even now I feel that she is not a matter of indifference to me. It is, therefore, a good thing for me that her husband is a jealous fool and lets her go nowhere, so that I seldom have an opportunity of seeing her."[69] As an old lady, she herself was not averse to declaring herself Mozart's eternal beloved: "She told me Mozart always loved her until the day of his death," wrote Mary Novello, "which to speak candidly she fears has occasioned a slight jealousy on the part of her sister."[70]

Rounding out the evidence with reports by less reliable witnesses, Karoline Pichler—who discerned in Mozart and Haydn "no trace of intellectual culture"—wrote of Mozart's "irresponsible way of life,"[71] and an anonymous note in the *Allgemeine Musikalische Zeitung* asserted, "To Mozart's contemporaries it is unfortunately all too well known that only over-exertion at his work, and fast living in ill-chosen company, shortened his precious days!"[72]

In the face of so many unsupported and sometimes contradictory allegations, it is tempting to give Mozart the benefit of every doubt. But individuals who knew him—some intimately, some casually—confirmed the main outlines of the story. His loving sister-in-law, Sophie Haibel, recalled that, "To keep him from intercourse of a hazardous kind his wife patiently took part in everything with him."[73] His pupil Hummel confirmed the stories of Mozart's excesses even as he denied them: "I declare it to be untrue that Mozart abandoned himself to excess, except on those rare occasions on which he was enticed by Schikaneder, which had chiefly to do with *Die Zauberflöte*."[74]

The theme of sin and forgiveness is sounded in several of these accounts. Nevertheless, Constanze did not automatically forgive her husband when he strayed. Jahn learned from one of her sisters that "Constanze was not always so patient, and that there were occasional violent outbreaks."[75] In the aftermath of the journey to Berlin, absolution was not readily given.

To anticipate our chronology somewhat, when Mozart went to Frankfurt in late September 1790, his first journey since Berlin, the still-ailing Constanze did not go with him, but he was not unchaperoned, for he was accompanied by his brother-in-law Franz de Paula Hofer and a servant. He wrote to his wife every few days—on 28 and 30 September, 3, 8, 15, 17, 23 and ca. 28 October, and before 4 November, and all of these letters managed to arrive safely in Vienna.[76] His reassurances have a familiar ring to those who have read his earlier letters to Salzburg; he feels optimistic that he will "make something in this place, but certainly not as much as you and some of my friends expect."[77] He longs to be with her and is overcome by melancholy at their separation: "If you could only look into my heart. . . . There a struggle is going on between my yearning and longing to see and embrace you once more and my desire to bring home a large sum of money," he wrote on 8 October.[78] "I am as excited as a child at the thought of seeing you again";[79] he told her that he wants nothing more than to "stay indoors in my hole of a bedroom and compose . . . but I fear that it will soon come to an end and that I am in for a restless life. Already I am being invited everywhere—and however tiresome it may be to let myself be on view, I see nevertheless how necessary it is. So in God's name I submit to it."[80] Above all, he continued to reassure her of his love, calling himself "your husband, who loves you with all his soul."[81] Still, Constanze was not altogether persuaded, and she reproached him from afar, so that he protested, "I seem to notice that you doubt my punctuality or rather my eagerness to write to you, and this pains me bitterly. Surely you ought to know me better. Good God! Only love me half as much as I love you, and I shall be content."[82] In this he was asking a great deal, for the crisis of the Berlin journey had left their marriage intact but far from contented. Having already lost his original family through death and estrangement, Mozart now has confronted the possibility of losing his new family, a prospect like a glimpse of the abyss. Whatever the compensations he received during those days in northern Germany, Mozart had deprived both himself and his wife of their peace of mind.

29

···

A "CONSTANT SADNESS"

Not long after arriving in Vienna, Mozart, using his considerable verbal gifts to charm her, cadged a fabulous red coat from his indulgent patroness, the Baroness Waldstätten:

> As for the beautiful red coat, which attracts me enormously, please, please let me know *where it is to be had and how much it costs*—for that I have completely forgotten, as I was so captivated by its splendor that I did not take note of its price. I must have a coat like that, for it is one that will really do justice to certain buttons which I have long been hankering after. I saw them once, when I was choosing some for a suit. They were in Brandau's button factory in the Kohlmarkt, opposite the Milano. They are mother-of-pearl with a few white stones round the edge and a fine yellow stone in the center. I should like all my things to be of good quality, genuine and beautiful.[1]

In closing he marveled, "Why is it, I wonder, that those who cannot afford it, would like to spend a fortune on such articles and those who can, do not do so?"[2] The engaging seductiveness of his appeal bore fruit: a few days later he thanked the "Dearest, Best and Loveliest of All, Gilt, Silvered and Sugared, Most Valued and Honored Gracious Lady Baroness!" for promising to satisfy his fancy for the red coat.[3] In return he sent her a rondo, probably K. 382.

Mozart honed his cadging abilities at an early age, for cadging was an essential requisite of the patronage setting in which his early journeys took

Mozart, 1789. Oil portrait by Joseph Lange. Mozart-Museum der Internationalen Stiftung Mozarteum, Salzburg.
© Mozarts Geburtshaus, Salzburg.

place, of which Empress Maria Theresa so heartily disapproved when she wrote of his family that "they go around Europe like beggars." In truth, the Mozarts, however refined the style they affected, knew that in the end they had to cultivate a manner that would encourage high-born music-lovers to maximize their gifts of cash and valuables. Naturally, one did not want to abase oneself in the process: a dignified, amused, even haughty style could be most effective. Surely Mozart, when he eventually took over this role from his father, played it better than most, certainly better than had Leopold Mozart, who was inherently incapable of successfully concealing his contempt for his social superiors.

Mozart's earliest requests for loans from Puchberg are candid and self-confident in tone: "Apart from the fact that at the moment I am not in a position to pay you back this sum, my confidence in you is so boundless that I dare to implore you to help me out with a hundred florins until next week."[4] Soon, as the summer of 1788 progressed, the letters revealed an underlying uneasiness, even anxiety, a tone that Mozart would have liked to suppress, for it could not strengthen his chances. He pleaded: "If you, my most worthy brother, do not help me in this predicament, I shall lose my honor and my *credit,* which of all things I wish to preserve." He told of being overcome by "black thoughts" that he could banish only "by a tremendous effort."[5]

Then, by mid–1789, soon after Mozart returned from Berlin, the tone of his letters to Puchberg took on a frankly desperate character, which continued into 1790. "Great God! I would not wish my worst enemy to be in my present position. And if you, most beloved friend and brother, forsake me, we are altogether lost, *both my unfortunate and blameless self* and my poor sick wife and child."[6] He refers to his "anguish" and expresses regret that he has been "obliged to beg so shamelessly from my only friend. Yet I hope for your forgiveness, for you know both the good *and the bad prospects of my situation.* The bad is temporary; the good will certainly persist, once the momentary evil has been alleviated."[7] Subsequent letters contain an outpouring of woes, fervently related: Mozart tells of his wife's illnesses, implying that she may die; he describes his own feelings of sadness, his illness, his inability to "sleep all night for pain."[8] And then he abandons all pretense of dignity and throws himself upon Puchberg's mercy: "Picture to yourself my condition—ill and consumed by worries and anxieties. Such a state quite definitely prevents me from recovering. . . . Can you not help me out with a trifle? The *smallest* sum would be very welcome just now."[9] From a sophisticated and elegant cadger, Mozart has become an outright wheedler whose need is so great that he is no longer sensible of the degrading implications of the beggar's appeal for small change: "Whatever you can easily spare will be welcome."[10]

The shift in tone from insinuatingly ironic cadging to blatant wheedling signals, of course, that Mozart's economic situation had reached bottom. But it also signals that Mozart had reached bottom in other ways as well, that he was in the grip of a despair that went beyond any need for ducats and florins. It was not money alone that Mozart called for; once again, he was calling for help in the most fundamental form, just as earlier—writing from Paris and then from Vienna—he had vainly called out to his father for love, understanding, and sympathy. The letters are so fraught with abjection and laden with emotion because this music-loving merchant now stood in the position of a father to Mozart: it is Puchberg whom he implores, to whom he explains his plight, whom he promises to repay for his generosity, and from whom he makes impossible demands for excessively large sums, demands that he knows cannot be satisfied. At the same time, by exhibiting the wretchedness of his state Mozart imitates his father, who had described himself as teetering on the edge of ruin in his own obsessively overwrought letters from Salzburg.

In either case, there is in these letters a sharp disparity between their febrile, confessional content and the actuality of Mozart's relationship with his Masonic creditor, who was his elder by fourteen years.[11] They were not intimate friends, but somehow, by virtue of his role as a dispenser of largesse, Michael Puchberg had become invested as an ideal father to whom Mozart could confess his weaknesses and ask for absolution, cry out for help and reveal his hopes without fear of reprisal or recrimination: "I now stand on the threshold of my fortune, but the opportunity will be lost for ever, if this time I cannot make use of it. . . . How delighted I shall be to discharge my debts to you! How glad I shall be to thank you and, in addition, to confess myself eternally your debtor! . . . In short!—my whole future happiness is in your hands. Act according to the dictates of your noble heart!"[12] On this letter Puchberg entered the simple notation "150 florins." From Puchberg Mozart received the tokens of comprehension and acceptance that his father had been unable freely to provide.

Beginning in 1787, Mozart had exerted every effort and utilized every possible strategy to ward off the looming crisis in his affairs. He had obtained an imperial post by making known his plans to leave Vienna permanently, he had become the music director of the Society of Associated Cavaliers, and he had succeeded for a full year in making Prague a major second source of income. Feeling the need to alter his direction as a composer, he wrote an ambitious opera that stretched the boundaries of the genre, and he infused the symphony with unheralded rhetorical content in the hope that it might substitute for the piano concerto as the staple of his subscription concerts. Growing increasingly desperate, he had borrowed money, pawned his silver plate, applied for new positions, sought out potential patrons, and even experimented with the possibility of resuming the composition of church music. Once again he had taken to the road, put himself on display as a virtuoso performer. He had accepted every commission, worked so hard, almost incessantly.

Despite these efforts, by early 1789 he had reached an impasse. He had no workable ideas for resolving his difficulties, and he opted instead for a restorative journey to north Germany that was half fantasy or more, a detour intended to give him breathing space and some relief from oppressive realities and family obligations. Upon his return the crisis had gotten out of control. By his flight he had placed serious strains upon the fabric of his marriage. His wife was pregnant, beset by jealousy, seriously ill, and requiring extended stays in expensive spas to restore her to health. Although economies were instituted, he still was living well beyond his means and was unable to pay off his debts.

With the failure of the Berlin journey the downward spiral intensified, striking now at his state of mind. "For some time you must have noticed my constant sadness," he wrote to Puchberg in early spring of 1790.[13] He had an ominous sense of an oppressive void within him. "If people could see into my heart," he wrote to Constanze from Frankfurt in September of the same year, "I should almost feel ashamed. To me everything is cold—cold as ice. Perhaps if you were with me I might possibly take more pleasure in the kindness of those I meet here. But, as it is, everything seems so empty."[14] His sister-in-law Sophie Haibel described the play of shifting affective states in him, his growing abstraction, implying that he had fallen into a state of melancholia: "He was always good-humored, but even at his most good-humored he was very pensive, looking one straight in the eye the while, pondering his answer to any question, whether it be gay or grave, and yet he seemed the while to be working away deep in thought at something quite different. Even when he was washing his hands when he rose in the morning, he walked up and down in the room the while, never standing still, tapped one heel against the other the while and was always deep in thought."[15] She had the feeling that he was removed from his surroundings, withdrawn into a private world: "At table he often took the corner of a napkin, crumpled it up tightly, rubbed it round below his nose, and seemed in his reflections to know nothing of what he was doing, and often he would grimace with his mouth the while."[16] Niemetschek observed that Mozart's "glance was unsteady and absent-minded, except when he was seated at the piano; then his whole face changed. A concentrated and serious look would come into his eyes."[17]

His actions and demeanor evidently now struck observers as verging on eccentricity. Constanze Mozart said that "he would greet acquaintances in the street with a finger to his lips, whispering sshh! and then doggedly move on," and she tried to explain away this singular conduct as a reflexive action carried over from when she had been ill and required hushed surroundings.[18] Elsewhere she described her husband's abstraction as the result of his preoccupation with his music: even when he played billiards or spoke with friends, "He always was at work in his mind," a "habit which evidently wore out the system."[19] Aloysia Lange's husband, Joseph, who knew Mozart intimately and was not one to be shocked by his antic moods, wrote that he often "spoke confusedly and disconnectedly" and "occasionally made jests of a nature which one did not expect of him, indeed he even deliberately forgot himself in his behavior."[20] Mozart himself began to feel that his friends had withdrawn from him, writing bitterly to Constanze from Frankfurt, "Give my greetings to the few friends who wish me well."[21] It seems clear that Mozart was now deep within a despondent condition from which he could not easily emerge.

A series of circumstances had converged to exert enormous pressure upon Mozart's defenses, undermining his adaptive abilities and for a time overwhelming his capacity to withstand the assaults of adversity. In 1787 death had taken from him his friends Count August Hatzfeld and Sigmund Barisani in rapid succession. Mozart was profoundly affected by these losses, describing each of them separately as his best and dearest friends ("liebster bester Freund"). Of Hatzfeld he wrote, "He was thirty-one—just my age. I do not mourn for *him,* but for myself and for all those who knew him as I did."[22] On the day of Barisani's death Mozart turned the pages of his souvenir album, found his friend's entry, and wrote beneath it, "Today, 3 September of this same year, I was so unfortunate as quite unexpectedly to lose by death this noble man, dearest, best of friends and preserver of my life."[23] The most painful loss was the death of his father on 28 May, an event sufficiently devastating in itself but whose impact was greatly magnified because it followed so closely on Leopold's crushing rejection of Mozart's children. And then, by virtue of the testamentary disclosures, Mozart suffered the further blow of receiving an unsatisfactory share of his father's estate, which in turn sealed his estrangement from his sister. All in all, the process of mourning for his father was permeated by a sense of helpless anger and disappointment. In his last letters to his sister, Mozart tried to conceal his hurt by affecting a distanced, offhand manner, trying to suggest that he was both unconcerned and untouched. But it did matter. Mozart had already achieved everything he had dreamed of—fame, family, love, friendship, a sense of being part of the social fabric, the knowledge that his creativity was unmatched, even the promise of immortality—and in the end these were not sufficient to counterbalance the loss of the family into which he had been born. Without its love and approval, he was not whole. And now he had to endure what appeared to be the certain knowledge that his father had died still resentful and unforgiving, that his sister regarded him as a traitor to the family ideal, that their repudiation of him and his wife and children was irrevocable.

Mozart could not know the unmistakable signs of Leopold Mozart's desperate longing for his son that fill his letters to Marianne, however grudgingly he gives voice to them. He could not know with what delight his father had recorded in one of those letters Haydn's description of Mozart as the greatest of all living composers. He could not know the eagerness and pride—and surely the sense of awe—with which his father studied each of his latest compositions, with never a word of criticism. And especially, he could not know that Leopold Mozart was utterly helpless to act differently, for he could not hold down the impulse to repeat his own mother's refusal to forgive him. In the end, a father and a son, trembling within a conflicting welter of disquieting emotions, weighed the compensations of their respective rebellions, wondered if they could have acted otherwise, tried to conceal their wounds, and were powerless to change course.

The fountain of financial and popular successes had begun to run dry. The relatively unalloyed adulation of his early Vienna years was encountering the powerful resistance of conservative critics and conventional music-lovers to Mozart's momentous mid-decade works, works that made unprecedented emotional and intellectual demands upon audiences. Just as Beethoven was later beset with complaints about the supposedly "bizarre" qualities of his music, Mozart was now charged with excess, caprice, and especially of composing only for an elite group of "connoisseurs." It was a charge with which he was familiar from earlier exchanges with his father, who once wrote, "If you compose something which is to be engraved, make it easy, suitable for amateurs and popular."[24] But in his hubris Mozart now actually chose to stress the rigorous, challenging aspects of his Vienna compositions, proudly introducing the engraved edition of his "Haydn" Quartets as "the fruit of a long and laborious labor" and referring to "compositions which I keep for myself or for a small circle of music-lovers and connoisseurs (who promise not to let them out of their hands)."[25] Experimental and learned styles were not previously unknown or unappreciated, especially in the Viennese string quartet, but Mozart had now dramatically enlarged the arena of experimentation and simultaneously raised the stakes, achieving what Warren Kirkendale calls the "most fruitful innovation in the history of fugue" through a "merger of fugato and sonata form" in such works as the G-major String Quartet, K. 387, the "Jupiter" Symphony, and the overture to *Le nozze di Figaro;* and a marriage of fugato and rondo form in such works as the Piano Concerto in F, K. 459, *Ein musikalischer Spass* (*A Musical Joke*), K. 522, and the String Quintets in D, K. 593, and E-flat, K. 614.[26] Beethoven understood the momentousness of the challenge that Mozart had laid down; he told his young pupil Carl Czerny that in the String Quartet, K. 464, which achieves a profound fusion of chromatic textures, contrapuntal techniques, and the sonata forms, "Mozart was telling the world: 'Look what I could do if you were ready for it!'"[27]

Clearly, in the flush of his success Mozart had no need for compromises, no inclination to accept impediments to the unhindered expression of his creativity. He had long been in full flight from the meretricious, from the circus atmosphere, the superficial virtuosity, the covered keyboards and the simple-minded musical fare of his childhood concert tours. Now he was a self-conscious artist, persuaded of his mission, who never again wanted to waste his gifts. It is worth repeating the imperious statement he made to his father from Mannheim in 1778: "I am a composer and was born to be a kapellmeister. I neither can nor ought to bury the talent for composition with which God in his goodness has so richly endowed me."[28]

As the decade of the 1780s wore on Mozart devoted himself largely to highly ambitious works, apart from the dances for the Redoutensaal required as a condition of his imperial employment, and with only rare additional exceptions. Even in a time of financial need, he appeared reluctant to fall back upon the popular genres of composition—sets of variations, sonatas, instrumental concertos, serenades, divertimentos—nor did he resort to writing facile keyboard or chamber music for the omnivorous market of musical amateurs. He well knew that by so doing he could have eased his situation. That is why he claimed to be writing a set of "easy clavier sonatas" for Princess Friederike; that is why he deferentially wrote a set of ornamental variations for Duport at Potsdam. He could shake such pieces out of his sleeve when he wished, but now he did not choose to do so. He had no objection to—and sometimes delighted in—writing such works for himself, for his friends or fellow artists, or even for the market, so long as no compulsion was involved. But when he did yield to the necessity of writing trivialities solely because he needed the money, it was with deep resentment. That is the plain meaning of "Too much for what I do, too little for what I could do," his contemptuous reference to his remuneration for the dances that he wrote so prolifically for the Redoutensaal. It was a matter of great discouragement that at the end of 1790 he was reduced to writing a work he despised ("It is a kind of composition which I detest") for an unsatisfactory instrument (a mechanical organ), simply so that he could "slip a few ducats into the hand of my dear little wife."[29] But even here he apparently determined to make the most of the task, refusing to allow the mediocrity of the occasion to limit the quality of his Adagio and Allegro in F minor, K. 594.

The issue of Mozart's unfettered creativity had always been surrounded by prohibitions. Now, a segment of his audience had turned away, disapprovingly; it was as though he were being struck down for violating old taboos or simply for being a superior child. To move from the psychological to a larger frame, it was as though a nostalgia for sobriety, order, and decorum—for a narrowly defined and conservative "classicism"—was beginning to overtake some members of Europe's elite audiences in the later 1780s, even as disintegrative and eruptive historical forces moved to threaten the social fabric.

In fact, the decline in Mozart's popularity was only temporary and involved the inevitable backlash against the almost unqualified acceptance of his music in the years up to about 1786. Growing numbers of music-lovers—and not only the connoisseurs—were and remained Mozart's faithful adherents. His music was now circulating via performances and publications throughout Europe, especially in German-speaking regions and in France, where his works were frequently listed on the programs of the Concert Spirituel. Even with caveats and critical reservations, his reputation as one of the foremost composers had been firmly established.

The later 1780s really were for him a period of consolidation, during which the splendors, challenges, and sometimes unbearable beauties of his works were being confronted and assimilated. This was not an easy process, even for sensitive or professional musicians, for whom Mozart's music was somehow profoundly disturbing in ways that could not be quite explained. "Mozart is unquestionably a great original genius," wrote Dittersdorf, "and I know of no composer who possesses such an astonishing wealth of ideas. I only wish he were a little less prodigal of them. He gives his hearers no time to breathe; as soon as one beautiful idea is grasped, it is succeeded by another and a finer one, which drives the first from the mind; and so it goes on, until at the end not one of these beauties remains in the memory."[30] Audiences needed a little more time to come to terms with Mozart, and indeed within only two or three years Europe was gripped by an extraordinary Mozart enthusiasm, the start of which he was still able to witness.

Nevertheless, while Mozart was in the downturn of his career he could not safely predict that he would soon emerge from it and its attendant distress. Mourning for friends and father, deeply concerned over his wife's illness, under great pressure to earn money to support an expensive lifestyle, subject to increasing tensions within his marriage, fissures began to develop in his defenses. Work had always been Mozart's most effective counterweight to sadness or external vicissitudes. And indeed, 1788 saw a flood of major compositions with which he aimed to solve his career problems. But after this most bountiful of his Vienna years, the crisis began to undermine Mozart's productivity itself.

During the closing months of 1788 Mozart wrote few works: the Divertimento for string trio in E-flat, K. 563, in September, was a token of gratitude for Michael Puchberg; the arrangement of Handel's *Acis and Galatea,* K. 566, was completed in November for Swieten's Society of Associated Cavaliers; over the winter, he furnished two dozen dances for the Redoutensaal, consisting of two sets of German Dances for orchestra, K. 567 and K. 571, and twelve Minuets for orchestra, K. 568. The Piano Sonata in B-flat, K. 570, in February and the arrangement of Handel's *Messiah* totally cleared Mozart's desk of work in progress before his departure for Berlin. At first it might have appeared that Mozart was simply experiencing an expectable letdown in productivity following the long sustained creative surge that had climaxed in the summer of 1788 with the three last symphonies. It also seemed only natural that there should be some decline, in view of the paucity of commissions or performance prospects to spur him to composition.

Even allowing for the distractions of the Berlin journey, however, he composed almost nothing of note between February and June 1789. After his return from Berlin in May his creativity stirred once again, so that by summer's end he had to his credit, if not a large number of works, at least several distinguished ones: the String Quartet in D, K. 575, the Piano Sonata in D, K. 576, and the Clarinet Quintet in A, K. 581, the last of which was entered in the thematic catalog on 19 September. He also wrote six assorted arias: several replacement arias, K. 577 and K. 579, for Adriana Ferrarese del Bene as Susanna in the revival of *Le nozze di Figaro* at the Burgtheater on 29 August; three insertion arias, K. 578, K. 582–83, for the soprano Louise Villeneuve's appearances in revivals of operas by Cimarosa and Martín y Soler; and one, "Schon lacht der holde Frühling," K. 580, for Josepha Hofer's role in an aborted revival of Paisiello's *Il barbiere di Siviglia.* Major projects were scarce. Fortunately, the revival of *Le nozze di Figaro* was a great success, sufficient, perhaps, to spur the commissioning from him of a new opera for the coming carnival season. Thus, for two or even three months the emperor's chamber composer was occupied, not only with the two dozen orchestral Minuets and German Dances, K. 585–86, required for the forthcoming carnival balls, but with *Così fan tutte,* the third and last of his Da Ponte operas, which was rehearsed on New Year's Eve and given its premiere at the Burgtheater on 26 January 1790. If evidence were required that Mozart was not out of official favor at this time, the commission of *Così fan tutte* and its favorable reception would be sufficient proof: the opera achieved its fifth performance by 11 February and reached ten during 1790.

Following *Così fan tutte,* however, Mozart's faltering productivity virtually collapsed. During the remainder of 1790 he entered only a handful of compositions into his thematic catalog: the Quartet in B-flat, K. 589, in May; the Quartet in F, K. 590, in June; arrangements of Handel's *Ode for St. Cecilia's Day* and *Alexander's Feast,* K. 592 and K. 591, in July; the String Quintet in D, K. 593, along with the Adagio and Allegro in F minor, K. 594, in December. To this list we can now add three newly discovered Masonic songs that were written in June, evidently his first Masonic music in four years.[31] Nothing at all was entered for the three months February through April or the four months August through November. He needed to work in order to earn money, but, he said, he found it difficult to work because he was not free from care. In May 1790 he wrote to Puchberg, "If only I had in hand 600 florins at least I should be able to compose with a fairly easy mind. And ah! I must have peace of mind."[32] Never before in his adult life had Mozart's productivity been so attenuated. It is worth noting that even during this, his most unproductive period, he continued to write music—the second and third "Prussian" Quartets, the D-major String Quintet—that was arguably only for an elite audience. In part this was because he now was relying wholly upon connoisseurs to support concerts at his home, which may have become a significant source of income. But it is also as though he had come to feel that the greater risk was the loss of his musical integrity, for this was the core of his selfhood. The issues were momentous ones that were not susceptible of easy resolution. It remained open whether this would be a temporary hiatus or a stage in a deepening descent into silence.

Thus, in the year and a half between the journey to Berlin and the end of 1790 the deterioration in Mozart's circumstances accelerated and came perilously close to something approaching a total breakdown involving his family, his finances, his career, and his productivity, leaving him in a state of dejection, anxiety, and partial creative paralysis. Ironically, in the end he had apparently succeeded in belatedly fulfilling his father's worst forecasts, shown himself to be irresponsible, negligent, wasteful, mendacious, unproductive, morally delinquent, incapable of properly managing either his household or his business affairs. In these years, desolated at being sundered from his father, guilt-ridden at having rejected him, Mozart—by wasting his money, his body, and his creative powers—seemed to have set out to prove that he was, after all, an eternal child.

That this might have had a self-punitive aspect goes without saying, for Mozart believed he had many things to atone for, especially his offenses against the Mozart family compact. But the issues went far beyond self-punishment: in fulfilling these old prophesies he was also resurrecting his father, not only so that he might fill the void left by Leopold's death but so that he could continue the contest between them. He was acting to restore the dynamic of nihilistic rebellion, exposure, shame, remorse, and submission. Perhaps, too, he sinned because, beyond all else, he was still in search of forgiveness.

Leopold Mozart was dead, but the struggle continued, except that its battleground was now located within the confines of Mozart's mind. It continued, and not only as an attempt to settle old differences retroactively by analysis and reflection. Rather, it was perpetuated in the present, white hot, as Mozart now warred against himself. Thus, he simultaneously assumed the roles of the righteous, censorious father whose stance has been vindicated and of the rebellious son still railing against injustice, demanding independence, and, reckless of the patricidal implications, needing to hammer home the evidence of his achievements. Riven by a variety of self-doubts and ambivalent conflicts, he also became the quiescent, self-reproaching son, persuaded that his father had been right all along; Leopold was even renovated as the benevolent ideal father of the early days and European journeys, utterly devoted to his son's welfare, a nurturing figure who brings both knowledge and beauty to a boy with an infinite hunger for both.

It may well have been the overpowering consciousness of what he owed to his father that made it so difficult for Mozart truly to savor the fruits of his creativity. After his flight to Vienna, each of Mozart's achievements unavoidably was pervaded by a painful sense that it had been purchased at his father's expense; every evidence of his genius, his acclaim, and his business acumen carried a tacit reproach to his father, underscored the old man's decline at the same time that it confirmed their alienation from one another and the permanence of their separation. Mozart's descent into melancholia may have to do with the immensity of his self-reproaches at having permitted himself to accomplish those things of which his father was incapable. It is as though he were perpetually asking himself why he should be permitted to take pleasure in anything that his father could not share in. Thus, because his achievements contained an admixture of contest and triumph, Mozart may inwardly have disavowed his right to rejoice in them, unable fully to taste the delights that his music, his marriage, and his friendships ought to have brought to him. Every joy was undermined by the sad knowledge that his father—to whom he owed everything—was excluded from it. Mozart knew the depth of his father's suffering and wanted somehow to assuage it: but in the end he could do so only by joining his father in suffering, by bringing suffering upon himself.

This penchant for suffering, this blighting of his potential to accept happiness, is but a special case—the most extreme one—of Mozart's impulse to merge with his father. Throughout his life Mozart took his father's role, emulating him, playing the little papa, echoing and parroting his attitudes. We have already quoted from his very first preserved letter, in which as a thirteen-year-old he gave virtuous, fatherly advice to a young girl, and we have seen how, later on, he taught Aloysia Weber principles of musical taste and feeling, and urged her to follow his very sound advice in all matters.[33] After his marriage there were familiar paternal cadences as he obsessively warned Constanze to guard her health and virtue:

> Dear little wife, I have a number of requests to make. I beg you
> (1) not to be melancholy.
> (2) *to take care of your health and to beware of the spring breezes.*
> (3) not to go out walking alone—and preferably not to *go out walking at all,*
> (4) to feel absolutely assured of my love. . . .
> (5) I beg you in your conduct not only to be careful of *your honor and mine,* but also to consider *appearances.* Do not be angry with me for asking this. You ought to love me even more for thus valuing our honor.[34]

We hear Leopold Mozart's voice also in Mozart's travel commentary, in his advice on medications, in his aesthetic ideas and observations on music and musicians, and in the mock-edifying banalities of the Zoroastran proverbs.

In fine, one suspects that Leopold Mozart's image had taken up residence within his son's mind, where the struggle for possession of Mozart's ego continued, but now as a contest within divided aspects of himself.[35] If in earlier days Mozart had freely taken into himself crucial aspects of the personality and attitudes of his father, after Leopold's death this introjection took on a darker, more ominous character. The grotesque scrounging (a caricature of the self-abasing beggar-father), the dread of betrayal, and the melancholia were the dark shadows that his dead father cast upon Mozart's ego. One part of Mozart's self had, defensively, fused with his father—imitating him, adopting his values, speaking in his voice. But to become host to his father's persona, with its seams of jealousy, mistrustfulness, and misogyny was to undermine the values—love, altruism, trust, a belief in beauty, a resistance to the commodification of music—that had kept Mozart's being intact.

If this sketch of a psychoanalytical reconstruction has any validity, it may follow that the split in Mozart's psyche eventually became intolerable. He wanted to rid himself of the intruder, but he also yearned to keep him inside, so as to undo his death. Part of him wanted to destroy his tormentor, another part wanted to be an obedient son, fetching and carrying, continuing to work in the service of God's deputy. Out of deference to power, the ill-used child turns to his persecutor for protection, at once fearing and worshipping that which can give both pain and pleasure. Or perhaps the child still cherishes the hope of a benevolent transformation, cleaves to the hope of a happy outcome.

Striving to expel the deeply rooted residues of his father's character and values, Mozart had the impossible task of trying somehow to rid himself of a malignant intruder without simultaneously annihilating himself. The repudiation would always remain incomplete, I suspect, because his identification with Leopold Mozart had always supported his sense of worth and mission. Moreover, there remained a good alternative to the annihilating contest—at last to find an accommodation, to rediscover the loving father within Leopold Mozart, to understand the reasons for his father's own pain, thereby to know that he had never been the true source of that agony, and to offer him forgiveness while finally forgiving himself. It is doubtful that Mozart could wholly achieve such an accommodation. And the strains of the effort took their toll on him in the closing years of his brief life.

There may be a more economical explanation for Mozart's depression and the breakdown of his creativity. His flight to Prussia in 1789 suggests that he was trying to escape from responsibilities that had become too onerous for him. His subsequent surrender to melancholia may be seen as a different kind of flight, an inward one, but one with the same purpose: to lay down the burden he had carried for so long. Having cared for others all his life, now he, at last, wanted to be cared for, to be a needy child. This more direct explanation does not necessarily exclude our earlier speculations, for in giving way to depression and in crying out for care Mozart did what his father had always freely done. Even Mozart's melancholia was a way of merging with his melancholic father.

In a sense, the clearest illustration of Mozart's dilemma is that he could resolve the issues neither by rebellion nor by submission. To maintain the status quo was to continue in fantasy Leopold Mozart's posthumous dominion. But to protest against the hardship of remaining always the family provider was to rebel against his own creativity. Unable to resolve such dilemmas, Mozart was now caught within a downward spiral in which a melancholic state of mind intertwined with a failure of productivity, the two trends reinforcing one another so powerfully that it seemed possible he would sink into a permanent condition of lethargy.

Weakened and shaken as he was, Mozart nevertheless was resolved to survive for the sake of his family and of his art, crying out to Puchberg for assistance, tearfully assuring his wife of his determination to work, formulating plans to extricate himself from his impasse. He tried to make the most of what little he composed. In May he led performances at his home of the first two "Prussian" quartets, and he informed Puchberg he was thinking of giving "subscription concerts at home during the three months of June, July, and August," perhaps intending to feature the three "Prussian" quartets as the nucleus of those concerts. These evidently were never given, for to Constanze he voiced a similar plan to give "quartet subscription concerts" at Advent.[36] On 12 June he conducted a performance of *Così fan tutte* at the Burgtheater, and his latest Handel arrangements were completed during the summer, probably so that he could perform them following his return from a journey to Frankfurt in the fall. For he had now worked out another restorative itinerary, one that was planned to coincide with the coronation of a new emperor. Although the main purpose of the journey was economic, it served the larger purpose of stirring Mozart to gather his inner forces and regain his creativity.

The death of Emperor Joseph II on 20 February 1790 deprived Mozart of his most significant patron and introduced a note of uncertainty as to his future prospects in Vienna. Yet it also opened up new opportunities, for Joseph's successor, Leopold II, the former grand duke of Tuscany, made numerous personnel changes to suit his very different tastes in music and theater. Within a few weeks after Leopold II's accession on 13 March, Mozart applied to Archduke Franz for the position of second kapellmeister, holding himself out as better suited for that post than Antonio Salieri, who, though a "very gifted kapellmeister, has never devoted himself to church music, whereas from my youth up I have made myself completely familiar with this style."[37] (Clearly, it was understood that Leopold II intended to revoke his predecessor's restrictions on church music.) In the same petition Mozart suggested that he be "entrusted with the musical education of the Royal Family," to teach music to the imperial princes. Despite his "great hopes of an appointment,"[38] Mozart did not obtain either of these positions, and he seems to have lost some ground at the imperial court, for— unlike Salieri, Weigl, Haydn, and others—he was not invited to participate in the great festivities held in September in Vienna to celebrate two royal weddings, of the Archdukes Franz and Ferdinand to the daughters of King Ferdinand of Naples. Perhaps his application for Salieri's post had been indiscreet, earning him some enmity among those in a position to affect his employment. Or perhaps the court had heard rumors of his financial and personal straits and was reluctant to extend its commitment to him beyond his existing post. He cautioned Puchberg: "You know how my present circumstances, were they to become known, would damage the chances of my application to the court, and how necessary it is that they should remain a secret; for unfortunately at court they do not judge by circumstances, but solely by appearances."[39]

Nor was Mozart among the imperial musicians who were asked to

Römerburgplatz, Frankfurt. Engraving by Delkeskamp.

accompany the emperor to Frankfurt for his coronation there on 9 October. In the absence of other performance opportunities, however, and perhaps piqued at having been slighted, he decided to travel to Frankfurt on his own, calculating that good money could be earned there while the city was crowded with sightseers. As the composer Ignaz von Seyfried later recalled, Mozart "visited the Frankfurt coronation on his own initiative, to give concerts in order to stop the little hole which kept draining his chaotic finances."[40] He lodged inexpensively, for only 30 florins per month, with the impresario Johann Böhm, whom we remember from Salzburg days and who was now director of the electoral theater at Trier. Once again, though, Mozart had miscalculated his chances. On 15 October, aided by Countess Hatzfeld and other local admirers, he presented a major concert at the Great Municipal Playhouse that featured the Piano Concertos in F, K. 459, and D, K. 537, an unidentified symphony, some arias sung by Margareta Louise Schick and the Salzburg castrato Francesco Cecarelli, and "a Fantasy improvised by Herr Mozart," according to the program.[41] Unfortunately the concert was only sparsely attended, and a second concert planned for the seventeenth did not materialize. "It was a splendid success from the point of view of honor and glory, but a failure as far as money was concerned," Mozart wrote home, blaming the difficulties on rival distractions—"Some Prince was giving a big déjeuner and the Hessian troops were holding a grand maneuver. But in any case some obstacle has arisen on every day during my stay here."[42] Better scheduling might have avoided these conflicts, but

Mozart's flair as an impresario was no longer fully in evidence. A performance of *Don Giovanni* was to have been given in his honor on 5 October, but at the last minute the theater company substituted an opera by Dittersdorf. The disappointment was partly made up by a performance of *Die Entführung aus dem Serail* on 12 October by Böhm's company.

Mozart left Frankfurt on the sixteenth for a five-day stay in Mainz, where he participated in several private performances and, on the twentieth, performed at the electoral palace for Elector Friedrich Karl Joseph von Erthal and Franz de Paula Gundaccar Prince Colloredo and his wife and sons, who were reported to have been highly satisfied. Writing to Constanze, Mozart called the elector's payment of 15 carolins (equivalent to 165 florins) a "meager sum," but there was nothing to be done about it except to hope for better fortune as he reversed directions and began the journey home.[43] On 23 October he arrived in Mannheim, where he was reunited with many old friends and where he was present at the first performance of *Figaro* in German translation on the twenty-fifth. He again stayed overnight at the White Lamb in Augsburg en route to Munich, which he reached on the twenty-ninth; it is doubtful that while in Augsberg he saw the Bäsle, his cousin Maria Anna Thekla, who was now an unmarried mother raising a young daughter. In Munich he visited the Cannabich, Marchand, Brochard, and Ramm families, who were connected to the Mozarts by so many old and binding strands: "You cannot conceive what a fuss they are making of me," he wrote to his wife. The reunions had so rejuvenating an effect upon him that he recommended a similar course of treatment for his wife in the coming year: "I am thinking of taking this very same journey with you, my love, at the end of next summer, so that you may try some other waters. At the same time the company, the exercise and the change of air will do you good, for it has agreed very well with me."[44] If it was not a financial success, the journey to Frankfurt was a signal nostalgic triumph and, perhaps, marked the beginning of Mozart's convalescence.

On 4 or 5 November, in Munich, Mozart took part in a concert at the electoral palace given by Elector Karl Theodor in honor of King Ferdinand IV of Naples and his wife, Maria Karolina. With some acridity, Mozart wrote to Constanze, "It is greatly to the credit of the Viennese Court that the King has to hear me in a foreign country."[45] Surely he received some evidence of the elector's generosity, but the amount of his remuneration has not come down to us. The route from Munich home could easily have taken Mozart through the province in which he was born. But nostalgia has both its limits and its prohibitions: he did not stop either in Salzburg or in St. Gilgen, his sister's home, on the way to Vienna, where he arrived on 10 November and was reunited with Constanze and their son, Karl Thomas, who was now six years old.

Mozart's sons, Karl and Franz Xaver, 1798–99. Oil portrait
by Hans Hansen. Mozart-Museum der Internationalen Stiftung
Mozarteum, Salzburg. © Mozarts Geburtshaus, Salzburg.

30

....

THE LAST YEAR

Mozart somehow managed to stem the drift into silence. Beginning in January 1791, his creative fires were rekindled and his productivity endured secure, protective, and triumphant for ten months, until the onset of his fatal illness in November. It was a mysterious renewal that may have had little to do with changes in his external circumstances, but perhaps simply with sheer strength of will. If the productivity downturn of 1790 suggested that his faith in the healing power of music had momentarily wavered, his recovery in 1791 may suggest that he again realized that, for him, there was no acceptable alternative to making music. The reawakening is marked by several entries in the thematic catalog: his first piano concerto in three years, the Concerto in B-flat, K. 595, dated 5 January and, on 14 January, three songs that the bookseller Ignaz Alberti had commissioned for a collection of songs for children. The first two are about the return of spring. "Sehnsucht nach dem Frühlinge" ("Komm, lieber Mai"), K. 596, opens with "Come, dear May, and clothe the trees in green once more"; "Im Frühlingsanfang" ("Erwacht zum neuen Leben"), K. 597, opens "At the beginning of spring, awaken to a new life."[1] It is as though, to mark his own renewal and to celebrate his convalescence, Mozart voiced his delight and expressed his sense of thanksgiving (Example 30.1). Tyson has proposed that Mozart may have written the first two movements of the B-flat Concerto at an earlier date and then left it as a suspended work in progress for a considerable time.[2] Thus, it may impart a special significance to the concerto that Mozart used the first of the spring songs in its rondo finale (Example 30.2).

Example 30.1. "Komm, lieber Mai," K. 596, mm. 1–8.

Example 30.2. Piano Concerto in B-flat, K. 595. Finale, mm. 1–8.

Entries in the thematic catalog show that by early March Mozart had once more fulfilled his annual obligations as imperial chamber composer by writing a great number of dances for the Redoutensaal, K. 599–607; other dances, K. 609–610, apparently originated earlier. By 12 April he completed his final String Quintet, in E-flat, K. 614, in addition to some smaller works, and in that same month he prepared a revision, with added clarinets, of the G-minor Symphony, K. 550, which was featured at the Tonkünstler-Societät concerts on 16 and 17 April. At those same concerts,

Title page, *Liedersammlung für Kinder und Kinderfreunde: Frühlingslieder*.
Vienna: Ignaz Alberti, 1791. Music Collection of the Österreichische
Nationalbibliothek, MS 27.064.

Aloysia Lange sang one of his arias, probably "No, no, che non sei capace,"
K. 419. Soon thereafter, probably beginning in May, he was fully occupied
with the composition of *Die Zauberflöte* for Emanuel Schikaneder's Freihaustheater. Most of the opera was done by July, and it was so entered in
his thematic catalog, although it was not fully revised and completed until
late September. He took time out from its composition to write an Adagio
and Rondo for glass harmonica, flute, oboe, viola, and cello, K. 617, for
the blind virtuoso Marianne Kirchgessner in May; the motet "Ave verum
corpus," K. 618, in June for the Baden choirmaster Anton Stoll; and a
Masonic work, the "Little German Cantata" ("Die ihr des unermesslichen
Weltalls Schöpfer ehrt") for solo voice and keyboard, K. 619, in July.
Sometime before then he was anonymously commissioned by Count Franz
Walsegg to write a requiem in remembrance of the Count's wife, Anna,
who had died earlier in the year, on 14 February 1791. Because he now
had several other pressing commitments, however, he could not immediately set to work on it.

Toward the middle of July he received a commission from Domenico
Guardasoni, impresario of the Prague National Theater, to compose the
opera *La clemenza di Tito* to a text by Caterino Mazzolà after Metastasio for

the festivities surrounding the coronation on 6 September of Leopold II as king of Bohemia.[3] Mozart was not the first choice as composer and the lateness of his appointment left little time for the actual composition of the opera, which was completed on 5 September after less than three weeks of nonstop writing. After his return to Vienna in mid-September, Mozart wrote the overture and Priests' March for *Die Zauberflöte* and revised several other numbers in time for its premiere on 30 September.[4] By 7 October he composed the Clarinet Concerto in A, K. 622, using 199 measures of an unfinished basset-horn concerto, K. 621b, that had been written a year or more earlier. Then, until the onset of his final illness on 20 November he worked mainly on the Requiem, but failed to complete it before his death. In addition, fragments survive from these last months for the Horn Concerto, K. 412 and 514/386b, and for music for glass harmonica, and he took time out to compose the Little Masonic Cantata, K. 623, by 15 November.

In sum, within just ten or eleven months, and with all due allowance for completion or recycling of earlier music, Mozart composed two full-length operas, a large part of a requiem mass, and a substantial number of other works. He was working at a colossal rate of speed, climaxed by the composition of *La clemenza di Tito,* written in just eighteen days. His productivity had been fully restored. He now had sufficient commissions that he was able to devote himself almost entirely to composition. His last public performance as a pianist had taken place on 4 March, when he played the new B-flat Piano Concerto in a concert given by clarinetist Joseph Beer at Jahn's Hall, though he continued to present concerts at home for invited guests and connoisseurs.[5]

Mozart's financial worries had already begun to ease considerably, although they were far from over. Only a few months earlier he had been compelled to pawn his wife's silver and jewels in order to raise funds for his journey to Frankfurt. While he was there arrangements were concluded in Vienna for the loan of 1,000 florins from Heinrich Lackenbacher, which somewhat relieved the urgency of his situation. Since earnings on the journey itself cannot have been very large, it is surprising to find that Mozart did not accept an extraordinarily favorable offer that he received from the British opera manager Robert May O'Reilly at the end of October 1790: "If you are . . . able to be in London towards the end of the month of December next, 1790, and to stay until the end of June 1791, and within that space of time to compose at least two Operas, serious or comic, according to the choice of the Directorate, I offer you three hundred pounds Sterling."[6] The fee of £300 was equivalent to 3,000 florins, a sum sufficient to discharge a considerable portion of Mozart's debts. Perhaps he did not accept this lucrative offer because he was unwilling to make an extended trip without his wife, who had by then been ailing for two years.

"I have often thought of travelling *farther afield,*" he wrote to her from Frankfurt, "but whenever I tried to bring myself to take the decision, the thought always came to me, how bitterly I should regret it, if I were to separate myself from my beloved wife for *such an uncertain prospect, perhaps even to no purpose whatever.*"[7]

Although we don't have the full details, it is more likely that Mozart already knew of significant sources or prospects of income in Vienna. Certainly, as Landon has shown, the publication and manuscript rights to his dances for the Redoutensaal must have brought substantial fees from his publishers, who hastened to put them on sale.[8] Perhaps even prior to his departure for Frankfurt, he had already agreed to compose an opera for Schikaneder. In December 1791 Constanze Mozart informed the emperor that her husband "was assured shortly before his death of an annual subscription of 1,000 florins from a member of the Hungarian nobility; while from Amsterdam he was advised of a still larger annual sum, for which he would have had to compose only a few works for the exclusive use of the subscribers."[9] It seems possible that Mozart already had begun to count on (and even to receive) the fruits of these annuities: the String Quintets in D, K. 593, and E-flat, K. 614, were published by Artaria in 1793 with the superscription "Composto per un Amatore Ongarese," indicating that these were commissioned works, perhaps for one of the unidentified Hungarian patrons (one of whom is thought to have been Johann Tost) who offered the annuity. In any event, by the spring of 1791 Mozart's requests to Puchberg were only for tiny sums and his letters had lost their note of desperate entreaty; indeed, so secure had Mozart's credit now become that when on 25 June he asked for 20 florins Puchberg actually sent him 30. In this same letter, Mozart, without specifying the source, announced the impending arrival of a very large sum of money: "In a few days . . . you will receive 2,000 florins in my name, from which you can then refund yourself."[10]

Mozart had an additional good reason for his new confidence. On 9 May 1791, the Vienna Municipal Council (*Magistrat der Stadt Wien*) approved his application and appointed him as assistant to Leopold Hofmann, the aged kapellmeister at St. Stephen's Cathedral; it was for the moment an unpaid appointment, but it carried the further provision that when the post of kapellmeister fell vacant, an event expected rather sooner than later, Mozart would be named kapellmeister at a salary of 2,000 florins.[11] Thus, including his salary as imperial chamber composer, he would soon enjoy the prospect of a minimum income of 2,800 florins— enough to guarantee his security—along with the coveted title of kapellmeister. And if the Dutch and Hungarian annuities were included, his basic annual income would have risen to the munificent sum of 4,800 florins. Of course, virtually all of this was yet to come, and Mozart did not actually live to see himself free of debt: it was as late as October that Lichnowsky obtained his court judgment and salary attachment against the composer for 1,415 florins, and although Mozart offered the intendant of the Mannheim theater a manuscript copy of *Die Zauberflöte* for 100 ducats, he was unable to finalize the sale.[12] Such ongoing frustrations may explain why, in mid-September, Count Andrey Razumovsky recommended Mozart to Prince Grigory Alexandrovich Potemkin for employment in Russia with the remark that Mozart is "somewhat discontented here" and "might be disposed to undertake such a journey."[13]

During the first months of 1791, which were so crowded with productive activities, Mozart was also much occupied with family matters. He arranged for Constanze, who was still suffering from a foot ailment that made it difficult for her to walk or to climb stairs, once again to spend the summer at the spas in nearby Baden. She arrived there with young Karl on 4 June and remained until mid-July, when they returned to Vienna, where she was to give birth to the couple's sixth and last child, Franz Xaver Wolfgang, on 26 July. Mozart visited her in Baden several times in six weeks—from 8 to 10 and about 15 to 23 June, and presumably from 9 to 11 July.

Her ailments were not entirely physical ones. After a few weeks she was in low spirits and wanted to cut short her stay, but Mozart wrote her on 5 July, "It is surely better for your foot that you should stay on at Baden" and promised to visit the following Saturday: "As soon as my business here is over, I shall be with you, for I mean to take a rest in your arms, and indeed I shall need it, for this mental worry and anxiety and all the running about connected with it is really exhausting me."[14] A few days later, however, after another distressed letter from her, he offered her the choice of immediately returning to Vienna or staying in Baden until he fetched her the following week. "Tell me quite frankly which you prefer."[15] He tried to allay his wife's anxieties by his solicitude and concern. "I am longing most ardently for news of you. . . . Farewell, dearest, most beloved little wife! Take care of your health, for as long as you are well and are kind to me, I don't care a fig if everything else goes wrong."[16] The tone of his letters is affectionate, caring, and loving—and occasionally passionate, as in his letter of 6 June 1791: "Adieu—my love—my only one. . . . Listen, I want to whisper something in your ear—and you in mine—and now we open and close our mouths—again—again—and again—at last we say: 'It is all about Plumpi—Strumpi—'"[17] He also tried to cajole her into contentment: "The greatest pleasure of all you can give me is to be happy and jolly. *And if I know for certain that you have everything you want,* then all my trouble is a joy and a delight. Indeed the most difficult and complicated situation, in which I can possibly find myself, becomes a trifle, if only I know that *you are well and in good spirits.*"[18] But though he repeatedly pleaded, "Do not be melancholy,"[19] and "Be as cheerful as possible," he did not succeed in altering her mood, and this in turn affected his own: "Your letter of yesterday made me feel so depressed that I almost made up my mind to let that business slide and drive out to you."[20] Some of the reasons for her downcast spirits are not hard to locate: her physical discomfort and her sense of isolation are quite evident. It seems equally likely, however, that painful questions about her husband's fidelity had surfaced once again.

The most persistent reports of Mozart's infidelities cluster in the last year of his life. In the main, these rumors centered on the period of the composition and production of *Die Zauberflöte,* for Mozart was said to have led a profligate existence during those months of his close association with members of Schikaneder's theatrical company, and Schikaneder, who was notoriously promiscuous, was later charged by biographers with introducing Mozart to the seductions of Viennese demimonde. It may well have been this circle of theater and music people that Sophie Weber (later Haibel) had in mind when she referred to Mozart's "false friends and undetected blood-suckers, worthless people, who served him as table buffoons." She said that "he rejoiced if they enjoyed their fare," even though "association with them injured his credit and reputation."[21] Mozart was reported, as we have already seen, to have had affairs with several members of the *Zauberflöte* troupe, notably Barbara Gerl and Anna Gottlieb, the original Papagena and Pamina, respectively. Of Gerl, Jahn wrote that "contemporaries affirmed that the very pretty and attractive woman had completely entangled Mozart in her coils."[22] Gottlieb herself hinted broadly about her romantic attachment to Mozart, in newspaper interviews in later years.[23] Furthermore, the rumored scandalous affair with Magdalena Hofdemel would have been at its height around this very time.

Jahn tried to explain Mozart's inability to resist temptation: "The pressure of external circumstances, of growing domestic troubles, and the bitter feeling of failure and disappointed hope, combined with his own excitable nature to cause Mozart to seek for distraction and forgetfulness in the whirl of a pleasure-loving life. His wife was at Baden . . . ; her absence deprived his home life of any comfort, and drove him to take refuge among his theatrical friends. Folly and dissipation were the inevitable accompaniments of such an existence."[24] Schikaneder had provided Mozart with a small garden house near the theater, where he worked during the day. It was a matter of dispute where he spent his nights. It did not necessarily calm Constanze's mind when her husband wrote from Vienna, joshing her about his sleeping arrangements: "And where did I sleep? At home, of course. And I slept very well, save that the mice kept me most excellent company."[25]

For all the attempted lightness of his tone, Mozart's mood readily turned somber, shifting rapidly from rollicking wit to deep dejection. His dejection is most poignantly expressed in his letter of 7 July, where he portrayed his love for Constanze as an infinite hunger that can never be assuaged, as though he were describing a Kleistian or Fichtean state of metaphysical longing: "You cannot imagine how I have been aching for you all this long while. I can't describe what I have been feeling—a kind of emptiness, which hurts me dreadfully—a kind of longing, which is never satisfied, which never ceases, and which persists, nay rather increases daily."[26] Separation from his wife adversely affected his work. The same letter continues: "When I think how merry we were together at Baden—like children—and what sad, weary hours I am spending here. Even my work gives me no pleasure, because I am accustomed to stop working now and then and exchange a few words with you. Alas! this pleasure is no longer possible. If I go to the piano and sing something out of my opera, I have to stop at once, for this stirs my emotions too deeply."[27] The darkness of this mood suggests that his underlying melancholy had persisted despite his renewed productivity and the favorable turn in his career.

Guilt over his infidelities—if such they were—may have augmented Mozart's melancholia, robbing him of the very pleasure and consolation he was seeking in them. And betrayal apparently begot a fear of retaliatory betrayal in an oscillating pendulum of discontent. Even though she was hobbled, ailing, and in the ninth month of her pregnancy, he was ever on the alert for the slightest indication that another man might be interested in Constanze, or for any hint that she encouraged such attentions. Beset by his own fantasies, he tried to wall her in with injunctions and cautions, urging her to be on guard against her innate frailty, seeking to instill in her his own wariness about the intentions of male visitors. "N.N. is with me at the moment," he writes. "He has a penchant for you and is perfectly certain that you must have noticed it."[28]

Mozart's letters tell of his malaise when he was separated from Constanze, and even of the encroachment of painful feelings of loneliness. He spent several nights at Leutgeb's, "because I had discharged [the maid] Leonore and I would have been all alone at home, which would not have been pleasant," he wrote.[29] And again: "If only I had someone to console me a little. It is not at all good for me to be alone, when I have something on my mind."[30] He reported that "In the evening I again took a meal at the 'Krone' simply in order not to be alone."[31] His was not the loneliness of the friendless, isolated individual, for he was not deprived of companionship; quite the contrary, his life was rich in friendships and associations, and he was very much in the world, not removed from it. His was what Melanie Klein once called "an inner sense of loneliness—the sense of being alone regardless of external circumstances, of feeling lonely even when among friends or receiving love."[32]

Mozart's driving sexuality sought to reconnect him to the world by finding a quickening validation in a woman's arms. We may want to see his apparent inability to remain faithful to Constanze, then, as a quest for reassurance and for love. We recall that the child Mozart sought love everywhere, and when it was denied, was bereft and in tears. But even when love was given and received, it always fell short of resolving his doubts. To Mozart, the ideas of love and betrayal, marriage and infidelity, unfortunately stood in close proximity to one another: five years before his marriage, he jestingly predicted that he would be a cuckolded husband, signing himself "Knight of the Golden Spur and, as soon as I marry, of the Double Horn."[33] Uncertainty was the fuel for what, in the end, became a restive quest. The pattern of an insatiable need meeting an insufficient response never found closure.

Nor was closure to be expected. In Mozart's last years we witness a struggle between creativity, love, friendship, rationality, and altruistic belief on one side and feelings of loss, woundedness, estrangement, passivity, and betrayal on the other. Whatever his sadness, his sense of mutilation, and his rage to mutilate in return, he does not fully give way to the disintegrating forces within him: in a hundred different ways he is constantly marshaling against them an array of powerful, though provisional counterweights. Instinctively, compulsively, Mozart explored every possible avenue to reinforce his sense of being in and of the world, ranging from his extraordinary productivity to his shadowy adventures in the Viennese halfworld. In his last year, too, he returned, rejuvenated, to some of the earlier sources of his strength—to the piano concerto, to German-language opera, to church music (the Ave verum corpus, K. 618, and the Requiem) and to Masonic music (two cantatas and Die Zauberflöte), all of which had been absent from his musical workshop for from three to ten years. The return to church music, though it can be explained in many ways, connotes a renewal of faith, a desire for grace, an appeal for relief from pain, and even an offer of expiation or repentance. And in the belated return to Masonic music it is as though Mozart were seeking to reestablish a wavering faith in utopian ideals and fraternal solidarity.[34]

None of these strategies by itself was sufficient to heal his afflictive melancholy, but each of them embodied Mozart's hunger for connectedness, for the reparation of loss. It may be tempting to portray Mozart's last years as a death-seeking plunge toward Nirvana, but self-destructiveness would not have sanctioned the writing of Così fan tutte, Die Zauberflöte, and the last B-flat Piano Concerto; would not have left Mozart's marriage intact; would not have permitted him to seek (and to find, if the scandalmongers are not wholly inaccurate) love in the arms of women other than his wife. An underlying melancholy may have driven him to a compulsive pursuit of felicity; to touch the body and the heart of another human being may have enabled him momentarily to skirt the deepest abysses of isolation, silence, and despair. The sadness of it all is unmistakable, but it is a sadness leavened by the realization that Mozart was always struggling to devise new strategies to overcome the pull toward oblivion.

31

....

THE FINAL JOURNEY

Franz Xaver Niemetschek, the first biographer to set down Constanze Mozart's account of the Requiem commission, observed that "the story of his last work . . . is as obscure as it is strange."[1] One day in the summer of 1791, an "unknown messenger" brought "a letter without signature," inquiring whether Mozart would be willing to undertake to write a Requiem mass, and, if so, to state his terms of payment and delivery. The fee was readily agreed upon, and Mozart was enjoined not to attempt "to find out who had given the order, as it would assuredly be in vain." Subsequently, as he was leaving Vienna for Prague at the end of August, Mozart was pursued by the impatient messenger, who "appeared like a ghost," asking, "What about the Requiem?" Eventually the dying Mozart came to identify his own mortality with the work, believing that "he was writing the Requiem for himself." At his death, recounts Niemetschek, the incomplete work was taken away by the "mysterious messenger," and all efforts to identify the patron "proved in vain." Clearly, the story of Mozart's last days had now entered the realm of the legendary: an uncanny messenger had delivered a summons from the underworld to prepare a doomed hero for an appointment in Samarra.

The story remains strange, but it is not as obscure as it once appeared. Count Walsegg had insisted upon the anonymity of his commission for a simple reason—his intention to pass off the work as his own composition. According to the memoirs left by one of his musicians, the count had an arrangement with "many composers . . . that they should supply him with works, of which he was to hold the exclusive ownership."[2] The composers,

Mozart, 1789. Silverpoint drawing by Doris Stock.

chief among them Franz Anton Hoffmeister, were generously paid, and probably they knew that at his biweekly private concerts Walsegg let it be understood that the works—mostly flute quartets—were of his own composition: "The scores he had obtained secretly he usually copied out with his own hand. . . . We had to guess the composer. Usually we guessed the count himself . . . ; he would smile at that and be pleased that he had (or so he believed) succeeded in mystifying us; but we laughed because he thought us so credulous."[3] Walsegg wanted to add Mozart to his stable of ghostwriters: Niemetschek saw a letter from the "unknown" patron to Mozart in which he asked him not only to send the Requiem but to state "a sum for which he would compose a certain number of quartets each year."[4] If we also consider that Hoffmeister was Mozart's close friend and publisher, and that Puchberg lived in the same house as Count Walsegg,[5] it may be that Mozart was well aware of the patron's identity and intention and that he acceded to the arrangement in return for a substantial fee. He is variously reported to have received 30 to 50 ducats in advance, and Constanze Mozart received an additional 100 ducats on delivery of the work. Probably Mozart was expected to deliver the manuscript in time for performance on the anniversary of Countess Walsegg's death the preceding February.[6] It was not until two years later, on 14 December 1793, that Walsegg's musicians, augmented by professionals, performed the Requiem in the choir of the Cistercian abbey and parish church at Wiener-Neustadt and again on 14 February 1794 at the church of Maria-Schutz at Semmering. Walsegg was mortified to the point of taking "serious measures" when later on the work was published and Mozart's authorship revealed.[7]

Mozart could not begin serious work on the Requiem until he had effectively brought his two opera commissions to completion, for even before he had quite finished *Die Zauberflöte* he found himself fully occupied with *La clemenza di Tito*.[8] On or about 25 August, after leaving his son Karl at W. B. Heeger's private school in Perchtoldsdorf, he set out for the coronation of Leopold II in Prague. Constanze may not have wanted him to travel unchaperoned, for she accompanied him only a month after giving birth. Mozart's pupil, the young composer Franz Xaver Süssmayr, also went along as Mozart's assistant and perhaps composed the unaccompanied recitatives for *La clemenza di Tito*.[9] On 28 August the trio arrived in Prague, where they probably stayed at the Duscheks' Villa Bertramka until it was time to return home on 15 September. Mozart's music was very widely heard during the coronation festivities: on 1 September an arrangement for wind band of *Don Giovanni* was performed, and the next day the opera itself was staged for the imperial retinue at Prague's National Theater (Ständetheater), where Mozart was seen in the auditorium, which was "crammed full."[10] The premiere of the coronation opera, *La clemenza di*

Tito, took place on 6 September at the National Theater, the performance led by Mozart in the presence of the emperor and empress. Meanwhile, at the churches, several of Mozart's masses appear to have been performed under Salieri's direction on the sixth, eighth, and twelfth of the month, and Mozart's dances were doubtless given at various balls, including one sponsored by the Bohemian Estates—the governing body of Bohemia—on the twelfth.[11]

The sheer quantity of performances failed to translate into an unalloyed triumph. *La clemenza di Tito* did not please: the Empress Maria Louisa was reported to have called it a "German swinishness" (*porcheria tedesca*) and in a letter she wrote of it, "The gala opera was not much and the music very bad so that almost all of us fell asleep."[12] A second performance failed to attract an audience and Guardasoni later petitioned to be reimbursed for his losses, which he attributed to competition from other coronation events and "a certain prejudice against Mozart's composition."[13] A contemporary "Coronation Journal" explained Mozart's failure: "The composition is by the famous Mozart, and does him honor, though he did not have much time for it and was also overtaken by an illness, during which he had to complete the last part of the same."[14] Niemetschek had a different explanation, suggesting that the public was so thoroughly "surfeited with dances, balls, and amusements" during the festivities that it "did

Leopold II's coronation procession in Prague, 1791. Engraving by Karl Pluth after Ph. and F. Heger. Reproduced from Oskar Schürer, *Prag* (Munich, 1935).

not find the simple beauties of Mozart's art much to its taste!"[15] On 10 September Mozart visited the Prague lodge "Truth and Unity" ("Zur Wahrheit und Einigkeit"), where his cantata *Die Maurerfreude*, K. 471, with its celebration of imperial wisdom was performed as an appropriate Masonic tribute to the coronation festivities. A few days later (perhaps on the fifteenth), the whirlwind tour came to an end and the homeward journey commenced.

In Prague, Mozart had indeed fallen ill. "While he was in Prague Mozart became ill and was continually receiving medical attention," wrote Niemetschek. "He was pale and his expression was sad, although his good humor was often shown in merry jest with his friends."[16] But he could not afford to be sick. He put the finishing touches on *Die Zauberflöte* by 28 September and participated in its premiere, which took place at the Freihaustheater on 30 September, Mozart himself conducting from the keyboard. Although there were no reviews of the first performances,[17] it was immediately evident that Mozart and Schikaneder had achieved a great success, the opera drawing immense crowds and reaching hundreds of performances during the 1790s. Mozart's delight is reflected in his last three letters, written to Constanze, who with her sister Sophie, was spending the second week of October in Baden. "I have this moment returned from the opera, which was as full as ever," he wrote on 7 October, listing the numbers that had to be encored. "But what always gives me most pleasure is the *silent approval!* You can see how this opera is becoming more and more esteemed."[18] He was in a euphoric state of mind, heightened because he had gotten a letter from Stadler in Prague with good news about *La clemenza di Tito:* "And the strangest thing of all is that on the very evening when my new opera was performed for the first time with such success, 'Tito' was given in Prague for the last time with tremendous applause."[19]

He went to hear his opera almost every night, taking along relatives and fellow musicians. "Leutgeb begged me to take him a second time and I did so. I am taking *Mama* tomorrow. Hofer has already given her the libretto to read. In her case what will probably happen will be that she will *see* the opera, but not *hear* it," a reference to her hearing difficulties.[20] On the thirteenth he and Hofer drove out to Perchtoldsdorf to bring home Karl from the Heeger school. After arriving in Vienna he "called in the carriage for Salieri and Madame Cavalieri—and drove them to my box. Then I drove back quickly to fetch Mama and Karl, whom I had left at Hofer's. You can hardly imagine how charming they [Salieri and Cavalieri] were and how much they liked not only my music, but the libretto and everything. They both said that it was a *grand opera,* worthy to be performed for the grandest festival and before the greatest monarch, and that they would often go to see it, as they had never seen a more beautiful or delightful show."[21] Afterward, Mozart drove his distinguished guests home and then had supper at the Hofers with Karl, before retiring at last, after a long day. "Karl was absolutely delighted at being taken to the opera."

In his letters to Constanze, Mozart gives an account of his daily activities: "Immediately after your departure I played two games of billiards with Herr von Mozart, the fellow who wrote the opera which is running at Schikaneder's theater; then I sold my nag for fourteen ducats; then I told Joseph [Preisinger, an innkeeper] to get Primus [a servant] to fetch me some black coffee, with which I smoked a splendid pipe of tobacco; and then I orchestrated almost the whole of Stadler's rondo."[22] He describes his day, from sunrise to bedtime, scrupulously accounting for his time, and assuring Constanze of his yearning and solicitude for her.

> The friseur came punctually at six o'clock. At half past five Primus had lit the fire and he then woke me up at a quarter to six. Why must it rain just now? I did so much hope that you would have lovely weather. Do keep very warm, so that you may not catch a cold. I hope that these baths will help you to keep well during the winter. For only the desire to see you in good health made me urge you to go to Baden. I already feel lonely without you. I knew I should. If I had had nothing to do, I should have gone off at once to spend the week with you; but I have *no facilities for working at Baden,* and I am anxious, as far as possible, to avoid all risk of *money difficulties.*[23]

Mozart was indeed very busy, working from early morning until evening. He explained that he preferred to sleep at home rather than at the Hofers because, to his intense annoyance, they slept far too late there. "I am happiest at home, for I am accustomed to my own hours."[24] And soon their separation would be over: "I shall certainly come out next Sunday, when we shall all visit the Casino and come home together on Monday."[25]

Clearly, Mozart was amazingly busy, not only with composition and operagoing, but with family matters as well—fetching Karl from one school, negotiating with the Piarists to admit him to another, visiting the Hofers, taking his mother-in-law to the theater, writing lengthy letters to Constanze, traveling to Baden to bring her home. In 1791, by a force of will that powered a colossal productivity, Mozart managed to make everything well, caring for his family, and dispelling the clouds of melancholy. *Liebe und Arbeit*—always he labored in the service of love: "I will work— work so hard—that no unforeseen accidents shall ever reduce us to such desperate straits again,"[26] he had written from Frankfurt.

This motif was still central in his last letters, where he insisted that he could only achieve "a mind at peace" by constant labor: "One must work hard; and I like hard work."[27] The miraculous child will—once again—rescue the family, offering up his own body for the sake of the larger organism that validated his identity and gave him his sense of purpose. He will do anything necessary to accomplish his goal of providing for his family: he will write an opera for an upstart theatrical troupe known primarily for farce and visual display, one devoted to gaudy stage entertainment in the vernacular;[28] he will exploit Masonic ritual for its exotic appeal to popular taste; he will compose a flattering portrait of one merciful emperor to celebrate the supposed benevolence of another; and he will even consent to ghost-write a Requiem for a vain count, an extraordinary act of self-abasement for a proud composer. Mozart had deeply resented his father's exhortations to compromise, felt humiliated that his primary duty as imperial chamber composer was to supply dance music for the masked balls, complained of the necessity to write a glorification of Field Marshal Laudon for a mechanical organ as part of a display in a wax museum. Now, however, he was uncomplaining, determined not to permit such issues to interfere with what he knew he must do. Mozart's efforts culminated in the presentation of two operatic premieres in two different capital cities within the span of three weeks. Without a moment's pause, he then wrote the Clarinet Concerto and immediately turned to the Requiem.

And then it was as though the flame had consumed itself. With the success of *Die Zauberflöte* he had achieved his goal, but now he was weakened and vulnerable, and his melancholy, which had remained dormant during his creative outpouring, overcame him again, and this time it could not be overridden by sheer effort or determination. Now all his energies were once more turned to defending himself against assaults from within. "On his return to Vienna," wrote Niemetschek,

> his indisposition increased visibly and made him gloomily depressed. His wife was truly distressed over this. One day when she was driving in the Prater with him, to give him a little distraction and amusement, and they were sitting by themselves, Mozart began to speak of death, and declared that he was writing the Requiem for himself. Tears came to the eyes of this sensitive man: "I feel definitely," he continued, "that I will not last much longer; I am sure I have been poisoned. I cannot rid myself of this idea."[29]

Many years later, Constanze Mozart told the Novellos that Mozart "was impressed with the horrid idea that someone had poisoned him with acqua toffana—he came to her one day and complained that he felt great pain in his loins and a general languor spreading over him by degrees."[30]

True, the imagined sensation of having a poisonous substance within his body may have been a medical symptom, perhaps of the disease that was to take his life, though Mozart's complaint preceded the sudden onset of that illness in late November.[31] More likely, he was trying to put into words the melancholiac's oppressive lethargy, his heaviness of body bordering on stupor, his loss of willpower and, beyond these, the feeling that his body has been invaded by a corrupting agent, a hidden persecutor whom he can visualize as a malignant fluid coursing through his veins or as a noxious mass in his bowels that can neither be disgorged nor digested. And this is what, according to Constanze Mozart's recounting of the story to the Novellos, he seems to have conveyed, in phrases suggestive of persecutory anxieties. Mary Novello's diary recorded Constanze's quotation of her husband's words: "'I know I must die,' he exclaimed, 'someone has given me acqua toffana and has calculated the precise time of my death—for which they have ordered a Requiem, it is for myself I am writing this.'"[32] Vincent Novello's own diary matched his wife's account; Mozart claimed "that some one of his enemies had succeeded in administering the deleterious mixture which would cause his death and . . . they could already calculate at what precise time it would infallibly take place."[33] The psychoanalyst Otto Fenichel writes, "In melancholic depressions the delusion of being poisoned is not rare, originating in the feeling of becoming destroyed by some orally introjected force."[34] An external enemy may be identified, confronted, and repulsed, but an enemy within—protean, hidden, masked—has taken one's very being hostage; to root him out one must take up arms against oneself.

Constanze was unable to console her husband "or to convince him that his melancholy imaginings were without foundation," and she felt that "the Requiem was getting on his over-sensitive nerves."[35] She therefore "entreated him to let her put it aside, saying that he was ill, otherwise he would not have such an absurd idea."[36] He did leave off writing the Requiem and instead, with a sure hand and very few corrections, wrote his last completed work, the Little Masonic Cantata, "Laut verkünde unsre Freude," K. 623, by 15 November, to celebrate the public consecration of a new temple for his lodge, "New Crowned Hope," on the seventeenth. The text was not, as has been thought, by Schikaneder, but most likely by the actor and playwright Karl Ludwig Gieseke, a member of the lodge. It was so enthusiastically received that he returned home quite elated, saying, according to Constanze, "Did I not know that I have written better I should think this is the best of my work, but I will put it in score. Yes I see I was ill to have had such an absurd idea of having taken poison, give me back the Requiem and I will go on with it."[37] Within a few days, however, continues Mary Novello, "he was . . . possessed with the same idea."[38]

Niemetschek writes, in a parallel description, "he became despondent once more, weaker and more listless, until he sank back in his sick-bed."[39]

Beleaguered by prohibitions, pursued by posthumous presences, overcome by constant sorrows, Mozart for a while had reached almost to the edge of silence. But somehow he had managed to harness his creative forces and the old imperatives to a new purpose—in a great effort to save his own family, which now included the Webers. Protected by a loving family—even if he may have sought solace beyond its borders—he had managed to erect a temporary bulwark against annihilation. He had resisted the pull to extinction through an amalgam of love and music. So long as he could write music, he could keep death at a distance. He composed a Requiem to mourn for a nobleman's wife, to express his feelings of grief over the death—or loss—of every beloved person, to propitiate his father and the gods. But now, once again, Mozart was unable to find an effective antidote to a toxic presence, either in work or in love. He no longer had the physical or emotional resources to resist the sacrificial summons.

Mozart's final illness set in on 20 November and lasted for fifteen days, during which he was bedridden and in great pain. "It began," wrote Nissen, "with swelling in the hands and feet, which were almost completely immobilized, followed later by sudden vomiting, which sickness was called acute miliary fever. Until two hours before his passing he remained completely conscious."[40] It is now widely accepted that Mozart died of acute rheumatic fever; he had had three or even four known attacks of it beginning in his childhood and it has a tendency to recur, with increasingly serious potential consequences, including rampant infection and cardiac valve damage.[41] The dying composer was treated by two leading Viennese physicians, Thomas Franz Closset and Matthias von Sallaba, who held a consultation on 28 November. A colleague of theirs, writing to refute rumors that Mozart had been poisoned by Salieri, subsequently described Mozart's condition:

> He fell sick in the late autumn of a rheumatic and inflammatory fever, which being fairly general among us at that time, attacked many people. . . . [Dr. Closset] considered Mozart's illness to be dangerous, and from the very beginning feared a fatal conclusion, namely a deposit on the brain. One day he met Dr. Sallaba and he said positively, "Mozart is lost, it is no longer possible to restrain the deposit." Sallaba communicated this information to me at once, and in fact Mozart died a few days later with the usual symptoms of a deposit on the brain. . . . This malady attacked at this time a great many of the inhabitants of Vienna, and for not a few of them it had the same fatal conclusion and the same symptoms as in the case of

Mozart. The statutory examination of the corpse did not reveal anything at all unusual.[42]

Mozart continued intermittently to work on the Requiem, but the pain of his swollen body and limbs eventually made it impossible for him to write.[43] Frau Weber and her youngest daughter, Sophie, fashioned a night jacket "which he could put on frontways, since on account of his swollen condition he was unable to turn in bed."[44] At one point he momentarily felt somewhat recovered, and asked, "Dear Sophie, do tell Mama that I am fairly well and that I shall be able to go and congratulate her on the octave of her name day"; but even as she communicated this "cheerful news" to her mother she had a presentiment of Mozart's death and hastened to return to him. When Sophie arrived at the Mozarts' lodgings, she was told by Constanze that Mozart's condition had become desperate: "Last night he was so ill that I thought he would not be alive this morning." He himself said, "Ah, dear Sophie, how glad I am that you have come. You must stay here tonight and see me die. . . . Why, I have already the taste of death on my tongue." She promised to remain, but first she ran to fetch a priest from St. Peter's: "For a long time they refused to come and I had a great deal of trouble to persuade one of those clerical brutes to go to him."[45] She arranged for her mother to spend the night at sister Josepha's apartment. "I then ran back as fast as I could to my distracted sister." Vincent Novello takes up the story as he had it from Sophie: Toward evening, Dr. Closset was sent for,

> but he was at the Theater and, on receiving the message, merely said that he would come "as soon as the opera was over." On his arrival he ordered Madame Haibl to bathe the temples and forehead of Mozart with vinegar and cold water. She expressed her fears that the sudden cold might be injurious to the sufferer, whose arms and limbs were much inflamed and swollen. But the Doctor persisted in his orders and Madame Haibl accordingly applied a damp towel to his forehead. Mozart immediately gave a slight shudder and in a very short time afterwards he expired in her arms. At this moment the only persons in the Room were Madame Mozart, the Medical Attendant and herself.[46]

Thus, at the end, Mozart received some shred of comfort from two of the beloved women in his family.

It is of course difficult to disentangle fact from legend here, where witnesses feel the impulse to participate in the mythic, to connect their own experience with ancient stories, tapping into underlying archaic verities. Several reports have it that Mozart, despite his imminent death and his swollen immobility, was much occupied with the Requiem on his dying day. Improbably, perhaps to bolster her sister's exaggerated accounts about Mozart's role in the completion of the Requiem, Sophie recalled Mozart giving Süssmayr instructions on completing the Requiem. More plausibly, she claimed that Mozart's last action "was an attempt to express with his mouth the drum passages in the Requiem." "That I can still hear," she wrote.[47] Mozart's friend the singer Benedict Schack claimed to remember that in the early afternoon of the day of his death Mozart "asked for the score of the Requiem to be brought to his bed" and that he, Schack, Gerl (the first Sarastro), and Hofer sang through it up to the first bars of the *Lacrymosa*, at which point Mozart "began to weep violently and the score was laid aside."[48] According to Niemetschek, "On the day of his death he asked for the score to be brought to his bedside. 'Did I not say before, that I was writing this Requiem for myself?' After saying this, he looked yet again with tears in his eyes through the whole work."[49] It was also reported that as Mozart lay delirious on the evening of 4 December, he imagined that he was attending *Die Zauberflöte* in the Freihaustheater and that he whispered to his wife as he visualized Josepha Hofer as the Queen of the Night: "Quiet, quiet! Hofer is just taking her top F;—now my sister-in-law is singing her second aria, 'Der Hölle Rache'; how strongly she strikes and holds the B-flat: 'Hört! hört! hört! der Mutter Schwur!' "[50]

Less than five years earlier, on hearing the news of his father's final ill-ness, Mozart had written his famous letter describing death as "the true goal of our existence," as the "best and truest friend of mankind," and as "the *key* which unlocks the door to our true happiness."[51] Thus, Mozart was one of those for whom death was an ontological opportunity, an affir-mation of faith, a release from pain, someone for whom, as Marcuse put it, "A brute biological fact, permeated with pain, horror, and despair, is trans-formed into an existential privilege."[52] It may be because early memoirists and biographers shared Mozart's own image of a consoling and transfigur-ing death that they suppressed two memoranda describing the wrenching materiality of his actual death throes. His son Karl, who was seven years old when he saw his father dying, reported: "Particularly remarkable is in my opinion the fact that a few days before he died, his whole body became so swollen that the patient was unable to make the smallest movement, more-over, there was a stench, which reflected an internal disintegration which, after death, increased to the extent that an autopsy was rendered impossible."[53] And Constanze Mozart told Nissen that just before the end Mozart asked her what Dr. Closset had said. When she answered with a soothing lie, he said, " 'It isn't true,' and he was very distressed: 'I shall die, now when I am able to take care of you and the children. Ah, now I will leave you unprovided for.' " And as he spoke these words, "Suddenly he vomited—it gushed out of him in an arc—it was brown, and he was dead."[54]

★ ★ ★

Now the Mozart residence became a place of delirium, filled with phantas-magoric scenes. Count Deym, owner of the wax museum, came and took a death mask of Mozart's face. Schikaneder walked about, crying, *"His spirit follows me everywhere; he stands constantly before my eyes."*[55] Sophie remembered how "his devoted wife in her utter misery threw herself on her knees and implored the Almighty for His aid. She simply could not tear herself away from Mozart, however much I begged her to do so."[56] Baron van Swieten arrived in the middle of the night, took the responsibility for making the funeral arrangements, and tried to console the grieving widow, "who had lain down in her sleeping husband's bed in order to become infected and to die with him."[57] Beside herself with grief, it is said that she—probably along with her sons—was taken from the house and looked after by two friends, the Freemason Joseph von Bauernfeld and the merchant Joseph Goldhahn. At 5:00 A.M. the innkeeper Joseph Deiner was fetched by Mozart's maid to dress the body, which "was laid on the bier and covered with a black drapery from the burial society, as was then the custom. . . . The corpse was taken into the study and placed near his pianoforte."[58] The musician Ludwig Gall, learning of Mozart's death, rushed to the apartment and was led—by Frau Mozart, he claimed, although more probably by one of her sisters—"into a small room on the left, where I saw the dead Master laid out in a coffin, wearing a black suit with a cowl down to his forehead veiling his blond hair and with his hands folded upon his breast!"[59] Meanwhile, people gathered in a vigil outside the house, weeping and wailing, and fluttering their handker-chiefs to express their grief and condolence.

The entry in the parish register of deaths at St. Stephen's Cathedral indi-cates that Mozart's burial was scheduled for 6 December.[60] His body remained on view at his apartment in the Rauhensteingasse for a day and then was carried to the cathedral, where it was examined and another, more detailed, entry made in the register:

	The 6th Xber.
Mozart 3rd class	Herr Wolfgang Amandeus Mozart, I. & R.
	[Imperial and Royal]
Parish St. Stephen's	Kapellmeister and Chamber Composer,
	in the Rauchensteingasse [sic], in the small
	Kaiserhaus No. 970, of severe miliary fever,
	examined, 36 years old.
	In the burial ground outside St. Marx

8 fl. 56 kr. Paid..............4.36. 4.20

Hearse f3.[61]

It has been claimed that the date on the death register is mistaken and that Mozart was actually taken to the cathedral on the seventh rather than the sixth,[62] this being an attempt to shift the date because the known fair weather on the sixth doesn't conform with several reports about bad weather en route to the cemetery, which in turn is said to explain the absence of mourners at the graveyard. But the anecdotal reports about bad weather are all either second-hand or by witnesses who are not always reliable, and it would be necessary to propose two separate slips of the pen by the registrar at St. Stephen's to assert that its dates are in error.[63]

Although it is evident that the body arrived at the cathedral on 6 December and that it was intended that the burial take place on the same day, it is not quite as certain that Mozart was actually buried on that day, for there was a prescribed interval of forty-eight hours between death and burial except in cases of death from epidemic or contagious diseases.[64] After examination, the body presumably was carried by a hearse on the night of the sixth through the Stubentor by way of the Landstrasse suburb to St. Marx Cemetery, some three miles from central Vienna. If not buried at once, it was kept in the mortuary there until the waiting period had ended so that it could be interred, along with five or six other bodies, in a common grave, which, Nissen found, was customarily "opened and cleaned out every seven years in order to make new funerals."[65] Thus, Mozart was buried either late in the day on the sixth or on the morning of 7 December. In either case, there were no witnesses to observe the moment when his body, which was sewn into a linen sack, was removed from the reusable wooden coffin in which it had been hauled, covered with quicklime to hasten decomposition, and placed in the grave among its neighbors.

According to the Deiner-Gottlieb memoirs published in 1856, Mozart's body received a ritual blessing at precisely three o'clock in the afternoon of the seventh in the Crucifix Chapel adjacent to the Capistrano pulpit in the cathedral.[66] According to this account, rain and snow were falling simultaneously on the day of the funeral, so that "only a few friends and three women accompanied the corpse" to the cathedral. "Mozart's wife was not present," it was pointedly observed. "These few people with their umbrellas stood round the bier, which was then taken via the Grosse Schullerstrasse to the St. Marx Cemetery. As the storm grew ever more violent, even these few friends determined to turn back at the Stuben Gate."[67] We don't know whether to believe this, for fantasies often have the ring of truth. The weather on the sixth was fair, and there was neither rain nor snow on the seventh, which started as a beautiful day. A light southerly wind came up in the afternoon, and by ten P.M. it had changed into a powerful southwesterly wind, though there was no precipitation. But there is no reason to believe that this confirms the story that inclement weather caused the mourners to turn back, and if the burial was, as is probable, either on the sixth or early on the seventh, the windy weather late in the evening of the latter day is altogether irrelevant.[68]

There are no contemporary or reliable reports describing either a funeral procession to St. Stephen's or a service in the cathedral. Nor is it really known who was present at the cathedral or who accompanied the body as far as the city limits before yielding to the weather.[69] If a few people gathered at the cathedral, they did so spontaneously rather than at the request of or with the sanction of Mozart's family. Years later, Constanze Mozart frankly acknowledged to an inquiring member of the Gesellschaft der Musikfreunde (Society of Friends of Music) that "none of *Mozart's* acquaintances and friends accompanied the body," explaining that "it was then the custom that the deceased would only be picked up by the hearse and driven to consecration in the church and then, without anything further, brought to the grave."[70] She added that she herself was prevented from "following the mortal remains of her inexpressibly beloved husband" because of her illness and the "severe" winter weather.

It was the least expensive funeral available, save a pauper's burial, to which it was identical in every respect except that paupers paid no fee. Nevertheless, such funerals were chosen by most Viennese citizens: of seventy-four burials listed on the St. Stephen's death register between mid-November and mid-December 1791, fifty-one—the great majority—were for third-class funerals, while only five were first-class and seven second-class, the remainder being of paupers.[71] Primarily this was a matter of money: first-class funerals cost 110 florins; second-class cost 40 florins; third-class only 8 florins 56 kreuzer.[72] Partly, though, it was a question of regulation and socially accepted practice: many citizens sympathized with Emperor Joseph's rationalist proposals for simplification of burials in the interest of hygiene and economy. Indeed, it was Joseph's decree of 20 December 1784, later largely withdrawn because of popular opposition, that prescribed sack burials in communal graves.[73] "That neither the widow nor close friends, nor yet any of the freemasons attended the procession is explicable only by the simplicity that became customary for funerals in Emperor Joseph's time," explained Deutsch.[74] Certainly it is true that, even under Leopold II, escorted processions to the cemetery were not customary and regulations continued to call for communal burial, although individual burials in coffins were available to those who wanted them.

Nevertheless, we are uncomfortable about Mozart's burial: the absence of a headstone or memorial tablet, the failure to mark the place where he lay, the impersonality of the interment. We fear that he had been neglected or ill-used, and that his burial was not only unconsecrated but supremely lonely. We wonder why Gluck, but not Mozart, received a ceremonial

funeral and was buried in an individual grave with an appropriate headstone in the Josephinian Vienna of 1787. Emperor Joseph's decrees forbade
memorial headstones but did not discourage memorial tablets on the
cemetery walls. And certainly there were no restrictions on attendance in
the chapel during the blessing of the corpse. It is not a question of blaming
anyone, certainly not a bereaved widow whose husband had died too
young, with too many issues unsettled between them. Surely, she had a
right to rage against a husband who had—with absolute finality—abandoned her and their children. For once again, Mozart had left home, emi-
grated, leaving behind much unfinished business, feelings of betrayal, and
reproaches that could never be properly voiced.

Against this it ought to be noted that no one has the right to override
Mozart's wishes, indeed that we ought to honor Mozart's deeply held beliefs
as perfectly as did his wife and his loyal friends, chief among them Baron van
Swieten, who was in charge of the funeral arrangements. As an enlightened
man of his time, Mozart surely sympathized with Emperor Joseph's proposals
for the simplification of burials; he would have disdained a ceremonious
funeral as a superstitious survival. We understand that Mozart might well
have considered it irrational to waste resources upon the decayed fleshly
envelope of the spirit. His faith was so profound that it had no room for
pomp, hypocrisy, and especially for the mediation of clerics between individuals and their God. His was the "pure, heartfelt religion" of the advanced
Viennese circles to which he belonged, which Georg Forster described as
"free from all superstition, the religion of gentle and innocent hearts familiar
with the secrets of nature and creation."[75] As her brother-in-law lay dying,
Sophie Haibel went to the priests and asked them to come—but a memorandum by Nissen written in the margin of her letter indicates that this was
done despite Mozart's wishes: "The priests declined to come because the sick
person himself did not send for them." And we are told that Mozart did not
receive the last rites in another memorandum Nissen wrote in the margin of
Sophie's account: "They didn't come."[76] Perhaps his anticlerical attitudes
were widely known. So it may be safe to assume that Mozart's family knew
what he wanted—an ordinary burial, a simple interment, without ceremony,
as an emblem of his beliefs. Perhaps, for him, to be buried without a coffin
in a common grave was to be returned to earth, to be merged into dust with
his fellow human beings, and was even a metaphor of the brotherhood of
souls, equal in death as they should have been in life. Mozart had chosen his
own way. Whether he also wanted all this without the presence of those
whom he loved and who loved him is another matter.

On the occasion of his father's last illness, Mozart had written: "I never lie
down at night without reflection that—young as I am—I may not live to

see another day. Yet no one of all my acquaintances could say that in company I am morose or disgruntled."[77] This was not a new idea for Mozart; when his mother died, he consoled himself with the thought that they would someday find blissful reunion: "We do not yet know when it will be—but that does not disturb me; when God wills it, I am ready."[78] Thus, Mozart thought he was ready; but he was not ready. "Like all people with tender disposition, he also feared death very much," wrote Nissen, perhaps on Constanze Mozart's authority.[79] On the occasion of his mother's death, Mozart had confessed that he had always wanted to see someone die, thereby implying the profound mixture of trepidation and curiosity that death aroused in him. When in a letter of 1778 to his father he denied that his mother had died, and when in 1787 he asked his father to regard death as our best friend, he was trying to quiet his own fears.

But the essence of the matter is that he was taken unawares, ambushed in the middle of the journey, before he had found the right way. He had not achieved a variety of fateful reconciliations. His melancholia, which was at bottom a despairing cry for love, had not yet been dispelled. He had not earned his wife's forgiveness. He had left a Requiem unfinished. He still had not delivered his birth certificate to the Tonkünstler-Societät. He had not seen his sister's children, nor she his. Mainly, he had not fulfilled the impossible task—to provide for his family so that it would be forever protected, forever beyond need. His last words, repeated and stressed by Sophie and Constanze, were his regret that he had not been able to fulfil his mission: "He also bitterly expressed his regret at leaving his wife and family so ill provided for."[80] Previously, he had failed his ancestral family because he would not altogether sacrifice himself; now he had failed his own family, even though he had made the ultimate sacrifice.

If his body was abandoned, Mozart's memory was not neglected by family, friends, and fellow citizens. We have already quoted the heartfelt editorial notice that appeared in the Wiener Zeitung on 7 December. On 10 December, a few days after the burial, the directors of the Freihaustheater presented a memorial for Mozart in the Church of St. Michael. A local newspaper reported that the Requiem, "which he composed in his last illness," was performed and it was announced that "Herr Schikaneder will give a performance of Die Zauberflöte in the next few days for the benefit of the widow."[81] It was also announced that Baron van Swieten "had taken over the care and upbringing" of Mozart's children, and the assembly expressed its determination that "Mozart's widow and children shall not be allowed to live in want in Vienna."[82] Later on Mozart was eulogized by his Masonic brethren as well: "It has pleased the Eternal Architect of the world to tear one of our most beloved, one of our most meritorious members from our brotherly chain," intoned the orator, asking, "Who did not know him? who did not esteem him? who did not love him?—our worthy brother Mozart."[83] In Prague, the most imposing of all memorial celebrations for Mozart was held on 15 December: it was a "solemn funeral ceremony" that began with the ringing of bells summoning mourners to the Nicolai Church "in such numbers that neither the church nor the adjacent, so-called Italian Square, could accommodate all of them." In the church itself a Requiem was performed by an orchestra and chorus of 120 under the direction of Josepha Duschek, "so nobly performed," according to the newspaper account, "that Mozart's spirit in Elysium must have rejoiced."[84]

On 11 December Constanze Mozart applied to the emperor for a pension and for permission to put on a benefit concert to pay Mozart's remaining debts, and soon she was able to earn considerable sums exploiting her position as Mozart's poverty-stricken widow, who, as one journalist put it, "sits sighing on a sack of straw amidst her needy children and under a sizeable burden of debt."[85] Not a few were eager to aid her. "Many noble benefactors are helping this unhappy woman," wrote one Viennese newspaper in 1793. After a Prague benefit, another paper reported that "Mozart's widow and son both wept tears of grief at their loss and of gratitude towards a noble nation."[86] In 1795, she continued to express her thanks to "Vienna's noble citizens, [who] have always followed their favorite inclination: to do good, whenever it was a question of supporting widows and orphaned children."[87] For several years she mounted additional benefit performances, in Graz, Linz, Dresden, Leipzig, and Berlin, winding up once more in Prague on 15 November 1797. Her earnings enabled her to lend Josepha Duschek the very large sum of 3,500 florins at 6 percent interest in 1797 and to leave the considerable fortune of 27,191 florins in cash at her death.[88] Nissen wrote to her son Karl in 1810: "By her tours, concert performances, as well as by the sale of your late father's original scores . . . your mother has been fortunate enough not only to pay the debts but also to amass a small capital."[89]

Thus, Mozart's family gained prosperity in the unprecedented wave of enthusiasm that commenced shortly after his death: soon, as A. Hyatt King has documented, he had become both "a household word" and "an object of veneration" among composers and music-lovers, with performances everywhere and numerous publishers issuing competing editions of his works.[90] By 1798, the most enterprising of these publishers, Breitkopf & Härtel, had commenced its *Œuvres complettes* of Mozart, a series that within eight years embraced more than 225 separate works, including comprehensive editions of his piano solos, piano duos, sonatas for violin and piano, and lieder, plus 12 concert arias, 12 string quartets, and 20 piano concertos in parts, and the Requiem, 2 masses, and *Don Giovanni* in full score.[91]

Meanwhile, the first lives of Mozart began to appear, with the rival branches of his family contending to have their stories told, demonstrating once again that biography is often a transparent contest for possession. By the spring of 1792, Marianne von Berchtold, scrupulously fulfilling her father's ambition to write Mozart's life, furnished her own and Schachtner's reminiscences and an outline biography of her brother to Schlichtegroll, aiming to buttress her father's views, emphasizing that Mozart's genius was a family enterprise and picturing the early journeys as his golden age. Constanze Mozart bought up and destroyed the entire second edition of Schlichtegroll's book because an offending passage portrayed her married life in a highly unfavorable light, and she soon balanced the scales by using Niemetschek's biography to tell Mozart's story from her own standpoint, furnishing "information, papers and letters" to its author, who was also her friend.[92] Subsequently, between 1798 and 1800, she engaged in a lengthy correspondence with Breitkopf & Härtel, whom she provided with materials for the purpose of preparing a full-scale biography of her husband.[93] Ten of her own anecdotes appeared in the Leipzig publisher's house journal, the *Allgemeine Musikalische Zeitung,*[94] and in 1828 she published the massive life of Mozart by her second husband, Georg Nissen, from notes and drafts left at his death in March 1826.

Breitkopf & Härtel also pursued a correspondence with Marianne von Berchtold (particularly after it became clear that Constanze Mozart was not about to accept the publisher's paltry offers for her husband's scores), and enlisted her aid in supplying Mozart manuscripts as well as materials for the projected biography. Marianne used the occasion to promote her own proxy biographer: "Concerning the biography of my brother," she wrote to Breitkopf & Härtel, "I find it remarkable that you have made no announcement of the *Nekrolog* of Professor Schlichtegroll, wherein is contained an authentic biography of my brother, for which, at the request of a friend, I provided an article . . . as well as excerpts from letters and writings and epigrams, written with much spice and humor."[95] She, too, wanted to be represented in the *Allgemeine Musikalische Zeitung:* "If you would like me to send you my article along with these writings, please let me know your pleasure."[96] Soon, four of her own anecdotes appeared in the journal, telling, among other things, of the child Mozart's reign over his "Kingdom of Back" and of his inexhaustible love for his father.[97]

Eventually, Mozart's widow and his sister seemed to be reconciled to the biographies of Mozart that the other had shaped. When the former offered Breitkopf & Härtel access to the documents in her possession, she acknowledged that these, together with "Niemetschek's work and the good part of [Schlichtegroll's] *Nekrolog* would permit one to make a whole."[98] And Marianne was deeply moved upon reading Niemetschek's book for the first time: "Herr Prof. Niemetschek's biography so completely reanimated my sisterly feelings toward my so ardently beloved brother that I was often dissolved in tears, since it is only now that I became acquainted with the sad condition in which my brother found himself."[99] Unfortunately, Constanze Mozart had developed an interest in exaggerating Mozart's generosity, poverty, and lack of recognition, and so, in Nissen's biography, she validated many false reports—primarily those originating with Friedrich Rochlitz—bearing on such matters, including those alleging that he was taken advantage of by impresarios, publishers, and fellow musicians. Thus, Rochlitz's fable about Mozart making an absurdly disadvantageous deal with Schikaneder for Die Zauberflöte ideally suited her purposes, just as it suited her to circulate and/or certify false accounts about the composition and completion of the Requiem. By the time Mary and Vincent Novello visited her in Salzburg in 1829, she avowed that "all Mozart's operas were either given, or stolen, the remainder of his music was sold for a mere trifle"; and she was ready to affirm Rochlitz's invention that Mozart had "refused an offer of the King of Prussia to reside at his court with a salary of 1,600 sequins [Rochlitz had written "3,000 Thaler," equivalent to 4,500 florins] because he would not leave [Emperor] Joseph," and expressed the hope that "this generous sacrifice will not go unrewarded to his family by the Austrian court."[100] Ironically, in this process Constanze joined forces with her father-in-law and sister-in-law, validating their opinions about Mozart's childish nature, irresponsibility, and naïveté in worldly affairs. In the end, the myth of the eternal child proved irresistible to everyone.

Marianne von Berchtold, whose eyesight began to fail toward 1820 and who became completely blind by 1826, died in Salzburg on 29 October 1829. In the first paragraph of her last will and testament, dated 20 October 1823, after commending her soul to God, she expressed her wish to "be buried in the consecrated earth at St. Sebastian in the grave of my father."[101] It was a fitting, even inevitable, request, all the more so since her daughter, Johanna (Jeanette), who had died in 1805 at the age of sixteen, was also buried in the family plot there. Remarkably, however, by a codicil to her will dated 1 July 1827, she altered this provision, specifying that she was to be "buried in the so-called community vault in St. Peter's instead of St. Sebastian."[102] No explanation was given, but the reason for the change is not difficult to find.

There had been so little contact between Mozart's wife and sister that in a letter of 1819 to a Viennese correspondent Marianne expressed her surprise to learn that Constanze was "still alive and in Vienna; I had looked for her to be in Denmark, since I was told several years ago that she married a legation secretary in Denmark. Since 1801 I have not had any letters from her subsequent to the one I received in which she sent me her condolences on the death of my husband."[103] The two women became cordial, though scarcely intimate, neighbors after Georg Nissen was pensioned from the diplomatic service, for he and his wife moved from Denmark to Salzburg in 1820, where she became an esteemed member of society and he assiduously worked on his biography of Mozart until his death in March 1826. To the Nissens' delight, Marianne even turned over to them about four hundred family letters, which contained the "correspondence between father and son . . . up to 1781," and had been completely unknown to biographers up to then.[104] But then, Constanze Nissen, asserting her rights as Mozart's widow, successfully made application to bury her second husband in the cemetery plot in St. Sebastian in which Leopold Mozart was buried and in which Marianne von Berchtold had expected to be buried.[105] It is now too late to decide whether this was an act of familial piety or a belated tender of reconciliation, rather than the raging usurpation that it appeared to be.

In August 1826, Mozart's younger son, Franz Xaver (now called Wolfgang Amadeus) came to Salzburg from Lemberg to pay tribute to Georg Nissen; he conducted Mozart's Requiem in the University Church and presented a concert at the town hall in memory of his stepfather.[106] A stately tombstone for Nissen was ordered and completed for installation by the summer of 1827, just at the time when Mozart's sister decided that she would rather give up the consolation of being buried in the family grave than to share that space with her brother's widow, who, by an inexplicable irony, had herself elected to spend eternity lying next to her father-in-law. Naturally, Constanze's own will specified that she be buried by Nissen's side, and so since her death on 6 March 1842, her remains lie in St. Sebastian's cemetery, adjoining the graves of Leopold Mozart and his mother-in-law, Eva Rosina Pertl.[107] The inscription on the tombstone reads, "Constanze von Nissen, widow of Mozart, born Weber."

The eldest of the Weber sisters, Josepha Hofer, had died in 1819 in Vienna, but the surviving sisters, Aloysia Lange and Sophie Haibel, both had joined Constanze in Salzburg and as aged widows lived out their long lives there. Aloysia died in 1839, in her late seventies, Sophie in 1846, aged eighty-three, and they, too, were buried in the St. Sebastian cemetery. We can only imagine Leopold Mozart's consternation at the thought of finding himself, in the end, resting among the women of the Weber family.

Autograph manuscript, *Requiem*, K. 626, Kyrie. Music Collection of the
Österreichische Nationalbibliothek. Mus. HS. 17.561a.

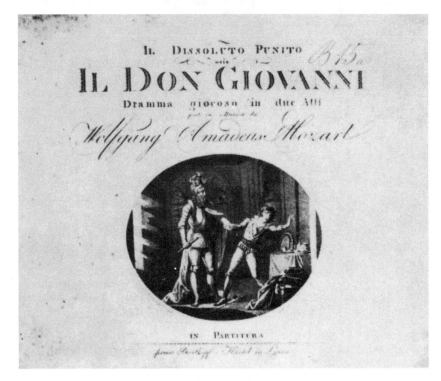

Title page of first edition, *Don Giovanni*, K. 527.
Breitkopf & Härtel, 1801.

32

··

THE POWER OF MUSIC

"Repent, change your life!" ("Pentiti, cianga vita!") insists the Commendatore's implacable ghost, and Don Giovanni knows that the price of refusal is death. Yet despite the implied offer of mercy he will not repent: "No, no, chio non mi pento!" But why not? Why doesn't he repent? Or rather, why doesn't he simply *say* that he has repented? For the lying, hypocritical, dissimulating Don Giovanni, whose every action heretofore has been based on deception, the Don Giovanni who masqueraded as Don Ottavio in order to seduce Donna Anna, the Don Giovanni who blamed Leporello for the attempted rape of Zerlina, the Don Giovanni who lured Donna Elvira into the arms of his servant, the Don Giovanni whose "lips are liars, whose eye is false," there should have been no difficulty in saying, "But of course, I do repent, and most sincerely! Long live repentance!" Moreover, he could readily have taken the occasion to beg for pardon as well as mercy, just as Count Almaviva had little difficulty in saying, "Contessa, perdono!" ("Countess, forgive me!") at the conclusion of *Le nozze di Figaro*. This would have been Don Giovanni's ultimate seduction—to be forgiven, loved, and graced by all, thus preparing the ground for further conquests. That he does not do so indicates that he has now gone beyond deception and is in search of something more. Whether that something is heroism, truth, knowledge, a desire for self-punishment, a drive to die, a need to descend to the mothers, a compulsion to submit to the marmoreal father-ghost, or a decision to continue his quest in a new territory, is completely open. What is not open is that Don Giovanni—first by his invitation to the Commendatore, then by unlatching the door for the supernatural visitor, by taking his hand, and finally by his refusal to repent—freely chooses his own fate. Perhaps, like Melmoth, the hero of Maturin's gothic novel, he needs to free himself of an impossible burden—the burden of life. Perhaps he is now taking seriously the ironic slogan of the Act I finale: "Viva la libertà!" Perhaps, he has concluded, "mille e tre" was enough.

In either event—repentance or refusal—we are left in disquietude. The refusal says there are unexpected depths of character here: we now need to consider that Don Giovanni may be a Faust, a Promethean rebel, a heretic willing to die for his beliefs, unwilling, he says, to be "falsely accused of cowardice!" And if so, what are we to make of all that went before? On the other hand, if he repents we know that he has won the game, that we cannot root out a seductive, dissimulating evil that plays by rules that are not ours. Crippled or potent, repentant or defiant, Don Giovanni departs in triumph. Appearances to the contrary, he may have escaped judgment, perhaps even begun a new quest. It was troubling enough to contemplate his ability to reach the hearts of good women—to know that noble Elvira retained her grand passion for him and would follow him to the ends of the earth despite his rejection of her redemptive love; that the spontaneous Zerlina could scarcely resist him: "Presto, non son più forte!" ("Quick, my strength is failing!"). Now, to envisage the probability that he operates on a higher moral plane than we do is for us to lose our moorings, even to glimpse the abyss.

We lose our moorings in *Die Zauberflöte* as well, where in a riot of carnivalesque metamorphoses, we are asked to validate the most improbable narrative detours and U-turns. Sarastro, a demonic kidnapper, is transformed into a fountainhead of benevolence; the Queen of the Night, a mother passionately seeking to recover her daughter, turns into the embodiment of malevolence; Papageno and Tamino become disciples of Sarastro, though both were initially in the service of the Queen of the Night; Monostatos too changes his allegiance, but in the other direction; Pamina, despite having been abducted by Sarastro and almost raped while in his charge, confesses her own criminality and to all appearances freely converts to the interests of her jailers. *Die Zauberflöte* is a rescue opera in which the hero arrives on the scene himself crying for help, trembling in fear, and fainting dead away. "Help! Help! Or else I am lost! . . . Ah, save me!"—this is a strange text for a chivalric hero. He has a bow but no arrows, yet despite his defenselessness he is chosen as the perfect knight, now armed with only a magic flute, to rescue Pamina. It is not Prince Tamino but the timorous bird catcher Papageno who twice saves Pamina from rape; and it is Papageno not Tamino who sings the great love duet with her, "Bei Männern, welche Liebe fühlen." An old crone says her age is eighteen years and two minutes; she turns out to be Papagena. The unpreparedness of these reversals, improbabilities, unmaskings, and remask-ings is what is so startling, like turning over a card, switching a lamp on and off, changing light into darkness and back again. Appropriately, the overarching design of the opera embodies the transition from star-flaming night to brilliant sun.

Le nozze di Figaro also confronts us with surprising and violent rever-sals, but of a quite different stamp: revelations of unanticipated passions that threaten both psychological equilibrium and the social order. It opens with the lovers Susanna and Figaro playfully preenacting their wedding night. She tries on her new hat and bids for Figaro's admiration, while he in turn measures the nuptial bed in what he expects will be their bridal chamber, measuring the space that will soon belong to them alone, a space that they have both earned by their labor and by steadfast devotion to the interests of their master, Count Almaviva. The space is inviolate, precious, it is Susanna's body. The hat is her own handiwork, which she wears to express her joy and as an offering to her bridegroom. Figaro is grateful to the Count, ready to leap to his service at the sound of a bell. But at the realization of their employer's designs upon Susanna, a convulsive alteration occurs, telling not only of the violence that lies hidden beneath Mozart's idyllic singspiel sur-face but of the readiness with which the apparently harmonious social fab-ric can be shredded. Feelings of betrayal, victimization, and jealousy surface and fantasies of revenge emerge as we watch and listen, transforming Figaro from jovial servant into single-minded pursuer of justice. "Se vuol ballare" is an enraged Hamlet-fantasy of making the Count—belittled by the diminutive attribute "Signor Contino," as Wye Jamison Allanbrook has remarked—dance to Figaro's tune:

> If you want to dance,
> My pretty little Count,
> I'll play the guitar
> For you. . . .

> If you want to come
> To my school,
> I'll teach you
> The capriole. . . .

He knows that it will be an unequal battle, so he will have to employ rapierlike cunning rather than sheer force:

> The art of fencing,
> The art of conniving,

Pricking from this side,
Tricking from that—
I'll upset
All your schemes.[1]

Figaro cloaks "his insolence in the noble *politesse* of the minuet," writes
Allanbrook, playing the dancing master so that his prey may be "lured into
the trap."[2] The singer retains a menacing, ironic distance, while the orchestra gives expression to his humiliation through cuckolding horn calls doubled by strings pizzicato to underscore his anger (Example 32.1).

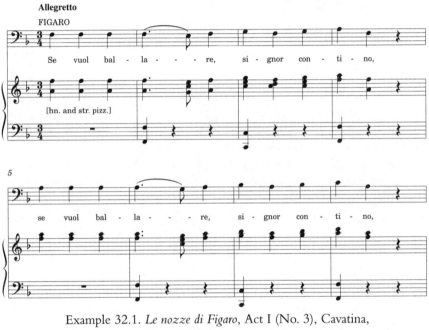

Example 32.1. *Le nozze di Figaro*, Act I (No. 3), Cavatina,
"Se vuol ballare," mm. 1–8.

As swiftly as the flip of a coin, Figaro thus reveals not simply the strength of
his feelings, but the dangerousness of which he is capable. Before he is
through, he will have inflamed the Count with morbid jealousy, played
Iago to his Othello, evened the score. Eventually, the Count will have been
reduced to utter impotence, stripped of all pretenses to authority. In the
end, he will continue to rule only by grace, by the mercy of women and
servants, rather than by moral right or personal power.

In *Così fan tutte,* our disquiet extends to the moral universe, overthrowing
traditional expectations of love and fidelity, valorizing irony as the *condition
humaine.* The social order remains intact, the marriages take place, but the
heart is permanently seared. Here the untangling at the close leaves a bitter

residue, a sense of love's uncertainty, a universal sense of betrayal and moral instability. And of ambiguity: Edward Dent thinks that it is not clear "from the libretto" whether the women pair off "with their original lovers or their new ones."[3] Joseph Kerman disagrees, giving several cogent reasons why "the original *status quo* is to stand."[4] He is surely right, but it may not make much difference how the couples are matched. The worm is deep within the apple: after the intervening betrayal and recognition scenes, none of the pairings can be satisfactory. The ending reinforces rather than relieves the anxiety that we all now feel about these alliances. Rather than a happy ending, perhaps, it is a sad beginning, which ratifies the death of innocence. Perhaps the happiest ending for all concerned would have been a clean break.

On the evidence of the Da Ponte operas and *Die Zauberflöte*, Mozart is one of those rare creative beings who comes to disturb the sleep of the world. He was put on earth, it seems, not merely to provide an anodyne to sorrow and an antidote to loss, but to trouble our rest, to remind us that all is not well, that neither the center nor the perimeter can hold, that things are not what they seem to be, that masquerade and reality may well be inter- changeable, that love is frail, life transient, faith unstable. The archaic myths and traditional stories had provided both certainty and assurance that we have a fixed place in the universe and some prospect of redemption. We knew what these old stories were and how they would turn out. And they did not disappoint us. But Mozart's universe is itself uncertain, a maze of doorways to the unknown and the unexpected. Everywhere there are dis- locations, fissures, tears, and weak spots; cynicism and disillusionment now permeate his resolutions, corrupt his happy endings.

Of course, a temporary disruption of the natural order of things is a pre- condition of dramatic action. What is so troubling in these operas—in con- trast to every form of Aristotelian drama and in contrast to Mozart's own instrumental cycles—is the jarring fragility and incompleteness of their cathartic effect, the impermanence and ambiguity of the transcendent residue with which we are left at the close. Mozart has succeeded in subverting the artist/patron/audience compact that provided an easy utopia of present con- tentment rather than an unreachable utopia of things that are not-yet. Unlike Haydn, for example, enlightened negotiation, comic reconciliation, and bri- dled emotions were not always sufficient for Mozart. For him, the benefi- cence of the Creation was not self-evident, or, at least, it was necessary to reconcile it with the stations of the Cross. Tranquillity must be earned, not ratified or colluded in. Evil persists even after music has had its say.

Allanbrook takes such issues seriously, viewing Mozart's works as divine commedias affirming integration and acceptance; of the happy end- ings in these operas she writes, "No matter what the depredations, proper orders were reestablished and their restoration celebrated," and asks, "Is it not in truth the braver, and the higher, act to assert that life goes on in the face of cruelty, disorder, and blighted hopes, rather than to delight in the titillation of prevailing melodrama and death?"[5] Elsewhere, she is not quite so certain that the circle has been successfully closed, that the "joyous commonality" of Die Zauberflöte's finale, for example, has successfully patched over the issues of despair, fear, and power that preoccupied its composer. She writes, "Comedy ends with the assertion of the proper orders, but this assertion may not necessarily be the crown of a serene and sane society; it may indeed be a lid clapped on disorder and despair."[6] If it were otherwise, Mozart's creative impulse would have satisfactorily completed its trajectory, for there would have been no need to continue. In any event, though Mozart is always in quest of reconciliation, it is not in his nature to be content with existing orders, especially ones that he has dismantled in so joyous a deconstructive spirit.

It is not merely circumvented catharses or the troubling residues of his endings that give Mozart's late operas their unsettling qualities. A sense of dislocation and disorientation rises from the use of distancing or estrangement effects, devices of which there are a variety, especially in Don Giovanni. On hearing Elvira's Act I account of her seduction and abandonment, Leporello comments, "It's just like a printed book!" thereby splitting himself into an observer of a twice-told traditional myth and an ironic participant in a reenactment of that myth. (The same device is used by Susanna and Figaro to wind up Le nozze di Figaro: "Let's end the comedy, my darling. Let's console this strange lover.") In the banquet scene of Don Giovanni a wind band plays fragments from three recent Italian operas—Martín y Soler's Una cosa rara, Sarti's I due litiganti, and Mozart's Le nozze di Figaro—and although Don Giovanni explains the intrusion as merely "a nice concert," the effect is to replant us in an uncertain geography that extends beyond Seville to Vienna, and to catapult us from the past into the opera's immediate present. Mozart has thereby undermined the historicity of the fable, placing it not only in a time-that-was but in the here-and-now, given us a doubleness of time and place, a doubleness of stage and reality at the intersection of two sonic universes. Leporello's casual depreciation of the music from Le nozze di Figaro—"I've heard that tune once too often!"—is low comedy, true, but it also throws into question the seriousness of impending climactic events. In Die Zauberflöte, a farrago of comic absurdities and descents into pure farce set up similar tensions by their contrast with the play's elevated purposes.

It is profoundly troubling to be drawn by the power of music into empathic collusion with murderers, tyrants, kidnappers, seducers, rapists, and misogynists. In Mozart's early operas, whether seria or buffa, he rarely if ever undermined the traditional stereotypicality of the characters or set up a dissonance between character type and music: in Lucio Silla, Mitridate, *rè di Ponto, Il rè pastore, La finta giardiniera,* and Mozart's last two efforts in opera seria, *Idomeneo* and *La clemenza di Tito,* the characters are closely synchronized with the mythological narrative, and their responses to the action are predetermined. From the moment they set foot upon the stage and introduce themselves by way of a characteristic set piece, we know within a relatively narrow range what we will feel about them as they make their way through a predictable universe.

But, though stock characters also populate the Da Ponte operas and *Die Zauberflöte* and create the illusion that they are performing according to expectations, we often encounter in them a disjunction between type and music, a revelation of unexpected ambiguities and apparently misplaced feelings. Sarastro is purged of his criminality (though not his misogyny) as he reveals the splendors of the Temples of Wisdom, Reason, and Nature; when she sings, "Batti Batti," Zerlina displays the all-too-human coexistence of betrayal and fidelity in a single individual, whose plea for forgiveness converts a desire for physical punishment into the anticipation of sensual pleasure; in his arias, as Ivan Nagel observed, Don Giovanni, "shockingly, still does not dissemble. Not a single note in his marriage vow to Zerlina, 'Là ci darem la mano,' or in his declaration of love to 'Elvira, idolo mio,' suggests that he does not believe what he is singing."[7] Resisting, we are swept into identification with a seducer.

As they slip into the timeless dimension where arias are sung, these characters strip away the limitations of their types; and when they reemerge onto the stage, it is as though they are stepping from that timeless world into the "real" world of adventitious character. We are asked for the moment to forget their limitations and to forgive their sins, disturbing prospects that stir unaccustomed emotional responses in us. The music upsets our composure, especially when it shows us redemptive qualities in scoundrels, desperate rage in an ordinarily accommodating manservant, the compulsion of an innocent to confess to a crime she never committed. If a villain is also capable of profound love, we may have difficulty in condemning his actions. If the Queen of the Night is evil, we may find ourselves condoning the theft of her child. These metamorphoses are far different from the routine narrative transformations (of Pasha Selim, Titus, Idomeneo, Almaviva) that testify to the workings of mercy, forgiveness, penitence, and reconciliation—not to mention the presumed ultimate beneficence of all misguided rulers—at the close of every exemplary drama. Like Ferrando and Guglielmo in *Così fan tutte* we find ourselves unable to differentiate between sham feeling and "real" feeling. And that may be Mozart's point: pretense, through the pulls of proximity and the asymmetrical logic of the emotions, may pass over into genuine feeling. The face of Max Beerbohm's "happy hypocrite" takes on the contours of his angelic mask: what, then, we wonder, lies beneath the mask of Don Giovanni?

★   ★   ★

Figaro pursues justice no less single-mindedly than does Kleist's Michael
Kohlhaas, with the difference that Figaro's is a preemptive strike against a
crime that has not yet been committed. In his fantasies he can already visualize Susanna's violation, imagining himself as Vulcan discovering Venus in
the embrace of Mars. He is driven by his own intense interior visions. To
prevent the seduction of Susanna he is willing to risk all—his position, his
prospects, his marriage—reckless of the odds, fearless of aristocratic privilege, scorning the alignments and prerogatives of power. For him destruction, even annihilation, is preferable to this injustice. Figaro's obsession is
only the most striking example of the intertwining themes of criminality,
justice, and the abuse of power in Mozart's late operas, which on an important level are narratives of crime and punishment (or absolution). That the
guilty are men in high places is an admonition that citizens of an enlightened society intend to hold aristocracy and kingship to rigorous standards
of behavior, to reject, in the interest of the social compact, the willful abuse
of power. Such abuses center not upon the wholly taboo issues of corruption of the state, but upon a panoply of sexual misdemeanors, and it is the
deep eroticism of these operas in the context of the critique of power that
provides much of their narrative tension and their disquieting effect.

Although Don Giovanni commits an incidental murder and Sarastro a
kidnapping, the cardinal crimes in the Da Ponte operas and *Die Zauberflöte*
are those aimed against virtue, in the first place seduction and rape. Indeed,
the threat of sexual violation is central to all of Mozart's opera buffas and
singspiels from *Zaide* to *Die Zauberflöte,* although it had been absent in his
earlier works in these genres. The threat of seduction or rape provides a
backdrop of menace in these operas which is quite at odds with their
comic surface. And the ambiguity in the range of feminine responses to
sexual threat adds another level of unease to the narrative tension. In all of
these operas, sexual violation remains imminent but is never actualized,
perhaps in order to avoid offense to conventional morality but also because
the frustration of the seducer's plans is a mainspring of the dramatic action
and a necessity of the comic mode. Despite imaginative efforts by commentators to convert Don Giovanni's failures into offstage conquests, it is
fairly unambiguous that he is literally thwarted in carrying out five
attempted seductions: "It seems that the devil amuses himself today by
impeding the progress of my pleasures; everything has gone badly." The
seeming exception among these operas, of course, is *Così fan tutte,* where
the seducers themselves want to prevent the seductions from taking place
but are unable to do so: themselves obsessed by thoughts of infidelity, they
cannot help betraying their loved ones. The successful commission of the
crime constitutes its own punishment, in a compulsive process of self-
humiliation. What gives *Così fan tutte* its melancholy aura is that seductions

that no one desired could not be prevented. Its saddest moment is perhaps when Dorabella says to Guglielmo, "Let us, too, go for a walk," and he responds, "Come vi piaco . . . " ("If you like") and adds in an aside, "Ahimè!" ("Alas!"). He would not have been consoled by what many know and few acknowledge, that Dorabella and Fiordiligi—or Ferrando and Guglielmo—are not the only ones who can love a second person without renouncing their first love.

In Mozart's hands, the endangered heroine is more than simply a usefully titillating dramatic trope fed by the confluent streams of classical mythology, the Richardsonian novel, gothic fiction, pornographic literature, Franco-Italian comedy, and Sturm und Drang antityrannical drama. Rather, this trope is an important means of focusing the deep eroticism that characterizes Mozart's late operas. Don Giovanni would rather die than give up his erotic quest—for impotence is to him a catastrophe worse than death. Not only Figaro but Masetto is transformed into a potential instrument of destruction by affronts to his sexuality: his "Capisco, sì signore!" ("I understand, yes, sir!") has the repressed rage and despair of a peasant's helplessness in face of his lord's hypocrisy, but soon he will be ready to kill for love—"Just touch her and your head will fall." In *Die Zauberflöte* the only reasonable alternative to love is "death and despair": Pamina will kill herself if she loses Tamino's love; Papageno will hang himself if he cannot find love; Tamino goes through fearsome ordeals to achieve love.

Pamina, subjected to a variety of horrors, of which kidnapping, captivity, coercion, and attempts at rape are only a beginning, is the paradigm of Mozart's endangered heroines. When we encounter the Hamletlike cruelty of Tamino toward Pamina/Ophelia during the ritual silence, and she asks, "And shalt thou then be my bridegroom?" as she looks at her dagger, we know, suddenly, that this is no idle fairy-tale entertainment. Tamino's (and Papageno's) silence is not the only reason why Pamina comes to the edge of suicide. Equally annihilating are her mother's insistence that she commit murder, her mother's curse ("Thou shalt nevermore be my daughter; be thou outcast forever, be thou forsaken forever"), and, finally, the knowledge that she has been offered by the Queen of the Night to Monostatos as the price of his treachery.

If Mozart's main themes are the critique of power, the protest against injustice, and the safeguarding of innocence, his main question is "How do we make things right?" On the surface, simple vengeance is an effective strategy of dealing with injustice, of balancing the scales. Except in *Così fan tutte,* where the loss of innocence leads to despair (some might say, wisdom), injustice generates a passion for revenge. "I ask for vengeance," cries Donna Anna to Don Ottavio, "your heart must also demand it. Remember the wound gaping in my father's breast! Recall his blood that covered the ground." The Queen of the Night joins in this call—"Hell's vengeance boils in my heart"—as she presses the knife into Pamina's hand. Sarastro, true to his practice of ideological hypocrisy (early on, Tamino grasped this when he exclaimed, "Then it is all duplicity!"—"alles Heuchelei!") explicitly disavows vengeance—"these sacred halls know not of revenge"—but takes it anyway. Figaro, Masetto, Leporello, and Monostatos are driven by fantasies of retribution. Even Susanna says, "I won't move a step from here, yet I'll have my revenge." But Mozart, despite his determination to get even when he himself has been mistreated, understands—at least, it is his rational/Masonic creed—that vengeance, because it indulges individual passion at the expense of objective reason, is an insufficient remedy for injustice.[8]

Die Zauberflöte offers an ideologically more appropriate response to cruelty and injustice: the rejection of violence, the acceptance of responsibility, the faith in love as a shield against evil. Although it was Sarastro's violent actions—his assertion of the droit de seigneur—that launched the perils of Pamina, she refuses the knife, acknowledges her own sins, and asks for forgiveness:

> Lord, I am indeed a criminal
> I wanted to flee from thy power.

Despite this abjection, however, she will not compromise her love and sacrifice herself to Sarastro. Pamina's "Lord, I am indeed a criminal!" is a simple echo of Zaide's plea to her captor, Soliman, "Forgive me—I cannot love you!" Pamina's crime is that she loves someone other than the totalitarian father. Sarastro is sufficiently explicit about the issue when he says,

> Arise, take courage, o beloved one!
> For without pressing thee further
> I know already what is in your heart.
> You love another dearly.
> I will not force you to love
> But I will not set you free.

The operas are not only about menace, but also about rescue—of Susanna from the Count's attentions; of Pamina (also Constanze and Zaide) from captivity; of Anna, Zerlina, and Elvira from seduction. The French revolutionary "rescue opera," which led to Fidelio, already had ample precedent in the operas of Mozart. Brigid Brophy showed that Die Zauberflöte combines two myths: the abduction of Demeter's daughter Persephone by Hades and the rescue of Eurydice from the underworld by the musician-hero Orpheus.[9] Nagel too wrote, "The rescue of a captive woman from the underworld by a loving man is the oldest plot in opera"; he observed further that with Goethe's Iphigenia, Mozart's Pamina, and Beethoven's Leonore "a different, clandestine plot-line asserts itself: how the woman in need of rescue becomes the rescuer."[10] Already in *Le nozze di Figaro,* Susanna plays a leading role in defending the sanctity of her betrothal; in *Don Giovanni,* Anna and Elvira cry out for justice even while Don Ottavio wavers; and in *Die Zauberflöte,* it is Pamina in the end who leads Tamino through the caverns of fire and darkness.

These operas try to make things right by bringing to bear every conceivable strategy of evasion and confrontation, opposing power with beauty, innocence, cunning, protest, evasion, irony, and carnivalesque inversion, and finally, by adapting the central formula of opera seria reconciliation, which is the transformation of a miscreant into a simultaneously repentant and forgiving ruler. The benevolent sun-priest dedicated to monogamous marriage, wisdom, and reason is no longer the lustful Sarastro who kidnapped and coerced Pamina and left her defenseless against his servant's assaults: he has been at once transfigured and neutralized. The primal father who had always ruled by fiat and terror has learned how to negotiate. In the end, Sarastro has no substantive power: he is an empty figurehead in a geometrical landscape; his authority is purely formal. Actual power resides in the married pair. Here, as in *Idomeneo* and *Le nozze di Figaro,* power passes through marriage to the younger generation. After a year of mourning and healing, Donna Anna and Don Ottavio will marry. The lovers in *Così fan tutte* will marry at once because there is no better alternative. The proper antidote to the misogyny of Don Alfonso and Sarastro is a joyous wedding. In all of the operas, the closest approximation to a satisfactory resolution resides in the marriage sacrament, where a consecrated private space replaces the social sphere as the locus of utopia, representing a leap of faith, the pledging of life, the promise of continuity, and even the microcosmic equivalent of the godhead:

> Man and Wife, and Wife and Man
> Reach even to divinity.

> Mann und Weib, und Weib und Mann
> Reichen an die Gottheit an.

Mozart's operas are dramas of desired transformations. If their happy endings nevertheless leave a residue of dissatisfaction and malaise, it is not for want of trying. Always Mozart strives for coherence, to overcome disquietude, spinning both traditional and imaginative strategies in hope of making things right. Naturally, he doesn't have equal faith in every modality of transcendence. He knows that there will remain unresolved issues of power and submission, that even the most felicitous denouements cannot erase memories of humiliation and terror. That is why, in Kerman's words,

"Cruelty and shame have their place in Mozart's picture of human fallibility."[11] Unlike Beethoven, Mozart cannot bring himself to validate the myth of a *bon prince:* his suspicion of kings, priests, and princes is too deeply engrained in him. He wavers between an extreme cynicism and a desire to believe in such eternal verities as benevolence, fidelity, and truth. The *lex talionis* is uncivilized, unenlightened; rescue is partial; accommodation is opportunistic; happy endings are vitiated by disillusionment, bitterness, and an excess of knowledge.

Certainly, Mozart subscribed to the conventional radicalisms of his time and place; the Three Boys speak on his behalf when they announce the coming of dawn:

> Soon shall superstition disappear
> Soon the wise man shall be victorious.
> As sweet tranquillity, descend here
> Return once more to grace men's hearts;
> Then shall the earth be a heavenly realm,
> And mortals shall be as gods.

Yes, but if the city of the sun turns out to be nothing more than a set of geometrical, astral, architectural blueprints for a new Sparta, without a hint of human warmth, do we really need it?[12] I harbor a fantasy that Mozart didn't really believe in this authoritarian utopia, for I would like to think that he could not suppress his innate mistrust of institutionalized power. I would even like to think that the greatest absurdity about *Die Zauberflöte's* patchwork of absurdities plagiarized and plundered from myth, Utopian fantasy, mystical tradition, and Masonic mummery is the subsequent appropriation of this bitterly satirical opera to the service of patriarchal imperatives that would have been very much to the liking of such rationalists as Don Alfonso, Sarastro, and Leopold Mozart.

When in doubt, as we know, Mozart always reverts to the comic mode, to farce, to carnival, to commedia dell'arte. Forget menace, forget the uncanny, forget philosophy and all excessively weighty questions. Ferrando and Guglielmo remove their mustaches while Don Alfonso forces an unaccustomed smile and counsels laughter. Papageno and Papagena stutter their way into happiness. The crazy day of "torment, caprice and folly" yields to gaiety. It's time to wrap up the story, which, after all, Mozart and Da Ponte dubbed a *dramma giocoso:* things are not as bad as we thought; perhaps with a hint of camp, Anna yet again asks Ottavio to postpone his longing for "another year, my darling, until my heart is ready"; Elvira is ready to retire to a convent; Zerlina and Masetto will go home to have their dinner; and Leporello heads for the inn in search of a better master. If a king's messenger on a white steed is really required, it can be arranged.

In the end, music remained Mozart's primary talisman against corruption, fear, and death. "Gladly, through the power of music, we wander through death's dark night," say the initiates, as *Die Zauberflöte* draws to a close. Mozart relies upon music—upon a flute, not a sword—to pursue his chivalric purposes. Pamina's captors flee from the sound of Papageno's chimes. "How powerful is your magic sound," marvels Tamino of his flute. "When you are played even the wild animals feel joy." Now we can see why a defenseless youth was chosen to carry out a heroic task: Mozart wants to demonstrate the power of innocence, love, and music. The improbable flute-playing hero overcomes his fear, transforms a representative of the underworld into a scion of the light, achieves a pure marriage of the heart. Cherubino, too, knows the power of music: he has written a little canzonetta, a love song—"Voi che sapete"—to be sung, he hopes, "to every woman in the palace." He wants to trade it for a consecrated ribbon from the Countess's nightcap. "You ladies who know what love is, see if it is what I have in my heart." Here, as in his Act I aria, "Non so più," he sings of his confusion, torment, and yearning: "I quiver and tremble without knowing it, I find no peace night or day, and yet it pleases me to languish this way." Thereupon he experiences the unhappy fate of all musicians: having poured out his heart to his beloved, he is judged solely by the quality of his performance. "Bravo!" says the Countess, "What a beautiful voice! I didn't know that you sang so well."

Autograph manuscript, *Le nozze di Figaro*, K. 492, Aria, "Non so più cosa son," Mozart's arrangement for voice, violin, and piano. The Pierpont Morgan Library, Dannie and Hettie Heineman Collection.

Cherubino—the composer, Eros, the tumescent eternal child—is himself a talisman against everything that is hurtful. And he is far from being the only musician in Mozart's operas. As Edward T. Cone has observed, when Susanna accompanies Cherubino, or Pedrillo sings his romance in *Die Entführung aus dem Serail,* or Don Giovanni picks up the guitar to serenade Elvira's maid, they too are musicians; and when Papageno plays his bells, he "reveals himself as an instrumental virtuoso as well; and Tamino similarly distinguishes himself on the flute."[13] Each of them is a carrier of music's potential transformational powers—whether intended to move the heart of another person, or to calm the wild beasts, or to establish a new kingdom. Sometimes its purposes are not benign: in the Act II trio of *Don Giovanni,* Don Giovanni succeeds in decoying Elvira into Leporello's arms solely through the seductive power of music, of his voice. And Mozart also shows us how music itself can effect transformations of a somewhat different kind. The churchyard scene of *Don Giovanni,* with its *ombra* style, gothic trappings, and nervous pacing, has created an unstoppable momentum that can only result in a destructive collision. But Anna's aria, "Non mi dir, bell'idol mio," with its sorrowful inwardness, interrupts the deathward plunge of the action and temporarily removes us to a region out of time where love holds sway (Example 32.2).

Example 32.2. *Don Giovanni,* Act II (No. 23), Aria, "Non mi dir, bell'idol mio," mm. 16–23.

Time stops. Anna declares her love, asking Ottavio to understand why she cannot yet give herself to him. Perhaps we can sense the action waiting to resume behind the scenes. But for a moment, by the beauty of a song, music has held back the rush to death.

Ultimately, we are left with the unexceptionable utopian affirmations—love, marriage, the good society, brotherhood, innocence, virtue, reconciliation—and a need to believe in the power of music. For a while, at least—and even longer, because music is endlessly repeatable—Mozart succeeds in offsetting the fears of separation, betrayal, and silence which his operas evoked in the first place. These affirmations may be defective, but they are all we have. We will have to make do.

Mozart's snuffbox with street scene and two young men. Oil on ivory. Göttweig, Stift. Reproduced from Selma Krasa et al., *Zaubertöne: Mozart in Wien.*

APPENDIX: MOZART'S VIENNA EARNINGS

In order to gauge Mozart's economic vicissitudes, we need to have an idea of how much money he earned during his Vienna years. The following is a listing of his estimated annual earnings, in florins, for the years 1781 through 1791. An "academy" is a public concert in a major theater, e.g., the Burgtheater or Kärntnertor Theater; a "subscription concert" is a public concert held in a smaller venue—e.g., in the Mehlgrube or Trattnerhof—for an audience mostly of subscribers; a "salon appearance" is a formal performance at a patron's residence, such as a court or palace.

1781	
Salzburg salary for first quarter	112
Idomeneo	450
Teaching	297
Competition with Clementi	225
Total	**1,084**
Other possible income	
Salon appearances	200
Earnings range	**1,084 to 1,284**

1782	
Entführung aus dem Serail	426
Teaching	648
Academies	600
Salon appearances	500
Total	**2,174**
Other possible income	
Benefit performance of *Entführung*	600
Augarten concerts	300
Earnings range	**2,174 to 3,074**

1783

Academies	1,400
Teaching	432
Publications	60
Total	**1,892**

Other possible income
Teaching	216
Salon appearances:	300
Earnings range	**1,892 to 2,408**

1784

Academies	600
Subscription concerts	600
Salon appearances	1,800
Teaching	540
Publications	180
Total	**3,720**

1785

Academies	559
Subscription concerts	1,500
Publications	900
Total	**2,959**

1786

Le nozze di Figaro	450
Der Schauspieldirektor	225
Academies	600
Subscription concerts	600
Publications	385
Scores for Prince Fürstenberg	119
Private performance, *Idomeneo*	225
Total	**2,604**

Other possible income
Benefit performance of *Figaro*	600
Salon appearances	500
Earnings range	**2,604 to 3,704**

1787

Don Giovanni (Prague)	450
Benefit performance of *Don Giovanni*	600
Personal appearances in Prague, including	
academy of 19 January	1,000
Publications	205
Inheritance	1,000
Salary (one month)	66
Total	**3,321**

1788

Don Giovanni (Vienna)	225
Salary	800
Subscription concert, Handel's *Acis and Galatea*	150
Publications	210
Total	**1,385**

Other possible income

Subscription concerts at the Casino	450
Fee for directing Swieten's Society of Associated Cavaliers	225
Earnings range	**1,385 to 2,060**

1789

Elector of Saxony	450
Salary	800
Publications	233
Total	**1,483**

Other possible income

Fee for directing Swieten's Society	225
100 ducats due "from abroad"	450
Earnings range	**1,483 to 2,158**

1790

Così fan tutte	450
Elector of Mainz	135
Salary	800
Teaching	324
Publications	141
Total	**1,850**

Other possible income

Così fan tutte extra fee	450
Frankfurt concert	200
Salon appearances and private concerts in Frankfurt, Mainz, Munich	500
Fee for directing Swieten's Society	225
Earnings range	**1,850 to 3,225**

1791

La clemenza di Tito	900
Die Zauberflöte	900
Requiem advance	225
Salary	800
Publications	550
Teaching	297
Total	**3,672**

Other possible income

Sum to be received late June	2,000
Earnings range	**3,672 to 5,672**

Because the documentary record is fragmentary, it is inevitable that we should have much more information about Mozart's money-producing activities than about the actual sums that he earned from those activities. Thus, in order to provide a useful survey of his earnings, I have estimated the probable fees or earnings from his known activities, basing my calculations on comparable fees or earnings for essentially similar activities by Mozart or his contemporaries. To complicate matters, there are conflicting ways to read the evidence about the actual amount that he earned on certain occasions, such as his fees for *Così fan tutte, Die Zauberflöte,* or the Requiem, reported cash presents from the elector of Mainz or the king of Prussia, or the amount of his teaching income. Similarly, there are lacunae in our knowledge of Mozart's activities as a performer after 1787, particularly since correspondence with his father, which until then had been the main source of such information, was no longer available. A particularly vexing issue is whether or not Mozart's planned "Casino concerts" of 1788 ever materialized; most recent scholarship holds for the affirmative.[1] Many of these conflicts cannot be satisfactorily resolved. Accordingly, there must be a considerable margin of error in my calculations. Estimates have not been used where the actual amount is known. The estimates are based on the following assumptions with respect to the various categories of income-producing activity.

- *600 florins per academy or per opera performance for Mozart's own benefit.* Mozart's actual receipts at his academy at the Burgtheater on 23 March 1783 were reported to be 1,600 florins, suggesting a profit after expenses of perhaps 1,400 florins, assuming costs of 200 florins.[2] Typical costs of presenting an orchestral concert in a major theater ranged from 115 florins for a concerto-size accompaniment to 240 florins for "the musical personnel" at a performance of *Don Giovanni.*[3] Mozart's profit on his academy at the Burgtheater on 10 March 1785 was 559 florins.[4] The Lebruns' profits at three successive academies at the Burgtheater in February–March 1785 were 1,100, 900, and 500 florins, respectively.[5] A single benefit performance of *Doktor und Apotheker* in Vienna brought Dittersdorf a profit of 900 florins.[6] The average profit on these six documented academies is 893 florins; the average on the two Mozart academies is 979 florins 50 kreuzer.
- *150 florins per subscription concert.* Mozart's receipts were 337 florins for each of six concerts (150 subscribers at 1 souverain d'or for the series = 2,025 florins) in the Mehlgrube in 1785;[7] I assume costs of 150 florins per concert, leaving a net profit per concert of 187 florins. Receipts were 334 florins for each of three concerts at the Trattnerhof in 1784 (a minimum of 167 subscribers at 6 florins for the series);[8] the profit after deducting estimated costs of 150 florins per concert amounted to 184 florins per concert. Receipts were 240 florins per concert for each of three concerts at Advent in 1785 (120 subscribers at 6 florins for the series);[9] deducting estimated costs of 150 florins, the net profit was 90 florins per concert. The average profit from these 12 concerts was 162 florins per concert.[10]
- *100 florins per salon appearance.* Mozart received 225 florins for his joint appearance with Clementi at the Viennese court in 1781;[11] 165 florins from the elec-

tor of Mainz in 1790;[12] 450 florins from the elector of Saxony in Dresden in 1789;[13] Archbishop Colloredo paid 18 to 22 florins to each of three court musicians, including Mozart, for salon appearances in 1781;[14] Countess Thun paid singers Adamberger and Madame Weigl 225 florin each in 1781.[15] In the years 1783 to 1785, Mozart probably received very high fees for such performances in accordance with his status as a celebrity artist. Kraemer's estimate of 200 florins per salon appearance seems high; Braunbehrens's 50 florins seems too low. Since no public announcements exist for such engagements, there are doubtless numerous undocumented salon appearances, especially during the years 1781–86. I have made no estimate of the number of undocumented salon appearances or the income from them.

- *27 florins per month per pupil.* Mozart repeatedly cited his fee of 6 ducats (ca. 27 florins) per month for a series of 12 clavier lessons.[16] Hamann has listed most of Mozart's clavier and composition students, and given the approximate dates of their studies.[17] Where the number of his pupils is known, I have estimated the probable number of total lesson-months (@ 27 florins) per year, allowing for summer holidays and Mozart's own absences from Vienna.

1781: 3 pupils, 11 lesson-months	297
1782: 3 pupils, 24 lesson-months	648
1783: 2 pupils, 16 lesson-months	432
(with possible third pupil for 8 months)	216
1784: 2 pupils, 20 lesson-months	540
1790: 2 pupils, 12 lesson-months	324
1791: 2 pupils, 11 lesson-months	297

I have made no estimate for the years 1785 to 1789, although Mozart is known to have had several composition students and perhaps a few clavier pupils during those years. We do not know whether he charged such gifted pupils as Hummel and Attwood for lessons; probably Hummel did not pay for either lessons or board. I assume that Mozart reluctantly returned to teaching as a source of income only in about 1790.[18] His lengthy absences from Vienna in the last years are also taken into account.

- *Estimated publication income.* This is limited to publications by the Viennese firms of Artaria, Hoffmeister, and Torricella, and is calculated at the rate of 75 florins per quartet or concerto;[19] 30 florins per symphony, overture, sonata, set of variations, trio, or quintet; 10 florins per smaller piano piece; and 4.5 florins per lied or dance. I use known fees paid by Viennese publishers to Mozart, Haydn, Beethoven, and Dittersdorf as a point of reference.[20] I multiply these fees by the number of publications in each genre, as follows:

1783: 2 sonatas = 60. Total: 60 florins.
1784: 6 sonatas = 180. Total: 180 florins.
1785: 2 symphonies = 60; 6 string quartets = 450; 1 piano quartet = 75; 3 concertos = 225; 1 sonata = 30; 2 sets of variations = 60. Total: 900 florins.

1786: 1 string quartet = 75; 9 sets of variations = 270; trio = 30; piano piece = 10. Total: 385 florins.

1787: 1 piano quartet = 75; 4 sonatas = 120; piano piece = 10. Total: 205 florins.

1788: 1 overture = 30; 4 trios = 120; 1 set of variations = 30; 3 piano pieces = 30. Total: 210 florins.

1789: 1 quintet = 30; 1 sonata = 30; 4 lieder = 18; 30 dances = 135; 2 piano pieces = 20. Total: 233 florins.

1790: 1 quintet, 1 trio = 60; 18 dances = 81. Total: 141 florins.

1791: 3 string quartets = 225; 1 concerto = 75; 1 set of variations = 30; 49 dances = 220.5 Total: 550.5 florins.

All of these appear to be authorized rather than unauthorized editions. In papers filed in connection with a lawsuit against the publishing firm of Cappi & Diabelli in 1818, Artaria claimed that, although it had no specific contractual assignment of rights from Mozart, its rights to its publications of his works could be confirmed by witnesses and by the firm's account books, which reflected fees paid to him for major works. As for minor works, the brief stated that "Mozart was much too generous to accept or to request anything for such trifles."[21] It is not clear what was meant by "trifles," for the lawsuit itself involved two of Mozart's lieder.

No estimate has been made for the sale of manuscript copies of Mozart's scores by reputable and presumably authorized dealers such as Torricella, Artaria, Lausch, and Traeg. Landon calculates that for the contredanses alone this could have been equivalent to as much as two thirds of the fee for engraving rights.[22] Also not estimated are fees for publication of arrangements of operatic numbers or for subscriptions to the six sonatas published by Artaria in November 1781; in the latter case Mozart received 229 florins' income from seventeen subscriptions at 3 ducats, but his expenses are not known.[23]

I have not estimated income from Mozart's numerous appearances at academies for other artists, although it is not certain that these were done gratis, inasmuch as the presence of a guest artist was for the purpose of increasing the box-office take, and, furthermore, such appearances tended to diminish, through overexposure, the income from an artist's own concerts, making compensation appropriate. A contemporary letter notes that at Josepha Duschek's special audience with the emperor in March 1786, "She was accompanied by the famous pianist Mozart and the virtuoso [violinist Johann Friedrich] Eck. . . . The accompaniment by the other musici cost Mme Duschek 100 thalers."[24] This is usually taken to refer to an orchestral accompaniment, but one way of reading the letter is that Mozart and Eck were paid as much as 100 florins each, somewhat less if there was actually an orchestra on hand.[25] Also not estimated is income from Mozart's regular Sunday-morning performances at his own home, although it is known that an admission fee was usually required, or for subscription concerts which may have been given there in later years.[26] And in the absence of clear data no estimate has been attempted for income from Mozart's sale of his opera scores to foreign companies. In light of the numerous productions of Le nozze di Figaro and Die Entführung aus dem

Serail in particular, this could have amounted to a substantial sum. Occasional sales of scores to patrons and admirers may also have added to Mozart's income.[27]

We must also allow for the possibility that Mozart had sources of income concerning which no information has survived, and that such income may have been substantial, for there are several references to windfall sums being paid for Mozart's compositions. Constanze Mozart related that a Polish count once paid Mozart 150 ducats (ca. 675 florins) as a token of admiration or as an advance on a flute trio, a substantial sum in either case, half as much again as the customary advance for an entire opera.[28] This report is not necessarily true, but it is certain that early in 1792 the king of Prussia paid Mozart's widow the astounding sum of 3,500 florins for eight of her husband's scores, at the rate of 100 ducats each.[29] Another sum, a mysterious 2,000 florins mentioned in Mozart's letter of 25 June 1791 to Puchberg, may belong in the category of windfall earnings.

A few miscellaneous observations relating to Mozart's finances: Mozart's payment in 1787 from his sister for his share of their father's inheritance amounted to a full 1,000 florins in Viennese currency, because his sister paid the 10 percent export tax levied by Salzburg as well as court costs.[30] Mozart was apparently a full partner with Philipp Jakob Martin in presenting the Augarten concerts in the summer of 1782: "Assuming that we get only a hundred subscribers [at 2 ducats], then each of us will have a profit of three hundred florins (even if the costs amount to two hundred florins),"[31] Mozart wrote to his father. The proceeds from the academy of 22 March 1783 at the Burgtheater were reported in Cramer's *Magazin der Musik*.[32] Mozart mentioned the amount of the proceeds from the first two performances of *Die Entführung aus dem Serail* in a letter to his father of 20 July 1782.[33] His earnings from an academy and perhaps other performances in Prague in January 1787 were reported to Leopold Mozart by Mozart's English friends.[34] The "100 Friedrich d'ors" (ca. 800 florins) from Friedrich Wilhelm II in 1789 is mentioned in Mozart's letter of 23 May 1789, but for reasons discussed in chapter 28 I do not believe the king actually made such a payment; accordingly, I have not included this reported sum in Mozart's income.[35] Possible sources of the unexplained "2,000 fl." about to arrive in late June or early July 1791 (see Mozart's letter to Puchberg of 25 June 1791)[36] include new loans taken by Mozart, repayments of loans made by Mozart, payments from the Hungarian or Amsterdam patrons who had supposedly guaranteed him an annual income,[37] advances from publishers, or payment of fees in connection with *Die Zauberflöte,* which had just been essentially completed.

Mozart himself specified the fee for *Così fan tutte* as 900 florins: "According to the present arrangement I am to receive from the management next month 200 ducats for my opera."[38] It has been argued, however, that despite his flat statement to Puchberg, he received only 100 ducats for the opera, because a surviving weekly ledger for 1789–90 shows for the week of 20–26 February 1790 a payment to him of 450 florins "for composing the music to the opera."[39] But the payment is listed under the heading "Extra Disbursements" and was paid more than a month after the premiere, suggesting that it may have been a payment supplementary to a previously paid advance, perhaps from the proceeds of the fifth and last performance, on 11 February. Mozart's letter to Puchberg indicates that the advance was expected in late December 1789 or early January 1790, i.e., before the premiere. The main account book for this period is missing.

Finally, I have not adjusted my calculations to take account of a recently redis-covered document in Mozart's hand, which at first glance gives what appears to be a tantalizing account of his cash position and expenses at an unspecified time in his late years:

> My cashbox for the past year contains 295 Imperial and Cremnitz ducats at 4 fl. 30 kr; 119 Salzburger Ducats at 4 fl. 20 kr; 88 Holland ducats at 4 fl. 18 kr; 101 souverains d'or at 13 florins 20 kr; 250 Thaler at 2 fl. 30 kr; 25 bank notes at 50 fl.; 18 bank notes at 25 fl.; 50 bank notes at 10 fl.; and 90 bank notes at 5 fl.
>
> In the course of this year have disbursed the following: 99 Imperial ducats; 55 Salzburger; 33 Holland; 66 Souverains; 88 thaler at 2 fl. 30; and beyond this another 539 fl. 56 kr.—The remainder has then been divided into five parts. Now the question is: how much did each one get?[40]

Despite the document's apparent practical function, in reality it is clearly an arith-metic problem: that is why the sums in the second paragraph are all divisible by 11 and the final amount is to be divided by five. Braunbehrens has found, by an anal-ysis of currency-exchange fluctuations, that the document must have been pre-pared after February 1786 and probably not later than February 1788. Braun-behrens and Ulrich Drüner would like to believe that Mozart based the exercise on actual income and disbursement amounts, but Ulrich Konrad demonstrates that the arithmetic problem is an amusing conundrum admitting of no precise answer in Viennese currency and he cogently holds that the document "does not allow us to draw any conclusions, direct or indirect, regarding Mozart's financial circum-stances."[41]

ABBREVIATIONS

Abert	Otto Jahn. *W. A. Mozart.* 5th ed. 2 vols. Ed. and enlarged by Hermann Abert. Leipzig, 1919–21; 9th ed., 1956.
AMZ	*Allgemeine Musikalische Zeitung.*
B&H	Breitkopf & Härtel.
Bär	Carl Bär. *Mozart: Krankheit, Tod, Begräbnis.* 2nd ed., Schriftenreihe der Internationalen Stiftung Mozarteum, vol. 1. Salzburg, 1972.
Blümml	E. K. Blümml. *Aus Mozarts Freundes- und Familienkreis.* Vienna, Prague, and Leipzig, 1923.
Briefe	Wilhelm A. Bauer, Otto Erich Deutsch, and Joseph Heinz Eibl, eds. *Wolfgang Amadeus Mozart: Briefe und Aufzeichnungen. Gesamtausgabe.* 7 vols. Kassel, 1962–75.
Chronik	Joseph Heinz Eibl. *Wolfgang Amadeus Mozart: Chronik eines Lebens.* Kassel, 1977.
Deutsch-Paumgartner	*Leopold Mozarts Briefe an seine Tochter.* Ed. Otto Erich Deutsch and Bernhard Paumgartner. Salzburg and Leipzig, 1936.
Dokumente	Otto Erich Deutsch, ed. *Mozart: Die Dokumente seines Lebens.* Neue Mozart-Ausgabe, X:34, *Dokumente aus dem Leben Mozarts.* Kassel, 1961.
Einstein	Alfred Einstein. *Mozart: His Character, His Work.* New York, 1945; reprint 1965.
ISM	Internationale Stiftung Mozarteum.
Jahn	Otto Jahn. *The Life of Mozart.* 3 vols. Trans. Pauline D. Townsend. London, 1882.
Jahn-Deiters	Otto Jahn. *W. A. Mozart.* 4th ed. 2 vols. Ed. and enlarged by Hermann Deiters. Leipzig, 1905–7.
K.	L. von Köchel. *Chronologisch-thematisches Verzeichnis der Werke W. A. Mozarts.* Leipzig, 1862.
K^6	L. von Köchel. *Chronologisch-thematisches Verzeichnis sämtlicher Tonwerke Wolfgang Amadè Mozarts.* 6th ed. Ed. F. Giegling, A. Weinmann, and G. Sievers. Wiesbaden, 1964.

Letters   Emily Anderson, trans. and ed. *The Letters of Mozart and His Family.* 3rd ed. (2 vols. in 1). London, 1985.

MDB   Otto Erich Deutsch. *Mozart: A Documentary Biography.* Trans. Eric Blom, Peter Branscombe, and Jeremy Noble. London, 1965.

MGG   *Die Musik in Geschichte und Gegenwart.* 17 vols. Ed. Friedrich Blume et al. Kassel, 1949–1986.

MJb   *Mozart-Jahrbuch.*

Niemetschek Franz Xaver Niemetschek. *Leben des k. k. Kapellmeisters Wolfgang Gottlieb Mozart, nach Originalquellen beschrieben.* Prague, 1798. Trans. Helen Mautner as *Life of Mozart.* London, 1956.

Nissen   Georg Nikolaus von Nissen. *Biographie W. A. Mozart's.* Ed. Constanze Nissen, with a foreword by Johann Heinrich Feuerstein. Leipzig, 1828. Reprinted with a foreword by Rudolph Angermüller. Hildesheim, 1984.

NMA   *Wolfgang Amadeus Mozart: Neue Ausgabe sämtlicher Werke.* Kassel, 1955–1993.

NMD   Cliff Eisen. *New Mozart Documents: A Supplement to O. E. Deutsch's Documentary Biography.* London and Stanford, 1991.

Novello   Nerina Medici di Marignano and Rosemary Hughes, eds. *A Mozart Pilgrimage: Being the Travel Diaries of Vincent and Mary Novello in the Year 1829.* London, 1955.

Plath   Wolfgang Plath. *Mozart-Schriften: Ausgewählte Aufsätze.* Ed. Marianne Danckwardt. Schriftenreihe der Internationalen Stiftung Mozarteum Salzburg, vol. 9. Kassel, 1991.

Schlichtegroll Friedrich Schlichtegroll. "Johannes Chrysostomus Wolfgang Gottlieb Mozart," in *Nekrolog auf dem Jahr 1791.* Gotha, 1793. Vol. 2, pp. 82–112 (entry for 5 December).

The New Grove Stanley Sadie, ed. *The New Grove Dictionary of Music and Musicians.* 20 vols. London, 1980.

Thematic
Catalogue   *Mozart's Thematic Catalogue: A Facsimile.* Ed. Albi Rosenthal and Alan Tyson. British Library, Stefan Zweig MS 63. Ithaca, 1990.

Tyson   Alan Tyson. *Mozart: Studies of the Autograph Scores.* Cambridge, Mass., and London, 1987.

NOTES

The Mozart correspondence is cited, with permission of the Macmillan Press Ltd., from the third edition of Emily Anderson's standard English translation of the Mozart family's letters, *The Letters of Mozart and His Family*, cited here as *Letters*. For materials that are not included in the Anderson edition, citations are from the definitive *Mozart: Briefe und Aufzeichnungen*, edited by Wilhelm A. Bauer, Otto Erich Deutsch, and Joseph Heinz Eibl, cited here as *Briefe*. In the latter case and that of other foreign-language sources, translations are mine unless otherwise noted.

In the case of English-language sources, American spelling and punctuation have been used throughout; my occasional emendations ("translation amended") and corrections ("translation revised") of Anderson's and others' translations are identified in the footnotes. All italics in quotations are original, unless otherwise noted.

Parenthetical number references are to number sequences in the various document collections.

References to currency have been standardized (see "Table of Money Values," p. xi).

References to *NMA* editions are divided into series, genres (*Werkgruppen*), and volumes. Thus, the reference *NMA* IX:25/1 (for the Piano Sonata in A minor, K. 310/300d), means: series IX (clavier music); genre or work group 25 (sonatas, fantasies, and rondos for clavier); volume 1.

Introduction

1. L. Hübner, *Beschreibung der hochfürstlich-erzbischöflichen Haupt- und Residenzstadt Salzburg und ihrer Gegenden* (Salzburg, 1792–93), vol. 1, pp. 27–28.

2. Ibid., p. 370.

3. *MDB*, pp. 425, 427, 442, 447, 467; *NMD*, p. 123 (no. 179).

4. For details, see Georg Abdon Pichler, *Salzburg's Landes-Geschichte* Part One: *Allgemeine Geschichte* (Salzburg, 1861), vol. 1, pp. 1036–37; Jahn-Deiters, vol. 2, p. 707; and Rudolph Angermüller, *Das Salzburger Mozart-Denkmal* (Bad Honnef, Germany, 1992). The proclamation of the Salzburg Mozart Monument Committee was published in September 1836.

5. Gernot Gruber, *Mozart und die Nachwelt* (Salzburg, 1985), p. 24.

6. *Letters*, pp. 896–97, Leopold Mozart to his daughter, 23 March 1786 (no. 538). There are authentic orchestral parts of several works, including the Piano Concerto in E-flat, K. 271, datable to the 1780s, which may have been prepared for local performances, perhaps given privately. By way of contrast, there were four known Salzburg performances of Mozart works in the years 1782–84: the "Haffner" Symphony, K. 385, on 29 July 1782 in connection with Sigmund Haffner's ennoblement; the *Litaniae de venerabili altaris sacramento*, K. 243, on 13 April 1783 at the cathedral; the C-minor Mass, K. 427, on 26 October 1783 at the church of St. Peter's Abbey under Mozart's own direction; and *Die Entführung aus dem Serail*, presented by Ludwig Schmidt's visiting theater company on 17 November 1784, with repetitions on 21 November and 9 December 1784.

7. Review of *Die Liebe im Narrenhause*, in *Oberdeutsche allgemeine Literaturzeitung*, 2 November 1791: *NMD*, p. 41 (no. 67). The reviewer discusses the difficulties of making piano reductions of operas: "How many operas have not already been ruined because of this? Consider

Mozart's masterpiece, *Die Entführung aus dem Serail,* and compare with it the keyboard arrangement, also published by *Schott,* made by *Abbé Stark.* Who would recognize *Mozart* in it?"

8. *MDB,* p. 268.

9. I say this with some reservations because previously unknown Mozart documents and references are being unearthed with unexpected frequency by archival researchers. See, moreover, the 1786 report about Mozart's Viennese activities in an unconventional newspaper that circulated briefly in Salzburg, *Pfeffer und Salz* (Salzburg [Vienna], 5 April 1786): *MDB,* p. 270.

10. *Oberdeutsche Staats-Zeitung,* 12 December 1791 (no. 99), columns 1961–62. The Salzburg obituary, previously unknown, was discovered in October 1992 by Cliff Eisen. *Wiener Zeitung,* 7 December 1791: *MDB,* p. 418; translation amended.

11. *NMD,* p. 76 (no. 119).

12. *Letters,* pp. 884–85, Leopold Mozart to his daughter, 19 November 1784 (no. 520); see also *Letters,* p. 884, after 21 November 1784 (no. 521).

13. Ernst Ludwig Gerber, *Historisch-biographisches Lexicon der Tonkünstler* (Leipzig, 1790): *MDB,* p. 383.

Prologue: The Myth of the Eternal Child

1. Daines Barrington, "Account of a Very Remarkable Young Musician": *MDB,* pp. 95–100.

2. Charles Burney, *The Present State of Music in France and Italy* (London, 1771): *MDB,* p. 140.

3. Barrington, "Account": *MDB,* p. 97. Mozart's age was usually understated by one year during his European journeys. See *MDB,* pp. 33–67, passim; *NMD,* pp. 8–9 (nos. 10–12).

4. Friedrich Melchior von Grimm, *Correspondance Littéraire,* 1 December 1763: *MDB,* pp. 26–27.

5. This and what follows are from the periodical *Aristide ou le citoyen,* 11 October 1766: *MDB,* pp. 61–62, 65. For Tissot and Mozart, see A. Hyatt King, "A Swiss Account of Mozart in 1766," in King, *Mozart in Retrospect: Studies in Criticism and Bibliography* (London, 1955), pp. 131–40, and *Briefe,* vol. 5, p. 165.

6. *MDB,* p. 140.

7. Ibid., p. 65.

8. Grimm, *Correspondance Littéraire,* 15 July 1766: *MDB,* pp. 56–57.

9. Among others, Padre Martini reportedly had a copy; see Jahn, vol. 1, p. 120 n. 37, and Arthur Hutchings, *Mozart: The Man, the Musician* (New York, 1976), vol. 2, p. 14. The *Miserere* story is further embroidered in Johann Friedrich Rochlitz, "Ein guter Rath Mozarts," in *Für Freunde der Tonkunst* (Leipzig, 1824–32), vol. 2, p. 284.

10. To test Mozart's abilities André-Ernest-Modeste Grétry "wrote him an Allegro in E-flat; difficult, but unpretentious; he played it, and everyone, except myself, believed that it was a miracle. The boy had not stopped; but following the modulations, he had substituted a quantity of passages for those which I had written." Grétry, *Mémoires ou essais sur la musique* (Paris, 1789 [not 1795]): *MDB,* p. 477; see also *NMD,* p. 15 (no. 22).

11. "I found likewise that most of the London musicians were of the same opinion with regard to his age." Barrington, "Account": *MDB,* p. 99.

12. Marianne von Berchtold, "Data for a biography of the late composer Wolfgang Mozart": *MDB,* p. 459; Ernst Ludwig Gerber, *Neues historisch-biographisches Lexikon der Tonkünstler* (Leipzig, 1812–14), col. 477.

13. Barrington "Account": *MDB,* p. 99; see also Erich Schenk, *Mozart and His Times,* trans. Richard and Clara Winston (New York, 1959), p. 98. The composition in question is thought to be the "Cantata on Christ's Grave" (*Grabmusik*), K. 42/35a. See K⁶, p. 36.

14. *Letters,* p. 89, 30 July 1768 (no. 62).

15. Nissen, pp. 48–49; Jahn, vol. 1, p. 35; Jahn-Deiters, vol. 1, p. 37. As Nissen remarks, there is no documentary support for this report. See Nissen, p. 48; *Briefe,* vol. 5, p. 92.

16. *Letters,* p. 6, Leopold Mozart to Lorenz Hagenauer, 16 October 1762 (no. 2); the anecdote was also recorded in the diary of Father Placidus Scharl, 6 January 1763: *MDB,* p. 19.

17. Johann Andreas Schachtner, letter to Marianne von Berchtold, 24 April 1792: *MDB,* p. 451. Niemetschek (p. 13) expands upon this: "He asked all with whom he came in contact whether they loved him, and burst into tears if they jokingly denied it."

18. *Letters,* p. 483, 16 February 1778 (no. 287).

19. Grimm, *Correspondance Littéraire*, 25 July 1766: *MDB*, p. 57.

20. Barrington "Account": *MDB*, p. 100. Cf. "He is really a most extraordinary effort of Nature, but our Professors in Physick don't think he will be long lived." Joseph Yorke to his brother Philip Yorke, second earl of Hardwicke, 1 October 1765: *NMD*, pp. 9–10 (no. 13). Similar fears were voiced by Tissot; see *MDB*, p. 64.

21. Quoted in C. Kerényi, "The Primordial Child in Primordial Times," in C. Jung and C. Kerényi, *Essays on a Science of Mythology* (Princeton, 1963), p. 26.

22. *Letters*, p. 67, 16 August 1766 (no. 43).

23. Ibid., pp. 68–69, to Lorenz Hagenauer, 10 November 1766 (no. 44).

24. Ibid., p. 85, to Lorenz Hagenauer, 11 May 1768 (no. 59); translation amended. See *Briefe*, vol. 1, p. 264 (no. 392).

25. *Letters*, p. 423, 18 December 1777 (no. 262).

26. Ibid., p. 620, 24 September 1778 (no. 333); p. 423, 18 December 1777 (no. 262); p. 567, 13 July 1778 (no. 314).

27. Ibid., p. 334, 18–20 October 1777 (no. 225).

28. Abert, vol. 1, p. 6.

29. *Letters*, p. 455, 29 January 1778 (no. 277).

30. Ibid., p. 465, 5 February 1778 (no. 282); translation amended.

31. Ibid., p. 476, [11]–12 February 1778 (no. 285).

32. Ibid., p. 475, [11]–12 February 1778 (no. 285).

33. Ibid., p. 463, 5 February 1778 (no. 281a).

34. Jean-Jacques Rousseau, *The Social Contract* and *Discourse on the Origin and Foundation of Inequality Among Mankind*, ed. Lester G. Crocker (New York, 1967), p. 233.

35. According to Lawrence Stone, *The Family, Sex and Marriage in England 1500–1800* (New York, 1977, p. 468), the class of lower artisans (into which Leopold Mozart was born) viewed children as "positive economic assets, primarily for their productive labor from the age of seven until their marriage, but also as supports for the parents in old age." Leopold Mozart followed the child-rearing practices of the wealthier artisans, who "rejected the use of physical punishment but substituted for it overwhelming psychological pressures of prayer, moralizing, and threats of damnation." They pursued "an unremitting and stern effort to break the child's will and so repress his impulses to sin." In eighteenth-century England, according to Sir William Blackstone, a child is maintained within "the empire of the father" until he reaches his majority, and thereafter his parents are "entitled to our protection in the infirmity of their age; they who by sustenance and education have enabled their offspring to prosper, ought in return to be supported by that offspring, in case they stand in need of assistance." Blackstone, *Commentaries on the Laws of England*, ed. William Draper Lewis (Philadelphia, 1897; reprint 1922), vol. 1, pp. 426–28 (Chapter 16, Sections 452–54).

36. *Briefe*, vol. 2, p. 464, 3 September 1778 (no. 482).

37. *Letters*, p. 494, 25–26 February 1778 (no. 291).

38. Leopold Mozart's finances are discussed in chaps. 5, 7, and 26.

39. *Letters*, p. 506, 7 March 1778 (no. 296).

40. Sigmund Freud, "Analysis, Terminable and Interminable," in *Standard Edition of the Complete Psychological Works of Sigmund Freud*, ed. and trans. James Strachey et al. (London, 1953–1974), vol. 23, p. 229. Quoted here from the Joan Riviere translation, in Freud, *Collected Papers* (New York, 1959), vol. 5, p. 331.

41. Karl Marx, preface to *Capital: A Critique of Political Economy*, vol. 1, trans. Samuel Moore and Edward Aveling (New York, 1947), p. xviii.

42. *Letters*, p. 496, 25–26 February 1778 (no. 291).

43. Ibid., p. 475, [11]–12 February 1778 (no. 285).

44. Ibid., p. 483, 16 February 1778 (no. 287).

45. Ibid., p. 483, 16 February 1778 (no. 287).

46. Letter of 7 July 1770: *MDB*, p. 124.

47. Letter to Charles Burney, 30 November 1772: *NMD*, p. 23 (no. 38).

48. *Letters*, p. 587, 31 July 1778 (no. 319).

49. Ibid., p. 698, Mozart to his father, 27 December 1780 (no. 381).

50. Ibid., p. 350, Mozart to his father, 31 October 1777 (no. 232a).

51. Postscript to Marianne von Berchtold, "Data for a biography of the late composer Wolfgang Mozart": *MDB*, p. 462. The passage almost surely stems from Marianne, even though it is in the hand of Albert von Mölk, who transmitted her reminiscences to the biographer

Friedrich von Schlichtegroll. She subsequently referred to the document as "my article" and sent it unaltered to B&H with the remark that it was "just as I extracted it from letters my father wrote," comments sufficient to establish her authorship—at the very least, her endorsement—of those passages that are not in her own handwriting. *Briefe,* vol. 4, p. 260, 4 August 1799 (no. 1250), and ibid., p. 296, 24 November 1799 (no. 1268).

52. Schlichtegroll, p. 109; see also, inter alia, Jean-Baptiste-Antoine Suard, "Anecdotes sur Mozart," in *Mélanges de littérature* 10 (1804): *MDB,* p. 498; Nissen, p. 529.

53. Jahn, vol. 2, p. 265 n.

54. Beethoven, too, was variously called "the great child," "very childlike," and "a wayward child." See Maynard Solomon, *Beethoven Essays* (Cambridge, Mass., 1988), pp. 145, 331 n. 37. See also A. B. Marx, *Ludwig van Beethoven: Leben und Schaffen* (Berlin, 1859), vol. 2, p. 120. Similar things were said about Goethe as well, but it is only with Mozart that the notion of a genius in a permanent state of childhood and childishness takes hold.

55. Arthur Schopenhauer, *The World as Will and Representation,* trans. E. F. J. Payne (New York, 1966), vol. 2, p. 395. See also Peter Kivy, "The Child Mozart as an Aesthetic Symbol," *Journal of the History of Ideas* 28 (1967), pp. 249–58.

56. G. W. F. Hegel, *The Philosophy of Fine Art,* trans. F. P. B. Osmaston (London, 1920), vol. 1, p. 37; translation amended.

57. Karl-Heinz Köhler and Grita Herre, eds., *Ludwig van Beethovens Konversationshefte,* vol. 8 (Leipzig, 1981), p. 85.

58. C. H. H. Parry, "Variations," in *A Dictionary of Music and Musicians,* ed. Sir George Grove (London, 1879–89), vol. 4, p. 224.

59. Wolfgang Hildesheimer, *Mozart,* trans. Marion Faber (New York, 1982), p. 252.

60. Hildesheimer, *Mozart,* pp. 243, 99. See also Maynard Solomon, review of *Mozart* by Wolfgang Hildesheimer, *Musical Quarterly* 69 (1983), pp. 274–76.

61. Peter Shaffer, letter to the *New York Times,* Sec. 2, 16 July 1989.

62. Jahn, vol. 1, pp. 329–30; translation amended. Jahn observed approvingly that "Wolfgang had neither the experience nor the practical shrewdness of his father; he felt secure of his art, in which alone he lived, and imagined the rest would come of itself" (p. 348).

63. Ludwig Nohl, *Mozart* (Leipzig, 1863); trans. Lady Wallace as *The Life of Mozart* (London, 1877), vol. 2, p. 23.

64. Arthur Schurig, *Wolfgang Amade Mozart* (Leipzig, 1913), vol. 1, pp. 43, 25; 2nd ed. (Leipzig, 1923), vol. 1, pp. 30, 43, 49.

65. Edward J. Dent, *Mozart's Operas: A Critical Study* (London, 1913; 2nd ed., 1947; reprint 1962), pp. 17, 15.

66. Ibid., p. 68.

67. Einstein, pp. 31, 27, and passim.

68. Erich Hertzmann, "Mozart's Creative Process," in *The Creative World of Mozart,* ed. Paul Henry Lang (New York, 1963), p. 25.

69. Søren Kierkegaard, *Either/Or: A Fragment of Life,* trans. David F. Swenson and Lillian Marvin Swenson (Princeton, 1944), vol. 1, p. 15.

70. Otto Erich Deutsch, *Schubert: A Documentary Biography,* trans. Eric Blom (London, 1946), p. 60.

Chapter 1: Leopold Mozart

1. Diary of Dominikus Hagenauer for 28 May 1787: *MDB,* p. 293; translation amended.

2. Nissen, p. 12.

3. Adolf Buff, "Mozart's Augsburger Vorfahren," *Zeitschrift des Historischen Vereins für Schwaben und Neuburg* 18 (Augsburg, 1891), p. 24; see also *MDB,* p. 3.

4. Adolf Layer, *Eine Jugend in Augsburg: Leopold Mozart 1719–1737* (Augsburg, [1975]), p. 32. For details, see Ernst Fritz Schmid, *Ein schwäbisches Mozartbuch* (Lorch, 1948), pp. 54–57.

5. For a complete list of the productions and Leopold Mozart's roles in them, see Layer, *Eine Jugend,* pp. 46–54, 89–91.

6. There is some dispute about this in the literature. Schmid regards a document from the early summer of 1728 on which Leopold Mozart was already listed as "Principista" as evidence that he enrolled in the fall of 1727. See Schmid. *Schwäbisches Mozartbuch,* pp. 56–57. Ludwig Wegele, "Leopold Mozart in Augsburg," in *Leopold Mozart, 1719–1787, Bild einer Persönlichkeit*

(Augsburg, 1969), ed. Wegele, p. 13, notes that in 1732–33 Leopold Mozart repeated the fourth class. Schmid (p. 81) writes, "He appears to have repeated two classes" and this is why his name was not found in the *personae musicae* of the school dramas in 1731 and 1732. Layer, however, speculates that Leopold Mozart may have taken several years of preliminary instruction at the gymnasium in 1727 and 1728, actually matriculating only in October 1729. See Layer, *Eine Jugend,* pp. 35, 90–91. Valentin tends to assume that Leopold was left back: "It would not be the last time that Leopold Mozart . . . behaved differently from the required rules and norms." Erich Valentin, *Leopold Mozart: Porträt einer Persönlichkeit* (Munich, 1987), p. 31. And Robert Münster thinks that Leopold Mozart at most repeated one year, and this, he believes, must have been caused by illness rather than inadequate scholastic accomplishment; see Robert Münster, "Neues zu Leopold Mozarts Augsburger Gymnasialjahren," *Acta Mozartiana* 12 (1965), pp. 57–60.

7. *Letters,* p. 307, 11 October 1777 (no. 219b); translation amended.

8. See Jahn, vol. 1, p. 6.

9. Layer, *Eine Jugend,* pp. 36–37; Wegele, "Leopold Mozart in Augsburg," p. 16.

10. Wegele, "Leopold Mozart in Augsburg," p. 15; Schmid, *Schwäbisches Mozartbuch,* p. 100.

11. Schmid, *Schwäbisches Mozartbuch,* pp. 101 and 473 n. 815; Franz Posch, "Leopold Mozart als Mensch, Vater und Erzieher der Aufklärung," *Neues MJb* 1 (1941), p. 59.

12. Erich Schenk, *Wolfgang Amadeus Mozart: Eine Biographie* (Zürich, 1955), p. 28; trans. Richard and Clara Winston as *Mozart and His Times* (New York, 1959), p. 12 n. 1.

13. According to Valentin, *Leopold Mozart,* p. 47, this took place at latest in 1740, perhaps as early as 1739. Leopold was probably guaranteed a position in advance of his forced departure from the university, for that carried "the risk of expulsion" from Salzburg as well. Josef Mančal, "Leopold Mozart und sein Verhältnis zu seinem Sohn," in *Zaubertöne—Mozart in Wien 1781–1791: Austellung des Historischen Museums der Stadt Wien im Künstlerhaus,* ed. Selma Krasa et al. (Vienna, 1990), p. 30.

14. Buff, "Mozart's Augsburger Vorfahren," pp. 26–27; Layer, *Eine Jugend,* p. 29; Wegele, "Leopold Mozart in Augsburg," p. 11. By the mid-1750s she had to borrow money to keep the property in repair and by 1763 she disposed of it altogether.

15. The petition, which was unaccountably overlooked by Buff and later researchers, is reproduced for the first time in Josef Mančal, "Vom 'Orden der geflickten Hosen,': Leopold Mozarts Heirat und Bürgerrecht," in *Leopold Mozart und Augsburg,* ed. Ottmar F. W. Beck (Augsburg, 1987), pp. 51–52. See also Josef Mančal, "Neues über Leopold Mozart," *Österreichische Musikzeitschrift* 42 (1987), pp. 282–91.

16. Mančal, "Vom 'Orden der geflickten Hosen,'" p. 39.

17. Mančal thinks that the town council, which included Leopold's schoolmate Jakob Wilhelm Benedikt Langenmantel von Westheim, colluded with him in his falsehoods ("Vom 'Orden der geflickten Hosen,'" p. 45).

18. Buff, "Mozart's Augsburger Vorfahren," pp. 27–28; the documents are reproduced in full in Mančal, "Vom 'Orden der geflickten Hosen,'" pp. 52–54. See also *MDB,* p. 5.

19. Buff, "Mozart's Augsburger Vorfahren," pp. 28–29; Heinz Schuler, "Die Hochzeit der Eltern Mozarts," *Acta Mozartiana* 28 (1981), p. 10. No further renewals have been located.

20. *Briefe,* vol. 1, pp. 10–11, 21 July 1755 (no. 6).

21. Ibid., p. 11, 21 July 1755 (no. 6).

22. Ibid., p. 16, 11 September 1755 (no. 9).

23. Ibid., p. 23, 15 December 1755 (no. 14).

24. See ibid., p. 40, 27 February 1756 (no. 26).

25. *Extract-Schreiben, oder . . . Europaeische Zeitung . . . ,* 19 July 1763: *MDB,* p. 23.

26. *Letters,* p. 22, 11 July 1763 (no. 12); translation amended. See *Briefe,* vol. 1, p. 75 (no. 53).

27. Marianne von Berchtold, "Data for a biography of the late composer Wolfgang Mozart": *MDB,* p. 454; *Dokumente,* p. 398; translation amended.

28. [Leopold Mozart], "Nachricht von dem gegenwärtigen Zustande der Musik Sr. Hochfürstl. Gnaden des Erzbischoffs zu Salzburg im Jahr 1757," in Friedrich Wilhelm Marpurg, ed., *Historisch-kritische Beyträge zur Aufnahme der Musik* (Berlin, 1757), vol. 3, p. 184; translation in Neal Zaslaw, *Mozart's Symphonies: Context, Performance Practice, Reception* (Oxford, 1989), pp. 550–51; see also *MDB,* p. 11.

29. *Briefe,* vol. 3, p. 52, 12–13 October 1777 (no. 348); *Letters,* p. 311 (no. 220); translation revised.

30. Marpurg, *Historisch-kritische Beyträge,* in Zaslaw, *Mozart's Symphonies,* p. 550.

31. Leopold Mozart, *A Treatise on the Fundamental Principles of Violin Playing,* ed. Alfred Einstein, trans. Editha Knocker (London, 1948; 2nd ed., 1951), p. 13; translation amended.

32. Ibid., p. 8.

33. Mančal, "Leopold Mozart und sein Verhältnis zu seinem Sohn," pp. 30–31.

34. *Letters,* p. 332, 18–20 October 1777 (no. 226).

35. Schenk, *Eine Biographie,* p. 55; Schenk, *Mozart,* p. 23. The pamphlet has not survived.

36. The standard work is C. Fr. Arnold, *Die Ausrottung des Protestantismus in Salzburg unter Erzbischof Firmian und seinen Nachfolgern: Ein Beitrag zur Kirchengeschichte des achtzehnten Jahrhunderts,* Schriften des Vereins für Reformationsgeschichte, nos. 67 and 69, vol. 18, nos. 2 and 4 (Halle, 1900–1901). See also Carl Mauelshagen, *The Salzburg Lutheran Expulsion and Its Impact* (New York, 1962).

37. *Briefe,* vol. 1, p. 5, 9 June 1755 (no. 2). Ibid., p. 14, 28 August 1755 (no. 8). Baron Grimm was a pupil of Gottsched.

38. Ibid., pp. 236–37, undated, presumably written between 1754 and 1766 (no. 115). Leopold Mozart's letter to Gellert is lost.

39. Letter of Friedrich Karl von Bose to Mozart, Paris, 1764: *MDB,* p. 28. Leopold mentions the gift in a letter to Hagenauer, *Briefe,* vol. 1, p. 140, 1 April 1764 (no. 83); *Letters,* p. 43 (no. 25). See *Briefe,* vol. 5, p. 108. In his letter Leopold Mozart writes of Bose and Baron von Hopfgart: "Here you will find two men who have everything which honest men should have in this world; and, although they are both Lutherans, yet they are Lutherans of a different type and men from whose conversation I have often profited much." *Letters,* pp. 42–43, 1 April 1764 (no. 25).

40. *Briefe,* vol. 1, p. 83, 3 August 1763 (no. 59).

41. Ibid., p. 103, 17 October 1763 (no. 67).

42. Abert, vol. 1, p. 7.

43. *Letters,* p. 422, 15 December 1777 (no. 261); translation amended.

44. Ibid., p. 91, 30 July 1768 (no. 62).

45. Ibid., p. 90, 30 July 1768 (no. 62). "It is an undeniable fact that everywhere you will have enemies, inasmuch as all men of great talent have them." Ibid., p. 535, 6 May 1778 (no. 304).

46. *Letters,* p. 406, 4 December 1777 (no. 255).

47. See Zaslaw, *Mozart's Symphonies,* pp. 128–38. See also Wolfgang Plath, "Leopold Mozart, 1987," in Plath, pp. 386–88.

48. Abert, vol. 1, p. 11. See also Max Friedlaender, "Leopold Mozarts Klaviersonaten," *Die Musik* 4, no. 1 (1904–5), pp. 38–40.

49. Einstein, pp. 10–12.

50. Cliff Eisen, "The Symphonies of Leopold Mozart and their Relationship to the Early Symphonies of Wolfgang Amadeus Mozart: A Bibliographical and Stylistic Study" (Ph.D. diss., Cornell University, 1986) p. 9. Zaslaw (*Mozart's Symphonies,* pp. 136, 279) agrees that Leopold Mozart was an "able, well-informed musician," whose "best works have genuine artistic merit."

51. Schmid, *Schwäbisches Mozartbuch,* p. 113.

52. Eisen, "Symphonies of Leopold Mozart," p. 2.

53. He writes of "the biography of our little one which I intend to publish later on." *Letters,* p. 77, 10 November 1767 (no. 51); translation amended. In the introduction to the second edition of his *Violinschule,* he wrote of his hope that "after my return from Italy, where I now intend to go with God's blessing," he would be able to "entertain the public with this story" of his son's life and travels. See *MDB,* p. 92.

54. *Letters,* pp. 548–49, 11 June 1778 (no. 308).

55. Leopold Mozart, *Fundamental Principles of Violin Playing,* p. 225 n. 1.

56. Wolfgang Plath, "Leopold Mozart" entry, *The New Grove,* vol. 5, p. 676.

57. Cliff Eisen, "The Symphonies of Leopold Mozart: Their Chronology, Style and Importance for the Study of Mozart's Early Symphonies," *MJb 1987/88,* p. 183. Leopold Mozart's contributions to his son's early compositions may be exceptions to this statement.

58. *Letters,* p. 266, 4 September 1776 (no. 205).

59. Marianne von Berchtold, "Data for a biography of the late composer Wolfgang Mozart": *MDB*, p. 454; translation amended.

60. *Letters*, p. 437, 29 December 1777 (no. 268).

Chapter 2: Early Days

1. *Letters*, p. 53, 27 November 1764 (no. 32).

2. *Letters*, p. 216, 21 November 1772 (no. 162). Mančal suggests that the courtship dated back to the beginning of the decade, if not earlier. See Josef Mančal, "Vom 'Orden der geflickten Hosen': Leopold Mozarts Heirat und Bürgerrecht," in Ottmar F. W. Beck, ed., *Leopold Mozart und Augsburg* (Augsburg, 1987), p. 32.

3. The following relies primarily upon Erich Schenk, "Mozarts Salzburger Vorfahren," *MJb* 3 (1929), pp. 83–105. See also Schenk, *Mozart and His Times* (New York, 1959), pp. 6–8; Schenk, "Mozarts mutterliche Familie," *Bericht über die musikwissenschaftliche Tagung der Internationalen Stiftung Mozarteum in Salzburg vom 2. bis 5. August 1931*, ed. Erich Schenk (Leipzig, 1932), pp. 45–68.

4. Marriage Register of the Parish of St. Gilgen, 22 November 1712: *MDB*, p. 3. See Heinz Schuler, "Mozarts Grossvater Pertl in St. Gilgen," *Mitteilungen der ISM* 23 (August 1975), p. 28.

5. Schenk, "Mozarts mutterliche Familie," p. 45.

6. Schenk points out that Pertl's financial debacle "was not exceptional, but a common everyday occurrence" in a principality where two thirds of the court's employees were considered by their employers to be superfluous and a burden to the state. Schenk, "Mozarts mutterliche Familie," p. 46.

7. Erich Valentin, *'Madame Mutter': Anna Maria Walburga Mozart (1720–1778)* (Augsburg, 1991), p. 18.

8. Schenk, "Salzburger Vorfahren," p. 92. The later document incorrectly gives Anna Maria's age as "fourteen."

9. Marriage Register of the Cathedral Parish, Salzburg, 21 November 1747: *MDB*, pp. 4–5. "Anna Maria" and "Maria Anna" were often interchanged in contemporary documents. It appears that here, too, Leopold Mozart gave the authorities the impression that his father was still alive.

10. Johann Leopold Joachim (18 August 1748–2 February 1749); Maria Anna Cordula (18 June 1749–24 June 1749); Maria Anna Nepomucena Walpurgis (13 May 1750–29 July 1750); Johann Karl Amadeus (4 November 1751–2 February 1753); and Maria Crescentia Franziska de Paula (9 May 1754–27 June 1754).

11. *Briefe*, vol. 3, p. 571, 12 August 1786 (no. 976).

12. Ibid., vol. 4, p. 303. See F. Breitinger, "Mutter Mozarts Badgasteiner Kur Anno 1750," *Salzburger Volksblatt*, 12 August 1964. The original reads:

"*Dem Höchsten, ach, ich dankh vor das was ich gefunden
Von diesem edlen Baad in fünfundneunzig Stunden.*"

13. *Briefe*, vol. 1, p. 23, 15 December 1755 (no. 14).

14. Ibid., p. 34, 9 February 1756 (no. 22). Trans. in *MDB*, p. 9; translation amended.

15. Baptismal Register of the Cathedral Parish, Salzburg, 28 January 1756: *MDB*, p. 9.

16. *Briefe*, vol. 2, p. 433, 3 August 1778 (no. 473); *Letters*, pp. 590–91, 3 August 1778 (no. 320); translation revised.

17. *Letters*, pp. 851–52, 18 June 1783 (no. 492).

18. Ibid., p. 852, 18 June 1783 (no. 492).

19. See *Briefe*, vol. 6, p. 145, with further references to "Gerstenwasser" in Leopold Mozart's letters to Mozart (see *Briefe*, vol. 3, p. 26, 20 November 1780 [no. 540] and pp. 45–46, 4 December 1780 [no. 553]). See also Johannes Dalchow, *W. A. Mozart's Krankheiten 1756–1763* (Bergisch Gladbach, Germany, 1955), p. 19. An otherwise sensitive psychoanalytic interpretation of this letter is undermined by the mistaken assumption that the infant Mozart was fed a diet of plain water. See Sara Sheftel, "Mozart: A Psychoanalytic Study" (Ph.D. diss., Union for Experimenting Colleges and Universities, 1982), p. 151.

20. Nannerl's "Notenbuch," presently in the Mozarteum, bears Leopold Mozart's heading: "Pour le Clavecin. Ce livre appartient à Marie Anne Mozart, 1759." For a complete edition, see *NMA*, IX:27/1 (*Die Notenbücher*), ed. Wolfgang Plath; see also Nissen, *Anhang*, following p. 16; *Briefe*, vol. 5, pp. 30–31; K⁶, p. 1; Alan Tyson, "A Reconstruction of Nannerl Mozart's Music Book (Notenbuch)," in Tyson, pp. 61–72.

21. Marianne von Berchtold, "Data for a biography of the late composer Wolfgang Mozart": *MDB*, p. 455; Schlichtegroll, p. 86.

22. For Leopold Mozart's notations in the Notenbuch see *Briefe*, vol. 1, p. 48, 1759–62 (no. 31).

23. Johann Andreas Schachtner to Marianne von Berchtold, 24 April 1792: *MDB*, p. 452; translation amended.

24. Schachtner to Berchtold: *MDB*, p. 451; Schlichtegroll, p. 87.

25. Schachtner to Berchtold: *MDB*, p. 451; translation amended.

26. Ibid., p. 452.

27. Ibid., p. 454; Schlichtegroll, p. 88.

28. Berchtold, "Data," *MDB*, p. 462.

29. *Briefe*, vol. 4, p. 201, draft of responses to questions submitted to Marianne von Berchtold by Schlichtegroll via Albert von Mölk (no. 1213).

30. Abert finds the absence of any formal schooling rather improbable and leaves this issue open. Abert, vol. 1, p. 79. A Salzburg lexicon published in 1821 referred to the court musician Franz Anton Spitzeder (1735–96) as "among the first music teachers of the great Mozart." Benedikt Pillwein, *Biographische Schilderungen oder Lexikon salzburgischer ... Künstler ...* (Salzburg, 1821), p. 226: *NMD*, p. 3 (no. 1).

31. Abert, vol. 1, p. 79 and n. 2.

32. Memoirs of Placidus Scharl, 1808: *MDB*, p. 512.

33. *Letters*, p. 4, 16 October 1762 (no. 2).

34. Ibid., p. 6, 16 October 1762 (no. 2).

35. Ibid., p. 5, 16 October 1762 (no. 2).

36. Niemetschek, p. 15.

37. Ibid., pp. 15–16; Schlichtegroll, p. 91.

38. Berchtold, "Data": *MDB*, p. 455; Schlichtegroll, p. 91.

39. *Briefe*, vol. 4, p. 201, draft of responses to questions submitted to Marianne von Berchtold by Schlichtegroll via Albert von Mölk (no. 1213); Schlichtegroll, pp. 91–92.

40. *Letters*, p. 8, 19 October 1762 (no. 3).

41. *Briefe*, vol. 1, p. 56, 30 October 1762 (no. 36); *Letters*, p. 9, 30 October 1762 (no. 4); translation amended.

42. *Letters*, pp. 13 and 14, 10 December 1762 (no. 8).

43. Ibid., p. 10, 30 October 1762 (no. 4).

44. *Briefe*, vol. 1, p. 57, 30 October 1762 (no. 36); *Letters*, p. 10, 30 October 1762 (no. 4); translation revised.

Chapter 3: The Grand Journey

1. *Letters*, p. 58, 19 September 1765 (no. 38).

2. Goethe, *Conversations with Eckermann*, trans. John Oxenford (New York and London, 1901), p. 318, entry for 3 February 1830.

3. See, for example, the advance notice and letter published in the *Augsburgischer Intelligenz-Zettel*, 19 May 1763: *MDB*, pp. 20–21.

4. *Letters*, p. 21, 21 June 1763 (no. 11).

5. Ibid., p. 31, 4 November 1763 (no. 18).

6. Ibid.

7. Ibid., p. 32, 8 December 1763 (no. 19).

8. Ibid., p. 43, 1 April 1764 (no. 25).

9. Ibid., p. 33, end of December 1763 (no. 20).

10. Ibid., pp. 34–35, 1 February 1764 (no. 22).

11. Ibid., p. 46, 28 May 1764 (no. 27).

12. Ibid., p. 48, 8 June 1764 (no. 28).

13. First advertisement for Frankfurt concerts, 16 August 1763: *MDB*, p. 24.

14. Second advertisement for Frankfurt concert, 30 August 1763: *MDB*, p. 25.

15. Notice in the *Public Advertiser*, 31 May, 1764: *MDB*, p. 34.

16. *Letters*, p. 52, 13 September 1764 (no. 31).

17. Notice in the *Public Advertiser*, 9 April 1765: *MDB*, p. 44.

18. Notice in the *Public Advertiser,* 8 July 1765: *MDB,* p. 45. Another announcement 9 July, repeated 11 July: *MDB,* pp. 45–46.

19. *The Kentish Post or Canterbury News-Letter,* 20 July 1765: *NMD,* p. 8 (no. 10).

20. *Letters,* p. 56, letter of 19 March 1765 (no. 35).

21. *Augsburgischer Intelligenz-Zettel,* 19 May 1763: *MDB,* p. 21. Mozart and his sister accompanied each other in arrangements for four hands or two keyboards. See, for example, *Gazette d'Utrecht,* 18 April 1766: *NMD,* p. 12 (no. 18).

22. *Augsburgischer Intelligenz-Zettel,* 19 May 1763: *MDB,* p. 21. In late 1762 in Vienna, the Mozarts acquired as many as twenty-two "new concertos" by Wagenseil for use on the forthcoming tour. *Briefe,* vol. 1, p. 61, 10 November 1761 (no. 41).

23. Friedrich Melchior von Grimm, *Correspondance littéraire,* 1 December 1763: *MDB,* p. 26; translation amended. One needs to bear in mind that Grimm had an interest: he sponsored the Mozarts' career and underwrote their concert appearances in Paris.

24. Ibid.: *MDB,* p. 26; see also notice in the *Avant-Coureur* (Paris), 5 March 1764: *MDB,* p. 30.

25. Schlichtegroll, p. 91; Schachtner to Marianne von Berchtold, 24 April 1792: *MDB,* p. 451. See also Niemetschek, p. 69. In later years, Mozart frequently expressed displeasure with inattentive audiences. See, for example, *Letters,* p. 531, 1 May 1778 (no. 303) and p. 736, 26 May 1781 (no. 406).

26. Schlichtegroll, p. 91.

27. *Letters,* p. 47, 28 May 1764 (no. 27).

28. Grimm, *Correspondance Littéraire,* 15 July 1766: *MDB,* p. 57.

29. *Letters,* p. 47, 28 May 1764 (no. 27).

30. Ibid., pp. 48–49, 8 June 1764 (no. 28).

31. Auguste Tissot, in *Aristide ou le Citoyen* (Lausanne), 11 October 1766: *MDB,* p. 64; translation from A. Hyatt King, *Mozart in Retrospect: Studies in Criticism and Bibliography* (London, 1955), pp. 135–36.

32. Daines Barrington, Report to the Royal Society in London, 15 February 1770: *MDB,* pp. 98, 96.

33. *Memoirs of Charles Burney 1726–1769,* ed. Slava Klima et al. (Lincoln, Neb., and London, 1987), p. 164: *NMD,* p. 4 (no. 4).

34. Donald Francis Tovey, "Mozart" entry, *Encyclopaedia Britannica,* 14th ed., vol. 17, p. 943.

35. *Letters,* p. 55, 8 February 1765 (no. 34).

36. Wolfgang Plath, "Beiträge zur Mozart-Autographie I: Die Handschrift Leopold Mozarts," *MJb 1960/61,* pp. 82–117; reprinted in Plath, pp. 28–73. Plath expands upon and refines handwriting studies that were begun by Otto Jahn but largely ignored for a century.

37. Abert did not overlook the extent of the father's participation in this composition, which was reminiscent of Leopold Mozart's own rustic orchestral music. Abert, vol. 1, p. 59. Mozart also wrote a set of keyboard variations on "Willem van Nassau," K. 25.

38. Plath, p. 40.

39. *Letters,* p. 53, 3 December 1764 (no. 33).

40. Ibid., pp. 40–41, 4 March 1764 (no. 24), and p. 45, 25 April 1764 (no. 26).

41. *Briefe,* vol. 1, p. 94, 26 September 1764 (no. 64); *Letters,* p. 29, 26 September 1763 (no. 17); translation amended.

42. Ibid.

43. *Letters,* p. 30, 17 October 1763 (no. 18).

44. Ibid., 36, 1 February 1764 to Frau Hagenauer (no. 22), and pp. 33–34, 1 February 1764 (no. 22).

45. For details of the surviving copies and their provenance, see *Briefe,* vol. 5, pp. 31–32.

46. *Letters,* pp. 36–37, 1 February 1764 (no. 22).

47. *Briefe,* vol. 1, pp. 186–87, 9 July 1765 (no. 98).

48. *Letters,* pp. 52–53, 27 November 1764 (no. 32).

49. Ibid., p. 38, 1 February 1764 (no. 22).

50. Ibid., p. 40, 22 February 1764 (no. 23); translation amended.

51. *Letters,* p. 60, 5 November 1765 (no. 39).

52. Ibid., p. 61, 5 November 1765 (no. 39).

53. Ibid., p. 63, 12 December 1765 (no. 40).

54. *Briefe,* vol. 1, p. 211, 12 December 1765 (no. 104).

55. *NMD,* pp. 11–12 (no. 17).

56. Marianne von Berchtold, "Data for a biography of the late composer Wolfgang Mozart": *MDB,* p. 457.

57. *Letters,* p. 69, 10 November 1766 (no. 44).

Chapter 4: The Family Treasure

1. *Letters,* pp. 167–68, Milan, 27 October 1770 (no. 118).

2. "The court is . . . compelled to make their appointments as slender as possible, that it may be able to keep them from starving; though above two-thirds of them are superfluous servants." Baron Caspar Riesbeck, *Travels Through Germany in a Series of Letters,* trans. Reverend Paul M. Maty (London, 1783), vol. 1, p. 183.

3. *Letters,* p. 464, 5 February 1778 (no. 282).

4. Ibid., p. 82, 30 January–3 February 1768 (no. 55); translation revised.

5. Ibid., p. 40, 22 February 1764 (no. 23); p. 69, 15 November 1766 (no. 45).

6. Ibid., p. 62, 5 November 1765 (no. 39).

7. Ibid., p. 63, 12 December 1765 (no. 40); translation amended.

8. Ibid., p. 7, 19 October 1762 (no. 3); p. 41, 1 April 1764 (no. 25); p. 49, 28 June 1764 (no. 29).

9. Ibid., pp. 55–56, 19 March 1765 (no. 35).

10. Ibid., p. 31, 4 November 1763 (no. 18).

11. Ibid., p. 48, 8 June 1764 (no. 28).

12. Diary of Father Beda Hübner, 29 November 1766: *MDB,* pp. 68–69.

13. Ibid., p. 69; translation amended.

14. *Letters,* p. 12, 24 November 1762 (no. 7).

15. Ibid., p. 29, 26 September 1763 (no. 17).

16. Ibid., p. 35, 1 February 1764 (no. 22).

17. Ibid., p. 52, 27 November 1764 (no. 32).

18. Ibid., p. 56, 19 March 1765 (no. 35).

19. Karl Benyovszky, *J. N. Hummel: Der Mensch und Künstler* (Bratislava, 1934), pp. 197–98; translation in H. C. Robbins Landon, *Mozart: The Golden Years* (New York, 1989), p. 201, where the expenses are greatly understated because "Aggregate Cost" is mistaken for "Gross Receipts." See also Erich Schenk, *Mozart and His Times* (New York, 1959), p. 367.

20. *Briefe,* vol. 1, p. 94, 26 September 1763 (no. 64). *Letters,* p. 29, 17 October 1763 (no. 17); translation amended. In addition to this letter, the archbishop's subsidy of the journeys is confirmed in Father Rupert von Gutrath's "Annales San-Petrenses seu variarum rerum notabilium . . . annotatio": *MDB,* p. 27; Ernst Hintermaier, *Die Salzburger Hofkapelle von 1700 bis 1806. Organisation und Personal* (Ph.D. diss., University of Salzburg, 1972), p. 268, cited in Cliff Eisen, "The Symphonies of Leopold Mozart and their Relationship to the Early Symphonies of Wolfgang Amadeus Mozart: A Bibliographical and Stylistic Study" (Ph.D. diss., Cornell University, 1986), p. 5 n. 7. Apart from the 600-florin subsidy of the first Italian journey (Register of the Salzburg Treasury: *MDB,* p. 94), the precise amount of the subsidies is not known. Father Beda Hübner reported that the Dutch government invited them "to Holland at its own expense." Diary of Father Beda Hübner, 26 April 1766: *MDB,* p. 55.

21. Diary of Father Beda Hübner, 8 December 1766: *MDB,* p. 70.

22. Ibid., pp. 70–71.

23. *Briefe,* vol. 1, pp. 108–9, 4 November 1763 (no. 68).

24. *MDB,* p. 23. The windowpane is preserved in the Historisches Museum, Frankfurt (see p. 61).

25. Leopold Mozart, "Preliminary Notice" to the 2nd edition of his *Violinschule,* 24 September 1769: *MDB,* pp. 91–92.

26. *Letters,* pp. 89, 90–91, 30 July 1768 (no. 62).

27. Schlichtegroll, p. 95; see also Niemetschek, p. 20.

28. Schlichtegroll, pp. 95–96. "He dared not eat even the slightest amount without his parents' permission, or take anything which one wanted to give to him." *Briefe,* vol. 4, p. 201, draft of responses to questions submitted to Marianne von Berchtold by Schlichtegroll via Albert von Mölk, 1792 (no. 1213).

29. Schachtner to Marianne von Berchtold, 24 April 1792: *MDB,* p. 452.

30. Ibid., p. 453. To Schachtner's report we may add the remarks of two other observers: Auguste Tissot, in *Aristide ou le Citoyen*, wrote that "aural sensibility and justness are so keen in young Mozart that wrong, harsh or too loud notes bring tears to his eyes": *MDB*, p. 64; and the Prior of Sternberg noted in his diary for 30 December 1767 that Mozart "could not endure the trumpets because they were incapable of playing completely in tune with one another": *MDB*, p. 77. Beethoven, too, had a fear of loud noises, and he told Karl Gottlieb Freudenberg that he had abandoned the organ because its overwhelming sound affected his nerves. Friedrich Kerst, ed., *Die Erinnerungen an Beethoven* (Stuttgart, 1913), vol. 2, p. 114.

31. Schachtner to Marianne von Berchtold, 24 April 1792: *MDB*, p. 453; translation amended.

32. Marianne von Berchtold, anecdotes about Mozart, *AMZ* 2 (1799–1800), columns 300ff.: *MDB*, p. 493.

33. *Letters*, p. 506, 7 March 1778 (no. 296).

34. Schachtner to Marianne von Berchtold, 24 April 1792: *MDB*, p. 452.

35. Wolfgang Plath, "Der gegenwärtige Stand der Mozart-Forschung," in Plath, p. 83.

36. Alfred Mann, "Leopold Mozart als Lehrer seines Sohnes," *MJb 1989/90*, p. 32.

37. Marianne von Berchtold, anecdotes about Mozart, *AMZ* 2 (1799–1800), columns 300ff.: *MDB*, p. 493; translation amended. As a grown man Mozart did not forget his imaginary kingdom. He wrote to the family's erstwhile servant, Sebastian Winter, who had mapped the Kingdom of Back for his young charge: "Companion of my youth! As I have often been in Rücken during these many years and yet have never had the pleasure of meeting you, my dearest wish indeed would be that you should visit me in Vienna." *Letters*, pp. 900–901, 30 September 1786 (no. 541).

Chapter 5: A Vienna Sojourn

1. Minutes of the Salzburg Gymnasium: *MDB*, p. 75.

2. Leopold Mozart's *Verzeichnis* of Mozart's early works, *Briefe*, vol. 1, p. 289, Vienna, 1768 (no. 144). See Neal Zaslaw, "Leopold Mozart's List of his Son's Works," in *Music in the Classical Period: Essays in Honor of Barry S. Brook*, ed. Alan W. Atlas (New York, 1985), pp. 323–58. Three Church Sonatas, K. 67–69/41h, i, k, formerly believed to date from these years are now assigned to 1771–72: see Plath, p. 231. It is not clear when the Offertory, K. 34, for which no authentic autograph or copy exists, was written.

3. Diary of Father Beda Hübner, 8 December 1766: *MDB*, p. 69.

4. *Briefe*, vol. 1, p. 240, 7 October 1767 (no. 118). See also *Letters*, p. 85, 11 May 1768 (no. 59).

5. *Briefe*, vol. 1, p. 241, 14 October 1767 (no. 119); *Letters*, p. 74, 14 October 1767 (no. 49); translation amended.

6. *Letters*, p. 76, 10 November 1767 (no. 51).

7. Marianne von Berchtold, anecdotes about Mozart, *AMZ* 2 (1799–1800), columns 300ff: *MDB*, p. 494.

8. *Letters*, p. 79, 23 January 1768 (no. 54).

9. Ibid., p. 81, 30 January–3 February 1768 (no. 55).

10. Ibid., p. 80, 30 January–3 February 1768 (no. 55).

11. Ibid.

12. Ibid., pp. 81–82, 30 January–3 February 1768 (no. 55).

13. Ibid.

14. Ibid., p. 82, 30 January–3 February 1768 (no. 55).

15. Ibid., p. 84, 30 March 1768 (no. 57).

16. Ibid., pp. 88–89, 30 July 1768 (no. 62).

17. Petition to Emperor Joseph II, 21 September 1768, "Species Facti": *MDB*, p. 82.

18. "Species Facti": *MDB*, p. 83.

19. *Letters*, p. 91, 30 July 1768 (no. 62).

20. "Species Facti": *MDB*, p. 83; see also *Letters*, p. 93, 14 September 1768 (no. 65).

21. *Letters*, p. 87, 29 June 1789 (no. 61).

22. *Briefe*, vol. 1, p. 247, 10 November 1767 (no. 121).

23. Letter of Marie-Thérèse Geoffrin to Prince Wenzel Kaunitz, 27 April 1768: *MDB*, p. 79.

24. *Letters*, p. 86 n. 1, 11 May 1768 (no. 59). The official instruction to the exchequer reads:

"His Serene Highness has graciously ordered by word of mouth, that the Court musicians at present absent by his most gracious permission, namely Kapellmeister Motzhard, Meissner, and Küffl, unless they report here again in the coming month of April, are not to be handed any further salary." Decree of 18 March 1768: *MDB*, p. 78.

25. *Letters*, p. 85, 11 May 1768 (no. 59). Leopold Mozart's salary was withheld from April 1768 through February 1769, but his salary for January and February 1769 was later refunded in response to his petition. See pp. 94–95, before 8 March 1769 (no. 69).

26. Leopold Mozart claims his expenses for four months were 160 ducats (= ca. 720 florins). "Species Facti": *MDB*, p. 83.

27. Jahn, vol. 1, p. 73. In contrast, Angermüller reckons that Mozart must have been paid "considerable sums" by the nobility. See Rudolph Angermüller, "'Auf Ehre und Credit': Die Finanzen des W. A. Mozart," *Ausstellung der Internationalen Stiftung Mozarteum Salzburg, der Staatlichen Münzsammlung München, und der Bayerischen Vereinsbank München* (Munich, 1983), p. 6.

28. "Species Facti": *MDB*, p. 81.

29. *Letters*, p. 84, 30 March 1768 (no. 57).

30. According to Nissen, p. 127; see also *MDB*, p. 84. Leopold Mozart's *Verzeichnis* confirmed that the work was written in Vienna. *Briefe*, vol. 1, p. 289 (no. 144); the work may have been amplified after the return to Salzburg.

31. *Letters*, p. 89, 30 July 1768 (no. 62).

32. Ibid., p. 91, 30 July 1768 (no. 62).

33. Marianne von Berchtold, "Data for a biography of the late composer Wolfgang Mozart": *MDB*, 458. There is some uncertainty about which works were composed for this occasion; most probably they are the Missa solemnis in C minor, K. 139/47a, an Offertorium, K. 47b (lost), and a Trumpet Concerto, K. 47c (lost).

34. *Wienerisches Diarium*, 10 December 1768: *MDB*, pp. 84–85.

35. *Letters*, p. 94, 14 December 1768 (no. 68).

36. Ibid., p. 89, 30 July 1768 (no. 62).

Chapter 6: The Italian Journeys

1. *Letters*, p. 118, 13 March 1770 (no. 83); see Marianne von Berchtold, "Data for a biography of the late composer Wolfgang Mozart": *MDB*, p. 459; see also *Notizie del Mondo*, Florence, 20 March 1770: *NMD*, p. 18 (no. 29).

2. A few months later, Leopold Mozart wrote: "If Wolfgang had not already the scrittura [contract] for the opera in Milan, he would have obtained one for Bologna, Rome or Naples, for he has received offers from all these places." *Letters*, p. 140, 29 May 1770 (no. 95). See also *Briefe*, vol. 5, p. 259.

3. *Staats- und gelehrte Zeitung . . .* , Hamburg, 22 May 1770: *NMD*, p. 19 (no. 31).

4. Papal Patent, 4 July 1770: *MDB*, p. 124.

5. *Letters*, p. 148, 4 July 1770 (no. 101).

6. Ibid., p. 177, Milan, 2 January 1771 (no. 128).

7. Ibid., p. 178, Milan, 5 January 1771 (no. 129).

8. Ibid., p. 197, 21 September 1771 (no. 144).

9. *Augspurgische Ordinari Postzeitung*, Augsburg, 28 September 1771: *NMD*, p. 20 (no. 34).

10. *Letters*, p. 202, 19 October 1771 (no. 148).

11. Ibid., p. 203, Milan, 26 October 1771 (no. 149).

12. "Questo ragazzo ci farà dimenticar tutti!" Jahn-Deiters, vol. 1, p. 156 and n. 75; Jahn, vol. 1, p. 136. "It really distresses me very greatly," wrote Leopold, "but Wolfgang's serenata has killed Hasse's opera." *Letters*, p. 202, 19 October 1771 (no. 148).

13. *Notizie del Mondo*, Florence, 26 October 1771: *NMD*, p. 21 (no. 35).

14. The contract is dated 4 March 1771: *MDB*, p. 133.

15. *Letters*, p. 219, Milan, 5 December 1772 (no. 164a).

16. Ibid., p. 223, 2 January 1773 (no. 168); translation amended.

17. Ibid., p. 224, 9 January 1773 (no. 169).

18. Ibid., p. 131, 25 April 1770 (no. 89).

19. Ibid., p. 153, 4 August 1770 (no. 106a). The "motet" is possibly the Miserere for alto, tenor, bass, and organ, K. 85/73s, composed probably at the end of July or beginning of August 1770 in Bologna.

20. Of these, authentic sources survive only for K. 74. For a discussion of the authenticity

of Mozart's Italian symphonies, see Neal Zaslaw, *Mozart's Symphonies: Context, Performance Practice, Reception* (Oxford, 1989), pp. 160–61; see also Cliff Eisen, "The Mozarts' Salzburg Copyists," in *Mozart Studies*, ed. Eisen (Oxford, 1991), p. 291: indeed, of the twenty-five symphonies attributed to Mozart between 1764 and 1771, "more than half of them lack authentic sources and there is no convincing evidence that any of them is by him. The authenticated repertory consists of K. 16, 19, Anh. 223/19a, 22, Anh. 221/45a, 43, 45, 73, 74, 110, and 112" (p. 292). For a summary, see also Eisen, "Symphonies," in H. C. Robbins Landon, *The Mozart Compendium: A Guide to Mozart's Life and Music* (New York, 1990), pp. 256, 258–59.

21. Stanley Sadie, "Wolfgang Amadeus Mozart" entry, *The New Grove*, vol. 12, p. 686.

22. Authentic sources are lacking for K. 96/111b.

23. *Letters*, p. 213, 28 October 1772 (no. 159).

24. Plath, pp. 229, 243–50.

25. Burney's travel notes for 30 August 1770, written immediately after a "long conversation" with Leopold Mozart, give Mozart's age as twelve. See *MDB*, p. 125.

26. *Gazzetta di Mantova*, 12 January 1770: *MDB*, p. 105.

27. Ibid.

28. *Gazzetta di Mantova*, 19 January 1770: *MDB*, p. 107; translation revised. (Facsimile in Guglielmo Barblan et al., eds, *Mozart in Italia* [Milan, 1956], Plate IX.)

29. *Gazzetta di Mantova*, 19 January 1770: *MDB*, p. 108.

30. *Letters*, p. 112, 10 February 1770 (no. 79); translation amended. See also Marianne von Berchtold, "Data for a biography of the late composer Wolfgang Mozart": *MDB*, p. 459.

31. *Letters*, p. 123, 27 March 1770 (no. 85).

32. Berchtold, "Data": *MDB*, p. 459; translation amended.

33. Ibid., *MDB*, p. 460. In fact, Padre Martini corrected Mozart's original draft of the Antiphon, K. 86/73v, which Mozart then reworked into a fair copy (see *NMA* I:3). Even his public concerts featured similar trials of his prowess: at his Venice concert on 5 March 1771, "An experienced musician gave him a fugue theme, which he worked out for more than an hour with such science, dexterity, harmony, and proper attention to rhythm, that even the greatest connoisseurs were astounded." Report of 27 March 1771: *NMD*, p. 20 (no. 33).

34. Nomination by the Accademia Filarmonica of Verona, 5 January 1771: *MDB*, pp. 131–32.

35. *Letters*, p. 177, 29 [not 22] December 1770 (no. 127); Berchtold, "Data": *MDB*, p. 460.

36. See Erich Schenk, "La sosta a Mantova," in Barblan et al., *Mozart in Italia*, p. 63.

37. *Briefe*, vol. 1, p. 303, 11 January 1770 (no. 155).

38. Ibid., p. 306, 26 January 1770 (no. 157).

39. Erich Schenk, *Mozart and His Times* (New York, 1959), pp. 126–27.

40. For Count Firmian, see Ernst Fritz Schmid, "Auf Mozarts Spuren in Italien," *MJb 1955*, p. 28.

41. See *Briefe*, vol. 5, pp. 234–35.

42. *Letters*, p. 146, 30 [June] 1770 (no. 100).

43. Eibl views the Neapolitan stay as a serious disappointment comparable to the last months in London and the Vienna stay of 1768. See Josef Eibl, "Mozart in Neapel," *MJb 1965/66*, pp. 94–95.

44. *Letters*, pp. 141–42, Naples, 5 June 1770 (no. 96).

45. Ibid., p. 114, Milan, 17 February 1770 (no. 80).

46. Ibid., p. 115, 27 February 1770 (no. 81). The original reads: "so haben wir doch immer ein wenig mehr als die Nothwendigkeit." *Briefe*, vol. 1, p. 316, 27 February 1770 (no. 162).

47. *Letters*, p. 120, Bologna, 24 March 1770 (no. 84).

48. Pallavicini account books, 26 March 1770: *MDB*, p. 112; see also Schenk, *Mozart*, p. 129.

49. Count Rosenberg's order of payment, 4 April 1770: *MDB*, pp. 114–15. Mozart was "frequently invited to gatherings in Rome," where he was reported to have received 20 scudi "for each appearance." P. Giovanni Biringucci, *Diario de' PP Biringucci e Romano*, Rome, 2 May 1770: *NMD*, p. 19 (no. 30). Because we do not know if these were gold scudi or silver scudi the value of these payments cannot be calculated.

50. *Letters*, p. 119, 24 March 1770 (no. 84).

51. See *Mozart in Italia*, p. 192.

52. *Letters*, p. 139, 26 May 1770 (no. 94).

53. *Briefe*, vol. 1, p. 354, 29 May 1770 (no. 188).

54. *Letters*, p. 139, 26 May 1770 (no. 94). In a letter of early September to Thomas Linley Mozart mentions the difficulties of making expenses during the summer, when the "season is over, for everyone is in the country and therefore we could not earn our expenses." *Letters*, p. 160, 10 September 1770 (no. 112).

55. Ibid., p. 108, Milan, 26 January 1770 (no. 77).

56. Ibid., p. 152, 4 August 1770 (no. 106); see also p. 120, 24 March 1770 (no. 84).

57. Register of the Salzburg Treasury, 27 November 1769: *MDB*, p. 94.

58. *Letters*, p. 154, 4 August 1770 (no. 106a).

59. Ibid., p. 129, 21 April 1770 (no. 88).

60. Ibid., p. 155, 11 August 1770 (no. 107).

61. Ibid., p. 145, 27 June 1770 (no. 99).

62. Ibid., p. 126, 14 April 1770 (no. 87).

63. Ibid., p. 135, 19 May 1770 (no. 92); see also p. 139, 26 May 1770 (no. 94).

64. Ibid., p. 137, 19 May 1770 (no. 92a).

65. Ibid., p. 175, 22 December 1770 (no. 126).

66. Ibid., p. 114, 17 February 1770 (no. 80).

67. Ibid., p. 127, 14 April 1770 (no. 87); see also Berchtold, "Data": *MDB*, p. 459.

68. *Letters*, p. 136, 19 May 1770 (no. 92); translation amended.

69. Ibid., p. 99, 14 December 1769 (no. 71a).

70. Ibid., p. 145, 16 June 1770 (no. 98a); p. 156, 21 August 1770 (no. 108a).

71. Ibid., p. 130, (no. 88).

72. Ibid., p. 183, 20 February 1771 (no. 133a).

73. Ibid., p. 186, 14 March 1771 (no. 136).

74. See Erich Valentin, "Mozart und die Dichtung seiner Zeit," *Neues MJb* 1 (1941), p. 90. Leopold Mozart visited the grave of "the great Fénelon" in 1766 in Paris (see *Briefe*, vol. 1, p. 220, 16 May 1766 [no. 108]).

75. *Letters*, p. 128, 14 April 1770 (no. 87a).

76. Ibid., p. 108, 26 January 1770 (no. 77).

77. Ibid., p. 127, 14 April 1770 (no. 87).

78. Ibid., p. 198, 21 September 1771 (no. 144).

79. Ibid., p. 200, 5 October 1771 (no. 146).

80. Ibid., p. 202, 19 October 1771 (no. 148).

81. Ibid., p. 161, 18 September 1770 (no. 113). Eibl comments, "This must not have been meant in earnest." *Briefe*, vol. 5, p. 278.

82. *Letters*, p. 201, 12 October 1771 (no. 147); p. 202, 19 October 1771 (no. 148).

83. Ibid., p. 191, 16 August 1771 (no. 138).

84. Ibid., p. 215, 14 November 1772 (no. 161).

85. Ibid., p. 217, 28 November 1772 (no. 163).

86. Ibid., p. 156, 11 August 1770 (no. 107).

87. Ibid., p. 170, 17 November 1770 (no. 121).

88. Ibid., p. 172, 1 December 1770 (no. 123).

89. Ibid., p. 114, 17 February 1770 (no. 80).

90. Ibid., p. 128, 14 April 1770 (no. 87a).

91. Ibid., p. 141, 29 May 1770 (no. 95a).

92. Ibid., p. 166, Milan, 20 October 1770 (no. 117a).

93. Ibid., p. 169, Milan, 3 November 1770 (no. 119a).

94. Ibid., p. 136, Naples, 19 May 1770 (no. 92).

95. Ibid., p. 231, Milan, 27 February 1773 (no. 176).

96. Letter to Archduke Ferdinand, 12 December 1771: *MDB*, p. 138; facsimile in Barblan et al., *Mozart in Italia*, Plate XXXI, following page 168. The empress was opposed to begging as a matter of economic as well as moral principle; she favored dissolution of the orders of mendicant monks because she believed that begging placed "an intolerable burden on the heavily taxed rural population." Ernst Wangermann, *The Austrian Achievement: 1700–1800* (London, 1973), p. 102.

97. Letter to Giovanni Maria Ortes, 23 March 1771: *MDB*, p. 134.

98. *Letters*, p. 208, 8 December 1771 (no. 155).

99. Ibid., p. 224, 9 January 1773 (no. 169).

100. Ibid., p. 225, 16 January 1773 (no. 170).

101. Ibid., p. 226, 23 January 1773 (no. 171).

102. Ibid.

103. *Letters,* p. 228, 30 January 1773 (no. 172).

104. *Briefe,* vol. 1, p. 480, 6 February 1773 (no. 283).

105. *Letters,* p. 231, 27 February 1773 (no. 176).

106. Ibid., pp. 226–27, 23 January 1773 (no. 171).

Chapter 7: The Favorite Son

1. Caspar Riesbeck, *Travels Through Germany in a Series of Letters,* trans. Rev. Mr. Maty (London, 1787), vol. 1, pp. 124–27.

2. *MDB,* p. 89.

3. See Judas Thaddäus Zauner and Corbinian Gärtner, *Neue Chronik von Salzburg,* vol. 5, part 1 (Salzburg, 1826).

4. It has recently been argued that the work may have remained unperformed, perhaps for reasons of economy. See *NMA* II:5/vi, ed. Josef-Horst Lederer. Eisen surveys the issues and suggests that it is likely the serenata was performed, perhaps at a documented gala celebration and dinner held at court on 29 April 1772. *NMD,* p. 22 (no. 37).

5. Beda Hübner, *Umständliche Geschichte, des allerersten feyerlichst gehaltenen Jahrhunderts, zu Maria Plain nächst Salzburg . . .* (Salzburg, 1774): *NMD,* p. 25 (no. 41).

6. Finales for a Symphony in C, K. 102/213c and a Symphony (or Divertimento) in D, K. 121/207a, both composed in 1775, are partial exceptions.

7. *Letters,* p. 619, 24 September 1778 (no. 333). Zaslaw interprets these remarks as "hypocritical" in light of Leopold Mozart's letters to Breitkopf of 7 February 1771, 6 October 1775, and 12 February 1781 offering his son's symphonies for publication. Neal Zaslaw, *Mozart's Symphonies: Context, Performance Practice, Reception* (Oxford, 1989), pp. 206–7.

8. A sixth divertimento in this series, in E-flat, K. 289/271g, ascribed to summer 1777, is not authentic.

9. *Letters,* p. 300, 6 October 1777 (no. 217b).

10. The autographs are dated, but the dates have been tampered with. Plath raised the possibility that K. 207 was originally dated 14 April 1773 (see *NMA* V:14/1, *Violinkonzerte und Einzelsätze,* p. xi), but in his recent republication of "Beiträge zur Mozart-Autographie II. Schriftchronologie 1770–1780," he leaves the dating of 1775 for all five concertos undisturbed. See Plath, pp. 253–54; see also Tyson, p. 25.

11. "What remains of K. 175, then, is the version used by Mozart in the early 1780s." Cliff Eisen, "The Mozarts' Salzburg Copyists: Aspects of Attribution, Chronology, Text, Style, and Performance Practice," in *Mozart Studies,* ed. Eisen (Oxford, 1991), p. 287. The Concerto for two pianos in E-flat, K. 365/316a, which also found its final form in Vienna in 1781, may have originated as a Salzburg vehicle of the mid-1770s for Mozart and his sister. Cadenzas for the concerto in Leopold Mozart's hand, with additions by Mozart, are on a paper type otherwise limited to use on autographs composed in the eighteen months ending January 1777. See Tyson, p. 172. Tyson, however, draws no specific inference from this data, perhaps because Plath accepts the received dating of 1779 on the basis of his handwriting analysis. See Plath, p. 259.

12. *Letters,* pp. 663–64, 13 November 1780 (no. 358).

13. Her name is given as "Jeunehomme" (or "Jenomé") in several letters of 1778: *Letters,* p. 521, 5 April 1778 (no. 300a); p. 530, 12–20 April 1778 (no. 303), and p. 615, 11 September 1778 (no. 331).

14. According to K[6] (pp. 269–70), the so-called "Spaur Mass" is the Missa brevis in C, K. 258, previously thought to have been dated December 1776; Tyson has shown that it really dates from December 1775. See Tyson, pp. 162–76, and p. 345 n. 16 for further literature on the problematical date of K. 262/246a.

15. K[6], pp. 254–55.

16. Jahn, vol. 1, p. 333.

17. Hübner, *Umständliche Geschichte.* See p. 100 above.

18. Archduke Maximilian's Travel Journal, 24 April 1775: *MDB,* pp. 152–53.

19. Baron Karl von Petermann to Count Prokop Adalbert Czernin, 13 December 1776: *MDB,* pp. 157–58. Although the Czernin archive in Czechoslovakia contains autographs with an

attribution to Mozart of four of the twelve dances of K. 269b, the autograph manuscript itself is in Michael Haydn's hand. See Cliff Eisen, "The Mozarts' Salzburg Copyists," in Eisen, *Mozart Studies*, pp. 269–70; see also *NMA* IV:13/1/1, p. vii. Perhaps Mozart "borrowed" these works from Haydn to fulfill his commission; conceivably the two composers occasionally had a reciprocal borrowing arrangement involving minor compositions.

20. See H. Klein, "Unbekannte Mozartiana von 1766/67, *MJb 1957*, pp. 171–72.

21. Carl Bär, "Die 'Musique vom Robinig,'" *Mitteilungen der ISM* 9, nos. 3/4 (1960), pp. 6–11.

22. For a listing of the orchestra's members, see *Letters*, pp. 526–27, 12 April 1778 (no. 302).

23. Ibid., p. 28, 20 August 1763 (no. 16).

24. Ibid., pp. 391–92, 26 November 1777 (no. 249a).

25. *Briefe*, vol. 2, pp. 190–91, 18 December 1777 (no. 392); *Letters*, pp. 422–23, 18 December 1777 (no. 422); translation amended.

26. *Letters*, p. 239, 21 August 1773 (no. 180).

27. Ibid., p. 236, 12 August 1773 (no. 178).

28. Ibid., p. 242, 4 September 1773 (no. 183).

29. Finscher writes that it is "evident that Mozart consciously and laboriously tried to imitate Haydn, and that his models were indeed Haydn's Opp. 9, 17, and 20," adding, however, that in the fugues his "model seems to be not Haydn so much as the special Viennese tradition of fugues for string ensembles, mostly for string quartet, by Gassmann, Albrechtsberger, and others. . . . Mozart reacted to Viennese musical fashion (probably hoping to gain access to the court) and to the challenge which Haydn's quartets must have posed for him." Ludwig Finscher, "Mozart's Indebtedness to Haydn: Some Remarks on K. 168–73," in Jens Peter Larsen, et al., eds., *Haydn Studies: Proceedings of the International Haydn Conference, Washington, D.C., 1975* (New York and London, 1981), pp. 408–10. Mozart's incorporation into these quartets of style elements of "those composers known to be aligned with Imperial tastes," is persuasively argued by A. Peter Brown, "Haydn and Mozart's 1773 Stay in Vienna: Weeding a Musicological Garden," *The Journal of Musicology* 10 (1992), pp. 192–230 (esp. pp. 221–30). For a brilliant overview of Mozart's fusion of fugato style with the sonata and rondo forms, see Warren Kirkendale, *Fugue and Fugato in Rococo and Classical Chamber Music*, trans. from the German by Margaret Bent and Warren Kirkendale (Durham, 1979), pp. 152–81.

30. *Letters*, p. 242, 8 September 1773 (no. 184).

31. Riesbeck, *Travels Through Germany*, vol. 1, p. 185. Colloredo's father was the Viennese Prince Rudolf Joseph Colloredo (1706–1788). See *Briefe*, vol. 5, p. 37.

32. *Letters*, p. 259, 14 January 1775 (no. 197).

33. Diary of J. F. Unger, 15 January 1775: *MDB*, p. 150.

34. Schubart's *Deutsche Chronik*, 27 April 1775: *MDB*, p. 153.

35. "There is every likelihood that Wolfgang will compose the grand opera here this time next year." *Letters*, p. 258, 11 January 1775 (no. 196a).

36. Ibid., pp. 261–62, 21 January 1775 (no. 199).

37. *Briefe*, vol. 1, p. 520, 21 January 1775 (no. 313).

38. *Letters*, p. 259, 14 January 1775 (no. 197).

39. Ibid., p. 260, 18 January 1775 (no. 198).

40. Ibid., p. 13, to Lorenz Hagenauer, 10 December 1762 (no. 8).

41. Ibid., p. 67, 16 August 1766 (no. 43).

42. L. Hübner, *Beschreibung der hochfürstlich-erzbischöflichen Haupt- und Residenzstadt Salzburg und ihrer Gegenden* (Salzburg, 1792–93), vol. 2, pp. 455–590.

43. Riesbeck, *Travels Through Germany*, vol. 1, p. 180.

44. Ibid., pp. 181–82.

45. Jahn, vol. 1, p. 332, from Joseph Mayr, *Die ehemalige Universität Salzburg* (Salzburg, 1859), p. 12.

46. Riesbeck, *Travels Through Germany*, vol. 1, p. 185.

47. For details and bibliography, see Cliff Eisen, "Salzburg under Church Rule," in *The Classical Era: From the 1740s to the End of the 18th Century*, ed. Neal Zaslaw (New York, 1989), pp. 167–68, 177–84.

48. *Briefe*, vol. 2, p. 482, 17 September 1778 (no. 490). See Jahn, vol. 1, p. 289.

49. *Letters*, p. 266, 4 September 1776 (no. 205).

50. Ibid., pp. 594–96, to Abbé Bullinger, 7 August 1778 (no. 322).

51. The petition does not survive. See *MDB*, p. 159.

52. "My father again humbly asked for this permission later," wrote Mozart, "but your Serene Highness refused him this and graciously observed that I, being in any case only on part-time service, might travel alone." *Letters*, p. 267, 1 August 1777 (no. 206); trans. from *MDB*, pp. 162–63.

53. *MDB*, p. 162.

54. Ibid., pp. 162–63; translation revised. There are no further known details about a proposed trip to Vienna in 1774; perhaps Mozart was referring to the Vienna journey of 1773.

55. Decree of 28 August 1777, communicated to Mozart on 1 September 1777: *MDB*, pp. 163–64.

56. Schiedenhofen's Diary, 6 September 1777: *MDB*, p. 164; translation amended.

57. *Letters*, p. 295, 4 October 1777 (no. 215); translation amended.

58. Ibid., p. 608, 31 August 1778 (no. 328).

59. Ibid., p. 365, 13 November 1777 (no. 240).

60. Ibid., p. 281, Leopold Mozart to his wife and son, 28 September 1777 (no. 211).

61. Response, 26 September 1777, to Petition of Leopold Mozart, quoted in ibid., p. 281, Leopold Mozart to his wife and son, 28 September 1777 (no. 211).

62. *Letters*, p. 266, Mozart to Padre Martini, 4 September 1776 (no. 205).

63. *AMZ* 23 (October 1821), column 685. I owe this reference to Cliff Eisen, who kindly brought it to my attention.

Chapter 8: A Composer's Voice

1. For probing discussions of the nature and complexities of musical style, see the following by Leonard Meyer: *Music, the Arts and Ideas: Patterns and Predictions in Twentieth-Century Culture* (Chicago and London, 1967), pp. 104–33; "Innovation, Choice, and the History of Music," *Critical Inquiry* 9 (1983), pp. 517–44; and *Style and Music: Theory, History and Ideology* (Philadelphia, 1989).

2. T. S. Eliot, "Tradition and the Individual Talent," in *Selected Essays* (New York, 1950), p. 7.

3. G. W. F. Hegel, *Philosophy of Fine Art,* trans. F. P. B. Osmaston (London, 1920), vol. 1, p. 405.

4. Niemetschek, p. 62.

5. "A Letter by Mozart to the Baron von . . . " *AMZ* 17 (1814–15), columns 561–66; see Maynard Solomon, "Beethoven's Creative Process: A Two-Part Invention," in his *Beethoven Essays* (Cambridge, Mass., 1988), pp. 126–38, and J. H. Eibl, "Ein Brief Mozarts über seine Schaffensweise," *Österreichische Musikzeitschrift* 35 (1980), pp. 578–93.

6. Goethe, *Conversations with Eckermann,* trans. John Oxenford (New York, 1901), p. 377 (conversation of 20 June 1831). See also Alfred Heuss, "Das dämonische Element in Mozart's Werken," *Zeitschrift der Internationalen Musik-Gesellschaft* 7 (1905–6), pp. 175–86. The historian H. Stuart Hughes wrote: "By 'demonic' the Germans meant a sudden welling-up of passion—whether creative or destructive or both together—that exceeded the bounds of 'normal' human behavior. Its ravages they found peculiar to their own national spirit. . . . It marked the Germans off from their neighbors as a people destined to special greatness and subject to unusual temptations." H. Stuart Hughes, *History as Art and as Science: Twin Vistas on the Past* (New York, 1964), p. 49.

7. For the classical sources of these ancient tropes of creativity, see Erwin Panofsky, *Idea: A Concept in Art Theory,* trans. Joseph J. S. Peake (New York, 1968), pp. 9–43; see also Solomon, "Beethoven's Creative Process," p. 132.

8. Dahlhaus sees the preoccupation with influences as stemming from a positivist "urge to locate tangible facts as a sort of surety for the scientific quality of music history." Carl Dahlhaus, *Foundations of Music History,* trans. J. B. Robinson (Cambridge, England, 1983), p. 26. There is also a nationalistic aspect to the preoccupation with influences, with emphasis often placed on their national origin. Of Mozart's violin concertos, Abert writes, ecumenically: "The French spirit is here at work. . . . Melodically German; technically Italian." Abert, vol. 1, p. 426.

9. Théodore de Wyzewa and Georges de Saint-Foix, "Un maître inconnu de Mozart," *Zeitschrift der Internationalen Musik-Gesellschaft* 10 (1908–9), p. 35.

10. *Letters*, p. 468, 7 February 1778 (no. 283a); p. 536, 6 May 1778 (no. 304).

11. Ibid., p. 300, 6 October 1777 (no. 217b). Joseph Schuster (1748–1812) was a composer in the service of the elector of Saxony.

12. Cited in Harold Bloom, *The Anxiety of Influence: A Theory of Poetry* (New York, 1973), p. 31. Bonds notes that "Mozart was also capable of covering his tracks, as it were, either avoiding or repressing all traceable connections to his original source." Mark Evan Bonds, "The Sincerest form of Flattery? Mozart's 'Haydn' Quartets and the Question of Influence," *Studi Musicali* 22 (1993), p. 406.

13. *Letters*, p. 497, 28 February 1778 (no. 292). Marshall demonstrates that Mozart was exaggerating somewhat the differences between Bach's aria and his own. See Robert L. Marshall, *Mozart Speaks: Views on Music, Musicians, and the World* (New York, 1991), pp. 26–28.

14. Leonard G. Ratner, "Topical Content in Mozart's Keyboard Sonatas," *Early Music* 19 (1991), p. 619.

15. Wye Jamison Allanbrook, *Rhythmic Gesture in Mozart: "Le nozze di Figaro" and "Don Giovanni"* (Chicago and London, 1983), p. 318.

16. Einstein, p. 110.

17. Ibid., p. 122.

18. Friedrich Blume, "Mozart's Style and Influence," in *The Mozart Companion*, ed. H. C. Robbins Landon and Donald Mitchell (New York, 1956, reprint 1969), p. 20.

19. Ibid.

20. Georges de Saint-Foix, *The Symphonies of Mozart*, trans. Leslie Orrey (New York, 1949), p. 99; Théodore de Wyzewa and Saint-Foix, *W. A. Mozart: Sa vie musicale et son oeuvre. Essai de biographie critique* (Paris, 1912–46), vol. 4, p. 225.

21. From *Greenes Groats-worth of Wit* (1592), in E. K. Chambers, *William Shakespeare: A Study of Facts and Problems* (Oxford, 1930), vol. 2, p. 188.

22. Charles Rosen, *The Classical Style: Haydn, Mozart, Beethoven* (New York, 1971), p. 53.

23. *Letters*, p. 867, 10 February 1784 (no. 503).

24. See Blume, "Mozart's Style and Influence," pp. 18–19.

25. See, for example, Stanley Sadie, "Wolfgang Amadeus Mozart" entry, *The New Grove*, vol. 12, p. 690.

26. Rosen, *Classical Style*, p. 265.

27. H. C. Robbins Landon, *Haydn: Chronicle and Works* (Bloomington and London, 1976–80), vol. 2, pp. 454–55, 578–82; Georg Feder, "Ein vergessener Haydn-Brief," *Haydn-Studien* 1 (1966), pp. 114–16. James Webster, following Jens Peter Larsen's lead, interprets Haydn's statement as a "declaration of stylistic novelty and an advertising slogan." See Webster, *Haydn's "Farewell" Symphony and the Idea of Classical Style* (Cambridge, England, 1991), p. 345.

28. The stage equivalents were "serenatas," e. g., Mozart's *Ascanio in Alba*.

29. J. A. P. Schulz, "Serenade," in Johann Georg Sulzer, *Allgemeine Theorie der schönen Künste* (Leipzig, 1771–74; 2nd ed. 1792–93), vol. 4, p. 369; translation in James Webster, "Towards a History of Viennese Chamber Music in the Early Classical Period," *Journal of the American Musicological Society* 27 (1974), p. 216. Walther in *Musicalisches Lexicon* (1732) calls the serenade "an evening piece; because such works are usually performed on quiet and pleasant nights." English translation in Hubert Unverricht, "Serenade" entry, *The New Grove*, vol. 17, p. 160.

30. For superb discussions of pastoral style in Mozart's later operas and of the conventional "meanings" associated with social dances used or alluded to in Mozart's music, see Allanbrook, *Rhythmic Gesture*, especially chapters 2–6.

31. *Briefe*, vol. 1, p. 526, diary of Marianne Mozart, 9 August 1775 (no. 319).

32. Günter Hausswald, *Mozarts Serenaden. Ein Beitrag zur Stilkritik des 18. Jahrhunderts* (Leipzig, 1951; reprint Wilhelmshaven, 1975), pp. 151–56.

33. Hausswald, *Mozarts Serenaden*, p. 152.

34. Cited in Werner Rainer, "Michael Haydns Orchesterserenaden," *MJb 1987/88*, p. 76.

35. For a summary of the Salzburg serenade repertory, see Andrew Kearns, "The Orchestral Serenade in Eighteenth-Century Salzburg," presented at the Annual Meeting of the American Musicological Society, Montreal, 5 November 1993.

36. Zaslaw, *Mozart's Symphonies*, p. 551. The surviving work is Leopold Mozart's nine-movement Serenata in D for orchestra (Zurich: Eulenberg, 1977), ed. Alexander Weinmann. For Michael Haydn's serenades, see Rainer, "Michael Haydns Orchesterserenaden."

37. For discussions, see Webster, "Viennese Chamber Music," pp. 212–31, Carl Bär, "Zum Begriff des 'Basso' in Mozarts Serenaden," *MJb 1960/61*, pp. 134–36, and Hausswald, *Mozarts Serenaden*, pp. 5–11.

38. Paul Henry Lang, *Music in Western Civilization* (New York, 1941), p. 648.

39. Allanbrook, *Rhythmic Gesture,* p. 128.

40. A. Hyatt King, *Mozart Wind and String Concertos* (Seattle, 1978), p. 24; H. C. Robbins Landon, "The Concertos: (2) Their Musical Origins and Development," in Landon and Mitchell, *Mozart Companion,* p. 248.

41. *Letters,* p. 615, 11 September 1778 (no. 331).

42. Ernst Bloch, *The Principle of Hope,* trans. Neville Plaice et al. (Cambridge, Mass., 1986), vol. 2, p. 797.

Chapter 9: A Fool's Errand

1. *Letters,* p. 286, 29–30 September 1777 (no. 212c).
2. Ibid., p. 283, 29–30 September 1777 (no. 212a).
3. Ibid., p. 284, 29–30 September 1777 (no. 212a).
4. Ibid., p. 292, 2 October 1777 (no. 214b).
5. Ibid., p. 284, 29–30 September 1777 (no. 212a).
6. Ibid. pp. 294–95, 4 October 1777 (no. 215).
7. Ibid., p. 290, 2 October 1777 (no. 214).
8. Ibid., p. 296, 6 October 1777 (no. 216).
9. Ibid., p. 298, 5 October 1777 (no. 216a).
10. Ibid., p. 395, 29 November 1777 (no. 251).
11. Ibid., p. 402, 3 December 1777 (no. 253).
12. Friedrich Heinrich Jacobi, letter to Christoph Martin Wieland, 8 June 1777, *Friedrich Heinrich Jacobi's auserlesener Briefwechsel* (Leipzig, 1825–27), vol. 1, p. 273, cited in Jahn, vol. 1, p. 369.
13. *Letters,* p. 353, 1 November 1777 (no. 234).
14. Ibid., p. 367, 13 November 1777 (no. 240).
15. Ibid., p. 376, 17 November 1777 (no. 244).
16. Ibid., p. 409, 7 December (no. 256a).
17. Ibid., p. 400, 3 December 1777 (no. 253).
18. Ibid., pp. 397 and 400, 29 November 1777 and 3 December 1777 (nos. 251, 253).
19. Ibid., p. 400, 3 December 1777 (no. 253). The Rondo for piano, K. 284f, does not survive.
20. Ibid., p. 414, 10 December 1777 (no. 258).
21. Ibid.
22. *Letters,* p. 420, 14 December 1777 (no. 260).
23. Apart from the Quartet in D, K. 285, all of these works are difficult to date with any precision, and the flute concertos and Quartet in G, K. 285a, are lacking in authentic sources. It is probable that Mozart exaggerated the amount of the promised fee. As of 14 February 1778, Dejean had paid him 96 florins, but he paid no additional amounts thereafter, apparently because Mozart did not fulfill the commission for three concertos and four quartets. See *Letters,* p. 481 (no. 286a). For a thorough discussion, see Wolf-Dieter Seiffert, "Schrieb Mozart drei Flötenquartette für Dejean?" *MJb 1987/88,* pp. 267–75. The Flute Quartet in C, K. Anh. 171/285b, the first movement of which was recently authenticated by Tyson, dates from 1781 or 1782; the Flute Quartet in A, K. 298, dates from 1786–87.
24. But see Plath, p. 257, where the possibility is raised that several of these were written in Paris.
25. *Letters,* p. 420, 14 December 1777 (no. 260).
26. Ibid., p. 429, 20 December 1777 (no. 264a).
27. Ibid., p. 426, 18 December 1777 (no. 263).
28. Ibid., p. 444, from Mannheim, 11 January 1778 (no. 271c).
29. Letter from Franz von Heufeld to Leopold Mozart, 23 January 1778: *MDB,* p. 170.
30. *Letters,* pp. 462–63, 4 February 1778 (no. 281).
31. Ibid., p. 435, 27 December 1777 (no. 267).
32. Ibid., p. 461, 4 February 1778 (no. 281).
33. All quotations in the above paragraph are from ibid., pp. 474–80, 11–12 February 1778 (no. 285); translation amended.
34. Ibid., p. 461, 4 February 1778 (no. 281).
35. Ibid., p. 462, 4 February 1778 (no. 281).
36. Ibid., p. 461, 4 February 1778 (no. 281).

37. Ibid., p. 485, 19 February 1778 (no. 288).

38. Ibid., p. 498, 28 February 1778 (no. 292).

39. Ibid., p. 486, 19 February 1778 (no. 288a).

40. Ibid., p. 499, 28 February 1778 (no. 292a).

41. Ibid., p. 487, 22 February 1778 (no. 289).

42. Ibid.

43. *Letters*, p. 640, 18 December 1778 (no. 345).

44. Ibid., p. 517, 24 March 1778 (no. 299).

45. Ibid., p. 518, 24 March 1778 (no. 299); translation amended.

46. Ibid., p. 518, 24 March 1778 (no. 299).

47. Ibid., p. 468, 7 February 1778 (no. 283a).

48. Two other sets, the Twelve Variations on "Ah, vous dirai-je, Maman," K. 265/300e, and Twelve Variations on "La belle Françoise," K. 353/300f, thought to have been written in Paris, have been shown by Plath to date at earliest from summer 1780 and probably from 1781 or 1782. See Plath, p. 258.

49. See Plath, pp. 316–31; Robert D. Levin, *Who Wrote the Mozart Four-wind Concertante?* (New York, 1988).

50. *Letters*, p. 622, 3 October 1778 (no. 335).

51. See Neal Zaslaw, *Mozart's Symphonies: Context, Performance Practice, Reception* (Oxford, 1989), pp. 333–34.

52. See *Letters*, pp. 552–53, 12 June 1778 (no. 309a), cited on p. 235 above.

53. An anonymous source reported that "the loving son" delayed his departure from Salzburg "in the hope that his father might be installed at his side with a salary as composer and director." *AMZ* 23 (1821), column 686.

54. Letter of 12 December 1771: *MDB*, p. 138.

55. *Letters*, pp. 336–37 (no. 227a).

56. Ibid., pp. 523–24, 6 April 1778 (no. 301).

57. Ibid., p. 489, 22 February 1778 (no. 289a).

58. Ibid., p. 533, 1 May 1778 (no. 303).

59. Ibid., p. 586, 31 July 1778 (no. 319).

60. Ibid., p. 454, 29 January 1778 (no. 277).

61. Ibid., p. 455, 29 January 1778 (no. 277).

62. Ibid., p. 539, 14 May 1778 (no. 305a); for an analysis of Mozart's calculations, see *Briefe*, vol. 5, p. 520.

63. *Letters*, p. 542, 28 May 1778 (no. 306).

64. Ibid., p. 547, 11 June 1778 (no. 308).

65. Ibid., p. 559, 3 July 1778 (no. 311).

66. Ibid.

67. *Letters*, p. 580, 29 July 1778 (no. 317).

68. Ibid., p. 573, 18 July 1778 (no. 315). "That I do not like being here, you must long ago have noticed. I have very many reasons, but, as I am here, it is useless to go into them." P. 558, 3 July 1778 (no. 311).

69. Ibid., p. 475, 11–12 February 1778 (no. 285).

70. Ibid., p. 431, 22 December 1777 (no. 265).

71. Ibid.

72. *Letters*, p. 437, 29 December 1777 (no. 268).

73. Ibid., p. 446, 12 January 1778 (no. 272); translation revised.

74. Ibid.

75. *Letters*, p. 547, 11 June 1778 (no. 308).

76. Ibid., p. 555, 29 June 1778 (no. 310).

77. Ibid., p. 562, 9 July 1778 (no. 313).

78. Ibid., p. 563, 9 July 1778 (no. 313).

79. Ibid., p. 562, 9 July 1778 (no. 313).

80. Ibid., p. 573, 18 July 1778 (no. 315).

81. Ibid., p. 608, 31 August 1778 (no. 328).

82. Petition and decree, 17 January 1779: *MDB*, pp. 181–82. Leopold Mozart's raise was putatively for additional duties consequent on the death, in early August, of Kapellmeister

Giuseppe Maria Lolli. Leopold had petitioned for the vacancy in mid-August but was refused; instead, he was granted the raise with the stipulation that "he appear diligently at the court and cathedral music, and additionally instruct others with regard to their obligations, and industriously supervise the instructors and students at the Kapellhaus." Decree of 30 August 1778: *NMD*, pp. 25–26 (no. 45); see also *Briefe*, vol. 5, p. 554. "Finally Lolli has died," Leopold wrote to Mozart on 3 September, "now things will be more serious. I have hopes that now my circumstances too may be improved and I believe that this would be the moment in time to bring your expectations to fruition." *Briefe*, vol. 2, p. 464, 3 September 1778 (no. 482).

83. *Letters*, p. 612, 11 September 1778 (no. 331); "I swear to you as your father and friend that you will not have to play violin at the court, rather only, like the late Adlgasser, if it is necessary to accompany singing." *Briefe*, vol. 2, pp. 466–67, 3 September 1778 (no. 482); see also Franz Anton Spitzeder to Archbishop Colloredo, ca. 20 February 1779: *MDB*, pp. 183–84. Only a few weeks later, Leopold Mozart wrote bluntly: "*As a lover of music* you will not consider it beneath you to play the violin in the opening symphony, any more than does the Archbishop himself." *Briefe*, vol. 2, p. 485, 24 September 1778 (no. 491); *Letters*, p. 620, 24 September 1778 (no. 333); translation amended.

84. *Letters*, p. 615, 11 September 1778 (no. 331), and p. 629, 26 October 1778 (no. 338).

85. Ibid., p. 613, 11 September 1778 (no. 331).

86. Ibid., pp. 593–94, 7 August 1778 (no. 322).

87. *Briefe*, vol. 2, p. 471, 10 September 1778 (no. 485).

88. Ibid., p. 463, 3 September 1778 (no. 482).

89. Ibid., p. 465, 3 September 1778 (no. 482).

90. *Letters*, p. 609, 3 September 1778 (no. 329).

91. Ibid., p. 610, 3 September 1778 (no. 329).

92. Ibid.

93. *Briefe*, vol. 2, p. 486, 24 September 1778 (no. 491); *Letters*, p. 620, 24 September 1778 (no. 333); translation revised.

94. *Letters*, p. 612, 11 September 1778 (no. 331).

95. Ibid., p. 624, 15 October 1778 (no. 336).

96. Ibid., p. 619, 24 September 1778 (no. 333).

97. K⁶, p. 332.

98. *Letters*, p. 630, 12 November 1778 (no. 339).

99. Ibid., pp. 633–34, 19 November 1778 (no. 340).

100. Ibid., p. 634, 19 November 1778 (no. 340).

101. *Briefe*, vol. 2, p. 510, 19 November 1778 (no. 505).

102. Jahn, vol. 1, p. 349. See *Letters*, p. 464, 5 February 1778 (no. 282).

103. For references to such loans, see *Briefe*, vol. 2, p. 132, 20 November 1777 (no. 375); *Letters*, p. 381, 20 November 1777 (no. 246); see also *Letters*, p. 490, 19 November 1777 (no. 290); *Letters*, p. 634, 19 November 1778 (no. 340); *Briefe*, vol. 5, p. 560. The letter of credit opened by Lorenz Hagenauer, the merchant-banker who frequently acted on Leopold's behalf in financial transactions, is not initially listed by Leopold among the debts.

104. *Letters*, p. 406, 4 December 1777 (no. 255).

105. Ibid., p. 418, 11 December 1777 (no. 259).

106. Ibid., p. 464, 5 February 1778 (no. 282); see also p. 459, 2 February 1778 (no. 280).

107. Ibid., p. 464, 5 February 1778 (no. 282).

108. Ibid., p. 535, 6 May 1778 (no. 304).

109. Ibid., p. 381, 20 November 1777 (no. 246).

110. Ibid., p. 634, 19 November 1778 (no. 340).

111. *Briefe*, vol. 2, p. 526, 28 December 1778 (no. 512).

112. *Letters*, p. 610, 3 September 1778 (no. 329).

113. *Briefe*, vol. 2, p. 515, 23 November 1778 (no. 506); *Letters*, p. 636, 23 November 1778 (no. 341); translation revised.

114. Ibid., p. 644, 28 December 1778 (no. 347).

115. Ibid., p. 645, 29 December 1778 (no. 348); Johann Baptist Becke to Leopold Mozart, 29 December 1778: *MDB*, p. 180.

116. *Letters*, pp. 644–45, 28 December 1778 (no. 347).

117. Ibid., p. 647, 31 December 1778 (no. 350).

118. Ibid.

119. *Letters,* p. 649, 8 January 1779 (no. 351).

120. *Briefe,* vol. 2, p. 512, 23 November 1778 (no. 506).

121. Ibid., vol. 2, p. 465, 3 September 1778 (no. 482), and p. 469, 10 September 1778 (no. 485).

Chapter 10: Mozart in Love

1. *Letters,* p. 649, 8 January 1779 (no. 351).

2. Ibid., p. 326, 16–17 October 1777 (no. 224).

3. Ibid., p. 327, 16 October 1777 (no. 224a); translation revised.

4. Ibid., pp. 334–35, 20 October 1777 (no. 226b).

5. Mozart entry in his cousin's album, 25 October 1777: *MDB,* p. 167.

6. *Letters,* p. 403, 3 December 1777 (no. 254).

7. Ibid.

8. *Letters,* p. 372, 13 November 1777 (no. 242). The original is in French.

9. *Briefe,* vol. 2, pp. 547–49, 10 May 1780 [not 1779] (no. 525); *Letters,* pp. 651–54, 10 May 1780 [not 1779] (no. 354).

10. *Letters,* p. 500, 28 February 1778 (no. 293).

11. Ibid., p. 501, 28 February 1778 (no. 293); translation revised.

12. See Blümml, pp. 170–71.

13. *Letters,* p. 138, 19 May 1770 (no. 92a).

14. Ibid., p. 359, 5 November 1777 (no. 236). See Wolfgang Hildesheimer, *Mozart,* trans. Marion Faber (New York, 1982), p. 107.

15. Hildesheimer, *Mozart,* p. 107. Eibl and Senn, seeking to preserve Mozart's claim that he was a virgin until his marriage, view the letters merely as verbal erotic and scatological byplay. See J. H. Eibl and Walter Senn, *Mozarts Bäsle-Briefe* (Kassel, 1978), p. 80 and passim. In his introduction to *Mozarts Bäsle-Briefe,* however, Hildesheimer argues for the sexual nature of the connection. Eibl and Senn, pp. 7–11.

16. *Letters,* p. 372, 13 November 1777 (no. 242).

17. Ibid.

18. *Letters,* p. 476, 11–12 February 1778 (no. 285).

19. Ibid., p. 485, 19 February 1778 (no. 288); translation amended.

20. Ibid., pp. 447–48, 17 January 1778 (no. 273a).

21. Ibid., pp. 467, 7 February 1778 (no. 283a).

22. Ibid., p. 478, 11–12 February 1778 (no. 285).

23. Ibid., pp. 499–500, 28 February 1778 (no. 293).

24. Ibid., pp. 500–501, 28 February 1778 (no. 293).

25. Ibid., pp. 582, 581, 30 July 1778 (no. 318).

26. Ibid., p. 581, 30 July 1778 (no. 318).

27. Ibid., p. 518, 24 March 1778 (no. 299).

28. Ibid., pp. 576, 581, 29 July 1778 (no. 317).

29. Nissen, pp. 414–15.

30. *Briefe,* vol. 5, p. 578; Blümml traces this to a traditional Bavarian quatrain, which concludes, "Leck mi da Bue im A—,/ Der mi net will." Blümml, p. 172.

31. *Letters,* p. 644, 23 December 1778 (no. 346).

32. Ibid., pp. 643–44, 23 December 1778 (no. 346).

33. Ibid., p. 651, 11 January 1779 (no. 352).

34. See *Briefe,* vol. 2, pp. 549–52, 10 May–15 June 1779 (no. 526).

35. Wegele thinks it certain that Mozart saw his cousin on that occasion. Ludwig Wegele, *Der Lebenslauf der Marianne Thekla Mozart* (Augsburg, 1967), p. 52.

36. *Letters,* pp. 774–75, 23 October 1781 (no. 429).

37. Ibid., p. 819, 31 August 1782 (no. 462).

38. See Leopold Mozart's letters to his daughter, 2 February and 21 February 1785, in Deutsch-Paumgartner, pp. 66, 73. See *Briefe,* vol. 3, p. 370 (no. 844), and p. 377 (no. 848).

39. *Briefe,* vol. 4, p. 269, Constanze Mozart to B&H, 28 August 1799 (no. 1256).

40. Hildesheimer viewed Aloysia and the Bäsle as occupying opposite ends of Mozart's "erotic scale," the former a remote "goddess" and the latter a "sex object." See Hildesheimer, *Mozart,* pp. 105, 122–23.

41. *Letters,* p. 927, 19 May 1789 (no. 564).

42. Ibid., p. 95, "1769" (no. 70). The addressee is now believed to have been Maria Anna Katharina Gilowsky von Urazowa (1753–1809). See Rudolph Angermüller, "Neuerwerbungen der Bibliotheca Mozartiana," *Mitteilungen der ISM* 41 (June 1993), p. 74.

43. Jahn, vol. 1, p. 348.

44. *Letters,* p. 424, 18 December 1777 (no. 262).

45. Ibid., p. 336, 23 October 1777 (no. 227).

46. Ibid.

47. *Letters,* p. 341, 25 October 1777 (no. 229).

48. Ibid., p. 422, 15 December 1777 (no. 261).

49. Ibid., p. 430, 20 December 1777 (no. 264a).

50. Ibid., pp. 465–66, 5 February 1778 (no. 282).

51. Ibid., pp. 475–77, 11–12 February 1778 (no. 285).

52. Ibid., p. 455, 29 January 1778 (no. 277).

Chapter 11: A Mother's Death

1. *Letters,* p. 277, 26 September 1777 (no. 209).

2. Ibid., pp. 271–72, 23–24 September 1777 (no. 207); translation amended.

3. *Briefe,* vol. 2, p. 14, 26 September 1777 (no. 333); see also *Letters,* p. 278, 26 September 1777 (no. 209a).

4. *Letters,* pp. 408–9, 7 December 1777 (no. 256a).

5. Ibid. On 11 December, she added, "Today I have a headache and I think I am in for a cold. It is bitterly cold here. I am so frozen that I can hardly hold my pen." P. 416 (no. 258a).

6. Ibid., p. 414, 10 December 1777 (no. 258).

7. Ibid., p. 416, 11 December 1777 (no. 258a).

8. Ibid., p. 420, 14 December 1777 (no. 260).

9. Ibid., pp. 421–22, 15 December 1777 (no. 261).

10. Ibid., pp. 424, 425, 18 December 1777 (no. 262).

11. Ibid., p. 453, 26 [recte 25] January 1778 (no. 276).

12. Ibid., p. 463, 5 February 1778 (no. 281a).

13. Ibid., p. 519, 24 March 1778 (no. 299a).

14. Ibid., p. 520, 5 April 1778 (no. 300).

15. Ibid.

16. *Letters,* p. 530, 12–20 April 1778 (no. 302).

17. Ibid. The reference is to the possibility of renewed hostilities between Russia and Turkey, which threatened to involve Germany and Austria as well.

18. *Letters,* p. 534, 1 May 1778 (no. 303a).

19. Ibid., p. 535, 6 May 1778 (no. 304).

20. Ibid., p. 536, 6 May 1778 (no. 304).

21. Ibid., pp. 550–51, 12 June 1778 (no. 309).

22. Church Register of Saint-Eustache, Paris, 4 July 1778: *MDB,* p. 176.

23. *Letters,* pp. 556–57, 3 July 1778 (no. 311).

24. Ibid., p. 585, 31 July 1778 (no. 319).

25. Ibid.

26. *Letters,* p. 560, 3 July 1778 (no. 312).

27. Ibid., p. 583, 31 July 1778 (no. 319).

28. Ibid., p. 561, 9 July 1778 (no. 313).

29. Ibid., p. 560, 3 July 1778 (no. 312); translation amended.

30. Ibid., p. 557, 3 July 1778 (no. 311).

31. Ibid., p. 561, 9 July 1778 (no. 313).

32. Ibid.

33. Ibid.

34. *Letters,* p. 567, 13 July 1778 (no. 314).

35. Ibid., pp. 567–68, 13 July 1778 (no. 314).

36. Ibid., p. 569, 13 July 1778 (no. 314).

37. Ibid., p. 584, 31 July 1778 (no. 319).

38. Ibid., p. 590, 3 August 1778 (no. 320).

39. Ibid.

40. *Letters,* pp. 590–91, 3 August 1778 (no. 320).

41. Ibid., p. 591, 3 August 1778 (no. 320).

42. Ibid., pp. 603–4, 27 August 1778 (no. 326).

43. Ibid., p. 480, 11–12 February 1778 (no. 285).

44. Ibid., p. 650, 8 January 1779 (no. 350).

45. Ibid., p. 586, 31 July 1778 (no. 319).

46. Ibid., p. 561, 9 July 1778 (no. 313).

47. Ibid., p. 569, 18 July 1778 (no. 315).

48. Ibid., p. 753, 25 July 1781 (no. 417), and p. 467, 7 February 1778 (no. 283a).

49. *Briefe,* vol. 2, p. 510, 19 November 1778 (no. 505).

Chapter 12: Trouble in Paradise

1. The theory is stated effectively by the British follower of Melanie Klein, Adrian Stokes, from whom I have adopted the phrase "the image in form." Stokes observes that any mode of feeling "takes to itself as a crowning attribute more general images of experience. Form, then, ultimately constructs an image or figure of which, in art, the expression of particular feeling avails itself. . . . Form in the widest sense of all, as the attempted organization that rules every experience, must obviously give rise to a strong and compelling imagery so generalized that it can hardly be absent from a consciousness in working order." *The Critical Writings of Adrian Stokes,* ed. Lawrence Gowing (London, 1978), vol. 3, p. 332.

2. John Dewey, *Art as Experience* (New York, 1934), pp. 147–48.

3. Ibid, p. 150.

4. Susanne Langer, *Feeling and Form* (New York, 1953), p. 242.

5. See Northrop Frye, *Anatomy of Criticism: Four Essays* (Princeton, 1957), and M. H. Abrams, *Natural Supernaturalism: Tradition and Revolution in Romantic Literature* (New York and London, 1971).

6. Rudolf Arnheim, *Art and Visual Perception: A Psychology of the Creative Eye* (Berkeley and Los Angeles, 1969), p. 376. See also Anton Ehrenzweig, *The Hidden Order of Art: A Study in the Psychology of Artistic Imagination* (Berkeley and Los Angeles, 1971), p. 174.

7. D. W. Winnicott, *The Maturational Processes and the Facilitating Environment: Studies in the Theory of Emotional Development* (London and New York, 1965), pp. 57–58.

8. Ernst Kris, *Psychoanalytic Explorations in Art* (New York, 1952), p. 50.

9. Ella Freeman Sharpe, *Collected Papers on Psycho-Analysis,* ed. Marjorie Brierley (London, 1950), p. 131.

10. Einstein, p. 255.

11. *Letters,* p. 573, 20 July 1778 (no. 315a), and p. 589, 31 July 1778 (no. 319a). It was formerly believed that Mozart was referring to the Sonatas, K. 330–332/300h, i, k and K. 333/315c, but these are now thought to have originated at later dates.

12. *Letters,* p. 599, 13 August 1778 (no. 323).

13. Three other works were also entered in the thematic catalog on 26 June 1788: the Symphony in E-flat, K. 543, the Adagio and Fugue in C minor for string orchestra, K. 546, and a March in D, K. 544, for string trio, flute, and horn.

Chapter 13: Parallel Lives

1. *Letters,* p. 319, 15 October 1777 (no. 222).

2. Ibid., p. 398, 1 December 1777 (no. 252).

3. Ibid., pp. 490–91, 23 February 1778 (no. 290).

4. Ibid., p. 591, 3 August 1778 (no. 320).

5. Ibid., p. 610, 3 September 1778 (no. 329).

6. Ibid., p. 626, 19 October 1778 (no. 337); translation amended.

7. Ibid., p. 524, 6 April 1778 (no. 301); translation amended.

8. Ibid., p. 278, 26 September 1777 (no. 209a).

9. Ibid., p. 292, 2 October 1777 (no. 214a).

10. Ibid., p. 278, 26 September 1777 (no. 209a).

11. Ibid., p. 338, 23 October 1777 (no. 228a).

12. Ibid., p. 518, 24 March 1778 (no. 299), and p. 522, 5 April 1778 (no. 300a).

13. Ibid., pp. 524–25, 6 April 1778 (no. 301). Occasional attempts to reassure Mozart and Frau Mozart—"If things go well with both of you, then I am in my best humor"—were quickly

nullified by renewed laments: "My very life depends on yours. I am your old deserted father and husband." *Briefe,* vol. 2, p. 16, 27 September 1777 (no. 335); *Letters,* p. 279, 27 September 1777 (no. 210); translation revised.

14. See Erich Schenk, "Mozarts Salzburger Vorfahren," *MJb* 3 (1928), p. 89.

15. *Letters,* pp. 583–84, 31 July 1778 (no. 319).

16. Ibid., p. 544, 29 May 1778 (no. 307a).

17. Ibid., p. 546, 11 June 1778 (no. 308).

18. Ibid.

19. *Letters,* p. 647, 31 December 1778 (no. 349).

20. Ibid., p. 644, 28 December 1778 (no. 347).

21. Ibid., p. 648, 31 December 1778 (no. 350).

22. Sara Sheftel, "Mozart: A Psychoanalytic Study" (Ph.D. dissertation, Graduate School of the Union for Experimenting Colleges and Universities, 1982), p. 58.

Chapter 14: Farewell to Salzburg

1. *Briefe,* vol. 3, p. 6, 24–31 May 1780 (no. 532). Entry for 28 May 1780.

2. Ibid., vol. 2, p. 549, 10 May–15 June 1779 (no. 526). Entry for 11 May 1779.

3. See ibid., pp. 554–55, 2–16 December 1779 (no. 528).

4. Ibid., p. 553, 15–28 September 1779 (no. 527). Entry for 16 September 1779.

5. *Briefe,* vol. 3, p. 5, 24–31 May 1780 (no. 532). Entry for 25 May 1780.

6. Ibid., vol. 2, p. 544, 26 March–9 May 1779 (no. 523). Entry for 20 April 1779.

7. The original reads, with the key letters underlined: "den 19ten: *um* scheissen, meine wenigkeit [= the letter I for "*Ich*"], ein *E*sel, ein *b*ruch, wider ein *E*sel, und endlich eine *N*ase, in der kirche, zu haus geblieben der *Pf*eif mir im *a*rsch, *pf*eif mir im *a*rsch ein wenig übel auf. Nachmittag die Katherl bey uns, und auch der Herr *F*uchs-schwanz, den *i*ch hernach brav im *a*rsch geleckt, habe, O köstlicher *A*rsch!—Doctor Barisani auch gekommen, den ganzen Tag geregnet." *Briefe,* vol. 3, pp. 7–8, 12 August–13 September 1780 (no. 533), entry for 19 August 1780. The German solution reads: "um sieben in der kirche. zu haus geblieben der Papa, ein wenig übel auf. Nachmittag die Katherl bey uns. und auch der Herr Fiala." *Briefe,* vol. 6, p. 11; J. H. Eibl and Walter Senn, *Mozarts Bäsle-Briefe* (Kassel, 1978), p. 68.

8. *Briefe,* vol. 3, p. 8, 12 August–13 September 1780 (no. 533). Entry for 26 August 1780.

9. Ibid., vol. 2, p. 482, 17 September 1778 (no. 490); *Letters,* p. 618, 17 September 1778 (no. 332); translation amended.

10. See Franz Anton Spitzeder to Archbishop Colloredo, ca. 20 February 1779: *MDB,* pp. 183–84. Apparently, Mozart was deputized to take over his father's responsibilities in the Kapellhaus; also apparent was that he was recalcitrant about fulfilling those responsibilities.

11. *Letters,* p. 678, 1 December 1780 (no. 367).

12. Ibid., p. 692, 19 December 1780 (no. 378), and p. 699, 27 December 1780 (no. 381).

13. Ibid., p. 701, 30 December 1780 (no. 382a).

14. Köchel places the first version of this work in 1773. As for the revised version, Plath suggests that the entr'actes date from ca. 1777, and the choruses from ca. 1779–80. Wolfgang Plath, "Beiträge zur Mozart-Autographie II. Schriftchronologie 1770–1780," *MJb 1976/77* (Basel, 1978), pp. 172–73; Plath, pp. 259–60.

15. The full program was punningly entered by Mozart into his sister's diary: it also included an Italian aria, a terzett by Salieri, a cello concerto, an aria by Grétry with oboe and harp accompaniment, a finale by Pasquale Anfossi. See *Briefe,* vol. 3, p. 3, 18 March 1780 (no. 529). For a free translation and reconstruction of the program, see Neal Zaslaw, *Mozart's Symphonies: Context, Performance Practice, Reception* (Oxford, 1989), pp. 341–42.

16. *Letters,* p. 290, 2 October 1777 (no. 214).

17. Ibid., p. 305, 11 October 1777 (no. 219).

18. Ibid., p. 462, 4 February 1778 (no. 281).

19. Caspar Riesbeck, *Travels Through Germany in a Series of Letters* (London, 1787), vol. 1, p. 183. For the Mozart family's absorption in Salzburg theater, see Ernst Lert, *Mozart auf dem Theater* (Berlin, 1918), pp. 67–78.

20. Böhm's Salzburg programs survive only in fragmentary form, but the repertory he presented in Augsburg between June and September 1779 is thoroughly documented. See Heinz Friedrich Deininger, "Die deutsche Schauspielergesellschaft unter der Direktion von Johann Heinrich Böhm, einem Freunde der Familie Mozart, in Augsburg in den Jahren 1779 und 1780."

Augsburger Mozartbuch 1942–43, pp. 386–92. For the troupe's history and membership, see Hans Georg Fellmann, *Die Böhmsche Theatertruppe und ihre Zeit,* Theatergeschichtliche Forschungen, ed. Julius Petersen, vol. 38 (Leipzig, 1928), with its complete repertory listed at pp. 79–86. Marianne Mozart's diary 2–16 December 1779 gives titles of the fifty-second to fifty-ninth productions; her diaries for the period prior to 2 December 1779, which probably listed the first 51 performances, are not extant. *Briefe,* vol. 2, p. 555, 2–16 December 1779 (no. 528). For Böhm, see also *Briefe,* vol. 5, pp. 573–74.

21. It lacks a finale. Zaslaw does not accept Einstein's conjecture that the Symphony in G, K. 318, was intended for *Zaide.* See Zaslaw, *Mozart's Symphonies,* p. 344; Einstein, p. 228; K⁶, p. 340. Böhm also used Mozart's Symphony in E-flat, K. 184/161a, as an overture to a play. The consensus of recent scholarship is that the work was intended for Vienna rather than Salzburg: see Walter Senn, "Mozarts *Zaide* und der Verfasser der vermutlichen Text-Vorlage," *Festschrift Alfred Orel zum 70. Geburtstag,* ed. Hellmut Federhofer (Vienna, 1960), pp. 174–78; Friedrich-Heinrich Neumann, "Zur Vorgeschichte der *Zaide,*" *MJb 1962/63,* pp. 244–46; Linda L. Tyler, "*Zaide* in the Development of Mozart's Operatic Language," *Music & Letters* 72 (1991), pp. 215–16.

22. *Letters,* p. 654, 24 April 1780 (no. 355).

23. Ibid., p. 668, 20 November 1780 (no. 361).

24. See "Schikaneder in Salzburg," in Blümml, pp. 140–62, 206–17, with tabular listings of all productions and income on pp. 210–16. It was a successful run, earning a minimum of 50 florins per night and a season's total of 8,269 florins.

25. *Letters,* p. 659, 8 November 1780 (no. 356).

26. Ibid., pp. 664–65, 15 November 1780 (no. 359).

27. The divertimento probably dates from the summer of 1780; the symphony is dated "29 August 1780," and the date of and occasion for the sinfonia concertante are unknown.

28. *Letters,* p. 663, 13 November 1780 (no. 358).

29. Ibid., p. 698, 27 December 1780 (no. 381).

30. Ibid., p. 701, 30 December 1780 (no. 383).

31. *Briefe,* vol. 3, pp. 26–27, 20 November 1780 (no. 540).

32. Ibid., p. 27, 20 November 1780 (no. 540); *Letters,* p. 668, 20 November 1780 (no. 361); translation revised.

33. *Letters,* p. 672, 24 November 1780 (no. 363).

34. Ibid.

35. *Letters,* p. 670, 24 November 1780 (no. 363).

36. Ibid., p. 676, 30 November 1780 (no. 366a).

37. "Wäre ich bey deiner Mutter gewesen, könnte ich hoffen, dass sie noch lebte: ihre Stunde war da, darum musste ich auch abwesend seyn." *Briefe,* vol. 3, pp. 38–39, 30 November 1780 (no. 547); *Letters,* p. 676, 30 November 1780 (no. 366a).

38. *Letters,* p. 690, 16 December 1780 (no. 376).

39. Ibid., pp. 691–92, 18 December 1780 (no. 377a).

40. Ibid., p. 693, 19 December 1780 (no. 378).

41. Ibid., p. 703, 3 January 1781 (no. 384).

42. Ibid., p. 662, 13 November 1780 (no. 358).

43. Ibid., p. 704, 3 January 1781 (no. 384).

44. *Briefe,* vol. 3, p. 33, 25 November 1780 (no. 543).

45. Ibid., vol. 3, pp. 46–47, 4 December 1780 (no. 553); *Letters,* p. 681, 4 December 1780 (no. 369).

46. *Letters,* p. 673, 25 November 1780 (no. 364); for more on Ceccarelli, see also *Briefe,* vol. 3, p. 84, 8 January 1781 (no. 576).

47. *Briefe,* vol. 3, p. 57, 15 December 1780 (no. 562); see also p. 46, 4 December 1780 (no. 553).

48. *Letters,* p. 681, 4 December 1780 (no. 369).

49. Ibid., p. 661, 11 November 1780 (no. 357).

50. Ibid., p. 707, 11 January 1781 (no. 388).

51. Ibid., p. 672, 24 November 1780 (no. 363).

52. Ibid., pp. 694–95, 22 December 1780 (no. 379).

53. Ibid., p. 700, 29 December 1780 (no. 382).

54. Ibid., p. 703, 3 January 1781 (no. 384).

55. Ibid., p. 354, 1 November 1777 (no. 234).

56. *Briefe,* vol. 2, p. 341, 12–20 April 1778 (no. 446); *Letters,* p. 529, 12–20 April 1778 (no. 302); translation amended.

57. *Letters,* p. 529, 12–20 April 1778 (no. 302).

58. Ibid., p. 536, 6 May 1778 (no. 304).

59. Ibid., pp. 552–53, 12 June 1778 (no. 309a).

60. Ibid., p. 599, 13 August 1778 (no. 323).

61. Ibid., p. 685, 11 December 1780 (no. 373).

62. Ibid., pp. 687–88, 15 December 1780 (no. 375).

63. *Münchner Stats-, Gelehrte, und Vermischte Nachrichten,* 1 February 1781: *MDB,* pp. 191–92.

64. *Annalen der Baierischen Litteratur vom Jahre 1781: MDB,* p. 192.

65. Plath, p. 260.

66. Alan Tyson, "Proposed New Dates for Many Works and Fragments Written by Mozart from March 1781 to December 1791," in *Mozart Studies,* ed. Cliff Eisen (Oxford, 1991), p. 217.

67. See Tyson, pp. 27–28; Tyson, "Proposed New Dates," p. 216. There is no physical or documentary evidence one way or the other, but it seems unlikely that Mozart would have failed to list a complete, orchestrated Kyrie in his thematic catalog of works written between 1784 and 1791, for, though he ordinarily does not include fragments, he does include completed individual movements such as an Andante for a violin concerto, K. 470, an Allegro and Andante for piano, K. 533, and an Adagio for piano in B minor, K. 540. The Munich date was first assigned by Jahn solely on the basis of style and orchestration. See Jahn, vol. 2, p. 166; Abert, vol. 1, p. 640.

Chapter 15: Arrival

1. *Letters,* p. 714, 17 March 1781 (no. 393).

2. Ibid., p. 716, 24 March 1781 (no. 395).

3. Ibid., p. 718, 24 March 1781 (no. 395).

4. Ibid.

5. *Letters,* p. 720, 4 April 1781 (no. 396).

6. Ibid.

7. *Letters,* p. 722, 8 April 1781 (no. 397). 1,000 Reichsthaler = 1,500 florins; 1,000 Laubthaler = 2,000 florins.

8. Ibid., p. 717, 24 March 1781 (no. 395).

9. Ibid., pp. 727–28, 9 May 1781 (no. 401); translation amended.

10. Ibid., p. 729, 9 May 1781 (no. 401).

11. Ibid., p. 730, 12 May 1781 (no. 402).

12. Ibid.

13. *Letters,* pp. 730–31, 12 May 1781 (no. 402).

14. Ibid., p. 733, 16 May 1781 (no. 404).

15. Ibid., pp. 733, 732, 16 May 1781 (no. 404).

16. Ibid., p. 735, 19 May 1781 (no. 405).

17. Ibid., pp. 733–34, 19 May 1781 (no. 405).

18. Ibid., pp. 734, 735, 19 May 1781 (no. 405).

19. Ibid., p. 738, between 26 May and 2 June 1781 (no. 407).

20. Ibid.

21. *Letters,* p. 739, 2 June 1781 (no. 408).

22. Ibid.

23. *Letters,* p. 741, 9 June 1781 (no. 409).

24. Ibid.

25. *Letters,* pp. 741–42, 9 June 1781 (no. 409).

26. Goethe, *Wilhelm Meister,* Book 5, in *Werke* (Weimar, 1887–1912), Part 1, vol. 22, p. 27; *Wilhelm Meister's Apprenticeship and Travels,* trans. Thomas Carlyle (Boston, 1851), vol. 1, p. 294.

27. *Letters,* p. 723, 11 April 1781 (no. 398).

28. Ibid., p. 731, 12 May 1781 (no. 403).

29. Ibid., p. 741, 9 June 1781 (no. 409); translation revised.

30. Ibid., p. 749, 4 July 1781 (no. 414); translation amended.

31. Ibid., p. 746, 20 June 1781 (no. 412).

32. Ibid., p. 718, 24 March 1781 (no. 395).

33. Ibid., p. 758, 10 August 1781 (no. 420).

34. Ibid., p. 731, 12 May 1781 (no. 403).

35. Ibid., p. 769, 26 September 1781 (no. 426).

36. Ibid., p. 735, 19 May 1781 (no. 405).

37. Ibid., p. 729, 9 May 1781 (no. 401).

38. Ibid., p. 763, 5 September 1781 (no. 423).

39. Ibid., p. 764, 5 September 1781 (no. 423).

40. *Briefe,* vol. 6, p. 81.

41. *Letters,* p. 743, 13 June 1781 (no. 410).

42. For Auernhammer, see O. E. Deutsch, "Das Fräulein von Auernhammer," *MJb 1958,* pp. 12–17; see also *Briefe,* vol. 6, p. 75.

43. *Letters,* p. 748, 27 June 1781 (no. 413).

44. Ibid., p. 761, 22 August 1781 (no. 421).

45. Ibid.

46. *Letters,* pp. 743–44, 13 June 1781 (no. 410).

47. Ibid., p. 772, 6 October 1781 (no. 427); see also p. 773, 13 October 1781 (no. 428).

48. "So I must ask you to send me another draft. It is just as well to have something in hand, as I really can't go about in a penniless condition." Ibid., p. 702, 30 December 1780 (no. 383).

49. Ibid., p. 721, 4 April 1781 (no. 396).

50. Ibid., p. 737, 26 May 1781 (no. 406).

51. Ibid., p. 763, 5 September 1781 (no. 423). See *Briefe,* vol. 6, p. 82.

52. *Letters,* pp. 789–90, 22 December 1781 (no. 438).

Chapter 16: Constanze

1. *Letters,* pp. 752–53, 25 July 1781 (no. 417).

2. Ibid., p. 753, 25 July 1781 (no. 417). Mozart left Frau Weber's lodgings at the end of August; in a letter of 5 September he gives his address as Graben 1175, third floor. See p. 763, 5 September 1781 (no. 423).

3. *Briefe,* vol. 3, p. 189, 1781 (no. 654).

4. *Letters,* p. 783, 15 December 1781 (no. 436).

5. Ibid., p. 784, 15 December 1781 (no. 436). For those who enjoy interpreting slips of the pen, Mozart adds inappropriate question marks after the two closing sentences.

6. Ibid., p. 784, 15 December 1781 (no. 436); p. 795, 23 January 1782 (no. 442); and p. 797, 13 February 1782 (no. 444).

7. Ibid., p. 589, 31 July 1778 (no. 319).

8. Ibid., p. 817, 24 August 1782 (no. 461).

9. Erich Valentin, "Das Testament der Constanze Mozart-Nissen. Mit biographischen Notizen über Constanze und Georg Nikolaus Nissen," *Neues MJb* 2 (1942), pp. 151–52. Previously it had been assumed that she was born on 5 October 1763. See also Arthur Schurig, ed., *Konstanze Mozart: Briefe, Aufzeichnungen, Dokumente, 1782–1842* (Dresden, 1922), and Erna Schwerin, *Constanze Mozart: Woman and Wife of a Genius* (New York, 1981).

10. Under its terms, if the marriage ended he would pay Aloysia 600 florins annually and Frau Weber 700 florins. He also agreed to assume a 900-florin debt for a loan taken by Frau Weber after her husband's death. See "Josef Lange und Maria Cäcilia Weber," in Blümml, pp. 21–35.

11. Valentin, "Das Testament," p. 153.

12. *Letters,* p. 784, 15 December 1781 (no. 436).

13. Ibid.

14. *Letters,* p. 790, 22 December 1781 (no. 438); *Briefe,* vol. 3, p. 188, 22 December 1781 (no. 651).

15. *Letters,* p. 787, 22 December 1781 (no. 438).

16. Ibid., p. 791, 9 January 1782 (no. 439).

17. For Thorwart, see Blümml, pp. 54–69; *Briefe,* vol. 6, p. 98.

18. *Letters,* pp. 787–88, 22 December 1781 (no. 438).

19. Ibid., p. 787, 22 December 1781 (no. 438).

20. Ibid., p. 802, 29 April 1782 (no. 448).

21. Ibid., pp. 802–3, 29 April 1782 (no. 448); translation amended. See *Briefe,* vol. 3, p. 206, 29 April 1782 (no. 670).

22. *Letters,* p. 803, 29 April 1782 (no. 448).

23. Ibid., p. 793, 16 January 1782 (no. 441).

24. Ibid.

25. *Letters,* p. 798, 23 March 1782 (no. 445).

26. Ibid., p. 810, 27 July 1782 (no. 455).

27. Ibid., p. 811, 31 July 1782 (no. 456).

28. Ibid.

29. *Letters,* p. 812, shortly before 4 August 1782 (no. 457).

30. Ibid.

31. *Letters,* p. 813, 7 August 1782 (no. 458).

32. Ibid., pp. 813, 812, 7 August 1782 (no. 458); translation revised. See *Briefe,* vol. 3, p. 218, 7 August 1782 (no. 684).

33. Jahn, vol. 2, p. 263.

34. *Letters,* pp. 812–13, 7 August 1782 (no. 458).

35. Ibid., p. 813, 7 August 1782 (no. 458).

36. Ibid., p. 816, 23 August 1782 (no. 460).

Chapter 17: Two Families

1. *Letters,* p. 818, 31 August 1782 (no. 462).

2. Ibid., p. 844, 3 April 1783 (no. 485).

3. Ibid., p. 846, 12 April 1783 (no. 486).

4. Ibid., p. 850, 7 June 1783 (no. 491).

5. Ibid., p. 852, 18 June 1783 (no. 492).

6. Ibid., p. 845, 12 April 1783 (no. 486).

7. Ibid., p. 849, 21 May 1783 (no. 490).

8. Ibid., p. 855, 5 July 1783 (no. 495).

9. Ibid., p. 856, 12 July 1783 (no. 496).

10. Ibid.

11. See Léon Grinberg and Rebeca Grinberg, *Psychoanalytic Perspectives on Migration and Exile,* trans. Nancy Festinger (New Haven and London, 1989).

12. Nissen, p. xviii.

13. *Briefe,* vol. 3, p. 225, 24 August 1782 (no. 689); *Letters,* p. 817, 24 August 1782 (no. 461).

14. *Letters,* p. 802, 20 April 1782 (no. 447a).

15. Ibid., p. 809, 24 July 1782 (no. 454a).

16. Rudolf Lewicki, "Aus Nissens Kollektaneen," *Mozarteums Mitteilungen* 2 (November 1919), p. 29.

17. Novello, p. 115; see also Jahn, vol. 2, p. 153.

18. *Letters,* pp. 852–53, 21 June 1783 (no. 493).

19. Ibid., p. 855, 5 July 1783 (no. 495).

20. Ibid., p. 863, 10 December 1783 (no. 501).

21. For the redating, see Tyson, pp. 231–32 and p. 30. The sonatas are on a rare paper type that is of no help in establishing their date of origin. Plath is inconclusive about their dating, although he is certain that the summer of 1780 is their earliest possible date. Plath, p. 258. Tyson therefore leaves the question open: "Since the handwriting evidence is not completely conclusive, we are left in doubt whether these four works [i.e., including the Sonata, K. 333] are from the last Salzburg years or from the first Viennese ones" (Tyson, p. 231).

22. Nissen, pp. 476–77.

23. *Letters,* p. 834, 4 January 1783 (no. 477).

24. Novello, p. 96.

25. Nissen, p. 476. Among Mozart's dedications to Constanze are an unfinished Violin Sonata in C, K. 403/385c (1782; 1784, according to Tyson), headed, "Sonate Première. Par moi W. A. Mozart pour ma très chère Epouse"; the first movement of a Sonata in B-flat, K. Anh. 43/375c (1782–83), headed, "Per la Signora Constanza Weber—ah—"; one of a collection of Solfeggios, K. 393/385b (1782), marked "per la mia cara Costanza" and "per la mia cara consorte." Also, according to her letter to B&H of 25 February 1798, he wrote the Aria, "In te spero, o spose amato" (fragment) for her, but Abert thinks it was for Aloysia because of the range. See Abert, vol. 1, p. 815.

26. Cliff Eisen, "Salzburg under Church Rule," in *The Classical Era: From the 1740s to the End of the 18th Century*, ed. Neal Zaslaw (New York, 1989), p. 180. Eisen cautions that the church reforms, which were primarily aimed at the provincial churches, may not have seriously handicapped cosmopolitan composers in the major cities or churches (personal communication).

27. *Briefe*, vol. 3, p. 290, 4 September–31 October 1783 (no. 765). Entry for 23 October 1783.

28. Ibid., p. 290, 4 September–31 October 1783 (no. 765). Entry for 27 October 1783. Gnigl is a suburb of Salzburg.

29. *Letters*, p. 859, 31 October 1783 (no. 499).

30. See Tyson, pp. 20, 73–81; Wolfgang Plath, "Beiträge zur Mozart-Autographie II. Schriftchronologie 1770–1780," *MJb 1976/77*, p. 171; Plath, p. 259.

31. *Letters*, p. 862, 6 December 1783 (no. 500).

32. Heinz Lichtenstein, *The Dilemma of Human Identity* (New York and London, 1983), p. 11. Lichtenstein calls this "the dilemma of symbiosis versus separateness" (p. 9). See also Hans W. Loewald, *Papers on Psychoanalysis* (New Haven, 1980), pp. 401–2.

33. For Cäcilia Weber, Josepha Weber-Hofer, Joseph Lange, and Franz de Paula Hofer, see the relevant chapters in Blümml, which, like most of the standard literature, treats Frau Weber ungenerously, even maliciously.

34. *Letters*, pp. 727–28, 9 May 1781 (no. 401).

35. Ibid., p. 733, 16 May 1781 (no. 404).

36. Ibid., p. 753, 25 July 1781 (no. 417).

37. Ibid., p. 796, 30 January 1782 (no. 443).

38. Ibid., p. 818, 31 August 1782 (no. 462). For Leopold Mozart's concern over this issue, see his letters to Baroness Waldstätten: *Letters*, p. 816, 23 August 1782 (no. 460) and p. 821, 13 September 1782 (no. 464).

39. Ibid., p. 851, 18 June 1783 (no. 492).

40. Ibid., p. 975, Sophie Haibel to Nissen, 7 April 1825; translation amended.

41. Lewicki, "Aus Nissens Kollektaneen," p. 29.

42. Sophie Haibel to Nissen, 7 April 1825: *MDB*, p. 526; Nissen, pp. 687–88. This passage is omitted from *Letters*.

43. *Letters*, pp. 902–3, 15 January 1787 (no. 544).

44. Ibid., p. 733, 16 May 1781 (no. 404).

45. Ibid., p. 784, 15 December 1781 (no. 436).

46. Blümml, p. 32. Blümml's account of Hofer's financial impoverishment is mistaken, for, in addition to several poorly remunerated posts he was also a member of the Nationaltheater orchestra as early as 1782–83 at a salary of 350 florins. See Dexter Edge, "Mozart's Viennese Orchestras," *Early Music* 20 (1992), pp. 72–73 (Tables 2 and 3).

47. *Letters*, p. 461, 4 February 1778 (no. 281).

Chapter 18: Adam

1. *Briefe*, vol. 1, p. 33, 9 February 1756, to Johann Jakob Lotter (no. 22).

2. Sonatas for clavier and violin (or, in some instances, for clavier and violin or flute), K. 6–15, and K. 26–31, published in 1764–66.

3. *Briefe*, vol. 1, p. 507, 16 December 1774 (no. 302); *Letters*, p. 251 (no. 191a). Leopold Mozart used the variant form "Amadée" as well. For further examples, see Wilhelm A. Bauer, "Amadeus?" in *Festschrift O. E. Deutsch zum 80. Geburtstag* (Kassel, 1963), pp. 105–9. See also Emanuel Winternitz, "Gnagflow Trazom: An Essay on Mozart's Script, Pastimes, and Nonsense Letters," *Journal of the American Musicological Society* 11 (1958), pp. 200–16.

4. Alexander Hajdecki, "Mozarts Taufnamen," in *Beethoven-Forschung*, ed. Theodor Frimmel, nos. 6–7 (August 1916), pp. 104–5. Mozart's petitions to the Police Administration and the Prince-Archbishop's Court have not survived.

5. *Dokumente*, p. 181; *MDB*, pp. 204–5; Otto Schneider, *Mozart in Wirklichkeit* (Vienna, 1955), p. 214.

6. Jahn-Deiters, vol. 2, p. 720; Hajdecki, "Mozarts Taufnamen," pp. 103–4.

7. O. E. Deutsch, ed., *Mozart und seine Welt in zeitgenössischen Bildern* (Basel, London, and New York, 1961), p. 334; *Dokumente*, p. 180; *MDB*, p. 203.

8. Hajdecki, "Mozarts Taufnamen," p. 105.

9. See chapter 22, "The Zoroastran Riddles."

10. Sir James Frazer, *The Golden Bough: A Study in Magic and Religion,* abridged ed. (New York, 1939), p. 244.

11. Ibid., p. 245.

12. Ernest Crawley, *The Mystic Rose: A Study of Primitive Marriage and of Primitive Thought in Its Bearing on Marriage,* ed. Theodore Besterman (London, 1927; reprint New York, 1960), pp. 323–24.

13. See Sigmund Freud, *Totem and Taboo* (1913), in *Standard Edition of the Complete Psychological Works of Sigmund Freud,* ed. James Strachey et al. (London, 1955–74), vol. 13, p. 81.

14. Otto Fenichel, *The Psychoanalytic Theory of Neurosis* (New York, 1945), p. 295. This notion is also central to religious and mythic thinking. See Ernst Cassirer, *Language and Myth,* trans. Susanne Langer (New York, 1946), pp. 49–50, 52.

15. Wilhelm Heinrich Wackenroder and Ludwig Tieck, *Outpourings of an Art-Loving Friar,* trans. Edward Mornin (New York, 1975), p. 59.

16. *Briefe,* vol. 4, p. 11, 15 January 1787; *Letters,* p. 904, 15 January 1787 (no. 544).

17. Members of the Order of Illuminati and Masons received code names in connection with their initiation and such adopted names were usually derived from classical or biblical sources. For example, the statutes of the Bonn Illuminati in the 1780s discloses: "One receives a name from the Order. And in order to use this in the service of scholarship, one must gather all the data concerning the life of the man whose name one bears." Alfred Becker, *Christian Gottlob Neefe und die Bonner Illuminaten,* Bonner Beiträge zur Bibliotheks- und Bücherkunde, vol. 21 (Bonn, 1969), p. 41. For code names of the founders of the Illuminati, see *Einige Originalschriften des Illuminatenordens* (Munich, 1787), passim. Mozart was proposed for membership in the Masons in November 1784 and admitted on 14 December 1784.

18. *Letters,* p. 868, 20 February 1784 (no. 504).

19. C. F. Pohl, *Denkschrift aus Anlass des 100jährigen Bestehens der Tonkünstler-Societät* (Vienna, 1871), pp. 17–18; see also *NMD,* p. 34 (no. 58). In general the requirement was stringently enforced, although occasional exceptions were made where furnishing the certificate was clearly impossible; but no exception was made for Mozart. See also *Briefe,* vol. 6, pp. 223, 430; *Dokumente,* pp. 209, 385; *MDB,* pp. 236, 439; Gustav Nottebohm, *Mozartiana* (Leipzig, 1880), p. 16.

20. Pohl, *Denkschrift,* p. 18. In her petition to the Emperor after Mozart's death, Constanze specifically referred to the absence of a pension from the Tonkünstler-Societät. See *MDB,* p. 421.

21. [Karl Friedrich Hensler], *Maurerrede auf Mozarts Tod* (Vienna, 1792), transcription and facsimile in O. E. Deutsch, "Die 'Maurerrede auf Mozarts Tod,'" *Schweizerische Musikzeitung* 96 (February 1956), pp. 50–60; also in Heinz Schuler, *Mozart und die Freimaurerei* (Wilhelmshaven, 1992), pp. 204–11; abridged in *Dokumente,* pp. 392–95 and *MDB,* pp. 447–50. Deutsch speculates that the "A" designates the biblical personage Adoniram, who is mentioned in the poem that closes the oration. See *Dokumente,* p. 395; *MDB,* p. 451. The "A" plus three asterisks, however, certainly designate a four-letter name, in the same way that Hensler's seven-letter name is given on the title page as "H . . . . . r."

Chapter 19: The Impresario

1. Although the last ten bars are not extant, Zaslaw does not regard the fantasia as a fragment, offering alternative explanations—that the last page of the score may have been lost or that "the final cadential coda may have been meant to be improvised like a cadenza" (personal communication). Two of the canons, K. 233/382d and K. 234/382e, were not written by Mozart. See *MJb 1992,* p. 240.

2. Robert L. Marshall, "Mozart's Unfinished: Some Lessons of the Fragments," *MJb 1991,* vol. 2, pp. 910–11.

3. *Letters,* p. 789, 22 December 1781 (no. 438).

4. See *MDB,* pp. 220–53, passim. For an extended list of first performances of *Die Entführung aus dem Serail* in various cities during Mozart's lifetime, see Thomas Bauman, *W. A. Mozart: Die Entführung aus dem Serial* (Cambridge, England, 1987), pp. 103–4. A famous anecdote reports Emperor Joseph's alleged remark about the opera: "Too beautiful for our ears and an extraordinary number of notes, dear Mozart," and Mozart's reply: "Just as many, Your Majesty, as are necessary." Niemetschek, p. 32; Nissen, p. 465. I share Bauman's skepticism about the anecdote's plausibility. See Bauman, *Die Entführung,* p. 89. On the other hand, it is worth noting that when imperial sponsorship of German-language opera recommenced, Mozart was not again employed except for *Der Schauspieldirektor.* See Jahn, vol. 3, pp. 45–47.

5. Cramer's *Magazin der Musik,* 27 March 1783: *MDB,* p. 214.

6. *Letters,* p. 793, 16 January 1782 (no. 441).

7. Ibid., p. 794, 23 January 1782 (no. 442).

8. *Briefe,* vol. 3, p. 201, 10 April 1782 (no. 667); *Letters,* pp. 799–800, 10 April 1782 (no. 446); translation amended.

9. *Letters,* p. 814, 17 August 1782 (no. 459).

10. Ibid.

11. *Letters,* p. 815, 17 August 1782 (no. 459).

12. Ibid., p. 816, 23 August 1782 (no. 460).

13. Ibid., p. 817, 24 August 1782 (no. 461).

14. Ibid., p. 832, 21 December 1782 (no. 475).

15. Ibid., pp. 837–38, 22 January 1783 (no. 479).

16. Ibid., p. 868, 20 February 1784 (no. 504).

17. Ibid., p. 826, 5 October 1782 (no. 469).

18. Ibid., p. 805, 8 May 1782 (no. 450).

19. Ibid.

20. *Letters,* p. 798, 23 March 1782 (no. 445).

21. For comprehensive listings of concerts and public concert locations in Vienna, see Mary Sue Morrow, *Concert Life in Haydn's Vienna: Aspects of a Developing Musical and Social Institution* (Stuyvesant, New York, 1989), pp. 237–411.

22. An ephemeral local periodical—apparently banned after two issues—commented on the frequency of his appearances: "He is uncommonly liked, and his expression has to be marveled at. He is also so agreeable as to give frequent public performances. His harvest season is not confined to Lent, for he also appears during Advent or, if the public so desires, in the summer." *Pfeffer und Salz,* Salzburg [Vienna], 1786, report dated 5 April 1786: *MDB,* p. 270; translation amended.

23. *Letters,* pp. 869–70, 3 March 1784 (no. 505).

24. For the annotated list, see *Briefe,* vol. 6, pp. 167–77. Mozart's list itself is in *Briefe,* vol. 3, pp. 305–7, 20 March 1784 (no. 780); see also *Letters,* pp. 870–72, 20 March 1784 (no. 506).

25. *Letters,* p. 872, 20 March 1784 (no. 506).

26. Ibid., p. 873, 10 April 1784 (no. 508).

27. Hermine Cloeter, *Johann Thomas Trattner: Ein Grossunternehmer im Theresianischen Wien* (Graz and Cologne, 1952), pp. 100–101: *MDB,* p. 222. For Mozart and the Trattners, see Cloeter, pp. 95–104.

28. Mozart wrote: "Richter, the clavier virtuoso, is giving six Saturday concerts in the said room." Mozart "promised" to appear as a guest in three of Richter's concerts, in addition to three solo concerts of his own. *Letters,* p. 869, 3 March 1784 (no. 505). There is no further documentary evidence that Richter's concerts, three of which were planned for 20 March, 27 March, and 3 April, actually took place. See *Briefe,* vol. 6, p. 166.

29. *Letters,* p. 833, 28 December 1782 (no. 476).

30. Hoffmeister featured Mozart's compositions in subscription offers for "an entire library of original music over the course of several years," including music by Haydn, Mozart, Vanhal, Pleyel, and himself. Advertisement in *Brünner Zeitung,* 2 July 1785: *NMD,* p. 36 (no. 61).

31. Tyson, pp. 246–47; see also Plath, pp. 191–92. The Romance (Sherman 806) was published under Michael Haydn's name in Vienna in 1802; we do not know which of them is the composer.

32. *Letters,* p. 795, 23 January 1782 (no. 442). According to a contemporary guidebook by Johann Pezzl, a bachelor could get by in Vienna in 1786 on an annual income of 464 florins, of which 180 went for food, 84 for rent and heat, 160 for clothing, and 40 for miscellaneous expenses. See H. C. Robbins Landon, *Mozart and Vienna* (New York, 1991), p. 74.

33. *Letters,* p. 889 n. 1, 19 March 1785; Deutsch-Paumgartner, p. 76.

34. Even as early as 20 November 1785 Mozart asked Hoffmeister for a small loan or advance: "I turn to you in my distress and beg you to help me out with some money, which I need very badly at the moment." *Letters,* p. 894, 20 November 1785 (no. 533).

35. *Letters,* p. 849, 21 May 1783 (no. 490), and p. 885, 16 February 1785 (no. 523). For Mozart's rent at the Trattnerhof, see *MDB,* p. 222, and *NMD,* p. 32 (no. 55).

36. Uwe Kraemer, "Wer hat Mozart verhungern lassen?" *Musica* 30 (1976), p. 206.

37. Carl Bär, " 'Er war . . . —kein guter Wirth'; Eine Studie über Mozarts Verhältnis zum

Geld," *Acta Mozartiana* 25 (April 1978), p. 37. According to his widow's testament, Mozart also owned several clavichords, which seem to have been withheld from the inventory of his effects. Erich Valentin, "Das Testament der Constanze Mozart-Nissen," *Neues MJb* 2 (1942), pp. 134, 136, 138. The organ advertised for sale at Mozart's address in the *Wiener Zeitung* during January 1791 (*NMD*, p. 65 [no. 105]) turns out to have belonged to someone else altogether. See Walther Brauneis, "Mozarts Hausorgel—Eine Mystifikation," *Mitteilungen der ISM* 41 (June 1993), pp. 59–63.

38. *Letters*, p. 764, 5 September 1781 (no. 423). In anticipation of a journey to Munich, Mozart and Aloysia Lange each had six pairs of shoes made, and to them this seemed altogether appropriate, while Leopold Mozart found it rather excessive, particularly when the tour was canceled. See *Briefe*, vol. 3, p. 387, Leopold Mozart to Marianne von Berchtold, 16 April 1785 (no. 861).

39. See n. 36, above. For anticipations of Kraemer's suggestion, see Josef Kreitmeier, S.J., *W. A. Mozart: Eine Charakterzeichnung des grossen Meisters nach literarischen Quellen* (Düsseldorf, 1919), p. 175, and Arthur Schurig, *Wolfgang Amade Mozart: Sein Leben, seine Persönlichkeit, sein Werk* (2nd ed., Leipzig, 1923), vol. 2, pp. 395–96. Kraemer's estimate that in his first Vienna years Mozart may have earned as much as 10,000 florins per year as a virtuoso is not without its supporters. See Rudolph Angermüller, "'Auf Ehre und Credit': Die Finanzen des W. A. Mozart," *Ausstellung der Internationalen Stiftung Mozarteum Salzburg, der Staatlichen Münzsammlung München, und der Bayerischen Vereinsbank München* (Munich, 1983), p. 8; see also p. 12. By contrast, Braunbehrens, making generous allowances for undocumented income, concludes that "Mozart's average income between 1782 and 1791 was 3,000 to 4,000 florins, at a very conservative estimate." Volkmar Braunbehrens, *Mozart in Vienna 1781–1791*, trans. Timothy Bell (New York, 1990), p. 140.

40. Henri Brunschwig, *Enlightenment and Romanticism in Eighteenth-Century Prussia* (Chicago, 1974), p. 204.

41. Friedrich Nicolai, *Beschreibung einer Reise durch Deutschland und die Schweiz, im Jahre 1781* (Berlin, 1784), vol. 4, p. 553; trans. in Jahn, vol. 2, p. 283 n. 43. In Salzburg, Leopold Mozart, who was opposed to gambling, wrote: "Yesterday the lottery pool was forbidden. . . . I wish that Faro playing would also be canceled. On Tuesday the Bank lost over 1,000 florins. . . . Bishop Schrattenbach won 100 ducats." *Briefe*, vol. 4, p. 16, 26 January 1787 (no. 1026); Deutsch-Paumgartner, pp. 434–44. The reference is to Count Vinzenz Joseph Schrattenbach, bishop of Lavant.

42. Quoted in Landon, *Mozart and Vienna*, p. 79.

43. *Letters*, p. 739, 2 June 1781 (no. 408).

44. Ibid.

45. Jahn, vol. 2, p. 308.

46. Robert Lindner, "The Psychodynamics of Gambling," in *Explorations in Psychoanalysis: Essays in Honor of Theodor Reik*, ed. Lindner (New York, 1953), p. 200.

47. *Letters*, p. 866, 10 February 1784 (no. 503).

48. Karl-Heinz Köhler and Grita Herre, eds., *Beethovens Konversationshefte*, vol. 5 (Leipzig, 1970), p. 179 (Heft 57, Folio 11).

49. Nissen's remark was noted in the margin of Mozart's letter to Constanze Mozart, 6 June 1791, cited in *Briefe*, vol. 6, p. 411.

50. Schlichtegroll, p. 111. It is conceivable that Karl van Beethoven had merely read the report in Schlichtegroll or one of his imitators, such as Winckler or Stendhal, whose life of Mozart (1814) included: "Mozart's hands were so specifically and categorically fashioned for the keyboard, that they were, if anything, clumsy when directed to any other task. At table, he would never cut the food that lay in front of him; or else, on the rare occasions when he did attempt this operation, he succeeded only at the cost of infinite difficulty and awkwardness. As a general rule, he would entreat his wife to perform this office in his place." Stendhal, *Haydn, Mozart and Metastasio*, trans. and ed. Richard N. Coe (New York, 1972), p. 182. See also Jahn-Deiters, vol. 1, p. 803; vol. 2, p. 157.

51. *Letters*, p. 69, 15 November 1766 (no. 45).

52. See Tim Carter, *W. A. Mozart: Le nozze di Figaro* (Cambridge, England, 1987), pp. 12–13.

53. Emperor Joseph II to Count Johann Anton Pergen, letter of 31 January 1785: *MDB*, p. 235.

54. Da Ponte's preface to the libretto of *Le nozze di Figaro: MDB*, p. 273; translation amended.

55. *Letters*, p. 897, 28 April 1786 (no. 539).

56. Emperor Joseph II to Count Rosenberg, letter of 9 May 1786: *MDB*, p. 275.

57. *Wiener Realzeitung*, 11 July 1786: *MDB*, p. 278. The quotation is from Beaumarchais's *Le Barbier de Séville*, Act I, scene 2.

58. We know of the concerts from a passing reference in a letter by Leopold Mozart to his daughter. See *Briefe*, vol. 3 p. 618, 8 December 1786 (no. 1010). See also *MDB*, p. 280. Eibl assumes the concerts, or some of them, actually took place. See *Chronik*, p. 91.

59. *Letters*, p. 901, 17 November 1786 (no. 542).

Chapter 20: Portrait of a Composer

1. Michael Kelly's *Reminiscences: MDB*, p. 530.

2. Marianne von Berchtold, "Data for a biography of the late composer Wolfgang Mozart": *MDB*, p. 462.

3. Niemetschek, pp. 52–53.

4. Paul Nettl, *Mozart and Masonry*, trans. Mrs. Robert Gold et al. (New York, 1957), p. 112.

5. Jahn-Deiters, vol. 2, p. 492; Jahn, vol. 3, p. 235.

6. Rudolf Köpke, *Ludwig Tieck: Erinnerungen aus dem Leben des Dichters nach dessen mündlichen und schriftlichen Mitteilungen* (Leipzig, 1855), vol. 1, p. 86: *MDB*, p. 562. See Erich Valentin, "Es war Mozart selbst gewesen," *Acta Mozartiana* 36 (May 1989), pp. 21–26, and Gernot Gruber, *Mozart und die Nachwelt* (Salzburg and Vienna, 1985), p. 95.

7. Wilhelm Backhaus, *Tagebuch der Mannheimer Schaubühne*, cited in Ludwig Nohl, *Musikalisches Skizzenbuch* (Munich, 1866), p. 190, and Jahn, vol. 3, p. 278.

8. Nissen, p. 692.

9. Kelly's *Reminiscences: MDB*, p. 533.

10. *MDB*, p. 542.

11. Niemetschek, p. 53; Joseph Frank, "Memoirs": *MDB*, p. 561.

12. Novello, p. 113.

13. From the papers of John Pettinger: *NMD*, p. 37 (no. 62).

14. Thomas Attwood, undated letter to an unidentified correspondent: *NMD*, p. 39 (no. 64).

15. *Letters*, p. 825, 2 October 1782 to Baroness Waldstätten (no. 467).

16. Ibid., p. 847, 3 May 1783 (no. 488).

17. Ibid., pp. 887–88, 21 February 1785 (no. 524).

18. Ibid., p. 942, 28 September 1790 (no. 584).

19. Ibid., p. 797, to Marianne Mozart, 13 February 1782 (no. 444).

20. Ibid.

21. *Letters*, p. 893, 11 November 1785, Leopold Mozart to Marianne von Berchtold (no. 532).

22. Ibid., p. 833, 28 December 1782 (no. 476).

23. Ibid., p. 669, 22 November 1780 (no. 362), and p. 833, 28 December 1782 (no. 476).

24. Ibid., p. 755, 1 August 1781 (no. 418).

25. Ibid, p. 756, 1 August 1781 (no. 418).

26. Novello, pp. 95–96.

27. *Letters*, p. 722, 8 April 1781 (no. 397).

28. Ibid., p. 886, 16 February 1785 (no. 523).

29. Wolfgang Amadé Mozart, *Verzeichnis aller meiner Werke*, conveniently available as *Mozart's Thematic Catalogue: A Facsimile*. British Library, Stefan Zweig MS 63, ed. Albi Rosenthal and Alan Tyson (Ithaca, 1990); see also Otto Erich Deutsch, *Mozart's Catalogue of his Works, 1784–1791* (New York, n.d [1956]). Tyson (*Thematic Catalogue*, p. 15) rejects a suggestion that the first ten works were entered retrospectively; see Daniel N. Leeson and David Whitwell, "Mozart's Thematic Catalogue," *Musical Times* 114 (1973), pp. 781–83.

30. Robert L. Marshall, "Mozart's Unfinished: Some Lessons of the Fragments," *MJb 1991*, vol. 2, p. 910; see also A. Hyatt King, *Mozart in Retrospect: Studies in Criticism and Bibliography* (Oxford, 1955), pp. 225–26.

31. Tyson, pp. 30, 32, 150–52, 157. Among such concertos are those in C, K. 503, A, K. 488, E-flat, K. 449, and perhaps the B-flat, K. 595.

32. Christoph Wolff, "Creative Exuberance vs. Critical Choice: Thoughts on Mozart's Quartet Fragments," in *The String Quartets of Haydn, Mozart and Beethoven: Studies of the Autograph Manuscripts,* ed. Christoph Wolff (Cambridge, Mass., 1980), p. 197.

33. *Briefe,* vol. 4, p. 324, 1 March 1800 to B&H (no. 1288). See also Erich Hertzmann, "Mozart's Creative Process," in *The Creative World of Mozart,* ed. Paul Henry Lang (New York, 1963), p. 21, with misidentification of addressee as André. For the first comprehensive list of the surviving sketches, see Ulrich Konrad, *Mozarts Schaffensweise: Studien zu den Werkautographen, Skizzen und Entwürfen* (Göttingen, 1992), pp. 104–338.

34. Ulrich Konrad, "Mozart's Sketches," *Early Music* 20 (1992), p. 119.

35. Mozart's transition from sequential "block composition" to "horizontal composition" of entire pieces is described in Marshall, "Mozart's Unfinished," pp. 913–16.

36. *Letters,* p. 794, 23 January 1782 (no. 442).

37. Erich Schenk, *Mozart and His Times* (New York, 1959), p. 365.

38. For details of Mozart's music for the Jacquins, see Hideo Noguchi, "Mozart: Musical Game in C, K. 516f," *Mitteilungen der ISM* 38 (July 1990), pp. 89–101. Also written for the Jacquins was "Musikalische Würfelspiele," K. Anh. 294d/516f, a musical game, which seems to have originated between 16 May 1787 and 28 October 1787. See also Hedwig Kraus, "W. A. Mozart und die Familie Jacquin," *Zeitschrift für Musikwissenschaft* 15 (1933), pp. 155–68.

39. *Letters,* p. 913, 4 November 1787 (no. 551).

40. *MDB,* p. 289.

41. *Letters,* p. 904, 15 January 1787 (no. 544).

42. Ibid., p. 905, 15 January 1787 (no. 544).

43. For Waldstätten, see *Briefe,* vol. 6, p. 91. For a previously unpublished letter dated 22 March 1783 inviting the baroness to Mozart's academy of 23 March 1783 at the Burgtheater, see Alfred Briellmann, " 'Hochschätzbareste Gnädige Frau Baronin!': Ein bisher unveröffentlichter Brief Mozarts," *MJb 1987/88,* pp. 233–48. See also Gustav Gugitz, "Von W. A. Mozarts kuriosen Schülerinnen," *Österreichische Musikzeitung* 11 (1956), pp. 261–69, which, as Briellmann notes (p. 239), confuses this Martha Elisabeth Waldstätten, who was the estranged wife of Baron Hugo Dominik Anton Waldstätten (1737–1800), with Baroness Maria Barbara Waldstätten, née Freiin von Rossi (1749–1823).

44. *Letters,* p. 776, 3 November 1781 (no. 431).

45. Ibid., p. 803, 29 April 1782 (no. 448).

46. Ibid., pp. 836–37, 8 January 1783 (no. 478).

47. *MDB,* p. 289.

48. Jahn, vol. 2, p. 337.

49. Ibid., p. 338.

50. *Letters,* p. 956, 25 June 1791 (no. 602).

51. Ibid., p. 886, 16 February 1785 (no. 523).

52. H. C. Robbins Landon, *Haydn: Chronicle and Works,* vol. 2 (Bloomington, 1978), p. 702, letter of December 1787 to Franz Roth (or Rott) in Prague, first published in Niemetschek, pp. 60–61.

53. Jahn, vol. 3, p. 4; vol. 2, pp. 351–52, cited from Th. G. von Karajan, "J. Haydn in London 1791 und 1792," *Jahrbuch für vaterländische Geschichte* 1 (Vienna, 1861), p. 97.

54. Haydn to Maria Anna von Genzinger, 30 May 1790: *MDB,* p. 367; for another translation, see Landon, *Haydn: Chronicle,* p. 742.

55. Haydn to Maria Anna von Genzinger, 9 February 1790: *MDB,* p. 363; for another translation, see Landon, *Haydn: Chronicle,* p. 737.

56. *Letters,* p. 885, 22 January 1785, Leopold Mozart to his daughter (no. 522); Nissen, p. 576.

57. Niemetschek, p. 32.

58. For a discussion, see Maynard Solomon, "The Rochlitz Anecdotes," in *Mozart Studies,* ed. Cliff Eisen (Oxford, 1991), pp. 15–16.

59. *Letters,* p. 891, 1 September 1785 (no. 529); translation amended.

60. Mark Evan Bonds, "The Sincerest Form of Flattery? Mozart's 'Haydn' Quartets and the Question of Influence," *Studi Musicali* 22 (1993), pp. 368–71.

61. *Letters,* p. 793, 16 January 1782 (no. 441), and p. 850, 7 June 1783 (no. 491).

62. Ibid., p. 839, 5 February 1783 (no. 480). For an annotated compilation of Mozart's remarks about composers, see Robert L. Marshall, ed., *Mozart Speaks: Views on Music, Musicians, and the World* (New York, 1991), pp. 319–54.

63. *Letters,* p. 374, 14 November 1777 (no. 243a), and p. 800, 10 April 1782 (no. 446).

64. Ibid., p. 875, 24 April 1784 (no. 510).

65. Ibid., p. 473, 9 February 1778 (no. 284b). But see ibid., p. 352 (no. 234).

66. "Several Further Bagatelles from Mozart's Life, Related by his Widow," *AMZ* 1 (1798–99), columns 854–56: *NMD,* p. 80 (no. 121).

67. Ibid.

68. "Several Further Bagatelles": *NMD,* p. 79 (no. 121).

69. Solomon, "Rochlitz Anecdotes," p. 18 (anecdote 9).

70. Ibid., p. 30 (anecdote 17).

71. *Letters,* p. 878, 26 May 1784 (no. 514).

72. Ibid., p. 879, 26 May 1784 (no. 514).

73. *Briefe,* vol. 3, p. 317, 27 May 1786 (no. 794).

Chapter 21: Freemasonry

1. "Rede bey der Aufnahme der Herren ** und M . . . . t, Den 14. Dezember 1784," in *Friedrich Hegrads vermischten Schriften* (Frankfurt and Leipzig, 1785), vol. 2, pp. 201–4. Reprinted in facsimile in Wilgert te Lindert, "Friedrich Hegrad, ein Logenbruder Mozarts," *Österreichische Musikzeitschrift* 48 (1993), pp. 3–11, quotation on p. 6.

2. For the possibility that Mozart reached the degree of Master Mason around 13 January 1785, see Philippe A. Autexier, *Mozart & Liszt sub Rosa* (Poitiers, 1984), p. 5.

3. The texts of these songs, by August Veit von Schlittlersberg, were discovered by Philippe A. Autexier and published in Autexier, *Mozart & Liszt: NMD,* pp. 38–39 (no. 63). See also Autexier, "Cinq Lieder inconnus de W. A. Mozart," *International Journal of Musicology* 1 (1992), pp. 67–79.

4. *MDB,* p. 231.

5. Masonic Oration on Mozart's Death: *MDB,* p. 448.

6. "Das kaiserliche Handbillet vom 11 Christmonat 1785," in *Joseph II. und die Freimaurerei im Lichte zeitgenössischer Broschüren,* ed. Helmut Reinalter (Vienna, Cologne, Graz, 1987), p. 64. An earlier stage in the institution of controls over Freemasonry was the founding by the government in April 1784 of the "Great National Lodge," which aimed to curb Bavarian and Prussian influence in the lodges. In protest, two thirds of the Rosicrucian "Saint Joseph" Lodge resigned from membership; after the *Freimaurerpatent,* "Saint Joseph" dissolved itself.

7. Including, among many others, Ignaz Born, Joseph von Sonnenfels, and Prince Dietrichstein. See Helmut Reinalter, "Ignaz von Born als Freimaurer und Illuminat," in *Die Aufklärung in Österreich: Ignaz von Born und seine Zeit,* ed. Helmut Reinalter. Schriftenreihe der Internationalen Forschungsstelle "Demokratische Bewegungen in Mitteleuropa 1770–1850," vol. 4 (Frankfurt, 1991), p. 55; Edith Rosenstrauch-Königsberg, "Illuminaten in der Habsburger Monarchie," *Quatuor Coronati Jahrbuch* 20 (1983), pp. 119–42; and Eberhard Weis, "Der Illuminatenorden (1776–1786)," in *Aufklärung und Geheimgesellschaften: Zur politischen Funktion und Sozialstruktur der Freimaurerlogen im 18. Jahrhundert,* ed. Helmut Reinalter. Ancien Régime: *Aufklärung und Revolution,* ed. Rolf Reichardt and Eberhard Schmitt, vol. 16 (Munich, 1989), pp. 87–108.

8. "That the Masonic Order is a state within a state is in my opinion, still not sufficiently remarked," wrote a prominent defender of the *Freimaurerpatent.* See Aloys Blumauer, *Was ist Gaukeley? oder vielmehr Was ist nicht Gaukeley?. . .* (Vienna, 1786), in Reinalter, *Joseph II,* p. 87; see also p. 21.

9. Georg Forster wrote to Christian Gottlob Heyne on 12 October 1786: "Born and Sonnenfels have completely fallen out over it." Cited in Reinalter, *Joseph II,* p. 17.

10. Letter of 16 August 1786 from Gottlieb Leon to his lodge brother Karl Leonhard Reinhold, in Heinz Schuler, " 'Mozart von der Wohlthätigkeit.' Die Mitglieder der gerechten und vollkommenen St.-Johannis-Freimaurer-Loge 'Zur Wohltätigkeit' im Orient von Wien," *Mitteilungen der ISM* 36 (1988), p. 19.

11. Paul Nettl, *Mozart and Masonry,* trans. Mrs. Robert Gold et al. (New York, 1957), p. 52; translation amended.

12. Ibid., p. 47; translation revised.

13. See Reinalter, *Joseph II,* pp. 80–81; see also p. 20. Reinalter observes that praise of the decree and its author was a tactic employed by some Freemasons, who hoped thereby to limit or even to reverse the restrictions.

14. Entry of 30 March 1787: *MDB*, p. 287. The entry, which is in English, reads:

Patience and tranquillity of mind contribute more to cure our distempers as the whole art of medecine.—

Your true, sincere friend and Brother
Wolfgang Amadé Mozart

15. Mozart's name appears upon the membership lists of "New Crowned Hope," which are complete for 1786–91. See Heinz Schuler, *Mozart und die Freimaurerei* (Wilhelmshaven, 1992), p. 32, and *NMD*, pp. 53, 63 (nos. 85, 100). For the membership lists for 1790 and 1791, see H. C. Robbins Landon, *Mozart and the Masons: New Light on the Lodge 'Crowned Hope'* (New York, 1983), pp. 65–72, and Gerald Fischer-Colbrie, "Die Mitgliederliste der Freimaurerloge 'Zur gekrönten Hoffnung' aus Mozarts Sterbejahr aufgefunden," *Mitteilungen der ISM* 41 (1993), pp. 41–47. The lodge's documents have otherwise not survived. See Heinz Schuler, "Die Mozart Loge 'Zur neugekrönten Hoffnung' im Orient von Wien: Eine Quellenstudie," *Mitteilungen des ISM* 37 (1989), p. 11.

16. Edith Rosenstrauch-Königsberg, *Freimaurerei im Josephinischen Wien: Aloys Blumauers Weg vom Jesuiten zum Jakobiner*. Wiener Arbeiten zur deutschen Literatur, vol. 6 (Vienna, 1975), pp. 52–55.

17. Edith Rosenstrauch-Königsberg, "Eine freimaurerische Akademie der Wissenschaften in Wien," in *Revolution und Demokratie in Geschichte und Literatur. Zum 60. Geburtstag von Walter Grab,* ed. Julius H. Schoeps and Imanuel Geiss (Duisburg, 1979), pp. 151–69. See also Reinalter, "Ignaz von Born," p. 43.

18. Rudolph Angermüller, "Friedrich Schlichtegrolls Nekrolog auf Ignaz von Born," *Mitteilungen der ISM* 35 (1987), p. 48.

19. Georg Forster to Samuel Thomas Sömmering, letter of 14 August 1784, quoted in Schuler, "'Mozart von der Wohlthätigkeit,'" p. 9.

20. It may have been this set of which Mozart's widow spoke: "One of [Mozart's] favorite authors is at present in her possession, and which she most frequently peruses, it is in 9 volumes but being a forbidden fruit in the Austrian states she did not name it." Novello, pp. 94–95.

21. See Schuler, "'Mozart von der Wohlthätigkeit,'" pp. 18–19.

22. Eva Huber, "Zur Sozialstruktur der Wiener Logen im Josephinischen Jahrzehnt," in Reinalter, *Aufklärung und Geheimgesellschaften*, pp. 179–80.

23. *Letters,* p. 908, 4 April 1787 (no. 546).

24. Cramer's *Magazin der Musik,* 14 February 1787, quoted in Ernst Fritz Schmid, "August Clemens Graf Hatzfeld," *MJb, 1954,* p. 26. For Hatzfeld's membership in the Order of Illuminati see Heinz Schuler, "Freimaurer und Illuminaten aus Alt-Bayern und Salzburg und ihre Beziehungen zu den Mozarts," *Mitteilungen der ISM* 35 (1987), p. 16; for his association with Masonic lodges, see Heinz Schuler, "Freimauerer im Rheingebiet zur Mozart-Zeit," *Mitteilungen der ISM* 35 (1987), p. 41.

25. His name appears on a 1792 police list of "famous Illuminati." See H. C. Robbins Landon, *Mozart: The Golden Years, 1781–1791* (New York, 1989), p. 258; see also p. 110. Hurwitz writes that there is much evidence of Swieten's "affinity with the Freemasons, or at least the rationalists within the brotherhood . . . [although] he was not demonstrably a member of any Austrian lodge." See Joachim Hurwitz, "Haydn and the Freemasons," *Haydn Yearbook* 16 (1985), pp. 78–79, which summarizes E. Wangermann, *Aufklärung und staatsbürgerliche Erziehung. Gottfried van Swieten als Reformator des österreichischen Unterrichtswesens 1781–1791* (Munich, 1978), pp. 12–16.

26. For details, see Schuler, "Freimaurer und Illuminaten," pp. 33–38, and Schuler, "'Mozart von der Wohlthätigkeit,'" pp. 18–19.

27. Richard Koch, *Br. Mozart, Freimaurer und Illuminat* (Bad Reichenhall, n.d. [1911]), pp. 34–35. Koch's title page claims he had access to "secret documents and sources in the Museum Carolineum Augusteum in Salzburg," but the museum cannot locate any of the documents in question. See Schuler, "Freimaurer und Illuminaten," p. 12. Koch's supposed "witness" is the editor Lorenz Hübner, but again no document supports the allegation, and Hübner did not arrive in Salzburg until 1783, more than two years after Mozart's departure. A reference to "Mr. Hübner" written by Mozart in his sister's diary for 24 September 1780 (*Briefe,* vol. 3, p. 11 [no. 534]) very likely has to do, not with Lorenz Hübner, but with Pater Beda (Georg) Hübner (1740–1811), the

librarian at St. Peter's Abbey Church who was known to the Mozarts, or with a member of the Joseph Hübner family mentioned in the family correspondence (*Briefe*, vol. 2, p. 351, 29 April–11 May 1778 [no. 448]). For unskeptical views of Koch's report, see Katherine Thomson, "Mozart and Freemasonry," *Music & Letters* 57 (1976), p. 27, and Georg Knepler, *Wolfgang Amadé Mozart: Annäherungen* (Berlin, 1991), pp. 188–90.

28. *Einige Originalschriften des Illuminatenordens* (Munich, 1787), p. 300. Leopold Mozart wholeheartedly approved of the suppression of the Bavarian Illuminati even though he recognized that most of the rumors about them were exaggerated: "The investigations undertaken are quite proper," he wrote to his daughter. "Some *stubborn* ones were sent away or went of their own accord. The rest, who made a clean breast of it to the Elector, remained. . . . The true Masons, of whom the Elector is one, are very much aroused about these peculiar people and for that reason these fanatics are again being strongly investigated." *Briefe*, vol. 3, p. 425, 14 October 1785 (no. 885); abridged translation in Nettl, *Mozart and Masonry*, p. 12.

29. See Alfons Rosenberg, *W. A. Mozart: Der verborgene Abgrund* (Zurich, 1976) and Hans-Josef Irmen, *Mozart: Mitglied geheimer Gesellschaften* ([Mechernich], 1988). Irmen claims that Mozart was a secret member of the Asiatic Brethren and that he concealed his preference for the so-called "high-grade system" of the Asiatic Brethren because "membership in any other than officially approved lodges was questionable and dangerous," especially for one who held an imperial post (p. 249). He asserts that Mozart's use, next to his signature in his entry in Kronauer's album, of a symbol consisting of two triangles interlocking to form a six-sided star is proof of his concealed membership (pp. 212–13; the triangles are not shown in *MDB*, p. 287). But Irmen offers no evidence of the significance of the symbol, nor does he demonstrate that this symbol is exclusive to the Asiatic Brethren; and he himself reproduces an album entry by Apfraim Joseph Hirschel, a noted member of the Brethren whom the Brethren's founder, Hans Heinrich Ecker, employed as his secretary, that omits the symbol (p. 219). Mozart uses two successive (not interlocking) triangles after his signature in his entry in Edmund Weber's album, 8 January 1787: *MDB*, p. 283. Knepler (*Mozart*, p. 192) points out that triangles are universal in Masonic symbolism. Irmen's main argument rests on an esoteric numerological analysis of the autograph score and first edition of the libretto of *Die Zauberflöte* (pp. 281–349).

30. Prince Dietrichstein became a member of the secret circle of the Viennese Rosicrucians in 1780 and from 1783 was the sovereign director of the Rosicrucians in Vienna. See Irmen, *Mozart: Mitglied*, p. 88; Huber, "Sozialstruktur der Wiener Logen," pp. 175, 177. According to G. Brabbée, Gemmingen was among a number of Asiatic Brethren appointed by Ecker to work within the Masonic lodges as "spies in the service of the order." G. Brabbée, "Die Asiatischen Brüder in Berlin und Wien," *Latomia* 22 (Leipzig, 1863), p. 27, cited in Irmen, *Mozart: Mitglied*, p. 208. See also Heinz Schuler, "Ein 'besonders guter Freund,'" *Acta Mozartiana* 36 (July 1989), p. 43, on Gemmingen's simultaneous membership in the Asiatic Brethren and the Order of Illuminati. Irmen (p. 202) suggests that Gemmingen's simultaneous adherence to the Illuminati and the Asiatic Brethren simply represents his ability to act as a "sensible seismograph of every change in trends."

31. *MDB*, pp. 589, 602; Irmen, *Mozart: Mitglied*, pp. 196–97. Ulrich Konrad and Martin Staehelin, eds., *"allzeit ein Buch": Die Bibliothek Wolfgang Amadeus Mozarts. Austellung im Maler-buchkabinett der Bibliotheca Augusta vom 5. December 1991 bis zum 15. März 1992* (Wolfenbüttl, 1991), pp. 73–75.

32. Hargrave Jennings, *The Rosicrucians: Their Rites and Mysteries* (5th ed., London, [1887]), p. 26.

33. Frances A. Yates, *The Rosicrucian Enlightenment* (London and Boston, 1972), p. 99.

34. See Hurwitz, "Haydn and the Freemasons," pp. 14–15, 44–45, and Huber, "Sozial-struktur der Wiener Logen," pp. 180, 181.

35. *Letters*, p. 718, 24 March 1781 (no. 395). *Briefe*, vol. 6, pp. 56–57. For Mozart and the Thun family, see Cornelius Preihs, "Mozarts Beziehungen zu den Familien von Thun-Hohenstein," *Neues MJb* 3 (1943), pp. 63–86. For details of Thun's esoteric leanings and Masonic ideas, see Irmen, *Mozart: Mitglied*, pp. 63–68.

36. Wolfgang Plath, "Beiträge zur Mozart-Autographie II: Schriftchronologie 1770–1780," *MJb 1976/77*, pp. 149–50; Plath, pp. 238–39. Autexier fixes the date of composition in 1773. See Autexier, "Cinq Lieder inconnus," p. 68 n. 3.

37. Jacques Chailley, *The Magic Flute, Masonic Opera*, trans. Herbert Weinstock (New York, 1971), pp. 66–67. For further indications of Mozart's pre-Vienna contacts with Freemasonry, see Schuler, "Freimaurer und Illuminaten."

38. *Letters,* p. 849, 21 May 1783 (no. 490).

39. "It would be an undoubted gain if the nunneries were dissolved," Leopold wrote to his daughter in 1785: "They exist neither by virtue of true vocation, nor supernatural calling, nor spiritual zeal, nor as the true discipline of devotion and abnegation of desires, but are the result of compulsion, hypocrisy, dissimulation, and childish folly, leading in the end to concealed wickedness." *Briefe,* vol. 3, p. 426, 14 October 1785 (no. 885); trans. (amended) in Jahn, vol. 2, p. 405. Earlier, Leopold Mozart had observed the dissolution of the Jesuit monasteries in 1773 with mixed emotions, approving of the expropriations while sympathizing with the ordinary Jesuit: "Now it is all up with the poor Jesuits! I call them poor, for only those who were the leaders, I mean, the rabbis and *corpus religionis* as a whole, could be called rich. The ordinary members had nothing. The Jesuit monastery Auf Dem Hof must be cleared out by September 16th. The church treasure, their wine-cellars and, in fact, their entire property have already been sealed up, for the Jesuit Order has been suppressed. But they may dress as secular priests and it is said that each priest will have three hundred florins a year, which is not so bad." *Letters,* p. 241, 4 September 1773 (no. 183). See Ernst Fritz Schmid, *Ein schwäbisches Mozartbuch* (Lorch and Stuttgart, 1948), p. 76.

40. See Yates, *Rosicrucian Enlightenment,* p. 231.

41. See Nettl, *Mozart and Masonry,* p. 55.

42. Trans. Robert Jordan, from program notes for the Philips *Complete Mozart Edition,* vol. 22.

43. Announcement in the *Wiener Zeitung,* 25 January 1792: *MDB,* p. 440.

44. Ignaz Seyfried to Georg Friedrich Treitschke, undated letter (1840?): *MDB,* p. 555; another translation in Chailley, *Magic Flute,* pp. 301–2. See also entry "Convivial Societies" in *Encyclopaedia of Freemasonry,* ed. Arthur Edward Waite (reprint New York, 1970), vol. 1, pp. 149–52.

45. See Leopold Alois Hoffmann, *Briefe eines Biedermannes an einen Biedermann ueber die Freymaeurer in Wien* (Munich, 1786), cited in Reinalter, *Joseph II,* p. 129. Caroline Pichler, who met Mozart and Haydn at her family's salon, wrote: "At that time it was not unadvantageous to belong to this brotherhood, which had members in every circle and had known how to entice leaders, presidents and governors into its bosom. For there, one brother helped the other." H. C. Robbins Landon, *Haydn: Chronicle and Works,* vol. 2 (Bloomington, 1978), p. 308.

46. Huber, "Sozialstruktur der Wiener Logen," p. 180. For detailed breakdowns of "Beneficence" members by occupation and class, see Schuler, " 'Mozart von der Wohlthätigkeit,' " p. 9. Only 7 to 8 percent were high nobles; 68 percent were bourgeois or professionals. For "New Crowned Hope," see Heinz Schuler, " 'Zur neugekrönten Hoffnung' " pp. 8–9. Fourteen percent of the members of "New Crowned Hope" were from the old or high nobility, 34 percent were from the lesser nobility, and 34 percent were from bourgeois backgrounds. Of the total of 700 Freemasons in 1785, 42 percent belonged to the nobility, including 14 percent to the high nobility (Huber, p. 183). See also Hurwitz, "Haydn and the Freemasons," p. 16, and Volkmar Braunbehrens, *Mozart in Vienna 1781–1791* (New York, 1990), p. 250.

47. Translated by Robert Jordan, from program notes for the Philips *Complete Mozart Edition,* vol. 22.

48. Mircea Eliade, *Rites and Symbols of Initiation: The Mysteries of Birth and Rebirth,* trans. Willard R. Trask (New York, 1958; reprint New York, 1965), p. 74. For excerpts from a typical Master Mason ritual at a Prague lodge, see Braunbehrens, *Mozart in Vienna,* pp. 229–31.

49. Leopold Mozart's name does not appear on the membership lists of the lodges after the *Freimaurerpatent,* suggesting that, like Haydn, he may have considered it indiscreet to continue his membership.

50. Speech by Joseph Holzmeister, cited in Landon, *Haydn: Chronicle,* vol. 2, p. 507.

51. Hoffmann, *Briefe eines Biedermannes,* p. 129. Hoffmann, himself a Mason, was a defender of the *Freimaurerpatent* and later became a bitter opponent of Freemasonry.

52. *Briefe,* vol. 4, pp. 299–300, 27 November 1799 (no. 1269).

53. Ibid., p. 360, 21 July 1800 (no. 1301).

54. Cited, from *Teutscher Merkur,* in Nettl, *Mozart and Masonry,* p. 79.

Chapter 22: The Zoroastran Riddles

1. *Briefe,* vol. 3, p. 521, 24 March 1786 (no. 943).

2. Ibid., pp. 506–7, before 19 February 1786 (no. 933); translation in *MDB,* p. 268. The

materials were first republished in Rudolf Lewicki, "Aus Nissens Kollektaneen," *Mozarteums Mit-teilungen* 2 (1919), p. 30.

3. The translations of the proverbs and riddles are my own.

4. *Briefe*, vol. 3, p. 524, 28 March 1786 (no. 946).

5. The rediscovery of the riddles was announced in 1970 and they were first published in 1971 in the appendix to the second "Commentary" volume of *Briefe* (vol. 6, pp. 713–15) as well as in a journal article by J. H. Eibl, "Mozartiana aus der Sammlung Hermann Härtel," *Musikforschung* 23 (1970), p. 445; see also Eibl, "Mozart verfasst Rätsel," *Österreichische Musikzeitschrift* 26 (1971), pp. 65–71. Mozart's putative "solutions" do not appear in the autograph, but he furnished his father with solutions to two of the riddles: no. 3 is "die Maulschelle" (the box on the ear) and the first of the two illegible riddles is "die Seufzer Allée" (the Avenue of Sighs), a narrow alley located next to Vienna's Redoutensaal and so named because it was a popular gathering place for lovers. See Leopold Mozart's letters to his daughter, *Briefe*, vol. 3, p. 521, 23 March 1786 (no. 943), and p. 546, 22 May 1786 (no. 959); see also *Briefe*, vol. 6, p. 283.

6. Paul Ricoeur, *Freud and Philosophy* (New Haven and London, 1970), pp. 7, 18.

7. J. B. Friedreich, *Geschichte des Rätsels* (Dresden, 1860), p. 2.

8. Michele de Filippis, *The Literary Riddle in Italy to the End of the Sixteenth Century* (Berkeley and Los Angeles, 1948), p. 14.

9. Aristotle, *Rhetoric*, Book III, cited in Frederick Tupper, Jr., *The Riddles of the Exeter Book* (Boston, 1910), pp. xii–xiii.

10. Shakespeare, *2 Henry IV*, Act I, scene 2, lines 48–50.

11. *Letters*, p. 403, 3 December 1777 (no. 254).

12. Frederick Thomas Elworthy, *Horns of Honour* (London, 1900), passim; Ruth Mellinkoff, *The Horned Moses in Medieval Art and Thought* (Berkeley and Los Angeles, 1970), pp. 121–24.

13. Archer Taylor, *English Riddles from Oral Tradition* (Berkeley and Los Angeles, 1951), pp. 316–17.

14. Ernst Kris observes that "the comic originates in the conflict between instinctual trends and the superego's repudiation of them," occupying a position "midway between pleasure and unpleasure." *Psychoanalytic Explorations in Art* (New York, 1952), p. 182.

15. See de Filippis, *Literary Riddle*, p. 66.

16. See Hugo Hayn, "Die Deutsche Räthsel-Litteratur," *Centralblatt für Bibliothekswesen* 17 (1890), pp. 526–28. See also Hugo Hayn, *Bibliotheca Germanorum Erotica*, 3rd ed. (Munich, 1914), vol. 6, pp. 348–58.

17. *Letters*, p. 500, 28 February 1778 (no. 293).

18. For some of the many carnival references in the Mozart correspondence, see *Letters*, p. 114, 17 February 1770 (no. 80); p. 116, 3 March 1770 (no. 82); p. 117, 3 March 1770 (no. 82a); p. 250, 14 December 1774 (no. 190); p. 262, 15 February 1775 (no. 201); p. 263, 21 February 1775 (no. 202); p. 500, 28 February 1778 (no. 293); pp. 837–38, 22 January 1783 (no. 479); p. 840, 15 February 1783 (no. 481); p. 842, 12 March 1782 (no. 483). See also Joachim Ferdinand von Schiedenhofen's diary for 18 February 1776: *MDB*, p. 155; see Ibid., p. 213, for cast and details of the 1783 pantomime.

19. *Letters*, p. 837, 22 January 1783 (no. 479).

20. Sir James Frazer, *The Golden Bough: A Study in Magic and Religion*, abridged ed. (New York, 1939), p. 583. Elaborating the implications of Frazer, Freud regarded the celebration of festivals as a periodic lifting of the "renunciations and limitations imposed upon the ego" (Freud, *Group Psychology and the Analysis of the Ego*, in *Standard Edition of the Complete Psychological Works of Sigmund Freud*, ed. and trans. James Strachey et al. [London, 1953–74], vol. 18, p. 131). A complementary hypothesis holds that the main purpose of the festivals was to safeguard the person of the king through vicarious sacrifice of a surrogate masquerader rather than to act out ritualized overthrow of authority. See Photeine P. Bourboulis, *Ancient Festivals of "Saturnalia" Type*, Hellenika no. 16 (Thessalonika, 1964), pp. 7–37.

21. *Letters*, p. 230, Milan, 27 February 1773 (no. 176).

22. See Eckehard Catholy, *Das Fastnachtspiel des Spätmittelalters: Gestalt und Funktion*, Hermaea Germanistische Forschungen, Neue Folge, vol. 8 (Tübingen, 1961). See also Eckehard Catholy, *Fastnachtspiel* (Stuttgart, 1966).

23. Mozart's brother-in-law, Joseph Lange, noted that Mozart "took delight" in "sudden outbursts of vulgar platitudes": *MDB*, p. 503.

24. Mikhail Bakhtin, *Rabelais and His World* (Cambridge, Mass., and London, 1968), p. 276.

25. Kris, *Psychoanalytic Explorations in Art,* p. 182.

26. Goethe, *Travels in Italy,* in *The Permanent Goethe,* ed. Thomas Mann (New York, 1956), pp. 542–43.

27. This and the following quotations in this paragraph are from *Letters,* pp. 886–87, 16 February 1785 (no. 523), and pp. 887–88, 21 February 1785 (no. 524).

28. Ibid., p. 888, 21 February 1785 (no. 524).

29. *Briefe,* vol. 3, p. 379, 12 March 1785 (no. 850); *Letters,* p. 888, 12 March 1785 (no. 525); translation amended.

30. Ibid.

31. *Briefe,* vol. 3, p. 385, 8 April 1785 (no. 860); Deutsch-Paumgartner, p. 80.

32. Karl Abraham, *Selected Papers,* trans. Douglas Bryan and Alix Strachey (London, 1942), p. 465.

33. Eric Partridge, *Shakespeare's Bawdy* (New York, 1960), p. 101; Robert Rogers, *Metaphor: A Psychoanalytic View* (Berkeley and Los Angeles, 1978), observes that "to die," in linguistic metaphor, "refers to death of the body, flatus, and orgasm" (p. 101).

34. *Much Ado About Nothing,* Act V, scene 2, lines 99–101.

35. Previously, Mozart's comic impulse had found its outlet in scatological anal obscenity, perhaps as his way to refute his father's cash- and morality-centered outlook. Riddle 3, whose unsatisfactory, "innocent" solution is "die Maulschelle" (the box on the ear) but whose more obscene solution is "a fart," shows that Mozart's wit remains at its best in anal humor. But phallic/genital humor predominates in the other riddles, a kind of braggadocio overlaying issues of potency, castration dread, and fear of homosexual incorporation.

36. *Letters,* p. 384, 22 November 1777 (no. 247).

37. Ibid., p. 398, 1 December 1777 (no. 252).

38. Sigmund Freud, *Introductory Lectures on Psycho-Analysis,* Strachey et al., *Standard Edition,* vol. 26, p. 376. Quoted here from Joan Riviere, trans., *A General Introduction to Psychoanalysis* (Garden City, N.Y., 1943), p. 328.

39. Ricoeur, *Freud and Philosophy,* pp. 175, 521.

Chapter 23: The Carnivalesque Dimension

1. *Letters,* p. 703, 30 December 1780 (no. 383); translation revised.

2. Ibid., pp. 757–58, 8 August 1781 (no. 419). Mozart gives the name as "Wiedmer." See *Briefe,* vol. 6, pp. 78–79.

3. *Letters,* p. 746, 16 June 1781 (no. 411).

4. Ibid., p. 747, 20 June 1781 (no. 412); see also p. 743, 13 June 1781 (no. 410).

5. Ibid., p. 779, 17 November 1781 (no. 433).

6. Ibid., p. 682, 5 December 1780 (no. 370).

7. Ibid., p. 826, 5 October 1782 (no. 469).

8. Ibid., p. 828, 12 October 1782 (no. 470).

9. Ibid., pp. 799–800, 10 April 1782 (no. 446), translation amended; and p. 828, 12 October 1782 (no. 470).

10. Ibid., p. 782, 5 December 1781 (no. 435).

11. Mikhail Bakhtin, *Rabelais and His World* (Cambridge, Mass., and London, 1968), pp. 88, 435.

12. Bakhtin, *Rabelais,* pp. 91–92.

13. *Briefe,* vol. 3, p. 232, 28 September 1782, to Baroness Waldstätten (no. 696); *Letters,* p. 823, 28 September 1782 (no. 466); translation revised.

14. *Briefe,* vol. 1, p. 458, 28 October 1772 (no. 264). The original reads in full:

botzen diess Sauloch.

Ein gedichte von einen der über botzen fuchs-teüfel
wild und harb war.
Soll ich noch komen nach botzen
so schlag ich mich lieber in d'fozen.

Anderson delicately renders this as, "If to Bozen I must come, Faith, I'd rather cut my thumb." *Letters,* p. 214, 28 October 1772 (no. 159a).

15. *Briefe,* vol. 3, pp. 7–8, 12 August–13 September 1780 (no. 533); *Briefe,* vol. 6, p. 11; J. H. Eibl and Walter Senn, *Mozarts Bäsle-Briefe* (Kassel, 1978), p. 68.

16. *Letters,* p. 672, 24 November 1780 (no. 363). "Nur der *Esel welcher einen Ring zereist, und*

durch die gewalt einen Bruch bekommet daβ ich ihn darüber scheissen höre wie einen Castraten mit hörner, und mit seinem langen ohr den fuchs-schwanz streicht, nicht so . . . " Briefe, vol. 3, p. 31, 24 November 1780 (no. 542). The solution is "Erzbischof."

17. "Dirty words, as a class, have special properties setting them apart from ordinary diction. For one thing, they have extraordinary power to excite people—with disgust, anger, laughter, desire, and so forth." Robert Rogers, *Metaphor: A Psychoanalytic View* (Berkeley and Los Angeles, 1978), p. 59.

18. *Letters,* p. 358, 5 November 1777 (no. 236).

19. Ibid., p. 372, 13 November 1777 (no. 242).

20. Ibid., p. 403, 3 December 1777 (no. 254).

21. Ibid., p. 652, 10 May 1780 [not 1779] (no. 354).

22. *Briefe,* vol. 2, p. 308, 28 February 1778 (no. 432); *Letters,* p. 500, 28 February 1778 (no. 293).

23. *Letters,* p. 457, 31 January 1777 (no. 278); translation amended.

24. John Middleton Murry, *Jonathan Swift* (London, 1954), p. 81, cited in Phyllis Greenacre, *Swift and Carroll: A Psychoanalytic Study of Two Lives* (New York, 1955), p. 276.

25. Bakhtin, *Rabelais,* p. 380.

26. Speech by Joseph Holzmeister, in H. C. Robbins Landon, *Haydn: Chronicle and Works,* vol. 2 (Bloomington, 1978), p. 507.

27. *Letters,* p. 372, 13 November 1777 (no. 242). Eibl and Senn, *Mozarts Bäsle-Briefe,* p. 70, suspect that this passage contains an as yet undeciphered code.

Chapter 24: Fearful Symmetries

1. Wye Jamison Allanbrook, *Rhythmic Gesture in Mozart: "Le nozze di Figaro" and "Don Giovanni"* (Chicago and London, 1983), p. 267.

2. Personal communication.

3. C. M. Girdlestone, *Mozart and His Piano Concertos* (New York, 1964), p. 345.

4. Approaching the theme from a rather different viewpoint, Agawu writes: "For a listener who has internalized the harmonic expectations generated by a half-cadence in eighteenth-century music, the onset of bar 6, despite—or rather because of—the intervening silence, fulfills the promise of resolution; it is a rebeginning as well as the resolution of an unresolved dominant." Kofi Agawu, "Does Music Theory Need Musicology," *Current Musicology* no. 53 (1993), p. 96.

5. Edward E. Lowinsky, "On Mozart's Rhythm," in *The Creative World of Mozart,* ed. Paul Henry Lang (New York, 1963), pp. 32–33.

6. Ibid., pp. 35, 37.

7. Ibid., pp. 33, 35.

8. Ibid., p. 33.

9. Plato, *Philebus,* in *The Dialogues of Plato,* trans. Benjamin Jowett (Boston and New York, n.d.), vol. 3, p. 191 (paragraph 51D).

10. Cited in Bernard Bosanquet, *A History of Aesthetic* (London, 1922), p. 247.

11. Plotinus, *The Six Enneads,* trans. Stephen MacKenna and B. S. Page (Chicago and London, 1952), p. 333 (Sixth Ennead, VII. 22).

12. "On Beauty," in *Francis Bacon: A Selection of His Works,* ed. Sidney Warhaft (Toronto and London, 1965), p. 157.

13. Charles Baudelaire, "The Exposition Universelle, 1855," in Baudelaire, *The Mirror of Art: Critical Studies,* trans. and ed. Jonathan Mayne (London, 1955), p. 195.

14. Mario Praz, *The Romantic Agony,* trans. Angus Davidson (2nd ed., Oxford, 1951; reprint New York, 1956), p. 26.

15. Cited in Hugh Honour, *Neo-classicism* (Harmondsworth, 1968; rev. ed., New York, 1977), p. 150.

16. Ibid., p. 149.

17. Hanns Sachs, *The Creative Unconscious: Studies in the Psychoanalysis of Art* (Cambridge, Mass., 1942), p. 240.

18. Herbert Marcuse, "The Affirmative Character of Culture," in *Negations: Essays in Critical Theory* (Boston, 1968), p. 118.

19. Sigmund Freud, *Beyond the Pleasure Principle,* in *Standard Edition of the Complete Psychological Works of Sigmund Freud,* trans. and ed. James Strachey et al. (London, 1955–1974), vol. 18, p. 36. Quoted here from C. J. M. Hubback, trans., *Beyond the Pleasure Principle* (London, 1948), p. 44.

20. Strachey et al., *Standard Edition*, vol. 18, p. 36; Hubback, *Pleasure Principle*, p. 45.

21. Sigmund Freud, *Civilization and Its Discontents*, Strachey et al., *Standard Edition*, vol. 21, pp. 118–19.

22. Paul Ricoeur, *Freud and Philosophy* (New Haven and London, 1970), p. 286. Ricoeur adds: "The work of art is also a *fort-da*, a disappearing of the archaic object as fantasy and its reappearing as a cultural object," p. 314.

23. Spinoza, *Ethics*, Part 3, Proposition 6, in *Improvement of the Understanding, Ethics and Correspondence*, trans. R. H. M. Elwes (New York and London, 1901), p. 135.

24. Freud, *Beyond the Pleasure Principle*, Strachey et al., *Standard Edition*, vol. 18, p. 59; Hubback, *Pleasure Principle*, p. 76.

25. *Letters*, p. 907, 4 April 1787 (no. 546).

26. Ibid., p. 561, 9 July 1778 (no. 313).

27. Henry James, *What Maisie Knew* (London, 1898; reprint 1947), p. 96.

28. Charles Rosen, *The Classical Style: Haydn, Mozart, Beethoven* (New York, 1971), p. 324.

29. Rosen, *Classical Style*, pp. 324–25.

30. Edgar Wind, *Art and Anarchy* (New York, 1964), pp. 10–11.

31. Herbert Marcuse, "The Affirmative Character of Culture," p. 115.

32. Rosen, *Classical Style*, p. 324.

Chapter 25: Little Leopold

1. *Letters*, p. 464, 5 February 1778 (no. 282).

2. *Briefe*, vol. 3, p. 205, 29 April 1782 (no. 669); *Letters*, p. 803 (no. 449); translation revised.

3. *Letters*, p. 750, 4 July 1781 (no. 414).

4. Ibid.

5. *Letters*, pp. 859–60, 31 October 1783 (no. 499).

6. *Briefe*, vol. 3, pp. 308–9, 3 April 1784 (no. 784); *Letters*, p. 873 (no. 507); translation amended.

7. *Briefe*, vol. 3, p. 596, 20 October 1786 (no. 992); Deutsch-Paumgartner, p. 377. For Leopold Mozart's letters to his daughter I give references both to *Briefe* as the standard edition and to Deutsch-Paumgartner as the most convenient edition. For Marchand's career, see *Briefe*, vol. 6, p. 314. Leopold Mozart seems not to have formed a similarly strong bond with his most talented later pupil, the accomplished Salzburg-born virtuoso Joseph Wölffl (1773–1812), who also studied with Michael Haydn and Marianne Mozart. See *NMD*, p. 63 (no. 101). Marianne's diaries for 1783 show that Wölffl was her pupil through the fall of that year. See esp. *Briefe*, vol. 3, pp. 286–91, 4 September–31 October 1783 (no. 765). Her father became the boy's teacher from December 1783 until February 1787, giving him a minimum of 236 lessons up to September 1785. See *Briefe*, vol. 3, p. 436, 29 October 1785 (no. 892).

8. *Briefe*, vol. 3, p. 378, 12 March 1785 (no. 850); Deutsch-Paumgartner, p. 74.

9. *Briefe*, vol. 3, p. 436, 28 October 1785 (no. 892); Deutsch-Paumgartner, p. 153.

10. This and the following quotations are from *Briefe*, vol. 3, pp. 404–6, 2 September 1785 (no. 875); Deutsch-Paumgartner, p. 103–5.

11. There is no question of illegitimacy; Marianne had been in St. Gilgen with her husband for eleven months prior to the birth of the child, and Leopoldl later received a full share of his father's inheritance.

12. *Briefe*, vol. 3, p. 407, 9 September 1785 (no. 876); Deutsch-Paumgartner, p. 107.

13. *Briefe*, vol. 3, p. 407, 9 September 1785 (no. 876); Deutsch-Paumgartner, p. 107.

14. *Briefe*, vol. 3, pp. 414–15, 22 September 1785 (no. 881); Deutsch-Paumgartner, pp. 118–20.

15. *Briefe*, vol. 3, p. 417, 29 September 1785 (no. 882); Deutsch-Paumgartner, p. 123.

16. E.g., *Briefe*, vol. 3, p. 443, 27 October 1785 (no. 892); Deutsch-Paumgartner, p. 147.

17. Jahn, vol. 3, p. 406; see also Deutsch-Paumgartner, p. vii.

18. *Briefe*, vol. 3, p. 512, between 11 February and 3 March 1786 (no. 938); Deutsch-Paumgartner, pp. 262–63.

19. *Briefe*, vol. 3, p. 517, 17 March 1786 (no. 940); Deutsch-Paumgartner, p. 275.

20. *Briefe*, vol. 3, p. 428, 14 October 1785 (no. 885); Deutsch-Paumgartner, p. 141.

21. *Briefe*, vol. 3, p. 446, 11 November 1785 (no. 897); Deutsch-Paumgartner, p. 170.

22. *Briefe*, vol. 3, p. 479, 29 December 1785 (no. 914); Deutsch-Paumgartner, p. 220.

23. *Briefe*, vol. 4, p. 5, 4 January 1787 (no. 1017); Deutsch-Paumgartner, p. 432.

24. *Briefe,* vol. 4, p. 22, 9 February 1787 (no. 1032); Deutsch-Paumgartner, p. 452.

25. *Briefe,* vol. 3, pp. 446–47, 11 November 1785 (no. 897); Deutsch-Paumgartner, p. 170.

26. *Briefe,* vol. 3, pp. 496–97, 27–28 January 1786 (no. 925); Deutsch-Paumgartner, pp. 248–49.

27. *Briefe,* vol. 3, p. 602, 2 November 1786 (no. 995); Deutsch-Paumgartner, p. 387. He describes similar symptoms in his letter of 7 November 1786: *Briefe,* vol. 3, p. 603 (no. 997); Deutsch-Paumgartner, p. 388.

28. *Briefe,* vol. 4, p. 15, 19 January 1787 (no. 1025); Deutsch-Paumgartner, p. 441.

29. *Briefe,* vol. 4, pp. 17–18, 26 January 1787 (no. 1026); Deutsch-Paumgartner, p. 446.

30. *Briefe,* vol. 4, p. 24, 13 February 1787 (no. 1033); Deutsch-Paumgartner, p. 455.

31. *Briefe,* vol. 4, p. 26, 24 February 1787 (no. 1034); Deutsch-Paumgartner, p. 458.

32. *Briefe,* vol. 4, p. 38, 16 March 1787 (no. 1041); Deutsch-Paumgartner, p. 477.

33. Theobold Marchand to Leopold Mozart, 29 May 1787, in Deutsch, "Ein Rezept für den sterbenden Vater Mozart," *Neues Augsburger Mozartbuch. Zeitschrift des historischen Vereins für Schwaben,* vols. 62–63 (Augsburg, 1962), pp. 329–31. The letter arrived after Leopold Mozart's death. The obituary notice attributed his death to consumption. *Salzburger Intelligenzblatt,* 2 June 1787: *MDB,* p. 293.

34. *Briefe,* vol. 4, pp. 43–44, 10–11 May 1787 (no. 1048); Deutsch-Paumgartner, pp. 481, 483.

35. *Briefe,* vol. 4, p. 44, 10–11 May 1787 (no. 1048); Deutsch-Paumgartner, p. 484; *Letters,* p. 908 n. 4.

36. With the exception of the letter of 4 April 1787, Mozart's letters to his father from 9 June 1784 until just before Leopold Mozart's death are missing; but their frequency and contents can be deduced from Leopold's letters to Marianne.

37. Walter Hummel, *Nannerl: Wolfgang Amadeus Mozarts Schwester* (Zurich, Leipzig, Vienna, 1952), p. 72.

38. *Letters,* p. 902, 17 November 1786 (no. 542).

39. *Briefe,* vol. 3, p. 612, 24 November 1786 (no. 1005); Deutsch-Paumgartner, p. 401.

40. The dates of instruction are not known precisely. Deutsch holds that "Hummel must have been a pupil of Mozart's in 1786 and 1787" (*MDB,* p. 570; see also p. 346); Robert Münster narrows the dates to the period between winter 1785–86 and September 1787. See Robert Münster, "Authentische Tempi zu den sechs letzten Sinfonien W. A. Mozarts?" *MJb 1962/63,* pp. 187–88.

41. *Briefe,* vol. 6, p. 590.

42. *Berlinische Nachrichten von Staats- und gelehrten Sachen,* 21 May 1789: *NMD,* p. 58 (commentary to no. 92).

43. A possible earlier example of Mozart's competitiveness—mingled with a strong sense of identification—is his declaration, knowing of his father's identical intention, that he is considering writing a book on musical pedagogy (see *Briefe,* vol. 2, p. 374, 11 June 1778 [no. 452]). Mozart wrote, "I should like to write a book, a short introduction to music, illustrated by examples, but, I need hardly add, not under my own name." *Letters,* p. 833, 28 December 1782 (no. 476).

44. *Letters,* p. 901, 17 November 1786 (no. 542). Mozart's letter has not survived.

45. Ibid., p. 902, 17 November 1786 (no. 542); translation amended. Nissen (or Constanze) reworded this letter to omit the rejection of Mozart's request to take the children. Nissen, p. 523.

46. *Briefe,* vol. 3, p. 613, 29 November 1786 (no. 1006); Deutsch-Paumgartner, p. 403.

47. *Letters,* p. 906, 1 March 1787 (no. 545).

48. Ibid.

49. *Briefe,* vol. 3, p. 405, 2 September 1785 (no. 875); Deutsch-Paumgartner, p. 103.

Chapter 26: "Carissima sorella mia"

1. *Letters,* p. 115, 17 February 1770 (no. 80a).

2. Ibid., p. 117, 3 March 1770 (no. 82a).

3. Ibid., p. 238, 14 August 1773 (no. 179a).

4. Ibid., p. 143, 5 June 1770 (no. 96a), and p. 115, 17 February 1770 (no. 80a). See also p. 221, 18 December 1772 (no. 166a).

5. Ibid., pp. 109–10, 26 January 1770 (no. 77a).

6. Ibid., p. 100, 14 December 1769 (no. 71b).

7. Ibid., p. 143, 5 June 1770 (no. 96a).

8. Ibid., p. 258 (no. 195a), and p. 283, 29 September 1777 (no. 211a).

9. Ibid., pp. 149–50, 21 July 1770 (no. 103b).

10. Ibid., p. 106, 7 January 1770 (no. 75a).

11. *Briefe,* vol. 1, p. 293, 14 December 1769 (no. 147); *Letters,* p. 100, 14 December 1769 (no. 71b); *Briefe,* vol. 1, p. 301, 7 January 1770 (no. 153); *Letters,* p. 104, 7 January 1770 (no. 75a).

12. *Letters,* p. 575, 20 July 1778 (no. 315b).

13. Ibid., pp. 589–90, 31 July 1778 (no. 319a).

14. Marianne von Berchtold, "Data for a biography of the late composer Wolfgang Mozart": *MDB,* p. 461. See also Gustav Nottebohm, *Mozartiana* (Leipzig, 1880), pp. 95–111.

15. *Letters,* p. 909, 16 June 1787 (no. 548).

16. Many of Marianne Mozart's performances at Salzburg have left no trace; among the documented performances are a joint appearance with Mozart on 15 October 1769; participation in Mozart's concert in the "Tanzmeistersaal" on 15 August 1777; performances for the visitors Anton Janitsch and Joseph Reicha on 25 and 26 January 1778; continuo accompaniments in a concert by Count Czernin's amateur orchestra on 12 April 1778; and accompanying Mozart at a concert at court in early September 1780. As noted earlier, in a letter of 24 March 1781 Mozart suggested that his sister "*demand* two ducats" each time she performed at court, but the details of such performances have not survived. See *Letters,* p. 718, 24 March 1781 (no. 395). Her final joint appearance with Mozart took place in Augsburg in early March 1781.

17. Diary of Marianne Mozart, in *Briefe,* vol. 2, p. 7, 23–24 September 1777 (no. 330). See also *Letters,* p. 296, 4 October 1777 (no. 215a).

18. *Letters,* pp. 273, 25 September 1777 (no. 208).

19. Ibid., p. 296, 4 October 1777 (no. 215a).

20. Ibid., p. 336, 23 October 1777 (no. 227a).

21. Ibid., p. 480, 13 February 1788 (no. 286).

22. Schwerin observed how few references there were to Marianne in her mother's letters, "despite the fact that her daughter's postscripts reflect the longing for her mother's presence." Erna Schwerin, "Anna Maria Mozart: A Profile of Mozart's Mother," *Friends of Mozart Newsletter,* no. 16 (Spring 1984), p. 3.

23. Jahn speculates that her earnings as a clavier teacher also helped to lighten "her father's pecuniary anxieties." Jahn, vol. 3, p. 402.

24. *Letters,* pp. 343–44, 27 October 1777 (no. 230a).

25. Ibid., p. 432, 22 December 1777 (no. 265a).

26. Ibid., p. 412, 8 December 1777 (no. 257a).

27. Ibid., p. 438, 29 December 1777 (no. 268a).

28. *Briefe,* vol. 2, p. 450, 27 August 1778 (no. 478). Even as he thus rejected an eligible suitor, Leopold complained emphatically in the same letter that "*your dear sister, who is already twenty-seven years of age . . . is not provided for, while I am growing old.*" *Letters,* p. 605, 27 August 1778 (no. 326).

29. D'Ippold had accumulated savings of 4,000 florins at his death. Eva Rieger, *Nannerl Mozart: Leben einer Künstlerin im 18. Jahrhundert* (Frankfurt, 1990), p. 182. He is usually identified in the Mozart literature as an imperial captain and a steward of the court pages. See Jahn-Deiters, vol. 2, p. 734; Erich Valentin, "Ein unbekannter Mozart-Brief," *Neues MJb* 3 (1943), p. 90. However, searches of the Salzburg archives have not confirmed this; see Rudolph Genée, "Mozarts Schwester Nannerl," *Mitteilungen für die Mozart-Gemeinde in Berlin* 3 (November 1896), p. 102n. Despite his name, d'Ippold was not of aristocratic origin, having himself added the particle to his name. The name is variously spelled d'Ippold, d'Yppold, and Diepold.

30. *Letters,* p. 751, 4 July 1781 (no. 415). Marianne Mozart's letters on this subject are not extant.

31. Ibid., pp. 766–67, 19 September 1781 (no. 425).

32. *Briefe,* vol. 3, p. 160, after 19 September 1781 (no. 626); *Letters,* p. 767, after 19 September 1781 (no. 425).

33. Walter Hummel, *Nannerl: Wolfgang Amadeus Mozarts Schwester* (Zurich, Leipzig, Vienna, 1952), p. 58; *Briefe,* vol. 6, p. 74; Rieger, *Nannerl Mozart,* pp. 181–83, 192–93. Erich Valentin, however, thinks the marriage plans came to nought because d'Ippold was unable to obtain the necessary consent from the authorities. Valentin, "Unbekannter Mozart-Brief," p. 89.

34. Hummel, *Nannerl*, p. 58.

35. He was described as a "tedious man" who "was often bad-tempered." Hummel, p. 69. Jahn writes: "Report said that Marianne had not always an easy time of it with her husband." Jahn, vol. 3, pp. 405–6. For a discussion of what Leopold Mozart in a letter to his daughter called Berchtold's "perhaps exaggerated parsimoniousness" (*Briefe*, vol. 3, 9 February 1786 [no. 931]), see J. H. Eibl, "Der 'Herr Sohn,'" *Mitteilungen der ISM* 14 (February 1966), p. 5.

36. *Letters*, p. 496, 25–26 February 1778 (no. 291).

37. Ibid., p. 495, 25–26 February 1778 (no. 291).

38. Friedrich Schlichtegroll to Albert Mölk, 25 May 1792, in Rudolph Angermüller, "'Das musikalische Kind Mozart': Ein Beitrag zur Biographie Mozarts im ausgehenden 18. Jahrhundert," *Wiener Figaro. Mitteilungen der Mozartgemeinde Wien* 42 (May 1975), p. 30. See also Angermüller, "Nissens Kollektaneen für seine Mozartbiographie," *MJb 1971/72*, pp. 221–22.

39. *Briefe*, vol. 4, p. 202, draft of responses to questions submitted to Marianne by Schlichtegroll via Albert von Mölk, 1792 (no. 1213).

40. *Letters*, p. 480, 11–12 February 1778 (no. 285).

41. Ibid., p. 486, 19 February 1778 (no. 288).

42. Ibid., p. 495, 25–26 February 1778 (no. 291).

43. Ibid., p. 471, 9 February 1778 (no. 284a).

44. Ibid., pp. 863–64, 10 December 1783 (no. 501).

45. Ibid., p. 882, 18 August 1784 (no. 517).

46. *Briefe*, vol. 3, p. 385, 8 April 1785 (no. 860); Deutsch-Paumgartner, p. 80. "The passage shows how deep was the rift between Leopold and Nannerl on one side and Wolfgang on the other." *Briefe*, vol. 6, p. 228.

47. *Letters*, p. 893, 11 November 1785 (no. 532). Occasionally, Mozart sent greetings to Marianne through their father, for example, in August of 1786: "Your brother sends his regards and writes that his wife will soon come to childbed." *Briefe*, vol. 3, p. 576, 23 August 1786 (no. 980); Deutsch-Paumgartner, p. 349.

48. *Briefe*, vol. 3, p. 557, 21 July 1786 (no. 968); Deutsch-Paumgartner, p. 325.

49. *Letters*, p. 908, end of May 1787 (no. 547).

50. Ibid., p. 909, 2 June 1787 (no. 547★).

51. Walter Senn, "Zur Erbteilung nach Leopold Mozart," *Neues Augsburger Mozartbuch. Zeitschrift des historischen Vereins für Schwaben*, vol. 62–63 (1962), p. 385. Senn concludes from several references to "the paternal inheritance" in the minutes of the princely council for 21 September 1787 that the testament actually existed. See pp. 393–94; *MDB*, pp. 297–98. See also Valentin, "Unbekannter Mozart-Brief," pp. 91–92.

52. *Briefe*, vol. 4, p. 167 (no. 1201). The scenario probably dates from early 1787. "This may be a sketch for one of Mozart's domestic carnival presentations." *Briefe*, vol. 6, p. 428.

53. Probably d'Ippold, who now turned down Mozart's request that he serve as his representative in the settlement of the estate.

54. *Letters*, p. 909, 16 June 1787 (no. 548).

55. Ibid., p. 910, 1 August 1787 (no. 549).

56. The auction list is transcribed in Rudolph Angermüller, "Leopold Mozarts Verlassenschaft," *Mitteilungen der ISM* 41 (November 1993), pp. 1–32. The auction was announced in the *Salzburger Intelligenzblatt*, 14 September 1787: *MDB*, pp. 296–97.

57. *MDB*, p. 298.

58. Senn, "Erbteilung," pp. 389–90. Deutsch comments: "Nannerl had probably already helped herself to a number of things before the auction." *MDB*, p. 298.

59. *Briefe*, vol. 4, p. 259, 4 August 1799, Marianne von Berchtold to B&H (no. 1251). In this letter, Marianne expressed regret that she had not withheld some of the early scores.

60. *MDB*, p. 297.

61. Deutsch-Paumgartner, p. xiii. A disbursement voucher confirms that Berchtold paid the 500 florins on the day after the wedding. Eibl, "Der 'Herr Sohn,'" p. 3.

62. Deutsch-Paumgartner, p. xiii; Hummel, *Nannerl*, p. 93.

63. See Johann Evangelist Engl, "Testament, Codicill, Nachtrag und Sperr-Relation der Schwester W. A. Mozarts," in *17. Jahresbericht der ISM* (Salzburg, 1897), pp. 29–34; this is now superseded by Rudolph Angermüller, "Testament, Kodizill, Nachtrag und Sperrelation der Freifrau Maria Anna von Berchtold zu Sonnenburg, geb. Mozart (1751–1829)," *MJb 1986*, pp. 97–132. See also Hummel, *Nannerl*, pp. 94–95, and Deutsch-Paumgartner, p. xiii.

64. *Letters,* p. 910, 1 August 1787 (no. 549), and p. 914, 19 December 1787 (no. 552).

65. Ibid., p. 918, 2 August 1788 (no. 557).

66. *Briefe,* vol. 4, p. 201, draft of responses to questions from Schlichtegroll, 1792 (no. 1213).

67. *Letters,* p. 507, 7 March 1778 (no. 296a).

68. Angermüller, "Testament," p. 107; Valentin, "Das Testament," *Neues MJb* 2 (1942), pp. 137–38.

69. *Letters,* p. 892, 16 September 1785 (no. 530).

70. *Briefe,* vol. 4, p. 38, 16 March 1787 (no. 1041); Deutsch-Paumgartner, p. 477.

71. *Briefe,* vol. 3, p. 589, 15–16 September 1786 (no. 987); Deutsch-Paumgartner, p. 368. "When Wolfgang . . . was away, the father, who could scarcely live without him, was often gloomy and preoccupied, and not even her tender ministrations could compensate him for the absence of his son." Jahn, vol. 3, p. 403.

Chapter 27: Prague and Beyond

1. Niemetschek, pp. 33, 35. Prague's enthusiasm for Mozart's music began with *Die Entführung aus dem Serail,* which was given there from as early as autumn 1782. See *MDB,* p. 219.

2. Lorenzo Da Ponte, *Memoirs: MDB,* pp. 549–50.

3. *Prager Oberpostamtszeitung,* 12 December 1786: *MDB,* pp. 280–81. At a performance on 4 January 1787, "The theater was so crowded . . . that people could hardly move." Ibid., 9 January 1787: *MDB,* p. 284. Other reports about *Le nozze di Figaro* from the *Prager Oberpostamtszeitung* are in Jiří Berkovec, *Musicalia v prazském periodickém tisku 18. století* (Prague, 1989), pp. 64, 65–66, and 139.

4. Niemetschek, p. 35.

5. *Letters,* p. 902, 12 January 1787, Leopold Mozart to Marianne von Berchtold (no. 543).

6. Ibid., p. 903, 15 January 1787, Mozart to Gottfried von Jacquin (no. 544).

7. Ibid., pp. 903–4, 15 January 1787 (no. 544); Paul Nettl, *Mozart in Böhmen* (Prague, 1938), pp. 88–89; Rudolf v. Procházka, *Mozart in Prag: Zum hundertjährigen Gedächtniss seines Todes* (Prague, 1892), p. 177.

8. Niemetschek, p. 36. A second concert may also have been given: "I shall probably have to give a second one," *Letters,* p. 904, 15 January 1787 (no. 544); Nissen, p. 517, note.

9. Niemetschek, p. 36.

10. Wilhelm Kuhe, *My Musical Recollections* (London, 1896), p. 8. The anecdote was told by double-bass player Wenzel Swoboda.

11. *Letters,* p. 904, 15 January 1787 (no. 544).

12. *Prager Oberpostamtszeitung,* 26 December 1786: *MDB,* p. 282. The report is reprinted from *Staats- und gelehrte Zeitung des hamburgischen unpartheyischen Correspondenten,* Hamburg, 15 December 1786: *NMD,* p. 47 (no. 75).

13. Tyson, p. 52.

14. The anecdote was first reported in Niemetschek, p. 64; Constanze later published it in *AMZ* 1 (1798–99), columns 290–91: *NMD,* p. 78 (no. 121); Mozart's remark is in Nissen, pp. 520–21.

15. *Prager Oberpostamtszeitung,* 16 October 1787: *MDB,* p. 300.

16. *Prager Oberpostamtszeitung,* 3 November 1787: *MDB,* pp. 303–4. There was also a favorable notice in a Hamburg periodical: "It is excellent beyond measure, and its equal has never before been given in Prague." *Staats- und gelehrte Zeitung,* 9 November 1787: *NMD,* p. 51 (no. 80).

17. Nissen, p. 514.

18. Abert, vol. 2, p. 360.

19. Niemetschek, p. 38.

20. H. C. Robbins Landon, *Haydn: Chronicle and Works,* vol. 2 (Bloomington, Ind., 1978), p. 702; translation amended. The autograph of Haydn's letter does not survive. There are few known Prague performances of Mozart's music between the *Don Giovanni* premiere and Josepha Duschek's concert of 26 April 1791 at the National Theater, which included a Mozart scene (probably K. 583), a rondo with bassett horn (perhaps Vitellia's aria from *La clemenza di Tito*) and a piano concerto (probably K. 595) played by Jan Vitásek; earlier in 1791 the Guardasoni company may have performed *Così fan tutte* in Italian in Prague.

21. *Letters,* p. 913, 4 November 1787 (no. 551).

22. Cited in H. C. Robbins Landon, *Mozart: The Golden Years* (New York, 1989), p. 200.

23. See Reinhold Bernhardt, "Aus der Umwelt der Wiener Klassiker: Freiherr van Swieten," *Der Bär*, 1929–30, pp. 74–164; Jahn, vol. 3, pp. 218–21; *MDB*, pp. 310–11, 331, 338; Mary Sue Morrow, *Concert Life in Haydn's Vienna: Aspects of a Developing Musical and Social Institution* (Stuyvesant, N.Y., 1989), pp. 10–13. Mozart took the place formerly held by Joseph Starzer, who died on 11 April 1787.

24. Report from Vienna, dated 26 February 1788, in Forkel's *Musikalischer Almanach* for 1789: *MDB*, p. 310.

25. The success of *Don Giovanni* in Prague "may have contributed to induce Joseph II. to retain Mozart in Vienna by appointing him Chamber-Musician." Jahn, vol. 3, p. 135.

26. F. Kasimir Kunz's *Allmanach der Kais. Königl. National-Schaubühne in Wien auf das Jahr 1789: MDB*, p. 332.

27. Count Johann Rudolf Chotek, head of the court finance department, to the lord high steward's office, 5 March 1792: *MDB*, p. 443.

28. Nissen, p. 539; *AMZ* 1 (1798–99), column 291: *NMD*, p. 78 (no. 121). During Lent, masked balls were given every Sunday, on Shrove Tuesday, and on the closing days of carnival. "Joseph II favored them as a means of drawing different classes together, and frequently appeared at them with his court; all ranks mixed freely, and considerable license was allowed." Jahn, vol. 3, p. 217.

29. *Letters*, p. 919, 2 August 1788 (no. 557).

30. For Mozart's use of the title "Kapellmeister," see *MDB*, pp. 306–7, and also p. 309.

31. Joseph II to Count Rosenberg, 16 May 1788: *Dokumente*, p. 277. Along similar lines, Da Ponte claimed that the emperor remarked, "The opera is divine, and perhaps it is finer than *Figaro*, but it is not food for the teeth of my Viennese." When he told Mozart of this, the composer allegedly responded, "Let us give them time to chew it." Da Ponte, *Memoirs: MDB*, p. 549.

32. Zinzendorf's Diary, 12 May 1788: *MDB*, p. 314.

33. Archduchess Elisabeth Wilhelmine, letter of 15 May 1788: *MDB*, p. 314.

34. Schink's *Dramaturgische Monate*, Schwerin, 1790 [Hamburg, 1789]: *MDB*, pp. 354–55.

35. *Chronik von Berlin*, 5 February 1791: *MDB*, p. 380.

36. Ibid., 2 October 1790, a review of the 14 September performance of *Le nozze di Figaro* at the National Theater: *MDB*, pp. 372–73; translation amended. A subsequent notice reads: "The house was not as full as on the day of the first performance, a proof that this grand heavenly music lies quite beyond the confines of the local public's perceptive faculty." *Chronik von Berlin*, 9 October 1790: *MDB*, p. 373.

37. Ernst Ludwig Gerber's *Historisch-biographisches Lexicon der Tonkünstler* (Leipzig, 1790): *MDB*, p. 383.

38. Jahn-Deiters, vol. 2, pp. 481–82; Jahn, vol. 3, p. 227.

39. See Peter Branscombe, "Mozart and the Theatre of His Time," in H. C. Robbins Landon, *The Mozart Compendium: A Guide to Mozart's Life and Music* (New York, 1990), pp. 366–70, and Tim Carter, *W. A. Mozart: Le nozze di Figaro* (Cambridge, England, 1987), pp. 11–12.

40. *Wiener Zeitung*, 25 June 1788: *MDB*, p. 319. The original advertisements appeared in the *Wiener Zeitung* for 2, 5, and 9 April.

41. *Letters*, p. 915, early June 1788, to Michael Puchberg (no. 553). It is worth noting that even successful concerts may leave no trace: Josepha Duschek's academy at the Burgtheater in March or early April 1786, given before an enthusiastic audience that included the emperor and the entire nobility, is known only through the accidental survival of a single private letter. See letter of Johann Thomas Kleinhardt to Count Franz Sternberg, 12–18 April 1786: *MDB*, pp. 271–72. For scholarly opinions on whether Mozart's concerts took place, see Appendix, note 1.

42. *MDB*, p. 320.

43. The schedule of what he owed to tradespeople at his death totaled only a bit more than 900 florins and showed no unusually extravagant items. See *MDB*, pp. 591–92.

44. *Letters*, p. 917, beginning of July 1788 (no. 556).

45. For Puchberg, see Gustav Gugitz, "Mozarts Finanzen und Freund Puchberg: Ein Beitrag zur Mozart-Biographie," *Österreichische Musikzeitschrift* 7 (1952), pp. 219–25; see also J. H. Eibl, "Ein 'ächter Bruder': Mozart und Johann Michael Puchberg," *Acta Mozartiana* 26 (August 1979), pp. 41–46.

46. Heinrich Beck to Friedrich Hildebrand von Einsiedel, 7 April 1791: *NMD*, p. 66 (no. 106).

47. Niemetschek, p. 39.

48. In 1785–86 he sued Mozart's friend, the clarinetist Anton Stadler, for repayment of 1,400 florins: *MDB*, p. 600.

49. *Letters*, p. 915, before 17 June 1788 (no. 554).

50. Ibid., p. 917, 27 June 1788 (no. 555).

51. Ibid., p. 931, 17 July 1789 (no. 568). "I shall pay back the whole sum with whatever interest you may demand." *Letters*, p. 930, 12 July 1789 (no. 567).

52. According to Nissen, Puchberg asked for and received repayment of his money "several years later from his widow." Nissen, p. 686; see also *MDB*, p. 600. Perhaps Puchberg had an agreement with Constanze to defer his claim in exchange for a promise of repayment out of her future earnings.

53. *Letters*, p. 957, 25 June 1791 (no. 603).

54. *MDB*, p. 338. Hofdemel lived far beyond his 400 florins salary. For details of several very large payments to him by Count Gottfried Ignaz von Walldorf, see Ernst Weizmann, "Der unbekannte Mozart," *Weltpresse* (Vienna) 12, (25 February 1956), p. 7.

55. Promissory note, 1 October 1790: *MDB*, pp. 371–72.

56. *MDB*, p. 372. One wonders whether Lackenbacher, about whom there are no particulars, is perhaps the Herr Lackenbauer who sponsored one of the few private theatrical companies in Vienna in the later 1780s, mounting numerous productions "of the best German works." See *NMD*, p. 44 (no. 70).

57. *Letters*, pp. 955, 962, 12 June 1791 and 6 July 1791 (nos. 600, 610).

58. Walther Brauneis, " '. . . wegen schuldigen 1435 f 32 xr': Neuer Archivfund zur Finanzmisere Mozarts im November 1791," *Mitteilungen der ISM* 39 (1991), pp. 159–63. See also Erna Schwerin, "Lichnowsky versus Mozart. The Enigma of a Lawsuit," *Friends of Mozart Newsletter*, no. 30 (1991), p. 1.

59. Niemetschek, p. 49.

60. It is conceivable that Lichnowsky here took over one of Mozart's debts, either the one to Puchberg or the one to Lackenbacher, both of which are for sums of over 1,000 florins. One may speculate that Lichnowsky formally assumed such a debt to relieve pressure on Mozart, and that judgment was entered only as a prudent precaution. Thus, Lichnowsky's claim does not necessarily signal a personal break between him and Mozart.

61. *Letters*, p. 945, 8 October 1790 (no. 587). Although Hoffmeister had published fifteen first editions of Mozart's works in the preceding four years, he published none thereafter. Apparently, Mozart paid off the loan in cash, so that Hoffmeister's pledge did not come into play.

62. Ibid., p. 942, 30 September 1790 (no. 585).

63. Ibid., p. 945, 8 October 1790 (no. 587).

64. Nissen, p. 683.

65. *Letters*, p. 939, ca. 17 May 1790 (no. 580).

66. Jahn, vol. 2, p. 301. Landon suggests that Mozart borrowed sums which "were larger and more frequent than hitherto realized." H. C. Robbins Landon, *1791: Mozart's Last Year*, p. 63.

67. Carl Bär, " 'Er war . . . —kein guter Wirth'; Eine Studie über Mozarts Verhältnis zum Geld," *Acta Mozartiana* 25 (1978), pp. 38–48.

68. *Briefe*, vol. 6, p. 426; Volkmar Braunbehrens, *Mozart in Vienna 1781–1791* (New York, 1990), pp. 368, 449 n. 4. The initial date of Karl Thomas's enrollment in Wenzel Heeger's school at Perchtoldsdorf is not known; it was no later than fall 1790 and may have been as early as 1787.

69. Niemetschek, p. 49; see Petition of 11 December 1791: *MDB*, pp. 421–22. Lichnowsky's 1,435 florins, the tradesmen's 918, and perhaps Puchberg's unpaid balance make the 3,000-florin figure appear to be a reasonable estimate.

70. See *MDB*, Appendix 2, p. 585; Franz Anton Gilowsky was advertised in the *Wiener Zeitung* for 2 May 1787 as having "absconded" insolvent: *MDB*, p. 291; see also Jahn, vol. 3, p. 360 n. 21. Additionally, Mozart, writing to his wife from Berlin in 1789, mentioned a loan to Prince Lichnowsky: "I had to lend him a hundred florins, as his purse was getting empty. I could not well refuse him: you will know why." *Letters*, p. 928, 23 May 1789 (no. 565).

71. Braunbehrens, *Mozart in Vienna*, p. 425.

72. Jahn, vol. 2, pp. 308, 310.

73. Niemetschek, p. 50.

74. Mortgage dated 22 November 1797: *MDB*, p. 485.

75. *Letters,* p. 945, 8 October 1790 (no. 587).

76. *MDB,* p. 311. Another patriotic song, entitled "Beim Auszug in das Feld," K. 552, was entered in the thematic catalog on 11 August 1788; and Mozart's Contredanse, "Der Sieg vom Helden Coburg," K. 587, is dated December 1789.

77. See Ernst Wangermann, *The Austrian Achievement, 1700–1800* (London, 1973), pp. 145, 171.

78. Hans Wagner, "Das Josephinische Wien und Mozart," *MJb 1978/79,* p. 9; Andrew Steptoe, *The Mozart–Da Ponte Operas* (Oxford, 1988), pp. 27–29; Braunbehrens, *Mozart in Vienna,* p. 315.

79. *MDB,* pp. 308, 310. Emperor Joseph wrote to Count Rosenberg on 23 July 1788: "The theater has a deficit of 80,000 florins. I believe that this is the moment to abandon the opera completely for the coming year." Cited in Hans-Josef Irmen, *Mozart: Mitglied geheimer Gesellschaften* ([Mechernich], 1988), p. 259.

80. *MDB,* p. 324.

81. The main source of the information in the table is Morrow, *Concert Life in Haydn's Vienna,* Appendixes 1 and 2. I have adjusted Morrow's totals by including additional concerts listed in Dexter Edge's review of Morrow's book in *Haydn Yearbook* 17 (1992), pp. 151–61. I have excluded Edge's listings of operas, operatic pasticci, *Tafelmusik,* entr'actes, and other musical performances that unnecessarily dilute the meaning of the term "concert." Naturally, there is some margin for error in such determinations.

82. [Joseph Richter], *Warum wird Kaiser Joseph von seinem Volke nicht geliebt?* (Vienna, 1787); trans. in Wangermann, *Austrian Achievement,* p. 142.

83. Journal of Joachim Daniel Preisler: *MDB,* p. 325; Michael Kelly, *Reminiscences: MDB,* p. 530. Kelly was in Vienna from 1783 to 1786. His *Reminiscences* were first published in 1826 in London.

84. Tyson, p. 142.

Chapter 28: The Journey to Berlin

1. *Letters,* p. 920, 8 April 1789 (no. 559).

2. *Briefe,* vol. 4, p. 78, before 8 April 1789 (no. 1088). For a rhymed translation, by Richard Winston, see Erich Schenk, *Mozart and His Times* (New York, 1959), p. 407.

3. *Letters,* p. 920, 10 April 1789 (no. 560).

4. Ibid., pp. 920–21, 10 April 1789 (no. 560).

5. Ibid., p. 923, 16 April 1789 to Constanze Mozart (no. 562). "Mozart received 100 ducats from the Elector," reported the *Magazin der Sächsischen Geschichte aufs Jahr 1789,* Dresden, April 1789: *NMD,* p. 56 (no. 90). Mozart did not specify the contents of the snuffbox, but this does not mean that he was concealing the amount from Constanze (as implied in *Chronik,* p. 100), for "very handsome" (*recht schene*) signifies that the box contained a substantial sum of money. See *MDB,* p. 339.

6. *Musikalische Real-Zeitung,* Speyer, 17 June 1789: *MDB,* p. 347.

7. *Berlinische Musikalische Zeitung* 1 (1805), p. 132. For another translation, see *NMD,* pp. 58–59 (no. 93).

8. *AMZ* 1 (21 November 1798), columns 116–17; trans. Maynard Solomon, "The Rochlitz Anecdotes," in *Mozart Studies,* ed. Cliff Eisen (Oxford, 1991), p. 28.

9. Proposal from the Cabinet to King Friedrich Wilhelm II, Potsdam, 26 April 1789: *MDB,* p. 340.

10. "I spent seventeen days in Potsdam," he wrote to Constanze. *Letters,* p. 926, 16 May 1789 (no. 563). The arithmetic is defective, for he was there at most from 24 April to ca. 6 May, a maximum of thirteen days. In his letter of 23 May he refers to "seventeen days" as the period during which "I was without a letter," that is from 21 April to 8 May. *Letters,* p. 928, 23 May 1789 (no. 565).

11. *Letters,* p. 925, 16 May 1789 (no. 563).

12. Probably the Scene with Rondo, "Ch'io mi scordi di te"—"Non temer, amato bene," K. 505, and perhaps the Scene, "Bella mia fiamma"—"Resta, o cara," K. 528. In his "Authentic Anecdotes," Rochlitz identified one of the concertos as the Concerto in C, K. 503. *AMZ* 1 (21 November 1798), columns 113–14; trans. Solomon, "Rochlitz Anecdotes," pp. 24–25; in a later publication he identified the other as the Concerto in B-flat, K. 456: "At his Leipzig academy,

three years before his death, he played two concertos: the cheerful and delightful B-flat major with the G-minor variations, which was engraved shortly thereafter, and the brilliant, glorious C major, which was published after his death." Johann Friedrich Rochlitz, *Für Freunde der Tonkunst* (Leipzig, 1824–32), vol. 2, p. 284 n. (at p. 287).

13. *Letters*, p. 925, 16 May 1789 (no. 563).

14. Ibid., p. 928, 23 May 1789 (no. 565).

15. Ibid., p. 925, 16 May 1789 (no. 563).

16. Karl August Varnhagen, manuscript notice: *NMD*, pp. 59–60 (no. 95).

17. *NMD*, p. 59 (no. 94).

18. Rochlitz's famous description of a conversation between Mozart and the king of Prussia, in which the king offered him a permanent post at a high salary but was refused with the words, "How can I leave my good Emperor," is wholly invented, as is his assertion that "almost every day, Mozart was required, so long as he was in Berlin, to improvise for him; in the King's chamber, he often performed quartets with several court musicians." *AMZ* 1 (10 October 1798), columns 22–23. See Solomon, "Rochlitz Anecdotes," p. 9.

19. Ernst Friedlaender, "Mozarts Beziehungen zu Berlin," in *Mitteilungen für die Mozartgemeinde in Berlin* 1 (1897), Heft 4, p. 115.

20. *Letters*, p. 928, 23 May 1789 (no. 565).

21. Ibid.

22. Anonymous ("Einem alten Veteran"), "Zur Säcularfeier Mozart's in Berlin," *Neue Berliner Musik Zeitung* (1856), column 35.

23. *Letters*, p. 930, 12 July 1789 (no. 567).

24. Ibid., p. 940, on or before 12 June 1790 (no. 582), as amended in Tyson, p. 46; see also Tyson, p. 37.

25. Tyson, p. 46; see also p. 37.

26. *Letters*, p. 922, 16 April 1789 (no. 562).

27. Ibid., p. 926, 16 May 1789 (no. 563).

28. Ibid. Mozart's arithmetic has gone somewhat awry.

29. *Letters*, p. 928, 23 May 1789 (no. 565).

30. *AMZ* 1 (10 October 1798), columns 20–22; trans. Solomon, "Rochlitz Anecdotes," pp. 7–8.

31. *MDB*, p. 379.

32. Anonymous, "Säcularfeier Mozart's," column 36. Mozart, writes Jahn, reportedly "became so deeply involved with her that it cost his friends much trouble to extricate him." Jahn, vol. 3, p. 234. See also Abert, vol. 2, p. 523.

33. *MDB*, p. 343.

34. See, for example, Théodore de Wyzewa and Georges de Saint-Foix, *Wolfgang Amédée Mozart: Sa vie musicale et son oeuvre*, vol. 2 (Paris, 1912), pp. 355, 392; Arthur Schurig, *Wolfgang Amade Mozart: Sein Leben und sein Werk* (Leipzig, 1913; 2nd ed. 1923), vol. 1, p. 19, vol. 2, p. 491; Ludwig Schiedermair, *Mozart: Sein Leben und seine Werke* (Munich, 1922), p. 326; Einstein, p. 362; Bernhard Paumgartner, *Mozart*, 6th ed. (Zurich and Freiburg im Breisgau, 1967), p. 375. Procházka was the first to raise this issue seriously, asserting that Mozart and Duschek used the intimate "Du" and that he gave her a gold ring as a sign of his affection. See Rudolf v. Procházka, *Mozart in Prag: Zum hundertjährigen Gedächtniss seines Todes* (Prague, 1892), p. 13. Jahn dismissed reports of Mozart's lovemaking with women singers in Prague in the autumn of 1787 as "professional fables." Jahn, vol. 3, pp. 130–31.

35. *Letters*, p. 280, to Mozart and his mother, 28 September 1777 (no. 211).

36. The dates of her academy and of the Hofburg recital are not known. See *MDB*, pp. 269, 271; her appearances in salons are known from Zinzendorf's diary. See Mary Sue Morrow, *Concert Life in Haydn's Vienna* (Stuyvesant, N.Y., 1989), p. 379; *MDB*, p. 269.

37. Jahn, vol. 3, p. 121.

38. *Briefe*, vol. 3, p. 532, 18–21 April 1786 (no. 950); pp. 530–31, 13 April 1786 (no. 949); p. 425, 14 October 1785 (no. 885); and p. 431, 21 October 1785 (no. 887).

39. Jahn, vol. 3, p. 135. The story was first told on the authority of Mozart's son Franz Xaver Wolfgang in *Berliner Musikzeitung Echo* (1856), no. 25, p. 198.

40. *Letters*, p. 920, 10 April 1789 (no. 560).

41. Ibid., p. 921, 13 April 1789 (no. 561).

42. Ibid.

43. 2 May is the date given by the *Berlinische Zeitungen* for Lichnowsky's departure from Potsdam for Leipzig: *MDB*, p. 341.

44. *Letters,* p. 925, 16 May 1789 (no. 563).

45. Ibid., pp. 928–29, 23 May 1789 (no. 565); see also p. 926, 16 May 1789 (no. 563).

46. Ibid., p. 925, 16 April 1789 (no. 562).

47. Ibid., p. 927, 19 May 1789 (no. 564).

48. Ibid., p. 928, 23 May 1789 (no. 565).

49. Ibid., p. 929, 23 May 1789 (no. 565).

50. Ibid., p. 921, 13 April 1789 (no. 561).

51. Ibid., p. 932, second half of July 1789 (no. 569). On 17 July he wrote to Puchberg: "My wife was wretchedly ill again yesterday. Today leeches were applied and she is, thank God, somewhat better." P. 932, 17 July 1789 (no. 568).

52. Ibid., p. 933, middle of August 1789 (no. 570). The initials "N.N." are used in the letters to avoid naming particular individuals.

53. Ibid., translation amended.

54. *Der heimliche Botschafter,* 13 December 1791: *MDB*, pp. 423–24. This report was reprinted in the *Stockholm-Posten* for 2 January 1792. See J. H. Eibl, ed., *Mozart: Die Dokumente seines Lebens, Addenda und Corrigenda* (Kassel, 1978), p. 76.

55. *Gratzer Zeitung,* 20 December 1791, reprinted in the *Pressburger Zeitung,* 21 December 1791: *MDB*, p. 426. For the contemporary documents concerning the Hofdemel affair, see Ernst Weizmann, "Der unbekannte Mozart," *Weltpresse* 12 (Vienna), nine weekly Saturday installments, from 4 February 1956 to 28 April 1956; see also *MDB*, p. 418, and Francis Carr, *Mozart & Constanze* (New York, 1984), pp. 144–56. Beethoven credited the rumors about Mozart and Frau Hofdemel: see Otto Jahn, "Mozart-Paralipomenon," *Gesammelte Aufsätze über Musik* (Leipzig, 1866), p. 231.

56. Schlichtegroll, p. 110; for another translation, see *MDB*, p. 469. These remarks do not derive from the notes and chronologies that Marianne von Berchtold supplied to Schlichtegroll, but evidently from an unidentified Viennese informant, perhaps Baron Joseph Friedrich Retzer. See Rudolph Angermüller, " 'Das musikalische Kind Mozart': Ein Beitrag zur Biographie Mozarts im ausgehenden 18. Jahrhundert," *Wiener Figaro. Mitteilungen der Mozartgemeinde Wien* 42 (May 1975), p. 30. Retzer was first identified in Henry Hausner, "Bemerkungen zu Schlichtegrolls Mozart-Biographie," *Mitteilungen der ISM* 26 (1978), p. 22.

57. Niemetschek, pp. 49, 71.

58. Ibid., p. 71. In the last phrase and in another comment that "the majority" of the scandalous stories circulating about Mozart are "bare-faced lies," Niemetschek brings the story to the edge of some significant revelation, but does not reward the curious with any details.

59. Ibid., p. 72.

60. Nissen, p. 690.

61. Ibid., pp. 688–89.

62. Johann Friedrich Rochlitz, "Anekdoten. Noch einige Kleinigkeiten aus Mozarts Leben," *AMZ* 3 (1800–1801), columns 494–97, trans. in Solomon, "Rochlitz Anecdotes," p. 40.

63. Jean-Baptiste-Antoine Suard, "Anecdotes sur Mozart," in *Mélanges de littérature* 10 (1804): *MDB*, p. 498.

64. Ignaz Ferdinand Cajetan Arnold, *Mozarts Geist* (Erfurt, 1803), trans. Jahn, vol. 2, p. 302 n. 91.

65. Jahn, vol. 2, p. 269.

66. Novello, p. 144. "Mozart taught his sister the Piano Forte. He thought him too gay in his manner, he was always in love with his pupils." Novello, p. 159.

67. Leopold Mozart wrote of her: "you were quite amazingly taken up with the little singer at the theater." *Letters,* p. 475, 11–12 February 1778 (no. 285).

68. On unstated evidence, Einstein thought she was the "only woman of whom Constanze would really have had a right to be jealous." Einstein, p. 73. Hildesheimer, too, considered her a "secret" love of Mozart's. Wolfgang Hildesheimer, *Mozart* (New York, 1982), pp. 99–100.

69. *Letters,* p. 733, 16 May 1781 (no. 404).

70. Novello, p. 150 (July 1829).

71. Karoline Pichler, *Denkwürdigkeiten aus meinem Leben* (Vienna, 1844): *MDB*, p. 557.

72. *AMZ* 27 (25 May 1825), column 349f.: *MDB*, p. 527. Surveying the issue in his customarily magisterial manner, Otto Jahn wrote that the many signs of the composer's "deep-seated

affection" for Constanze "causes us to be more surprised to hear that Mozart, whose unmarried life had been without a blemish, was, nevertheless, unfaithful to his wife." Jahn, vol. 2, p. 269.

73. Nissen, p. 628; trans. in *MDB*, p. 537.

74. Karl Benyovszky, *J. N. Hummel: Der Mensch und Künstler* (Bratislava, 1934), p. 188; trans. in Jahn, vol. 2, p. 271.

75. Jahn, vol. 2, p. 269. Jahn does not specify which of the Weber sisters made this statement.

76. His letter of 28 or 29 October from Augsburg no longer survives, but there is no reason to think it was undelivered.

77. *Letters,* p. 942, 30 September 1790 (no. 585).

78. Ibid., p. 945, 8 October 1790 (no. 587).

79. Ibid., p. 943, 30 September 1790 (no. 585).

80. Ibid., p. 944, 3 October 1790 (no. 586).

81. Ibid., p. 943, 30 September 1790 (no. 585).

82. Ibid., p. 946, 15 October 1790 (no. 588).

Chapter 29: A "Constant Sadness"

1. *Letters,* p. 823, to Baroness von Waldstätten, 28 September 1782 (no. 466).

2. Ibid.

3. *Letters,* p. 824, 2 October 1782 (no. 467).

4. Ibid., pp. 914–15, early June 1788 (no. 553).

5. Ibid., p. 917, 27 June 1788 (no. 555).

6. Ibid., pp. 929–30, 12 July 1789 (no. 567).

7. Ibid., p. 931, 12 July 1789 (no. 567).

8. Ibid., p. 941, ca. 14 August 1790 (no. 941).

9. Ibid.

10. *Letters,* p. 937, on or before 8 April 1790 (no. 576).

11. For biographical details, see Gustav Gugitz, "Mozarts Finanzen und Freund Puchberg: Ein Beitrag zur Mozart-Biographie," *Österreichische Musikzeitschrift* 7 (1952), pp. 219–25.

12. *Letters,* p. 936, end of March or beginning of April 1790 (no. 575).

13. Ibid.

14. *Letters,* p. 943, 30 September 1790 (no. 585).

15. Sophie Haibel's memoirs, Nissen, pp. 627–28; trans. in *MDB,* p. 537.

16. Ibid.

17. Niemetschek, pp. 52–53.

18. *AMZ* 1 (1798–99), column 291: *NMD,* p. 79 (no. 121).

19. Novello, p. 95.

20. Reminiscences of Joseph Lange: *MDB,* p. 503.

21. *Letters,* p. 944, 3 October 1790 (no. 586).

22. *Briefe,* vol. 4, p. 41, 4 April 1787 (no. 1044); *Letters,* p. 908, 4 April 1787 (no. 546); trans. from Jahn, vol. 2, p. 292.

23. *MDB,* p. 296.

24. *Letters,* p. 536, 6 May 1778 (no. 304); translation amended.

25. Dedication of the "Haydn" Quartets, *Letters,* p. 891, 1 September 1785 (no. 529), translation revised; p. 900, 30 September 1786 (no. 541). Similarly, Beethoven wrote of his String Quartet in F, op. 95, to Sir George Smart: "The Quartet is written for a small circle of connoisseurs and is never to be performed in public." Emily Anderson, ed. and trans., *The Letters of Beethoven* (New York, 1961), vol. 2, p. 606, ca. 11 October 1816 (no. 664).

26. Warren Kirkendale, *Fugue and Fugato in Rococo and Classical Chamber Music* (Durham, 1979), p. 163.

27. Friedrich Kerst, ed., *Die Erinnerungen an Beethoven* (Stuttgart, 1913), vol. 1, p. 51; Carl Czerny, *On the Proper Performance of All Beethoven's Works for the Piano,* ed. Paul Badura-Skoda (Vienna, 1970), p. 8; translation amended.

28. *Letters,* p. 468, 7 February 1778 (no. 283a).

29. Ibid., p. 943, Mozart to his wife, 3 October 1790 (no. 586).

30. Carl Ditters von Dittersdorf, *Lebensbeschreibung* (Leipzig, 1801), p. 237, cited in Jahn, vol. 2, p. 454. In a letter to Artaria & Co., 18 August 1788, Dittersdorf wrote of the "overwhelming and unrelenting artfulness" of Mozart's "Haydn" Quartets: *NMD,* p. 54 (no. 86). In

the later 1780s, Mozart was frequently criticized for departing from classical norms of decorum, coherence, and proportion. A leading music journal preferred Pleyel, finding his "agreeable melodies . . . not as difficult as Clementi's and Mozart's sorcery; he is more true to nature, without, however, violating the rules of composition." Cramer's *Magazin der Musik,* Hamburg, 26 July 1787: *NMD,* p. 48 (no. 76). For further examples of classicizing critiques of Mozart dating from 1789, see *NMD,* pp. 56 (no. 89), 57 (no. 91), and 57–58 (no. 92).

31. Discovered by Philippe A. Autexier, these are "Bey Eröffnung der Tafelloge," "Lied im Nahmen der Armen," and "Kettenlied." See Autexier, "Cinq Lieder inconnus de W. A. Mozart," *International Journal of Musicology* 1 (1992), pp. 67–79. The texts are by Gottlieb Leon; the music is not extant.

32. *Letters,* p. 938, beginning of May 1790 (no. 578).

33. Ibid., p. 95, to an unknown young girl, 1769 (no. 70); *Letters,* pp. 581–83, 30 July 1778 (no. 318).

34. *Letters,* p. 924, 16 April 1789 (no. 562); translation amended. For Mozart's emulation of his father, see also Florian Langegger, *Mozart: Vater und Sohn. Eine psychologische Untersuchung* (Zurich, 1978), pp. 119–21.

35. Freud observed that when an ambivalently loved object has been lost in reality and then taken into the ego, there occurs in the melancholiac "a cruel self-depreciation of the ego combined with relentless self-criticism and bitter self-reproaches." These self-reproaches are to be regarded as an attempt to dislodge the intruder, or at least to diminish its dominion. Hopelessly divided, one part of the ego rages relentlessly against the other, which "is the one which has been altered by introjection and which contains the lost object." Freud, *Group Psychology and the Analysis of the Ego,* in *Standard Edition of the Complete Psychological Works of Sigmund Freud,* ed. and trans. James Strachey (London, 1953–74), vol 18, p. 109; see also p. 133.

36. *Letters,* p. 938, beginning of May 1790 (no. 578), and p. 945, 8 October 1790 (no. 587).

37. Ibid., pp. 938–39, first half of May 1790 (no. 579).

38. Ibid., p. 939, on or before 17 May 1790 (no. 580).

39. Ibid., p. 936, end of March or beginning of April 1790 (no. 575).

40. Ignaz von Seyfried to Georg Friedrich Treitschke, ca. 1840: *MDB,* p. 556.

41. Program of Mozart's Frankfurt Concert, 15 October 1790: *MDB,* p. 374.

42. *Letters,* p. 946, 15 October 1790 (no. 588).

43. Ibid., p. 947, 23 October 1790 (no. 590).

44. Ibid., p. 948, before 4 November 1790 (no. 591).

45. Ibid., pp. 947–48, before 4 November 1790 (no. 591).

Chapter 30: The Last Year

1. The songs, and a third entitled "Das Kinderspiel," K. 598, were published in 1791 in *Liedersammlung für Kinder und Kinderfreunde am Clavier: Frühlingslieder* (Vienna, 1791).

2. Tyson, pp. 134–35, 156. Without pretending to certainty, Tyson suggests that the autograph score of the concerto, written on music paper that otherwise is primarily used on works that are datable to the period between late 1787 and early 1789, may have been started as early as 1788, perhaps, like the three last symphonies, in expectation of a concert performance (p. 156). Plath's handwriting analyses do not confirm the early date, and Tyson (p. 51) cautions that, on average, a given watermark occurs in Mozart scores extending over a time span of somewhat more than two years.

3. For a thorough discussion of the opera's commission and composition, see H.C. Robbins Landon, *1791: Mozart's Last Year* (New York, 1988), pp. 84–101.

4. For details of the chronology and order of composition, see Peter Branscombe, *W. A. Mozart: "Die Zauberflöte"* (Cambridge, England, 1991), pp. 84–86, summarizing findings by Alan Tyson and Karl-Heinz Köhler.

5. For example, in April he wrote to Puchberg, "Come to our little concert in the evening." *Letters,* p. 949, between 21 and 27 April 1791 (no. 593).

6. Letter of 26 October 1790: *MDB,* p. 378.

7. *Letters,* p. 945, 8 October 1790 (no. 587).

8. See Landon, *1791,* pp. 42–46. Manuscript copies of piano reductions were advertised by Lausch as early as 12 March, Artaria by 16 March, Traeg by 23 March; on 10 August Artaria advertised engraved editions of four volumes each containing twelve German dances or minuets arranged for piano. See *MDB,* pp. 387–88, 395–96, 397, and 399. Tyson proposes earlier dates

for K. 609 and K. 610 (Tyson, pp. 33, 35, 227–28). The Concerto in B-flat, K. 595, was also published in parts by Artaria & Co., on 10 August.

9. Constanze Mozart, petition to Emperor Leopold II, 11 December 1791: *MDB*, pp. 421–22.

10. *Letters*, p. 957, 25 June 1791 (no. 603). He also alludes to his favorable prospects in a letter to Constanze Mozart of the following week: p. 959, 3 July 1791 (no. 606).

11. *Letters*, pp. 949–50, Mozart to the Vienna Municipal Council (*Magistrat*), beginning of May 1791 (no. 594). (Deutsch dates the letter "about 25 April," *MDB*, p. 393.) Decree of the Council, 9 May 1791: *MDB*, p. 395.

12. Johann Haibel to Wolfgang Heribert von Dalberg, 10 December 1791: *NMD*, p. 73 (no. 117).

13. Letter of 15 September 1791: *MDB*, pp. 406–7.

14. *Letters*, p. 961, 5 July 1791 (no. 609).

15. Ibid., p. 965, 9 July 1791 (no. 612). If the date of this letter is correct, he did not reach Baden before 10 July.

16. Ibid., p. 959, 2 July 1791 (no. 605).

17. Ibid., p. 952, 6 June 1791 (no. 597).

18. Ibid., p. 963, 6 July 1791 (no. 610).

19. Ibid., p. 961, 5 July 1791 (no. 609).

20. Ibid., p. 965, 9 July 1791 (no. 612).

21. Nissen, p. 673.

22. Jahn, vol. 3, p. 282, without any further documentation.

23. See Ursula Mauthe, *Mozarts "Pamina": Anna Gottlieb* (Augsburg, 1986), pp. 16, 19–20; see especially the anonymous, unreliable memoirs attributed to Joseph Deiner: *MDB*, p. 564. The memoirs, which were published in the Vienna *Morgen-Post* for 28 January 1856, may well derive from Anna Gottlieb, who died one week later, on 4 February 1856. It may be that she herself had interviewed Deiner before his death in 1823 or that she had in her possession his written reminiscences of Mozart, which she furnished, together with her own, to a journalist-interviewer. The misprint "Elossek" for "Closset" (p. 564) suggests a misreading from a manuscript. Gottlieb tended to grandiosity in later years, introducing herself to strangers with the words, "Ich bin die erste Pamina." See Wilhelm Kuhe, *My Musical Recollections* (London, 1896), pp. 11–12.

24. Jahn, vol. 3, p. 285.

25. *Briefe*, vol. 4, p. 140, 25 June 1791 (no. 1170); *Letters*, p. 956, 25 June 1791 (unnumbered letter).

26. *Letters*, pp. 963–64, 7 July 1791 (no. 611).

27. Ibid., p. 964, 7 July 1791 (no. 611).

28. Ibid., p. 961, 5 July 1791 (no. 609).

29. Ibid., p. 951, 6 June 1791 (no. 597). The passage is written in French.

30. Ibid., p. 954, 12 June 1791 (no. 600).

31. Ibid.

32. "On the Sense of Loneliness," in Melanie Klein, *Envy and Gratitude and Other Works 1946–1963* (London, 1975), p. 300.

33. *Letters*, p. 385, 22 November 1777 (no. 247).

34. In the slow recovery from melancholia, the "punishing superego gradually lost its destructive features, while exalted ideals, social interests, cultural strivings, and love relationships were built up again, which the strengthened and elated ego then pursued successfully and enjoyed intensely." Edith Jacobson, *Depression: Comparative Studies of Normal, Neurotic, and Psychotic Conditions* (New York, 1971), p. 227.

Chapter 31: The Final Journey

1. This and the following quotations are from Niemetschek, pp. 41–44. Rochlitz's even more melodramatic account of the same events has not been utilized because it is merely an elaboration of Niemetschek's, without any verifiable independent source. See Maynard Solomon, "The Rochlitz Anecdotes," *Mozart Studies*, ed. Cliff Eisen (Oxford, 1991), pp. 31–36.

2. Anton Herzog, "Wahre und ausführliche Geschichte des Requiems von W. A. Mozart": *MDB*, p. 551. For several manuscripts to which Walsegg appended his name, see Otto Biba, "Par Monsieur François Comte de Walsegg," *Mitteilungen der ISM*, September 1981, pp. 34–40. For

Walsegg's background and marriage, see Walther Brauneis, "'Dies irae, dies illa—Tag des Zornes, Tag der Klage': Auftrag, Enstehung und Vollendung von Mozarts *Requiem*," *Jahrbuch des Vereins für Geschichte der Stadt Wien* 47–48 (1991–92), pp. 33–39.

3. Herzog, "Geschichte des Requiems": *MDB*, p. 552.

4. Niemetschek, p. 44 n. 8.

5. *MDB*, pp. 312 and 583. Gugitz suggests that Puchberg may have "mediated between Walsegg and Mozart in order that the latter might earn something." Gustav Gugitz, *Mozartiana* (Vienna, 1964), p. 48. Niemetschek (p. 44 n. 8) discreetly questioned the veracity of the account of the Requiem commission, writing that he "speaks of the event as he has often heard it from the lips of Mozart's widow, and leaves it to the reader to draw his own conclusions."

6. Maunder suggests that the date "1792" on the autograph of the score represents Mozart's own anticipated completion date. Richard Maunder, *Mozart's Requiem: On Preparing a New Edition* (Oxford, 1988), p. 10. A Munich handwriting expert concluded, however, that the inscription "di me W: A: Mozart mpr. ./ 1792" is actually in Süssmayr's hand. See Johannes Dalchow et al., *Mozart's Tod, 1791–1971* (Pähl, 1971), pp. 284–87. For the complicated matter of the posthumous completion of the Requiem, see Christoph Wolff, *Mozart's Requiem: Historical and Analytical Studies, Documents, Score* (Berkeley and Los Angeles, 1993); Wolff, "The Composition and Completion of Mozart's Requiem, 1791–1792," in Eisen, *Mozart Studies*, pp. 61–82; Maunder, *Mozart's Requiem;* and Paul Moseley, "Mozart's Requiem: A Revaluation of the Evidence," *Journal of the Royal Musical Association* 114 (1989), pp. 203–37.

7. Herzog, "Geschichte des Requiems". *MDB*, p. 553.

8. Plath found it "highly probable that the first sketches fell in September 1791." Wolfgang Plath, "Über Skizzen zu Mozarts 'Requiem,'" *Bericht über den Internationalen Musikwissenschaftlichen Kongress Kassel 1962,* ed. Georg Reichert and Martin Just (Kassel, 1963), p. 185; Plath, p. 74; Alan Tyson, personal communication, cited in Maunder, *Mozart's Requiem,* p. 206 n. 17.

9. See Niemetschek, p. 82; F. Giegling, "Zu den Recitativen von Mozarts oper 'Titus,'" *MJb 1967,* pp. 121–26. Maunder questions whether Süssmayr traveled to Prague and wrote the recitatives: see Maunder, review of *Mozart's Requiem: Geschichte, Musik, Dokumente* by Christoph Wolff, in *Music & Letters* 74 (1993), p. 442.

10. *Prager Oberpostamtszeitung,* 6 September 1791: *MDB*, p. 403.

11. See Karl Pfannhauser, "Mozarts Krönungsmesse," *Mitteilungen der ISM* 11, nos. 3–4 (1963), pp. 3–11; for Mozart's music during the coronation festivities, see H. C. Robbins Landon, *1791: Mozart's Last Year* (New York, 1989), pp. 103–4, 111–14, 118–20.

12. *Chronik,* p. 112; Empress Maria Louisa to her daughter-in-law Empress Maria Theresa, Prague, 7 September 1791: *NMD,* p. 70 (no. 109). See J. H. Eibl, "'. . . Una porcheria tedesca'? Zur Uraufführung von Mozarts *La clemenza di Tito*," *Österreichische Musikzeitung* 31 (1976), pp. 329–34.

13. Count Heinrich Rottenhan on Guardasoni's Petition, 29 October 1791: *MDB*, p. 411.

14. *Krönungsjournal für Prag,* 1791: *MDB*, p. 405; translation amended.

15. Niemetschek, p. 82. In an earlier report, Niemetschek wrote: "The subject is too simple to be able to interest the mass of people busy with coronation festivities, balls and illuminations. . . . There is a certain Grecian simplicity, a still sublimity, which strike a sensitive heart gently but none the less profoundly." Cited in Paul Nettl, "Prager Mozartiana," *Mitteilungen der ISM* 9, nos. 3–4 (1960), pp. 4–5; trans. Landon, *1791,* pp. 117–18.

16. Niemetschek, p. 43. In the second edition of his book (1808), Niemetschek, perhaps influenced by Rochlitz's fictionalized account, added: "A foreboding sense of his approaching death seemed to have produced this melancholy mood—for at this time he already had the seed of the disease which was so soon to carry him off." *MDB*, p. 510. After Mozart's death, a Berlin newspaper reported that "he returned home from Prague a sick man, and continued to get worse." *Musikalisches Wochenblatt* (Berlin), ?31 December 1791, no. 12, p. 94: *MDB*, p. 432.

17. See, however, the later review in *Vertraute Briefe zur Charakteristik von Wien* (Görlitz, 1793), vol. 2, pp. 50–53, translated in Peter Branscombe, *W. A. Mozart: "Die Zauberflöte"* (Cambridge, England, 1991), pp. 158–59.

18. *Letters,* pp. 966–67, 7–8 October 1791 (no. 614).

19. Ibid., p. 967, 7–8 October 1791 (no. 614).

20. Ibid., p. 969, 8–9 October 1791 (no. 615).

21. Ibid., p. 970, 14 October 1791 (no. 616); translation amended.

22. Ibid., p. 967, 7–8 October 1791 (no. 614). The reference is to the last movement of the Clarinet Concerto, K. 622.

23. Ibid., p. 968, 7–8 October 1791 (no. 614).

24. Ibid., p. 971, 14 October 1791 (no. 616).

25. Ibid., p. 970, 8–9 October 1791 (no. 615).

26. Ibid., p. 942, 28 September 1790 (no. 584).

27. Ibid., p. 968, 7–8 October 1791 (no. 614).

28. For the terms of Josepha Weber Hofer's contract with Schikaneder's troupe, see Blümml, pp. 128–30; see also pp. 32–33. Dent observed: "It was hardly dignified for a musician who had been constantly associated with court life at Vienna and elsewhere, both as composer and pianist, to undertake to collaborate in a fairy play to be acted in what was little more than a wooden barn, to an audience that cared only for trivial and vulgar melody, 'gag' and 'business' of the silliest kind, crude spectacular effects and the introduction of a whole menagerie of animals on the stage." Edward J. Dent, *Mozart's Operas: A Critical Study*, 2nd ed. (London, 1962), p. 211. Whatever the justice of these observations, Dent fails to credit Schikaneder's innovative contributions to repertory and stagecraft in the German theater of his time.

29. Niemetschek, *Leben des K. K. Kapellmeisters Wolfgang Gottlieb Mozart* (Prague, 1798), p. 34; trans. Niemetschek, p. 43; translation amended. Niemetschek's account is taken over verbatim by Nissen, pp. 563–64.

30. Novello, p. 128.

31. According to the Novellos, Constanze Mozart placed this conversation as early as "six months" before her husband's death (Novello, p. 125), which, although it gets the chronology of the Requiem's composition wrong, is not necessarily an error, for Mozart's melancholia was not a sudden development, but a condition of long standing, one that affected him even during periods of great productivity.

32. Novello, p. 125. Mozart's poisoning fantasy has given rise to many speculations that he was murdered—by a range of potential assassins, including Antonio Salieri, the Jews and Freemasons, and a jealous husband. For a refutation of the assassination theories, see Otto Erich Deutsch, "Die Legende von Mozarts Vergiftung," *MJb 1964*, pp. 7–18, and William Stafford, *Mozart's Death* [U.S. title: *The Mozart Myths*] (London, 1991), pp. 31–55. For a conspiratorial view involving the Freemasons in Mozart's death, see Dalchow et al., *Mozarts Tod*.

33. Novello, p. 128. The outline of the Requiem legend began to emerge only a month after Mozart's death: "So Mozart had to write it, which he did, often with tears in his eyes, constantly saying: I fear that I am writing a Requiem for myself; he completed it a few days before his death." *Salzburger Intelligenzblatt*, 7 January 1792: *NMD*, p. 76 (no. 119). For a later version of this anecdote, see *MDB*, p. 439.

34. Otto Fenichel, *The Psychoanalytic Theory of Neurosis* (New York, 1945), p. 398: "The feeling of being poisoned contains a piece of psychological truth. The patient has introjected an object that now disturbs him from within." See Edoardo Weiss, "Der Vergiftungswahn im Lichte der Introjektions- und Projektionsvorgänge," *Zeitschrift für Psychoanalyse* 12 (1926), pp. 466–77. Persecutory anxieties or delusions, often involving feelings of having been poisoned, have long been noted by observers of melancholia, beginning with the ancients. Aretaeus (ca. 150 A.D.) was one of the first to note that the melancholiac is "suspicious of poisoning." See Stanley W. Jackson, *Melancholia and Depression from Hippocratic Times to Modern Times* (New Haven and London, 1986), pp. 39, 251; see also pp. 302 (Thomas Arnold) and 321 (Freud).

35. Niemetschek, p. 43.

36. Novello, p. 125.

37. Ibid.

38. Ibid. The parallel passage in Vincent Novello's diary reads: "His melancholy forebodings again returned in a few days, when he again set to work on the Requiem." Novello, p. 128.

39. Niemetschek, p. 44.

40. Nissen, p. 572.

41. The standard work is Carl Bär, *Mozart: Krankheit, Tod, Begräbnis*, Schriftenreihe der ISM, 1 (2nd ed., Salzburg, 1972), esp. pp. 88–118. Bär's diagnosis of rheumatic fever, which accounts for most of Mozart's reported symptoms, is augmented by Boissevain's suggestion of bacterial endocarditis with cardiac valve damage. See Willem Boissevain, "Neue Erklärung der Todesursache Mozarts: 'Hitziges Frieselfieber' war bakterielle Herzklappenentzündung," *Mitteilungen der ISM* 38 (1990), pp. 139–44. In one of the first obituaries, Mozart's death was

attributed to "Herzwassersucht" (dropsy of the heart), suggesting that the inflammatory miliary fever ("Hitziger Frieselfieber") that was given as the official cause of death also had cardiac sequelae. See Walther Brauneis, "Unveröffentlichte Nachrichten zum Dezember 1791 aus einer Wiener Lokalzeitung," *Mitteilungen der ISM* 39 (July 1991), pp. 165–66; see also *Musikalische Korrespondenz der teutschen filharmonischen Gesellschaft,* Speyer, 28 December 1791: *MDB,* p. 428, and *Musikalisches Wochenblatt,* Berlin, for ?31 December 1791: *MDB,* p. 432. Davies proposes that Mozart died from Henoch-Schönlein syndrome: see Peter J. Davies, "Mozart's Illnesses and Death," *Journal of the Royal Society of Medicine* 76 (1983), pp. 776–85; Davies, *Mozart in Person: His Character and Health* (New York, 1989), passim. The evidence adduced in support of Davies's hypothesis has not been found universally persuasive; see, for example, John Stone, "Mozart's Illnesses and Death," in H. C. Robbins Landon, *The Mozart Compendium: A Guide to Mozart's Life and Music* (New York, 1990), p. 138.

42. Dr. Eduard Guldener von Lobes to Giuseppe Carpani, 10 June 1824: *MDB,* pp. 522–23. Guldener wrote a very similar letter in English to Sigismund Neukomm at about the same time, which has some important variants. See Bär, pp. 59–60. It should be noted that contemporary death registers do not confirm Guldener's assertion that deaths from rheumatic or inflammatory fever were widespread. See Dalchow et al., *Mozarts Tod,* p. 222.

43. According to a belated report, after Mozart "could no longer write himself, because his hands were crippled, he dictated to Süssmayr up to the day of his death." J. P. Lyser, in 1856, allegedly on the authority of Sophie Weber Haibel. Cited in Stafford, *Mozart's Death,* p. 62, from Johann Friedrich Kayser, *Mozart-Album* (Hamburg, 1856), p. 64.

44. Nissen, pp. 573–75; this and the following are cited from *Letters,* pp. 975–77, Sophie Weber Haibel to Nissen, 7 April 1825.

45. Mozart probably did not receive the last rites. See page 497 and note 76, below.

46. Novello, p. 215. The Anna Gottlieb–Joseph Deiner memoirs tell the story somewhat differently and less reliably: "As Mozart's illness took on a graver character with each minute, his wife summoned Dr. Sallaba again on 5 December 1791. He came, soon followed by Kapellmeister Süssmeyer, to whom Sallaba secretly confided that Mozart would not survive the coming night. Dr. Sallaba also prescribed a medicine for Mozart's wife, as she too was unwell. . . . Süssmeyer remained at the side of the dying composer. At 12 o'clock in the night Mozart raised himself in his bed, his eyes staring, then he sank back with his head towards the wall, and seemed to fall asleep again. At 4 o'clock in the morning he was a corpse": *MDB,* pp. 564–65.

47. *Letters,* p. 977, 7 April 1825.

48. Nissen, Anhang (Appendix), p. 168 n.

49. Niemetschek, p. 44.

50. Seyfried to Treitschke, ca. 1840 (?): *MDB,* p. 556.

51. *Letters,* p. 907, 4 April 1787 (no. 546).

52. Herbert Marcuse, "The Ideology of Death," in *The Meaning of Death,* ed. Herman Feifel (New York, 1959), p. 67.

53. Karl Thomas Mozart, undated memorandum, in Dalchow et al., *Mozarts Tod,* p. 231; trans. Landon, *1791,* p. 159.

54. Nissen, memorandum, in Dalchow et al., *Mozarts Tod,* p. 30.

55. Nissen, p. 572.

56. *Letters,* p. 977, Sophie Weber Haibel to Nissen, 7 April 1825.

57. Nissen, p. 572. Constanze told the Novellos how she "threw herself on the bed and sought to catch the fever of which he died, but it was not to be. There were moments, she declared, when she not only prayed sincerely to die but that she did not love her children, every thing was hateful to her in the world, yet here I am still and have gone through all this suffering." Novello, pp. 97–98.

58. *MDB,* p. 565.

59. Karl Pfannhauser, "Epilegomena Mozartiana," *MJb 1971/72,* p. 284; trans. Landon, *1791,* p. 168; translation amended.

60. Register of Deaths of St. Stephen's Cathedral, 5 December 1791: *MDB,* p. 416.

61. Register of Deaths of St. Stephen's Parish, 6 December 1791: *MDB,* p. 417; translation amended.

62. Bär, pp. 127–34; Volkmar Braunbehrens, *Mozart in Vienna 1781–1791* (New York, 1990), p. 418.

63. See Bär, pp. 127–30.

64. Ibid., pp. 134–36. See note 42 above.

65. Rudolf Lewicki, "Aus Nissens Kollektaneen," *Mozarteums Mitteilungen* 2, (November 1919), p. 29. The scenario of a burial on the morning of the seventh is outlined in *Briefe*, vol. 6, p. 663.

66. *MDB*, p. 565. Scholars dispute whether the blessing took place in the Chapel of the Cross (*Kreuzkapelle*) or the Crucifix Chapel. See Bär, pp. 132–34; Walther Brauneis, "Mozarts Begräbnis," in *Zaubertöne—Mozart in Wien: Ausstellungskatalog* (Vienna, 1990), pp. 542–43; Brauneis, " 'Dies irae, dies illa,' " p. 42.

67. *MDB*, p. 565.

68. "It is therefore quite evident . . . that if a strong wind was approaching or was already measuring maximum, the friends would abandon their plan to accompany Mozart's funeral procession on foot to St. Marx." Bär, p. 130. Bär escalates the windy conditions into a sand- or dust-storm.

69. For speculations on their identities, see Jahn, vol. 3, p. 359; Bär, pp. 153–54. Salieri told Hüttenbrenner that he had accompanied Mozart's corpse in the funeral procession. See *AMZ* 27 (1825), column 797: *NMD*, p. 71 (no. 113). "No original sources exist for the funeral procession from Mozart's house to the Cathedral, the consecration, the accompanying of the hearse to the cemetery, the burial." Dalchow et al., *Mozarts Tod*, p. 162. Although their explanation—an esoteric conspiracy of Masonic assassins—does not hold, Dalchow, Duda, and Kerner are right to raise questions about the obscurities surrounding Mozart's death, to ask why there is no contemporary report of a funeral procession from the house in the Rauhensteingasse to St. Stephen's Cathedral; no authentic description of the blessing at St. Stephen's; no believable memoir by anyone accompanying the body en route to the cemetery; and no witness to the burial.

70. *Briefe*, vol. 4, p. 520, Constanze Nissen to Johann Ritter von Lucam, 14 October 1841 (no. 1472). It speaks for at least the partial accuracy of Deiner and Gottlieb that they knew that Constanze Mozart was not present at the cathedral.

71. Bär, p. 149.

72. Dalchow et al., *Mozarts Tod*, p. 128.

73. Bär, p. 140; Erich Schenk, *Mozart and His Times* (New York, 1959), p. 446 n. 2 (translator's note); Braunbehrens, *Mozart in Vienna*, pp. 413–18. Brauneis argues that Mozart was buried in an "ordinary individual grave" rather than in a communal grave. See Walther Brauneis, "Mozarts Begräbnis," pp. 544–45; Brauneis, " 'Dies irae, dies illa,' " p. 42.

74. *MDB*, p. 417.

75. Letter of 1 September 1784 to Therese Heyne, in Georg Forster, *Sämmtliche Schriften*, ed. by his daughter (Leipzig, 1843), vol. 7, p. 275; trans. in Jahn, vol. 2, p. 354.

76. "Die Geistlichen weigerten sich zu kommen, da der Kranke sie nicht selbst rufen liess." Lewicki, "Aus Nissens Kolakteneen," p. 28. A further note by Nissen says: "If he hadn't been neglected, he would have received the last rites." Ibid.

77. *Letters*, p. 907, 4 April 1787 (no. 546).

78. Ibid., p. 561, 9 July 1778 (no. 313).

79. Nissen, p. 572.

80. Novello, p. 215.

81. *Der heimliche Botschafter*, 16 December 1791: *MDB*, p. 425; see also *Musikalisches Wochenblatt*, Berlin, ?31 December 1791: *MDB*, p. 432.

82. *Auszug aller europäischen Zeitungen*, Vienna, 13 December 1791, cited in Walther Brauneis, "Unveröffentlichte Nachrichten zum Dezember 1791 aus einer Wiener Lokalzeitung," *Mitteilungen der ISM* 39 (July 1991), p. 166.

83. Karl Friedrich Hensler, Masonic Oration on Mozart's Death: *MDB*, p. 448.

84. *Prager Oberpostamtszeitung*, 17 December 1791: *NMD*, p. 123 (no. 179).

85. *Der heimliche Botschafter*, 13 December 1791: *MDB*, pp. 423–24.

86. *Magyar Hírmondó*, 4 January 1793; *Prager Neue Zeitung*, ?9 February 1794: *MDB*, pp. 467, 470.

87. *Wiener Zeitung*, 18 March 1795: *MDB*, p. 473.

88. *MDB*, p. 485; Erich Valentin, "Das Testament der Constanze Mozart-Nissen," *Neues MJb* 2 (1942), p. 137. The total includes 7,449 florins that she inherited from Nissen.

89. *Briefe*, vol. 4, p. 454, Georg and Constanze Nissen to Karl Thomas Mozart, 13 June 1810 (no. 1388); translation in *MDB*, p. 513; translation revised.

90. A. Hyatt King, *Mozart in Retrospect: Studies in Criticism and Bibliography* (London, 1955), p. 17; see Gernot Gruber, *Mozart und die Nachwelt* (Salzburg and Vienna, 1985), chapters 1 and 2.

91. K⁶, Anhang D, pp. 915–17.

92. Niemetschek, p. 87.

93. These materials, along with additional documents furnished by Marianne von Berchtold, were retained in the B&H archives; they were first published in Gustav Nottebohm, *Mozartiana* (Leipzig, 1880). During her negotiations with B&H, Constanze Mozart considered appointing Friedrich Rochlitz, the editor of B&H's house journal, the *AMZ,* as Mozart's biographer: "Please give my best regards to the intelligent Herr Rochlitz, whom I regard as the future biographer of my late husband." *Briefe,* vol. 4, p. 275, Constanze to B&H, 10 October 1799 (no. 1259).

94. *AMZ* 1 (6 February 1799, columns 289–91, and 11 September 1799, columns 854–56): *NMD,* pp. 77–80 (no. 121).

95. *Briefe,* vol. 4, p. 260, 4 August 1799 (no. 1250).

96. Ibid.

97. *AMZ* 2 (22 January 1800), columns 300–301: *MDB,* pp. 493–94.

98. *Briefe,* vol. 4, p. 263, Constanze Mozart to B&H, 13 August 1799 (no. 1253).

99. Ibid., vol. 4, p. 312, 8 February 1800 (no. 1280).

100. Novello, pp. 98, 81–82; Solomon, "Rochlitz Anecdotes," pp. 9–11.

101. Rudolph Angermüller, "Testament, Kodizill, Nachtrag und Sperrelation der Freifrau Maria Anna von Berchtold zu Sonnenburg, geb. Mozart (1751–1829)," *MJb 1986,* p. 102.

102. Ibid., p. 106.

103. *Briefe,* vol. 4, p. 456, to Joseph Sonnleithner, 2 July 1819 (no. 1391).

104. Ibid., p. 477, Constanze Nissen [actually Nissen himself writing under his wife's name] to Benedikt Schack, 16 February 1826 (no. 1407).

105. See Walter Hummel, *Nannerl: Wolfgang Amadeus Mozarts Schwester* (Zurich, Leipzig, and Vienna, 1952), pp. 83–84; Eva Rieger, *Nannerl Mozart: Leben einer Künstlerin im 18. Jahrhundert* (Frankfurt, 1990), pp. 269–70.

106. See Nissen, pp. 595–96.

107. Valentin, "Das Testament der Constanze Mozart-Nissen," p. 129.

Chapter 32: The Power of Music

1. Translation from Wye Jamison Allanbrook, *Rhythmic Gesture in Mozart: "Le nozze di Figaro" and "Don Giovanni"* (Chicago and London, 1983), pp. 341–42.

2. Allanbrook, *Rhythmic Gesture,* p. 80.

3. Edward J. Dent, *Mozart's Operas: A Critical Study,* 2nd ed. (London, 1947; reprint 1962), p. 206.

4. Joseph Kerman, *Opera as Drama* (New York, 1956; rev. ed., Berkeley and Los Angeles, 1988), p. 94.

5. Allanbrook, *Rhythmic Gesture,* pp. 324–25.

6. Wye Jamison Allanbrook, "Mozart's Happy Endings: A New Look at the 'Convention' of the 'lieto fine,'" *MJb 1984/85,* pp. 4–5.

7. Ivan Nagel, *Autonomy and Mercy: Reflections on Mozart's Operas,* trans. Marion Faber and Ivan Nagel (Cambridge, Mass., 1991), p. 36.

8. Jean Starobinski writes: "Vengeance is nothing other than the expression of personal wish. The initiate has abdicated this wish or passion," whereas the Queen of the Night and her followers "know only selfish passion: jealousy, anger, murder, revenge." Jean Starobinski, "Light and Power in *The Magic Flute,*" in *1789: The Emblems of Reason,* trans. Barbara Bray (Charlottesville, 1982), p. 220.

9. See Brigid Brophy, *Mozart the Dramatist* (London, 1964; rev. ed., 1988), pp. 152–56. Brophy uncovers other Orpheus parallels: Orpheus's lute is transformed into a flute, and just as Orpheus may not look at Eurydice, Tamino may not speak to Pamina.

10. Nagel, *Autonomy and Mercy,* p. 82.

11. Kerman, *Opera as Drama,* p. 90.

12. *Die Zauberflöte* is firmly in the tradition of authoritarian utopian literature: one of the main sources of its libretto is Abbé Jean Terrasson's *Séthos* (1731), which in turn was heavily influenced by Fénelon's *Les Aventures de Télémaque* (1699), a favorite book in the Mozart family. And I think it likely that Tommaso Campanella's *City of the Sun* (1623), with its priesthood of

"Solarians" and its temples of Wisdom and Reason, provided the model for *Die Zauberflöte's* misogynist heliopolis, either directly or through the mediation of Campanella's numerous imitators. See Frank E. Manuel and Fritzie P. Manuel, *Utopian Thought in the Western World* (Cambridge, Mass., 1979), and Glenn Negley and J. Max Patrick, eds., *The Quest for Utopia: An Anthology of Imaginary Societies* (New York, 1952; reprint Garden City, 1962). Of course, many aspects of Masonic social thought are a subspecies of this brand of utopianism and it has been argued that *Die Zauberflöte*, with its depiction of a crusading "missionary order" dedicated to "the moral education of humanity," is the "dramatic expression of the political hopes, humanitarian ideals, and educational aspirations of Illuminist Freemasonry." Ernst Wangermann, *The Austrian Achievement, 1700–1800* (London, 1973), pp. 152–53.

13. Edward T. Cone, "The World of Opera and Its Inhabitants," in *Music: A View from Delft—Selected Essays,* ed. Robert P. Morgan (Chicago and London, 1989), p. 131.

Appendix: Mozart's Vienna Earnings

1. Mozart refers to the planned concerts in *Letters,* p. 915, to Puchberg, early June 1788 (no. 553). See H. C. Robbins Landon, *1791: Mozart's Last Year* (New York, 1989), pp. 31–33; Mary Sue Morrow, "Mozart and Viennese Concert Life," *Musical Times* 126 (1985), pp. 453–54; Volkmar Braunbehrens, *Mozart in Vienna 1781–1791* (New York, 1990), pp. 323–24; Neal Zaslaw, *Mozart's Symphonies: Context, Performance Practice, Reception* (Oxford, 1989), pp. 421–22. For a dissenting view, see Andrew Steptoe, "Mozart and his last three symphonies—a myth laid to rest?" *Musical Times* 132 (1991), pp. 550–51.

2. Cramer's *Magazin der Musik,* 9 May 1783: *MDB,* p. 215.

3. Costs were 115 florins at Heinrich Marchand's academy at the Burgtheater on 2 March 1785: *Briefe,* vol. 3, p. 378, 12 March 1785 (no. 850). Deutsch believes that the figure of 240 florins for the *Don Giovanni* performance is for the "stage band." *MDB,* p. 314. For expenses, receipts, and profits of concerts in Vienna, see Mary Sue Morrow, *Concert Life in Haydn's Vienna: Aspects of a Developing Musical and Social Institution* (Stuyvesant, N.Y., 1989), pp. 126–39.

4. *Letters,* p. 888, 12 March 1785 (no. 525).

5. *Briefe,* vol. 3, p. 378, 12 March 1785 (no. 850).

6. *Autobiography of Karl von Dittersdorf, Dictated to His Son,* trans. A. D. Coleridge (London, 1896; reprint New York, 1970), pp. 256, 257–58.

7. One souverain d'or = 13.5 florins. *Letters,* p. 888, 12 March 1785 (no. 525).

8. *Briefe,* vol. 6, p. 177.

9. *Letters,* p. 895, 13 January 1786 (no. 536).

10. Morrow, using a figure of ca. 100 florins in expenses per concert, arrives at somewhat higher profits. Morrow, *Concert Life in Haydn's Vienna,* p. 135.

11. *Letters,* pp. 789–90, 22 December 1781 (no. 438).

12. Ibid., p. 947, 23 October 1790 (no. 590).

13. "Mozart received 100 ducats from the Elector, Kraft 50." *Magazin der Sächsischen Geschichte aufs Jahr 1789,* Dresden, April 1789: *NMD,* p. 56 (no. 90); "I received a very handsome snuffbox," wrote Mozart, *Letters,* p. 923, 16 April 1789 (no. 562); see also *MDB,* p. 339 (14 April 1789).

14. *Letters,* p. 720, 24–28 March 1781 (no. 395), and p. 723, 11 April 1781 (no. 398).

15. Ibid., p. 723, 11 April 1781 (no. 398).

16. Ibid., pp. 744–45, 16 June 1781 (no. 411), and p. 795, 23 January 1782 (no. 442).

17. See Heinz Wolfgang Hamann, "Mozarts Schülerkreis," *MJb 1962/63,* pp. 115–39, as expanded and corrected in Carl Bär, "Mozarts Schülerkreis," *Acta Mozartiana* 11 (1964), pp. 58–64.

18. *Letters,* p. 939, to Puchberg, on or before 17 May 1790 (no. 580).

19. See O. E. Deutsch, "Mozarts Verleger," *MJb 1955,* pp. 49–55; Deutsch and Cecil B. Oldman, "Mozart-Drucke. Eine bibliographische Ergänzung zu Köchels Werkverzeichnis," *Zeitschrift für Musikwissenschaft* 14 (1931–32), pp. 135–50, 337–51; A. Hyatt King, *Mozart in Retrospect: Studies in Criticism and Bibliography* (London, 1955), pp. 8–10; Gertraut Haberkamp, *Die Erstdrucke der Werke von Wolfgang Amadeus Mozart,* 2 vols. (Tutzing, 1986).

20. See H. C. Robbins Landon, *1791: Mozart's Last Year,* pp. 43–46, for a cogent calculation of Mozart's probable income from publishing and sales of manuscript rights in his last year.

21. Otto Erich Deutsch, "Mozarts Verlagshonorare," *Börsenblatt für den Deutschen Buchhandel,* no. 86, 11 April 1933, p. 263. Beethoven refers to this issue in a letter of 1820 to Tobias

Haslinger: see Emily Anderson, ed., *The Letters of Beethoven* (New York, 1961), vol. 2, p. 895, ca. May 1820 (no. 1025).

22. Landon, *1791*, pp. 45–46.

23. *Letters*, p. 734, 19 May 1781 (no. 405); p. 753, 25 July 1781 (no. 417); p. 762, 29 August 1781 (no. 422).

24. Letter of Johann Thomas Kleinhardt to Count Franz Sternberg, 12–18 April 1786: *MDB*, p. 271.

25. Morrow observes that the stated amount of 100 thalers is three to six times higher than what an orchestra of 35 musicians would have cost. Morrow, *Concert Life in Haydn's Vienna*, pp. 127–28. Mozart did sometimes contribute his services out of friendship—"as a favor"—or in exchange for appearances at his own concerts. See Morrow, pp. 128–29; *Letters*, p. 888, 12 March 1785 (no. 525).

26. See Michael Kelly, *Reminiscences: MDB*, p. 530, and Jahn, vol. 2, p. 292; Constanze Mozart, "Anecdotes from Mozart's life," *AMZ* 1 (1798–99), column 290: *NMD*, p. 77 (no. 121, Anecdote 1); *Letters*, p. 938, to Puchberg, beginning of May 1790 (no. 578); *Letters*, p. 945, 8 October 1790 (no. 587).

27. Note the sale to Prince Fürstenberg in 1786 and the negotiations for a sale to Franz Deyerkauf in 1791. See *Letters*, pp. 900–901, 30 September 1786 (no. 541), and p. 962, ? summer 1791 (no. 609).

28. *AMZ* 1 (1798–99), column 290: *NMD*, p. 77 (no. 121, Anecdote 1).

29. Dispatch to Friedrich Wilhelm II from Prussia's ambassador in Vienna, Konstantin Philipp Wilhelm Jacobi, Baron Klöst, dated 18 February 1792: "In conformity with your majesty's very gracious order of the 7th of this month, I have made the arrangements with the widow Mozzart to acquire at a price of 100 ducats per piece, the eight designated pieces of music. I hope to be in possession of them during the first days of next week, after which I shall have them dispatched to Berlin with the first post-coach, which will leave here next Friday, the 24th." Ernst Friedlaender, "Mozarts Beziehungen zu Berlin," in *Mitteilungen für die Mozartgemeinde in Berlin* 1 (1897), Heft 4, pp. 119–20; see *MDB*, pp. 440–41. The letter of agreement survives, and identifies several of the works, including the Oratorio *La Betulia liberata*, K. 118/74c, and two Litanies, K. 125 and K. 243, and perhaps the Requiem. See *Briefe*, vol. 4, p. 178, Constanze Mozart contract with Baron Konstantin Philipp Wilhelm Jacobi, 4 March 1792 (no. 1207); see also *Briefe*, vol. 6, pp. 431–32.

30. See *Briefe*, vol. 6, pp. 357–58; Walter Senn, "Zur Erbteilung nach Leopold Mozart," *Neues Augsburger Mozartbuch. Zeitschrift des historischen Vereins für Schwaben*, vol. 62–63 (1962), pp. 387–88.

31. *Letters*, p. 805, 8 May 1782 (no. 450). Mozart here calculates 1 ducat = 4 florins instead of 4.5 florins.

32. Cramer's *Magazin der Musik*, 9 May 1783: *MDB*, p. 215.

33. "My opera has brought in 1,200 florins in the two days." *Letters*, p. 808, 20 July 1782 (no. 453).

34. "The English company told me that he made a thousand florins there." *Letters*, p. 906, 1 March 1787 (no. 545).

35. *Letters*, p. 928, 23 May 1789 (no. 565).

36. Ibid., p. 957, 25 June 1791 (no. 603).

37. Constanze Mozart Petition to Emperor Leopold II, 11 December 1791: *MDB*, pp. 421–22.

38. *Letters*, p. 934, December 1789 (no. 572).

39. Dexter Edge, "Mozart's Fee for *Così fan tutte*," *Journal of the Royal Musical Association* 116 (1991), p. 215. See also Rudolph Angermüller, " 'Seine Fehler waren, dass er das Geld nicht zu dirigieren wuste': Mozarts finanzielle Verhältnisse," in Cordula Roleff, ed., *Collectanea Mozartiana* (Tutzing, 1988), p. 35.

40. See Ulrich Drüner, "Wohin geht unser Mozart-Bild?" *Festschrift des 42. Deutschen Mozartfestes der Deutschen Mozart-Gesellschaft* (Augsburg, 1993), pp. 18–34. Rediscovered in 1992, the document had previously been auctioned in 1929 and its first line appears in *Briefe*, vol. 4, p. 174 (no. 1203). See *Briefe*, vol. 6, p. 429.

41. The matter is debated in *MJb 1993*, pp. 65–82. Translation by Bruce Cooper Clarke, who kindly provided me with the relevant materials.

SELECTED BIBLIOGRAPHY

The bibliography is arranged by topic, as follows:

For full bibliographical information on abbreviated items, see "Abbreviations," pp. 529–30.

I. MOZART'S WORKS AND WRITINGS
Collected Works

Wolfgang Amadeus Mozarts Werke: Kritisch durchgesehen. Gesamtausgabe (Leipzig, 1877–1910, various reprints), the sturdy Breitkopf & Härtel complete edition, has now been replaced by *Wolfgang Amadeus Mozart: Neue Ausgabe sämtlicher Werke* (= *Neue Mozart-Ausgabe,* hereinafter *NMA)* (Kassel, 1955–1991). For the relative merits of these editions, see Cliff Eisen, "The Old and New Mozart Editions," *Early Music* 19 (1991), pp. 513–32. See also L. von Köchel, *Chronologisch-thematisches Verzeichnis* (see CATALOGS, below).

Early Published Editions

Gertraut Haberkamp, *Die Erstdrucke der Werke von Wolfgang Amadeus Mozart,* 2 vols. (Tutzing, 1986), provides title pages in facsimile of 131 authentic works in 78 editions published during Mozart's lifetime. A minor blemish is that the book does not clearly differentiate between authorized and unauthorized editions.

The basic literature includes Otto Erich Deutsch, "Mozarts Verleger," *Mozart-Jahrbuch 1955,* pp. 49–55; Otto Erich Deutsch and Cecil B. Oldman, "Mozart-Drucke. Eine bibliographische Ergänzung zu Köchels Werkverzeichnis," *Zeitschrift für Musikwissenschaft* 14 (1931–32), pp. 135–50, 337–51; Otto Erich Deutsch, "Mozarts Verlagshonorare," *Börsenblatt für den Deutschen Buchhandel,* no. 86, 11 April 1933, pp. 262–63; A. Hyatt King, *Mozart in Retrospect: Studies in Criticism and Bibliography* (London, 1955), pp. 10–15. See also Wolfgang Rehm in *Mozart Compendium* (see HANDBOOKS AND DICTIONARIES, below), pp. 422–25.

Letters and Other Personal Documents

The definitive edition of the letters of Mozart and his family, including his sister's and father's diaries and other family writings, comprehensively annotated and indexed, is Wilhelm Bauer, Otto Erich Deutsch, and Joseph Heinz Eibl, eds., *Mozart: Briefe und Aufzeichnungen,* 7 vols. (Kassel, 1962–1975). The standard English edition—essentially complete for Mozart's own letters but otherwise far from complete—is Emily Anderson, ed. and trans., *The Letters of Mozart and His Family,* 3 vols. (London, 1938; 2nd ed., 2 vols., revised by A. Hyatt King and Monica Carolan, London and New York, 1966; 3rd ed., revised by Stanley Sadie and Fiona Smart, London, 1985).

The first collected edition of Mozart's letters was Ludwig Nohl, ed., *Mozarts Briefe* (Salzburg, 1865), translated by Lady Wallace as *The Letters of Wolfgang Amadeus Mozart,* 2 vols. (New York, 1866). The first critical edition was Ludwig Schiedermair, *Die Briefe W. A. Mozarts und seiner Familie,* 5 vols. (Munich and Leipzig, 1914); see also Erich H. Müller von Asow, ed., *Briefe Wolfgang Amadeus Mozarts,* 2 vols. (Berlin, 1942; reprint, Lindau, 1949).

Selections from Mozart's letters to his cousin Maria Anna Thekla Mozart and Constanze Mozart's letters to Breitkopf & Härtel were first published in Gustav Nottebohm, *Mozartiana* (Leipzig, 1880; reprint, 1972). Many of Constanze Mozart's letters were collected in Arthur Schurig, ed., *Konstanze Mozart's Briefe, Aufzeichnungen, Dokumente* (Dresden, 1922). Her correspondence with the publisher Johann Anton André appears in translation as a supplement to the 1st edition of Anderson, *Letters* (see above). Leopold Mozart's letters to his daughter between 1784 and 1787 were first collected in Otto Erich Deutsch and Bernhard Paumgartner, eds., *Leopold Mozarts Briefe an seine Töchter* (Salzburg and Leipzig, 1936). See also Wilhelm Hitzig, "Die

Briefe Franz Xaver Niemetscheks und der Marianne Mozarts an Breitkopf & Härtel," in *Der Bär: Jahrbuch von Breitkopf & Härtel auf das Jahr 1927* (Leipzig, 1928), pp. 101–16.

Song texts and librettos written by Mozart, along with poems embedded in his letters, are collected in Richard Batka, *W. A. Mozarts gesammelte Poesien* (Prague, 1906). Excerpts from Mozart's letters in Anderson's translation are skillfully arranged by topic with copious commentary in Robert L. Marshall, ed., *Mozart Speaks: Views on Music, Musicians, and the World* (New York, 1991).

II. REFERENCE WORKS
Catalogs

Mozart's thematic listing of compositions completed between February 1784 and November 1791—his *Verzeichnis aller meiner Werke (Catalog of All My Works)*—is available in a fine new edition, *Mozart's Thematic Catalogue: A Facsimile*. British Library, Stefan Zweig MS 63, ed. Albi Rosenthal and Alan Tyson (Ithaca, 1990); see also Otto Erich Deutsch, *Mozart's Catalogue of his Works, 1784–1791* (New York, [1956]). A convenient edition combines Mozart's *Verzeichnis aller meiner Werke* and Leopold Mozart's *Verzeichnis der Jugendwerke W. A. Mozarts*, ed. Erich Müller von Asow (Vienna and Wiesbaden, 1956).

The definitive chronological thematic catalog, constantly in process of revision as the chronology is refined, is Ludwig Ritter von Köchel, *Chronologisch-thematisches Verzeichnis sämtlicher Tonwerke Wolfgang Amadé Mozarts* (Leipzig, 1862, reprint, 1905); 3rd–5th editions, ed. Alfred Einstein (Leipzig, 1937–47); 6th edition, ed. F. Giegling, A. Weinmann, and G. Sievers (Wiesbaden, 1964; reprinted as 7th edition, 1984). *Koechel ABC* (Wiesbaden, 1965), ed. Hellmuth von Hase, offers an abbreviation of the 6th ed. of the Köchel listings. An accurate and convenient summary of the Köchel numbers, taking account of recent work on authenticity and chronology, is in Neal Zaslaw and William Cowdery, *The Compleat Mozart* (see CRITICISM: SURVEYS AND OVERVIEWS, below), pp. 343–50. For a work list classified by genre see *The New Grove*, vol. 12, pp. 725–47.

Alan Tyson's superb illustrated catalog of the watermarks of Mozart's autographs, *Wasserzeichen-Katalog*, 2 vols., published in the *NMA*, X:33/2 (Salzburg, 1992 [1993]), is also an indispensable guide to the current location of the autographs.

For detailed listings of holdings of Mozart autographs and documents see: Karl-Heinz Köhler, "Die Erwerbung der Mozart-Autographe der Berliner Staatsbibliothek—ein Beitrag zur Geschichte des Nachlasses," *Mozart-Jahrbuch 1962/63*, pp. 55–67; Hans-Günter Klein, *Wolfgang Amadeus Mozart: Autographe und Abschriften. Katalog* (Berlin, 1982); A. Hyatt King, *A Mozart Legacy: Aspects of the British Library Collections* (London, 1984); Leopold Nowak, "Die Wiener Mozart-Autographen," *Österreichische Musikzeitschrift* 11 (1956), pp. 180–87; Günter Brosche, "Die Originalhandschriften Wolfgang Amadeus Mozarts in der Österreichischen Nationalbibliothek," in *Collectanea Mozartiana*, ed. Cordulia Roleff (Tutzing, 1988), pp. 177–88; Otto Biba, "Musikautographe von W. A. Mozart im Archiv der Gesellschaft der Musikfreunde in Wien," in *Collectanea Mozartiana*, pp. 193–200; Rudolph Angermüller, "Mozart-Autographe im Besitz der Internationalen Stiftung Mozarteum Salzburg," in *Collectanea Mozartiana*, pp. 165–76; Manfred Hermann Schmid, *Die Musikaliensammlung der Erzabtei St. Peter in Salzburg. Katalog, Part 1: Leopold und Wolfgang Amadeus Mozart, Joseph und Michael Haydn*. Schriftenreihe der Internationalen Stiftung Mozarteum, 3.4 (Kassel, 1970); Manfred Hermann Schmid, "Musikalien des Mozartschen Familienarchivs im Stift St. Peter," in *Das Benediktinerstift St. Peter in Salzburg zur Zeit Mozarts*. Musik und Musiker—Kunst und Kultur, ed. P. Petrus Eder OSB and Gerhard Walterskirchen (Salzburg, 1991), pp. 173–85; E. H. Müller von Asow, "Die Mozarthandschriften der Stadtbibliothek Leipzig," *Neues Mozart-Jahrbuch* 2 (1942), pp. 243–65; François Lesure, "Mozartiana Gallica," *Revue de Musicologie* 38 (1956), pp. 115–24; Ervin Major, "Magyarországi Mozart-kéziratok" ("Mozart Manuscripts in Hungary") in *Mozart és Magyarország* (Budapest, 1956), pp. 10–13; Hans Moldenhauer, "Übersicht der Musikmanuskripte W. A. Mozarts in den Vereinigten Staaten von Amerika," *Mozart-Jahrbuch 1956*, pp. 88–99; Dimitri Kolbin, "Autographe Mozarts und seiner Familie in der UdSSR," *Mozart-Jahrbuch 1968/70*, pp. 281–303.

For Mozart holdings of the Morgan Library and the British Library, see C. A. Banks and J. Rigbie Turner, eds., *Mozart: Prodigy of Nature* (New York, 1991), pp. 86–87.

The Biblioteka Jagiellónska in Kraków, Poland, houses 151 Mozart autographs from the Berlin Staatsbibliothek Preussischer Kulturbesitz. See Tyson, *Wasserzeichen-Katalog* (see above); see also "Verzeichnis der verschollenen Mozart-Autographe der ehemaligen Preussischen Staatsbibliothek

Berlin (BB)," in *Neue Mozart-Ausgabe: Bericht über die Mitarbeitertagung in Kassel 29.–30. Mai 1981* (Salzburg, 1984), pp. 75–78.

Bibliographies

The authoritative ongoing bibliography, though with inevitable lacunae, arranged alphabetically by author, is Rudolph Angermüller and Otto Schneider, eds., "Mozart Bibliographie bis 1970," occupying the entire issue of *Mozart-Jahrbuch 1975,* with subsequent supplements and corrections covering 1971–75, 1976–80, 1981–85, 1986–91 (Kassel, 1978, 1982, 1987, 1992), the last of these coedited by Angermüller and Johanna Senigl.

Still extremely useful for the older literature, both for its sometimes unique listings and its convenient topical arrangement, is Otto Keller, ed., *Wolfgang Amadeus Mozart: Bibliographie und Ikonographie* (Berlin and Leipzig, 1927). Another extensive bibliography is in O. Schneider and A. Algatzy, *Mozart Handbuch* (see HANDBOOKS AND DICTIONARIES, below).

For sturdy selective bibliographies, see *The New Grove,* vol. 12, pp. 747–52; *Die Musik in Geschichte und Gegenwart,* vol. 9, columns 826–39, and Landon, ed., *Mozart Compendium* (see HANDBOOKS AND DICTIONARIES, below), pp. 429–34. The *Mozart Compendium* also contains several illuminating bibliographical essays by A. Hyatt King (pp. 404–20).

Documentary Collections

The fundamental collection of Mozart documents is Otto Erich Deutsch, ed., *Mozart: Die Dokumente seines Lebens* (published as part of the *NMA,* X:34) (Kassel, 1961). It, and a volume of *Addenda und Corrigenda* (*NMA,* X:31/1), ed. Joseph Heinz Eibl (Kassel, 1978), are translated by Eric Blom, Peter Branscombe, and Jeremy Noble as *Mozart: A Documentary Biography,* called here *MDB* (London, 1965); the translations are not always reliable.

An indispensable supplement to *MDB* is Cliff Eisen, ed. and trans., *New Mozart Documents: A Supplement to O. E. Deutsch's Documentary Biography* (London and Stanford, 1991). Rudolf Lewicki, "Aus Nissens Kollektaneen," *Mozarteums Mitteilungen* 2 (November 1919), contains some documentary materials omitted from Nissen. Jiří Berkovec, *Musicalia v prazském periodické tisku 18. století* (Prague, 1989) lists about forty references to Mozart in the *Prager Oberpostamtszeitung* from 30 May 1786 to 17 December 1791, including eight reports not yet in *MDB* or its supplements. For other newly discovered documents see especially later issues of *Mozart-Jahrbuch* and *Mitteilungen der ISM.*

Handbooks and Dictionaries

O. Schneider and A. Algatzy, *Mozart-Handbuch: Chronik-Werk-Bibliographie* (Vienna, 1962), and H. C. Robbins Landon, *The Mozart Compendium: A Guide to Mozart's Life and Music* (New York, 1990), are extremely useful handbooks, the latter remarkably accurate and with outstanding special contributions by Peter Branscombe, Cliff Eisen, A. Hyatt King, Robert Levin, Andrew Steptoe, John Stone, and others. Also useful, but far from comprehensive, is Erich Valentin, *Lübbes Mozart Lexikon* (rev. ed., Bergisch Gladbach, Germany, 1985). See also Neal Zaslaw and Fiona Morgan Fein, *The Mozart Repertory: A Guide for Musicians, Programmers, and Researchers* (Cornell, 1991).

Iconographies and Illustrated Catalogs

The standard work is Otto Erich Deutsch, ed., *Mozart and His World in Contemporary Pictures* (Kassel, 1961), published in the *NMA,* X:32, based on the collection of Maximilian Zenger and printed in black and white. Less comprehensive pictorial collections include Robert Bory's pathbreaking black-and-white *The Life and Works of Wolfgang Amadeus Mozart in Pictures* (Geneva, 1948) and Arthur Hutchings, *Mozart: The Man, the Musician,* 2 vols. in 1 (London, 1976), which is reproduced mostly in color.

Selma Krasa et al., eds., *Zaubertöne—Mozart in Wien 1781–1791: Austellung des historischen Museums der Stadt Wien im Künstlerhaus* (Vienna, 1990), offers a wide variety of rare pictorial materials, many in color. Two important illustrated catalogs are Hans-Günter Klein, ed., *Wolfgang Amadeus Mozart: "Componiern—meine einzige freude und Passion." Autographe und frühe Drucke aus dem Besitz der Berliner Staatsbibliotheken* (Wiesbaden, 1991), and Rudolph Angermüller and Geneviève Geffray, eds., *Mozart, Bilder und Klänge.* Salzburger Landesausstellung (Salzburg, 1991).

A joint exhibition primarily of autograph scores in the collections of the Morgan Library and the British Library is documented in C. A. Banks and J. Rigbie Turner, eds., *Mozart: Prodigy of Nature* (New York, 1991). Another fine catalog, edited by Albi Rosenthal and Peter Ward Jones, is *Mozart: A Bicentennial Loan Exhibition* (Oxford, 1991), documenting an exhibition at the Bodleian Library. A valuable aid to understanding Mozart's intellectual interests is Ulrich Konrad and Martin Staehelin, eds., *"allzeit ein Buch": Die Bibliothek Wolfgang Amadeus Mozarts,* Austellung im Malerbuchkabinett der Bibliotheca Augusta vom 5. December 1991 bis zum 15. März 1992 (Wolfenbüttl, Germany, 1991).

Serials, Periodicals, Yearbooks

Main periodicals devoted exclusively to Mozart studies:

Mitteilungen für die Mozartgemeinde in Berlin (1895–1925)
Mozarteums-Mitteilungen (1918–21)
Mozart-Jahrbuch (1923–29), 3 vols.
Neues Mozart-Jahrbuch (1941–43), 3 vols.
Mozart-Jahrbuch (1950–), 27 vols. to 1993
Mitteilungen der Internationalen Stiftung Mozarteum [ISM] (1952–).
Acta Mozartiana (Mitteilungen der Deutschen Mozart-Gesellschaft) (1954–).

Essays, Special Issues, and Congress Reports

Important collections of essays by individual scholars include: E. K. Blümml, *Aus Mozarts Freundes- und Familienkreis* (Vienna, Prague, and Leipzig, 1923); Ernst Fritz Schmid, *Ein schwäbisches Mozartbuch* (Lorch and Stuttgart, 1948); A. Hyatt King, *Mozart in Retrospect: Studies in Criticism and Bibliography* (Oxford, 1955); Alfred Einstein, *Essays on Music* (New York, 1956; rev. ed., London, 1958); Gustav Gugitz, *Mozartiana* (Vienna, 1963); Alan Tyson, *Mozart: Studies of the Autograph Scores* (Cambridge, Mass., 1986); Wolfgang Plath, *Mozart-Schriften: Ausgewählte Aufsätze*, ed. Marianne Danckwardt, Schriftenreihe der Internationalen Stiftung Mozarteum Salzburg, vol. 9 (Kassel, 1991).

The uncollected papers of Hermann Abert, Carl Bär, Rudolph Angermüller, Otto Erich Deutsch, Joseph Heinz Eibl, Rudolph Genée, Erich Schenk, Heinz Schuler, and other prominent Mozart scholars must be consulted in the journals.

Significant symposiums and congress reports include: *Bericht über die musikwissenschaftliche Tagung der Internationalen Stiftung Mozarteum in Salzburg*, ed. Erich Schenk (Leipzig, 1931); *Augsburger Mozartbuch*, special issue of *Zeitschrift des historischen Vereins für Schwaben*, vol. 55–56 (Augsburg, 1942–43); *Internationale Konferenz über das Leben und Werk W. A. Mozarts*, ed. Pavel Eckstein (Prague, [1956]); *Bericht über den Internationalen Musikwissenschaftlichen Kongress Wien: Mozartjahr 1956*, ed. Erich Schenk (Graz and Cologne, 1958); *Les Influences étrangères dans l'oeuvre de W. A. Mozart*, Internationales Colloquium, Paris, 1956, ed. André Verchaly (Paris, 1958); *Neues Augsburger Mozartbuch*, special issue of *Zeitschrift des historischen Vereins für Schwaben*, vol. 62–63 (Augsburg, 1962); Cordula Roleff, ed., *Collectanea Mozartiana* (Tutzing, 1988); Cliff Eisen, ed., *Mozart Studies* (Oxford, 1991); Rudolph Angermüller et al., eds., *Bericht über den Internationalen Mozart-Kongress Salzburg 1991*, 2 vols., as *Mozart-Jahrbuch 1991*; Manfred Hermann Schmid, ed., *Mozart Studien*, 2 vols. (Tutzing, 1992–93).

For the Lincoln Center 1991 conference, "Performing Mozart's Music," see PERFORMANCE PRACTICE, below.

III. LIFE

Reminiscences of Contemporaries

The main reminiscences and documentary references are in Otto Erich Deutsch's monumental *Mozart: A Documentary Biography,* which, however, is somewhat selective and arbitrary in its inclusion of the early anecdotal materials and early biographical literature. A convenient but outdated collection of the memoirs and early anecdotal materials is Albert Leitzmann, ed., *Mozarts Persönlichkeit* (Leipzig, 1914). This superseded Ludwig Nohl, ed., *Mozart nach den Schilderungen seiner Zeitgenossen* (Leipzig, 1880). A belated publication of unique interviews with Mozart's sister, widow, and sister-in-law is in Rosemary Hughes, ed., *A Mozart Pilgrimage: Being the Travel Diaries of Vincent and Mary Novello in the year 1829,* transcribed and compiled by Nerina Medici di Marignano (London, 1955). For a guide to Mozart references in the Beethoven circle, see Karl-Heinz Köhler, "Die Konversationshefte Ludwig van Beethovens als retrospektive Quelle der Mozartforschung," *Mozart-Jahrbuch 1971/72,* pp. 120–39.

Early Biographies

The first important biographies, written with the aid of Mozart's sister and widow, respectively, are Friedrich Schlichtegroll, "Johannes Chrysostomus Wolfgang Gottlieb Mozart," in *Nekrolog auf dem Jahr 1791* (Gotha, 1793), vol. 2, pp. 82–112 (entry for 5 December) and Franz Xaver Niemetschek, *Leben des k.k. Kapellmeisters Wolfgang Gottlieb Mozart nach Originalquellen beschrieben* (Prague, 1798; 2nd ed. 1808). A modern facsimile reprint of Schlichtegroll was edited by Joseph Heinz Eibl (Kassel, 1974), and a facsimile reprint of the 1808 edition of Niemetschek was edited by Peter Krause (Leipzig, 1978). Another reprint, which relied heavily on Krause, appeared as *Ich kannte Mozart,* ed. Jost Perfahl (Munich, 1984). The 1798 edition of Niemetschek was translated by Helen Mautner and titled *Life of Mozart* (London, 1956).

Almost wholly unreliable is the influential Johann Friedrich Rochlitz, "Verbürgte Anekdoten aus Wolfgang Gottlieb Mozarts Leben. Ein Beitrag zur richtigeren Kenntnis dieses Mannes, als Mensch und Künstler" ("Authentic Anecdotes from Wolfgang Gottlieb Mozart's Life. A Contribution to a Better Understanding of this Man as Human Being and Artist") *AMZ* 1–3, from 10 October 1798 to 27 May 1801. An English translation is in Maynard Solomon, "The Rochlitz Anecdotes," in *Mozart Studies,* ed. Cliff Eisen (Oxford, 1991), pp. 1–59.

Heavily derivative of these three sources are such early biographies as the following: Carl Friedrich Cramer, *Anecdotes sur W. G. Mozart* (Paris and Hamburg, 1801); Théophile Frédéric Winckler, *Notice bibliographique sur Jean-Chrysostome-Wolfgang-Théophile Mozart: extrait du "Magazin Encyclopédique"* (Paris, 1801); Ignaz Ferdinand Cajetan Arnold, *Mozarts Geist: seine kurze Biographie und ästhetische Darstellung* (Erfurt, 1803); Jean-Baptiste-Antoine Suard, "Anecdotes sur Mozart," in *Mélanges de littérature* 10 (1804), pp. 337–47; Louis-Alexandre-César Bombet [pseud. for Henri Beyle, known as Stendhal], *Lettres écrites de Vienne en Autriche, sur le célèbre compositeur Joseph Haydn, suivies d'une vie de Mozart . . .* (Paris, 1814); rev. ed. 1817, as *Vies de Haydn, de Mozart et de Métastase.* Translated as Henri Stendhal, *Lives of Haydn, Mozart and Metastasio,* ed. Richard N. Coe (New York, 1972). See also Johann Aloys Schlosser, *W. A. Mozarts Biographie* (Prague, 1828; reprinted Prague, 1993).

Georg Nikolaus von Nissen, *Biographie W. A. Mozart's,* ed. Constanze Nissen, with a foreword by Johann Heinrich Feuerstein (Leipzig, 1828; reprint with a foreword by Rudolph Angermüller, Hildesheim, 1984) is a vast, uncritical compendium of the earlier sources supplemented by valuable information from Mozart's wife and Sophie Haibel that includes the first publication (abridged, altered, and somewhat bowdlerized) of large numbers of the family letters. A consummately crafted Romantic life distilled from Nissen's voluminous materials and the Novellos' travel diaries is Edward Holmes, *Life of Mozart* (London, 1845; numerous reprints). A once-influential hagiography is Alexandre D. Oulibicheff, *Nouvelle biographie de Mozart* (Moscow, 1843).

Later Biographies

The only biography of Mozart that may be called definitive is Otto Jahn, *W. A. Mozart,* 4 vols. (Leipzig, 1856; 2nd ed. 1867). The 3rd and 4th editions were revised by Hermann Deiters, who also enlarged the 4th edition (2 vols. [Leipzig, 1905–7]). The 2nd edition appeared in translation by Pauline D. Townsend as *The Life of Mozart,* 3 vols. (London, 1882). The 5th edition of Jahn's work, published by Hermann Abert as *W. A. Mozart* (Leipzig, 1919–21; reprint 1955–56), contains important further discussions of the music, but Abert's additions and revisions disturb the balanced structure of Jahn's masterpiece.

Subsequent biographies are often heavily derivative of Jahn or are attempts to return to earlier positions that he had attempted to displace by his evolutionist Victorian perspective, which viewed Mozart as embodying the classical ideal of a gifted and harmonious being organically fulfilling his creative potential.

Among the most significant of the post-Jahn biographies are Ludwig Nohl, *Mozart* (Leipzig, 1863; rev. ed., *Mozarts Leben,* 1877), translated by Lady Wallace as *The Life of Mozart,* 2 vols. (London, 1877); Constantin von Wurzbach, *Mozart-Buch* (Vienna, 1869); Arthur Schurig, *Wolfgang Amade Mozart,* 2 vols. (Leipzig, 1913; 2nd ed., 1923); and Josef Kreitmeier, S.J., *W. A. Mozart: Eine Charakterzeichnung des grossen Meisters nach literarischen Quellen* (Düsseldorf, 1919). Théodore de Wyzewa and Georges de Saint-Foix, *Wolfgang Amédée Mozart: Sa vie musicale et son oeuvre,* 5 vols. (Paris, 1912–46), is notable less as a life than as a study of the music and especially its formative influences.

Other notable or once-influential biographies of Mozart include: Ludwig Schiedermair, *Mozart: Sein Leben und seine Werke* (Munich, 1922; 2nd ed., 1948); Bernhard Paumgartner, *Mozart* (Berlin, 1927, rev. ed. 1993); Henri Ghéon, *Promenades avec Mozart* (Paris, 1932), translated by Alexander Dru as *In Search of Mozart* (New York, 1934); Eric Blom, *Mozart* (London, 1935); W. J. Turner, *Mozart: The Man and His Works* (London, 1938).

A reliable but impersonal chronological biography is Erich Schenk, *Wolfgang Amadeus Mozart: Eine Biographie* (Vienna, 1955, revised 1975 as *Mozart: sein Leben—seine Welt*). The translation by Richard and Clara Winston was somewhat abridged as *Mozart and His Times* (New York, 1959).

Wolfgang Hildesheimer, *Mozart* (Frankfurt, 1977), trans. Marion Faber (New York, 1982), is a loosely structured meditation, written with sensitivity and insight, but reckless of historical constraints. Partly in reaction against the extravagant revival of early Romantic tropes in Hildesheimer—and in Peter Shaffer's *Amadeus,* which it partially inspired—several later books make excellent use of the specialized literature to emphasize the more prosaic aspects of Mozart's Vienna years. Volkmar Braunbehrens, *Mozart in Wien 1781–1791* (Munich, 1986), trans. Timothy Bell as *Mozart in Vienna 1781–1791* (New York, 1990), shifts the focus to Mozart's bourgeois status and associations and to the details of his daily life. In Braunbehrens and in H. C. Robbins Landon, *1791: Mozart's Last Year* (New York, 1989) and Landon's *Mozart: The Golden Years* (New York, 1991), a more sober, industrious, entrepreneurial Mozart emerges to replace the image of the willful, wastrel, scatological, and doomed composer that had begun to dominate Mozart biography in the wake of Uwe Kraemer, "Wer hat Mozart verhungern lassen?" of 1976 (see FINANCES, below) and Hildesheimer's *Mozart* of 1977.

Jean and Brigitte Massin, *Wolfgang Amadeus Mozart: Biographie, Histoire de l'oeuvre* (Paris, 1959; 3rd ed., 1990) is a conventional biography with a keen eye for social and political issues. Georg Knepler, *Wolfgang Amadé Mozart: Annäherungen* (Berlin, 1991), translated by J. Bradford Robinson as *Wolfgang Amadé Mozart* (Cambridge, England, 1993) contains insightful reflections by an outstanding Marxist historian on Mozart's creativity in the context of the social and intellectual background. Stanley Sadie, "Wolfgang Amadeus Mozart" entry in *The New Grove,* vol. 12, pp. 680–753, published separately as *The New Grove Mozart* (New York, 1983), is a reliable and perceptive account of Mozart's life and productivity. Other biographies of recent decades include Stanley Sadie, *Mozart* (New York, 1965); Michael Levey, *The Life and Death of Mozart* (London, 1971); Ivor Keys, *Mozart: His Life in His Music* (London, 1980), and Konrad Küster, *Mozart: Eine musikalische Biographie* (Stuttgart, 1990). An indispensable outline chronicle of Mozart's life, abstracted from *MDB,* is Joseph Heinz Eibl, *W. A. Mozart: Chronik eines Lebens* (Kassel, 1975).

Psychoanalytic and Related Views

The following all center on implications of the father-son psychological constellation, raising issues of links between oedipal conflict, depression, and creativity: Aaron Esman, "Mozart: A Study in Genius," *Psychoanalytic Quarterly* 20 (1951), pp. 603–12; Jan Ehrenwald, "Mozart, Father and Son: Patterns of Sharing and Compliance in Genius," in his *Neurosis in the Family and Patterns of Psychosocial Defense* (New York, 1963), pp. 94–108; Brigid Brophy, *Mozart the Dramatist* (London, 1964; rev. ed., 1988); and Florian Langegger, *Mozart: Vater und Sohn: Eine psychologische Untersuchung* (Zurich, 1978).

Sara Sheftel, "Mozart: A Psychoanalytic Study" (Ph.D. dissertation, Graduate School of the Union for Experimenting Colleges and Universities, 1982), is broad-ranging and sensitive, proposing a failure of Mozart's connection to his mother but portraying him as a raging, ungrateful child. Peter J. Davies, in "Mozart's Manic-Depressive Tendencies," *Musical Times,* 128 (1987), pp. 123–26 and 191–96, and *Mozart in Person* (see MEDICAL HISTORY, below), pp. 145–60, attempts a reductive clinical diagnosis. Hildesheimer in *Mozart* argues that Mozart is emotionally incapable of real human ties. See also various articles and brochures by Erna Schwerin on Mozart's family members (see next section).

IV. MOZART'S FAMILY

Genealogy and Family Background

A comprehensive source is Heinz Schuler, *Wolfgang Amadeus Mozart. Vorfahren und Verwandte, Genealogie und Landesgeschichte,* Publikation der Zentralstelle für Personen- und Familiengeschichte, Institut für Genealogie, 34 (Neustadt an der Aisch, 1980).

For the maternal line, see Erich Schenk, "Mozarts Salzburger Vorfahren," *Mozart-Jahrbuch,* vol. 3 (1929), pp. 81–93. For the paternal line, see Adolf Buff, "Mozart's Augsburger Vorfahren," *Zeitschrift des historischen Vereins für Schwaben und Neuburg* 8 (1891), pp. 1–36; Heinz Friedrich Deininger and Josef Herz, "Beiträge zur Genealogie der ältesten schwäbischen Vorfahren Wolfgang Amadeus Mozarts," *Neue Augsburger Mozartbuch* (see ESSAYS, SPECIAL ISSUES, AND CONGRESS REPORTS, above), pp. 1–76; and Schmid, *Ein schwäbisches Mozartbuch* (see ESSAYS, SPECIAL ISSUES, AND CONGRESS REPORTS, above), pp. 28–52; Adolf Layer, *Die Augsburger Künstlerfamilie Mozart* (Augsburg, [1971]); and Adolf Layer, "Künstlerische und geistige Begabung in der Augsburger Mozart-Sippe," *Neue Augsburger Mozartbuch,* pp. 227–39. A detailed family tree for the paternal line is E. H. Müller v. Asow, "Nachkommentafel David Mozarts," *Augsburger Mozartbuch* (see ESSAYS, SPECIAL ISSUES, AND CONGRESS REPORTS, above), following p. 504. Convenient family trees for the more immediate Mozart and Weber families are in Eibl, *Chronik* (see LATER BIOGRA-PHIES, above), pp. 115–17 and Landon, *Mozart Compendium* (see HANDBOOKS AND DICTIONARIES, above), pp. 36–37. See also listings for Anna Maria Mozart (below).

Leopold Mozart

Leopold Mozart's *Versuch einer gründlichen Violinschule* (Augsburg, 1756) is available in a facsimile reprint of the 3rd edition of 1789, ed. Hans Joachim Moser (Leipzig, 1956) and in translation as Leopold Mozart, *A Treatise on the Fundamental Principles of Violin Playing,* ed. Alfred Einstein, trans. Editha Knocker (London, 1948; 2nd ed., 1951). His "Report on the Present State of the Musical Establishment at the Court of His Serene Highness the Archbishop of Salzburg in the year 1757" is translated in Zaslaw, *Mozart's Symphonies* (see SYMPHONIES, below), pp. 550–57. His *Reise-Aufzeichnungen 1763–1771,* facsimile edition, ed. Arthur Schurig (Dresden, 1920), are also conveniently available in *Briefe.*

In addition to the standard Mozart biographies, the basic literature on Leopold Mozart's life includes: Adolf Buff, "Mozart's Augsburger Vorfahren," *Zeitschrift des historischen Vereins für Schwaben und Neuburg* 8 (1891), pp. 1–36; Ernst Fritz Schmid, *Ein schwäbisches Mozartbuch* (Lorch-Stuttgart, 1948); Ernst Fritz Schmid, "Neues zu Leopold Mozarts Bildungsgang," in *Neues Augsburger Mozartbuch* (see ESSAYS, SPECIAL ISSUES, AND CONGRESS REPORTS, above), pp. 191–227; Ernst Fritz Schmid, "Leopold Mozart" entry in *MGG,* vol. 9 (1961), columns 692–98; Ludwig Wegele, ed., *Leopold Mozart 1719–1787. Bild einer Persönlichkeit,* with essays by Werner Egk, Adolf Layer, Géza Rech, Hans Schurich, Erich Valentin, Hans E. Valentin, and Wegele (Augsburg, 1969); Adolf Layer, *Eine Jugend in Augsburg: Leopold Mozart 1719–1737* (Augsburg, [1975]); Erich Valentin, *Leopold Mozart: Porträt einer Persönlichkeit* (Munich, 1987). See also Erna Schwerin, *Leopold Mozart: Profile of a Personality* (New York, 1987).

Three recent papers by Josef Mančal are of special importance: "Vom 'Orden der geflickten hosen': Leopold Mozarts Heirat und Bürgerrecht," in *Leopold Mozart und Augsburg,* ed. Ottmar F. W. Beck (Augsburg, 1987), pp. 31–54; "Neues über Leopold Mozart," *Österreichische Musikzeitschrift* 42 (1987), pp. 282–91; and "Leopold Mozart und sein Verhältnis zu seinem Sohn," in Krasa et al., *Zaubertöne* (see ICONOGRAPHIES AND ILLUSTRATED CATALOGS, above), pp. 30–37.

For Leopold Mozart's estate, see Walter Senn, "Zur Erbteilung nach Leopold Mozart," *Neues Augsburger Mozartbuch,* pp. 383–95; Anna Hamerníková, " 'Licitations-Protocoll über die Leopold Mozartische Verlassenschaft' im Familienarchiv Berchtold," *Mozart-Jahrbuch 1991,* vol. 1, pp. 122–25; and Rudolph Angermüller, "Leopold Mozarts Verlassenschaft," *Mitteilungen der ISM* 41 (November 1993), pp. 1–32.

Marianne (Nannerl) Mozart

Walter Hummel, ed., *Nannerl Mozarts Tagebuchblätter* (Salzburg and Stuttgart, 1958), is an elegant facsimile edition of Marianne Mozart's diaries; its several misdated entries are corrected in *Briefe.* The standard life is Walter Hummel, *Nannerl: Wolfgang Amadeus Mozarts Schwester* (Zurich, Leipzig, and Vienna, 1952), which now is significantly supplemented by Eva Rieger's feminist reading, *Nannerl Mozart: Leben einer Künstlerin im 18. Jahrhundert* (Frankfurt, 1990). The earliest biographical essay on her is in Otto Jahn, *Life of Mozart* (London, 1882), vol. 3, pp. 401–7. See also Erna Schwerin, "Maria Anna ('Nannerl') Mozart: A Profile of Mozart's Sister," *Friends of Mozart Newsletter,* no. 19 (1985), pp. 1–4 and no. 20 (1986), pp. 1–5.

Important documentary materials are in Rudolph Genée, "Mozarts Schwester Nannerl," *Mitteilungen für die Mozart-Gemeinde in Berlin* 3 (November, 1896), pp. 98–103, and Johann Evangelist Engl, "Testament, Codicill, Nachtrag und Sperr-Relation der Schwester W. A. Mozarts," in *17. Jahresbericht der Internationalen Stiftung Mozarteum* (Salzburg, 1897), pp. 29–34. The latter is now superseded by Rudolph Angermüller, "Testament, Kodizill, Nachtrag und Sperrelation der Freifrau Maria Anna von Berchtold zu Sonnenburg, geb. Mozart (1751–1829)," *Mozart-Jahrbuch 1986,* pp. 97–132.

Anna Maria Mozart

Erich Valentin, *'Madame Mutter': Anna Maria Walburga Mozart (1720–1778)* (Augsburg, 1991) is an informed essay on Mozart's mother. The fundamental papers on her early life and genealogy are Erich Schenk, "Mozarts mütterliche Familie," *Bericht über die musikwissenschaftliche Tagung der Internationalen Stiftung Mozarteum in Salzburg vom 2. bis 5. August 1931,* ed. Schenk (Leipzig, 1932), pp. 45–68, and Erich Schenk, "Mozarts Salzburger Vorfahren," *Mozart-Jahrbuch* 3 (1929), pp. 81–93. See also Schenk, *Mozart and His Times* (see LATER BIOGRAPHIES, above), pp. 6–8.

Two essential papers by Heinz Schuler are "Mozarts Grossvater Pertl in St. Gilgen," *Mitteilungen der ISM* 23 (1975), pp. 27–36, and "Die Hochzeit der Eltern Mozarts," *Acta Mozartiana* 28

(1981), pp. 3–11. See also Erna Schwerin, "Anna Maria Mozart: A Profile of Mozart's Mother," *Friends of Mozart Newsletter*, no. 16 (Spring 1984), pp. 1–6.

Maria Anna Thekla (the Bäsle)

The only extended account is Ludwig Wegele, *Der Lebenslauf der Marianne Thekla Mozart* (Augsburg, 1967). See Ernst Fritz Schmid, "Aus Mozarts schwäbischer Sippe," *Mozart-Jahrbuch 1950*, pp. 99–115 and 128–34. See also articles by Hermann Endrös, E. H. Müller von Asow, Arnold Kühn, Ernst Fritz Schmid, and Karl Meier-Gesees in *Augsburger Mozartbuch* and *Neues Augsburger Mozartbuch* (see ESSAYS, SPECIAL ISSUES, AND CONGRESS REPORTS, above). The most telling discussion is in Wolfgang Hildesheimer, *Mozart* (New York, 1982), pp. 105–24. J. H. Eibl and Walter Senn, *Mozarts Bäsle-Briefe* (Kassel, 1978), with an incisive introduction by Hildesheimer, analyzes Mozart's bawdy language.

A neglected but classic analysis of Mozart's verbal techniques and other aspects of Mozart as *homo ludens* is Emanuel Winternitz, "Gnagflow Trazom: An Essay on Mozart's Script, Pastimes, and Nonsense Letters," *Journal of the American Musicological Society* 11 (1958), pp. 200–216.

Constanze Mozart

Constanze Mozart's letters and documents are conveniently collected in Arthur Schurig, ed., *Konstanze Mozart: Briefe, Aufzeichnungen, Dokumente, 1782–1842* (Dresden, 1922). Her testament is reprinted in Erich Valentin, "Das Testament der Constanze Mozart-Nissen. Mit biographischen Notizen über Constanze und Georg Nikolaus Nissen," *Neues Mozart-Jahrbuch* 2 (1942), pp. 128–75. For defenses of her character, see Volkmar Braunbehrens, *Mozart in Vienna*, pp. 92–108, and H. C. Robbins Landon, *1791* (see LATER BIOGRAPHIES, above), pp. 182–99.

For a profile, see Erna Schwerin, *Constanze Mozart: Woman and Wife of a Genius* (New York, 1981). See also Heinz Gärtner, *Mozarts Requiem und die Geschäfte der Constanze M.* (Munich and Vienna, 1986), trans. Reinard G. Pauly as *Constanze Mozart: After the Requiem* (Seattle, 1991).

Walter Hummel, *W. A. Mozarts Söhne* (Kassel and Basel, 1956) is the authoritative book on Mozart's and Constanze's two sons.

V. SPECIAL TOPICS

Medical History, Death, and Burial

The standard work is Carl Bär, *Mozart: Krankheit, Tod, Begräbnis,* Schriftenreihe der Internationalen Stiftung Mozarteum, 1 (2nd ed., Salzburg, 1972). A fine survey of competing theories, though marred by inaccurate documentation, is William Stafford, *Mozart's Death: A Corrective Survey of the Legends* (London, 1991), U.S. title, *The Mozart Myths: A Critical Reassessment* (Stanford, 1991). See also Peter J. Davies, *Mozart in Person: His Character and His Health* (Westport and London, 1989). Otto Erich Deutsch offers a skeptical view of conspiracy theories in "Die Legende von Mozarts Vergiftung," *Mozart-Jahrbuch 1964,* pp. 7–18. Advocates of conspiracy theories include Johannes Dalchow, *Mozarts Krankheiten 1756–1763* (Bergisch Gladbach, Germany, 1955) and Johannes Dalchow, Gunther Duda, and Dieter Kerner, *Mozarts Tod 1791–1971* (Pähl, Germany, 1971), the latter containing first publications of several important documents. An account of Mozart's burial and related matters is in Walther Brauneis, "Mozarts Begräbnis," in *Zaubertöne* (see ICONOGRAPHIES AND ILLUSTRATED CATALOGS, above), pp. 542–47.

Freemasonry

The standard literature on Mozart and Freemasonry includes: Otto Erich Deutsch, *Mozart und die Wiener Logen: Zur Geschichte seiner Freimaurer-Kompositionen* (Vienna, 1932); Paul Nettl, *Mozart und die königliche Kunst* (Berlin, 1932), trans. Mrs. Robert Gold and enlarged by the author as *Mozart and Masonry* (New York, 1957); H. C. Robbins Landon, *Mozart and the Masons: New Light on the Lodge 'Crowned Hope'* (New York, 1983); Philippe A. Autexier, *Mozart & Liszt sub Rosa* (Poitiers, 1984); Heinz Schuler, "Freimaurer und Illuminaten aus Alt-Bayern und Salzburg und ihre Beziehungen zu den Mozarts," *Mitteilungen der ISM* 35 (1987), pp. 11–39; Heinz Schuler, "'Mozart von der Wohlthätigkeit.' Die Mitglieder der gerechten und vollkommenen St.-Johannis-Freimaurer-Loge 'Zur Wohltätigkeit' im Orient von Wien," *Mitteilungen der ISM* 36 (1988), pp. 1–56; Heinz Schuler, "Die Mozart-Loge: 'Zur neugekrönten Hoffnung' im Orient von Wien: Eine Quellenstudie," *Mitteilungen der ISM* 37 (1989), pp. 1–44; Heinz Schuler, "Freimaurer im Rheingebiet zur Mozart-Zeit," *Mitteilungen der ISM* 35 (1987), pp. 40–41.

For a convenient summary of Heinz Schuler's researches, including a thorough collection of the relevant documents on Mozart and Freemasonry, see his *Mozart und die Freimaurerei: Daten, Fakten, Biographien,* Taschenbücher zur Musikwissenschaft (Wilhelmshaven, 1992). Harald Strebel, *Der Freimaurer Wolfgang Amadé Mozart* (Stäfa, 1991) is another serious documentation of the subject. For a sturdy overview, see Joachim Hurwitz, "Haydn and the Freemasons," *Haydn Yearbook* 16 (1985), pp. 5–98. See also Braunbehrens, *Mozart in Vienna* (see LATER BIOGRAPHIES, above), pp. 226–66.

For speculations that Mozart adhered to esoteric tendencies in Freemasonry and that these are reflected in his works, see: Hans-Josef Irmen, *Mozart: Mitglied geheimer Gesellschaften* ([Mechernich], 1988); Alfons Rosenberg, *W. A. Mozart: Der verborgene Abgrund* (Zurich, 1976); Alfons Rosenberg, "Alchemie und Zauberflöte," *Mozart-Jahrbuch 1971/72*, pp. 402–14; Jacques Henry, *Mozart Frère Maçon: La Symbolique Maçonnique dans l'oeuvre de Mozart* (Aix-en-Provence, 1991); and Walther Brauneis, "Das Frontispiz im Alberti-Libretto von 1791 als Schlüssel zu Mozarts 'Zauberflöte,'" *Mitteilungen der ISM* 41 (1993), pp. 49–60.

A questionable source is Richard Koch, *Br. Mozart, Freimaurer und Illuminat* (Bad Reichenhall, n.d. [1911]). See also Katherine Thomson's "Mozart and Freemasonry," *Music & Letters* 57 (1976), pp. 25–46, and her *The Masonic Thread in Mozart* (London, 1977).

For some of the recent scholarship on the historical background, see the following: Edith Rosenstrauch-Königsberg, *Freimaurerei im Josephinischen Wien: Aloys Blumauer's Weg vom Jesuiten zum Jakobiner,* Wiener Arbeiten zur deutschen Literatur, vol. 6 (Vienna and Stuttgart, 1975); Helmut Reinalter, ed., *Joseph II. und die Freimaurerei im Lichte zeitgenössischer Broschüren* (Vienna, Cologne, Graz, 1987); Helmut Reinalter, ed., *Die Aufklärung in Österreich: Ignaz von Born und seine Zeit,* Schriftenreihe der Internationalen Forschungsstelle "Demokratische Bewegungen in Mitteleuropa 1770–1850," vol. 4 (Frankfurt, 1991); Helmut Reinalter, ed., *Aufklärung und Geheimgesellschaften: Zur politischen Funktion und Sozialstruktur der Freimaurerlogen im 18. Jahrhundert.* Ancien Régime: Aufklärung und Revolution, vol. 16 (Munich, 1989).

Aufklärung und Geheimgesellschaften includes Eva Huber's "Zur Sozialstruktur der Wiener Logen im Josephinischen Jahrzehnt," pp. 173–88. For a fuller documentation, see Huber, "Sozialstruktur der Wiener Freimaurer 1780–1790" (Ph.D. dissertation, University of Vienna, 1991).

Relationships with Significant Individuals

The two commentary volumes of *Briefe* contain reliable biographical notes on the main characters in Mozart's biography, with further bibliographical references. These have been extensively drawn upon in Peter Clive, *Mozart and his Circle: A Biographical Dictionary* (New Haven, 1993). Landon, *Mozart Compendium* (see HANDBOOKS AND DICTIONARIES, above) contains a "Who's Who" section, pp. 41–55; see also the listings in *Lübbes Mozart Lexikon* (see HANDBOOKS AND DICTIONARIES, above). For individual Freemasons, see Heinz Schuler, *Mozart und die Freimaurerei* (see FREEMASONRY, above), pp. 71–153.

Among typical or exemplary studies of some of the leading personages are: O. E. Deutsch, "Das Fräulein von Auernhammer," *Mozart-Jahrbuch 1958,* pp. 12–18; Heinz Friedrich Deininger, "Die deutsche Schauspielergesellschaft unter der Direktion von Johann Heinrich Böhm, einem Freunde der Familie Mozart, in Augsburg in den Jahren 1779 und 1780," *Augsburger Mozartbuch* (see ESSAYS, SPECIAL ISSUES, AND CONGRESS REPORTS, above), pp. 299–397; Ernst Fritz Schmid, "Der Mozartfreund Joseph Bullinger," *Mozart-Jahrbuch 1952,* pp. 17–23; Rudolph Angermüller, "Lorenzo Da Ponte" entry in *The New Grove*, vol. 5, pp. 235–38; Heinz Schuler, "Ein 'besonders guter Freund' [Gemmingen]," *Acta Mozartiana* 36 (1989), pp. 41–45; Ursula Mauthe, *Mozarts "Pamina": Anna Gottlieb* (Augsburg, 1986); Ernst Fritz Schmid, "August Clemens Graf Hatzfeld," *Mozart-Jahrbuch 1954,* pp. 14–33; Hedwig Kraus, "W. A. Mozart und die Familie Jacquin," *Zeitschrift für Musikwissenschaft* 15 (1933), pp. 155–68. H. C. Robbins Landon, *Haydn: Chronicle and Works,* 5 vols. (Bloomington and London, 1976–80); Ernst Fritz Schmid, "Mozart and Haydn," in *The Creative World of Mozart,* ed. Paul Henry Lang (New York, 1963), pp. 86–102; Jens Peter Larsen, "Haydn und Mozart," *Österreichische Musikzeitschrift* 14 (1959), pp. 216–22; Gerhard Croll, "Johann Michael Haydn in seinen Beziehungen zu Leopold und Wolfgang Amadeus Mozart," *Mozart-Jahrbuch 1987/88,* pp. 97–106; Otto Erich Deutsch, "Die Mesmers und die Mozarts," *Mozart-Jahrbuch 1954,* pp. 54–64; Walter Senn, "Barbara Ployer, Mozarts Klavierschülerin," *Österreichische Musikzeitschrift* 33 (1978), pp. 18–28; Gustav Gugitz, "Mozarts Finanzen und Freund Puchberg: Ein Beitrag zur Mozart-Biographie," *Österreichische Musikzeitschrift* 7, 1952, pp. 219–25; Heinz Freiberger, *Anton Raaff. Sein Leben und sein Wirken* (Bonn, 1929); Volkmar Braunbehrens, *Salieri: Ein Musiker im Schatten Mozarts* (Munich, 1989), trans. Eveline L. Kanes as *Maligned Master: The Real Story of Antonio Salieri* (New York, 1992); Egon Komorzynski, *Der Vater der Zauberflöte: Emanuel Schikaneders Leben* (Vienna, 1948); Kurt Honolka, *Papageno: Emanuel Schikaneder, Man of the Theater in Mozart's Time,* trans. Jane Mary Wilde (Portland, 1990); Reinhold Bernhardt, "Aus der Umwelt der Wiener Klassiker: Freiherr

Gottfried van Swieten," *Der Bär, Jahrbuch auf die Jahre 1929–30* (Leipzig, 1930), pp. 74–164; Gustav Gugitz, "Von W. A. Mozarts kuriosen Schülerinnen," *Österreichische Musikzeitschrift* 11 (1956), pp. 261–69 [re Therese von Trattner and Baroness Waldstätten]; Cornelius Preihs, "Mozarts Beziehungen zu den Familien von Thun-Hohenstein," *Neues Mozart-Jahrbuch* 3 (1943), pp. 63–86; Alfred Orel, "Gräfin Wilhelmine Thun," *Mozart-Jahrbuch 1954,* pp. 89–101; Alfred Briellmann, " 'Hochschätzbareste Gnädige Frau Baronin!': Ein bisher unveröffentlichter Brief Mozarts," *Mozart-Jahrbuch 1987/88,* pp. 233–48.

Count Walsegg is covered in Otto Biba, "Par Monsieur François Comte de Walsegg," *Mitteilungen der ISM* 29 (September 1981), pp. 34–50, and Walther Brauneis, " 'Dies irae, dies illa,' " *Jahrbuch des Vereins für Geschichte der Stadt Wien* 47–48 (1991–92), pp. 33–50.

For the members of the Weber family, their spouses, and Johann Thorwart the standard work remains Blümml, *Aus Mozarts Freundes- und Familienkreis* (see ESSAYS, SPECIAL ISSUES, AND CONGRESS REPORTS, above), now strongly in need of updating. For Mozart's pupils, see Heinz Wolfgang Hamann, "Mozarts Schülerkreis," *Mozart-Jahrbuch 1962/63,* pp. 115–39; Carl Bär, "Mozarts Schülerkreis," *Acta Mozartiana* 11 (1964), pp. 58–64; and Erich Hertzmann, "Mozart and Attwood," *Journal of the American Musicological Society* 12 (1959), pp. 178–84.

For Franz and Magdalena Hofdemel, see Ernst Weizmann, "Der unbekannte Mozart," *Weltpresse* (Vienna), vol. 12, nine weekly Saturday installments from 4 February 1956 to 28 April 1956; Otto Jahn, *Gesammelte Aufsätze über Musik* (Leipzig, 1866), p. 231; and Francis Carr, *Mozart and Constanze* (New York, 1984), pp. 144–56.

For a discussion of reciprocal influences of Haydn and Mozart, see Jens Peter Larsen, et al., eds., *Haydn Studies: Proceedings of the International Haydn Conference, Washington, D.C., 1975* (New York and London, 1981), pp. 404–20, with contributions by Georg Feder, Ludwig Finscher, Charles Rosen, James Webster, and others.

For other musicians, composers, librettists, music publishers, and patrons, see the index and commentary volumes of *Briefe* and the relevant entries in *The New Grove* and *MGG*. See also Meredith J. West and Andrew P. King, "Mozart's Starling," *American Scientist* 78 (March–April 1990), pp. 106–14.

Reputation and Reception

A. Hyatt King, *Mozart in Retrospect: Studies in Criticism and Bibliography* (Oxford, 1955), pp. 1–65, contains an exemplary account of the trajectory of Mozart's repute, measured by publications, performances, and critical opinion. Gernot Gruber, *Mozart und die Nachwelt* (Salzburg and Vienna, 1985), trans. R. S. Furness as *Mozart and Posterity* (London, 1991), is a first-rate monograph on evolving views of Mozart. For a convenient collection of extracted opinions about Mozart, see Willi Reich, ed., *Bekenntnis zu Mozart* (Lucerne, 1945).

Finances

The modern reappraisal of Mozart's finances was initiated by Uwe Kraemer, "Wer hat Mozart verhungern lassen?" *Musica* 30 (1976), pp. 203–11, in which Kraemer proposed extremely high estimated earnings and draining gambling expenses. A sober but overly cautious response is Carl Bär, " 'Er war . . . —kein guter Wirth': Eine Studie über Mozarts Verhältnis zum Geld," *Acta Mozartiana* 25 (1978), pp. 31–53. A middle ground is sought in Rudolph Angermüller, " 'Auf Ehre und Credit': Die Finanzen des W. A. Mozart," Ausstellung der Internationalen Stiftung Mozarteum Salzburg, der Staatlichen Münzsammlung München, und der Bayerischen Vereinsbank München (Munich, 1983), and Angermüller's " 'Seine Fehler waren, dass er das Geld nicht zu dirigieren wuste': Mozarts finanzielle Verhältnisse," in *Collectanea Mozartiana* (see ESSAYS, SPECIAL ISSUES, AND CONGRESS REPORTS, above), pp. 19–39.

Braunbehrens, *Mozart in Vienna* (see LATER BIOGRAPHIES, above), pp. 124–41, refines Bär's figures and offers cogent estimates of some undocumented earnings. Landon, *1791* (see LATER BIOGRAPHIES, above) offers the soundest appraisal of Mozart's earnings in his last year (see pp. 27–30, 43–47, 60–63). Roman Sandgruber, "Wirtschaftsentwicklung, Einkommensverteilung und Alltagsleben zur Zeit Haydns," in Gerda Mraz et al., eds., *Joseph Haydn in seiner Zeit.* (catalog for exhibition in Eisenstadt, 20 May–26 October 1982) (Eisenstadt, 1982), pp. 72–90, presents a survey of comparative earnings and expenses by Mozart's contemporaries. Julia Moore, "Mozart in the Market-Place," *Journal of the Royal Musical Association* 114 (1989), 18–42, provides comparative data on other composers' estates but does not take into account Mozart's potential earnings from documented activities. Stafford, *Mozart's Death* (see MEDICAL HISTORY, DEATH, AND BURIAL, above) surveys the contradictory evidence (see pp. 100–105, 230–33, 242–49, 252–60). Dexter

Edge, "Mozart's Fee for *Così fan tutte*," *Journal of the Royal Musical Association* 116 (1991), pp. 211–35, contains valuable information but draws one-sided conclusions.

A useful special study is Rudolf Haas, "Die Finanzierung von Mozarts Mannheimer Aufenthalt 1777/1778," in Roland Würtz, ed., *Das Mannheimer Mozart-Buch* (Wilhelmshaven, 1977), pp. 89–103. The documents detailing Prince Lichnowsky's lawsuit against Mozart were first published in Walther Brauneis, "'. . . wegen schuldigen 1435 32 xr': Neuer Archivfund zur Finanzmisere Mozarts im November 1791," *Mitteilungen der ISM* 39 (1991), pp. 159–63. For discussion of the lawsuit's implications, see the issues of *The Prince Lichnowsky Newsletter*, ed. Bruce Cooper Clarke (Vienna, privately printed, 1992–93).

Travels and Local Studies

A reliable guide to Mozart sites, arranged by city and country, is Harrison James Wignall, *In Mozart's Footsteps: A Travel Guide for Music Lovers* (New York, 1991).

Exemplary special studies of Mozart and various localities include: Ludwig Wegele, *Mozart und Augsburg* (2nd ed., Augsburg, 1960); Josef Mančal, *Die Mozarts in Augsburg und Schwaben* (Augsburg, 1991); Fons de Haas and Irène Smets, eds., *Mozart in Belgien. Ein Wunderkind unterwegs durch die Südlichen Niederlande, 1763–1766* (Antwerp, 1990); Paul Nettl, *Mozart in Böhmen* (Prague, 1938); Rudolf Procházka, *Mozart in Prag* (Prague, 1892); Albert Richard Mohr, *Das Frankfurter Mozart-Buch* (Frankfurt, 1968); C. F. Pohl, *Mozart und Haydn in London*, 2 vols. (Vienna, 1867); Guglielmo Barblan et al., eds., *Mozart in Italia* (Milan, 1956). Willy Lievense, *De Familie Mozart op Bezoek in Nederlands: een Reisverslag* (Helfenshoen, 1965); Adam Bernhard Gottron, *Mozart und Mainz* (Mainz, 1951); Roland Würtz, ed., *Das Mannheimer Mozart-Buch* (Wilhelmshaven, 1977); Géza Rech, *Das Salzburger Mozartbuch* (Salzburg, 1964); Lucas Staehelin, *Die Reise der Familie Mozart durch die Schweiz* (Bern, 1968); Max Fehr and Leonhard Caflisch, *Der junge Mozart in Zürich* (Zurich, 1952).

Among important shorter studies, see Ernst Fritz Schmid, "Auf Mozarts Spuren in Italien," *Mozart-Jahrbuch 1955*, pp. 17–48; Josef Eibl, "Mozart in Neapel," *Mozart-Jahrbuch 1965/66*, pp. 94–120; and Ernst Friedlaender, "Mozarts Beziehungen zu Berlin," *Mitteilungen für die Mozartgemeinde in Berlin* 1 (1897), pp. 115–21.

Rudolph Angermüller, ed., *W. A. Mozarts musikalische Umwelt in Paris (1778): Eine Dokumentation* (Munich, 1982) contains a wealth of background documentation. For Vienna, see Braunbehrens, *Mozart in Vienna* (see LATER BIOGRAPHIES, above); H. C. Robbins Landon, *Mozart: The Golden Years* (New York, 1989); and Selma Krasa et al., eds., *Zaubertöne—Mozart in Wien 1781–1791: Austellung des historischen Museums der Stadt Wien im Künstlerhaus* (Vienna, 1990).

VI. CRITICISM

Surveys and Overviews

Illustrious extended overviews of Mozart's oeuvre are in Hermann Abert's revision of Otto Jahn's *W. A. Mozart* (see LATER BIOGRAPHIES, above), Wyzewa and Saint-Foix (see LATER BIOGRAPHIES, above); and Alfred Einstein, *Mozart: His Character, His Work* (New York, 1945; reprint 1965). Because of their sensitivity to analytic and affective issues, the chapters on Mozart in Charles Rosen, *The Classical Style: Haydn, Mozart, Beethoven* (New York, 1971) have become the touchstone of Mozart criticism in our time. Highly informed surveys include Arthur Hutchings, *Mozart: The Man, The Musician*, 2 vols. in 1 (New York, 1976), and Stanley Sadie, "Wolfgang Amadeus Mozart" entry in *The New Grove*, vol. 12, pp. 680–753, reprinted separately as Sadie, *The New Grove Mozart* (New York, 1983). Neal Zaslaw and William Cowdery, eds., *The Compleat Mozart: A Guide to the Musical Works of Wolfgang Amadeus Mozart* (New York and London, 1990) contains program notes for all of the authentic compositions. Paul Henry Lang, ed., *The Creative World of Mozart* (New York, 1963) includes classic essays by Lang, Edward E. Lowinsky, Erich Hertzmann, Friedrich Blume, and Ernst Fritz Schmid. An influential essay emphasizing anticlassical strands in Mozart is Alfred Heuss, "Das dämonische Element in Mozart's Werken," *Zeitschrift der Internationalen Musikgesellschaft* 7 (1905–6), pp. 175–86. An exemplary study is Ludwig Finscher, "Mozart und Mannheim," in *Die Mannheimer Hofkapelle im Zeitalter Carl Theodors*, ed. Finscher (Mannheim, 1992), pp. 71–96. H. C. Robbins Landon and Donald Mitchell, eds., *The Mozart Companion* (2nd ed., New York, 1969) remains a vital survey. See also the prefaces and critical reports to the individual volumes of *NMA*.

Symphonies

The standard work is Neal Zaslaw, *Mozart's Symphonies: Context, Performance Practice, Reception* (Oxford, 1989). Shorter studies are Georges de Saint-Foix, *The Symphonies of Mozart*, trans. Leslie

Orrey (New York, 1949) and Stanley Sadie, *Mozart's Symphonies* (London, 1986).

Among significant treatments of individual symphonies or groups of symphonies are: Heinrich Schenker, "Mozart: Sinfonie g-Moll," *Das Meisterwerk in der Musik,* vol. 2 (Munich, 1926), pp. 105–57; Donald Francis Tovey, *Essays in Musical Analysis,* vol. 1 (London, 1935), pp. 181–201, and vol. 6 (London, 1939), pp. 19–24; Hans Engel, "Über Mozarts Jugendsinfonien," *Mozart-Jahrbuch 1951,* pp. 22–33; Elaine Sisman, *Mozart: The "Jupiter" Symphony.* A Cambridge Music Handbook (Cambridge, England, 1993); Stefan Kunze, *Mozart: Sinfonie in C-Dur KV 551, Jupiter-Sinfonie.* Meisterwerke der Musik, no. 50 (Munich, 1988); Nathan Broder, ed., *Mozart: Symphony in G minor, K. 550,* Norton Critical Scores (New York and London, 1967).

For a subtle reading of narrative implications in the Symphony no. 39 in E-flat, K. 543, see Leo Treitler, "Mozart and the Idea of Absolute Music," in his *Music and the Historical Imagination* (Cambridge, Mass., 1989), pp. 176–214. A challenging ideological reading is Rose Rosengard Subotnik, "Evidence of a Critical World View in Mozart's Last Three Symphonies," in Edward Strainchamps et al., eds., *Music and Civilization: Essays in Honor of Paul Henry Lang* (New York, 1984), pp. 29–43. Cliff Eisen, "New Light on Mozart's 'Linz' Symphony," *Journal of the Royal Musical Association* 113 (1988), pp. 81–96, suggests that the Salzburg copy of the score documents Mozart's second thoughts.

The standard work on Leopold Mozart's symphonies is Cliff Eisen, "The Symphonies of Leopold Mozart and Their Relationship to the Early Symphonies of Wolfgang Amadeus Mozart: A Bibliographical and Stylistic Study" (Ph.D. dissertation, Cornell University, 1986); its data and conclusions are summarized in *Mozart-Jahrbuch 1987/88,* pp. 181–93.

Concertos

The classic study is Cuthbert M. Girdlestone, *Mozart's Piano Concertos* (London, 1948; 2nd ed. London, 1958), reprinted as *Mozart and His Piano Concertos* (New York, 1964). See also Arthur Hutchings, *A Companion to Mozart's Piano Concertos* (2nd ed., London, 1958), and Philip Radcliffe, *Mozart Piano Concertos* (London, 1978). For an overview, see H. C. Robbins Landon, "The Concertos (II): Their Musical Origin and Development," in Landon and Mitchell, *The Mozart Companion* (see SURVEYS AND OVERVIEWS, above), pp. 234–82. Somewhat outdated but still useful, though marred by its unaccountable validation of the spurious "Adelaide" Concerto, is Friedrich Blume, "The Concertos (I): Their Sources," in *The Mozart Companion,* pp. 200–33.

Special studies include: Denis Forman, *Mozart's Concerto Form: The First Movements of the Piano Concertos* (London and New York, 1971); Hans Tischler, *A Structural Analysis of Mozart's Piano Concertos,* Musicological Studies, 10 (Brooklyn, 1966); Susan McClary, "A Musical Dialectic from the Enlightenment: Mozart's Piano Concerto in G Major, K. 453, Movement 2," *Cultural Critique* 4 (1986), pp. 129–69; Joseph Kerman, "Mozart's Concertos and Their Audiences," paper presented at the Mozart Symposium at the Woodrow Wilson Center, Washington, D. C., December 1991, published in James M. Morris, ed., *Observing Mozart* (Cambridge, England, 1994).

For Donald Francis Tovey on the piano concertos, see his *Essays in Musical Analysis,* vol. 3 (London, 1936), pp. 3–46. Tovey's analysis of the C-major Concerto, K. 503, is among a group of essays reprinted in Joseph Kerman, ed., *Mozart: Piano Concerto in C major, K. 503,* Norton Critical Scores (New York and London, 1970). A forthcoming symposium, Neal Zaslaw, ed., *Mozart's Piano Concertos: Text, Context, Interpretation* (Ann Arbor, in press), contains twenty-three papers, including contributions by Zaslaw, Wye J. Allanbrook, Karol Berger, Dexter Edge, Cliff Eisen, William Kinderman, Robert D. Levin, Carl Schachter, Alan Tyson, James Webster, and Christoph Wolff. An excellent survey is A. Hyatt King, *Mozart String and Wind Concertos* (London, 1978; 2nd ed., 1986); see also Tovey on several of these concertos in *Essays in Musical Analysis,* vol. 3, pp. 47–63. For an advocate's view of the questionably authentic Symphonie Concertante, K. Anh. C 14.01/297B, see Robert D. Levin, *Who Wrote the Mozart Four-wind Concertante?* (New York, 1988).

Chamber Music

Two insightful surveys are A. Hyatt King, *Mozart Chamber Music* (London, 1968, rev. ed., 1986), and Hermann Abert, "Mozart" entry in Walter Wilson Cobbett, ed., *Cobbett's Cyclopedic Survey of Chamber Music,* 2 vols. (London, 1929), vol. 2, pp. 150–81. A major symposium is documented in *The String Quartets of Haydn, Mozart and Beethoven: Studies of the Autograph Manuscripts,* ed. Christoph Wolff, Isham Library Papers, 3 (Cambridge, Mass., 1980) with contributions by Wolff, Ludwig Finscher, Marius Flothuis, and Alan Tyson. An exemplary paper is Finscher, "Mozarts 'Mailänder' Streichquartette," *Die Musikforschung* 19 (1966), pp. 270–83. See Marius Flothuis, *Wolfgang Amadeus Mozart: Streichquintett g-Moll KV 516.* Meisterwerke der

Musik, no. 44 (Munich, 1987). Tovey's masterly analysis of the Quintet for Piano and Winds in E-flat, K. 452, is in his *Essays in Musical Analysis: Chamber Music* (London, 1944), pp. 106–20.

Sonatas and Other Keyboard Music

Hanns Dennerlein, *Der unbekannte Mozart. Die Welt seiner Klavierwerke* (Leipzig, 1951), appears to be the only book solely devoted to Mozart's keyboard music. For surveys, see Einstein, pp. 252–60; A. Hyatt King, "Mozart's Piano Music," *Music Review* 5 (1944), pp. 163–91; and Abert, "Mozart" (see CHAMBER MUSIC, above), pp. 170–77. See Heinrich Schenker, "Mozart: Sonate A-Moll," *Der Tonwille,* no. 2 (1922), pp. 7–24. The standard work on the evolution, style, and form of the sonata, William S. Newman, *The Sonata in the Classic Era* (Chapel Hill, 1963), contains an overview of Mozart's solo and duo sonatas at pp. 477–500. For the church sonatas, see Hanns Dennerlein, "Zur Problematik von Mozarts Kirchensonaten," *Mozart-Jahrbuch 1953,* pp. 95–104.

Operas and Singspiels

Edward J. Dent, *Mozart's Operas: A Critical Study* (London, 1962) is a classic work, first published in 1913 and revised in 1947. Wye Jamison Allanbrook, *Rhythmic Gesture in Mozart: "Le nozze di Figaro" and "Don Giovanni"* (Chicago and London, 1983), is challenging and evocative, opening new perspectives; see also Allanbrook's "Mozart's Happy Endings: A New Look at the 'Convention' of the 'lieto fine,'" *Mozart-Jahrbuch 1984/85,* pp. 1–5. Rudolph Angermüller, *Mozart's Operas* (New York, 1988), is a reliable, illustrated conspectus, with a useful bibliography. Daniel Heartz, *Mozart's Operas,* ed. and with additional essays contributed by Thomas Bauman (Berkeley and Los Angeles, 1990), is an insightful collection by a leading scholar, and includes several exemplary papers.

Reliable overviews of Mozart's operas include Stefan Kunze, *Mozarts Opern* (Stuttgart, 1984), William Mann, *The Operas of Mozart* (London, 1977), and Charles Osborne, *The Complete Operas of Mozart: A Critical Guide* (London, 1978). Joachim Kaiser, *Who's Who in Mozart's Operas: From Alfonso to Zerlina,* trans. Charles Kessler (London, 1986), contains keen descriptions of the opera characters. Ernst Lert, *Mozart auf dem Theater* (Berlin, 1918), remains a standard study of Mozart's dramaturgy. See also Christopher Benn, *Mozart on the Stage* (London, 1946), with an introduction by Richard Capell.

The volumes in the Cambridge Opera Handbooks series provide ready access to the biographical context, literary and musical sources, performance history, reception, and interpretation of all the later operas except *Così fan tutte:* Julian Rushton, *Don Giovanni* (1981); Tim Carter, *Le nozze di Figaro* (1987); Thomas Bauman, *Die Entführung aus dem Serail* (1987); John A. Rice, *La clemenza di Tito* (1991); Peter Branscombe, *Die Zauberflöte* (1991); and Julian Rushton, *Idomeneo* (1993). Rushton's *Don Giovanni* is especially fine.

Other books and catalogs wholly devoted to individual operas include: Hermann Abert, *Mozart's Don Giovanni,* extracted from Abert's revision of Jahn's biography, trans. Peter Gellhorn (London, 1976); Rudolph Angermüller and Robert Münster, eds., *Bayerische Staatsbibliothek, Wolfgang Amadeus Mozart: Idomeneo 1781–1981* (Munich, 1981); Rudolph Angermüller, ed., *Figaro—Mit einem Beitrag von Wolfgang Pütz: 'Le Nozze di Figaro' auf dem Theater* (Salzburg, 1986). Jacques Chailley, *The Magic Flute: Masonic Opera,* trans. Herbert Weinstock (New York, 1971), emphasizes Masonic symbolism in *Die Zauberflöte.* Siegmund Levarie, *Mozart's "Le nozze di Figaro": A Critical Analysis* (Chicago, 1952), makes a powerful case for the structural coherence of *Le nozze di Figaro.*

A seminal work is Joseph Kerman, *Opera as Drama* (New York, 1956; rev. ed., Berkeley and Los Angeles, 1988), chaps. 4 and 5. See also his "Reading Don Giovanni," in Jonathan Miller, ed., *Don Giovanni: Myths of Seduction and Betrayal* (New York, 1990), pp. 108–25; also in Kerman, *Write All These Down: Essays on Music* (Berkeley, 1994), pp. 307–21. Recent important challenges to organicist and Wagnerian readings are Carolyn Abbate and Roger Parker, "Dismembering Mozart," *Cambridge Opera Journal* 2 (1990), pp. 187–95, and James Webster, "Mozart's Operas and the Myth of Musical Unity," *Cambridge Opera Journal* 2 (1990), pp. 197–218. For unsettling qualities in Mozart's Da Ponte operas, see Bernard Williams, "Don Giovanni as an Idea," in Rushton's Cambridge Opera Handbook *Don Giovanni,* pp. 81–91.

Brigid Brophy, *Mozart the Dramatist* (New York, 1964; rev. ed., 1988), views the operas against the biographical and Enlightenment background. Ivan Nagel, *Autonomy and Mercy: Reflections on Mozart's Operas,* trans. Marion Faber and Ivan Nagel (Cambridge, Mass., 1991), is a profound discourse on the ideological dimension of the operas. See also Fritz Noske, *The Signifier and the Signified: Studies in the Operas of Mozart and Verdi* (Oxford, 1990), and Nicholas Till, *Mozart and the*

Enlightenment: Truth, Virtue and Beauty in Mozart's Operas (New York, 1993). For the historical and cultural context of the later operas, see Andrew Steptoe, *The Mozart–Da Ponte Operas* (Oxford, 1988) and Steptoe's "Joseph II and Social Sensitivity," *Music Review* 43 (1982), pp. 109–20. For some musical contexts of the operas, see: John Platoff, "Music and Drama in the 'Opera buffa'-Finale: Mozart and his Contemporaries in Vienna, 1781–1790" (Ph.D. dissertation, University of Pennsylvania, 1984); John Platoff, "The Buffa Aria in Mozart's Vienna," *Cambridge Opera Journal* 2 (1990), pp. 99–120; John Platoff, "Musical and Dramatic Structure in the Opera Buffa Finale," *Journal of Musicology* 7 (1989), pp. 191–230; Linda Louise Tyler-Schmidt, "Mozart and Operatic Conventions in Austria and Southern Germany, 1760–1800" (Ph.D. dissertation, Princeton University, 1988); and Mary Hunter, "Some Representations of *opera seria* in *opera buffa*," *Cambridge Opera Journal* 3 (1991), pp. 89–108.

A worthy special study is Linda L. Tyler, "*Zaide* in the Development of Mozart's Operatic Language," *Music & Letters* 72 (1991), pp. 214–35. James Webster argues persuasively for the dramatic significance of the arias in his "The Analysis of Mozart's Arias," in *Mozart Studies,* ed. Eisen, pp. 101–99. Donald Francis Tovey's "A Note on Opera," *The Main Stream of Music and Other Essays* (Oxford, 1949; reprinted Cleveland, 1959), pp. 353–60, is a fine essay on Mozart's gifts as a dramatist. Edward T. Cone, "The World of Opera and Its Inhabitants," in *Music: A View from Delft, Selected Essays,* ed. Robert P. Morgan (Chicago and London, 1989), pp. 125–38, imaginatively constructs the multiple dimensions in which Mozart's characters are realized.

Editions of the collected librettos include a German-language edition by Rudolph Angermüller, ed., *Mozart: Sämtliche Opernlibretti* (Stuttgart, 1990); an Italian-language edition by Marco Beghelli, ed., *Tutti i libretti di Mozart* (Milan, 1990); and an original language–English bilingual edition of the last seven operas, Paul Gruber, ed., *The Metropolitan Opera Book of Mozart Operas* (New York, 1991).

Serenades and Divertimentos

The standard work is Günter Hausswald, *Mozarts Serenaden. Ein Beitrag zur Stilkritik des 18. Jahrhunderts* (Leipzig, 1951; reprint Wilhelmshaven, 1975). Two other studies are Werner Rainer, "Michael Haydns Orchesterserenaden," *Mozart-Jahrbuch 1987/88,* pp. 73–79; and Carl Bär, "Zum Begriff des 'Basso' in Mozarts Serenaden," *Mozart-Jahrbuch 1960/61,* pp. 133–55. Erik Smith, *Mozart Serenades, Divertimenti and Dances* (London, 1982), is a rapid survey. For recent scholarship on the serenade genre, see Andrew Kearns, "The Eighteenth-Century Orchestral Serenade in South Germany" (Ph.D. dissertation, University of Illinois, 1993).

Church Music

K. G. Fellerer, *Die Kirchenmusik W. A. Mozarts* (Laaber, Germany, 1985), is a comprehensive monograph. Arthur Hutchings, *Mozart: The Man, the Musician* (London, 1976), vol. 2, pp. 26–32, has important things to say about the church music and the Salzburg masses in particular. See also Karl Pfannhauser, "Mozarts *Krönungsmesse*," *Mitteilungen der ISM* 11 (1963), pp. 3–11.

The Requiem

The issues are cogently surveyed in Christoph Wolff's *Mozart's Requiem: Historical and Analytical Studies, Documents, Score* (Berkeley and Los Angeles, 1993), and "The Composition and Completion of Mozart's Requiem, 1791–1792," in Eisen, *Mozart Studies* (see ESSAYS, SPECIAL ISSUES, AND CONGRESS REPORTS, above), pp. 61–82; and in Paul Moseley, "Mozart's Requiem: A Revaluation of the Evidence," *Journal of the Royal Musical Association* 114 (1989), pp. 203–37.

An influential earlier study is Friedrich Blume, "Requiem but no Peace," in Lang, *Creative World of Mozart* (see SURVEYS AND OVERVIEWS, above), pp. 103–26.

A serious attempt to deconstruct Süssmayr's contributions is Richard Maunder, *Mozart's Requiem: On Preparing a New Edition* (Oxford, 1988). Re dating, see Wolfgang Plath, "Über Skizzen zu Mozarts 'Requiem,'" in *Bericht über den Internationalen Musikwissenschaftlichen Kongress Kassel 1962,* ed. Georg Reichert and Martin Just (Kassel, 1963), pp. 184–87 (reprinted in Plath, pp. 74–77). An important exhibition of materials from the music collection of the Österreichische Nationalbibliothek is documented in Günter Brosche et al., eds., *Requiem: Wolfgang Amadeus Mozart 1791/1991* (Graz, 1991).

Variations

Elaine R. Sisman, *Haydn and the Classical Variation* (Cambridge, Mass., 1993), pp. 196–234, contains an informed treatment of Mozart's variations.

Style and Tradition

A rigorous demonstration of the persistence of traditional contrapuntal procedures in Mozart's music is in Warren Kirkendale's *Fuge und Fugato in der Kammermusik des Rokoko und der Klassik* (Tutzing, 1966), trans. Margaret Bent and the author as *Fugue and Fugato in Rococo and Classical Chamber Music* (Durham, 1979), pp. 152–81. See also Reinhold Hammerstein, "Der Gesange geharnischten Männer. Eine Studie zu Mozarts Bachbild," *Archiv für Musikwissenschaft* 13 (1956), pp. 1–24, and Robert Lach, *Mozart als Theoretiker* (Vienna, 1918). In his *Classic Music: Expression, Form, and Style* (New York, 1980), Leonard G. Ratner views Mozart's music within the context of eighteenth-century music theory.

Formal and Analytical Issues

Several exemplary papers include: Friedrich Blume, "Mozart's Style and Influence," in Landon and Mitchell, *Mozart Companion* (see SURVEYS AND OVERVIEWS, above), pp. 10–31; Edward E. Lowinsky, "On Mozart's Rhythm," in Lang, *Creative World of Mozart*, pp. 31–55; Leonard Meyer, "Grammatical Simplicity and Relationship Richness: The Trio of Mozart's G minor Symphony," *Critical Inquiry* 2 (1976), pp. 693–761; Jane R. Stevens, "An 18th Century Description of Concerto First-Movement Form," *Journal of the American Musicological Society* 24 (1971), pp. 85–95; Robert S. Winter, "The Bifocal Close and the Evolution of the Viennese Classical Style," *Journal of the American Musicological Society* 42 (1989), pp. 275–337.

For hierarchical cadential organization in Mozart's concerto form, see Karol Berger's "The First-Movement Punctuation Form in Mozart's Piano Concertos," in Neal Zaslaw, ed., *Mozart's Piano Concertos: Text, Context, Interpretation* (Ann Arbor, in press), and Berger's "The Second-Movement Punctuation Form in Mozart's Piano Concertos: The Andantino of K. 449," *Mozart-Jahrbuch 1991*, pp. 168–72. See also the dissertation by Konrad Küster, "Formale Aspekte des ersten Allegros in Mozarts Konzerten" (Kassel, 1991).

Classicism and Romanticism

The problems inherent in attempting to differentiate these decisive style periods in music are discussed in Friedrich Blume, *Classic and Romantic Music: A Comprehensive Survey*, trans. M. D. Herter Norton (New York, 1970); Ludwig Finscher, "Zum Begriff der Klassik in der Musik," *Deutsches Jahrbuch der Musikwissenschaft* 11 (1966), pp. 9–34; and Rosen, *The Classical Style*, passim. For Mozart and romanticism, see Leo Schrade, "Mozart und die Romantiker," in *Bericht über die musikwissenschaftliche Tagung der Internationalen Stiftung Mozarteum in Salzburg*, ed. Erich Schenk (Leipzig, 1931), pp. 22–38; and Ludwig Schiedermair, "Mozart und die Romantik," *Neues Mozart-Jahrbuch* 3 (1943), pp. 9–21.

See also Neal Zaslaw, ed., *The Classical Era from the 1740s to the End of the 18th Century* (Englewood Cliffs, 1989).

Issues of Chronology and Authenticity

Two momentous projects for refining the chronology of Mozart's works by means of paper studies and handwriting analysis respectively are codified in Alan Tyson, *Mozart: Studies of the Autograph Scores* (Cambridge, Mass., 1987) and Wolfgang Plath, *Mozart-Schriften: Ausgewählte Aufsätze*, ed. Marianne Danckwardt, Schriftenreihe der ISM Salzburg, vol. 9 (Kassel, 1991). The former gathers together eighteen of Tyson's papers and lectures written between 1975 and 1986, detailing his analyses of the watermarks and other physical properties of Mozart's autograph scores. The latter reprints twenty-one of Plath's papers, written between 1959 and 1987, including his fundamental studies of Leopold Mozart's and Mozart's handwriting: "Beiträge zur Mozart-Autographie I: Die Handschrift Leopold Mozarts," *Mozart-Jahrbuch 1960/61*, pp. 82–117, and "Beiträge zur Mozart-Autographie II: Schriftchronologie 1770–1780," *Mozart-Jahrbuch 1976/77*, pp. 131–73.

Tyson systematizes his findings on the watermarks in his *Wasserzeichen-Katalog* (see CATALOGS, above) and summarizes his suggested redatings in "Proposed New Dates for Many Works and Fragments Written by Mozart from March 1781 to December 1791," in *Mozart Studies*, ed. Eisen, pp. 213–26. For a discussion of inherent difficulties in dating Mozart's music by means of analysis of the paper types he used, see A. Hyatt King, Review of Alan Tyson, *Mozart: Studies of the Autograph Scores*, in *Journal of Musicological Research* 8 (1989), pp. 386–95.

A valuable study of the Salzburg copyists is Cliff Eisen, "The Mozarts' Salzburg Copyists: Aspects of Attribution, Chronology, Text, Style, and Performance Practice," in *Mozart Studies*, ed. Eisen, pp. 253–308. Issues of authenticity are addressed in Wolfgang Plath, "Echtheitsfragen bei Mozart," in Hanspeter Bennwitz, et al., eds., *Opera incerta: Echtheitsfragen als Problem musikwissenschaftlicher Gesamtausgaben*. Kolloquium Mainz 1988 (Mainz, 1991), pp. 207–14, 237–70, and 271–84. Issues of authenticity were also the subject of a panel held at the Conference of the Central Institute for Mozart Research in 1971, with papers by Jens Peter Larsen, Wolfgang Plath, Jan

LaRue, Martin Staehelin, and others, subsequently published in *Mozart-Jahrbuch 1971/72*, pp. 7–67.

Fragments and Sketches

The primary literature on Mozart's fragments includes: Mena Blaschitz, "Die Salzburger Mozart-Fragmente" (Ph.D. dissertation, University of Bonn, 1926); Alfred Einstein, Preface to 3rd ed. of *Köchel-Verzeichnis*, reprinted in K⁶, pp. xliii–xlv; King, *Mozart in Retrospect* (see ESSAYS, SPECIAL ISSUES, AND CONGRESS REPORTS, above), pp. 216–27; K⁶, pp. 941–49; Christoph Wolff, "Creative Exuberance vs. Critical Choice: Thoughts on Mozart's Quartet Fragments," in Wolff, ed., *The String Quartets of Haydn, Mozart and Beethoven: Studies of the Autograph Manuscripts* (Cambridge, Mass., 1980), pp. 191–210; Alan Tyson, "The Mozart Fragments," in Tyson, *Mozart: Studies of the Autograph Scores*, pp. 125–61; and Robert L. Marshall, "Mozart's Unfinished: Some Lessons of the Fragments," *Mozart-Jahrbuch 1991*, vol. 2, pp. 910–21.

A pioneering essay on Mozart's compositional practice is Erich Hertzmann, "Mozart's Creative Process," in Lang, *Creative World of Mozart* (see SURVEYS AND OVERVIEWS, above), pp. 17–30. Mozart's sketches have now been surveyed and cataloged in Ulrich Konrad, *Mozarts Schaffensweise: Studien zu den Werkautographen, Skizzen und Entwürfen*, Abhandlungen der Akademie der Wissenschaften in Göttingen, Philologisch-historische Klasse, dritte Folge, Nr. 201 (Göttingen, 1992), a pioneering monograph with an indispensable listing of Mozart's sketches (pp. 104–338). For an introduction to the subject, see Konrad's "Mozart's Sketches," *Early Music* 20 (1992), pp. 119–30.

Topics and Rhetoric

The groundbreaking book on eighteenth-century musical topics, rhetoric, and characteristic styles is Leonard G. Ratner, *Classic Music: Expression, Form, and Style* (New York, 1980). Further implications of considering the embedded, conventional "meanings" of Mozart's music through Ratner's approach have been elaborated in Wye Jamison Allanbrook's *Rhythmic Gesture in Mozart: "Le nozze di Figaro" and "Don Giovanni"* (Chicago and London, 1983), and "'Ear-Tickling Nonsense': A New Context for Musical Expression in Mozart's 'Haydn' Quartets," *The St. John's Review* 38 (1988), pp. 1–24, as well as in V. Kofi Agawu's *Playing with Signs: A Semiotic Interpretation of Classic Music* (Princeton, 1991), which also examines a potential fusion of Ratnerian and Schenkerian approaches.

For an important appraisal of Ratner, see Joseph Kerman, "Theories of Late Eighteenth-Century Music," in *Studies in Eighteenth-Century British Art and Aesthetics*, ed. Ralph Cohen (Berkeley, 1985), pp. 217–44, reprinted as "Critics and the Classics," in Kerman, *Write All These Down: Essays on Music* (Berkeley, 1994), pp. 51–72. Analogies between musical expression and classical rhetoric are lucidly discussed in Mark Evan Bonds, *Wordless Rhetoric: Musical Form and the Metaphor of the Oration* (Cambridge, Mass., 1991). Brian Vickers, "Figures of Rhetoric/Figures of Music?" *Rhetorica* 2 (1984), pp. 1–44, is rigorously skeptical of music's ability to convey equivalents of linguistic rhetorical tropes.

Performance Practice

Some examples of the lively literature reflecting the burgeoning interest in performance practice are: Eva and Paul Badura-Skoda, *Interpreting Mozart on the Keyboard*, trans. Leo Black (London, 1962); Frederick Neumann, *Ornamentation and Improvisation in Mozart* (Princeton, 1986); Jean-Pierre Marty, *The Tempo Indications of Mozart* (New Haven and London, 1989); and Robert D. Levin, "Instrumental Ornamentation, Improvisation and Cadenzas," in *Performance Practice: Music after 1660*, ed. Howard Mayer Brown and Stanley Sadie (New York, 1990), pp. 267–91.

The proceedings of the Lincoln Center conference, "Performing Mozart's Music," held at the Juilliard School, New York, 19–24 May 1991, under the direction of Neal Zaslaw, are published as three issues of *Early Music* 19 (November 1991), and 20 (February and May 1992). Of particular interest are articles on Mozart's orchestras by Dexter Edge, Cliff Eisen, and Zaslaw, and on Mozart and the violin (Peter Walls) and the flute (Jane Bowers).

See also R. Larry Todd and Peter Williams, eds., *Perspectives on Mozart Performance*, Cambridge Studies in Performance Practice (Cambridge, England, 1991), particularly Katalin Komlós, "'Ich praeludirte und spielte Variazionen': Mozart the Fortepianist," pp. 27–54, and Jean-Pierre Marty, "Mozart's Tempo Indications and the Problems of Interpretation," pp. 55–73.

Other important papers on this subject include Robert Münster, "Authentische Tempi zu den sechs letzten Sinfonien W. A. Mozarts," *Mozart-Jahrbuch 1962/63*, pp. 185–99; Will Crutchfield, "The Prosodic Appoggiatura in the Music of Mozart and His Contemporaries," *Journal of the American Musicological Society* 42 (1989), pp. 229–74; and several by Max Rudolf, including "Inner

Repeats in the Da Capo of Classical Minuets and Scherzos," *Journal of the Conductors' Guild* 3 (1982), pp. 145–50; and "Ein Beitrag zur Geschichte der Temponahme bei Mozart," *Mozart-Jahrbuch 1976/77,* pp. 204–24.

For a concise survey, see Robin Stowell, in Landon, *Mozart Compendium,* pp. 372–83.

VII. HISTORICAL BACKGROUND
Salzburg
An important contemporary source is Caspar Riesbeck, *Travels Through Germany in a Series of Letters,* trans. Rev. Mr. Maty, 3 vols. (London, 1787). For a detailed history of Salzburg under Archbishops Schrattenbach and Colloredo, see Judas Thaddäus Zauner, continued by Corbinian Gärtner, *Neue Chronik von Salzburg,* vol. 5, part 1 (Salzburg, 1826), and also Georg Abdon Pichler, *Salzburg's Landes-Geschichte,* part 1, vol. 1 (Salzburg, 1861). A thorough Salzburg guidebook is L. Hübner, *Beschreibung der hochfürstlich-erzbischöflichen Haupt- und Residenzstadt Salzburg und ihrer Gegenden,* 2 vols. (Salzburg, 1792–93). See numerous works by Franz Martin, including *Kleine Landesgeschichte von Salzburg* (Salzburg, 1971) and *Hundert Salzburg Familien* (Salzburg, 1946). For the musical context the soundest synoptic treatment is Cliff Eisen, "Salzburg under Church Rule," in *The Classical Era: From the 1740s to the End of the 18th century,* ed. Neal Zaslaw (Englewood Cliffs, 1989), pp. 166–87.

Vienna
A handful of listings includes: Ilse Barea, *Vienna* (New York, 1966); Felix Czeike, *Das grosse Groner Wien Lexikon* (Vienna, 1974); Ernst Wangermann, *The Austrian Achievement: 1700–1800* (London, 1973); Ernst Wangermann, *From Joseph II to the Jacobin Trials,* Oxford Historical Series, 2nd series (London, 1959), pp. 133–87; Hans Wagner, "Das Josephinische Wien und Mozart," *Mozart-Jahrbuch 1978/79,* pp. 1–13; and Johann Pezzl, *Skizze von Wien,* 2 vols. (Vienna, 1786–90), abridged translation in H. C. Robbins Landon, *Mozart and Vienna* (New York, 1991), pp. 53–191.

See also FREEMASONRY (above).

The pioneering work on Viennese concert life from the founding of the Tonkünstler-Societät in 1771 until the 1860s is music critic Eduard Hanslick's *Geschichte des Concertwesens in Wien* (Vienna, 1869). The study of concert performances during Mozart's Vienna years has now been placed on a sound footing in Mary Sue Morrow's ambitious *Concert Life in Haydn's Vienna: Aspects of a Developing Musical and Social Institution* (Stuyvesant, N.Y., 1989).

LIST OF ILLUSTRATIONS

"Mozart Enfant."
Statue in bronze,
1883, by Ernest
Barrias. Louvre.

INDEX OF COMPOSITIONS

Classified List of Compositions, with Köchel Numbers

K. numbers given here are those assigned to Mozart's compositions in the first edition of Köchel.

Requiem: K. 626

Masses and Kyries: K. 33, 90, 115, 116, 139, 167, 192, 220, 257, 258, 259, 262, 275, 296a–c, 317, 337, 341, 427

Litanies and Vespers: K. 109, 125, 193, 243, 321, 339

Shorter Sacred Works: K. 34, 85, 86, 108, 127, 165, 198, 222, 260, 273, 277, 343, 618

Church Sonatas: K. 67–69, 328–29, 336

Oratorios, Sacred Dramas, and Cantatas: K. 35, 42, 118, 429, 469, 471, 619, 623

Operas, Singpiels, and Dramatic Cantatas: K. 38, 50, 51, 87, 111, 126, 135, 196, 208, 344, 366, 384, 422, 430, 486, 492, 527, 588, 620, 621

Ballet and Incidental Music: K. 345, 367, Anh. 10–11

Soprano Arias and Scenes: K. 77, 82–83, 88, 119, 272, 294, 316, 368–69, 374, 383, 416, 418–19, 440, 486a, 505, 528, 538, 540c, 577–80, 582–83

Alto Arias and Scenes: K. 255

Tenor Arias and Scenes: K. 36, 295, 420, 431, 490, 540a

Bass Arias and Scenes: K. 432, 512–13, Anh. 245

Vocal Duets, Trios, Quartets: K. 479–80, 489, 540b

Lieder: K. 148, 307, 308, 349, 468, 483–84, 517–20, 523–24, 529, 530, 552, 596–98

Canons: K. 73i, 73r, 229–34, 347–48

Symphonies: K. 16, 19, 22, 43, 45, 45a, 48, 73, 74, 110, 112, 114, 121, 124, 128, 129, 130, 132, 133, 134, 135, 162, 181, 183, 184, 199, 201, 202, 297, 318, 319, 338, 385, 425, 504, 543, 550, 551, K. *deest*, Anh. 221

Divertimentos of various genres: K. 32, 41a, 131, 136–38, 166, 186, 205, 213, 240, 247, 251–54, 270, 287, 289, 334, 439b, 563

Serenades: K. 185, 203, 204, 239, 250, 320, 361, 375, 388, 525

Cassations: K. 99

Dances: K. 267, 269b, 534–36, 567–68, 571, 585–87, 599–607, 609, 610

Piano Concertos: K. 37, 39–41, 107, 175, 238, 242, 246, 271, 365, 413–15, 449–51, 453, 456, 459, 466–67, 482, 488, 491, 503, 537, 595

String Concertos: K. 190, 207, 211, 216, 218, 219, 268, 271i, 364

Wind Concertos: K. 191, 271k, 299, 313, 314, 412, 417, 447, 495, 621b, 622, Anh. 9

Quartets and Quintets for strings and wind: K. 285, 285a, 298, 370, 407, 581, Anh. 171

String Quintets: K. 174, 406, 515, 516, 593, 614

String Quartets: K. 80, 136–38, 155–60, 168–73, 387, 421, 428, 458, 464–65, 499, 546, 575, 589–90

Duos and Trios: K. 423–24, 563

Piano Trios and Quartets: K. 10–15, 254, 478, 493, 496, 502, 542, 548, 564

Piano and Wind: K. 452, 498

Violin and Piano Sonatas: K. 6–9, 10–15, 26–31, 296, 301–6, 376–80, 403, 454, 481, 526, 547

Violin and Piano Variations: K. 359–60

Piano Sonatas: K. 279–84, 309–11, 312, 330–33, 457, 494, 533, 545, 570, 576

Piano four hands and two pianos: K. 358, 381, 448, 497, 521

Piano Variations: K. 25, 179–80, 264–65, 352–54, 398, 455, 460, 500, 501, 573

Works for Mechanical Organ or Harmonica: K. 356, 594
Masonic Music: K. 148, 429, 468, 471, 477, 483–84, 619, 623, K. *deest.*

Operas and Other Stage Works, Listed Alphabetically

Apollo et Hyacinthus: K. 38
Ascanio in Alba: K. 111
Bastien und Bastienne: K. 50
La Betulia liberata: K. 118
Clemenza di Tito, La: K. 621
Così fan tutte: K. 588
Davidde penitente: K. 469
Don Giovanni: K. 527
Die Entführung aus dem Serail: K. 384
La finta giardiniera: K. 196
La finta semplice: K. 51
Idomeneo: K. 366
Lucio Silla: K. 135
Mitridate, rè di Ponto: K. 87
Le nozze di Figaro: K. 492
L'oca del Cairo: K. 422
Les Petits Riens: K. Anh. 10
Il rè pastore: K. 208
Der Schauspieldirektor: K. 486
Die Schuldigkeit des ersten Gebots: K. 35
Il sogno di Scipione: K. 126
Lo sposo deluso: K. 430
Thamos, König in Ägypten: K. 345
Zaide: K. 344
Die Zauberflöte: K. 620

Other Titled or Nicknamed Works, Listed Alphabetically

"Andretter" Serenade: K. 185
"Coronation" Concertos: K. 459, 537
"Coronation" Mass: K. 317
"Credo" Mass: K. 257
"Dissonance" String Quartet: K. 465
Eine kleine Nachtmusik: K. 525
Galimathias musicum: K. 32
"Gran Partita" Serenade: K. 361
"Haffner" Serenade: K. 250
"Haffner" Symphony: K. 385
"Haydn" Quartets: K. 387, 421, 428, 458, 464, 465
"Hoffmeister" Quartet: K. 499
"Holy Trinity" Mass: K. 167
"Hunt" String Quartet: K. 458
"Jeunehomme" Concerto: K. 271
"Jupiter" Symphony: K. 551
"Kegelstatt" Trio: K. 498
"Lambach" Symphony: K. 45a
"Linz" Symphony: K. 425
"Lodron" Concerto: K. 242
Masonic Funeral Music: K. 477
Die Maurerfreude: K. 471
Musical Joke, A (Ein Musikalischer Spass): K. 522
"Organ Solo" Mass: K. 259
"Palatine" Sonatas: K. 301–306
"Paris" Symphony: K. 297
"Piccolomini" Mass: K. 258
"Posthorn" Serenade: K. 320
"Prague" Symphony: K. 504

Index of Compositions, Listed by Köchel Number

For an explanation of the notation of Köchel listings, see "A Note on Köchel Numbers," p. xii.
In this index minor keys are designated by lowercase letters.

K. *Anhang*

K. *deest* (not in Köchel)

GENERAL INDEX